Paul Cobley and Peter J. Schulz (Eds.)
Theories and Models of Communication

CW00742269

Handbooks of Communication Science

Edited by
Peter J. Schulz and Paul Cobley

Volume 1

Theories and Models of Communication

Edited by
Paul Cobley and Peter J. Schulz

DE GRUYTER
MOUTON

The publication of this series has been partly funded by the Università della Svizzera italiana – University of Lugano.

ISBN: 978-3-11-029480-4
e-ISBN: 978-3-11-024045-0

Library of Congress Cataloging-in-Publication Data
A CIP catalog record for this book has been applied for at the Library of Congress

Bibliographic information published by the Deutsche Nationalbibliothek
The Deutsche Nationalbibliothek lists this publication in the Deutsche Nationalbibliografie; detailed bibliographic data are available in the Internet at http://dnb.dnb.de.

© 2013 Walter de Gruyter GmbH, Berlin/Boston
Cover image: Oliver Rossi/Photographer's Choice RF/Gettyimages
Typesetting: Meta Systems, Wustermark
Printing: Hubert & Co. GmbH & Co. KG, Göttingen

Printed in Germany

www.degruyter.com

Preface to *Handbooks of Communication Science* series

This volume is part of the series *Handbooks of Communication Science*, published from 2012 onwards by de Gruyter Mouton. When our generation of scholars was in their undergraduate years, and one happened to be studying communication, a series like this one was hard to imagine. There was, in fact, such a dearth of basic and reference literature that trying to make one's way in communication studies as our generation did would be unimaginable to today's undergraduates in the field. In truth, there was simply nothing much to turn to when you needed to cast a first glance at the key objects in the field of communication. The situation in the United States was slightly different; nevertheless, it is only within the last generation that the basic literature has really proliferated there.

What one did when looking for an overview or just a quick reference was to turn to social science books in general, or to the handbooks or textbooks from the neighbouring disciplines such as psychology, sociology, political science, linguistics, and probably other fields. That situation has changed dramatically. There are more textbooks available on some subjects than even the most industrious undergraduate can read. The representative key multi-volume *International Encyclopedia of Communication* has now been available for some years. Overviews of subfields of communication exist in abundance. There is no longer a dearth for the curious undergraduate, who might nevertheless overlook the abundance of printed material and Google whatever he or she wants to know, to find a suitable Wikipedia entry within seconds.

'Overview literature' in an academic discipline serves to draw a balance. There has been a demand and a necessity to draw that balance in the field of communication and it is an indicator of the maturing of the discipline. Our project of a multi-volume series of *Handbooks of Communication Science* is a part of this coming-of-age movement of the field. It is certainly one of the largest endeavours of its kind within communication sciences, with almost two dozen volumes already planned. But it is also unique in its combination of several things.

The series is a major publishing venture which aims to offer a portrait of the current state of the art in the study of communication. But it seeks to do more than just assemble our knowledge of communication structures and processes; it seeks to *integrate* this knowledge. It does so by offering comprehensive articles in all the volumes instead of small entries in the style of an encyclopedia. An extensive index in each *Handbook* in the series, serves the encyclopedic task of find relevant specific pieces of information. There are already several handbooks in sub-disciplines of communication sciences such as political communication, methodology, organisational communication – but none so far has tried to comprehensively cover the discipline as a whole.

For all that it is maturing, communication as a discipline is still young and one of its benefits is that it derives its theories and methods from a great variety of work in other, and often older, disciplines. One consequence of this is that there is a variety of approaches and traditions in the field. For the *Handbooks* in this series, this has created two necessities: commitment to a pluralism of approaches, and a commitment to honour the scholarly traditions of current work and its intellectual roots in the knowledge in earlier times.

There is really no single object of communication sciences. However, if one were to posit one possible object it might be the human communicative act – often conceived as "someone communicates something to someone else." This is the departure point for much study of communication and, in consonance with such study, it is also the departure point for this series of *Handbooks*. As such, the series does not attempt to adopt the untenable position of understanding communication sciences as the study of everything that can be conceived as communicating. Rather, while acknowledging that the study of communication must be multifaceted or fragmented, it also recognizes two very general approaches to communication which can be distinguished as: a) the semiotic or linguistic approach associated particularly with the humanities and developed especially where the Romance languages have been dominant and b) a quantitative approach associated with the hard and the social sciences and developed, especially, within an Anglo-German tradition. Although the relationship between these two approaches and between theory and research has not always been straightforward, the series does not privilege one above the other. In being committed to a plurality of approaches it assumes that different camps have something to tell each other. In this way, the *Handbooks* aspire to be relevant for all approaches to communication. The specific designation "communication science" for the *Handbooks* should be taken to indicate this commitment to plurality; like "the study of communication," it merely designates the disciplined, methodologically informed, institutionalized study of (human) communication.

On an operational level, the series aims at meeting the needs of undergraduates, postgraduates, academics and researchers across the area of communication studies. Integrating knowledge of communication structures and processes, it is dedicated to cultural and epistemological diversity, covering work originating from around the globe and applying very different scholarly approaches. To this end, the series is divided into 6 sections: "Theories and Models of Communication", "Messages, Codes and Channels", "Mode of Address, Communicative Situations and Contexts", "Methodologies", "Application areas" and "Futures". As readers will see, the first four sections are fixed; yet it is in the nature of our field that the "Application areas" will expand. It is inevitable that the futures for the field promise to be intriguing with their proximity to the key concerns of human existence on this planet (and even beyond), with the continuing prospect in communication sciences that that future is increasingly susceptible of prediction.

Note: administration on this series has been funded by the Università della Svizzera italiana – University of Lugano. Thanks go to the president of the university, Professor Piero Martinoli, as well as to the administration director, Albino Zgraggen.

Peter J. Schulz, Università della Svizzera italiana, Lugano
Paul Cobley, London Metropolitan University

Contents

Paul Cobley and Peter J. Schulz
1 Introduction

Abstract: This essay introduces the current volume and also gives a sense of its contents in relation to the entire series of *Handbooks of Communication Science*. It considers two broad definitions of communication and the problems of the 'objects' of communication science. It gives a sense of how the terms 'theory' and 'model' are used in the volume as well as some of the dilemmas that have existed in the field in respect of theory.

Keywords: Communication, definitions, theories, theory, models, research, object, science, interdisciplinarity

1 Defining communication and defining communication sciences

This volume is the inaugural handbook in the multiple-volume *Handbooks of Communication Science* – a major publishing venture which aims to offer a portrait of the current 'state of the art' in the study of communication. It was thought appropriate, then, that the first volume in the series of handbooks presented the main models and theories of communication, thus producing a sense of the frame in which much of the study of communication takes place. Yet, even before theories and models are considered, there needs to be an awareness of the problems involved in defining the object of communication science, in delineating the breadth of the domain of study and even the naming of the discipline which is devoted to research in that domain.

Definitions of communication commonly refer to etymology. Usually, this involves noting that the Latin root of 'communication' – *communicare* – means 'to share' or 'to be in relation with' and has its own relations in English to 'common,' 'commune,' and 'community,' suggesting an act of 'bringing together.' (cf. Cobley 2008, Rosengren 2000: 1; Schement 1993: 11; Beattie 1981: 34). Yet, this seemingly inclusive and broad definition of communication is not the only one that arises from the invocation of etymology. Peters (2008; cf. Peters 1996 and Craig 2000), somewhat differently, notes that 'communication' arises from the Latin noun *communicatio*, meaning a 'sharing' or 'imparting': arguably, this has little relation to terms such as *union* or *unity*, but rather links to the Latin *munus* (duty, gift). As such, its root senses have to do with change, exchange, and goods possessed by a number of people. These differently inflected senses of the roots of 'communication' have consequences for the way that the object of 'communication science' is conceived; but before expanding on this, let us consider how communication study has been understood.

Communication study is very much a modern discipline; yet it also has a long tradition and deep roots in philosophy and rhetoric. It was only in the twentieth century that it developed into an organized field with its own institutional history, its own appointed professors and academic journals. At this point, 'communication science' developed out of several traditions, including those of the also recently developing psychology and sociology. Like these disciplines, it has a proliferation of foci. The National Communication Association (NCA) in the United States sees communication study as a discipline focusing on:

> how humans use verbal and nonverbal messages to create meaning in various contexts (from two person groups to mass audiences) across cultures using a variety of channels and media. The discipline is especially interested in the impact of those messages on human behavior. Communication as a discipline includes the study of communication in interpersonal relationships, groups, organizations, and across cultures; rhetorical theory and criticism; performance studies; argumentation and persuasion; technologically mediated communication; and popular culture. (http://www.natcom.org, accessed 20 April 2012)

What is important here, firstly, is that communication study is envisaged as a *discipline* in its own right, in the same way that psychology and sociology have become. This status was not achieved without struggle – Donsbach (2006: 439) cites the famous 1930 statement by Tönnies on the proposal for the establishment of 'press research' alongside sociology in the German academic system: "Why would we need press research within sociology? We don't need a chicken or duck science within biology." Contemplating this leads to two further observations about communication study as a field – its interdisciplinarity (Cooren 2012; Livingstone 2009) and its similarities with sociology – which will be considered further below. Secondly, the range of communication, the proliferation of communication science's foci – across interpersonal relationships, groups, organizations, cultures – is crucial: communication study is no more to be defined solely as the study of mass media as it is to be depicted as focused on isolated linguistic exchanges between individuals.

Although it is already a broad church and may have to become ever more Catholic in its embrace of communicative phenomena in the future, communication science is not the study of everything that can be conceived as communicating. Instead, it can be described in terms of two very general approaches to its object which have come to a head in the last 100 years:
- a semiotic or linguistic approach associated particularly with the humanities and developed especially where the Romance languages have been dominant;
- a quantitative approach associated with the hard and the social sciences and developed, especially, within an Anglo-German tradition.

These two broad approaches have informed investigation into communication both at the level of forming the discipline's *theory* as well as its actual *collection of data*. Yet, the relationship between these approaches and between theory and research has not always been straightforward. Furthermore, the relationship has unfolded in the West largely independent of Asiatic culture and its different conceptions of the act of communication. The key factors in this uneven development are inherent in communication study and intimately connected; they concern both communication study's fragmentation and its object.

Before considering these, a few words should be offered on the designation 'communication science.' In the last century and a half, many disciplines have claimed 'scientific' status for themselves. Often, the claim is made to bolster that discipline, giving it a reputation for truth and rigour that it may not necessarily deserve. The claim has sometimes assisted institutionalization of disciplines, underpinning the establishment of university departments and the winning of grants for research in the area. On the other hand, and often as a backlash, the term 'science' has sometimes been considered derogatory or precisely indicative of an undeserved status. Particularly in the 'postmodern' moment in which science has been one of the 'grand' or 'metanarratives' (Lyotard 1984) to which people have expressed credulity, it has been assumed not only that science does not embody a narrative of progress but that it is open to question for its self-justifications, its vacillations, its uncertainty, its sexist and other ideological pre-dispositions. There is understandable resistance, therefore, to the term 'communication science.' Yet, the study of communication has not just been the province of Anglophone academia. Indeed, arguably its major constituency is in Germany. Certainly, communication study is pursued at a consolidated institutional level not just in the UK and North America but in a number of European countries and, increasingly, in Asia. In these areas 'science' tends to have a connotation which differs from that of the English term and is associated, instead, simply with disciplinary rigour and the virtues of the higher learning in general, in contrast to, say, anecdotal or journalistic accounts of phenomena. As such, 'communication science,' like 'the study of communication,' designates the disciplined, methodologically informed, institutionalized study of communication rather than the guaranteed path to truth and progress (see also Craig, Chapter 3). However, it is clear that one problem regarding how communication science derives or constructs its models – a problem that informs the concern over the designation 'science' – arises over communication study's object and its fragmentation.

1.1 Communication science and its objects

A concern about communication science as a discipline is its very fragmentation. It is a domain made up of many sub-domains and sub-disciplines. This is undeniable; yet the domain of communication has all the attributes that render it an established discipline. It is an institutionalized field, with journals, associations, departmental structures, professorial chairs and all the paraphernalia contributing to the organization of attempts to maintain quality of investigation and scientific status. As with any other rigorous discipline, one can find out about its key issues by consulting a large number of core journals, esteemed and peer-reviewed, as well as journals that may have less esteem for varying reasons. The discipline, like any other, monitors rigour in its research methods which are recognized by numerous national research councils. In Europe, the subject area is well embedded in universities in countries such as Germany, Denmark, the Netherlands, Belgium, Sweden, Norway, Spain, parts of Italy, Switzerland, Austria (with the UK as an anomalous case where, notwithstanding the London School of Economics, communication study has not formally embedded itself in the elite universities, although media studies is strong in a number of other UK universities). The European Communication and Research Association (ECREA), is the result of a merger of a number of relatively powerful communication associations across Europe. In the USA, communication science is professionally organized by the National Communication Association (NCA) and international organizations, including the International Communication Association (ICA). In Africa, the most prominent communication association is probably the South African Communication Association (SACOMM). In Asia, besides several national organizations, there is the Pacific and Asian Communication Association (PACA). It should be remembered, though, that communication study is not just concentrated in the work of professional societies and institutional structures. At the margins of the field and domain there is much work that is not easily assimilated into professional concerns and, in some cases, is not currently easy to assimilate into the project of communication science as a whole. Examples might include the output of researchers and teachers working on scripts, some journalism, creative writing, some aspects of communicative efficiency, and so on.

This last point has a direct bearing on the conceptualizing of communication science and how it develops theories and models in that it raises the issue of what might be the object of this discipline. If we were to compare communication science with medicine, the immediate impression is that the latter seems to have a clearer, defined sense of its object – there may be some local debate about what medicine's object is, but there is a clear consensus regarding what medicine is *not* about. Communication study is different: there is no clear consensus regarding its object and, indeed, it is constantly compelled to chase new objects. In a case of appendicitis, medicine will employ such procedures as diagnosis, prognosis, surgery, medical and biochemical analysis of the inflammation and so on (notwithstanding the possibility of interrogating the matter with reference to medical sociology, health psychology and other means allied to medicine). What is outstanding is that in such cases medicine has a clear sense of pathology (one can say this to an extent about psychology, too). As such, appendicitis is palpably 'bad,' an 'evil' that demands cure or amelioration. However, the equivalent situation does not hold in communication science. Many people, including communication researchers and teachers, may believe that the communication phenomenon of pornography is 'bad'; but there is certainly no consensus on this issue. For communication science, it is still difficult to arrive at a foolproof definition of pornography. In the second place, a definitive account of the 'effects' – if any – of pornography on all people, of all different kinds, is a long way away. The object of communication science is therefore underdetermined and inescapably so. Furthermore, there are numerous reasons for this. If we take an example from the foundation of medicine, we know that Hippocrates (1983 [c. 430–330 BC]: 185) advanced medical science by observing that a symptom exists as such when it is found to be identical in Delos, Scythia and in Libya. Where the object of communications is concerned, the opposite is the case: the object will be subject to sometimes significantly different degrees of difference according to geography and context. This is the reason, too, that the study of communication can never be organized according to the implementation of just one method, typically either adopted from a social science template or from a humanities one. The frequently extreme variation and richness of the cultural context in which communication takes place dictates that a diverse set of methods is crucial to the task of attempting to unravel the nature of communication in different places and contexts. This is not to say that the object of communication science can be simply summed up as 'cultural signs' or 'signs in context.' Whilst these are dominant in communication science, there are also endeavours which serve to illustrate the illusory basis of the nature/culture divide. One of these is the investigation of communication disorders (Rieber 1981; Damico et al. 2010); another is biosemiotics (see Cobley, Chapter 12).

Unlike medicine, then, it is difficult to say what communication science is *not* about. Communication is sufficiently general that it suffuses other disciplines or objects. This is so to the extent that it is even easy to find examples in which the interaction of cells or other organic entities are said to be involved in 'communication.' Often, this term is used in a self-consciously metaphorical way. Yet, on the same level, it would be strange to encounter a sociology of neurons or the philosophy of metals. Communication science, of course, is not alone in having a diverse profusion of objects. Because of their focus on objects which change according to issues of sociality, geography, time, and context, both communication and sociology, despite their many differences, are fragmented. Communication science and psychology, again with many differences, have a slightly different experience of fragmentation, with the latter discipline being fragmented in some areas and unified in others. There is really no single object of communication science. However, if one were to posit one possible object it might be the human communicative act – often conceived as "someone communicates something to someone else". This, of course, is the thread of one of the most fundamental models of communication offered by Lasswell (1948: 37): "Who says what to whom in what channel and with what effect?" Of course, it is well known that Lasswell's model leaves out all manner of noise and contextual matters as well as embedding assumptions such as that there is necessarily any 'effect' in communications. The contributions in Section 2 of this volume, 'Components of communication,' are very much alive to this fact and point out the most salient shortcomings of the model where relevant. Indeed, we might add that in addition to questioning the character of the 'who,' 'what,' 'whom,' 'channel' and 'effect,' it would not be impossible to make a credible argument about the way in which the elements in between – 'says' (glottocentric), 'to' (attributing intentionality), 'in' (a spatial metaphor privileging dissemination over representation), 'and with what' (assuming an attuned destination) – are open to criticism because they do not account for the entirety of the vicissitudes of communications. Nevertheless, as a hook for discussion and as a short mnemonic for recalling the general object of communication science, Lasswell's formula still serves.

There is a problem, though, with too great a degree of generality in the study of communication. The idea of 'pan-communication,' for example – the belief that *everything* communicates in some way or another – is one possible position that could be taken in communication. However, it is not desirable for this series of Handbooks nor, we believe, for communication science as a whole. There are a number of reasons for this. Firstly, it is not clear that everything *does* communicate. There are some objects which harbour the potential to communicate but seldom do play a part in the world of communication; there are also things which remain resolutely on the fringes of experience and are not considered in their capacity – however limited – to communicate. More importantly, a pan-communication perspective tends to prevent rather than promote investigation; it presents an unlimited array of objects about which it is difficult say anything regarding what unifies them or in what way they are related. As with all academic work, communication science is compelled to identify common features and patterns which will illuminate the workings of its objects. Indeed, in the etymologically-inflected definitions at the commencement of this Introduction, there are clear imperatives with respect to this task. One definition – invoking 'community' and 'bringing together' – tends towards a proliferation of communication science's objects; the other – focusing on exchange, gift, participation and the way that a municipal impulse creates an event – lends itself to a more specific set of contextualized objects or processes. At the root of communication science, to be sure, it is possible that a broad conception of communication would be tenable. This would include communication among animals and plants. However, communication scientists have been mindful of the fact that the entire field would be untenable if its central conception of communication was too broad. The way that communication science has so far manifested itself has meant that the key concern has been with human communication. There remains a residual concern about the extent to which there is continuity of communication, from plants, through animals, to humans, plus a concomitant concern that 'communication' as applied to say, cells, is merely 'metaphorical' but, as yet, this has not been developed. Yet, it should be qualified that, insofar as communication science takes as its object human communication, the act of 'communication' is not reified. What the study of communication is concerned with is *not* communication as a material and 'finished' entity. Rather, it is concerned with the manifold nature of human behaviour in communication. Stating this does not amount to sympathy with the discredited project of 'behaviourism,' nor is it an alignment with the so-called behavioural sciences. Instead, it indicates that the object of communication science is an empirical entity which, far from being stable and consisting of matter, is susceptible to the vagaries of changes in human behaviour and historical forces.

1.2 Defining communication theories and models

One of the great achievements in the definition of communication science in recent years has been the *International Encyclopedia of Communication* in 12 volumes (2008) edited by Wolfgang Donsbach. It represents a major step in the task of establishing a sense of the range of objects of communication science. However, in its definition of terms and outlining of topics, it is not necessarily designed to offer a sense of ongoing research, the 'state of the art' in communication science or an overview of the materials that will equip the field to meet future challenges. We see the present series of Handbooks of which the current volume is the first as the next step in the *Encyclopedia*'s synoptic work. Important to the current project is the constitution of the field – for this reason, the editors of the other Handbooks and the contributors to this volume are leading and agenda-setting scholars. The task for this volume, ahead of the other Handbooks, is to consider the rough structure for the field that arises from the range of its pursuits (intercultural communication, organizational communication, broadcasting and so forth), to set this against the areas of communication science that are established globally (the study of communicative competence, rhetoric, political communication including 'influence,' 'persuasion,' etc., commercial communication, also including 'influence,' 'persuasion,' etc., the study of media) and rising fields such as the study of communication technology or health communication, and to focus on the key models/theories that have developed sometimes from specific areas but have had consequences for communication study as a whole. To do this, of course, we need to have an understanding of what constitutes a 'model' or 'theory.' As a field, communication science has been very profligate in its spawning and naming of theories locally. Part of this volume's remit is to decide what a 'theory' or 'model' is as well as presenting the most important of these.

As a start, we can describe a model as a simplified picture of a part of the real world. It represents characteristics of reality, but only *some of them*. Like a picture, a model is much simpler than the phenomena it is supposed to represent or explain. For example, a model of an aeroplane resembles the real aeroplane with respect to some parts of an aeroplane – wings, tail, wheels, etc. – although it is likely to miss other characteristics – for example, wing flaps and slats. Considering the model, we can learn something about the size or the proportion of wings and fuselage, but this would not necessarily tell us anything about its speed (see also Lanigan, Chapter 4).

In a similar manner, a theory is supposed to represent or explain the phenomena to which it refers. There are plenty of definitions of what a theory is. Some scholars describe theory as a symbolic construction (Kaplan 1964: 296), others as "a set of interrelated constructs (concepts), definitions, and propositions that present a systematic view of phenomena by specifying relations among variables, with the purpose of explaining and predicting the phenomena" (Kerlinger and Lee 2000: 11). What is common in these as well as in other definitions is the fundamental idea that a theory consists of abstract or concrete concepts or constructs that function as representations or means by which we are able to understand and handle the complex reality. Concepts are "building blocks" (Jaccard and Jacoby 2010: 10) for all thinking and understanding of the physical and social world around us, regardless of whether these blocks are used by scientists or non-scientists. In addition, a theory implies a *statement* about relationships between the concepts or constructs that are inherent to it. There are different types of such statements. These may connect concepts and constructs; in addition, many theories in the social sciences include either relational or causal statements. A relational statement describes the association or correlation between concepts. In practice, it means that the existence of one concept conveys information about the existence of another concept. A causal statement, in contrast, means that one concept is considered to be the cause of a second concept. Despite the fact that theories differ in many respects and have been classified in different types of theories, at the core of all theories stands the fundamental idea of a set of statements about the relationship between concepts or constructs (Jaccard and Jacoby 2010: 28). Something very similar applies also to models: they always include concepts, constructs and the relations between them. This is why, in this volume, both terms, theory and model, are used interchangeably.

From this perspective, scientific knowledge of a discipline is basically nothing more than a corpus of theoretical statements in the aforementioned sense. Theorizing or modelling includes the conceptualization of phenomena in terms of a set of concepts or constructs and relationships among them. Learning what a discipline is about and what is the common wisdom in this field means studying its major theories and models. That is what this first volume of the Handbooks series intends to do.

Yet, it should be acknowledged that while theories have arisen in different areas of communication science, the work of forging theory is far from over. In an essay that has lost none of its acumen since it was written more than 20 years ago, Charles Berger (1991) asked (and answered!) the question of why there have been so few genuine communication theories. He found that certain historical legacies, a fixation on methodology at the expense of theory and risk aversion on the part of researchers had made theory parochial and almost utterly context-dependent. Not that much has changed since Berger's essay and scholars in the field still struggle with the shortage of theories, for which new explanations were found since Berger described his. Many theories in the field have been borrowed from other disciplines, mainly from sociology, social psychology and political science, and adapted to the needs and interests of communication science. And, as Berger notes, communication science has not yet exported as much as it has imported from other fields; as such, communication research has not yet become an autonomous scientific enterprise with its own theoretical frameworks. What often happened was that communication theorists refined existing theoretical frameworks from other disciplines rather than developing their own which then could have been embraced by other disciplines.

The question of why theories are so important in the field leads us to one additional observation. Communication science provides us with extensive knowledge about the world in which we live. Such knowledge of what happened in the past, what is happening right now and what will happen in the future would, however, be incomplete if it did not also tell us *why* certain events are likely to happen. So, communication theories provide us with an *explanation* for the phenomena they also describe (hopefully accurately). In fact, the explanation of observed phenomena is at the core of any theory. Once we are able to explain why certain things happen, this will also allow us, at least to a certain extent, to predict what is likely to happen in the future (see also Cobley, Chapter 12). Both explanation and prediction are constitutive parts of a theory. Both function as guidance regarding our understanding of some aspects of our experience: they allow us to say, with a high degree of probability, what is going to occur and re-occur. With respect to this explanatory power it is not difficult to understand why communication science continues to claim that the field needs mainly theory-based research.

Theories are good or useful to the extent that they explain, allow us to predict and to the extent that they *fit* our experience of events and reality. Theories may be rejected simply because they do not fit, meaning they do not make sense in light of our experience, or lack credibility. In the 1990s especially, postmodernism questioned the basic assumption in communication theory, which is based on the idea of fit – that is, the correspondence between the relations of concepts and constructs as conceived in theories, on the one side, and the empirical data that more or less fit these concepts and relations on the other side. Postmodern thinking, in opposition to this idea, holds that correspondence or 'consensus' are intrinsically modernist notions that lead to totalitarian and totalizing ways of thinking. Indeed, postmodernism implies that there cannot be *one* correspondence or consensus but, instead, that there are many possible correspondences which are often in conflict with others. Additionally, postmodernism rejects the idea of a reasoning, rational subject at the centre of any theory and replaces it with an 'individual' that is conceived of as a product of various discursive practices and knowledge structures. Without discussing the details of this critical approach toward theory, it should be sufficient to mention at this point that by the same token that postmodernism criticizes the traditional idea of theory, it also tends to imply that its own approach – based on the recognition of numerous contingent forces – is somehow more 'fitting'. Ultimately, this prevents communication science from developing sounder theories and 'fits' in the future. It threatens to be the end of a number of fields, but especially communication science. This is the case not so much because of postmodernism's critique of consensus and empirical certainty; rather, it is because of the way that postmodernism has attempted to encourage communication theory to shut up shop and to fall back on the risk aversion and fixation on methodology that Berger so cogently delineated. One of the objectives of the current book is to contribute to ensuring that this does not happen.

1.3 Theories and models in the field

The way that theories and models are figured in this volume corresponds to the way in which the series of Handbooks has been conceived. The series aims to *integrate* knowledge of communication structures and processes, not to split them into little pieces. It is committed to a pluralistic approach to the field, both in terms of theories and methods. It is supposed to document the current state of knowledge in the field, whilst also describing the intellectual roots of that knowledge. It seeks a coherent terminology whilst acknowledging that this is not possible in all instances. And it embraces any theory or model that can enlighten communication processes.

Following the present volume on theories and models of communication, the Handbooks are divided into five areas, the last being a single volume on the futures for communication science. The first area of volumes is on messages, codes and channels. Issues to do with these feature strongly in the current volume: the essays in this volume loosely arranged around Lasswell's formula for communication study necessarily consider the message (especially 'What') and channel. The channel, of course, takes in communication technology, verbality, nonverbality, and other visual communication. Code is particularly important in considering communication because it has common and specialized definitions, involving either a very specific function or a more varied one associated with the many different forms of communication – verbal, nonverbal, specifically visual and connected to different communication technologies (see also Cobley, Chapter 12). Moreover, we must consider where and how the messages, channels and codes of communication are studied. The centrality of verbal communication to communication science derives to a great extent from its institutionalization. The history of the study of nonverbal communication is marked by its almost total lack of institutionalization globally. Visual communication (as opposed to, say, auditory communication) is an example of an area that has become institutionalized for specific historical reasons. The study of communication technology is remarkable for its rapid institutionalization and the fact that it is related to other endeavours by virtue of involving investigation of the extensions of human processes.

Models and theories of communication also need to attempt to account for the matters in the third section of volumes within this series: mode of address, communicative situations and contexts. Any kind of communication takes place in a given context – narrow, broad, intermediate, rule-bound – its mode. It is through mode (conceived in this way) that some traditions in communication science come together: interpersonal communication, small group communication, mass communication. Additionally, if one compares speech communication and mass communication, it is notable that they have much in common and study can be carried out on this basis. Yet, if the communication situation changes – for example, if the communication is taking place during a war – the comparison can be rendered invalid. Thus, there are fluctuating differences and similarities in interpersonal communication, mass communication and organizational communication that theories and models must take into account.

Communication is also studied according to a range of methodologies which have been developed in the history of communication science for their honed ability to address questions that arise from both communication in specific areas and communication across a number of areas. Commonly in research the object and method are intertwined. However, it should be remembered that what one finds is not always *entirely* determined by how one looks for it – sometimes research in a specific area of communications throws up unanticipated empirical developments. Some developments in some areas (obvious examples are developing technologies or burgeoning social networks) will create new research areas. So, whether one is carrying out research using quantitative or qualitative research methods in a particular area of the communication landscape, theories and models are not extraneous. If studying the rapid growth of online social networks in the last decade, then the body of work on network theory (see Chapters 4, 5, 12 and 19 by Lanigan, Baecker, Cobley and Self respectively) should have enabled at least some contextualizing projection regarding the growth of contemporary social networking. In line with theory, as well as with new objects, research methods sometimes have to be adjusted. This may go hand-in-hand with the development of new (sub)fields and with consequent effects on the methodology of research in those (sub)fields. Journals and publications in the field are usually taxed with the task of representing new methods and developments.

As has been noted, one of the dilemmas facing theories and models of communication is that the objects of communications seem to proliferate to such an extent that they have created the impression of a very fragmented field. Even with the task of successfully representing the 'state of the art,' which is central to this Handbooks series, there is the problem of rapidly developing (sub)fields or 'application areas' before the series is finally complete. The growth of new areas with features that have not been anticipated can undermine communication models. This is especially the case in the present when it is clear that communication technology and its availability has meant that there are 'amateur' or 'domestic' producers of prominent communications (for example, citizen journalists) who would, in previous decades, be considered as mere consumers. This upsets, among other things, models of the audience in communications (see Chapter 21, Shoemaker, Riccio and Johnson). Thus, the 'application areas' in this series of Handbooks will be covered by volumes on Health Communication, Educational/Instructional Communication, Science Communication, Journalism and others. However, it may be necessary to supplement these in the coming years with volumes on such fast developing areas as crisis communication.

Even at this stage, communication science is still a youthful field and the fact that vibrancy is problematic for the development of completely watertight theories and models is a small price to pay for the knowledge of human behaviour that its research yields. Ultimately, while theory is a conceptualization of phenomena in terms of a set of concepts or constructs and relationships among them, it is also a map helping those outside and within the field to find their way round.

2 Organization of the volume

Each of the essays in this volume begins with an abstract foreshadowing what is to follow. For quicker reference, still, on the collection of essays as a whole and how to use the volume, some comments are offered here.

Following this Introduction which has focused on communication study and its objects as a *theoretical* foundational matter for theories and models, Eadie and Goret's Chapter 2 presents a historically-orientated overview of that matter. The volume is then divided into two sections. The first of these features 17 contributions which present the key theories or models of communication. The second section is made up of some short and more focused chapters on 'components' of communication. The classic, five-point model of Lasswell has been taken as the departure point for this project: so there are chapters on how 'Who' has been conceived in communication study, as well as 'What,' 'Whom,' 'Channel' and 'Effect.' As has been seen, Lasswell's model is far from being the final word on the components of communication and, as the chapters will show, even while serving as a basis, the model has had to be adapted or pronounced as lacking full adequacy in the face of communication's mutability, fragmentation, geographical and contextual situatedness.

The section on 'Theories and models' begins with Craig's (Chapter 3) discussion of how theories and models are actually constructed in communication science. It gives a strong sense of the way that this takes place in the context of different disciplines. This is then followed by chapters that discuss particular models from specific areas of the study of communication or that have fed into contemporary communication science. Lanigan's chapter (Chapter 4) pits information theory and its model of signification against communication theory with its model of meaning. Following this, Baecker's chapter (Chapter 5) outlines systemic theories of communication in the wake of Shannon and Weaver's 1949 model.

The next three chapters find models in the 'bases' of communication. Lieberman's (Chapter 6) is concerned with the motor control, cognitive flexibility and creativity that give rise to communication in primates. Siegert and von Rimscha (Chapter 7) review networks and regulation as well as their consequences in considering the economic bases of communication while Hamelink (Chapter 8) gives an overview of the key issues that make up the normative bases of human communication: fairness in speech, freedom of speech, responsibility, confidentiality and truth in communication.

In Chapter 9, Tindale considers the ways in which communication has been shown to be 'efficient' by way of the traditions of argumentation and rhetoric, plus more recent evaluations of the communication process by research into Artificial Intelligence. Chapter 10, by Greene and Dorrance Hall surveys the range of cognitive theories of communication, showing how they have sometimes been complementary and sometimes competing, and offering some syntheses. Then Trevarthen and Delafield-Butt (Chapter 11), consider the evidence in human development which indicates that learning of communication, particularly 'language,' takes place from the ante-natal stage onwards.

The three chapters that follow outline traditions that have had a considerable (sometimes unacknowledged) influence on communication. Chapter 12 by Cobley traces the way in which models of communication in semiotics, especially those giving rise to 'code' and 'text,' have contributed to communication science. Wharton (Chapter 13) discusses the bases of pragmatics or action-orientated theories of communication. Bangerter and Mayor (Chapter 14) then go on to consider the influence of the action-orientation in attempts in communication science to understand the relations of communication and cognition.

In the more demonstrably public environment of communication are the following four chapters. Through the consideration of a range of findings from areas including cognitive dissonance, computational theories, dual process models and affectively-orientated theories, Shen (Chapter 15) discusses the way in which communication has been conceived in terms of its possibility to shape, reinforce, or change the responses others. Moy and Bosch (Chapter 16) discuss not only how public communication is theorized but also how it might be underpinned by normative models of what constitutes 'the public.' Chapter 17 concentrates more on media, with Crowley's essay on meditation theories as explorations not just of media but also symbolic exchange and interaction. Finally in this section, Chapter 18 by Schrøder gives an account of socio-cultural models of communication in which the central exemplar is so-called 'British cultural studies' and, within that, Hall's formulation of the encoding/decoding model.

Section 2 addresses the components of communication within a loosely Lasswellian frame. Chapter 19 by Self considers 'Who' in relation to 'strong effects,' 'limited effects,' 'structural effects' and 'semiotic effects' models. Chapter 20 on 'What' sees Hample considering the message in terms of the way that arguments are constructed. 'Whom' (Chapter 21) by Shoemaker, Riccio and Johnson looks at the ways in which audiences have been conceptualized over the last century and points to the way that models of audiences proposed by researchers have often been problematic because they have paid too little attention to change. In the essay on 'Channel' (Chapter 22), Bolchini and Lu see their subject in terms of the 'instrumentation' of communication and they analyse it in general terms and with reference to contemporary interactive media and the internet. Finally, Oliver, Limperos and Woolley (Chapter 23) interrogate models of 'effect,' identifying three broad classes: cumulative, immediate and interpretative.

The chapters in the volume have been designed to be read on their own or in groups with other chapters in the volume or as a whole statement, along with the Introduction, of the current constitution of theory in communication science. The chapters cross-reference each other at different stages in order to reduce repetition and to provide easy access to fuller discussions of various issues. However, there is some necessary repetition – for example, the topic of 'effects' crops up in a number of places because it has played such a key role in 'who,' 'what,' 'whom,' 'channel' and fields such as 'public communication.' Each chapter encourages research beyond the confines of this volume by offering suggestions for further reading.

References

Beattie, Earle. 1981. Confused terminology in the field of communication, information and mass media: brillig but mimsy. *Canadian Journal of Communication* 8 (1). 32–55.

Berger, Charles. 1991. Chautauqua: Why are there so few communication theories? *Communication Monographs* 58. 101–113.

Cobley, Paul. 2008. Communication: definition and concepts. In: Wolfgang Donsbach (ed.), *International encyclopedia of communication, Vol. II*, 660–666. Malden, MA: Blackwell.

Craig, Robert T. 2000. Communication. In: Thomas O. Sloane (ed.), *Encyclopedia of rhetoric*. New York: Oxford University Press.

Cooren, François. 2012. Communication theory at the center. Ventriloquism and the communicative constitution of reality. *Communication Theory* 62 (1). 1–20.

Damico, Jack S., Nicole Müller & Martin J. Ball. 2010. *The handbook of language and speech disorders*. New York: WileyBlackwell.

Donsbach, Wolfgang. 2006. The identity of communication research. *Journal of Communication* 56. 437–448

Donsbach, Wolfgang (ed.). 2008. *International encyclopedia of communication*. 12 vols. Malden, MA: Blackwell.

Hippocrates. 1983. [c. 430–330 bc]. *Hippocratic writings*. Chadwick, J. and Mann, W. N. (trans.). Harmondsworth: Penguin.

Jaccard, James & Jacob Jacoby. 2010. *Theory construction and model-building skills*. New York and London: The Guilford Press

Kaplan, Abraham. 1964. *The conduct of inquiry. Methodology for behavioral science*. New Brunswick and London: Transaction.

Kerlinger, Fred N. & H. B. Lee. 2000. *Foundations of behavioral research*. Wadsworth: Thomson Learning.

Lasswell, Harold D. 1948. The structure and function of communication in society. In: Lymon Bryson (ed.), *The communication of ideas*, 37–51. New York: Institute for Religious and Social Studies.

Livingstone, Sonia. 2009. On the mediation of everything. ICA Presidential address 2008. *Journal of Communication* 59 (1). 1–18.

Lyotard, Jean. 1984. *The postmodern condition: A report on knowledge*. Bennington Geoffrey and Massumi, Brian (trans.). Minneapolis, MN: University of Minnesota Press.

Mumby, Dennis K. 1997. Modernism, postmodernism, and communication studies: A rereading of an ongoing debate. *Communication Theory* 7 (1). 1–28.

Peters, John Durham. 1996. Sharing of thoughts or recognizing otherness? Reply to Logue and Miller. *Critical Studies in Mass Communication* 13 (4). 373–380.

Peters, John Durham. 2008. Communication: history of the idea. In: Wolfgang Donsbach (ed.) *International encyclopedia of communication. Vol. II*, 689–693. Malden, MA: Blackwell.

Rosengren, Karl Erik. 2000. *Communication: an introduction*. London and Thousand Oaks: Sage.

Rieber, Robert W. 1981. *Communication disorders*. Dordrecht: Springer.

Schement, Jorge Reina. 1993. Communication and information. In: Jorge R. Schement and Brent D. Ruben (eds.), *Between communication and information. Information and behaviour, Vol. 4*, 3–34. New York: Transaction.

William F. Eadie and Robin Goret
2 Theories and models of communication: foundations and heritage

Abstract: This chapter charts the historical influences on the theories and models that shaped the communication discipline. It illustrates the importance of U.S. and European scholars from not only the beginnings of the communication discipline, but including those who were pre-eminent in other academic disciplines such as sociology, psychology, political science and journalism, as well as examining emerging scholarship from Asia that focuses on understanding cultural differences through communication theories. The chapter traces the foundations and heritage of communication study from five perspectives: (1) communication as shaper of public opinion; (2) communication as language use; (3) communication as information transmission; (4) communication as developer of relationships; and (5) communication as definer, interpreter, and critic of culture.

Keywords: Public opinion, media messages, agenda setting theory, cultivation theory, language, cultural studies, rhetoric, general semantics, symbolic interactionism, relational communication

Communication study seems inherently multi-disciplinary, drawing theory and sharing concepts from psychology, sociology, political science and other social sciences. Indeed, many of the scholars who are considered pre-eminent in communication were not from the discipline of communication itself and the fact that their work shaped communication theory was a by-product and not the original intent of their work (Delia 1987; Rogers 1994).

Communication has deep roots as an area of inquiry, but its history as an academic discipline is relatively brief. The most comprehensive ancient texts on communication to which we have access are those of the Greek and Roman societies. In both societies, communication is defined as synonymous with rhetoric, although that term was contested between Plato and Aristotle. Plato, according to Peters's (1999) analysis, defined rhetoric as fostering the ability for humans to connect as *eros*, or at a soulful level through stylish and poetic language, while Aristotle's ideas about rhetoric are generally seen as explaining how humans influence each other ethically in public *fora*. Aristotle's ideas were frequently seen as cornerstones of democratic deliberation, while Plato's ideas provided a foundation for the study of literature. The differences between them were sometimes simplified to style ("mere rhetoric") vs. substance (rhetoric as an ancient and noble art). Nevertheless, major philosophers tended to write about rhetoric at least in passing. Rhetoric evolved distinctly from communication for at least half of the twentieth century, but eventually the two areas of study came to rival each other.

Communication's history is also somewhat contentious, as a communication disciplinary story starts with sociology and social psychology and then co-mingles with the study of journalism and speech before emerging as the dominant force in the stories of both of the latter (Eadie 2011). The study of communication developed primarily in the United States, though with considerable influence from European thinkers. In this chapter, we will trace some of the historical influences on contemporary thought in the communication discipline. In doing so, we will draw on the influence of U. S. and European scholars on the development of our ideas about communication phenomena, and we will touch on some emerging scholarship from Asia that shows potential for understanding cultural differences through communication ideas.

In structuring this chapter, we need to take into account differing ideas about the nature of communication. So, we will organize our survey around five broad categories of communication phenomena: (1) communication as shaper of public opinion; (2) communication as language use; (3) communication as information transmission; (4) communication as developer of relationships; and (5) communication as definer, interpreter, and critic of culture.

1 Communication as shaper of public opinion

Communication's roots in the formation of public opinion stem from the development of sociology as a discipline, primarily at the University of Chicago. Deliberately located in the midst of a working class urban neighborhood, the university took as its mission the study of its surroundings as a laboratory for societal improvement. Robert Park, the head of the nascent program that would come to define the university's mission, recognized early the role that communication technology could play in society. Park's (1922, 1952) theories of mass communication became the basis for his colleagues to begin to think, from a variety of perspectives, about how a variety of communication phenomena interacted with the formation and maintenance of society.

It was a journalist who brought the idea of public opinion into focus, however. Newspaper columnist Walter Lippmann chose to write for public, rather than scholarly consumption, but the thorough and eloquent manner in which he expressed his ideas led scholars to value his work. Lippmann's (1922) book, *Public Opinion*, became a touchstone for scholarship for many years to come.

Following World War I, concern arose in particular about the role of propaganda in shaping public opinion. Political scientist Harold Lasswell (1927) became an early advocate for studying how media could be used, particularly by governments, to influence public opinion through biased or incomplete messages. Media were looked on as powerful forces that could potentially affect large numbers of people in similar ways. The wide-spread panic that set in following the Halloween radio broadcast of, *The War of the Worlds,* H. G. Wells' story re-told as a series of radio news broadcasts, was seen as an example of the power of media to act as a "hypodermic needle" (Lowery and DeFleur 1995; Pooley 2006; Rogers 1994), injecting a powerful drug into the public consciousness.

Concern about the rise of Nazism and Fascism in Europe led to the first concerted research efforts in both mediated and face-to-face communication, in the 1930s. Interestingly, many of the scholars who participated in these efforts were European émigrés who sought to escape those two political movements. As outsiders (including Jews, who suffered under anti-Semitic attitudes then prevalent at major U. S. universities) these scholars found ways of supporting themselves by doing practical research on problems deemed to be of great interest either to U. S. corporations or to the government. From this research, which eventually was identified with social psychology, came a tradition of quantitative study of communication behavior.

During World War II, the U. S. government gathered scholars together in Washington, DC, to provide collective brainpower for managing the war effort and the sacrifices that were necessary at home. Research on propaganda and public opinion had already been underway in the 1920s and 1930s, and Paul Lazarsfeld and his associates' (1944) study of the 1940 election (see below for details) had debunked the idea that mass media messages had direct effects on voting behavior. Rather, these effects were often modulated by pre-existing attitudes, such as political party allegiances, and by interactions with influential people (who were labeled "opinion leaders"). Research conducted on group interaction as a tool of persuasion (e.g., Lewin 1943) demonstrated that commonly-held attitudes could be modified if "good of the whole" pressures were applied. All in all, research efforts during World War II set the stage for an explosion of communication study in the years following the end of the war.

Lazarsfeld and the Office of Radio Research studied how political advertisements during the presidential campaign of 1940 affected voters in Erie County, Ohio. This study, according to Lazarsfeld (1969: 330), was not originally intended to focus on voting habits but, instead, to test "a program of the Department of Agriculture, since its innovations made major changes in American behavior and … this Department … developed the most extensive use of the radio in support of its policies."

The Erie County study examined the changes in voters' opinions over a period of several months, expecting to find that the media messages they were exposed to had a direct effect on their voting behavior. Instead of showing a direct effect, however, the analysis of the results showed that voting decisions were completely unrelated to the messages the audience had heard (Barton 2001; Jeřábek 2001; Rogers 1994). These findings completely contradicted the prevailing thought of the day. The study further showed that opinion leaders developed their ideas through a variety of sources that included the media, and then influenced the members of their community through their social interactions. The voters who Lazarsfeld interviewed inevitably pointed to these influential individuals as the source of their information and the main influence on their voting decisions. This finding led Lazarsfeld to propose that there was another level of communication other than the media (Lowery and DeFleur 1995), a process he called the two-step flow of communication.

After Lazarsfeld's large-scale case study demonstrated that media messages played only a small role in directly influencing election results, research in this area for a number of years focused on conditions where media messages would play more or less of a role than face-to-face influence in the formation of public opinion. It was not until McCombs and Shaw (1972) produced data causing the re-thinking of the small-effects paradigm that research shifted to what these authors dubbed "the agenda-setting function of media." This function links press coverage with public ratings of importance with issues, and a study of the 1968 U. S. presidential election found a high correlation between these two items, given a three-week lag time. While these findings did not negate Lazarsfeld's idea of two-step flow, they identified for the first time a powerful direct effect for media messages on public opinion. Rather than persuade people or tell them what to think, argued the researchers, media tell them what is important to think *about*.

A companion theory, Cultivation (Gerbner 1973), argued that large effects from media could be generated based on the amount of time spent consuming media. Heavy users of media tended to distort perceptions of society to fit with media content to a far greater extent than did light users. For example, individuals who heavily consume news and news analysis from a particular point of view (e.g., in the U. S., Fox News or MSNBC) will be likely to distort news events to a greater extent than those who spent little to no time consuming content from these stations. While Cultivation Theory had uses outside of public opinion research, it, too, was a crack in the formulation that media had but small effect on public opinion.

In later developments, agenda-setting theorists demonstrated that media messages also had the capability to influence *how* individuals think about topics. In particular, these theorists developed the concepts of "framing" and "priming" to describe this process. Framing refers to the means by which media messages are presented. Frames provide salience for particular aspects of the message that have been selected by its creator to shape it from a specific perspective (Entman 1993). So, a news story about a crime can be framed from the perspectives of the victim, the perpetrator, or the investigating police officer and the same details can yield different impressions of the event. Priming, on the other hand, relates to how media messages are constructed to indicate to audiences what elements are important to use in judging the value of an object. To provide an example, a news analysis is priming its readers when its author states that performance on maintaining a healthy national economy is the most important element for forming judgments about the performance of U. S. presidents when they run for re-election. Such an analysis may cause its readers to overlook other measures of presidential performance and focus only on economic viability. President Ronald Reagan, who was a master of priming rhetoric, famously asked American voters whether they were better off than four years previously as a cornerstone of his campaign for a second term. Americans agreed overwhelmingly that they were and returned Mr. Reagan to office in a landslide vote.

The study of communication as a shaper of public opinion has focused primarily on means by which media messages influence the public's perceptions of issues and events. Research on how mediated and face-to-face communication combine to change behavior has integrated public opinion research with other communication phenomena to produce promising means for promoting individual and social good. These models have been used primarily to create campaigns for the betterment of individual and public health (e.g., Cappella 2006; Donohew et al. 1998).

2 Communication as language use

The turn of the twentieth century brought with it not only the investigation of stimulus and response as a direct cause of behavior but also an interest in philosophical quarters in how language is constructed and used. Early twentieth century interest in language use developed in both Europe and in the U.S. The study of language represented the variety of interests of the day, including interest in the nature of reality and the relationship of language to culture.

For example, Ferdinand de Saussure, working in Europe, and Charles Sanders Peirce, working in the U. S., are credited with formulating the theory of semiotics. Saussure was a Professor of Linguistics at the University of Geneva in the first decade of the twentieth century. He posited that linguistics would eventually be incorporated into a then unheard of science called semiology (later named semiotics), the term being derived from the Greek word *semeion*. Saussure argued that language is a system made up of linguistic signs that join a concept and a sound image. The sign, according to Saussure (1916/2000), is a psychological construct with a number of distinct properties which include arbitrariness.

Another approach to semiotics was undertaken by Roland Barthes who acted as an influential filter for Saussure's teachings. In particular, Barthes extended Saussure, developing the dual nature of the sign for the study of nonverbal communication, as well as language. In Barthes's (1957) volume, *Mythologies*, the overarching theme is that the majority of experiences a person has at a social or personal level begin with the linguistic sign – media artifacts, identity, narrative, communication with others, and so on. But linguistic behavior as a structure of experience derives far less from personal exchange than with how language is conveyed to the personal level from the public level, where lies the locus of social control, including control over language itself (Barthes 2000).

In fact, according to Barthes, linguistic signs with a forceful social meaning are not necessarily 'clear' but are rather ambiguous or deceptive in some way. Thus linguistic signs, as attributes of culture, lend themselves to 'myth', a 'language' devoted to the "decorative display of the *what-goes-without-saying*" which prevents the imposing "at the outset [of] a full meaning which it is impossible to distort" (Barthes 2000: 11, 132). Language may be unclear in a variety of ways, either because it is poetic or because it works by analogy. The key idea, for Barthes, is that language "lends itself to multiple contingencies" (132). Semiologists engage in this interpretive act, and it is up to the reader of myths to reveal their necessary function. That is because "in a language, the sign is arbitrary: nothing compels the acoustic image tree 'naturally' to mean the concept tree" (126). Instead, Barthes posited, there is a motivation for the sign to mean whatever it means from the habits and the traditions of the community of language users in which the word appears.

Where language use is intent on signifying a cultural meaning there is undoubtedly intent to affect the psychological experience of that meaning (Barthes 2000). Motivation, Barthes argued, is essential "to the very duplicity of myth: myth plays on the analogy between meaning and form, there is no myth without motivated form" (126). Barthes cited the innumerable images that the media use to convey a social message, to imply, without directly pronouncing, the superiority of a Eurocentric and bourgeois worldview. The communicated image conforms to what Barthes termed the "very principle of myth: it transforms history into nature ...[and] is not read as a motive, but as a reason" (129). In due course, he argued, values get conveyed with the authority of facts, all in the service of social control. Only when the receivers that would be recognized as decoders of language themselves effect language change is social control likely to shift. Thus, the "bourgeoisie hides the fact that it is the bourgeoisie and thereby produces myth; revolution announces itself openly as revolution and thereby abolishes myth" (146). (See also Chapter 12, Cobley.)

Somewhat in contrast to Barthes, interest in language use by Vygotsky (1971: originally published in 1934) and Ayer (1936) drew upon logical positivism and empiricism as a means of explaining the relationship of language to reality. Vygotsky saw language development as a function of experience with one's environment, using language to associate objects with thoughts and feelings. Ayer proposed the use of language as a means of verifying the logic of one's environment. Language in itself is not verifiable, but it can be used to understand what may be verified empirically.

A desire for empirical verification also pervaded the development of General Semantics, which started out as a theory of language use and became more a philosophy of communication than anything else. Begun by a Polish engineer named Alfred Korzybski (1933) and popularized in the U. S. by S. I. Hayakawa (1941), General Semantics began with the observation that language was not a logical system and ended by advocating for a series of devices designed to make communication based on language that was concrete, as opposed to abstract. General Semanticists envisioned a communication system with as little ambiguity as possible so as to promote understanding and thereby reduce conflict, particularly conflict between nations. The proposed system was based on a set of tools that would continually remind language users to aim for the lowest possible level of abstraction in both speech and writing.

Peirce's (cf. 1878) work on the philosophical movement known as pragmatism influenced a number of U. S. scholars interested in language use. Among those were John Dewey, whose book, *How We Think* (1910), became the basis for teaching generations of students the basics of collective decision-making, and George Herbert Mead, whose book, *Mind, Self, and Society* (1934, a posthumous rendering of his theory, based on lecture notes and working papers) became a basis for understanding how individuals interact with society through the use of signs and symbols. Mead and Dewey were colleagues at the University of Chicago for a time, and their interactions with each other and with colleagues were instrumental in developing the perspective that became known as the Chicago School of Sociology.

Communication scholars eventually pursued with gusto Mead's ideas about what was eventually called symbolic interactionism (Blumer 1969). Symbolic interactionism held that individual behavior was a function of the repertoire of roles available to an individual, as well as how that person diagnosed what role might be appropriate for a particular situation. Hart and Burks's (1972) concept of rhetorical sensitivity provided an early example of the influence of symbolic interactionism in communication study, as these authors combined rhetorical message-generation principles with symbolic interaction's emphasis on role-taking and adaptation. Eventually, symbolic interactionism gave way to social construction, as communication scholars adapted the work of psychologist Kenneth Gergen (1992, 1999) for use in communication research. Social construction derived from the work of Berger and Luckmann (1966), who argued that communication is dependent on intersubjective meaning that operates at a societal level but is subject to re-negotiation within individual and group relationships.

Kenneth Burke was a literary theorist whose ideas would prove to be highly influential in understanding of the rhetorical aspects of language use. Burke described language as a tool used by people to communicate and rationalize at a far deeper level than could be done by words themselves. Burke focused on the symbols people created to name things in his understanding of language. According to Holland (1955) when rhetoricians analyzed speeches, they tended to look at three aspects – what was said, why it was said and how it was said. Burke however, would argue that Holland's formulation did not go far enough and that a primary goal of criticism was to use "all [language instruments] that there is to use" (Burke,

1941: 23). For Burke, speeches were only one aspect of language instruments and he argued that a rhetoricians should not limit themselves to spoken text.

Burke proposed the Dramatist Pentad Theory, which analyzes events through five essential elements: "what was done (act), when or where it was done (scene), who did it (agent), how he did it (agency), and why (purpose)" (Burke 1945: xv). He adapted his terms of analysis from the theater in order to account for motivation, which he took to be a decisive category for the explanation of rhetorical events. Burke held that language is created hierarchically, that it reinforces hierarchies, and that humans cling to hierarchies to bring order to their lives through symbolic actions. Language for Burke is always layered with emotion. Every word is layered with judgment, attitude and feelings, and Burke further argued that because of this complexity, language functions either to bring people together or to separate them. When people identify with the language and symbols that a speaker is using, this bringing-together process creates what Burke called "consubstantiality." Like many scholars of language use, Burke's influence crossed disciplines. Communication scholars poring over Burke's work continue to find insights that reveal how language use not only communicates but can also influence communicators.

Of course, the study of language use overlaps with linguistics, including both its sub-fields of psycholinguistics and sociolinguistics. Yet, communication scholarship tends to focus more on the pragmatics of language use, as well as the effects of such use, while linguistics often focuses more on structure and function of language.

3 Communication as information transmission

Major strands of theory and research appeared in the U. S. following World War II. Most of them focused on information and transmission, or in other words, how to get a message from Point A to Point B in the most intact fashion possible. The key works associated with this perspective came from engineering, and the technological problems that drove the theorizing concerned the modernizing of the telephone system and the development of high speed computers that could process a great deal of information in a short span of time. Two books stood out in particular: Claude Shannon and Warren Weaver's (1949) *The Mathematical Theory of Communication* and Norbert Wiener's (1948) *Cybernetics*. Shannon and Weaver developed a theory that defined information as the reduction of uncertainty, and their primary concern revolved around how much "noise" (pure uncertainty) in any transmission could be tolerated before the message would be transmitted inaccurately. Wiener's work described the reduction of uncertainty in systems through feedback that would indicate a change of course was needed. Wiener's scholarship on the control of systems was instrumental in developing computers, which were popularly known as "thinking machines." Scholars who built on Shannon and Wiener's work attempted to model communication based on transmission of information, moderated by feedback. Some scholars (cf. Dupuy 2000) believed that these theories could be used to model thought, about which little was then known.

Indeed, a great deal of theory and research in communication and media based itself on the transmission model and continued to do so after the appearance of information theory and cybernetics. Two post-World War II research programs illustrated this approach. The first was the Yale Communication and Attitude Change Program, directed by Carl Hovland. Hovland had been one of the scholars who worked on propaganda research for the Federal government during World War II, and after the war he focused his efforts on understanding how people were influenced by other people and their messages to change their attitudes. According to McGuire's (1996) review of that period, Hovland succeeded because he was able to attract top-notch faculty and graduate students to work on the project and because his management style allowed for creativity of theory development while still keeping research focused on the overriding goal. Hovland's efforts made attitude change the major topic for social psychological research during the 1950s and 1960s.

The second came via the leadership of Wilbur Schramm, another veteran of the Federal government's propaganda research program. Schramm moved to Washington, DC, from the University of Iowa, where he was head of the famed Iowa Writers' Workshop. When the propaganda project ended, Schramm wanted to return to Iowa, but his position with the Writers' Workshop had been filled. Instead, Iowa asked Schramm to head its journalism school, and Schramm accepted the position with the condition that he be allowed to start an institute for communication research. Schramm's institute spurred the beginning of the field of journalism's association with mass communication scholarship, as opposed to scholarship about journalism itself. Under Schramm's tutelage, Iowa scholars and others attempted to take the theoretical work from information theory and social psychology and apply it more directly to understanding communication phenomena. Journalism scholars were joined in this effort by scholars from the field of speech who were energized both by Kurt Lewin's work on group dynamics and the Yale Group's scholarship on individual credibility in promoting attitude change. Schramm became a proselytizer for communication scholarship, and he began institutes at the University of Illinois and Stanford before affiliating with an institute in Hawaii after retirement (Rogers 1994).

Such models of communication as transmission began to break down in the 1960s. David Berlo's (1960) book, *The Process of Communication*, for example, presented what was then a traditionally linear transmission model of information flow but added the idea that communication was dynamic and cyclical and that research efforts to measure simple effects would ultimately fall short. Berlo urged scholars to account for process in their research, but he did not provide a clear means for so doing. It would take some years before scholars began to devise ways to measure communication as interaction and thus to downplay effects research. Indeed, measuring process can be a complex task, as illustrated by Luhmann's (2000) mathematical theorizing about the cyclic nature of media news.

In media research, the transmission model found continued life as part of research using Social Learning Theory and later, Social Cognitive Theory (Bandura 1986). Research conducted under the theme of learning the audience's uses and gratifications of media (Blumler and Katz 1974) later found the transmission model amenable for some time before succumbing to criticism that audiences were more active than the approach gave them credit (e.g., Reinhard and Dervin 2009).

But, the information transmission approach was not only about movement of data from one point to another. Shannon and Weaver's (1949) theory, for example, also focused on how information functioned either to increase or decrease entropy, or the level of uncertainty within a system. As Wiener (1948) noted, uncertainty is present in every system and is a healthy element, causing the system to self-correct via the use of negative feedback. Two different theorists applied this principle to specific situations, creating examples of a turn away from the development of grand theories of communication and moving toward more contained theories that provided more focused opportunities for testing. The first was Berger's Uncertainty Reduction Theory (Berger and Calabrese 1975), which was focused on communication between individuals who were just beginning a relationship. Drawing on information theory's central tenet that individuals process information for the purpose of reducing uncertainty, Berger and Calabrese laid out a set of variables such as amount of verbal communication, nonverbal affiliative expressiveness, information-seeking behavior, intimacy content of messages, reciprocity of information sharing, perceived similarity and liking between communicators, and degree of perceived shared communication networks. From these variables, the authors drew eight axioms and twenty-one theorems that served as the basis for a program of research that has continued through the present day.

A second use of the uncertainty principle emerged from the work of Karl Weick. An organizational psychologist, Weick (1969) proposed that organizing is a process that involves reducing uncertainty through the negotiation of organizational goals and routines. While previous theorists had assumed that organizations were formed to achieve goals, Weick contended that organizational goals evolved out of interaction among the organization's members. Weick called the process of individual negotiation with the organization and its members "sensemaking," and he proposed that organizations were loosely-coupled systems where collective meanings of messages and actions evolved over time. Weick's notions were radical in that they ignored organizational hierarchies in favor of the power of informal networks to define and influence collective thought and actions. Communication scholars eagerly embraced Weick's ideas about organizations and have used his sensemaking principle as a means of studying organizational culture, oftentimes employing qualitative data such as stories (e.g., Smircich and Calás 1987).

The information transmission model remains a dominant one in communication scholarship, though its nature has become more process-like and less linear over time.

4 Communication as developer of relationships

Relational communication scholarship emerged from a variety of sources, including anthropology, social and clinical psychology, social work and family studies, and systems analysis. It is likely that scholars from a number of disciplines influenced each other as common problems overlapped. For example, Schramm (1997), who was working on propaganda research during World War II in Washington, DC, shared a carpool with anthropologist Margaret Mead, who was working on conserving food for the war effort and whose program funded Kurt Lewin's (1948) work on using groups to solidify cooperation from homemakers to use what they might consider to be "inferior" cuts of meat in preparing meals for their families. Mead, in turn, was married to Gregory Bateson, whose work on family systems in the post-World War II era would develop the idea that double binds (communications where meaning was made deliberately unclear) were a basis for relational pathology (Bateson, et al. 1956).

Behavioral researchers approached relationships as a matter of perception (e.g., Heider 1946; Thibaut and Kelley 1959), while clinical psychologists defined relational intimacy in terms of degrees of authenticity (e.g., Buber 1947; Rogers 1961) and degree to which being in relationship with others allowed individuals to self-actualize (Maslow 1943) (see also Chapter 14, Bangerter and Mayor). In fact, Peters (1999), in his intellectual history of the idea of communication, argued that all curiosity about communication arises from a desire for connection at a number of levels: another's soul and/or intellect, which we cannot directly experience; those entities (such as plants and animals) that do not use symbols; and connection that is distinguished by authenticity that the participants do experience. The two groups often found themselves at cross-purposes, and they disagreed substantially about the nature of the phenomena they were studying.

Building on Bateson's work, Watzlawick et al. (1967) devised the basis of a formal theory of relational communication. In particular, the group's five axioms became the cornerstone of a number of research programs: (1) "one cannot not communicate"; (2) "every communication has a content and relationship aspect such that the latter classifies the former and is therefore a meta-communication"; (3) "the nature of a relationship is dependent on the punctuation of the partners' communication procedures"; (4) "human communication involves both digital and analogic modalities"; and (5) "inter-human communication procedures are either symmetric or complementary, depending on whether the relationship of the partners is based on differences or parity". Dubbed "the interactional view," Watzlawick et al.'s work led the study of communication in relationships away from both competing emphases: variable analysis and psychic connection.

The end of variable analysis did not spell the end of quantitative approaches to relational communication, however. Instead, quantitative research sought to blend verbal and nonverbal elements of communication behavior so as to demonstrate how those elements combine to produce interactive meaning. An exemplar of such an approach, Burgoon's (1978) Expectancy Violations Theory, proved to be a model of the genre. Burgoon revised her theory often and sometimes substantially based on the data she collected (c.f., Burgoon and Hale 1988), and the result of persistence and a willingness to reinterpret her findings has made the theory one of the most respected and robust of its type.

Relational communication has also been studied qualitatively, through interviews, personal narratives, and ethnographic approaches. An exemplar of a theory emerging from such study is Relational Dialectics Theory, which was developed by Leslie Baxter and her associates (e.g., Baxter and Montgomery 1996). Derived from the work of philosopher Mikhail Bakhtin (1986), the theory proposed that relationships are developed out of the push and pull of interaction. Some of the contradictory dynamics that the theory has studied are: (1) autonomy vs. connectedness (i.e., how much "I" and how much "we" are needed by relational partners); (2) favoritism vs. impartiality (i.e., how much is each partner treated "fairly," as opposed to how much each partner is valued as "special"); (3) openness vs. closedness (i.e., how much information is disclosed between partners, as opposed to how much information is kept private); (4) novelty vs. predictability (i.e., how much the relationship feels exciting and new, as opposed to how much it feels comfortable and old); and (5) instrumentality vs. affection (i.e., how much continuing the relationship is based on tangible rewards, as opposed to how much continuing the relationship is based on emotional rewards).

Relational communication replaced the former "interpersonal communication" as the designator for communication in face-to-face settings. The term implies that it is the relationship that is being studied, not the face-to-face context, and this subtle change in focus has made a great deal of difference in how theorizing in this approach to communication study has proceeded.

5 Communication as definer, interpreter, and critic of culture

The early works of the Frankfurt School, specifically critical theory, laid the foundation that led toward one of several paradigm shifts in communication theory during the post-World War II era. According to Jay (1973, 1980), Rogers (1994), Tar (1977) and others, critical theory is the term that refers to a specific tradition of thought that originated with Herbert Marcuse, Theodor Adorno, Max Horkheimer, and Walter Benjamin in the 1930s at the Frankfurt School and the Institute of Social Research in Germany. This theory synthesizes ideas advanced by Karl Marx and Sigmund Freud and positions media as having the potential to advance the agenda of the bourgeois while controlling the proletariat (Jay 1973; Tar 1977). Celikates (2006) posited that critical theory makes it possible for one to understand what is really happening in social reality and to explain these actions in terms of such constructs as socioeconomic structures and who in society has the power. Critical theory, Celikates (2006) further argued, questions and analyzes media, the production of media, and its agents (see also Chapter 18, Schrøder).

Not all critical models of communication followed the Frankfurt School line. In the early 1960s at the University of Birmingham in the United Kingdom, a group of scholars founded the Centre for Contemporary Cultural Studies (producing a body of work that later became synonymous with British Cultural Studies) because they had a desire to understand the changes in post-war British society within the structure of "a long retrospective historical glance" (Hall, 1992: 16). Hall (1980) argued that Cultural Studies "defines 'culture' as both the meanings and values which arise amongst distinctive social groups and classes on the basis of their given historical conditions and relationships, through which they 'handle' and respond to the conditions of existence" (63). An essential element of the new paradigm was to redefine and refocus the meaning of communication itself. Hall (1992) cited the practice of analyzing communication as similar to a circle of activity. The emerging idea was to think of communication as "structure produced and sustained through the articulation of linked but distinctive moments – production, circulation, distribution/consumption, reproduction" (128). This idea came to be known as structuralism (not to be confused with the same term applied to anthropology and linguistics) and had its roots not just in Marxist theory but in early semiotic theory, particularly the code-semiotics of Eco (Hall, 1980) (see also Chapter 12, Cobley). For Hall, though, there were inherent problems in the idea of structuralism such that the content of ideas gives way to patterns of ideas that may be contained in a communication, as well as the means or conventions, whether literary, linguistic, or social, by which the ideas are encoded and function toward making meaning.

The encoding of a communication event is only part of the process of communication itself, carrying no essential meaning without an audience (or receiver) to decode what the meaning is and, by decoding the message, the audience constructs the meaning. Hall (1992) provided the example of a TV news broadcast, which has an impact on the society in which the encoded message is transmitted only when the meanings are decoded. Drawing on the work of sociologist Frank Parkin, as well as semiotician Umberto Eco, Hall posited that there were three types of readings of meanings of a message when it was decoded. The dominant or preferred reading is produced by those whose status favors the preferred readings and therefore do not question the dominant ideology; the negotiated readings are produced by those who interpret the preferred reading as it is aligned with their societal status; and the oppositional readings are produced by those whose social status puts them in direct conflict with the dominant ideology.

Embedded in the foundation of British Cultural Studies is the work of Antonio Gramsci, specifically Gramsci's extension of the Marxist concept of hegemony. Gramsci argued that the bourgeois retained power not just through political, economic or violent control of the masses but ideologically through a cultural power that conveyed that the values of the "haves" are common sense values for all of society. If the working class believed they have the same values as the "haves" in society, they would maintain the status quo and not work to change society for the betterment of the working class. Gramsci also noted that "common sense is not something rigid and immobile, but is continually transforming itself" (Hall 1982: 73). Stuart Hall and the British Centre for Cultural Studies applied Gramsci's theory of cultural hegemony to the examination of racial representations in the media by illustrating racist stereotypes that Hall called the "grammar of race" embedded in early films of the twentieth century (Hall 1995: 21) (see also Chapter 18, Schrøder).

Jürgen Habermas, a student of Theodor Adorno, added further to the foundation laid by the Frankfurt School and the British Centre for Contemporary Cultural Studies. During his tenure at the Frankfurt School, Habermas focused his research on how a new public sphere materialized during both the age of Enlightenment and the French Revolution in Europe and the American Revolution in the United States and how this new public sphere encouraged political discourse and closely examined language, meaning, and understanding during political discourse (Habermas 1973, 1974, 1984, 1989; Jay 1973; Kellner 2000; Wiggerhaus 1994). Habermas (1974) posited that access to the public sphere was granted to all citizens and that the dialogue about political power did not always exist, it "grew out of a specific phase of bourgeois society and could enter into the order of the bourgeois constitutional state only as a result of a particular constellation of interests" (50). Using the U.S. wars in both Vietnam and the Gulf Wars as examples, Habermas developed the view that public opinion and understanding of the wars were primarily shaped by "the demonstrative rationality of the military planning, and the unparalleled presence of the media" (Habermas, 1994: 6). The "encoding" objectives of those in power were, in Habermas' view, involved in managing how much information and precisely what information to dispense to the general public in a way that was meant to influence public opinion and to install a "staged reality" that existed not just for the general public, but for the "mediators" of public information as well. The act of installing a staged reality, Habermas argued, transformed media from a place that aided rational discourse to one that limited such discourse to what media corporations wished to discuss (see also Chapter 5, Lanigan). Habermas also examined early theories of semantics and put forth the theory of meaning. He argued that the "meaning of sentences, the understanding of sentence meanings cannot be separated from language's interest in relation to the validity of statements" (1984: 276). Habermas further argued that by understanding the validity of statements, a communicative action occurs. Habermas posited that communicative action occurs when at least two parties "reach an understanding about the action situation and their plans of action in order to coordinate their actions by way of agreement" (86).

Besides the cultural studies approach, which often took societal critique as a given (see also Chapter 18, Schrøder), theorizing and scholarship have also been devoted to understanding communication across cultures or across groups within cultures. Cultural anthropologist Edward T. Hall (1959, 1966) provided the genesis of this scholarship with his sweeping ideas of types of culture (high context, low context), space (Hall introduced the concept of proxemics and documented how cultures vary in their use of space), and time (Hall originated the ideas of polychromic and monochromic time). Much of the theorizing in this area of study built on either the information transmission or the relational approach (c. f., Gudykunst 2005), but one attempt to develop a unique cultural perspective on communication has come from the work of Guo Ming Chen. Chen, who splits his time between the University of Rhode Island and the South China University of Technology, has outlined in a series of articles (Chen 2001, 2002a, 2002b, 2002c, 2004, 2005, 2006) a vision of communication based in several Asian concepts: harmony, the polarity of the yin and the yang, the Tao, the I Ching, and Confucian spirituality. Assuming Chen's formulation is developed further through research, it could provide a new direction for theorizing about how communication is culture-specific.

6 Concluding remarks

In 1999, Robert T. Craig summarized different theoretical strands in communication scholarship into seven "traditions:" rhetorical, semiotic, phenomenological, cybernetic, sociopsychological, sociocultural, and critical. Craig (1999) defined the rhetorical tradition as considering communication to be a practical art; the semiotic tradition as considering communication to be intersubjective mediation via signs; the phenomenological tradition as considering communication to be the capacity of experiencing otherness through authentic dialogue; the cybernetic tradition as considering communication to be synonymous with information processing; the sociopsychological tradition as considering communication to be expression, interaction and influence; the sociocultural tradition as considering communication to be the means by which the social order may be (re)produced; and the critical tradition as considering communication to be discursive reflection, particularly on hegemonic ideological forces and how these might be critiqued. Each of these traditions combines ontology and epistemology differently (Anderson and Baym 2004), making communication theory truly a "big tent" encompassing social sciences, humanities, and arts (see also Chapter 3, Craig).

Craig (1999) worried that scholars adhering to each of his traditions were sufficiently different from each other that they potentially could not engage in dialogue about what issues were important to communication as a discipline. Disciplinary dialogue, Craig argued, is essential to growth, development, and ultimately to disciplinary health. While we have defined the major intellectual strands of communication in a slightly different manner than did Craig, we do not have the same worries. There may be no such thing as COMMUNICATION THEORY, but there may be many communication theories, each proceeding from a different understanding of communication phenomena and each contributing to scholarship proceeding from that understanding. There may be quarrels about which of these understandings is "correct" (or, more likely, which might be considered "incorrect" or "inadequate"), but ultimately we find commonality through appreciating the variety of different approaches and the scholarship they have produced. "Communication" may turn out to be the wrong term to define what we are studying, but for the moment it is good enough.

Further reading

Anderson, James A. & Geoffrey Baym. 2004. Philosophies and philosophic issues in communication, 1994–2004. *Journal of Communication* 54. 589–615. doi:10.1093/joc/54.4.589

Craig, Robert T. 1999. Communication theory as a field. *Communication Theory* 9. 117–161. doi:10.1111/j.1468-2885.1999.tb00355.x

Eadie, William F. 2011. Stories we tell: Fragmentation and convergence in communication disciplinary history. *The Review of Communication* 11. 161–176.

Peters, John Durham. 1999. *Speaking into the air: A history of the idea of communication.* Chicago, London: University of Chicago Press

Rogers, Everett M. 1994. *A history of communication study: A biographical approach.* New York: Free Press.

References

Anderson, J. A. & G. Baym. 2004. Philosophies and philosophic issues in communication, 1994–2004. *Journal of Communication* 54. 589–615. doi:10.1093/joc/54.4.589

Ayer, A. J. 1936. *Language, truth and logic.* London: Victor Gollancz [Reprinted by Penguin Books, 1990].

Bakhtin, M. M. 1986. *Speech genres and other late essays,* McGee, Vern W. (trans.). Austin, TX: University of Texas Press.

Bandura, A. 1986. *Social foundations of thought and action: A social cognitive theory.* Englewood Cliffs, NJ: Prentice-Hall.

Barthes, R. 2000. *Mythologies,* Lavers, A. (trans.). New York: Hill and Wang. [Originally published 1957].

Barton, A. H. 2001. Paul Lazarsfeld as institutional inventor. *International Journal of Public Opinion Research* 13. 245–269. doi:10.1093/ijpor/13.3.245

Bateson, G., D. D. Jackson, J. Haley & J. Weakland. 1956. Toward a theory of schizophrenia. *Behavioral Science* 1. 251–264. doi:10.1002/bs.3830010402

Baxter, L. A. & B. M. Montgomery. 1996. *Relating: Dialogues and dialectics*. New York: Guilford.

Berlo, D. 1960. *The process of communication*. New York: Holt, Rinehart and Winston.

Berger, C. R. & R. J. Calabrese. 1975. Some exploration in initial interaction and beyond: Toward a developmental theory of communication. *Human Communication Research* 1. 99–112. doi:10.1111/j.1468–2958.1975.tb00258.x

Berger, P. L. & T. Luckmann. 1966. *The social construction of reality: A treatise in the sociology of knowledge*. Garden City, NY: Anchor Books.

Blumer, H. 1969. *Symbolic interactionism: Perspective and method*. Englewood Cliffs, NJ: Prentice-Hall.

Blumler, J. G. & E. Katz. 1974. *The uses of mass communication*. Newbury Park, CA: Sage.

Buber, M. 1947. *Between man and man*. London: Routledge.

Burgoon, J. K. 1978. A communication model of personal space violation: Explication and an initial test. *Human Communication Research* 4. 129–142. doi:10.1111/j.1468–2958.1978.tb00603.x

Burgoon, J. K. & J. L. Hale. 1988. Nonverbal expectancy violations: Model elaboration and application to immediacy behaviors. *Communication Monographs* 55. 58–79. doi:10.1080/03637758809376158

Burke, K. 1941. *The philosophies of literary form; Studies in symbolic action*. Baton Rouge, LA: Louisiana State University Press.

Burke, K. 1945. *A grammar of motives*. New York: Prentice-Hall, Inc.

Cappella, J. N. 2006. Integrating message effects and behavior change theories: Organizing comments and unanswered questions. *Journal of Communication* 56. 265–279. doi:10.1111/j.1460–2466.2006.00293.x

Celikates, R. 2006. From critical social theory to a social theory of critique: On the critique of ideology after the pragmatic turn. *Constellations* 31. 21–40.

Chen, G. M. 2001. Toward transcultural understanding: A harmony theory of Chinese communication. In: V. H. Milhouse, M. K. Asante and P. O. Nwosu (eds.), *Transcultural realities: Interdisciplinary perspectives on cross-cultural relations*, 55–70). Thousand Oaks, CA: Sage.

Chen, G. M. 2002a. Problems and prospect of Chinese communication study. In: W. Jia, X. Lu, and D. R. Heisey (eds.), *Chinese communication theory and research: Reflections, new frontiers, and new directions*, 255–268. Westport, CT: Ablex.

Chen, G. M. (ed.). 2002b. Culture and communication: An East Asian perspective [Special issue]. *Intercultural Communication Studies* 11. 1–171.

Chen, G. M. 2002c. The impact of harmony on Chinese conflict management. In: G. M. Chen and R. Ma (eds.), *Chinese conflict management and resolution*, 3–19. Westport, CT: Ablex.

Chen, G. M. 2004. The two faces of Chinese communication. *Human Communication: A Journal of the Pacific and Asian Communication Association* 7: 25–36.

Chen, G. M. 2005. A model of global communication competence. *China Media Research* 1. 3–11.

Chen, G. M. 2006. Asian communication studies: What and where to now. *The Review of Communication* 6. 295–311.

Craig, R. T. 1999. Communication theory as a field. *Communication Theory* 9. 117–161. doi:10.1111/j.1468–2885.1999.tb00355.x

de Saussure, F. 1916/2000. The nature of linguistic sign. In: L. Burke, T. Crowley and A. Girvin (eds), *The Routledge language and cultural theory reader*, 21–31. New York: Routledge.

Delia, J. G. 1987. Communication research: A history. In: C. Berger and S. Chaffee (eds.), *Handbook of Communication Science*, 20–99. London: Sage.

Dewey, J. 1910. *How we think*. Boston, NY, Chicago: D. C. Heath and Company.

Donohew, L., E. P. Lorch & P. Palmgreen. 1998. Applications of a theoretic model of information exposure to health interventions. *Human Communication Research* 24: 454–468. doi:10.1111/j.1468-2958.1998.tb00425.x

Dupuy, J. P. 2000. *The mechanization of the mind: On the origins of cognitive science*, DeBevoise, M. B. (trans.). Princeton: Princeton University Press

Eadie, W. F. 2011. Stories we tell: Fragmentation and convergence in communication disciplinary history. *The Review of Communication* 11. 161–176.

Entman, R. 1993. Framing: toward clarification of a fractured paradigm. *Journal of Communication* 43 (4). 51–58. doi:10.1111/j.1460-2466.1993.tb01304.x

Gerbner, G. 1973. Cultural indicators: The third voice. In: G. Gerbner, L. P. Gross and W. Melody (eds.), *Communication, technology and social policy*, 555–573. New York: Wiley.

Gergen, K. J. 1992. Organizational Theory in the Post-Modern Era. In: M. Reed and M. Hughes (eds.), *Rethinking organizations: new directions in organization theory and analysis*, 207–226. London: Sage Publications.

Gergen, K. J. 1999. *An invitation to social constructionism*. London: Sage Publications.

Gudykunst, W. B. 2005. *Theorizing about intercultural communication*. Thousand Oaks, CA: Sage.

Habermas, J. 1973. *Theory and practice*. Boston: Beacon Press.

Habermas, J. 1974. The public sphere: An encyclopedia article 1964, Lennox, S. and Lennox, F. (trans.). *New German Critique* 3. 49–55. http://www.jstor.org/stable/487737 (accessed 23 April 2012).

Habermas, J. 1984. *Theory of communicative action: Reason and the rationalization of society*. Vol. 1, McCarthy, T. (trans.). Boston: Beacon Press.

Habermas, J. 1989. *Structural transformation of the public sphere*, Burger, T. and Lawrence, F. (trans.). Cambridge, MA: MIT Press.

Habermas, J. 1994. *The past as future: Vergangenheit als zukunft*, Pensky, M. (trans. and ed.). Lincoln: University of Nebraska Press.

Hall, E. T. 1959. *The silent language*. Greenwich, CT: Fawcett Publications.

Hall, E. T. 1966. *The hidden dimension*. Garden City, NY: Doubleday.

Hall, S. 1980. Cultural studies: Two paradigms. *Media, Culture and Society* 2. 57–72. doi:10.1177/016344378000200106

Hall, S. 1982. The rediscovery of "ideology": Return of the repressed in media studies. In: M. Gurevitch, T. Bennett, J. Curran and J. Wollacott (eds.), *Culture, society and the media*, 52–86. London: Methuen.

Hall, S. 1992. *Culture, media, language: Working papers in cultural studies, 1972–79*. London: Routledge.

Hall, S. 1995. The whites of their eyes: Racist ideologies and the media. In: G. Dines and J. Humez (eds.), *Gender, race and class in media – A text reader*, 89–93) Thousand Oaks, CA: Sage.

Hart, R. P. & D. M. Burks. 1972. Rhetorical sensitivity and social interaction. *Speech Monograph*, 39: 75–91. doi:10.1080/03637757209375742

Hayakawa, S. I. 1941. *Language in action: A guide to accurate thinking, reading and writing*. New York: Harcourt, Brace and Company.

Heider, F. 1946. Attitudes and cognitive organization. *Journal of Psychology*, 21. 107–112. doi:10.1080/00223980.1946.9917275

Holland, L. V. 1955. Kenneth Burke's dramatistic approach in speech criticism. *Quarterly Journal of Speech* 41. 352–358. doi:10.1080/00335635509382094

Jay, M. 1973. *The dialectical imagination: A history of the Frankfurt School and the Institute of Social Research, 1923-1950*. Berkeley, CA: University of California Press.

Jay, M. 1980. The Jews and the Frankfurt School: Critical theory's analysis of Anti-Semitism. *New German Critique* 19. 137–149.

Jeřábek, H. 2001. Paul Lazarsfeld – the founder of modern empirical sociology: A research biography. *International Journal of Public Opinion Research* 13. 229–244. doi:10.1093/ijpor/13.3.229

Kellner, D. 2000. Habermas, the public sphere and democracy: A critical intervention. In: L. E. Hahn (ed.), *Perspectives on Habermas*, 259–288. Peru, IL: Open Court Press

Korzybski, A. 1933. *Science and sanity: An introduction to non-Aristotelian systems and general semantics.* New York: International Non-Aristotelian Library Publishing Company.

Lasswell, H. D. 1927. *Propaganda technique in the world war.* New York: A. A. Knopf.

Lazarsfeld, P. F., B. Berelson & H. Gaudet. 1944. *The people's choice: How the voter makes up his mind in a presidential campaign.* New York: Duell, Sloan and Pearce.

Lazarsfeld, P. F. 1969. An episode in the history of social research: A memoir. In: D. Fleming and B. Bailyn (eds.), *Intellectual migration: Europe and American 1930–1960*, 270–337. Cambridge, MA: Belknap Press.

Lewin, K. 1943. Cultural reconstruction. *Journal of Abnormal and Social Psychology* 38 (2). 166–173. doi:10.1037/h0062523

Lewin, K. 1948. *Resolving social conflicts, selected papers on group dynamics [1935–1946]*, Lewin, G. W. (ed.). New York: Harper.

Lippmann, W. 1922. *Public opinion.* New York: Macmillan.

Lowery, S. A. & M. L. DeFleur. 1995. *Milestones in mass communication research.* New York: Longman.

Luhmann, N. 2000. *The reality of the mass media*, Cross, K. (trans.). Stanford, CA: Stanford University Press.

Maslow, A. 1943. A theory of human motivation. *Psychological Review* 50. 370–396. doi:10.1037/h0054346

Mead, G. H. 1934. *Mind, self and society.* Chicago: University of Chicago Press.

McCombs, M. E. & D. Shaw. 1972. The agenda-setting function of mass media. *Public Opinion Quarterly* 36. 176–187. doi:10.1086/267990

McGuire, W. J. 1996. The Yale communication and attitude-change program in the 1950s. In: E. E. Dennis and E. Wartella (eds.), *American communication research: The remembered history*, 39–60. Mahwah: Lawrence Erlbaum Associates.

Park, R. E. 1922. *The immigrant press and its control.* New York: Harper and Brothers.

Park, R. E. 1952. *Human communities: The city and human ecology.* Glencoe, IL: Free Press.

Peirce, C. S. 1878, January. How to make our ideas clear. *Popular Science Monthly* 12. 286–302.

Peters, J. D. 1999. *Speaking into the air: A history of the idea of communication.* Chicago, London: University of Chicago Press

Pooley, J. 2006. Fifteen pages that shook the field: Personal influence, Edward Shils, and the remembered history of mass communication research. *The ANNALS of the American Academy of Political and Social Science* 608. 130–156. doi:10.1177/0002716206292460

Reinhard, C. D. & B. Dervin. 2009. Media uses and gratifications. In: W. F. Eadie (ed.), *21st Century communication: A reference handbook, Vol. 2*, 506–515. Thousand Oaks, CA: Sage Publications.

Rogers, C. 1961. *On becoming a person: A therapist's view of psychotherapy.* Boston: Houghton Mifflin.

Rogers, E. M. 1994. *A history of communication study: A biographical approach.* New York: Free Press.

Schramm, W. L. 1997. *The beginnings of communication study in America: A personal memoir*, Chaffee, S. H. and Rogers, E. M. (eds.). Thousand Oaks, CA: Sage Publications.

Shannon, C. E. & W. Weaver. 1949. *The mathematical theory of communication.* Urbana, IL: University of Illinois Press.

Smircich, L. & M. B. Calás. 1987. Organizational culture: A critical assessment. In: F. M. Jablin, L. L. Putnam, K. H. Roberts and L. W. Porter (eds.), *Handbook of organizational communication: An interdisciplinary perspective*, 228–263. Thousand Oaks, CA: Sage Publications.

Tar, Z. 1977. *The Frankfurt school: The critical theories of Max Horkheimer and Theodor W. Adorno*. New York: John Wiley and Sons.

Thibaut, J. W. & H. H. Kelley. 1959. *The social psychology of groups*. New York: Wiley.

Vygotsky, L. S. 1971. *Denken und sprechen*, 2nd edn. Frankfurt: S. Fischer.

Watzlawick, P., J. H. Beavin & D. D. Jackson. 1967. *Pragmatics of human communication*. New York: Norton.

Weick, K. 1969. *The social psychology of organizing*. New York: McGraw Hill.

Wiener, N. 1948. *Cybernetics*. New York: John Wiley and Sons.

Wiggerhaus, R. 1994. *The Frankfurt school. Its history, theories, and political significance*, Robertson, M. (trans.). Cambridge, MA: The MIT Press.

I Theories and models

Robert T. Craig

3 Constructing theories in communication research

Abstract: Diverse approaches to theory construction are distinguished by different metatheoretical assumptions of epistemology, ontology, axiology and praxeology. Two broad approaches are the empirical-scientific and critical-interpretive. A scientific theory is a logically connected set of abstract statements from which empirically testable hypotheses and explanations can be derived. Models and paradigms are distinguished from theories. Several approaches to scientific explanation and theory development are discussed. Critical-interpretive approaches represent a convergence of humanities and social science. Interpretive approaches emphasize the heuristic function of theory, while critical approaches emphasize social change. Postmodern critical-interpretive theory intervenes in societal discourses to deconstruct or reconstruct social practices.

Keywords: Metatheory, epistemology, ontology, axiology, praxeology, empirical-scientific approaches, scientific explanation, models and paradigms, critical-interpretive approaches, practical theory

1 Introduction

This chapter presents an overview of theory construction in communication research. The diversity of ideas in the field makes this a challenging task. Not only are there many theories about communication and media, those theories represent radically different intellectual styles, reflecting different assumptions about the object of study, the nature of theory and the process of inquiry in general (Craig 1993, 1999). Indeed, the very idea that theories are discrete conceptual objects "constructed" in some systematic way makes more sense in some views of communication theory than in others.

The diversity of theories in communication research has been influenced by recent interdisciplinary trends; however, it is not only a product of recent developments. Theories relevant to communication and media sprang up independently across the humanities and social sciences before a distinct field of communication research took shape in the second half of the twentieth century. Rather than appearing all at once ex nihilo or branching off from a single limb of the academic tree, communication research developed lines of inquiry from many sources, and even now the field continues to grow, in part, by incorporating new interdisciplinary areas with their sometimes distinct theoretical approaches.

The fragmented state of the field calls for broad awareness and careful reflection on practices of theory construction. This chapter introduces metatheory as an effort to achieve a critical understanding of the diversity of theories in the field and the fundamental choices involved in constructing theories. Following a general introduction to metatheory, two current issues for communication theory are discussed, and diverse methods of theory construction are sketched within two broad approaches.

2 Metatheory

Metatheory is a branch of theory that articulates and critiques the assumptions underlying particular theories or kinds of theory. Every work of theory relies on assumptions, some of which may be stated explicitly in the theory but most of which are usually left implicit. Following Anderson (1996: 2; see also: Anderson and Baym 2004; Craig 2009; Craig and Müller 2007: 55–62; cf. Fiske and Shweder 1986: 3), four kinds of metatheoretical assumptions can be distinguished: assumptions about fundamental characteristics of the objects that are theorized (ontology), about the basis for claims regarding a theory's truth or validity (epistemology), about normative practices for generating, presenting and using theories (praxeology), and about the values that determine the worth of a theory (axiology).

Approaches to theory construction that are often loosely described as "epistemologies" can be shown to differ complexly across all types of metatheoretical assumptions (Craig 2009). As a matter of convenience, this chapter distinguishes two broad approaches: empirical-scientific and critical-interpretive, each of which spans many differences. However, there can be no single, all-purpose scheme for classifying theories. Theories can be distinguished and grouped to highlight particular metatheoretical issues important for theory construction. Two of those important issues for communication theory will be introduced before surveying the major approaches to theory construction. The first issue concerns communication's ontological status as a process of information transmission or as the social constitution of meaning. The second issue concerns communication theory's epistemological status as either universal or culturally specific.

2.1 An ontological issue: what is a *communication* theory?

Communication is still commonly understood as a process in which some content (thought, information) is *transmitted* from a sender through a medium or channel to a receiver. Although a transmitted message may be called "a communication," it acquires that status only by virtue of being transmitted. In this common view, communication can also refer to the activity of communicating, which consists entirely of transmitting and receiving messages. Communication is "successful" insofar as the content is not lost or distorted in the transmission process (the message received equals the message sent). From a transmission view it thus makes perfect sense to say that two parties in conflict are communicating successfully if they decode each other's messages correctly, even though they continue to disagree. If communication *is* transmission, then theories of communication should explain the sources, processes and effects of transmission, or in Harold Lasswell's classic formula, "Who Says What in Which Channel to Whom With What Effect?" (Lasswell 1948: 37).

The transmission model has been critiqued by communication theorists who propose instead versions of what can be called a *constitutive* model of communication. By separating content from transmission and limiting communication to the latter, the transmission model reduces communication to a merely technical process. This, the critics argue, is an *ontological* mistake. It fails to acknowledge the essentially symbolic and dialogical quality of human existence (Shepherd 1993). It assumes that senders, receivers, and meaningful content all exist independently prior to the event of transmission, ignoring that all of these elements are actually *produced* (constituted) symbolically in ongoing human interaction (Deetz 1994; Pearce 2007). Accordingly, and in contrast to Lasswell's linear model, James W. Carey famously defined communication as "a symbolic process whereby reality is produced, maintained, repaired, and transformed" (Carey 2009: 19).

The ontological difference between transmission and constitutive models of communication makes a significant difference for the role of theory construction. In the transmission view, the primary role of theory is to explain the causes and effects of message exchange, often by reference to psychological mechanisms that influence behavior. In a constitutive view, the role of theory is to conceptualize symbolic models that not only describe the communication process but also operate *within* the communication process to produce the reality of communication itself. Communication exists in varied cultural forms, which are *in*-formed by models of communication that formal theories can explicate, develop, critique, and potentially transform. Hence, the relation between communication theory and practice is reflexive, or mutually constitutive, and the role of theory is "to create a particular corner of culture – culture that determines, in part, the kind of communicative world we inhabit" (Carey 2009: 29).

Further developing this idea, Craig (1999; see also: Craig 2007a; Craig and Müller 2007) has contributed a "constitutive metamodel" of communication theory in which seven main traditions are distinguished with regard to their *ontological* assumptions concerning the form in which communication exists as a lifeworld phenomenon. For theories in the *rhetorical* tradition, communication is a practical art of discourse that can be cultivated by study and practice. Theories in the *semiotic* tradition take communication to be a process of signification that mediates subjectivities. In the *phenomenological* tradition, communication is an experiential encounter of self and other. In the *cybernetic* tradition, communication exists in the flow of information. In the *sociopsychological* tradition, it exists in the behavioral interaction among cognitively advanced biological organisms. In the *sociocultural* tradition, it exists in social and cultural patterns that allow coordinated interaction among members. Finally, in the *critical* tradition, it exists in the potential for discursive reflection, the questioning of assumptions. From the standpoint of the constitutive metamodel, each tradition of communication theory provides resources for both *describing* and *producing* the reality of communication in practical discourse.

2.2 An epistemological issue: universal or culture-specific theories?

The problem of Eurocentric cultural bias in communication theory has received increasing attention in recent years (Miike and Chen 2007; Wang 2011; Wang and Kuo 2010). The traditions of communication theory identified by Craig (1999) all originated in European thought, and most current theories of communication and media have been developed by North American and European scholars working in those traditions. Although it has been understood for some time that distinct theories of communication can be derived from nonwestern thought traditions (Dissanayake 1988; Kincaid 1987) those ideas have received relatively little attention, even by Asian communication scholars. Communication research around the world has relied on western theories and methods. On a superficial interpretation, the problem is simply that Asian and non-Asian scholars both should be more attentive to the potential contributions of nonwestern ideas. The deeper problem of epistemology becomes apparent when we ask what the nature of those contributions might be.

The fundamental question is whether theories of communication can express universal principles that apply to all cultures, or whether the phenomenon of communication is so culturally variable (an ontological assumption) that specific theories are needed for each culture. If theories can be universally valid, then the problem of cultural bias is simply a neglect of relevant ideas, and nonwestern theories potentially contribute to a body of communication theory that applies everywhere. If theories must be culture-specific, then the current reliance on western theories and methods by nonwestern communication researchers represents a form of cultural domination that can only be overcome by replacing those alien theories with ones that are grounded in local cultures, such as "Asiacentric" (Miike 2010) theories for Asian cultures.

Of course, several intermediate positions between these two extremes are both conceivable and well represented in the recent debates. The impulse of theory is always to generalize, but generalizations can be broader or narrower in scope.

From an empirical-scientific standpoint, cross-cultural comparative research may capture generalizations that apply broadly, perhaps even universally, and may also capture differences that require different theoretical explanations. Kim (2002) argued in this vein that several scientific communication theories largely developed in North America simply fail to explain Asian communication behavior because they are based on culture-bound western individualistic assumptions about the psychology of self-construal.

Everyone in the recent debates tends to agree that we must avoid essentializing cultures. Cultures are not uniform, static, or permanently walled off from one another. Critical-interpretive approaches, which tend to embrace the ontology of communication as constitutive, see communication theory as contributing to ongoing discourses in which culture is not just explained but also *created*. In that view, the problem of cultural bias in communication theory (Craig 2007b) is not that theories must be restricted to particular cultures but that the global discourse on communication theory has been excessively one-sided. If our knowledge of communication cannot take the form of a universal theory, it can still be informed by a multicultural conversation in which all would have much to learn.

2.3 Theory construction: two themes with variations

Theory construction is a practical activity that takes different forms according to the praxeological conventions of institutionalized academic fields and networks of scholars. Thus, "theory" has a very different range of meanings in physics than it does in sociology or literary studies. The family resemblance among these forms of theory is marked by characteristics such as abstractness, generality, relevance to an object of study, and careful argumentation. The differences among fields can be attributed in part to their different objects of study: a theory of black holes differs from a theory of hip-hop culture by virtue of the different ways we can know those objects. In this regard, the praxeology of theory expresses principles of ontology and epistemology. However, the differences among disciplines are also due to the specific interests with which they approach any object of study: black holes can be theorized as a cultural metaphor, and something of hip-hop dancing can be explained by laws of physics. Interests can be articulated in terms of *value*, and so practices of theory construction are also expressions of *axiology*: by what values should we judge the worth of a theory? What, then, are the purposes of theory, and the goals of theory construction? The conventional practices of scientific and scholarly communities make some assumptions about existence, knowledge and value more relevant than others to problems of theory construction.

Communication research follows a wide range of approaches, as we have noted. It is useful for present purposes to group those approaches under the two main headings of empirical-scientific and critical-interpretive inquiry, while recognizing that there is much variety in each category, that the two categories overlap (interpretive social science traditionally straddles the two), and that some theoretical approaches are not easily placed with either. A strong case can be made that there are three main types of theory oriented respectively to fundamental human interests in goal-directed action, intersubjective understanding, and emancipation (Habermas 1971). One can argue further for *practical theory* as a fourth main approach that integrates the other three with the distinct purpose of cultivating communicative praxis (Craig 1989, 2009). However, as was just illustrated by the debates over transmission versus constitutive models and universal versus cultural-specific theories, the distinction between empirical-scientific and critical-interpretive approaches captures what is undoubtedly an important dimension on which the field of communication theory tends to polarize (Craig and Müller 2007: 496; see also Anderson 1996).

3 Empirical-scientific approaches

The term *communication science* connotes a conception of communication research as an autonomous empirical social science discipline distinct from the broader field of communication and media, which also includes humanistic studies (Berger et al. 2010: 6). Commentaries on the state of communication science over the last several decades have continued to note the relative paucity of original scientific theories contributed by communication scientists themselves (e.g., Berger 1991; Wiemann et al. 1988). Instead, communication science has tended to import theories from other disciplines, a pattern that is understandable in light of the field's interdisciplinary origins but needs to be overcome in order to achieve theoretical integration as a scientific discipline (Berger et al. 2010: 7). The perceived need for original theories in the field has stimulated interest in explicit methods of theory construction, an interest that is not unique to communication science but one that has cyclically waxed and waned among the social sciences for more than half a century.

Although we have been using the term theory construction in a broad sense that includes all forms of theory, there is a long established literature on theory construction that has accumulated a body of principles, models, and methods specifically for the creation of scientific theory in the social sciences (some prominent examples: Bell 2008; Blalock 1969; Dubin 1969; Kaplan 1964; Weick 1989; Zetterberg 1965). Trends in the philosophy of science around the middle of the last century emphasized the importance of systematic theory development, rather than sheer fact gathering, in the growth of scientific knowledge. Spectacular advances in natural science, especially theoretical physics, revealed by comparison the relative absence or weakness of theories in the social sciences. In response to the apparent need for better theories, theory building began to have a more prominent role in the methodological training of some social scientists. The literature on theory construction grew rapidly in the 1960s but tapered off in the following decades. Little new material appeared in sociology after 1990, according to Murray and Markovsky (2007), who anticipated, however, a revival of interest in the topic. Interest among communication scientists has continued since the 1970s, and they have contributed several texts (Anderson 1996; Casmir 1994; Hawes 1975; Pavitt 2001; Shoemaker et al. 2004).

The following sections draw upon the literature of scientific theory construction to outline the characteristics and functions of theory, the role of models and paradigms in theory development, and variations and disputes within the empirical-scientific approach.

3.1 Theories and explanations

A *scientific theory* can be defined as a logically connected set of abstract statements from which empirically testable hypotheses and explanations can be derived. Social science theories vary in formality from relatively discursive verbal presentations to formal axiomatic or mathematical systems. An important function of theories is to explain the regularity of empirical phenomena with reference to the functional or causal processes that produce them. Successful scientific explanations enable researchers to understand, statistically predict, and potentially control the occurrence of empirical events. The *sine qua non* of scientific theory is testability or *falsifiability* (Popper 1959): the concepts and statements comprising a theory must be explicated with sufficient operational clarity to allow empirical testing of derived hypotheses. Careful explication of theoretical concepts is thus a key element in scientific theory construction (Chaffee 1996). Scientific knowledge is expected to grow as research reveals gaps and errors in existing theories, thus stimulating the invention of new and better theories.

Scientific theories are distinguished both from isolated empirical generalizations and speculative philosophical theories. Isolated generalizations (e.g., stating that media exposure correlates with some demographic variable) fail to provide understanding with reference to general explanatory principles, while all-encompassing philosophical systems, famously characterized by C. Wright Mills as "grand theory" (Mills 1959: 25–49), tend to be vague and untestable by empirical methods. In response to this problem, Merton (1957) called for *theories of the middle range* that would be optimally designed to guide empirical inquiry. Such theories provide explanations that are both sufficiently abstract to cover a wide range of phenomena and yet sufficiently clear and logically structured to suggest an abundance of empirical hypotheses for researchers to test. *Cultivation theory* (Gerbner 1969) in mass communication and *uncertainty reduction theory* (Berger and Calabrese 1975) in interpersonal communication can be mentioned as home-grown examples of middle-range theory in communication science, both of which have been highly fertile for empirical research and subsequent theorizing. Notably, uncertainty reduction theory was originally presented in the form of an axiomatic system comprising seven axioms and 21 formally derived theorems (Berger and Calabrese 1975).

Among the *functions* of scientific theory are description, prediction, explanation, and control. *Explanation* is arguably the most important function but philosophers of science have disputed over how to define it. Pavitt (2000, 2001: 133–154, 2010) has reviewed this debate and proposed a *realist* approach to explanation, which will be summarized briefly. A good *scientific* explanation makes patterns of events understandable by showing that they conform to a general principle that also explains a wide range of other events. A realist explanation is one that goes beyond variable analysis or logical deduction to describe the actual process that produces events. This realist epistemology recognizes two main kinds of explanations: causal (*how* events are produced by underlying micro-structures and processes) and functional (what events accomplish for the larger systems in which they occur). Pavitt (2010) goes on to distinguish several explanatory principles and models typically used in communication science. Communication theories are classified by explanatory principles as hedonistic (pleasure seeking), understanding-driven, consistency-driven, goal-driven, process-driven, or functional. Pavitt (2010: 41) maintains that the underlying micro-processes that explain communication behavior must be psychological, sociological, or biological because "communication cannot explain itself", but this conclusion can be questioned on the grounds that communication occurs at multiple levels so that one level can potentially be explained by another level. For example, underlying micro-processes of interpersonal communication have traditionally been used to explain media effects and diffusion phenomena (e.g., Katz and Lazarsfeld 1955).

Several *criteria* can be used to assess the quality of an empirical-scientific theory. *Empirical support* is essential, of course: to what extent have predictive hypotheses derived from the theory been confirmed by methodologically sound empirical research? Additional criteria include *scope* (the range of phenomena the theory explains), and *precision* (the exactness of the theory's predictions). Theories are also evaluated by *aesthetic* criteria such as simplicity and elegance: given two theories of equivalent scope, precision, and empirical support, the simplest explanation is preferred. A final criterion to be mentioned here is *heuristic value*. That is, even a theory that is somewhat weak by other standards may be valued for its fertility as a source of concepts and questions to stimulate further inquiry.

3.2 Models and paradigms

Although the terms model and theory are sometimes treated as equivalent, this usage occludes an important distinction. A *model* is a *representation* of a phenomenon. An empirical-scientific *theory* is an *explanation* of a phenomenon. How the two are related has been a matter of dispute (Hawes 1975: 109–123; Kaplan 1964: 263–266; Pavitt 2000: 130–131). Insofar as a theory must represent the phenomenon of interest in some way, it can be said that every theory includes a model or at least has a conceptual form that can be modeled. However, not every model is a theory because not every model provides a principled explanation for the structure or process represented.

Several *types of models* can be distinguished. Pavitt (2010: 38) provides a recent classification. *Physical* models that reproduce the physical appearance or functioning of something (like a model airplane) are rarely used in communication research. (Network models that physically correspond to actual message flows might be an exception.) Much more common are *conceptual* models such as structural path diagrams that model the relations among a set of variables or process diagrams that depict the main components and stages of a process. Finally there are *formal* models that simulate processes through mathematical equations or computational algorithms. Formal models tend to be highly valued in theoretical approaches that place more value on predictive accuracy than realist explanation (e.g., Blalock 1969; Fink 1993; Woelfel and Fink 1980).

Conceptual models are often constructed in early phases of inquiry as *heuristic devices*, rough representations designed to suggest important components, relationships, and processes for study. Several heuristic models of communication were published in the 1940s through 60s. The components of communication in Lasswell's (1948) classic verbal model organize one part of this handbook. Other early and influential models were those of Shannon and Weaver, Berlo, Gerbner, Westley and MacLean, and Dance (McQuail 2008: 3144–3145).

A concept related to models is that of a *paradigm*. This term is often used to refer to standard research frameworks (concepts, methods, procedures) that are used in particular fields or programs of research (e.g., the diffusion paradigm). Kuhn's (1970) influential work in the history and philosophy of science gave the concept of paradigm a deeper theoretical significance. Kuhn argued that scientific disciplines develop through a cyclical series of stages, punctuated by "revolutions" in which a single paradigm (a coherent set of fundamental assumptions, theories, and research exemplars) comes to dominate the field. A new, *pre-paradigmatic science* is typically preoccupied with random fact gathering and philosophical arguments. A mature, *normal science* is dominated by a single paradigm that facilitates rapid advances in the field. Critics may point out *anomalies* (such as inconsistent empirical findings) in the dominant paradigm but most of their proposed alternatives do not gain wide acceptance. Occasionally, however, a new proposal begins to pose a serious challenge and the science then enters a crisis stage of intense conflict, a *scientific revolution*, in which the new paradigm is adopted en masse by younger scientists and eventually takes over the field.

A Kuhnian interpretation of communication science would suggest that we are still an immature, pre-paradigmatic field that will become a more productive and rapidly advancing normal science discipline only if we are able to agree on a single paradigm. In the 1980s this idea inspired a push for theoretical integration, but agreement on a paradigm has been an elusive goal. Instead, the "paradigm dialogues" (theme of the International Communication Association's 1985 annual conference; see Dervin et al. 1989) only intensified the conflicts among theoretical perspectives, some of which challenged the very idea of an empirical science. Communication scientists seem to have largely abandoned the search for a single disciplinary paradigm, opting instead for what Craig (1999: 123) referred to as *productive fragmentation*: many middle-range theories, models, and paradigms, both home-grown and borrowed from other fields, guiding many productive programs of empirical research that may have little in common beyond a shared commitment to scientific method.

3.3 Metatheoretical issues and approaches

While there is broad agreement on many aspects of scientific theory construction, various theoretical approaches to communication science can be distinguished. Some differences arise from epistemological assumptions. A *realist* epistemology, as was mentioned, assumes that the underlying causal mechanisms that produce events can be known. Realism can be distinguished from more skeptical alternatives such as instrumentalism and perspectivism (or constructivism). *Instrumentalism* rejects the assumption that scientific concepts (e.g., "attitude") correspond to real entities in the world and assumes only that concepts can be useful for explaining and predicting empirical observations. Influenced by Kuhn and others, *perspectivism* holds that phenomena cannot be known independently of our theories because the perspective (paradigm) in which a theory is constructed determines how empirical data will be interpreted.

A classic ontological issue in social scientific theory construction concerns the reality of collective social entities. Do "societies" or "groups" or "networks" really exist and function as distinct units (*holism*) or are these merely collections of individuals that can only be understood in terms of individual behavior (*reductionism, or more specifically, methodological individualism*)? Reductionist assumptions favor cognitive, psychological or biological strategies of theoretical explanation, whereas holist assumptions favor macro-structural, systems, or group process explanations. In an interesting example of the last-mentioned approach, Poole (2007) has argued that the *small group* should be the fundamental unit of communication research.

A final difference to be mentioned concerns an issue in the praxeology of theory construction: whether theories should be constructed as coherent wholes and then tested empirically or whether they should be built up inductively through a course of empirical studies. An example of the latter approach that has been extensively used in some areas of communication research is the *grounded theory* methodology first presented by Glaser and Strauss (1967), and developed in various ways by them and others (Bryant and Charmaz 2007). Those developments include postmodern and social constructionist forms of grounded theory that would better be regarded as critical-interpretive in orientation, rather than empirical-scientific.

4 Critical-interpretive approaches

To the extent that theory construction goes on in humanistic studies, it generally follows what we are calling critical-interpretive approaches, but those approaches are not limited to the humanities. The category also includes critical-interpretive theorizing by social scientists. The distinction between humanities and critical-interpretive social science is a matter partly of traditional subject matter and partly of intellectual style but is increasingly unclear in many fields as the two traditions converge in subject matter, method, and theory.

Traditionally, the *humanities* have engaged in the documentation, interpretation, and appreciation of historically significant events and artifacts. In this enterprise they have sometimes had trade with philosophical theories and methods of hermeneutics (interpretation), poetics (aesthetics), semiotics, and rhetoric, among others, but the humanities typically have not been regarded as fields of substantive theory in their own right. Some areas of humanistic scholarship have been rigorously scientific in their use of technical methods such as textual criticism and stylistic analysis. Their purpose, however, has usually been *ideographic* (understanding historical particulars) rather than *nomothetic* (discovering universal laws). They have often been (and sometimes still are) disdainful of theory for its tendency to reduce the rich texture of historical experience to thin and poorly grounded abstractions.

Interpretive social science similarly has tended to downplay the role of theory as a goal of inquiry, in contrast to empirical-scientific approaches for which explanatory theory is the ultimate goal. Like humanistic studies, interpretive social science is predominately ideographic rather than nomothetic in purpose; it seeks intersubjective understanding (*verstehen*), rather than causal explanation (*erklären*). In contrast to the humanities, interpretive social science has primarily studied ordinary life in contemporary societies rather than prominent historical events or works of art, often uses explicitly elaborated qualitative empirical methods (such as ethnography and, more recently, discourse analysis) rather than historiographic or less formalized critical methods, and tends to favor empirical description and to shy away from normative critical judgment. However, the overlap between humanities and social science has increased greatly in the last several decades as social scientists have turned to humanistic cultural theory and textual methods while both have turned to critical and postmodern social theory and studies of contemporary culture. In much of current critical/cultural studies of communication and media, the distinction no longer seems very relevant (see, for examples: Durham and Kellner 2006).

The following sections draw upon previous formulations (Craig 1989; 2009; Craig and Müller 2007) to distinguish several critical-interpretive approaches to theory construction, including traditional interpretive and critical approaches, newer approaches that blend interpretive and critical inquiry from a stance of postmodern reflexivity, and practical theory approaches that extend postmodern reflexivity from critical deconstruction to positive reconstruction of communicative practices.

4.1 Interpretive approaches

The roots of the interpretive tradition can be traced to the distinction between the human sciences (*Geisteswissenschaften*) and natural sciences (*Naturwissenschaften*) introduced by the German historian and philosopher Wilhelm Dilthey (1883/ 1989: 56–72) and further developed in the sociological theory of Max Weber (1904/ 1949). In this view, human action cannot be explained by reducing it to simple causal mechanisms like chemical reactions. Humans are self-interpreting beings who act on the basis of some understanding of what they are doing. Those understandings vary among individuals and groups and change over time but are not random. A particular action or product of action (artifact) can be interpreted by seeing how it participates in a patterned whole, such as a plan of action, a culture, an artistic genre, or an historical movement. The human sciences (including both the humanities and non-positivistic social science) can be thought of as formalized extensions of the everyday interpretive practices by which humans make sense of each other's words and actions in order to coordinate their activities (Habermas 1971). Whereas everyday interpretation serves immediate practical needs, the human sciences extend the scope of human understanding to encompass the widest possible range of cultures, social situations, texts, and artifacts of the past and present.

Numerous praxeological traditions of interpretive inquiry (such as conversation analysis, ethnography, ethnomethodology, historiography, narrative inquiry, psychoanalysis, and rhetorical criticism) all relate to theory in different ways and rely on different metatheoretical assumptions. The following discussion of interpretive theory construction necessarily glosses over most of those differences.

Interpretive approaches to theory construction primarily emphasize the *heuristic* functions of theory. Although theories do not provide generalizable causal explanations, they do provide conceptual frames or reference points that can assist in interpreting particular situations. Weber (1904/1949: 89–112) referred to these theoretical reference points as *ideal types*. The symbolic interactionist Herbert Blumer (1954: 7) proposed a related idea of *sensitizing concepts*. The ideal type of bureaucracy will serve as an example. Every organization has a unique structure and culture that requires interpretation, but the theoretical concept of bureaucracy provides a useful reference point for characterizing that uniqueness with regard to the specific ways in which a particular organization resembles or deviates from the ideal type.

Rather than seeking a single best explanation, interpretative approaches tend to see value in multiple theories that can illuminate different aspects of a situation. For example, cultural studies scholars Durham and Kellner (2006) characterize theories as "optics, or ways of seeing" that "center attention on phenomena and their connections to the broader society and a wide range of institutions, discourses, and practices" (2006: xi). They go on to argue, "Multiplying theories and methods at one's disposal aids in grasping diverse dimensions of an object, in making more and better connections, and thus provides a richer and more comprehensive understanding of cultural artifacts or practices under scrutiny" (Durham and Kellner 2006: xii; see also Craig 1999).

One other interpretive approach to theory building will be mentioned. Because interpretation works by placing particular objects in patterned wholes, abstract concepts (theories) of those larger patterns can serve as both starting points and outcomes of inquiry. Among the hoped-for contributions of nonwestern communication theories is to conceptualize the distinct communicative practices of Asian cultures, thus rendering their meaning sharable and universalizable (Miike 2010). Carbaugh and Hastings (1992) proposed a four-phase model of theory construction for ethnographies of communication: (1) developing a basic orientation to communication, (2) conceptualizing specific kinds of communicative activity, (3) formulating the general way in which communication is patterned within a socioculturally situated community, and (4) evaluating the general theory (basic orientation or communicative activity type) from the vantage point of the situated case.

4.2 Critical approaches

The essential purpose of *critical theory* is social change, which in Max Horkheimer's (1937/2002) classic neo-Marxist formulation, it hopes to achieve by pursuing a critical analysis of society as a whole, revealing systems of class domination and the ideologies that uphold them, thus showing the way to political resistance by the dominated groups. Theories of political economy in the Marxist tradition critique unjust conditions masked by the ideology of capitalism. The neo-Marxist Frankfurt School, of which Horkheimer was a leading member, contributed to critical theories of media and culture (e.g., Horkheimer and Adorno 1947/1976). Jürgen Habermas (1984–1987, and in many other works), the most prominent current theorist in the Frankfurt School tradition, has developed a different critical theory based on an ideal of free and open rational discourse that reveals the ways in which actual communication processes are distorted by power.

Recent work by Fuchs (2009) has sought to revive a Marxist approach to communication and media theory. Jansen (2002) approaches classic critical theory from a feminist stance. Other current strands of critical scholarship depart from classic critical theory to critique the oppressive consequences of dominant ideologies of race, ethnicity, gender, sexuality, and other social identity attributions, with varying emphasis – all forms of theory committed to social change as a primary goal (Durham and Kellner 2006 provide a range of exemplars). However, many of these current strands disagree with neo-Marxist materialism as well as Habermas's ontology of rational discourse. Instead, they embrace postmodern metatheoretical assumptions.

4.3 Postmodern reflexivity and practical theory

Postmodern theory has taken a radically reflexive turn that rejects modernist assumptions such as the ontology of the autonomous rational mind, the epistemological separation between truth and power, and the ontological assumption that language can express stable meanings and personal identities (Mumby 1997). Critical and interpretive work across the humanities and social sciences has converged toward a range of metatheoretical stances that Anderson (1996: 55–60) has characterized as *constructive empiricism* and *postmodern empiricism*. While the latter involves a more radical deconstruction of knowledge claims, both stances regard theory as a form of *discursive intervention* that goes beyond explanation and interpretation to *influence* society, potentially inducing change (the postmodern turn of interpretive social science can be traced through many of the chapters in Rabinow and Sullivan 1987).

The idea that theory influences the phenomena theorized characterizes the critical tradition in general. Horkheimer's original statement affirmed that critical theory "is part of the development of society" and consciously works to change the reality that it theorizes (Horkheimer 1937/2002: 229). This assumes, however, that critical theory must provide a correct description of the material reality of society in order to promote change, whereas postmodern critical-interpretive approaches assume that the meaning of a material reality can be influenced by the very act of describing it. Rather than one correct description there can be many, more or less adequate interpretations that not only give different views of reality but constitute different practical orientations to it (Craig 1999). Works of theory are rhetorical interventions in societal discourses, the influence of which depends on their reception.

While holding on to the axiological assumption that the worth of a theory is determined by its potential to *change* society in valued ways, postmodern critical-interpretive approaches tend to adopt one of two broad strategies of theory construction that will be labeled *deconstruction* and *reconstruction*, albeit with the caveat that other writers have used these terms differently.

The typical postmodernist approach is *deconstruction*. Deconstruction is not generally accomplished by crafting discrete conceptual objects known as *theories*, but rather by discursive interventions that question and undermine the dominant assumptions of any practice. As the literary theorist Jonathan Culler defines it, theory is "an open-ended corpus of writings," the purpose of which is "to undo, through a contesting of premises and postulates, what you thought you knew, so that there may appear to be no real accumulation of knowledge or expertise" (Culler 1994: 15). Another prominent literary theorist, Terry Eagleton, similarly defines theory as "critical self-reflection" which forces us "into a new self-consciousness of what we are doing … because we can no longer take these practices for granted" (Eagleton 2004: 27).

The larger purpose of deconstruction is not confusion for its own sake but rather to liberate us from unexamined assumptions, thereby opening avenues of change. Deconstructive theory does not assert normative claims; its purpose is emancipatory, not prescriptive. Society is bound by dominant ideological assumptions about matters such as race, class, and gender that have to be undermined so that other views, now suppressed, can flourish. As other assumptions become dominant, they too must be questioned, for liberation is only sustained by endless reflexive questioning.

The less common postmodern critical-interpretive strategy is *reconstruction*. Rather than only offering a negative critique of assumptions, reconstruction offers *positive alternatives*, critical interpretations that envision possible ways in which a social practice could be normatively better than it is. Taylor's (1985) idea of *self-defining theory* is consistent with this strategy, as is Carey's (2009) reflexive view of theory. Craig (1989, 1999) and others have pursued this strategy in the form of *practical theory*. Craig and Tracy (1995) have developed a theory construction method of *grounded practical theory*, which builds from critical-interpretive studies of communicative practices toward a normative reconstruction of practices on three interrelated levels of problems, techniques, and situated philosophical ideals. A closely related approach is *design theory* (Aakhus and Jackson 2005), which is an effort to design communicative practices in line with normative theoretical models.

Barge and Craig (2009) treat grounded practical theory and design theory as exemplars of a broader approach to practical theory as *engaged reflection*, which they distinguish from two other approaches. Practical theory as *mapping* (which can be pursued from empirical-scientific as well as critical-interpretive approaches) conceptualizes practical problems, communicative strategies, and the empirical consequences of performing particular communicative strategies. Finally, practical theory as *transformative practice* approaches theorizing as a process of elaborating the communication abilities of both practical theorists and research participants through the practical theorist's own active participation in helping others to solve communication problems. The theory of coordinated management of meaning (Pearce and Cronen 1980; Pearce 2007) exemplifies practical theory as transformative practice.

5 Conclusion

We have seen that many diverse approaches to theory construction are pursued in communication and media studies. Each approach has its metatheoretical rationale but many of them are incompatible. A great divide seems to separate empirical-scientific from interpretive-critical approaches, which polarize the field. The development of specialized expertise would seem to require that each scholar concentrate on one approach and have limited knowledge of others. Even with some awareness of other approaches, intellectual disagreements along with temperamental and political differences may tend to promote polarization. While this tendency may be likely, there is good reason to resist it and to cultivate some appreciation of work that goes on across the great divide, based on recognition of the limitations and occasional fallibility of one's own assumptions and the plausible merit of others for occasionally learning something of interest.

Further reading

Anderson, James A. 1996. *Communication Theory: Epistemological Foundations*. New York: The Guilford Press.

Craig, Robert T. & Heidi L. Müller (eds.). 2007. *Theorizing Communication: Readings Across Traditions*. Thousand Oaks, CA: Sage.

Littlejohn, Stephen W. & Karen A. Foss (eds.). 2009. *Encyclopedia of Communication Theory*. 2 volumes. Thousand Oaks, CA: Sage.

Pavitt, Charles. 2001. *The Philosophy of Science and Communication Theory*. Huntington, NY: Nova Science Publishers.

Reed, Isaac Ariail. 2011. *Interpretation and Social Knowledge: On the Use of Theory in the Human Sciences*. Chicago: University of Chicago Press.

References

Aakhus, Mark & Sally Jackson. 2005. Technology, interaction, and design. In: Kristine L. Fitch and Robert E. Sanders (eds.), *Handbook of Language and Social Interaction*, 411–435. Mahwah, NJ: Lawrence Erlbaum Associates.

Anderson, James A. 1996. *Communication Theory: Epistemological Foundations*. New York: The Guilford Press.

Anderson, James A. & Geoffrey Baym. 2004. Philosophies and philosophic issues in communication, 1995–2004. *Journal of Communication* 54. 589–615.

Barge, Kevin J. & Robert T. Craig. 2009. Practical theory in applied communication scholarship. In: Lawrence R. Frey and Kenneth N. Cissna (eds.), *Routledge Handbook of Applied Communication Research*, 55–78. New York: Routledge.

Bell, David C. 2008. *Constructing Social Theory*. Lanham, MD: Rowman and Littlefield.

Berger, Charles R. 1991. Communication theories and other curios. *Communication Monographs* 58. 101–113.

Berger, Charles R. & Richard J. Calabrese. 1975. Some explorations in initial interaction and beyond: Toward a developmental theory of interpersonal communication. *Human Communication Research* 1. 99–112.

Berger, Charles R., Michael E. Roloff & David R. Ewoldsen. 2010. What is communication science? In: Charles R. Berger, Michael E. Roloff and David Roskos-Ewoldsen (eds.), *The Handbook of Communication Science*, 2nd edn, 3–20. Thousand Oaks, CA: Sage.

Blalock, Hubert M Jr. 1969. *Theory Construction: From Verbal to Mathematical Formulations*. Englewood Cliffs, NJ: Prentice-Hall.

Blumer, Herbert. 1954. What is wrong with social theory? *American Sociological Review* 18. 3–10.

Bryant, Antony & Kathy Charmaz (eds.). 2007. *The SAGE Handbook of Grounded Theory*. Thousand Oaks and London: Sage.

Carbaugh, Donal & Sally O. Hastings. 1992. A role for communication theory in ethnography and cultural analysis. *Communication Theory* 2. 156–165.

Carey, James W. 2009. *Communication as Culture: Essays on Media And Society*. Revised edn. New York and London: Routledge.

Casmir, Fred L. (ed.). 1994. *Building Communication Theories: A Socio/Cultural Approach*. Hillsdale, NJ: Lawrence Erlbaum Associates.

Chaffee, Steven H. 1996. Thinking about theory. In: Michael B. Salwen and Don W. Stacks (eds.), *An Integrated Approach to Communication Theory and Research*, 15–32. Mahwah, NJ: Lawrence Erlbaum Associates.

Craig, Robert T. 1989. Communication as a practical discipline. In: Brenda Dervin, Lawrence Grossberg, Barbara J. O'Keefe and Ellen Wartella (eds.), *Rethinking Communication; Volume 1: Paradigm Issues*, 97–122. Newbury Park, CA: Sage.

Craig, Robert T. 1993. Why are there so *many* communication theories? *Journal of Communication* 43 (3). 26–33.

Craig, Robert T. 1999. Communication theory as a field. *Communication Theory* 9. 119–161.

Craig, Robert T. 2007a. Pragmatism in the field of communication theory. *Communication Theory* 17. 125–145.

Craig, Robert T. (ed.). 2007b. Issue forum: Cultural bias in communication theory. *Communication Monographs* 74. 256–285

Craig, Robert T. 2009. Metatheory. In: Stephen W. Littlejohn and Karen A. Foss (eds.), *Encyclopedia of Communication Theory*, 657–661. Thousand Oaks, CA: Sage.

Craig, Robert T. & Heidi L. Müller (eds.). 2007. *Theorizing Communication: Readings Across Traditions*. Thousand Oaks, CA: Sage.

Craig, Robert T. & Karen Tracy. 1995. Grounded practical theory: The case of intellectual discussion. *Communication Theory* 5. 248–272.

Culler, Jonathan. 1994. Introduction: What's the point? In: Mieke Bal and Inge E. Boer (eds.), *The Point of Theory: Practices of Cultural Analysis*, 13–17. New York: Continuum.

Deetz, Stanley A. 1994. Future of the discipline: The challenges, the research, and the social contribution. In: Stanley A. Deetz (ed.), *Communication Yearbook 17*, 565–600. Thousand Oaks, CA: Sage.

Dervin, Brenda, Lawrence Grossberg, Barbara J. O'Keefe & Ellen Wartella (eds.). 1989. *Rethinking Communication*. 2 volumes. Newbury Park, CA: Sage.

Dilthey, Wilhelm. 1883/1989. *Introduction to the Human Sciences; Selected Works, Volume 1*. Makkreel, Rudolf A. and Rodi, Frithjof (eds.). Princeton, NJ: Princeton University Press.

Dissanayake, Wimal (ed.). 1988. *Communication Theory: The Asian Perspective*. Singapore: Asian Media, Information and Communication Center.

Durham, Meenakshi Gigi & Douglas Kellner (eds.). 2006. *Media and Cultural Studies: Keyworks*. Revised edn. Malden, MA: Blackwell.

Eagleton, Terry. 2004. *After Theory*. New York: Basic Books.

Fink, Edward L. (ed.). 1993. Symposium: Communication theory, mathematical models, and social policy. *Journal of Communication*, 43 (1). 4–100.

Fiske, Donald W. & Richard A. Shweder (eds.). 1986. *Metatheory in Social Science: Pluralisms and Subjectivities*. Chicago: University of Chicago Press.

Fuchs, Christian. 2009. A contribution to theoretical foundations of critical media and communication studies. *Javnost-The Public* 16 (2). 5–24.

Gerbner, George. 1969. Toward "Cultural Indicators": The analysis of mass mediated message systems. *AV Communication Review* 17 (2). 137–148.

Glaser, Barney G. & Anselm L. Strauss. 1967. *The Discovery of Grounded Theory: Strategies for Qualitative Research*. Hawthorne, NY: Aldine.

Habermas, Jürgen. 1971. *Knowledge and Human Interests*. Translated by Shapiro, J. J. Boston, MA: Beacon Press.

Habermas, Jürgen. 1984–1987. *The Theory of Communicative Action*. 2 volumes. Translated by McCarthy, Thomas. Boston: Beacon Press.

Hawes, Leonard C. 1975. *Pragmatics of Analoguing: Theory and Model Construction in Communication*. Reading, MA: Addison-Wesley.

Horkheimer, Max. 1937/2002. Traditional and critical theory. In: *Critical Theory: Selected Essays*, 188–243. New York: Continuum.

Horkheimer, Max & Theodor W. Adorno. 1947/1976. *Dialectic of Enlightenment*. Translated by Cumming, J. London and New York: Continuum International Publishing Group.

Jansen, Sue Curry. 2002. *Critical Communication Theory: Power, Media, Gender, and Technology*. Lanham, MD: Rowman and Littlefield.

Kaplan, Abraham. 1964. *The Conduct of Inquiry: Methodology for Behavioral Science*. San Francisco, CA: Chandler.

Katz, Elihu & Paul F. Lazarsfeld. 1955. *Personal Influence: The Part Played by People in the Flow of Mass Communications*. New York: The Free Press.

Kim, Min-Sun. 2002. *Non-western Perspectives on Human Communication*. Thousand Oaks, CA: Sage.

Kincaid, Lawrence D. (ed.). 1987. *Communication Theory: Eastern and Western Perspectives*. San Diego, CA: Academic Press.

Kuhn, Thomas S. 1970. *The Structure of Scientific Revolutions*, 2nd edn. Chicago: University of Chicago Press.

Lasswell, Harold D. 1948. The structure and function of communication in society. In: Lyman Bryson (ed.), *The Communication of Ideas: A Series of Addresses*, 37–51. New York, NY: Harper and Brothers.

McQuail, Denis. 2008. Models of communication. In: Wolfgang Donsbach (ed.), *International Encyclopedia of Communication, Volume VII*, 3143–3150. Oxford, UK and Malden, MA: Blackwell Publishing.

Merton, Robert K. 1957. *Social Theory and Social Structure*. Glencoe, IL: The Free Press.

Miike, Yoshitaka. 2010. An anatomy of eurocentrism in communication scholarship: The role of asiacentricity in de-westernizing theory and research. *China Media Research* 6 (1). 1–11.

Miike, Yoshitaka & Guo-Ming Chen (eds.). 2007. Special Issue: Asian Contributions to Communication Theory. *China Media Research* 3. 1–109. Retrieved from http://www.chinamediaresearch.net (accessed 20 April 2012)

Mills, C. Wright. 1959. *The Sociological Imagination*. London, Oxford, New York: Oxford University Press.

Mumby, Dennis K. 1997. Modernism, postmodernism, and communication studies: A rereading of an ongoing debate. *Communication Theory* 7. 1–28.

Murray, Webster Jr. & Barry Markovsky. 2007. Theory construction. In: George Ritzer (ed.), *Blackwell Encyclopedia of Sociology*. Malden, MA and Oxford, UK: Blackwell Publishing.

Pavitt, Charles. 2000. Answering questions requesting scientific explanations for communication. *Communication Theory* 10. 379–404.

Pavitt, Charles. 2001. *The Philosophy of Science and Communication Theory*. Huntington, NY: Nova Science Publishers.

Pavitt, Charles. 2010. Alternative approaches to theorizing in communication science. In: Charles R. Berger, Michael E. Roloff and David Roskos-Ewoldsen (eds.), *The Handbook of Communication Science*, 2nd edn., 37–54. Thousand Oaks, CA: Sage.

Pearce, W. Barnett. 2007. *Making Social Worlds: A Communication Perspective*. Malden, MA and Oxford, UK: *Blackwell*.

Pearce, W. Barnett & Vernon E. Cronen. 1980. *Communication, Action, and Meaning: The Creation of Social Realities*. New York: Praeger.

Poole, Marshall Scott. 2007. The small group should be *the* fundamental unit of communication research. In: Robert T. Craig and Heidi L. Müller (eds.), *Theorizing Communication: Readings Across Traditions*, 357–360. Thousand Oaks, CA: Sage.

Popper, Karl R. 1959. *The Logic of Scientific Inquiry*. London: Hutchinson.

Rabinow, Paul & William M. Sullivan (eds.). 1987. *Interpretive Social Science: A Second Look*. Berkeley, CA: University of California Press.

Shepherd, Gregory J. 1993. Building a discipline of communication. *Journal of Communication* 43 (3). 83–91.

Shoemaker, Pamela J., James William Tankard Jr. & Dominic L. Lasorsa. 2004. *How to Build Social Science Theories*. Thousand Oaks, CA: Sage Publications.

Taylor, Charles. 1985. Social theory as practice. In: *Philosophy and the Human Sciences; Philosophical papers 2*, 91–115. Cambridge: Cambridge University Press.

Wang, Georgette (ed.). 2011. *De-Westernizing Communication Research: Altering Questions and Changing Frameworks*. New York: Routledge.

Wang, Georgette & Eddie C. Y. Kuo. 2010. The Asian communication debate: culture-specificity, culture-generality, and beyond. *Asian Journal of Communication* 20 (2). 152–165.

Weber, Max. 1904/1949. 'Objectivity' in social science and social policy. In: Edward Shils and Henry Finch (eds.), *Max Weber: The Methodology of the Social Sciences*, 50–113. Glencoe, IL: The Free Press.

Weick, Karl E. 1989. Theory construction as disciplined imagination. *Academy of Management Review* 14. 516–531.

Wiemann, John M., Robert P. Hawkins & Suzanne Pingree. 1988. Fragmentation in the field—and the movement toward integration in communication science. *Human Communication Research* 15. 304–310.

Woelfel, Joseph & Edward L. Fink. 1980. *The Measurement of Communication Processes: Galileo Theory and Method*. New York: Academic Press.

Zetterberg, Hans L. 1965. *On Theory and Verification in Sociology*. 3rd enlarged edn. Totowa, NJ: The Bedminster Press. (1st edn. 1954).

Richard L. Lanigan

4 Information theories

Abstract: This chapter describes information theory and signification in comparison to communication theory and meaning by looking at a number of definitions offered through semiotics, linguistics, and mathematics. Information theory used by machines is compared to communication theory used by humans by looking at historically evolved models. Each of these key models explain the evolving relation of information to human, animal and machine, particularly in respect to consciousness and embodiment. Finally, the essay offers some comments on the status of information in the development of what is often taken to be the pinnacle of contemporary communication technology, the internet.

Keywords: Communicology, model and theory, phenomenology, semiotics, signs, signals, signification, meaning, Roman Jakobson

1 Definitions

The concept of "information" ranges from facts we reference in conversation to the mathematical specification of electrical impulses in computers. To gain a general understanding of the varying uses of the term, we can define basic concepts and then examine some key theories of how these ideas are organized into explanations of the most basic of all human behaviors: *communication*. We communicate with one another because we surmise basic human values (decisions displayed in behavior) from the things we say and do with others. Our speech and gestures convey meanings, so the most fundamental understanding of information is the *meaning* we interpret in human comportment.

The *meaning* of human interaction is the paradigm for all theories and models of communication. Yet semantics – interpreted meaning – is irrelevant for studying information as a mathematical phenomenon – signal behavior – in electrical engineering. Unfortunately, the warning by mathematician Claude Shannon (1948, 1993a,b,c), inventor of information theory, against drawing analogies between information and communication *processes* has been ignored for decades (Gleick 2011: 242, 416). The meaning problem was suggested to Shannon by Margaret Mead during his first public lecture on the theory at the Macy Foundation Conference on Cybernetics held 22–23 March 1950 in New York City. In short, information theory studies the signifying physical properties of electrical signals, whereas communication theory studies the meaning of human interaction. Note, however, that this *signification – meaning* distinction is only one of 52 basic differentiations identified between information and communication (Marcus 1974). The most relevant of these distinctions are discussed in the Roman Jakobson model below.

This chapter will address information theory by looking at a number of definitions offered through semiotics, linguistics, and mathematics. It will then consider information theory and a number of information/communication models. Each of these sheds light on the relations of information to human, animal and machine, particularly in respect of consciousness and embodiment. Finally, the chapter will offers some comments on the status of information in the development of what is often taken to be the pinnacle of contemporary communication technology, the internet.

1.1 Semiotics: semantics, syntactics, pragmatics

The field pre-eminently associated with signification is semiotics (Krampen 1997). Semiotics is the science of understanding representation, i.e., how human beings express their thoughts and feelings in an external form perceptible to others. What is perceived constitutes a *sign* that stands in place of an idea or emotion. The sign codes or re-presents the original item. Charles S. Peirce (1931, 2: 247) suggests there are three basic ways to do this: (1) an *icon* is a sign that denotes the whole character of the original perception, e.g., a statue of a person; (2) an *index* is a sign that points to the original characteristics of a perception, e.g., dark clouds that suggest rain; and (3) a *symbol* is a sign that we associate, by cultural rule, with the original perception, e.g., your name reminds us of you.

One major division of semiotics is *semantics*, the interpretation of the meaning we associate with any type of sign. In communication, we cross-check all codes used and not used to preform this complex human cognition (Cherry [1957] 1978: 233). *Syntactics* is the relation or structure that articulates strings of signs into systems, e.g., words into sentences into paragraphs. Last, *pragmatics* is the way we use sign-systems for various purposes, e.g., making a statement into a question by tone of voice: "You are doing WHAT?".

1.1.1 Signs versus signals

One fundamental difference between information theory and communication theory is the basic unit being studied, the thing perceived in its behavior. First, let's remember that a human being is the *observer,* the source of *perception*. We use our bodies to perceive ourselves (internally and externally) and our environmental world (Merleau-Ponty 1945). What we perceive are signs. These signs are never isolated, but are part of sign-systems or *codes* (see Chapter 12, Cobley). Human codes are (1) *synergistic* (the whole is greater than the sum of its parts) and (2) embodied (all our body senses are integrated simultaneously) at three logical levels: the expression and perception of (1) *Affect* or emotion, (2) *Cognition* or thought, and (3) *Conation* or purposeful action. We have a *signal* when we perceive the presence and absence of signs, and their movement to determine if they are static or dynamic. Electrical signals are a good example. They constitute the physical system in the human brain and we use our mind to symbolically measure them, often with the mediation of machines. For example, computing machines use electrical impulses or their absence (icon) to indicate (index) a meaning assigned to them (symbol) by a human observer. Once properly programmed by a person, one machine can mediate another machine, and so on, to *simulate* simple items of human memory and action. In short, computers and similar machines manipulate meaningless signal units, whereas human beings use signs to code meaning, i.e., make information into communication by creating complex relationships among represented signs. "Signs become necessary when the circulation of information *within* an organism is replaced by communication *between* organisms" (Lotman 1990: 68). There are two fundamental ways to code such meanings: Linguistics and Mathematics.

1.1.2 Language: grammar, rhetoric, logic

The modern discursive foundations of language and mathematics were elaborated in the Middle Ages and the Renaissance with the development of the famous Seven Liberal Arts, linguistically marked in most universities today as the "College of Arts and Sciences." The Scholastics taught as primary the *human science* pedagogy of the *Trivium* (Grammar, Rhetoric, Logic) followed secondarily by the *natural science* practices of the *Quadrivium* (Arithmetic, Geometry, Music, Astronomy) in the Medieval universities, principally at L'Université de Paris.

Because Greek and Latin were the languages of literate people at this time, their characteristics and structure became the guideline for writing rules about the socially effective use of ordinary speech, whether spoken or written. Hence, social rules of usage emerged at three levels of thought (Kristeva 1989). The first level meaning rules were called *grammar* and specified what classes or types of words could be used, especially in relation to each other. Second level meaning rules of *rhetoric* concern the articulation of words into utterances or sentences for effective expression to a listener or reader (Lanigan 1984). When the phonetics of speech (tone) are employed, the articulation is a focus on *tropes of speech*. Whereas perceptual impression in writing (style) refers to *figures of language* (Lotman 1990: 49). Third level meaning rules in *logic* consist of combining the rules of grammar and rhetoric as metarules. This is to say, the articulation of words is compared (as a structural process) to the articulation of sentences. In writing, the paragraph is such a product of articulation. These metalinguistic functions are the basis of all human reasoning about choices and contexts: "Rhetoric, therefore (like logic, from another point of view), reflects a universal principle both of the individual consciousness and of the collective consciousness (culture)" (Lotman 1990: 48).

Effectively, what was taught was a concept of information as *symbolic logic,* while the logic of meaningful utterances is known as *rhetorical logic*. Where there is no meaning reference to language, but only the use of numbers or algebraic notation, it is known as *mathematical logic*.

1.2 Mathematics: signals, information modeling, informatics

From a mathematical point of view, information is an algorithm, i.e., a step by step procedure that solves a probability problem in a finite linear sequence of steps (Cherry [1957] 1978: 228–231). Each step is a "bit" of information that indicates a binary (either/or) choice by means of the presence or absence of an electrical signal in a machine circuit. The critical signification of such a bit is that we understand its *probable place in the sequence* of choices, not whether the choice was right or wrong, meaningful or not! Thus, a "no" (incorrect) answer gives just as much "information" as a "yes" (correct) answer. In short, signal information is merely a syntax of signals without any semantics or pragmatics that could make it equal to a human language. To make the signal into a sign with meaning and use value, a human being must code the signal by making it represent a sign, e.g., a *symbol* in the Latin alphabet like "Y" (meaning "Yes") or "N" (meaning "No"). Umberto Eco's (1976: 32–55) famous "Watergate Model" demonstrates how human beings need to convert information theory into communication theory by adding sign semantics and pragmatics to such a signal syntax.

2 Theories

2.1 Information Theory (IT)

IT is technically a mathematical algorithm and specifies the constraints on a signal mediation as the number of mediations increases. This is simply a capacity problem applied to a particular physical channel, such as the capacity of a metal or fiber optic telephone line to carry multiple signals (phone calls) at the same time. In fact, Claude Shannon (1948; 1993a) was concerned with this electrical engineering problem while working at the Bell Telephone Laboratories when he formulated the advanced mathematics of IT.

For our purposes, IT is best described as an *applied logic* and is easier to understand in non-mathematical terms as the *signification* problem of making choices and understanding the context for those decisions. Simply put, IT only allows *choices in a given context*. IT is based on a discrete *Closed System of Signal Rules:* (1) Context is already given as *data;* (2) All choices are *digital* (either/or logic) and must be signaled by *either* "Yes" *or* "No"; and (3) Choices have no meaning, they just reduce uncertainty in signifying the next choice. Thus, signification "informs" how to choose, not what a choice means. The system signification rules for the operation of IT are illustrated by a conversation between Warren and Claude:

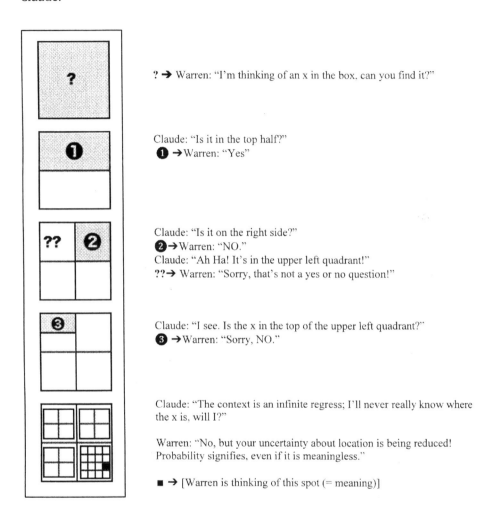

? → Warren: "I'm thinking of an x in the box, can you find it?"

Claude: "Is it in the top half?"
❶ → Warren: "Yes"

Claude: "Is it on the right side?"
❷ → Warren: "NO."
Claude: "Ah Ha! It's in the upper left quadrant!"
?? → Warren: "Sorry, that's not a yes or no question!"

Claude: "I see. Is the x in the top of the upper left quadrant?"
❸ → Warren: "Sorry, NO."

Claude: "The context is an infinite regress; I'll never really know where the x is, will I?"

Warren: "No, but your uncertainty about location is being reduced! Probability signifies, even if it is meaningless."

■ → [Warren is thinking of this spot (= meaning)]

2.2 Communication Theory (CT)

Communication is technically an account of how human beings use *semiotic systems,* especially language, to symbolize their interactive thinking, speaking, and bodily practices, i.e., behavior as culture. Keep in mind that there are "verbal systems" or eidetic codes (linguistics, mathematics, and logics) as well as "nonverbal systems" or empirical codes: proxemics (space), chronemics (time), ocularics (sight), kinesics (action), haptics (tactile), vocalics (sound), and olfactorics (smell/taste); all codes are explicated in Lanigan (2010b,c).

Following the same approach that was used for the discussion of information theory, Communication Theory is best explicated as an *applied logic* and is easier to understand in language terms as the *meaning* problem of making choices and understanding the context for those discourse decisions. Simply put, CT allows the *choice of a context*. CT is based on a discrete System of Sign Rules: (1) Context is taken by Choice made; (2) Normal analog rules (both/and logic) of discourse operate; (3) Answers have meaning, they constitute intentionality (consciousness) about *both* the choice made *and* those not made. Thus, interactive discourse communicates *what* a choice means in its context, not how to choose. Most importantly, human beings simultaneously know all the choices *not* made that are still available to make (we can *take* another choice, i.e., change our mind, reverse course, etc.). "To speak essentially is not to say yes or no, but to make something exist linguistically. To speak supposes the use of contingency and the absurd" (Merleau-Ponty 2003: 164).

The system meaning rules of logic application for CT are illustrated by a conversation between Roman and Juri:

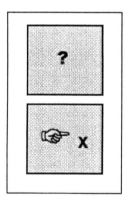

? Roman: "I'm thinking of an x in the box, can you find it?"
Juri: "Please point to it with your finger."

☞ Roman: "OK, look carefully! I'll point to it"

Juri: "That's really easy for a human being! Let's name it **X** and talk about it. I'll also remember where it was not located!

3 Models

Models are abbreviated, usually diagrammed, presentations of theories. While the pictorial presentation is a useful visual aid to comprehension, it is critical to remember there is a large body of published research that explains the conceptual content of the model. Assuming what visual models mean, as opposed to understanding the published theory, is a major problem in the diffusion of misinformation about the nature and process of human communication behavior. There are hundreds of models of communication that specify individual formats and events of communication, many associated with the history of mass media. But, there are very few theories of communication that comprehensively explain all possibilities of communication at the intrapersonal, interpersonal, group, and cultural levels. The key historical developmental of modern *theories* is explicated in the following models.

3.1 Karl Bühler: 1934 Model

Bühler's ([1934] 1982a: 30; 1982b) *Organon Model* of human communication derives from Plato's argument in the *Cratylus* "that language is an *organum* for the one to inform the other of something about the things." Bühler's ([1934] 1982a: 13) approach builds linguistic science into the logic foundation constituted by Edmund Husserl's ([1922] 1970) intersubjective phenomenology as articulated in the *Logical Investigations* and especially in the *Cartesian Meditations*.

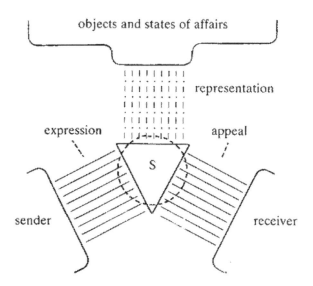

Figure 1: Bühler's *Organon Model*

Bühler (1982b: 34–37) specifies the concepts in the Fig. 1:

> The circle in the middle symbolizes the concrete acoustic phenomenon. Three variable factors in it go to give it the rank of a sign [= s] in three different manners. The sides of the inscribed triangle symbolize these three factors. In one way the triangle encloses less than the circle

(thus illustrating the principle of abstractive relevance). In another way it goes beyond the circle to indicate that what is given to the senses always receives an apperceptive complement. The parallel lines symbolize the semantic functions of the (complex) language sign [= s]. It is a *symbol* by virtue of its coordination to objects and states of affairs, a *symptom* (*Anzeichen, indicium:* index) by virtue of its dependence on the sender, whose inner state it expresses, and a *signal* by virtue of its appeal to the hearer, whose inner or outer behaviour it directs as do other communicative signs.

The semantic relations are indicated by "the terms *expression* (*Ausdruck), appeal* (*Appell*) and *representation.*" Bühler (1982b: 37–38) is describing interpersonal communication where

each of the two participants has his own position in the make-up of the speech situation, namely the sender as the agent of the act of speaking, as the *subject* of the speech action on the one hand, and the receiver as the one spoken to, as the *addressee* of the speech action on the other hand. They are not simply a part of what the message is about, rather they are the partners in an exchange, and ultimately this is the reason why it is possible that the sound as a medial product has a specific significative relationship to each, to the one and to the other severally.

Up until 1982, the only account of Bühler's model available in English was that by Leo Zawadowski (1975). Per Durst-Andersen (2009) provides a clear linguistic explication of Bühler's model in terms of a correlation to C. S. Peirce's semiotics that expands the previous discussion of grammar, rhetoric, and logic as elements of communication theory.

3.2 Claude Elwood Shannon: 1948 model

James Gleick (2011) offers a comprehensive history of the notion of information articulated by Claude Shannon (1948, 1993a,b,c). The model we know as information theory (IT) stimulated many subsequent variations that appear in all manner of books on just about every topic of communication and media. All are variations on the following diagram that Shannon (1948: 31, 34, 35) specifies as a "schematic diagram of a general communication system" as found in "computing machines" or "telephone exchanges." Shannon's model is directed at solving the problem of "noise in the channel" when an electrical signal is transmitted from one machine to another. The small unlabeled box in the middle of the diagram represents the physical *channel*, such as a telephone line, fiber optic cable, or computer chip. By comparison in human communication (CT), "when we use the term '*medium*', rather than '*channel*', we are concerned not with the actual transmission of signals, but with the systematic functional and structural differences between written and spoken language" (Lyons 1977: I, 69) or network levels of language use, such as human *groups* (McFeat 1974: 22, 40).

Shannon begins his technical presentation of the mathematical model with this warning:

The fundamental problem of communication is that of reproducing at one point either exactly or approximately a message selected at another point. Frequently the messages have *meaning;* that is they refer to or are correlated according to some system with certain physical or conceptual entities. These semantic aspects of communication are irrelevant to the engineering problem. The significant aspect is that the actual message is one *selected from a set* of possible messages. The system must be designed to operate for each possible selection, not just the one which will be actually chosen since this is unknown at the time of design (Shannon 1948: 31).

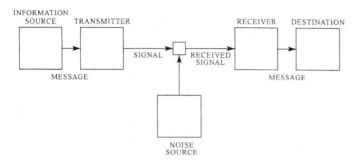

Figure 2: Claude Elwood Shannon's model

There are two important facts here: (1) meaning is not part of the theory and (2) the chosen message is unknown. Here, also, we must understand that "certain physical or conceptual entities" refers to *human writing/speaking or language,* the system of *meaning.* When we take the requirement for meaning into account, the diagram must be modified to account for a *human observer* who has a command of a natural language. While it is possible to have one machine monitor another machine (e.g., the internet) there will always have to be a *human observer* to build, maintain, use, and supply language to the machine (Ruesch 1953: 55). Ultimately, the "correction data" will always be a natural human language (syntactics, semantics, pragmatics) as specified in Figure 3 by Shannon (1949: 68).

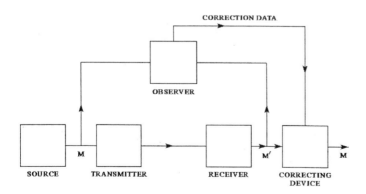

Figure 3: Shannon's "correction data"

3.3 Jürgen Ruesch and Gregory Bateson: 1951 model

The human science response to the Shannon IT model was made initially by Jürgen Ruesch and Gregory Bateson (1951), a psychiatrist and an anthropologist respectively, with an explicit CT account of the *human observer* – the language using human being. Ruesch and Bateson specify that human communication operates on four ascending embedded network levels of complexity: Level I is intrapersonal communication (embodied consciousness), Level II is interpersonal communication (dyadic interaction), Level III group communication (social interaction), and Level IV cultural communication (inter-group culture). As a direct comparison to the Shannon model, Ruesch and Bateson (1951: 277, Table D.) designate each network according to (1) Origin of the Message, (2) Sender, (3) Channels (4) Receiver, and (5) Destination of Message. The communication *process* involves (1) evaluating, (2) sending, (3) "channel" [= medium] chosen, and (4) receiving. Note that the process begins with the *observer evaluating the message* (the part external to the Shannon model). All these elements of the model are presented in Fig. 2 (1951: 275). A summary version of the theory is Ruesch (1953).

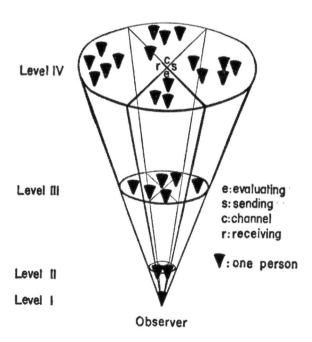

THE LEVELS OF COMMUNICATION

Level IV

Level III   e:evaluating
                     s:sending
                     c:channel
                     r:receiving

Level II   ▼:one person

Level I

Observer

Figure 4: Jürgen Ruesch and Gregory Bateson's 1951 model

3.4 Roman Osipovîch Jakobson: 1958 model

Jakobson's communication theory is the most comprehensive ever developed, ranging from phonology in consciousness to practice in culture. The theory builds on the "rhetorical branch of linguistics" because "distinctiveness and redundancy, far from being arbitrary assumptions of the investigator [as in IT], are objectively present and delimited in language [as in CT]" and thereby "establishes a clear-cut demarcation between the theory of communication and of information" (Jakobson 1960b: 571–573). By this time, as Gleick (2011: 268) notes, "In the social sciences, the direct influence of information theorists had passed it peak. The specialized mathematics had less and less to contribute to psychology and more and more to computer science."

Jakobson's (1960a: 21–27) model of communication (Fig. 5) presents both six ELEMENTS and six respective *[functions]*. Note that the Addresser – Addressee are horizontal to indicate a primary syntagmatic relationship, whereas the paradigmatic relationship is shown vertically by the Context and Message pair in opposition to the Contact and Code pair. Note that the functions and elements are also incorporated into the *Alexander Model* which is seen in Fig. 6 below.

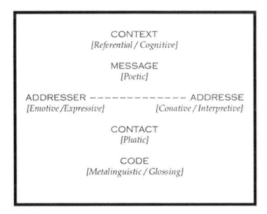

Figure 5: Jakobson's human communication model

The *Addresser* is the human, embodied origin of communication and in consequence is not a mechanical "sender" or "signal source," but the *expressive constitution of emotion*. In linguistic terms, the Addresser is the verbal 1st Person (*persona) who is speaking*. The person may be the psychic voice the Greeks called *mythos,* or the persona whose oral speaking is audible as the interpretant *logos* of a person. As such, the Addresser *gives* (data) a Message that constitutes a Code and selects a Context for Contact ("choice of context" or analogue logic). Lotman (1994: 22) provides a detailed analysis of the motivation that occurs between message and code, code and message, in the formation of discourse as practice and communication as culture.

The *Addressee* element of communication is basically the reverse phenomenological intentionality of the Addresser. The Addressee is the human, embodied origin of culture and, in consequence, is not a mechanical "receiver" or "signal destination," but the *interpretive constitution of conation*. In linguistic terms, the Addressee is the verbal 2nd Person (persona) *who is spoken to*. The person for whom aural listening is audible (oral) becomes the interpretant *logos* (a preconscious social practice or *habitus*) for the psychic voice that the Greeks called *hexis*, or the self embodied practice of culture. As such, the Addressee *takes* (capta) a Code that constitutes a Message and selects a Contact for Context ("context of choice" or digital logic).

Context is the *referential function* of the communicative act in which signification is denotative within a cognitive system of meaning. In linguistic terms, Context is the 3rd person, *someone or something spoken of*. It is crucial to recall that Jakobson rejects Saussure's notion of an arbitrary sign (signifier in *opposition* to signified). Rather, Jakobson demonstrates that communication is a "choice of context" such that signs have a relative, but necessary, motivation to one another (signifier in *apposition* to signified). As Holenstein (1974: 157) explains Jakobson's use of Peircian semiotics, a sign's "own constitution reflects the relational structure of the thing represented," Hence we have Peirce's preferred name for the sign as a *representamen*. The notion of "representation" is a key problematic and thematic in all Postmodern discussions of intentionality in the human sciences.

Contact is the *phatic function* operating in human communication such that a physical (interpersonal) and psychological (embodied, intrapersonal) connection is established between the Addresser and the Addressee. The best eidetic/empirical example in linguistics is the concept of an *emblem*. An emblem is the anthropologist's name for a word that stands in place of a gesture, or, the gesture that replaces a verbal message (this is also an example of code switching). The emblem is a sign with a culturally known interpretant that moves from (1) physical contact (signification) between Addresser and Addressee to (2) mutual psychic sharing (meaning).

The *Message* displays the phenomenology of the *poetic function* in communication. Rather than a mundane reference to poetry, the essence of *poiesis* is the shifting of verbal elements exterior to the system of language in which case you have *rhetoric*, or, interior to the system of language in which case you have *poetic*. While there is a long, detailed phonological analysis that is relevant at this point (i.e., the nature of distinctive and redundancy phonetic features), we must be content to explain the poetic function in verbal communication as paradigmatic and syntagmatic *reversal* of words as units in sentences.

For example, once you know the words in a sentence by grammatical function, any word in that category can replace any other word. In the sentence, "The cat ate the dog." you immediately see that if you are a dog lover the message can be reversed as "The dog ate the cat." Moreover, you immediately also know that any noun in the sentence can be replaced by a pronoun, and, any verb can substitute for any other verb. The vertical (paradigmatic) and horizontal (syntagmatic) word shifts can be remembered as a whole set, what Jakobson calls the "Prague Prism" (Holenstein 1974: 31, 139) or ever expanding matrix, hence, Ruesch and Bateson's (1951) use of "social matrix" in the subtitle of their book.

Jakobson concludes that messages are unique in language because human speaking (*parole*) consists of: (1) a linguistic utterance, (2) language as an individual, private property, and (3) the individualizing, centrifugal aspect of language (where *centrifugal* means the agency of moving from individual out to group, from person into culture). Message interpretation relies on perceiving the diachronic ("then and there" historical sequences) of verbal or nonverbal usage. Egocentric cultures, typically Western, stress the importance of messages over codes, individuals over groups (Lanigan 2011b).

The concept of a *Code* entails the understanding of the *metalinguistic, glossing, or rubric function* in communication. Every communication system, verbal or nonverbal, has both an object language (discourse about extralinguistic entities) and a metalanguage (discourse about linguistic entities) that specify synchronic relationships ("here and now" existential moments). Linguists refer to this code phenomenon as "double articulation," since an utterance or gesture refers both to itself as an entity (the *agency* function) and beyond itself to its context in a system (the *efficacy* function). Jakobson also judges that codes are unique in language because social language (*langue*) consists of (1) linguistic norm, (2) language as supraindividual, social endowment, and (3) the unifying, centripetal aspect of language (where *centripetal* means the efficacy of moving from group to individual, from culture to person). Sociocentric cultures, typically Eastern, stress the importance of codes over messages, groups over individuals (Lanigan 2011b).

Most people experience the complexity of the metalinguistic function when they look up a word (message) in a dictionary (code) only to find themselves referred to other words (message in the same code), thus acting to no avail in an unknown code. With an encyclopedia, the name (code) of a concept, person, place is described in a narrative (message) where the sought after name becomes a concept among related ideas. The *Dictionary* or *IT Model* of the message-to-code processing is often compared to the *Encyclopedia* or *CT Model* of code-to-message processing (Eco 1976: 98–100).

3.5 Hubert Griggs Alexander: 1967 model

Alexander's ([1967] 1988, 1968, 1969) communication model is philosophic in orientation with the goal of explicating how human thinking operates as *rational-*

ity through the agency of language and logic as suggested by leading Western philosophers and linguists. At Yale University for his Ph.D., his teachers were Wilbur Urban, Edward Sapir (1931), and Ernst Cassirer ([1957] 1995) and he was a classmate of Benjamin Lee Whorf (1952) which helps explain this orientation (Lanigan 2011a). The model is formalized with notation to show all the complex semiotic relationships being considered, especially the connection between *symbol* and *referent*. The diagram, Fig. 6, is modified to show the corresponding elements and functions of the *Roman Jakobson Model* which are indicated as *[bracketed terms]*.

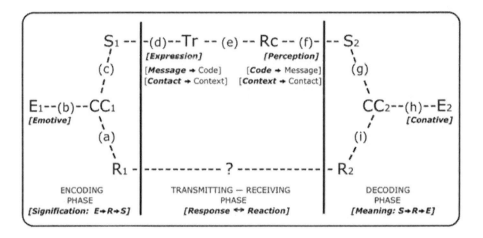

Figure 6: Hubert Griggs Alexander's model

Symbolic Notation:

E1   = The Background Experience and Attitude of the Communicator.
CC1 = The Concept of the Communicator.
S1   = The Symbol(s) used by the Communicator.
R1   = The Referent(s) as Perceived or Imagined by the Communicator.
S2   = The Symbol(s) as Understood by the Communicatee.
R2   = The Referent(s) as Perceived or Imagined by the Communicatee.
CC2 = The Concept of the Communicatee.
E2   = The Background Experience and Attitude of the Communicatee.
Tr   = The Transmitting Device, Mechanism, Medium of Expression.
Rc   = The Receiving Device, Mechanism, Medium of Perception.
?   = The Mediation Possibility of a Relationship as Response (Verbal), Reaction (Nonverbal).
a – i = Specific Boundary Relationships that are Necessary (validity) and Sufficient (reliability) Conditions in the Communicological Process.
···· = Space/Place and Time/Moment Link, Connection, Relationship.

Alexander focuses on the *communication concept* that is a complex semiotic relationship moving from human *experience* (awareness) to *referents* for that experience (awareness of awareness) on to the *symbols* (representation of awareness of awareness) *used* as a *signification* of the experience. A special focus of the model is the fact, first noted by Jakobson, that the Communicator *encoding* process is *reversed* in *decoding* by the Communicatee. Decoding involves moving from symbol to referent to experience as the constitution of *meaning*. This reversal (poetic function) is a key component of Jakobson's idea of motivated redundancy in which the symbol is *psychologically distinct* in every usage (CT) for a human being as opposed to *physically identical* repetition that is arbitrary (IT) for a machine. Jakobson's new definition of redundancy also resolves many classic philosophical paradoxes based on the hypostatization of ideal referents.

The explanatory power of Alexander's model is best understood by an examination of the key relations points marked (a) through (i) in the Encoding, Transmitting, and Decoding phases. These are points at which a *functional failure* in human communication can take place which we recognize as misunderstanding – the failure of proper concept formation. The failure points are examined in order together with suggestive examples.

3.5.1 Failures in communicator conceiving and encoding

Encoding is primarily the *process* of creating a *signification* in the language system and contextual nonverbal behavior where a personal *message* is constructed using synergistic parts of the cultural *code*. The signification is often referred to as a *denotation* or extensional term (Alexander [1967] 1988: 85–88).

(a) Referent: Epistemic-Pragmatic Failure occurs by the Communicator forming the *wrong idea* which maybe due to [1] unclear perceptions (e.g., mistaking a "cat" for a "dog"), [2] improper conceptualizing (e.g., mistaking a cardinal ["1"] for an ordinal ["first"] number), or [3] the wrong application of a properly conceived Idea (e.g., taking the planet Earth to be a perfect sphere).

(b) Experience: Epistemic-Emotive Failure because of *preconceptions* on the part of the Communicator that may be due to [1] a lack of appropriate background experience or [2] an inadequate education.

(c) Symbol: Semiotic-Semantic Failure in Encoding (using the *wrong symbols*) may be due to: [1] an inadequate knowledge of the symbol system (e.g., saying "dog" when one means "cat") or [2] using ambiguous symbols, or symbols that are apt to be unfamiliar to the Communicatee, either intentionally (deception) or not (mistake).

3.5.2 Failures due to expression (Transmitting) and perception (Receiving)

(d) Physiological Failures of the Communicator (e.g., mis-articulation, stuttering).

(e) Mechanical Failures in Transmitting and Receiving (e.g., mispronunciation, aberrant sounds, background noise, static).

(f) Physiological Failures of the Communicatee (e.g., being hard of hearing, confused by an unfamiliar accent, contradiction between word and gesture).

3.5.3 Failures in Decoding and discovering the correct Referent

Decoding is primarily the Communicatee *process* of creating a *meaning* in the language system and contextual nonverbal behavior where the cultural *code* is used to construct a personal *message*. The meaning is typically referred to as a *connotation* or intensional term (Alexander [1967] 1988: 85–88). Among human beings, this open system process is curvilinear, while in machines the closed system process is linear (Ruesch 1953: 50). Hence, encoding as a *channel code signification* is never an equivalent process to decoding *medium message meaning* – as Margaret Mead and Claude Shannon warned!

(g) Symbol: Semiotic-Semantic Failure in Decoding (using the *wrong concept* for the symbols received) may be due to: [1] Inadequate knowledge of the symbol system used by the Communicator (e.g., hearing a foreign or unfamiliar language); or, [2] Not recognizing all of the implications of the symbols used (e.g., not detecting irony in the speaker's tone of voice).

(h) Experience: Epistemic-Emotive Failure because of *preconceptions* on the part of the Communicatee (e.g., having a misconception of geographical orientation, which leads to a failure to understand directions; or, having no experience with an object which is being described to one).

(i) Referent: Epistemic-Pragmatic Failure in Finding the Correct Referent (e.g., failure to get from the correct, but too general, concept to a *specific referent* such as not knowing that "Betty" refers to a pet dog, not a person).

4 Communication

Communication science is fundamentally the study of organisms and their environment. On that premise, a distinction is made on the basis of systems complexity among humans, animal, and machines. The complexity levels are best characterized semiotically in the sense that human beings synergistically embody iconic, indexical, and symbolic systems in both time and space (Merleau-Ponty 2003). Animals and machines do not (Dreyfus [1972] 1992).

4.1 Human

Throughout history there has been an enduring consensus about human communication that is captured by Jürgen Ruesch (1972: 127):

> The word 'communication' will be used here in a very broad sense to include all the procedures by which one mind affects another. This, of course, involves not only written and oral speech, but also music, the pictorial arts, the theatre, the ballet, and in fact, all human behavior.

The unique human ability to use symbols to hold meaning in consciousness is referred to as "time binding" and our parallel ability to locate that same meaning in language (speech and writing) is called "space binding" (Korzybski 1926; Lanigan 1997b).

4.2 Animal

Research on animal communication is generally known as *zoosemiotics* (Sebeok 1977). In the case of animals, various species display a range of specific capacities to use iconic or indexical signs, but not both. None have symbol capacity, primarily because of the inability to pass specific signs from one generation to the next. While there is evidence of passing a general biological capacity for sign production/recognition from one to a second generation only, there is no intergenerational learning and no *doutero learning* (the symbol capacity of learning how to learn). Thus Margaret Mead (1970: 2) specifies "that the continuity of all cultures depends on the living presence of at least three generations."

4.3 Machine

Machine communication is usually associated with current technologies for manipulating indexical signs. Beginning first with the primitive technology of drum beats, then hand held flags, and then the electrical signals of Morse Code on the telegraph or sound simulation on the telephone, human technology is now at the computer stage with "wireless" signal connections on a global scale. While technology forms continue to evolve and integrate (e.g., iMac computer, iPhone, and iTablet synchronized as Mobile.me in the iCloud), the major contribution of machine communication to human users is the increased opportunity for technologically extended interaction using existing symbol systems (i.e., language and audio-visual records).

5 Communicology

Communicology is the science of human communication (DeVito 1978: v; Lanigan 1988, 1992, 2008a,b; Flusser 1996, 2002). This theoretical and applied approach to the study of human communication uses the combination of semiotics (cultural codes) and phenomenology (embodied consciousness) to explicate communication theory (CT) and information theory (IT) as logics of verbal and nonverbal interaction (Lanigan 1997a,b). The approach stresses the priority of CT as the logical context for IT. This is to say as a theorem of logic, (1) a Choice of Context as a *combinatory analog apposition* always precedes (2) a Context of Choice as a *disjunctive digital opposition* is the distinguishing characteristic of human thought and speech (Wilden [1972] 1980, 1987).

Communicology can be summarized easily as a semiotic logic of discourse and practice:

> IF the *formation rules* are DISCOURSE:
> *Rule 1:* Things included in the system (Both—And analog logic).
> *Rule 2:* Things excluded from the system (Either—Or digital logic).
> THEN the *transformation rules* are PRACTICE:
> *Rule 3:* Things excluded from the system can be Things included in the system (Paradigmatic Axis of poetic function).
> *Rule 4:* Things included in the system can be Things excluded from the system. (Syntagmatic axis of poetic function) (cf. Lanigan (2005: 421–435).

Note that discourse and practice constitute an *open curvilinear system* in human thought, whereas a closed machine memory system must always be *linear,* hence cannot simultaneously process an analog and digital logic in *apposition* – which is what human cognition does (Lanigan 1988: 184–193; Ruesch 1953: 50).

It is a fact that only the human mind can engage this theorem in which *both the* chosen *and* not chosen are the binary boundary condition (analog logic) for choosing to *either* choose *or* not choose (digital logic) as the choice made. In CT the binary combination choice is an *apposition* of meaning that constitutes the context, whereas the binary disjunction context is an *opposition* that constitutes the choice as a signification (Durst-Andersen 2009: 59). Bühler ([1934] 1982a: 438–451) defines the linguistic *apposition* as *anaphoric deixis*: a continuous structure of relationship in which the sign presence (*words* in a sentence) projects a combination with the sign absence (words not used, but in paradigmatic and syntagmatic relation) in a synergism which we reduce to the concept of "contexts" (words in *specific possible sentences* that are recognized as *intended* by the speaker).

A simple conversation example of anaphoric deixis is a person (listener) who *finishes* the sentences of another person (deixis) after only the first few words (anaphora) are spoken by the speaker. Edmund Husserl ([1922] 1970: 18) refers to this communicological phenomenon as a case of "transcendental sociological [intersubjective] phenomenology having reference to a manifest multiplicity of conscious subjects communicating with one another." Roman Jakobson (1962–2002; Holenstein [1974] 1976: 138–139) specifies these same communicological characteristics of all human discourse, that he calls *poetic function,* as the *reversibility* potential of (1) vertical *paradigmatic* distinctive features (selection, substitution, similarity, metaphor) and (2) horizontal *syntagmatic* redundancy features (combination, contexture, contiguity, metonymy).

In Western cultures this communicology logic of apposition prior to opposition is described as *non-Aristotelian* or postmodern logic (Lanigan 2008a) and in Asia it is known as *correlation logic* (Chang 1938, 1946; Jiang 2002; Lanigan 2011b; Nisbett 2003). To summarize, human symbolic capacity (represented empirically in spoken language) is the ability to make time and space binding logics by *combining an analog and digital logic at the same time in the same place* – a physical impossibility for an animal or machine because an electrical signal cannot both be and not be at the same time and place, but that is the very definition of a *symbol!* And, symbolic capacity is the very definition of being human (Urban [1939] 1971: 21).

5.1 Consciousness

The human mind has consciousness as a product of pre-consciousness, which we have discussed as time and space binding in verbal and nonverbal communication. Human beings, unlike animals and machines, function on three simultaneous levels of consciousness that integrate *both expression and perception* of (1) *Affect* or emotion, (2) *Cognition* or thought, and (3) *Conation* or purposeful action. The scholastic philosophers in the Middle Ages designated the three levels by the respective Latin terms: (1) *Capta*, (2) *Data*, and (3) *Acta*, which today are still in use to varying extents. In the specific context of communication, human consciousness thus functions as a simultaneous integration of (1) Awareness, or Preconsciousness, (2) Awareness of Awareness, or Consciousness, and (3) Representation of Awareness of Awareness, or variously, Nonconsciousness, Subconsciousness, Unconsciousness. Charles S. Peirce (1931–1958: 1.530–544) provides a useful reference system for these three levels by referring to them as *Firstness, Secondness,* and *Thirdness.* Thus from the perspective of the cultural development of speech as language, human Awareness becomes the syntactic code of "grammar" in verbal communication expressing iconic signs of expression-perception. In turn, Awareness of Awareness becomes the semantic code of "rhetoric" illustrating indexical signs of expression-perception. Last, the Representation of Awareness of Awareness becomes the pragmatic code of the "logic" expression of the symbolic signs of perception. Peirce (1931–1958: 7.585) provides a simple, but explicit summary": "A man has consciousness; a word has not."

5.2 Embodiment

Following the proofs offered by Merleau-Ponty (1945) for human embodiment as the source of human expression and perception, Hubert Dreyfus ([1972] 1992 : 236) reminds us that communication interaction and meaning is founded on our understanding of the *practical activity* of the human body: "what distinguishes persons from machines, no matter how cleverly constructed, is not a detached, universal immaterial soul but an involved, situated, material body." Consciousness as the human mind in the synergistic body is the source and context for communication (Lanigan 2010a; Weiss and Haber 1999).

5.3 Information, Communication, and the Future of 'Intelligent' Machines

Machines can be programmed by creating artificial "languages" (mathematical algorithms) to match *closed system signals* to the *symbol open systems* that we know as human languages (Ruesch 1953: 49–50). This is *information modeling*. Once such a model is in place (e.g., a machine version of "English"), another model can be constructed for "French." Then a third model can be constructed to translate the machine "English" into machine "French." This process is known as primary, secondary, and tertiary modeling in *general systems theory* (Kull 2010; Lanigan 1988: 184).

Once you start to create models for "searching" specific terms in the combined models, you need a complex hierarchy and network of computers to store, sort, classify, and retrieve bits. *Complexity studies* is concerned with how to do this and is most familiar to us as the *Internet* system of models called the World Wide Web. Of course, we can do the same thing with internets that we do with models and this level of metacoding is called *Informatics*. We are presently at the point of developing Internet 2.0 to work with Internet 1.0. If we can continue to develop high order complex systems in this way to achieve an even higher level of complexity, then it will be called "Internet 3.0." Whether or not this level of development is possible at all is a matter of great controversy and is referred to as the problem of the *Semantic Web*. So far, basic negative critiques of the attempt to move from machine syntax to the level of human semantics (by computers) and pragmatics (by robotics) dominate the debate by demonstrating that the key requirements of synergism and embodiment cannot be represented in machines (Dreyfus [1972] 1992: 165, 237, 2001; Searle 1983, 1984, 1995). As Merleau-Ponty (2003: 163) summarizes: "The enumeration of possible combinations does nothing to help us understand the very act by which language takes on a meaning."

The Semantic Web is still confronting the original problems faced by information theory: "Level A. How accurately can the symbols of communication be transmitted? (The technical problem). Level B. How precisely do the transmitted symbols convey the desired meaning? (The semantic problem). Level C. How effectively does the received meaning affect conduct in the desired way? (The effectiveness problem)." (Weaver 1949: 4). In semiotic terms, (A) is the *signal transmission* problem as a matter of Syntactics, (B) is the *sign meaning* problem of Semantics, and (C) is the *symbol expression and perception* effectiveness problem of Pragmatics.

Despite the extraordinary advances that have been made in computer technology in terms of storage capacity and signal transmission efficiency, computer science and the associated "cognitive sciences" are still working at Level A on fundamental issues of signal accuracy. By comparison, the paradigm discussed in this essay is the one we are currently using: *human language* (verbal and nonverbal communication) that already functions at Levels A, B, and C with an embodied, synergistic, analog logic base that simply cannot be duplicated by a machine or an animal.

Further reading

Alexander, Hubert G. [1967]. 1988. *The Language and Logic of Philosophy*. Lanham, MD: University Press of America.

Krampen, Martin. 1997. Communication Models and Semiosis. In: Roland Posner, Klaus Robering, Thomas A. Sebeok (eds.), *"Model of Semiotik:", Ein Handbuch zu den zeichentheoretischen Grundlagen von Natur und Kultur, Vol. 1*, 4 vols. 247–287. Berlin: Walter de Gruyter & Co.

Lanigan, Richard L. 1992. *The Human Science of Communicology: A Phenomenology of Discourse in Foucault and Merleau-Ponty*. Pittsburgh, PA: Duquesne University Press.

Ruesch, Jürgen & Gregory Bateson. 1951. *Communication: The Social Matrix of Psychiatry*. New York: W. W. Norton, reprint edn. 1968, 1987.

References

Alexander, Hubert G. 1968. Communication, Technology, and Culture. *The Philosophy Forum* (Special Volume 7: Communication), 7 (1). 1–40.

Alexander, Hubert G. [1967]. 1988. *The Language and Logic of Philosophy*. Lanham, MD: University Press of America. Reprint of revised and enlarged edition by University of New Mexico Press, 1972. Originally published as *Language and Thinking: A Philosophical Introduction*. Princeton, NJ: D. Van Nostrand Co. Inc., 1967.

Alexander, Hubert G. 1969. *Meaning in Language*. Glenview, IL: Scott, Foresman, and Co.

Bühler, Karl. [1934]. 1982a. *Sprachtheorie: Die Darstellungsfunktion der Sprache*. Jena/Stuttgart: Gustav Fischer Verlag, 2nd edn. 1982. Goodwin, Donald Fraser (trans.). *Theory of Language: The Representational Function of Language*. (Foundations of Semiotics: Vol. 25). Amsterdam and Philadelphia: John Benjamins Publishing Co., 1990.

Bühler, Karl. 1982b. The Axiomatization of the Language Sciences. In: Robert E. Innis (ed.), *Karl Bühler: Semiotic Foundations of Language Theory*. New York and London: Plenum Press.

Cassirer, Ernst. [1957]. 1995. *The Philosophy of Symbolic Forms: Vol. 1: Language, Vol. 2: Mythical Thought; Vol. 3: Phenomenology of Knowledge; Vol. 4: The Metaphysics of Symbolic Forms*. Manheim, R. (trans.). New Haven: Yale University Press. Original works published 1923, 1925, 1929.

Chang, Tung-Sun [= transliteration of Zhang Dongsun 张东荪 (1886–1973)]. 1938. Thought, Language and Culture. An-Che, Li (trans.), *Yenching Journal of Social Studies (Peking)* I (2) (1939). Originally published in Chinese in Sociological World X (June 1938). Trans. reprinted as: *A Chinese Philosopher's Theory of Knowledge, Et cetera* IX (3); reprinted in Berman, Sanford I. (ed.) *Logic and General Semantics: Writings of Oliver L. Reiser and Others*.

San Francisco, CA: International Society for General Semantics, 1989. , 111–132. Page references are to the 1989 edition.

Chang, Tung-Sun [Zhang Dongsun 张东荪 (1886–1973)]. 1946. *Zhishi yu wenchua* [Knowledge and Culture]. Shanghai: Commercial Press.

Cherry, Colin. [1957]. 1978. *On Human Communication: A Review, A Survey, and A Criticism*, 3rd edn. Cambridge and London: The MIT Press.

DeVito, Joseph A. 1978. *Communicology: An Introduction to the Study of Communication*. New York: Harper and Row, Publishers, Inc.

Durst-Andersen, Per. 2009. The Grammar of Linguistic Semiotics: Reading Peirce in a Modern Linguistic Light. *Cybernetics and Human Knowing* 16 (3–4). 37–79.

Dreyfus, Hubert L. [1972]. 1992. *What Computer's Still Can't Do: A Critique of Artificial Reason*. Cambridge, MA: The MIT Press. First published as *What Computer's Can't Do: The Limits of Artificial Intelligence*.

Dreyfus, Hubert L. 2001. *On the Internet*. New York, NY: Routledge; Taylor and Francis Group.

Eco, Umberto. 1976. *A Theory of Semiotics*. Bloomington and London: Indiana University Press.

Flusser, Vilém. 1996. *Kommunikologie. Schriften 4*. Eckstein, V. and Bollman, S. (eds.). Mannheim: Bollmann.

Flusser, Vilém. 2002. *Writings*. Ströhl, A. (ed.), Eisel, E. (trans.). Minneapolis: University of Minnesota Press.

Gleick, James. 2011. *The Information: A History, A Theory, A Flood*. New York: Pantheon.

Holenstein, Elmar. [1974]. 1976. *Roman Jakobson's Approach to Language: Phenomenological Structuralism*. Schelbert, Catherine and Schelbert, Tarcisius (trans. [from German Habilitationschrift, Zurich 1974].). Bloomington and London: Indiana University Press. [Edited in French 1974 *Jakobson, ou sur le structuralisme phénoménologique*. Paris: Editions Seghers].

Husserl, Edmund. [1922]. 1970. Syllabus of a Course of Four Lectures on "Phenomenological Method and Phenomenological Philosophy". *JBSP: The Journal of the British Society for Phenomenology* 1 (1). 18 23. [Trans. of the lecture series syllabus given in German at the University College, London, UK on June 6, 8, 9, 12, 1922].

Innis, Robert. 1994. *Consciousness and the Play of Signs*. Bloomington: Indiana University Press.

Jakobson, Roman. [1958. , rev. 1959]. 1960a. Linguistics and Poetics, vol. 3, revised edn, 18–51. In: Jakobson 1962–2002.

Jakobson, Roman. 1960b. [1961]. Linguistics and Communication Theory, vol. 2, 570–579. In: Jakobson 1962–2002.

Jakobson, Roman Osipovîch. 1962–2002. *Selected Writings*, 9 vols. *Vol. 1, Phonological Studies*, 1962, 2nd edn. 1971, 3rd edn. 2002; *Vol. 2, Word and Language*, 1971; *Vol. 3, Poetry of Grammar and Grammar of Poetry*, Rudy, Stephen (ed.), 1981; *Vol. 4, Slavic Epic Studies*, 1966; *Vol. 5, On Verse, Its Masters and Explorers*, Rudy, Stephen and Taylor, Martha (eds.), 1979; *Vol. 6, Early Slavic Paths and Crossroads: Part 1 and Part 2*, Rudy, Stephen (ed.), 1985: *Vol. 7, Contributions to Comparative Mythology; Studies in Linguistics and Philology, 1972–1982*, Rudy, Stephen (ed.), 1985; *Vol. 8, Completion Volume One: Major Works, 1976– 1980*, Rudy, Stephen (ed.), 1988; *Vol. 9, A Complete Bibliography of his Writings*, Rudy, Stephen (ed. and compiler), 1990. Berlin: Mouton de Gruyter. [Unless noted, volumes were edited by Jakobson.]

Jiang, Xinyan. 2002. Zhang Dongsun: Pluralist Epistemology and Chinese Philosophy. In: Chung-Ying Cheng and Nicholas Bunnin (eds), *Contemporary Chinese Philosophy*, 57–81. Oxford: Blackwell Publishers.

Korzybski, Alfred. 1926. *Time-Binding: The General Theory*. Lakeville, CN: Institute of General Semantics.

Krampen, Martin. 1997. Communication Models and Semiosis. In: Roland Posner, Klaus Robering, Thomas A. Sebeok (eds.), *"Model of Semiotik:", Ein Handbuch zu den zeichentheoretischen Grundlagen von Natur und Kultur, Vol. 1*, 4 vols. 247–287. Berlin: Walter de Gruyter & Co.

Kristeva, Julia. 1989. *Language, the Unknown: An Invitation to Linguistics.* Menke, A. M. (trans.). New York: Columbia University Press. First published Paris: Seuil, [1981].

Kull, Kalevi. 2010. Umwelt and Modelling. In: Paul Cobley (ed.) *The Routledge Companion to Semiotics*, 43–56. London and New York: Routledge; Taylor and Francis Group

Lanigan, Richard L. 1984. *Semiotic Phenomenology of Rhetoric: Eidetic Practice in Henry Grattan's Discourse on Tolerance.* Washington, DC: Center for Advanced Research in Phenomenology and University Press of America.

Lanigan, Richard L. 1988. *Phenomenology of Communication: Merleau-Ponty's Thematics in Communicology and Semiology.* Pittsburgh, PA: Duquesne University Press.

Lanigan, Richard L. 1992. *The Human Science of Communicology: A Phenomenology of Discourse in Foucault and Merleau-Ponty.* Pittsburgh, PA: Duquesne University Press.

Lanigan, Richard L. 1995a. A Good Rhetoric Is Possible: Ricoeur's Philosophy of Language as a Phenomenology of Discourse in the Human Sciences. In Lewis Hahn (ed.): *The Philosophy of Paul Ricoeur* (The Library of Living Philosophers), 309–326. Chicago: The Open Court Publishing Co. [A reply by Ricoeur occurs on pp. 327–329].

Lanigan, Richard L. 1995b. From Enthymeme to Abduction: The Classical Law of Logic and the Postmodern Rule of Rhetoric. In: Lenore Langsdorf and Andrew R. Smith (eds.), *Recovering Pragmaticism's Voice: The Classical Tradition, Rorty, and the Philosophy of Communication*, 49–70. Albany: State University of New York Press.

Lanigan, Richard L. 1997a. Communicology. In: Lester Embree (ed.), *Encyclopedia of Phenomenology*, 104–110. Boston, Norwell, MA: Kluwer Academic Publishers.

Lanigan, Richard L. 1997b. Structuralism. In: Lester Embree (ed.), *Encyclopedia of Phenomenology*, 683–689. Boston, Norwell, MA: Kluwer Academic Publishers

Lanigan, Richard L. 2001. Charles Sanders Peirce (1839–1914). In: Jorge Reina Schement (ed.) *Encyclopedia of Communication and Information, Vol. 3*: 705–707. New York: Macmillan Library Reference USA.

Lanigan, Richard L. 2005. Fabulous Political Semiotic: The Case of George Orwell's *Animal Farm.* In: Rodney Williamson, Leonard G. Sbrocchi, and John Deely (eds.), *Semiotics 2003: "Semiotics and National Identity"*, 421–435. Ottawa, Canada: Legas Publishing [appeared 2006].

Lanigan, Richard L. 2007. Communicology: The French Tradition in Human Science. In: Pat Arneson (ed.), *Perspectives on the Philosophy of Communication*, 168–184. West Lafayette, IN: Purdue University Press.

Lanigan, Richard L. 2008a. Communicology. In: Wolfgang Donsbach (ed.), *International Encyclopedia of Communication, vol. 3*, 12 vols: 855–857. Oxford, UK and Malden, MA: Wiley-Blackwell Publishing Co.; International Communication Association.

Lanigan, Richard L. 2008b. Phenomenology. In: Wolfgang Donsbach (ed.), *International Encyclopedia of Communication, Vol. 8*, 12 vols: 3595–3597. Oxford, UK and Malden, MA: Wiley-Blackwell Publishing Co.; International Communication Association.

Lanigan, Richard L. 2010a. Mind-Body Problem. In: Ronald L. Jackson II (ed.), *Encyclopedia of Identity, Vol. 1*, 2 vols, 450–454. Thousand Oaks, CA: Sage Publications, Inc.

Lanigan, Richard L. 2010b. Theoretical and Applied Aspects of Communicology. In: Zdzisław Wąsik (ed.), *Consultant Assembly III: In Search of Innovatory Subjects for Language and Culture Courses*, 7–32. Wrocław, Poland: Philological School of Higher Education in Wrocław Publishing.

Lanigan, Richard L. 2010c. The Verbal and Nonverbal Codes of Communicology: The Foundation of Interpersonal Agency and Efficacy. In: Deborah Eicher-Catt and Isaac E. Catt (eds.),

Communicology: The New Science of Embodied Discourse, 102–128. Madison, NJ: Fairleigh Dickinson University Press

Lanigan, Richard L. 2011a. Husserl's Phenomenology in America (USA): The Human Science Legacy of Wilbur Marshall Urban and the Yale School of Communicology. *Schutzian Research* 3. 199–213.

Lanigan, Richard L. 2011b. The Logic of Phenomena: Semiotic Structures of West and East in Communicology and Culture. *Chinese Semiotic Studies* [Journal of the Nanjing University International Institute of Semiotic Studies], 6 (2).

Lotman, Yuri. 1990. *The Universe of Mind: A Semiotic Approach to Culture.* Bloomington: Indiana University Press.

Lotman, Yuri. 1994. The text within the text. Leo, Jerry and Mandelker, Amy (trans). *Publications of the Modern Language Association* 109 (3). 377–384.

Lyons, John. 1977. *Semantics*, 2 vols. Cambridge and New York: Cambridge University Press.

Marcus, Solomon. 1974. Fifty-Two Oppositions Between Scientific and Poetic Communication. In: Colin Cherry (ed.), *Pragmatic Aspects of Human Communication*, 83–96. Dordrecht and Boston: D. Reidel Publishing Co.

McFeat, Tom. 1974. *Small-Group Cultures.* New York, NY: Pergamon Press, Inc.

Mead, Margaret. 1970. *Culture and Commitment: A Study of the Generation Gap.* Garden City, NY: Nat Hist Press; Doubleday and Co. Inc.

Merleau-Ponty, Maurice. 1945. *Phénoménologie de la Perception.* Paris: Éditions Gallimard. Smith (trans.), Colin, 1962; corrections by Williams, Forrest and Guerrière, David, 1981, *Phenomenology of Perception.* London: Routledge and Kegan Paul.

Merleau-Ponty, Maurice. 2003. The Notions of Information and Communication. In: *Nature: Course Notes from the Collége de France*, 158–166. Vallier, Robert (trans.). Evanston, IL: Northwestern University Press. Originally published as *La Nature: Notes, cours du Collége de France.* Paris: Éditions du Seuil, 1957. ; Éditions Gallimard,1995.

Nisbett, Richard E. 2003. *The Geography of Thought: How Asians and Westerners Think Differently … and Why.* New York: Free Press.

Peirce, Charles Sanders. 1931–1958. *Collected Papers of Charles Sanders Peirce. Vol. 1: Principles of Philosophy; Vol. 2: Elements of Logic; Vol. 3: Exact Logic (Published Papers); Vol. 4: The Simplest Mathematics; Vol. 5: Pragmatism and Pragmaticism; Vol. 6: Scientific Metaphysics*, Hartshorne, Charles and Weiss, Paul (eds.). Cambridge, MA: Harvard University Press, 1931–1935; *Vol. 7: Science and Philosophy; Vol. 8: Reviews, Correspondence, and Bibliography*, Burks, Arthur W. (ed.) (Cambridge, MA: Harvard University Press, 1958.). [All eight vols. in electronic form Deely, John (ed.), Charlottesville, VA: Intelex Corporation, 1994. Dating within the CP (which covers the period in Peirce's life, 1839–1914) is based principally on the Burks Bibliography at the end of CP 8. Reference by codex custom is to volume and paragraph number(s) with a period in between.]

Ruesch, Jürgen. 1953. Synopsis of the Theory of Human Communication. In Ruesch 1972, 47–94.

Ruesch, Jürgen. 1972. *Semiotic Approaches to Human Relations.* The Hague and Paris: Mouton.

Ruesch, Jürgen & Gregory Bateson. 1951. *Communication: The Social Matrix of Psychiatry.* New York: W. W. Norton, reprint edn. 1968, 1987.

Sapir, Edward. 1931. Communication. In: *Encyclopedia of the Social Sciences*, 78–81. New York: Macmillan. [Page references are to the reprint in *Selected Writings*.].

Sapir, Edward. 1949. *Selected Writings of Edward Sapir in Language, Culture and Personality*, 104–109. Berkeley: University of California Press.

Searle, John. 1983. *Intentionality: An Essay in the Philosophy of Mind.* New York: Cambridge University Press.

Searle, John. 1984. *Minds, Brains, and Science.* Cambridge, MA: Harvard University Press.

Searle, John. 1995. *The Construction of Social Reality.* New York: The Free Press.

Sebeok, Thomas A. 1977. Zoosemiotic Components of Human Communication. In: Thomas A. Sebeok (ed.), *How Animals Communicate*, 1055–1075. Bloomington and London: Indiana University Press.

Shannon, Claude Elwood. 1948. A Mathematical Theory of Communication, Part I, Part II, *Bell Systems Technical Journal* 27 (3) (July), 4 (October). 379–423; reprinted in Shannon, Claude E. and Weaver, Warren, *A Mathematical Model of Communication*. Urbana: University of Illinois Press, 1949. Reprinted in Shannon 1993b. 5–83.

Shannon, Claude Elwood. 1993a. Information Theory. In: Shannon 1993b, 212–220.

Shannon, Claude Elwood. 1993b. *Collected Papers*. Sloane, N. J. A. and Wyner, Aaron D. (eds.). New York: IEEE Press.

Shannon, Claude Elwood. 1993c. *Miscellaneous Writings*. Sloane, N. J. A. and Wyner, Aaron D. (eds). Murray Hill, NJ: Mathematical Sciences Research Center, AT&T Bell Laboratories.

Urban, Wilbur M. [1939]. 1971. *Language and Reality: The Philosophy of Language and the Principles of Symbolism*. New York: Books of Libraries Press Reprint; Arno Books.

Weaver, Warren. 1949. The Mathematics of Communication, *Scientific American* 181 (1). 11–15; revised as Recent Contributions to the Mathematical Theory of Communication. In: Claude E. Shannon and Warren Weaver, *A Mathematical Model of Communication*, 1–28. Urbana: University of Illinois Press, 1949.

Weiss, Gail & Honi Fern Haber (eds.). 1999. *Perspectives on Embodiment: The Intersections of Nature and Culture*. New York and London: Routledge.

Wilden, Anthony. [1972]. 1980. *System and Structure: Essays in Communication and Exchange* 2nd edn. London, UK: Tavistock Publications Ltd.

Wilden, Anthony. 1987. *The Rules Are No Game: The Strategy of Communication*. New York, NY: Routledge and Kegan Paul.

Whorf, Benjamin Lee. 1952. Language, Mind, and Reality. *Et cetera* IX (3). 203–226.

Zawadowski, Leo. 1975. *Inductive Semantics and Syntax: Foundations of Empirical Linguistics*. The Hague and Paris: Mouton.

Dirk Baecker
5 Systemic theories of communication

Abstract: Systemic theories of communication proceed from a deconstruction of Shannon's and Weaver's mathematical theory and transmission model of communication. Referring to the unresolved question of the identity of a message for different observers they instead develop a selection model of communication. In order to overcome the engineering model of signaling (rather than communication) offered by Shannon and Weaver systemic theories drop the assumption of a given set of possible messages any one message is considered to be selected from, and instead assume that the set of possible messages is to be constructed by the participants in communication as much as the single message then to be selected from that constructed set, also known as the context.

Keywords: Autology, communication, form, message, network, observer, selection, society, systemic theory

1 Transmission

Systemic theories of communication proceed from a deconstruction of Claude E. Shannon's and Warren Weaver's transmission model of communication (Shannon and Weaver 1948: 7 and 34) (Fig. 1):

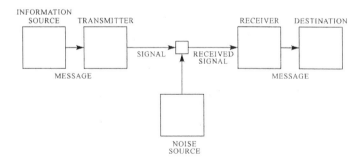

Figure 1: Shannon's and Weaver's schematic diagram of a general communication system

There are few models in science that have caused more misunderstandings than this one. The model is to be found in Weaver's introduction and the opening pages of Shannon's first chapter. The purpose of the model seems to be to enable the reader to focus on the engineering question of how to make sure that a signal transmitted can be received as that signal by a receiver, despite noise from a noise source. Shannon's core idea had been to use concepts of statistical mechanics for ensuring that possible distortions by interference from the noise source can be corrected by the receiver. Any message reaching the receiver was to be understood as "one *selected from a set* of possible messages" (Shannon and Weaver 1948: 31) so that the receiver had only to calculate the probabilities of possible messages in order to substitute a possibly distorted one by a probably correct one.

Shannon's stroke of genius was to waive any attempt to let receivers know the substantial 'meaning' of a message, letting them focus instead on the relational 'information' supplied by it with respect to other messages already received or still expected. There is therefore never just one message but always many, all from a "set of possible messages" (Shannon and Weaver 1948) so that one is to be determined by the probability of all others. Norbert Wiener, a close collaborator of Shannon at the time, insisted on the fundamentality of this idea. He underlined that cybernetics takes its starting point from the same concept of statistical mechanics, which for him consists in "the resolution of a complex contingency into an infinite sequence of more special contingencies – a first, a second, a third, and so on – each of which has a known probability" (Wiener 1948: 46). There is a nice paradox hidden in this formula, namely that sums of probability zero lead to probability one (Wiener 1948; 46/7), but we will not go into that here.

Shannon emphasized that his 'mathematical theory of communication' is relevant only for understanding and solving the engineering problem of signal transmission. He refrained from any implication the solution of this problem could have for understanding the 'semantic aspects of communication'. Indeed, he originally presented not 'the' but 'a' mathematical theory of communication (Shannon 1948), leaving the selection of the bolder definite article to Weaver, who put the book together out of Shannon's papers. But Shannon's reluctance to generalize his theory could not prevent his and Weaver's ideas on 'communication' from being quickly and enthusiastically received as well as fervently rejected by social scientists (e.g., as regards reception, Jakobson 1981; Bense 1969; and with respect to rejection, Hayles 1999). The same happened to Wiener. He rejected the application of cybernetics to social systems due to the lack of sufficiently long runs of statistical data describing such systems (Wiener 1948: 24–5). But this warning could not prevent cybernetic ideas about 'communication and control' based on a calculus of contingencies, as it were, becoming prominent in many areas of the social sciences, much as Shannon's and Weaver's model had.

The problem with Shannon's and Weaver's diagram was that 'transmitter' and 'receiver' are personalized as the 'sender' and 'receiver' of messages, thus picturing communication as the transmission of messages from one person to another using a channel, which even though posing problems about choosing the right code in encoding and decoding messages and, although possibly distorted by unknown noise, nevertheless let messages travel in orderly fashion from one point to the other. The two boxes representing 'information source' and 'destination' were meanwhile discarded as rather enigmatic references, possibly to the 'consciousness' of the people involved in communication. Weaver, to be sure, did his best to foster the misunderstanding by saying, for instance, that 'communication' is one of several "procedures by which one mind may affect another" (Shannon and Weaver 1948: 3) and, in distinction to Shannon, by addressing not only 'technical,' but also 'semantic' and 'effectiveness problems' (Shannon and Weaver 1948: 4). He even mused about selecting not just a message but a "desired" one out of a set of possible messages (Shannon and Weaver 1948: 7). This he considered a point worth coming back to, for it showed the way beyond selection and statistical calculation to 'desires', to the receiver's purposes, aims, and motives. Not least, he emphasized that Shannon's warning to treat the semantic aspect as irrelevant to the engineering aspect does not necessarily mean that the engineering problems are irrelevant to the semantics (Shannon and Weaver 1948: 8).

I think that he was right in this emphasis. But the engineering problems are not relevant to semantics since in engineering we are concerned only with messages as signals traveling along a channel. They become relevant when we consider the possibility of generalizing the selection model of communication inherent in Shannon's statistical definition of information (Baecker 1997).

2 The observer

In the co-authored book, Shannon quotes two papers in the first paragraph of his chapter, one on 'telegraph speed' (Harry Nyquist), the other on 'transmission of information' (Ralph Hartley), both of which had already looked at the 'signal-to-noise ratio,' leaving him only to add some ideas on noise and, *nota bene*, on the statistical structure of the original message. In what is possibly the most important and most deceptive statement in the chapter, he goes on to say in the second paragraph: "The fundamental problem of communication is that of reproducing at one point either exactly or approximately a message selected at another point" (Shannon and Weaver 1948: 31). One could write volumes about any of the words in this exposition, and Michel Serres in fact did so (Serres 1968–1980; 1982), but we will focus only on 'reproduction.' That the problem of communication is one of reproduction could have been the most obvious indicator of the theory dealing with the engineering problem of how to make sure that the signal sent is the same as the signal received. As a matter of fact, however, this statement, even if not quoted literally, became the mantra of all communication theorists in search of ways to ensure that communication successfully transmits the meaning the sender has in mind to the receiver seeking to understand this meaning. Keep the channel clean or, better, domination-free (Habermas 1984), make sure that everybody is both reasonably enlightened and well-intentioned, and everything will be just fine. Communication will be possible and will be able to sort out the fate of mankind, or so the reasoning went (see also Chapter 2, Eadie and Goret, Chapter 13, Wharton and Chapter 14, Bangerter and Mayor).

The problem of this well-meaning reading of the sentence is that it neglects what any philosopher and any cognitive scientist knows: that minds and hearts are closed to one another (if not to themselves as well) (see only Locke 1959, vol. II: 8–14), that communication is there to replace understanding (thus enabling it, even if at the price of possible mendacity and deception) (Schleiermacher 1995; Schlegel 1997), and that the fascinating questions arise when we begin to inquire into how minds (and bodies) participate in communication (see only, possibly after having read about Johannes Peter Müller's or similar neurophysiological research, Nietzsche 2006). Even worse, this reading overlooks a more fundamental conceptual issue implied by the sentence. The 'reproduction' of a message selected at one point at another would mean that someone knows what the message is if its identical reproduction is to be verified. Who is in this position? Who can state that the message reproduced here is identical to that selected there? Certainly not the sender and not the receiver, if for a moment we maintain this misleading personalization, for both know only about their own selections. It may be an external observer, but who is this external observer, and how is s/he involved in the transmission of the information? Do we need some divine or secular authority invented precisely for the purpose of telling us that we have indeed correctly reproduced our messages, let alone understood each other well?

Shannon's genius, once again, consists in anticipating the very problem of the impossibility of verifying the identity of the two messages–the first selected at one point, the second at another–transmitted via a possibly distorted channel and chancing on a receiver who is possibly uncertain about how to deal with decoding. Indeed, Shannon explicitly states the problem without offering a solution. In his second chapter, where he introduces the concept of channels containing noise, he presents us with a 'correction system' whose key innovation may indeed be the introduction of the observer (Shannon and Weaver 1948: 68):

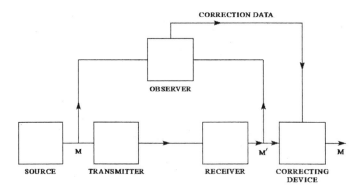

Figure 2: Shannon's schematic diagram of a correction system

This is a prime example of self-deconstruction of a model, if there ever was one. The most interesting detail apart from the introduction of the observer is the correction of M' to M by a 'correcting device' instructed by the 'observer.' The corrected M, however, then exits to the right of the diagram and off the page with no indication of who could be interested in it, who the receiver, let alone the destination, is. Note, however, that the riddle of this diagram in parts at least is to be unlocked easily as soon as one looks at the scheme of a "general secrecy system" which Shannon had pictured in his classified 1946 paper on 'A Mathematical Theory of Cryptography' (declassified as Shannon 1949). Here (Shannon 1949: 661) the observer is the enemy cryptanalyst and the question is how to avoid being deciphered and how to pass on the message:

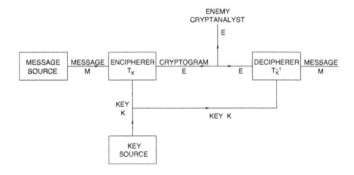

Figure 3: Shannon's schematic of a general secrecy system

It should also be noted that in Fig. 2 (as in Fig. 3) the noise source has disappeared, leaving the observer in a position to state the difference between M and M' without necessarily having to explain how this difference, let alone its detection, came about. It is the 'observer' (whether he, she or it) that states and corrects the difference and also has the means to do so: a 'correction device' operating within the transmission channel, whoever may then be interested in the outcome of its operations.

The deconstruction of the schematic general communication system diagram consists in singling out that the diagram presupposes the identity of two messages nobody within the system can verify to the effect that it becomes impossible to know whether any transmission, let alone the transmission of a message reproduced at one point as the message selected at another point, has in fact taken place.

An observer is needed to know about the difference between the message selected and the message reproduced. A correction device is needed to correct a distorted message. And no-one knows who is involved in receiving the corrected message, or who might want to know about the whole process of sending, distorting, and correcting the message, if not the ominous observer again.

3 Selection

Systemic theories of communication replace transmission with selection (MacKay 1969) and the identity of the message with recursivity (von Foerster 1980). To do this, they introduce a notion of 'system,' which is necessary to show how messages relate to information source, transmitter, receiver, and destination through recursive instead of causal connection (Pask 1970; Krippendorff 1994). 'System' is to be distinguished from 'environment,' which is a proxy for the noise source. The notion of channel then involves structural coupling instead of operational coupling between the distinctions which the transmitter and receiver use to encode and decode messages. Structural coupling occurs when complex units relate to each other to deal with their own complexity; operational coupling is where the operations of one system recursively reproduce each other (Maturana 1975; Luhmann 1992a). The one observer presented by Shannon's correction system is multiplied and distributed throughout the system. And the notion of technically given sets of possible messages ('alphabets') is considered a particular case of the more general case of the systemic construction, production, and reproduction of sets of possible messages ('frames') (Baecker 2005).

However, the one condition for doing all this is to keep Shannon's seminal concept, namely the statistical mechanics notion that information is the relation of one message to a set of possible other messages. The information content of any message is given by the change in the probability of all other possible messages in relation with the first. This decisive step from a substantial to a relational definition of information – much in line with both Gottlob Frege's notion of the meaning of a word residing in the proposition using that word and Ferdinand de Saussure's notion of the semantic elements of language being differences with other elements (Frege 1980; de Saussure 1986) – was grasped early on by Gregory Bateson, who made a first attempt at generalizing Shannon's theory, claiming that communication was not the transmission of information but "the creation of redundancy or patterning" (Bateson 1972: 412; see also Watzlawick et al. 1967).

The relational concept of information is all important because it is the relationship of redundancy to variety (or the signal-to-noise ratio) that is both produced by the system of communication and guides it. A system of communication can thus be defined in terms of the following concepts:

- A *message* is one selected from a set of possible messages.
- Any *unit* participating in a system of communication is an *observer* using its own *distinctions* to identify messages and sets of possible messages they can be selected from.
- The *system* of communication is produced by a message identified by a unit participating in that system and selectively and recursively attributed to another unit, to a set of possible messages, and to possible sources of noise, all three constituting a *network* without boundaries.

- The *reproduction* of the system consists in dealing with variety in such a way that redundancy is maintained. This redundancy distinguishes the system from everything else, i.e. from the environment. Variety and redundancy describe the relation of any message to sets of possible messages distributed with the *network* of messages, units, sets of possible messages, and noise sources.

This definition does not stipulate what kinds of message are produced by the system, whether gestures in facial and bodily expression, images within other images, words within sentences, numbers within calculations, or any mix of these within a multimedia combination. Note that a definition of 'things' consisting of rigid couplings of some elements within 'media' consisting of loose couplings of the same elements (Heider 1926) fits neatly with this definition of systemic communication but has the advantage of not requiring a statistical definition of the set of possible messages, or 'medium.'

The definition does not stipulate what kinds of entity or unit participate as long as they are able to make their distinctions and select their messages, be they spirits, devils, animals, plants, humans, or machines. There is an interesting terminological choice to be made: to talk about 'entities' means to assume something substantial brought with them to communication, while the notion of 'unit' takes those to depend on further units and their common class to actually turn them into a 'unit.' On the one hand, we are dealing with a circular definition of communication, and on the other with entities taking part in communication while not being reducible to that communication. This is why Georg Simmel, for instance, posited that individuals had in part to be non-sociable to take part in processes of socialization (Simmel 1950).

Moreover, the given definition of a system of communication is open with respect to the emergence of a system of communication; any message can start it as long as there is a set of possible messages from which the initiating message can be considered to have been selected, and thus further, related messages. Luhmann emphasizes that any selection whatsoever of information, utterance or understanding can start a communication as long as it finds the two elements with which to synthesize, even if this start necessarily and paradoxically refers back to some previous communication (thus highlighting its link to, and switch from, 'society') (Luhmann 1995). Note that this idea combines high arbitrariness of initiative with strict constraint of constitution. The bootstrapping of communication is due to communication being its own bottleneck.

Finally, our definition does not stipulate a specific balance between redundancy and variety; rigidly repeating almost the same meaning is just as possible as the most flexible dynamics of almost always different meaning. The little word 'almost' is decisive since without it the system would become either a machine or chaos, both of which are defined by a lack of any possibility for selection.

The definition of a system of communication given here is therefore autological because it is as relational as the system it defines. It fulfills Heinz von Foerster's demand for any formalism of communication not to contain symbols representing *communicabilia*: communication cannot be proved by the existence of anything that demands communication (von Foerster 1974). Instead, communication may be proved by proving the production and reproduction of messages to be possible. This production and reproduction relying on a relationship of redundancy to variety, or signal to noise, is called the 'system.'

If the definition of a system of communication is not substantial but relational, two other features are essential. We can call them 'recursivity' and 'sociality.' 'Recursivity' means that there is never just one message to be communicated and never just one unit of communication participating but always an indefinite number of messages and an indefinite number of units, even if most structuring and cultivating of communication (i.e. building expectations to produce 'structure' and valuing and revaluing expectations to constitute 'culture') consists in restricting the number of both possible messages and possible units. But without the recursivity of a message referring via selective memory to previous messages and via selective anticipation and expectation to coming messages, there would be no set of possible messages from which to select in order to identify the message in the first place.

It is thus interesting to use the mathematics of recursive functions, including non-linear dynamics, to prove the general possibility of communication in terms of *eigen*-values or attractors appearing within these recursions. What the vernacular calls the 'objects' and 'subjects' of communication, and the purpose and frames, and indeed the sets of possible messages, are examples of these *eigen*-values (von Foerster 1974, 1980).

'Sociality' means that the interplay of units participating in communication as observers making their distinctions and selections is characterized by both independence and dependence of and among these units. Any communication (production of a message relating to possible other messages) necessarily begins by both accepting another unit to make its selections in accordance with its own distinctions and by trying to restrict these selections by offering frames that define the set of possible messages desired by the first unit. A system of communication as defined here presupposes that the units participating in it are free to choose and nevertheless choose to participate. Communication presupposes units that do not have to communicate. This is why structures and cultures have to emerge that make it both attractive to participate, i.e. which recruit the units participating in communication, and that make it possible at any time to either leave communication or give it a completely unexpected turn, which nevertheless has to be recursively reconnected.

Because of this principle of 'sociality' Heinz von Foerster calls for any systemic theory of communication to accept a basic hermeneutic principle: that the listener not the speaker determines the information of the message (von Foerster and Pörksen 2002). And Niklas Luhmann speaks about the 'improbability' of any communication, whose social, i.e. multiple, constitution compels it to find, define, negotiate, and maintain its attractiveness for all units participating all on its own to make a generally improbable communication specifically, situationally, and temporarily probable (Luhmann 1992b, 1995). Communication comes about if there is the possibility to reject it, or, demonstrating indifference, to avoid, neglect, and ignore it.

4 Error correction

Such a relational rather than substantial definition of communication brings with it the difficulty of empirically determining whether communication takes place or not. Certainly, no single message causes the set of possible messages from which it is selected to be produced, let alone the next message that might refer to it. There is therefore no option to prove communication empirically by determining its causal mechanism, since there is none. If there is any mechanism at all, it is again a selective and relational one, involving the loose coupling of organisms that always have their range of choice and not the tight coupling that, as it were, links cause and effect.

Donald MacKay, for instance, assumes that there is a mechanism of communication which ensures that any communication refers to both individuals taking part, as there is never a change in the 'goal-complex' of the one, induced by communication, that is not linked to a change in the 'goal-complex' of the other (MacKay 1969). But that means that empirical research so important for evidence-based sciences encounters some difficulties with the notion of communication. How is one to ascertain a change in the goal-complex of an individual? It certainly does not help that systemic theories ever since Gregory Bateson's epistemological inquiries doubt the empirical provability of causality as well, since any causality depends on an observer selecting certain causes (but which ones?) to cause (but how?) certain selected effects (again, which ones?) (Bateson 1972). The concern provoked by this objection among the various schools of empirical research prompts them to insist even more strongly on evidence to back assumptions that theoretical notions have reference to some reality.

Systemic theories of communication do not assume that communication is something one can point out to skeptical observers to 'see for themselves.' Instead, the concept of communication is an explanatory principle, or 'metadatum' (Bagley 1968), which helps to frame and order observations into more ambitious and sophisticated descriptions that declare an observer's perspective on some complex reality. The same holds for all other concepts of systems theory, beginning with 'system' and 'environment,' not to mention 'function,' 'boundary,' 'code,' or 'form.' To assume that any word, just because it is there, must refer to a real thing would be to fall victim to the "fallacy of misplaced concreteness," as Alfred North White-head put it (Whitehead 1967: 19–20). In fact, once again, words are determined relationally, not substantially.

Yet, this does not mean that systems theorists are not themselves interested in evidence. Pure belief is satisfactory only in resignation. Systems theories ask for evidence that consists in a description organized on these explanatory principles that tells more about the world and enhances our ability to deal with it. But such a criterion can soon turn into a self-serving ideology, enabling a school to celebrate its proceedings without anybody else understanding what the gains may be. Thus, even systems theorists, in pursuing their research, need some more tangible clue as to whether they are on track or not. In their early attempt to introduce Shannon's insights to the social sciences and, in fact, to psychiatry, Jürgen Ruesch and Gregory Bateson have been among the few to identify such a clue (Ruesch and Bateson 1951). It is very simple. They ask for error correction. As soon as an observer is able to watch two units possibly engaged in communication who refer to each others' behavior by first addressing errors and then correcting them, they may indeed be correctly assumed to be engaged in communication. Of course, this criterion presupposes that Shannon's observer watching the 'transmission' of messages is in fact to be multiplied such that the position of this observer describes the position of any unit engaged in this communication, including that of external observers engaged in research.

5 Unities of difference

We conclude this chapter with a look at a few concepts of communication that have the advantage of keeping in touch with Shannon's relational definition of information and with Wiener's idea of a system referring to many and possibly recursively interlinked contingencies to deal with this world.

The concepts in question are double closure, autopoiesis, social system, and form. Each deals differently with the fundamental challenge of any systemic theory of communication that is, to combine the operation of a message changing the state of the world with the distribution of elements that are both produced by this operation and necessary to support it.

Take 'double closure' first. The concept of double closure was introduced by von Foerster to describe the self-organization of a complex system that reproduces operationally (first closure) because it is able to regulate or program how this reproduction proceeds (second closure) (von Foerster 1973). While first closure eliminates an element of freedom in the system by requiring any end to an operation to be the beginning of another, second closure adds an element of freedom in the choice of structures and cultures for determining the next operation. As far as communication is concerned, this means that messages must indeed be selected to reproduce a system, but (in relation to the facticity of the selection) the system is relatively free in choosing the sets of possible messages from which one is to be selected. Programs or – in more sociological terms – structures and cultures emerge that describe what has proved helpful in reproduction and what is valued as still desirable over other possible structures. Note that possible self-descriptions of the system are established on the level of second closure, allowing confusions, illusions, ideologies, discourses, and semantics to develop that take a rather simplistic stance towards the complexity of the sheer reproduction of operations on the first closure level. Since first and second closure are loosely coupled, it is interesting for communication research to inquire into the function of structures and cultures, to compare them, and, in its own illusory and delusory account, to highlight their contingency.

The concept of 'autopoiesis' invented by Humberto R. Maturana and Francisco J. Varela is closely related to this idea of double closure (Maturana and Varela 1980). It distinguishes between the elements of a system producing the network of elements of the system, on the one hand, and the network of the elements of the system, on the other. This way a distinction can be drawn between the elements operationally reproducing, via 'organizational closure,' the system, on one hand, and the 'structures' contributing to this reproduction while being materialized in most diverse empirical forms, on the other. Operational reproduction, that is the actual linking of one element to another to bring forth a third, remains inaccessible to both the system and the observer because it involves a self-reference that is still systems theory's most axiomatic assumption. Yet the network structuring reproduction is fairly well observable empirically. The network of elements playing some role in reproduction is accessible to an observer who can even try to become involved in this reproduction.

In communication, the network consists of observers and of links between them which, because they change what the observer can see, may be considered observers themselves. Harrison C. White (1992) proposed a corresponding network concept – albeit without reference to systems theories of communication – emphasizing that any element of the network gets its identity from both successful and failed attempts at controlling other elements. Moreover, the overall dynamics of networks are switching operations since no element fails to gain a different perspective on both itself and its connecting links when it switches to another element or link from where to observe the network.

The 'social system' is Niklas Luhmann's version of a systemic theory of communication. It is much in line with the ideas of double closure and of autopoiesis, yet looks more closely at the 'social' conditions of an emerging system of communication. 'Communication' is taken to be the basic element of the system, emerging as the both improbable and fragile synthesis of utterance, information, and understanding, all attributions of the system itself, producing self-simplifying descriptions of 'actions' (including 'individuals' and their 'intentions') whose recurrence is taken to infer 'structures' and 'cultures,' 'traditions' and 'conventions,' if not the 'system' itself. The message together with the set of possible messages and the selection from this set is called 'meaning,' meaning being the possibility to switch from an actual meaningful state of the world to potential other meaningful states of the world (Luhmann 1990).

At least four features assure the internal restlessness of the social system. There is, first, the multiple constitution of communication always addressing several participants who can only artificially be taken as one (i.e. a 'collectivity', for instance a 'class' in school) and all of whom can withdraw at any time. There is, second, the self-reference of communication addressing an always elusive self. Third, there is the temporal nature of the elements, which appear and disappear as events, emphasizing the inherent improbability of the communication and the necessity to assure continuation right now.

The fourth feature is called 'society.' 'Society' is Luhmann's term for all kinds of disturbances of and by communication to be expected while society organizes itself into recurrent patterns and frames (Luhmann 1997). He chooses this term to draw attention to the reflexive nature of a theory of social systems, since it is a theory elaborated inside society, analyzing society from a distance even while participating in it. The theory is developed in communication even if author and reader may feel quite alone in their world; it must therefore exhibit an understanding of the nature of a society that allows such a thing, i.e. the writing and reading of such a theory. To quote Warren McCulloch (1965; see Luhmann 1997): 'What is a society such that it has a theory describing it?'

Society is also a term that draws attention to the fact that, contrary to a widespread belief in the communication sciences, not all communication is either face-to-face or mass or strategic communication, such that, apart from face-to-face communication, most communication, as this belief would have it, is "speaking into the air" and must be reminded of its not only fleeting but disembodied and thus somehow inhuman nature (Peters 1999). Quite to the contrary, most communication mixes indexicality and contextuality, present and absent references and participants, bodies and ideas, stories and projects, giving ample space to distinctions in communication research between interaction, organization, and society. If switching is pervasive, present references to other, absent, and potential meaning must come first; it must therefore be asked what structures and cultures enable communication agencies such as families, groups of peers, couples, people in line, offices, firms, schools, armies, parties, and others to produce and handle this mixing, crossing, and switching (see, also, Chapter 2, Eadie and Goret).

Finally, a last concept to capture the both operational and distributive nature of communication is George Spencer-Brown's notion of form (Spencer-Brown 1969). 'Form' is the answer to the question of how one operation can encompass the focus on itself, the problem of finding a next operation, and the knowledge of a world in which this operation takes place. The answer to this question is that we are dealing with operations of distinction whose form we can describe. They have an inside, an outside, a dividing line between inside and outside, and a space in which they occur. Thus, any one-valued or, to quote Gordon Pask (1981: 270, albeit with respect to 'understanding'), "sharp-valued" operation of distinction has, in its simplest form, four values to it: indicated inside, unmarked outside, severance, and space. There are more complicated forms of form possible, since distinctions may concatenate in different ways and also re-enter into themselves, producing forms that produce and live in recursive functions. The value of severance, not being among the things indicated nor part of the unmarked outside, indicates the observer actually drawing the distinction (Bateson 1972: 454–471), thus turning the whole calculus of form into a calculus of self-reference.

Luhmann introduced this notion of form into social systems theory and started to rebuild his theory of society according to its scheme (Luhmann 1997). With regard to communication, this means that any communication can be considered an operation of distinction (a selective message) that indicates something in difference to something else, which may or not be specified, so that further operations of distinction can choose to affirm or reject the indication, crossing the distinction to look at its outside, or re-entering the distinction into itself to inquire about the observer drawing it or about the possibility of distinguishing what had not previously been distinguished.

Using Spencer-Brown's notation, this reads as follows. Any simple operation of communication (if it ever is simple) draws a distinction which indicates on its inside a distinguished term, m:

$$\text{Communication (first-order)} = \overline{m\,|}$$

This communication attracts the attention of a second-order observer (who may be the first observer observing himself) either to the included indication, m, or to the excluded outside of the distinction, the unmarked state, n:

$$\text{Communication (second-order)} = \overline{m\,|}\,n$$

The second-order observer seeking communication with the first-order observer may then invite the latter or some third party to reflect on the possibility of distinguishing m from n, thus re-entering the distinction into the distinction:

Communication (re-entry) = m | n

Note that Spencer-Brown's form matches precisely the relational understanding of information put forward by Shannon, since any indication (or message) *m* is to be considered a distinction (or selection) from a set of possible other messages, either to be determined, *n*, or to be left unmarked. With Spencer-Brown, however, the mathematical theory of communication becomes self-contained. Any distinction tells us about the observer drawing it, a marked state indicated by it, and an unmarked state necessarily accompanying it, such that the marked state may at any moment become uneasily informed by the ignorance that comes with it.

Systemic theories of communication may then go on to consider further forms of communication as operational, structural, or cultural specifications of the first form (Baecker 2005), thus venturing into a kind of empirical communication research always seeking contact with some complexity out there and reflecting on the distinctions of its own being used.

If systemic theories of communication consist in deconstructing the transmission model of communication, emphasizing the selection model instead, and if the statistical mechanics theory of communication can reliably be generalized towards a systems theory of communication by dropping the assumption of given sets of possible messages, then Spencer-Brown's form seems the appropriate candidate to underline what systemic theories of communication are about and to foster the next generation of communication models. This 'form' seems fit to model operation, context, and switch without ever losing sight of the elusive self of the observer doing the operation.

Acknowledgment: English language editing by Rhodes Barrett.

Further reading

Bateson, Gregory. 1972. *Steps to an Ecology of Mind*. New York: Ballantine. Reprint Chicago, IL: Chicago UP, 2000.

Luhmann, Niklas. 1995. *Social Systems*, Bednarz, John (trans.). Stanford, CA: Stanford UP.

Serres, Michel. 1982. *The Parasite*, Schehr, Lawrence R. (trans.). Baltimore, MD: Johns Hopkins UP.

Shannon, Claude E. & Warren Weaver. 1948. *The Mathematical Theory of Communication*. Urbana, IL: Illinois UP. Reprint 1963.

Watzlawick, Paul, Janet H. Beavin & Don D. Jackson. 1967. *Pragmatics of Human Communication: A Study of Interactional Patterns, Pathologies, and Paradoxes*. New York: Norton.

References

Ashby, W. Ross. 1958. Requisite Variety and Its Implications for the Control of Complex Systems. *Cybernetica* 1 (2). 83–99.

Baecker, Dirk. 1997. Bringing Communication Back into Cybernetics. *Systemica: Journal of the Dutch Systems Group* 11. 11–28.

Baecker, Dirk. 2005. *Form und Formen der Kommunikation*. Frankfurt am Main: Suhrkamp.

Bagley, Philip. 1968. *Extension of Programming Language Concepts*. Philadelphia, PA: University of City Science Center.

Bateson, Gregory. 1972. *Steps to an Ecology of Mind*. New York: Ballantine. Reprint Chicago, IL: Chicago UP, 2000.

Bense, Max. 1969. *Einführung in die informationstheoretische Ästhetik: Grundlegung und Anwendung der Texttheorie*. Reinbek b. Hamburg: Rowohlt.

de Saussure, Ferdinand. 1986. *Course in General Linguistics*. Harris, Roy (trans. and annotation). La Salle, IL: Open Court.

Frege, Gottlob. 1980. *Translations from the Philosophical Writings of Gottlob Frege*, 3rd edn. Geach, P. and Black, M. (eds. and trans.). Oxford: Blackwell.

Habermas, Jürgen. 1984. *The Theory of Communicative Action*. McCarthy, Thomas (trans.), Boston, MA: Beacon Press.

Hayles, N. Katherine. 1999. *How We Became Posthuman: Virtual Bodies in Cybernetics, Literature, and Informatics*. Chicago, IL: Chicago UP.

Heider, Fritz. 1926. Thing and Medium. In: Fritz Heider, *On Perception, Event Structure, and Psychological Environment: Selected Papers*, 1–34 [Psychological Issues 1 (3)]. New York: International University Press, 1959.

Hirschman, Alfred O. 1970. *Exit, Voice, and Loyalty: Responses to Decline in Firms, Organizations, and States*. Cambridge, MA: Harvard UP.

Jakobson, Roman. 1981. Linguistics and Poetics. *Selected Writings, vol. III: Poetry of Grammar and Grammar of Poetry*, 18–51. Rudy, Stephan (ed.). The Hague: Mouton.

Krippendorff, Klaus. 1994. A Recursive Theory of Communication. In: David Crowley and David Mitchell (eds.), *Communication Theory Today*, 78–104. Cambridge: Polity Press.

Locke, John. 1959. *An Essay Concerning Human Understanding*. Fraser, Alexander Campbell (ed.), 2 vols. New York: Dover.

Luhmann, Niklas. 1990. Meaning as Sociology's Basic Concept. In: Niklas Luhmann, *Essays on Self-Reference*, 21–79. New York: Columbia UP.

Luhmann, Niklas. 1992a. Operational Closure and Structural Coupling: The Differentiation of the Legal System. *Cardozo Law Review* 13. 1419–1441.

Luhmann, Niklas. 1992b. What Is Communication? *Communication Theory* 2. 251–259.

Luhmann, Niklas. 1995. *Social Systems*. Bednarz, John (trans.). Stanford, CA: Stanford UP.

Luhmann, Niklas. 1997. *Die Gesellschaft der Gesellschaft*. Frankfurt am Main: Suhrkamp.

MacKay, Donald M. 1969. *Information, Mechanism and Meaning*. Cambridge, MA: MIT Press.

Maturana, Humberto R. 1975. The Organization of the Living: A Theory of the Living Organization. *International Journal of Man-Machine Studies* 7. 313–332.

Maturana, Humberto R. & Francisco J. Varela. 1980. *Autopoiesis and Cognition: The Realization of the Living*. Dordrecht: Reidel.

McCulloch, Warren. 1965. *Embodiments of Mind*. Cambridge, MA: MIT Press.

Nietzsche, Friedrich. 2006. On Truth and Lies in a Nonmoral Sense. Ansell-Pearson, Keith and Large, Duncan (eds.), *The Nietzsche Reader*, 114–123. Malden, MA: Blackwell.

Pask, Gordon. 1970. The Cybernetics of Behaviour and Cognition Extending the Meaning of 'Goal'. *Cybernetica* 13. 139–159 and 250–250.

Pask, Gordon. 1981. Organizational Closure of Potentially Conscious Systems. In: Milan Zeleny (ed.), *Autopoiesis: A Theory of Living Organization*, 265–308. Amsterdam: North-Holland.

Peters, John Durham. 1999. *Speaking into the Air: A History of the Idea of Communication*. Chicago, IL: Chicago UP.

Ruesch, Jürgen & Gregory Bateson. 1951. *Communication: The Social Matrix of Psychiatry*. New York: Norton. Reprint 1987.

Schlegel, Friedrich. 1997. On Incomprehensibility. In: J. Schulte-Sasse (eds. and trans.), *Theory as Practice: A Critical Anthology of Early German Romantic Writings*, 118–127. Minneapolis: University of Minnesota Press.

Schleiermacher, Friedrich. 1995. *Friedrich Schleiermacher's 'Toward a Theory of Sociable Conduct', and Essays in Its Intellectual-Cultural Context*. Richardson, Ruth Drucilla (ed. and trans.). Lewiston, NY: Edwin Mellen Press.

Serres, Michel. 1968–1980. *Hermès. Vol. 1: La communication. Vol. 2: L'interférence. Vol. 3: La traduction. Vol. 4: La distribution. Vol. 5: Le passage du nord-ouest*. Paris: Le Seuil.

Serres, Michel. 1982. *The Parasite*. Schehr, Lawrence R. (trans.). Baltimore, MD: Johns Hopkins UP.

Shannon, Claude E. 1948. A Mathematical Theory of Communication. *Bell System Technical Journal* 27 (July and October 1948). 379–423 and 623–656.

Shannon, Claude E. 1949. Communication Theory of Secrecy Systems. *Bell System Technical Journal* 28: 656–715.

Shannon, Claude E. & Warren Weaver. 1948. *The Mathematical Theory of Communication*. Urbana, IL: Illinois UP. Reprint 1963.

Simmel, Georg. 1950. *The Sociology of Georg Simmel*. Wolff, Kurt H. (ed., trans. and introduction). Glencoe, IL: Free Press.

Spencer-Brown, George. 1969. *Laws of Form*. London: Allen & Unwin.

von Foerster, Heinz. 1973. On Constructing a Reality. Reprinted in: Heinz von Foerster, *Understanding Understanding: Essays on Cybernetics and Cognition*, 211–227. New York: Springer, 2003.

von Foerster, Heinz. 1974. Notes on an Epistemology for Living Things. Reprinted in: Heinz von Foerster, *Understanding Understanding: Essays on Cybernetics and Cognition*, 247–259. New York: Springer, 2003.

von Foerster, Heinz. 1980. Epistemology of Communication. In: Kathleen Woodward (ed.), *The Myths of Information, Technology and Post-Industrial Culture*, 18–27. Madison, WI: Coda.

von Foerster, Heinz. 1993. For Niklas Luhmann: 'How Recursive is Communication?' Reprinted in: Heinz von Foerster, *Understanding Understanding: Essays on Cybernetics and Cognition*, 305–323. New York: Springer, 2003.

von Foerster, Heinz & Bernhard Pörksen. 2002. *Understanding Systems: Conversations on Epistemology and Ethics*. New York: Plenum Press.

Watzlawick, Paul, Janet H. Beavin & Don D. Jackson. 1967. *Pragmatics of Human Communication: A Study of Interactional Patterns, Pathologies, and Paradoxes*. New York: Norton.

White, Harrison C. 1992. *Identity and Control: A Structural Theory of Action*. Princeton, NJ: Princeton UP.

Whitehead, Alfred North. 1967. *Science and the Modern World*. New York: Free Press.

Wiener, Norbert. 1948. *Cybernetics, or Control and Communication in the Animal and the Machine*, 2nd edn. Cambridge, MA: MIT Press, 1961.

Philip Lieberman

6 Biological and neurological bases of communication

Abstract: The unique human tongue permits the production of "quantal" sounds that enhance the robustness of human speech. Neural circuits linking areas of the cortex with the basal ganglia and other subcortical structures regulate motor control, including speech. Similar circuits involving prefrontal cortex regulate language and aspects of cognition involving "executive control" – including working memory and cognitive flexibility. These circuits are similar to those of non-human primates. The evolution of enhanced human motor control, cognitive flexibility, and creativity 260,000 years ago appears to derive from a selective sweep of the FOXP2 human transcriptional factor that increased synaptic plasticity and connectivity in the basal ganglia.

Keywords: Basal ganglia, human tongue, neural circuits, speech, language, cognitive flexibility, evolution, FOXP2

The biological and neurological bases of human communication derive from attributes that we share with other species, modifications of organs that had different functions in other species, and novel factors that differentiate humans from all other species.

1 Gesture

Charles Darwin (1872) called attention to the expression of emotion in humans and other species using similar means. The facial musculature of apes and humans is similar and many innate facial expressions of emotion are similar. Darwin also called attention to body movement such as shrugs. Humans and apes both employ manual gestures as communicative elements. The anatomy, physiology, and neural control necessary to produce these gestures is shared by humans and chimpanzees. Chimpanzees raised from birth in a human setting were able to produce about 150 words using the dynamic manual gestures of American Sign Language (Gardner and Gardner 1969, 1984). Studies, such as those of McNeill (1985), demonstrate that manual gestures complement linguistic information constituting a manual signal keyed to phrase structure and salience. Darwin and many subsequent investigators have stressed the innate nature of these communicative signals. However, as McNeill pointed out other 'emblematic' gestures, such as signaling 'yes' by either vertical or horizontal head movements are culturally transmitted and vary from one culture to the next.

2 Vocal communication and speech

Darwin (1872) also emphasized the role of vocal signals in conveying emotion. A brief explanation of how human speech is produced is in order to understand both the aspects of vocal communication shared by humans and other species, such as the 'isolation cries' produced by mammalian infants, other vocal signals that signal distress, positive affect or stress, and the unique characteristics of human speech.

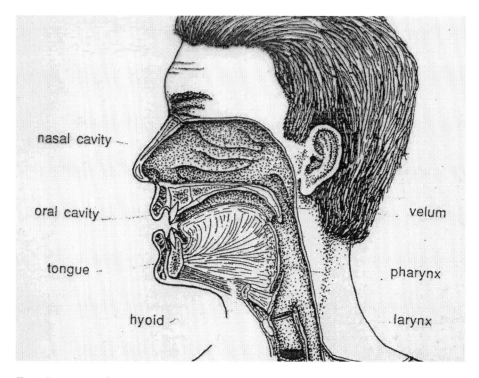

Fig. 1: Human speech anatomy

Explicit studies of speech production can be traced back to the closing years of the eighteenth century and are summarized in Johannes Müller's 1848 *Physiology of the sense, voice and muscular motion with the mental faculties*. The title of Müller's book was prescient. As we shall see, current studies show that similar neural circuits regulate speech motor control and the range of cognitive capacities subsumed by the term 'executive control' – comprehending the meaning of a sentence, short-term 'working memory,' planning ahead, and cognitive flexibility.

Although speech anatomy is often equated with the larynx, that is not the case. The human larynx (often called the 'voice-box') generates a periodic source of energy for vowels and consonants such as [m] and [v]. The larynx is a complex structure that sits on top of the trachea – the 'windpipe' that leads upwards from the lungs. The vocal 'cords' (sometimes called 'vocal folds') act as valves that can interrupt the flow of air from or into your lungs. They are moved apart to open the air passage during quiet respiration. Phonation occurs when the vocal cords are moved closer together and are tensioned by the laryngeal muscles. The airflow out from the lungs then sets them into motion and the vocal cords rapidly close and open, producing puffs of air that are the source of acoustic energy for phonated vowels, such as those normally occurring in English and 'voiced' consonants such as [m] and [v] of the words *ma* and *vat*. The rate, i.e. the 'fundamental frequency' (F_0), at which the vocal cords open and close depends on the pressure of alveolar air in the lungs, the tension placed on the vocal cords and the mass of the vocal cords.

The average F_0 is perceived as the 'pitch' of a speaker's voice. The fundamental frequency of phonation for adult males, who generally have larger larynges than most adult women, can vary from about 60 Hz to 200 Hz. The unit 'hertz' (Hz) is a measure of frequency – the number of events per second. Adult women and children can have F_0s ranging up to and exceeding 500 Hz. Periodic (actually quasi-periodic phonation) has acoustic energy at 'harmonics,' integral multiples of the fundamental frequency of phonation. For example, if F_0 were 100 Hz, acoustic energy could be present at 200Hz, 300 Hz, 400 Hz, 500 Hz, and so on. Depending on how abruptly the vocal cords open and close, energy falls off as frequency increases to a greater or lesser degree.

But the larynx would not produce any sound, without the alveolar air pressure generated in the lungs. Our lungs are the result of evolutionary tinkering. As Darwin pointed out, our lungs reflect the evolutionary process by which an organ is modified for some other purpose. Deep in *On the origin of species* Darwin notes that an,

> organ might be modified for some other and quite distinct purpose. The illustration of the swimbladder in fishes is a good one, because it shows us that an organ originally constructed for one purpose, namely flotation, may be converted into one for a wholly different purpose, namely respiration. (Darwin [1859] 1964: 190)

Advanced fish, such as those that are usually seen in fishbowls, have internal swimbladders that are inflated or deflated by transferring air from the fish's gills. This increases or decreases the fish's body size so as to change the quantity of water displaced at a given depth allowing the fish to hover, with minimal movements of its flippers. The net result of the evolutionary process that crafted our lungs is that when we talk, we must execute a complex set of motor gestures that entails having neural capacities that take into account the length of the sentence that we intend to say, before we utter a sound.

3 Control of alveolar air pressure

Darwin on his voyage on the British survey ship, Beagle, to South America observed lungfish, living fossils, close in form to the starting point of the swim-bladder to lung conversion process. We have two elastic lung sacks that are inflated indirectly so as to increase the water that we would displace if we were aquatic. There is no direct connection between any of the muscles that inflate the two elastic lung sacks that take in air during inspiration or expel air during expiration. Inspiratory muscles in your abdomen and chest can act to increase the volume of your body. In turn, the lung sacks expand, lowering their internal air pressure so that atmospheric air at a higher pressure flows into them during inspiration. The 'elastic recoil' of the two expanded lung sacks then forces air out during expiration (Bouhuys 1974).

During quiet respiration the elastic lung sacks act as springs, generating maximum alveolar pressure at the start of expiration. The alveolar air pressure then gradually falls. It's as though you blew up a balloon and then let it go. The balloon would start by flying around fast, then slow down as it deflates, and finally fall to the ground. Talking or singing would be problematic if the alveolar pressure pattern that occurs during quiet respiration was not modulated. The high initial pressure would blow the vocal cords apart, precluding phonation. As the alveolar air pressure fell, the fundamental frequency of phonation would fall. What instead occurs when people talk is that before uttering a word, they 'program' an inspiratory muscle command plan that starts by maximally opposing (holding back) the elastic lung-sack spring force using the same 'inspiratory' muscles that expand their lungs during inspiration. The hold-back, braking function gradually falls, matching the falling lung-sack elastic force to achieve relative stable, level alveolar air pressure. The elastic lung sack hold-back function depends on the length of the sentence that you intend to say. People also anticipate the length of the sentence that they intend to say by inflating their lungs to a greater degree before the start of a long sentence (Lieberman and Lieberman 1973). Similar maneuvers occur during singing. Complicated? It is the result of evolutionary tinkering with swim bladders to 'make' lungs.

4 The larynx

The human larynx also has a long evolutionary history. In lungfish it sealed the pathway into the lungs when the fish swam under water. Victor Negus's 1949 book summarizes his studies of the many changes that modified larynges for phonation. The larynx essentially is a 'transducer,' converting the almost inaudible flow of air out of the lungs into an acoustic source that is within the range of frequencies that the human auditory system can hear. The normal human respiratory rate is about 12 cycles per minute. This equals a frequency of 0.2 Hz, far below the 15 to 20 Hz lower frequency limit of the human auditory system. Frogs and virtually all mammals communicate vocally using acoustic signals generated by their larynges.

The F_0 contour and amplitude of phonation typically varies as a person speaks, yielding a *prosodic* signal that can transmit both emotional and referential linguistic information. Prosody also provides information that identifies a specific language, dialect or individual.

5 Formant frequencies

Although short F_0 contours, *lexical* tones, play a role in specifying words in many languages, for example, the Chinese languages, the vowels and consonants that make up words are largely determined by *formant frequencies*. As Müller (1848) pointed out, the airway above the larynx selectively allows maximum energy through it at certain frequencies, termed formant frequencies. This airway, the *supralaryngeal vocal tract* (SVT), acts as an acoustic filter, similar to an organ pipe. The difference between an organ and human speech producing anatomy is that we have one 'pipe' – the SVT – that continually changes its shape as we move our lips, tongue, and move our larynx up or down when we talk. The different shapes change the SVT's filtering characteristics, producing a continual change in the formant frequency pattern (Chiba and Kayiyama 1941; Fant 1960). We'll return to this critical aspect of human speech, which yields its signal advantage over other vocal signals – a data transmission rate that is about ten times faster.

Pipe organs work in much the same manner. The note that you hear when the organist presses a key is the product of the organ pipe acting as an acoustic filter on a source of sound energy. The energy source is similar for all the pipes. You can produce any vowel or phonated consonant with the same laryngeal source. The phonetic distinctions result from setting up diferent SVT shapes.

A useful analogy is to consider the manner by which tinted sunglasses color the world. The tint of the sunglasses results from a 'source' of light (electromagnetic) energy being 'filtered' by the sunglasses' colored lenses. The dye in the sunglasses' lenses acts as a filter, allowing maximum light energy to pass through at specific frequencies that result in your seeing the world before you tinted yellow, green, or whatever sunglass color you selected. The sunglasses' lenses don't provide any light energy; the 'source' of light energy is sunlight that has equal energy across range of electromagnetic frequencies that our visual system sees as white. If the sunglasses' lenses remove light energy at high electromagnetic frequencies, the result is a reddish tint. If energy is removed at low frequencies, the result is a bluish tint.

6 The unique human tongue

The human tongue is very peculiar. Charles Darwin first raised the question of why we have peculiar tongues. In the first edition of *On the Origin of Species,* he noted "The strange fact that every particle of food and drink which we swallow has to pass over the orifice of the trachea, with some risk of falling into the lungs ..." (Darwin [1859] 1964: 191).

The reason for our being susceptible to choking on food when we swallow is that the shape and position of the human tongue has been modified in the course of evolution to produce vowels that minimize errors in understanding what someone is trying to communicate. Your tongue also allows you to be somewhat sloppier when you produce the vowel sounds that make speech communication less susceptible to confusion. The human tongue has moved down into the throat, carrying the larynx down with it into a position that makes us uniquely susceptible to choking when we eat. Victor Negus's (1949) studies showed that at birth your tongue was similar to an ape's. It was adapted for swallowing. The human tongue's shape and position in the neck gradually changes until sometime between age six and eight years it is unlike that of any other creature on earth and has the capability to produce the full range of human speech (Lieberman et al. 2001).

7 Drinking and eating

If you cannot drink or eat, being able to talk is irrelevant. At birth, in newborn humans the tongue is positioned almost entirely in the mouth and the larynx is close to the opening into the nose. This arrangement allows newborn infants to simultaneously suckle milk and breathe. The infant larynx rises and locks in the nasal passageway like a small periscope, sealed off from the liquid pathway while water, milk and soft solids move past on either side of the raised larynx. Apes, dogs, cats, and other mammals have similar tongues and mouths throughout life. That's why dogs and cats can slurp away without stopping to breathe until their bowls are emptied. Newborn humans are obligate nose breathers until about the age of three or four months when tongue, throat, and skull anatomy begin to change. Anatomy and neural control are matched to facilitate an infant's being able to feed without risking choking.

When it comes to swallowing solid food, apes and other animals have an advantage over adult humans. Their tongues first propel food along the roof of the mouth, past the larynx and into the esophageal pathway leading to the stomach. Swallowing and breathing patterns differ profoundly in humans and nonhuman primates (Lieberman 2011: 295–302). In nonhuman primates the pharynx forms a 'tube within a tube' in which air flows directly from the lungs through the nose. The larynx, the entry to the inner air pathway lies within the opening to the nose, sealed off from the outer tube through which liquids and soft solids are swallowed. Two soft tissue 'flaps' – the epiglottis and velum which overlap each other, seal off the raised larynx from the food pathway when drinking. When swallowing solid food, the epiglottis is flipped down and breathing stops momentarily for all adult mammals, including humans. The increased risk of choking faced by humans derives from the human tongue gradually changing its shape and migrating down into the pharynx in the first six to eight years of life, carrying the larynx down with it. Humans older than eight must pull the larynx and the hyoid bone which supports the larynx forward and upwards to get it out of the trajectory of solid bits of food that are forcefully propelled down our pharyngeal air-food pathway – while simultaneously moving the epiglottis down to cover the larynx. About 500,000 people in the United States suffer from swallowing disorders (*dysphagia*) which results from failing to coordinate these complex maneuvers. Despite the introduction of the Heimlich maneuver, which attempts to clear the larynx by applying pressure to the abdomen to compress the lungs, 'popping-out' a blocked larynx, asphyxiation from food lodging in the larynx still remains the fourth largest cause of accidental death in the United States (National Safety Council 2009).

8 The human supralaryngeal vocal tract

The ontogenetic development of the human SVT was first studied by Negus (1949). Subsequent studies (e.g., Crelin 1973; Bosma, 1975; Lieberman and McCarthy 1999; Lieberman et al. 2001; Vorperian et al. 2005; Lieberman and McCarthy 2007) show that the length of the oral cavity is reduced in the first two years after birth by a process of differential bone growth that moved the hard palate (the roof of the mouth) backwards. The tongue begins to move down into the pharynx carrying the hyoid bone and the larynx down with it. (The larynx is suspended from the hyoid.) As the tongue descends into the pharynx, the length of the neck gradually increases to accommodate the lower position of the larynx. A short neck and a low larynx would preclude swallowing (Lieberman 2006; Lieberman and McCarthy 2007).

This developmental process yields the species-specific human vocal tract in which half of the tongue is positioned in the mouth, half in the pharynx. The posterior, back contour of the human tongue has become circular and the oral 'horizontal' SVTh and pharyngeal 'vertical' SVTv segments of the tongue meet at a right angle. In contrast, at the start of the developmental process in newborn human infants, the proportion of the tongue, SVTh, in the oral 'horizontal' part of the infant oral cavity, relative to the part of the tongue, SVTv, in the short 'vertical' pharynx is 1.5 when the larynx is at its lowest position during forceful vocalizations in the Truby et al. (1965) cineradiographic study of human infant cry.

9 Quantal vowels

Computer-modeling studies reveal the functional significance of the developmental changes that occur in humans. They show that newborn human and non-human SVTs cannot produce the full range of human speech (Lieberman et al. 1969, 1972; Carre et al. 1995; de Boer 2010). It is impossible to produce the vowels [i], [u], and [a] (the vowels of the words *see, do,* and *ma*). These vowels are among the few attested 'universals' of human language (Greenberg 1963). Experiments aimed at establishing the least error prone vowels for computer-implemented speech recognition systems showed that [i] and [u] had the lowest chance of being confused with other vowels when human listeners were unfamiliar with the voice of the speaker to whom they were listening. In 10,000 trials [i] was confused two times, [u] six times (Peterson and Barney 1952). Other vowels were confused hundreds of times in the 1950 study and in Hillenbrand et al. (1995), which replicated it using computer-implemented acoustic analysis that did not exist in the 1950s.

Kenneth Stevens (1972) provided part of the answer to why the vowels [i], [u], and [a] make human speech a more effective means of vocal communication. Stevens showed that the species-specific human SVT produce the ten-to-one midpoint area function discontinuities that are necessary to produce the vowels [i], [u], and [a], which Stevens termed 'quantal.' In the species-specific human vocal tract, the back contour of the tongue is almost circular. Half of the tongue, SVTv is positioned in the pharynx, half of the tongue SVTh is positioned in the oral cavity. SVTv and SVTh meet at an approximate right angle, owing to the tongue's posterior circular shape. The extrinsic muscles of the tongue, muscles firmly anchored in bone, thus can move the undeformed tongue to form abrupt midpoint ten-to-one discontinuities in the cross-sectional area of the SVT. Stevens, using both computer-modeling and physical models of the SVT having the shapes of strange woodwind instruments, showed that these abrupt midpoint discontinuities were necessary to produce the quantal vowels.

Fig. 1 presents a sketch of an adult human supralaryngeal vocal tract. The quantal vowels are perceptually salient owing to the convergence of two formant frequencies which yields spectral peaks to differentiate spoken words. A visual analogy would be using signal flags that had saturated colors in place of the pale colors equivalent to other vowels. The formant frequency patterns of quantal vowels also do not shift when tongue position varies slightly about the midpoint – speakers can be sloppy and produce the 'same' vowel. In 1978 Terrance Nearey showed that the vowel [i], and to a lesser degree the vowel [u], had another property that explained why they were almost never confused with another vowel. The vowel [i] is an optimal signal for determining the length of a speaker's vocal tract – a necessary step in the complex process of recovering the linguistic content from the acoustic signals that convey speech (Nearey 1978). Human listeners, as well as the computer systems used in telephone systems that attempt to recognize what you're saying on a telephone, have to guess at the length of your SVT. This is necessary because the formant frequencies for a speaker having a very short SVT will differ from those produced by a speaker having a long SVT for the same word. We don't notice this. A person who has a short SVT will produce the same words as a person having a long SVT with higher formant frequencies, but our brains unconsciously compensate for the frequency differences and we 'hear' the same words. Nearey (1978) showed that we unconsciously estimate the length of a speaker's SVT to accomplish this feat. The vowel [i] is the optimal vowel for doing this.

The 'quantal' vowels [i], [u], and [a], cannot be produced unless SVTv and SVTh have equal lengths and can meet at a right angle. That entails having an adult-like human tongue. In contrast, all other non-quantal vowels can be produced by the 'normal' non-human primate SVTs first described by Negus (1949). Properly designed computer modeling studies calculate the formant frequency patterns that would result from changing the shape of a SVT so as to produce a particular cross-sectional area function. The SVT's cross-sectional area function determines the formant frequency pattern (Chiba and Kajiyama 1941; Fant 1960). The constraints imposed by tongue shape and SVT proportions, the limits on the deformation of a relatively thin tongue located in the oral cavity, preclude producing the 10:1 midpoint changes in cross-sectional area that are necessary to produce quantal vowels (Stevens, 1972). In the case of humans, X-ray data that reveal the midsaggital shape of the airway and MRIs (images formed using Magnetic Resonance Imaging technology) that yield the cross-sectional area function are used to determine the range of possible SVT shapes. The computed SVT shaped can then be compared with these data. The resulting computed range of vowels then can be compared with actual acoustic measurements to validate the modeling technique. Vowels are most often modeled because subjects can hold still to obtain MRI images of the cross-sectional SVT area function.

In contrast, as de Boer and Fitch (2010) point out, the computer modeling studies of L-J Boe and his colleagues which have disputed the unique properties of the human tongue are inherently flawed because the modeling technique used in these studies, the VLAM procedure, fails to take account of the anatomical constraints imposed on the SVTs ostensibly modeled. The VLAM computer algorithms inherently reshape any SVT whatsoever into that of an adult human (specifically those of the elderly Frenchwomen who form the VLAM database). When the VLAM computed vowel range for infants and young children is compared with the vowels that are actually produced, it is apparent that it incorrectly includes quantal vowels that never occur (Buhr 1980) This discrepancy is also apparent in data of the Serkhane et al. (2007) study which attempted to use the VLAM technique to study the vowel repertoires of human infants and young children.

10 Consonants and speech encoding

The mix of consonants and vowels that marks human speech provides the basis for one of its central advantages over the vocal communications of other living species – its high rate of data transmission. Studies of the acoustic cues that specify stop consonants, such as the sounds [b] or [p] of words *bat* and *pat,* or [t], [d] (of the words *to* and *do)* and the initial consonants of the words *cat* and *go* revealed this effect – termed *encoding* in the seminal paper, *Perception of the speech code,* published in 1967 by Alvin Liberman and his colleagues.

Stop consonants are formed by the lips or tongue closing off the SVT (stopping it up) and then abruptly releasing the closure. English has three series of stop consonants, labial which involve lip movements, tongue blade, or tongue body movements momentarily obstructing the SVT. The distinction between the labial (lip-produced) stop consonants [b] and [p], rests on the time that elapses between the 'burst' of sound that occurs when the lips open and the start of phonation. The interval between the burst and phonation for the 'short-lag' [b] is less than 25 msec. (a msec. = 1/1000 of a second). The interval for the long lag [p] exceeds 25 msec. Leigh Lisker and Arthur Abramson, in 1964, had analyzed the stop consonants of many languages from around the world. They found that every language used similar time intervals, which they termed *voice-onset-time* (VOT), to differentiate stop consonants. In English, VOT differences differentiate short lag [b], [d], and [g] from long-lag [p], [t], and [k]. The stop consonants [t] [d], [g], and [k] of the words *to, do, go,* and *come* are formed by obstructing the VOT with the tongue. A third VOT category 'prevoicing,' which isn't used in English, involves starting phonation before the stop consonant's release-burst. Spanish, for example, uses prevoicing for the stop consonant of words beginning with the letter *b.*

Other *continuent* consonants, such as the sounds [s] and [f] of the words *sat* and *fat,* involve constricting the SVT to the degree that air turbulence results in a 'noise-source' being generated at the constriction. Distinctions in duration also play a part in specifying other consonants and all vowels. The vowel of the word *bat,* for example, is much longer than the vowel of the word *bit.*

As we talk, we merge the formant frequency patterns that define individual consonants and vowels. This process is not a deficiency – it instead provides the high data transmission rate that makes speech the default phonetic mode of human language. This became apparent when the Haskins Laboratories was attempting to build a machine that would 'read' printed texts aloud to blind people. Linguists for thousands of years, since the time of Sanskrit scholars, had conceived of speech consisting of a string of 'phonemes,' segments that defined words.

It was thought that words were composed of phonemes (roughly equivalent to the letters of the alphabet) similar to beads on a string. Much to everyone's surprise, it proved impossible to isolate any sounds that corresponded to letters that could be permuted to form words. It, for example, should have been possible to isolate the phoneme [t] from a tape recording of someone saying the word *too*, where it occurs before the sound [u] (the phonetic symbol used by linguists that is the equivalent of the letters *oo*). However, when the segment of recording tape that should have corresponded to the 'pure' [t] was isolated and linked to the vowel [i] segmented from the word *tea*, the resulting signal was incomprehensible. It became evident that there were no 'pure' speech sounds because formant frequency patterns of the hypothetical independent phonemes were melded together into syllables and words.

For example, the formant frequency patterns that convey the 'phonemes' [t], [ɪ], and [p] of the word *tip* are melded together into one syllable. As the tongue moves from its position against the roof of the mouth (the palate) to produce the syllable-initial 'stop' consonant [t], a formant frequency pattern is produced that transitions into that of the [ɪ] vowel, and then to the final stop consonant [p]. Human speakers plan ahead. If you instead say the word *too* (in phonetic notation [tu]) your lips are already protruding and narrowing for the [u] vowel. But this apparent sloppiness of speech is its inherent communicative value. When people listen to a stream of individual sounds, the sounds fuse into a buzz at rates exceeding 15 sounds per second. At slower rates it still is almost impossible to make out what the sounds are (Lieberman et al. 1967). The Haskins speech research group found that formant frequency melding, which they termed 'encoding' speech, allows humans to transmit phonetic distinctions at rates of up to 20 to 30 'segments' per second.

Human speech is an 'encoded' signal in which information is transmitted at the slower syllable rate and then decoded into phonemes. At the slow non-speech rate, you would forget the beginning of this sentence if it were spoken, before you came to its end. Speech thus plays a critical role in human language, making it possible to communicate thoughts in long sentences having complex syntax productive. Encoding appears to differ somewhat from language to language. For example, Swedish speakers plan ahead for a longer interval at the start of a syllable than English speakers (Lubker and Gay 1982). The minimal encoding unit for speech is a syllable, but encoding effects have longer spans. Alphabetic orthography perhaps leads us to believe that words can be formed by permutable phonemes, but orthography that codes entire words, such as Chinese, are used by more than a billion people.

11 When did the human tongue evolve?

The time depth for the evolution of the human tongue must extend well before the period before humans migrated out of Africa at least 80,000 years ago. The fully modern humans who settled in Eurrope in the Upper Paleolithic era some 40,000 years ago had fully modern human tongues and SVTs. However, sub-Saharan Africans also have fully modern tongues and SVTs, placing its evolution in Africa well before the Upper Paleolithic (Lieberman and McCarthy 2007). In light of the negative consequences of having a human tongue, the neural bases for speech motor control must have been present before the mutations that resulted in the species-specific human tongue were retained. Thus as Lieberman and Crelin noted in 1971, Neanderthals who did not have human tongues and SVTs must have talked, albeit with less indelibility.

12 The neural bases of speech and language

The neural bases of speech and language reflect the gradual aggregation of Natural Selection, which involves small steps, plus the abrupt changes that can result from mutations as well as the process that Darwin noted, where an 'organ' can take up a new function. Both cortical and subcortical structures regulate human speech production and are involved in speech perception and in producing and comprehending sentences. As is the case in anatomy, some of the neural bases of human speech have a long evolutionary history. The anterior cingulate cortex (ACC) can be traced back to Therapsids, mammal-like reptiles who appeared in the age of the dinosaurs. The ACC, as is the case for other neural structures, is connected to other parts of the brain in neural circuits. When neural circuits involving the ACC are cut in infant monkeys, the monkeys are unable to produce the mammalian 'isolation call' that signals their need for attention. Lesions in monkey mothers cause them to be inattentive to their infants (Newman and Maclean 1982). Studies of the effects of Parkinson disease (PD), which affects the basal ganglia, largely sparing cortex (Jellinger 1990), show that the role of the ACC has shifted in humans to more general aspects of attention and laryngeal control. The neural circuit linking the ACC and basal ganglia can degrade in PD, resulting in hypophonation, reduced laryngeal output, and apathy – a general loss of intentional resources (Cummings 1993).

The effects of PD also refutes claims for humans having a unique neural circuit for laryngeal control that bypasses the basal ganglia (Deacon 1997; Fitch 2010). The claim is based on two flawed studies that attempted to study human subjects using a tracer techniques developed for studies on animals that involves sacrificing the animal (c.f. Lieberman 2012). If this hypothetical neural circuit that bypassed the basal ganglia pathway actually existed, Parkinson disease would have no effect on laryngeal control or attention. The issue had been resolved by Noninvasive Diffusion Tenor Imaging (DTI) which traces out neural pathways. DTI shows that humans make use of the cortical to basal ganglia neural circuits similar to those found in other species (Lehericy et al. 2004) to control motor behavior, including laryngeal activity, as well as a range of cognitive tasks, and other aspects of behavior.

13 Cortical-basal ganglia circuits and human speech, language, and cognition

Over the course of three centuries, repeated attempts to teach apes to talk have failed. As noted above this cannot be ascribed to any anatomical limitations. The computer modeling studies of Lieberman et al. (1969, 1972) showed that monkeys and apes had SVTs that were capable of producing the formant frequency patterns that specify all non-quantal vowels and most consonants. However, acoustic analyses (e.g., Lieberman 1968) show that they don't.

It thus is clear that non-human primates must lack the neural mechanisms that allow humans to learn and produce the complex motor commands that are necessary to produce speech. The conclusion that might follow is that monkeys and apes don't have a functioning Broca's area, the traditional language speech organ. However, it has become clear that the traditional Broca-Wernicke language organ theory is wrong.

The traditional Broca-Wernicke theory, which has been repeated in book after book, paper after paper, claims that Broca's area in the left hemisphere of the frontal part of neocortex (the outer layer of the human brain) controls speech production. Wernicke's area, a posterior (rear) part of the neocortex, is the brain's hypothetical speech comprehension organ. The evidence for this theory was flawed from the start. In 1861 Paul Broca published his study of a stroke victim, nick-named 'Tan' by Broca because he was unable to utter more than a single syllable that to Broca's ear sounded like word 'tan.' The patient soon died. Though Broca never performed a post-mortem autopsy of the patient's brain he ascribed Tan's inability to talk to damage to a particular area of the patient's cortex, that has since been termed Broca's area.

Broca also had examined a second patient who had similar speech deficits. In this case, Broca performed an autopsy that revealed damage extending into the basal ganglia. The brains of both patients were preserved in alcohol. A high-resolution postmortem MRI (Dronkers et al. 2007) of patient Tan's brain shows cortical damage extending well beyond the part of the brain identified by Broca as the seat of language, and massive damage to the basal ganglia, other subcortical structures and pathways connecting cortical and subcortical neural structures.

In 1874, Karl Wernicke studied a stroke patient who had difficulty comprehending speech and had damage to the rear, posterior temporal, region of the cortex. Wernicke decided that this area was the brain's speech comprehension organ. Since spoken language entails both comprehending and producing speech, Lichtheim in 1885 proposed a cortical pathway linking Broca's and Wernicke's area. Thus Brocas and Wernicke's cortical areas became the neural bases of human language, supposedly devoted to language and language alone.

Doubts were expressed from the 1920s onwards. Marie (1926), basing his conclusions on autopsies of stroke victims, proposed that Broca's syndrome instead derived from damage to the basal ganglia. In the 1970s CT scans allowed neurologists to readily establish the pattern of brain damage that resulted in Broca's and Wernicke's aphasic syndromes. The syndromes – the patterns of possible deficits are real – but they do not derive from brain damage localized to these cortical areas. Patients typically recovered or had minor problems, when Broca's and Wernicke's areas were completely destroyed, so long as the subcortical structures of the brain were intact. Naeser et al. (1982) noted the aphasic symptoms and signs of patients who had suffered brain damage that spared cortex altogether, but damaged the basal ganglia and pathways to it in neural circuits that link cortical areas through the basal ganglia, thalamus and other subcortical structures. The position expressed by Stuss and Benson in their 1986 book, *The frontal lobes*, directed at aphasiologists, is that aphasia never occurs, absent subcortical damage.

Over the course of the twentieth century, it also became apparent that patients who had suffered brain damage that resulted in aphasia, permanent loss of some aspect of linguistic ability, also had cognitive deficits. Kurt Goldstein, in his 1948 book, based on observations of patients over the course of decades, characterized aphasia as a loss of the 'abstract capacity.' Aphasic patients lost cognitive flexibility as well as language. Converging evidence from studies of the effects of Parkinson disease, focal damage to the basal ganglia, and neuroimaging studies of neurologically intact 'normal' subjects, shows that neural circuits linking activity in cortical areas through the basal ganglia provide the basis for many of the qualities that differentiate us from animals.

The basal ganglia are buried deep within the human brain. The caudate nucleus and putamen, two adjacent structures, are the principal input structures of the basal ganglia. The putamen receives a stream of sensory information from other parts of the brain. It also monitors the completion of motor and cognitive acts. The caudate nucleus is active in a range of cognitive tasks. The globus pallidus is the output structure for information. The information stream then is channeled to the thalamus and other subcortical structures.

Neuroimaging studies of intact 'normal' subjects are gradually resolving the manner by which these circuits regulate both complex motor activity such as that involved in talking, cognitive tasks, and emotional regulation. For example, medial ventrolateral and dorsolateral prefrontal cortex participate in the range of cognitive tasks subsumed under the term 'executive control' (Duncan and Owen 2000). The 'local' operations in different cortical areas and subcortical structures differ. However, the circuits are not domain-specific – they are not *modules* devoted solely to language motor control or emotion. Functional Magnetic Resonance Imaging (fMRI) studies such as those of Oury Monchi's research group (Monchi et al. 2001, 2006, 2007; Simard et al. 2011) show these that basal-ganglia circuits involving ventrolateral and dorsolateral prefrontal cortex participate in the cognitive behaviors subsumed under the cover term 'executive control.' These include working memory tasks involving recalling information, semantic association tasks, judg-

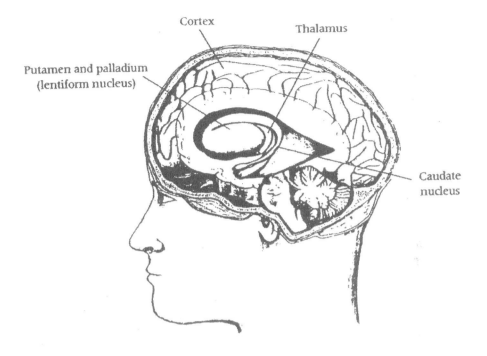

Cortex

Thalamus

Putamen and palladium (lentiform nucleus)

Caudate nucleus

Fig. 2: The basal ganglia

ments of phonetic similarity, matching cards to different criteria such as color or shape, planning ahead, and cognitive flexibility – changing the direction of a thought process. Similar circuits linking motor cortex and the basal ganglia control motor acts, including the rapid, coordinated sequences that are necessary to produce speech.

The local operations of the basal ganglia in circuits regulating motor control and cognitive executive control became apparent in studies of Parkinson disease (PD). Marsden and Obeso (1994: 889), reviewing the results of brain surgery intended to alleviate the motor and cognitive deficits of PD concluded that the basal ganglia perform several local operations. "They first... promote automatic execution of routine movement by facilitating the desired cortically driven movements and suppressing unwanted muscular activity." The basal ganglia act as a controller that ensures that each step of a motor act is carried out, before activating and monitoring the next step. Studies using micro-electrodes in monkeys and mice confirm this local motor control operations (Aldridge and Berridge 2003).

Marsden and Obeso (1994: 889) also observed a second local basal ganglia operation in, "... unusual circumstances to reorder the cortical control of movement." Noting the cognitive inflexibility that frequently marks PD (Flowers and Robertson 1985), Marsden and Obeso (1994: 893) concluded that, "...the basal ganglia are an elaborate machine, within the overall frontal lobe distributed system, that allow routine thought and action, but which respond to new circumstances to allow a change in direction of ideas and movement."

13.1 Transcriptional factors

But this leads to seeming mystery – if it is the case that humans and apes have similar cortical-basal ganglia circuits, why can we talk and why is a human writing this essay, instead of an ape? Why are humans so unpredictable? Why do humans spend a good deal of time on seemingly unproductive activates such as art and music? The answer to all of these questions is beginning to emerge from studies of the effects of transcriptional factors, genes that affect the expression of other genes during development.

About 98–99% of human and chimpanzee genes are identical (The Chimpanzee Sequencing and Analysis Consortium 2005). However, the remaining 1–2% appear to be transcriptional factors. One that has received a great deal of attention is, FOXP2 human, a gene that differs from the version found in chimpanzees, FOXP2 chimp. A 'selective sweep' which resulted in FOXP2 human spreading throughout the human population was initially thought to have occurred in the last 200,000 years (Enard et al. 2002). Selective sweeps occur when a gene results in a significant advantage in the Darwinian 'struggle for existence' – an individual's having more surviving children. Subsequently, the human form of FOXP2 was found in one Neanderthal fossil (Krause et al. 2007) which may push the date back to between 370–450,000 years ago when humans and Neanderthals last share a common ancestor (Green et al. 2010).

The behavioral and neural effects of FOXP2 human on humans have gradually becoming clear. A pattern of speech, language and cognitive deficits was first discovered in the K E family, a large multigenerational family living in London in which some members had only one functional copy of the FOXP2 gene. It was almost impossible to understand the affected members of the family. Deficits occurred in comprehending English sentences such as *Tom was kissed by Susan,* or sentences that had relative clauses. Neuroimaging studies showed anomalies in subcortical brain structures. The basal ganglia's putamin was abnormally small.

Different versions of the FOXP2 gene are present in all mammals and birds. The human and mouse versions of FOXP2 act on similar parts of the body and brain during embryological development (Lai et al. 2001). FOXP2 affects the formation of the lungs, various muscles, and in the brain, the basal ganglia, other subcortical structures, and layer VI of the cortex. Further studies show that the human version of FOXP2 ramps up information transfer and associative learning in the basal ganglia. Increased synaptic plasticity in the neurons affected by FOXP2 human (medium spiny neurons) in the basal ganglia and substantia nigra, another structure in cortical-basal circuits (Alexander et al 1986; Cummings 1993), enhances associative motor learning in mice (Jin and Costa 2010).

The effect of increased synaptic plasticity in enhancing learning is consistent with our general knowledge of the bases of associative learning. The synapses that transfer information from one neuron to another are the mechanism by which the brain learns the relations that hold between seemingly unrelated phenomena (Hebb 1949). Studies, ranging from electrophysiologic recordings of neuronal activity in the basal ganglia of mice and other animals as they learn tasks (Graybiel 1995; Mirenowicz and Schultz 1996; Jin and Costa 2010) to studies of PD patients (Lange et al. 1992, Monchi et al. 2007) and birds (Brainard and Doupe 2000), show that the basal ganglia play a critical role in associative learning, planning and executing motor acts including motor control for vocal communication.

Other transcriptional factors are involved in upgrading information transfer in the human brain. Konopka et al. (2009) found that the greatest effect of FOXP2 on human genes was to 'upregulate' genes in the caudate nucleus – the basal ganglia structure that fMRI studies of the Monchi group in Montreal show is the neural 'engine' involved in changing the direction of a thought process. The Konopka study concluded that 61 human genes whose expression was 'upregulated' by the human form of FOXP2 act on the human brain. Pruess et al. (2004) noted that most or all of the genes expressed in the brain that are known to differ between chimpanzees and humans are 'upregulated.' Green et al. (2010) identified 'highly accelerated regions' (HAR) of the human genome that differ from the Neanderthal genome that appear to be associated with cognition, as well as with mental illness

The neural bases of speech and language are commingled with other aspects of human behavior – cognition and emotional regulation. Determining these neural substrates remains a work in progress.

Further reading

Lieberman, P. 2006. *Toward an evolutionary biology of language*. Cambridge, MA: Harvard
    University Press
Lieberman, P. 2012. Vocal tract anatomy and the neural bases of talking. *Journal of Phonetics*.
Lieberman, P. 2013. *The Unpredictable Species: How Our Brains Evolved so that We, Not Genes,
    Control How We Think and Behave*. Princeton NJ: Princeton University Press.
Reimers-Kipping, S., S. Hevers, S. Paabo & W. Enard. 2011. Humanized Foxp2 specifically allects
    cortico-basal ganglia circuits. *Neuroscience* 175. 75–84.

References

Aldridge, J. W. & K. C. Berridge. 2003. Basal ganglia neural coding of natural action sequences. In: A. M. Graybiel, S. T. Kitai, and M. DeLong (eds.), *The basal ganglia IV*, 279–287. New York: Plenum.

Alexander, G.E., M.R. DeLong & P. L. Strick. 1986. Parallel organization of segregated circuits linking basal ganglia and cortex. *Annual Review of Neuroscience 9*. 357–381.

Bosma, J.F. 1975. Anatomic and physiologic development of the speech apparatus. In: D. B. Towers (ed.), *Human communication and its disorders*, 469–481. New York: Raven.

Bouhuys, A. 1974. *Breathing: physiology, environment and breathing*. Grune and Stratton: New York.

Broca, P. 1861. Nouvelle observation d'aphémie produite par une lésion de la moitié postérieure des deuxième et troisième circonvolutions frontales. *Bulletin Societé Anatomie, 2nd ser.* 6. 398–407.

Brainard, A. S. & A. J. Doupe. 2000. Interruption of a basal ganglia-forebrain circuit prevents the plasticity of learned vocalizations. *Nature 404.* 762–766.

Buhr, R. D. 1980. The emergence of vowels in an infant. *Journal of Speech and Hearing Research* 23. 75–94.

Carre, R., B. Lindblom & P. MacNeilage. 1995. Acoustic factors in the evolution of the human vocal tract. *C. R. Academie des Sciences Paris* t320(Serie IIb). 471–476.

Chiba, T. & M. Kajiyama. 1941. *The Vowel: Its Nature and Structure*. Tokyo: Tokyo-Kaiseikan. Reprinted 1958. Tokyo: Phonetic Society of Japan.

Crelin, E. S. 1969. *Anatomy of the newborn; an atlas*. Philadelphia: Lea and Febiger.

Crelin, E. S. 1973. *Functional Anatomy of the Newborn*. New Haven: Yale University Press.

Cummings, J. L. 1993. Frontal-subcortical circuits and human behavior. *Archives of Neurology 50.* 873–880.

Darwin, C. [1859]. 1964. *On the origin of species*. Cambridge, MA: Harvard University Press.

Darwin, C. 1872. *The expression of the emotions in man and animals*. London: John Murray.

Deacon, T.W. 1997. *The symbolic species: The co-evolution of language and the brain*. New York: Norton.

de Boer, B. 2010. Modeling vocal anatomy's significant effect on speech. *Journal of Evolutionary Psychology* 8. 351–366.

de Boer, B. & W. T. Fitch. 2010. Computer models of vocal tract evolution: An overview and critique. *Adaptive Behavior* 18 (1). 36–47.

Dronkers, N. F., O. Plaisant, M. T. Iba-Zizain & E. A. Cananis. 2007. Paul Broca's historic cases: high resolution MR imaging of the brains of Leborgne and Lelong. *Brain* 130. 143–1441.

Duncan, J. & A. M. Owen. 2000. Common regions of the human frontal lobe recruited by diverse cognitive demands. *TINS* 10. 475–483.

Enard, W., M. Przeworski, S. E. Fisher, C. S. L. Lai, V. Wiebe, T. Kitano, A. P. Monaco & S. Paabo. 2002. Molecular evolution of FOXP2, a gene involved in speech and language. *Nature* 41. 869–872.

Fant, G. 1960. *Acoustic theory of speech production*. Mouton: The Hague.

Fitch, W. T. 2010. *The evolution of language*. New York: Cambridge University Press.

Flowers, K. A. & C. Robertson. 1985. The effects of Parkinson's disease on the ability to maintain a mental set. *Journal of Neurology, Neurosurgery, and Psychiatry* 48. 517–529.

Gardner, R. A. & B. T. Gardner . 1969. Teaching sign language to a chimpanzee. *Science* 165. 664–672.

Gardner, R. A. & B. T. Gardner. 1984. A vocabulary test for chimpanzees. *Journal of Comparative Psychology* 98. 381–404.

Goldstein, K. 1948. *Language and language disturbances*. New York: Grune and Stratton.

Graybiel, A. M. 1995. Building action repertoires: Memory and learning functions of the basal ganglia. *Current Opinion in Neurobiology* 5. 733–741.

Green, R. E. & J. Krause. 2010. A draft sequence of the Neandertal genome. *Science* 328. 710–722.

Greenberg, J. 1963. *Universals of language*. Cambridge, MA: MIT Press.

Hebb, D. O. 1949. *The organization of behavior: A neuropsychological theory*. New York: Wiley.

Hillenbrand, J. L., A. Getty, M. J. Clark & K. Wheeler. 1995. Acoustic characteristics of American English vowels. *Journal of the Acoustical Society of America* 97. 3099–3111.

Jellinger, K. 1990. New developments in the pathology of Parkinson's disease. In: M. B. Streifler, A. D. Korezyn, J. Melamed and M. B. H. Youdim (eds.), 1–15. *Advances in neurology. Vol. 53, Parkinson's disease: Anatomy, pathology and therapy*. New York: Raven.

Jin, X. & R. M. Costa . 2010. Start/stop signals emerge in nigrostriatal circuits during sequence learning. *Nature* 466. 457–462.

Konopka, G., J. Bomar, K. Winden, G. Coppola, Z. O. Jonsson, F. Gao, S. Peng & T.M. Preuss. 2009. CNS development genes by FOXP2, 2009 *Nature* 462. 213–217.

Krause, J., C. Lalueza-Fox, L. Orlando, W. Enard, R. E. Green, H.A. Burbano, J. J. Hublin, C. Hänni, J. Fortea, M. d.l. Rasilla, J. Bertranpetit, A. Rosas & S. Pääbo. 2007. The derived FOXP2 variant of modern humans was shared with Neandertals. *Curr Biol* 17. 1908–1912.

Lai, C. S. L., S. E. Fisher, J. A. Hurst, F. Vargha-Khadem & A. P. Monaco. 2001. A forkhead-domain gene is mutated in a severe speech and language disorder. *Nature* 413. 519–23.

Lange, K. W., T. W. Robbins, C. D. Marsden, M. James, A. M. Owen & G. M. Paul. 1992. L-dopa withdrawal in Parkinson's disease selectively impairs cognitive performance in tests sensitive to frontal lobe dysfunction. *Psychopharmacology* 107. 394–404.

Lehericy, S. 2004. Diffusion tensor fiber tracking shows distinct corticostriatal circuits in humans. *Annals Neurology* 55. 522–527.

Liberman, A. M., F. S. Cooper, D. P. Shankweiler & M. Studert-Kennedy. 1967. Perception of the speech code. *Psychological Review* 74. 431–461.

Lichtheim, L. 1885. On aphasia. *Brain* 7. 433–484.

Lieberman, D. E. 2011. *The evolution of the human head*. Cambridge, MA: Harvard University Press.

Lieberman, D. E. & R. C. McCarthy. 1999. The ontogeny of cranial base angulation in humans and chimpanzees and its implications for reconstructing pharyngeal dimensions. *J Hum Evol* 36. 487–517.

Lieberman, D. E., R. C. McCarthy, K. M. Hiiemae & J. B. Palmer. 2001. Ontogeny of postnatal hyoid and laryngeal descent: Implications for deglutition and vocalization. *Arch Oral Biol* 46. 117–128.

Lieberman, M. R. & P. Lieberman. 1973. Olson's "projective verse" and the use of breath control as a structural element. *Language and Style* 5. 287–298.

Lieberman, P. 1968. Primate vocalizations and human linguistic ability. *Journal of the Acoustical Society of America* 44. 1157–1164.

Lieberman, P. 1984. *The biology and evolution of language*. Cambridge, MA: Harvard University Press.

Lieberman, P. 2006. *Toward an evolutionary biology of language*. Cambridge MA: Harvard University Press.

Lieberman, P. 2009. FOXP2 and Human Cognition. *Cell* 137. 800–802

Lieberman, P., D. H. Klatt & W. H. Wilson. 1969. Vocal tract limitations on the vowel repertoires of rhesus monkey and other nonhuman primates. *Science* 164. 1185–1187.

Lieberman, P. & E. S. Crelin. 1971. On the speech of Neanderthal man. *Linguistic Inquiry* 2. 203–222.

Lieberman, P., E. S. Crelin & D. H. Klatt. 1972. Phonetic ability and related anatomy of the newborn, adult human, Neanderthal man and the chimpanzee. *American Anthropologist* 74. 287–307.

Lieberman, P. & R. M. McCarthy. 2007. Tracking the evolution of language and speech. *Expedition* 49. 15–20.

Lisker, L. & A. S. Abramson. 1964. A cross language study of voicing in initial stops: Acoustical measurements. *Word* 20. 384–442.

Lubker, J. & T. Gay. 1982. Anticipatory labial coarticulation Experimental, biological, and linguistic variables. *Journal of the Acoustical Society of America* 71. 437–448.

Marie, P. 1926. *Traveaux et mémoires*. Paris: Masson.

Marsden, C.D. & J. A. Obeso. 1994. The functions of the basal ganglia and the paradox of sterotaxic surgery in Parkinson's disease. *Brain* 117. 877–897

McNeill, D. 1985. So you think gestures are nonverbal? *Psychological Review* 92. 350–371

Mirenowicz, J. & W. Schultz. 1996. Preferential activation of midbrain dopamine neurons by appetitive rather than aversive stimuli. *Nature* 379. 449–451.

Monchi, O., M. Petrides, V. Petre, K. Worsley & A. Dagher. 2001. Wisconsin card sorting revisited; Distinct neural circuits participating in different stages of the test as evidenced by event-related functional magnetic resonance imaging. *The Journal of Neuroscience* 21. 7739–7741.

Monchi, O., M. Petrides, A. P. Strafella, K. J. Worsely & A. Doyon. 2006. Functional role of the basal ganglia in the planning and execution of actions. *Annals of Neurology* 59. 257–264.

Monchi, O., J. H. Ko & A. P. Strafella. 2006. Striatal dopamine release during performance of executive function: A [^{11}C] raclopride PET study. *Neuroimage* 33. 907–912.

Monchi, O. M., M. Petrides, B. Meja-Constain & A. P. Strafella. 2007. Cortical activity in Parkinson disease during executive processing depends on striatal involvement. *Brain* 130. 233–244.

Müller, J. 1848. *The physiology of the senses, voice and muscular motion with the mental faculties*. Baly, W. (trans.). London: Walton and Maberly.

Naeser, M.A., M. Alexander, P. N. Helms-Estabrooks, H. L. Levine, S. A. Laughlin & N. Geschwind. 1982. Aphasia with predominantly subcortical lesion sites: Description of three capsular/putaminal aphasia syndromes. *Arch Neurol* 39. 2–14.

National Safety Council. 2009. *Highlights from Injury Facts*. www.nsc.org/news_resources/injury and _death_statistics/Pages/HighlightsFromInjuryFacts.aspx (accessed May 2010).

Nearey, T. 1978. *Phonetic features for vowels*. Bloomington: Indiana University Linguistics Club.

Negus, V. 1949. *The comparative anatomy and physiology of the larynx*. London: Heinemann.

Newman, J.D. & P. D. Maclean. 1982. Effects of tegmental lesions on the isolation call of squirrel monkeys. *Brain Res* 232. 317–329.

Peterson, G. E. & H. L. Barney. 1952. Control methods used in a study of the vowels. *Journal of the Acoustical Society of America* 24. 175–184.

Preuss, T. M., M. Cáceres, M. C. Oldham & D. H. Geschwind. 2004. Human brain evolution: Insights from microarrays (Review). *Nature Reviews Genetics* 5 (11). 850–860.

Reimers-Kipping, S., S. Hevers, S. Paabo & W. Enard. 2011. Humanized Foxp2 specifically allects cortico-basal ganglia circuits. *Neuroscience* 175. 75–84

Serkhane, J. E., J-L. Schwartz, J-L. Boe, B. L. Davis & C. L. Matyear. 2007. Infants' vocalizations analyzed with an articulatory model: A preliminary report. *Journal of Phonetics* 35. 321–340.

Simard, F., Y. Joanette, M. Petrides, T. Jubault, C Madjar & O. Monchi. 2011. Fronto-striatal contributions to lexical set-shifting. *Cerebral Cortex* 21 (5). 1084–1093.

Stuss, D.T. & D. F. Benson. 1986. *The frontal lobes*. New York: Raven Press.

Stevens, K. N. 1972. Quantal nature of speech. In: E. E. David Jr. and P. B. Denes (eds.), *Human communication: A unified view*, 51–66. New York: McGraw Hill.

The Chimpanzee Sequencing and Analysis Consortium. 2005. Initial sequence of the chimpanzee genome and comparison with the human genome. *Nature* 437. 69–87.

Truby, H. L., J. F. Bosma & J. Lind. 1965. *Newborn infant cry*. Uppsala: Almquist and Wiksell.

Vorperian, H. K., R. D. Kent, M. Lindstrom, C. M. Kalina, L. R. Gentry & B. S. Yandell. 2005. Development of vocal tract length during early childhood: A magnetic resonance imaging study. *Journal of the Acoustical Society of America* 117. 338–350.

Gabriele Siegert and Bjørn von Rimscha

7 Economic bases of communication

Abstract: This chapter provides a general introduction to the essential economic issues of communication, both interpersonal and mediated. It covers economic concepts and methods relevant to the field. The focus is on mass communication and media economics, however featured concepts such as network effects and issues of regulation are also relevant for interpersonal communication. Furthermore it discusses concentration, internationalization, and convergence as three fundamental developments in media systems that tend to blur clear cut distinctions between media technologies and areas of research.

Keywords: Media markets, good characteristics, media regulation, business models, value-chain, network effects, media concentration, convergence, internationalization

Economic considerations related to communication generally focus on mass communication and mass media. Media economics has a long research tradition, although different periods were dominated by different theoretical approaches. For example, in Europe, critical political theory approaches dominated the 1970s through the late 1980s. In the 1990s, though, media economics research started to use traditional economic and management theories, models, and concepts of neoclassical and institutional economics. Economic considerations are less common in the context of interpersonal or group communication. For a long time, research on telecommunications did not refer to communication science explicitly.

Taking the research history into account, the following article focuses on media economics but also briefly covers aspects of interpersonal communication. The article is divided into four sections and starts with a general introduction to the essential economic issues of communication, both interpersonal and mediated. Section 2 covers economic concepts and methods relevant to the field. The discussion will focus on mass communication and media economics, although concepts such as network effects and issues of regulation are also relevant for interpersonal communication. Section 3 discusses concentration, internationalization, and convergence as three fundamental developments in media systems that tend to blur clear cut distinctions between media technologies research. Section 4 provides an overview and outlook to conclude the article.

1 Fundamental economic challenges in communication

Interpersonal communication is a precondition of any economic activity. Before any kind of transaction can take place, individuals must communicate even if they do so as the representative of a larger corporate body. Information must be available for markets to be functional (Baumol and Blinder 2006: 195), and more often than not, it is gathered through interpersonal communication be it face-to-face or mediated through a carrier medium. Individuals negotiate prices or discuss how a task is to be carried out. The expectancy-value theory (Fishbein and Ajzen 1975) addresses the question of how much effort should be made to make a persuasive message credible. It suggests that the persuasiveness of a suggestion equals the promised value (or harm) multiplied by the perceived probability of its occurrence. The Harvard concept (Fisher and Ury 1981) also offers an economic perspective on interpersonal communication as it tries to make personal negotiations both successful and efficient. However, usually interpersonal communication itself is not the traded matter; only personal counselors or psychologists get paid for the act of interpersonal communication. Thus, when analyzing communication, economists usually concentrate on mediated communication, or mass communication.

In modern societies, successful mass communication relies on mass media systems that meet important socio-political and cultural expectations. Society expects the media to provide information, to entertain people, to create publicity for various issues, to criticize, and, to a certain extent, control activities and protagonists, in particular those concerning politics and the economy. Some researchers doubt a commercial media system relying on free markets and market-oriented media companies can meet these expectations. Instead of quality news coverage that supports the political debate, society might then have to face "news that's fit to sell" (Hamilton 2004) or "market-driven journalism" (McManus 1994). The debate on the commercialization of the media (Croteau and Hoynes 2001; Gandy 2004; Picard 2004, 2005a; Siegert 2001b, 2003; McQuail 1998; Bagdikian 2000; Napoli and Gillis 2006) addresses this issue and discusses the consequences of market considerations becoming ever more important in the daily work of media organizations. Following the arguments of the commercialization debate tends to result in media production that does not serve the public interest. However, it is also discussed whether media brand reputation as an institutional arrangement could help media markets to better work in respect of the public interest (Siegert et al. 2008; Siegert et al. 2011).

In addition, the importance of a functioning mass media system is only partly reflected in the economic size of the industry. The percentage that the media contributes to the gross domestic product (GDP) differs according to the market definition (see Section 2.2) from 0.21% for broadcast media in Germany in 2009 (ALM

2010) to 6.0% for copyright-based industries in the United States in 2002 (Siwek 2004: 3). These numbers only represent the economic dimension of the media, and thus tremendously underestimate the significance of the industry for society. Luhmann (1996: 9) stated: "What we know about our society, indeed the world in which we live, we learn from the mass media". Therefore, any account of the media as economic good must also pay respect to the importance of the media as a cultural good that shapes our opinions, influences our values and norms, and provides us with conversation topics to build social capital. The dual character as economic and cultural good poses a challenge to regulation (see Section 2.4).[1]

Both interpersonal and mass communication markets show large externalities due to network effects (see Section 2.6). Thus, business models in communication are routinely based on two-sided markets and mixed funding (see Section 2.5).

2 Economic concepts and models

In this section, we will discuss economic concepts and models mainly focusing on mass communication. However, many of the presented concepts are relevant for interpersonal communication too, and this will be pointed out where appropriate.

2.1 Media as economic good

Most introductions to media economics mention the unique characteristics of media goods, which exert major influence on how media markets work and what kinds of strategies fit in media business (Doyle 2002: 11; Kiefer 2005: 130–160; Picard 1989: 17–19, 2005b; Heinrich 2010: 25–43).[2]

Taking 'packaged and delivered content' as a starting point, it is discussed throughout the literature whether media goods are public goods and/or merit goods and how to handle externalities. These characteristics are sources of the inefficiency of resource allocation and consequential of market failure (see Section 2.4). Public goods are non-excludable (exclusion of potential users is either

---

1 The difference between media as economic and as cultural good is also important in the production of media. A special characteristic about media products is the level of dedication and commitment that the content producers – be it journalists or film directors – show toward their work. Creative workers care about their product (Caves 2000: 3), and thus value not only the monetary compensation, but also a creative satisfaction.

2 Most authors refer to the packaged and delivered content as media good. Only a few contributions include access to audiences as marketed service, and almost none consider that the key characteristics change along the value chain. We like to address this problem simply by mentioning that on the business-to-business market, where content producers deal with media distributors, the traded good does not feature most of the listed unique characteristics.

impractical or impossible), which leads to free rider problems, and are non-rivalrous (consumption by one person does not lessen the amount available for others), which makes exclusion inefficient. In particular, free-to-air broadcasting is said to be a public good.

Putatively, the consumption of media content can have positive external effects, such as citizens being well-informed and making enlightened choices, as well as negative external effects, such as citizens exhibiting violent behavior. Both effects are not included in the price of media content: society either benefits from it or has to pay for it. Society expects the media to provide content with positive external effects, but unfortunately this content often does not generate a great consumer demand. In a normal market relationship, profit-maximizing suppliers therefore would fail to meet society's demand for such a service. This does not mean that merit goods will not be offered in a market with profit-maximizing suppliers, but the socially desirable output level will be higher than the market efficient output level (Demsetz 1970). That makes part of the media content a merit good.

Furthermore, the media industry is characterized by high first copy costs, economies of scale, and economies of scope. High first copy costs imply that fixed costs of media production are high and independent of the amount of copies made, while variable costs are relatively low. This tends to result in decreasing the average fixed costs by increasing output (economies of scale). Due to the costs of physical production and distribution of copies, this effect is stronger in the audiovisual industry than in the print publishing industry and is most powerful concerning digital production and distribution. To sum up, large scale production is more efficient than small-scale production (Picard 1989: 62). Economies of scope "arise when there are some shared overheads for two or more related products to be produced and sold jointly, rather than separately. Savings may arise if specialist inputs gathered for one product can be re-used in another" (Doyle 2002: 13–14).

Additionally, media goods are characterized as experience and credence goods. Entertainment is regarded as an experience good, or a good with unknown characteristics whose quality and utility can only be judged after being used several times (Nelson 1970). Journalistic information, however, is regarded as a credence good. Credence good markets are characterized by asymmetric information between sellers and consumers (Darby and Karni 1973). Users are unable to fully measure the quality of media content. For example, they cannot judge whether information provided by a news broadcast meets journalistic quality standards because the background work, selection, investigation, and effective workload remain 'invisible,' or cannot be accessed for monitoring, and could only be evaluated by completely repeating the journalistic inquiry. Altogether, media users tend to rely on external information and market signals such as reputation and brand (Heinrich and Lobigs 2003; Lobigs 2004; Siegert 2001a, 2006a). Charging users for an experience good or a credence good is difficult. People might not be willing to pay before they can access the good, and if they have experienced it they most likely will not want to pay for something they already experienced. This renders indirect financing through advertising an expeditious alternative.

Last but not least, uncertainty in the media production process and copyright problems are also characteristics that lead to imitation rather than innovation as a preferred strategy of media companies. The characteristics of media content do have consequences regarding financing. In the media business, frequently revenue is not immediately connected to transactions. Readers often pay a subscription fee for their newspaper; advertisers pay for advertising space and assumed attention but cannot be sure that anybody will see it. The license fee for public service broadcasters has to be paid independently from the use of the public channels.

2.2 Defining relevant media markets

Defining the relevant market involves clarifying the market structure and is closely related to the state of competition. Usually four types of competitive market structure are differentiated: perfect competition, monopolistic competition, oligopoly, and monopoly. Following the Structure-Conduct-Performance (SCP) paradigm, analyzing the market structure includes at least the number of sellers and buyers, product differentiation, cost structures, vertical integration, and barriers to entry for new competitors. The market structure determines the state of competition, the context for strategies, and the resulting performance of companies (Scherer 1980; Chan-Olmsted 2006: 163).

It is essential to define the relevant market in order to assess its market power and the intensity of competition in a (media) market, as well as to align (media) strategies with the competitive environment. "Defining a market involves specifying the good/service markets involved and combining that description with a specific geographic market description" (Picard 1989: 17). The generally used 'relevant market concept' is based on the substitutability of goods or services; from the average consumer's perspective, (media) products and services can easily replace one another and compete in the same market.

Throughout the literature on media economics and media management, it is given that most media companies operate in a dual-product market by participating in an audience market as well as in an advertising market (see Section 2.3). However, the different media are not fully interchangeable with one another due to technological standards, product differences, and usage patterns. Therefore, it once was assumed that different media technologies (newspaper, magazines, television, and radio) do not compete with each other, whereas companies dealing with the same media do (intramedia competition). Among changing technological standards, though, consumer tastes and usage patterns have led to increasing intermedia competition and also challenged the precise definition of the relevant market. The topics covered and the corresponding target groups increasingly determine the boundaries of media markets rather than media technologies.

In addition, it is important to clarify the geographical dimension of media markets. Due to the interests of audiences, some media firms market their outlets locally or regionally, yet others sell them nationwide or, in some cases, internationally. Global media outlets are an exception, although the activities of transnational corporations force competition on an international level (Gershon 2006; Sánchez-Tabernero 2006). The geographical dimension is only one factor that influences the size of a media market; it refers partly to the size of the audience that could be interested in a certain media outlet. However, media outlets are also closely connected to certain geographical areas for cultural and political reasons. They relate to a certain political system's events and actors, to languages, to different patterns of media usage, and to a common cultural identity. The market size, on the other hand, is important because of the effectiveness of key economic characteristics of media products (fixed cost degression, economies of scale, partly economies of scope). The bigger the market in which a media company operates, the more effective are these characteristics – operating in a big market is a competitive advantage. Small media markets are a key characteristic of so-called small countries and therefore foster regulation (see Section 2.4).

2.3 Dual-product market

Some media technologies such as books or recorded music rely almost entirely on direct sales to recipients. Producers offer one product in one market and the audience's interest should be their only benchmark. However, more often than not, media are financed simultaneously from several different sources. A newspaper publisher derives revenue from the copy price as well as from advertising sales. A public broadcaster might add some advertising revenue to its license fee, but a free-to-air TV channel might rely almost entirely on advertising revenue. In these cases, media firms operate in a dual-product market (Picard 1989), which means that media firms produce and market one product – content – in an effort to simultaneously produce and market a second product – audience attention. Economists speak of a two-sided market (Rochet and Tirole 2006) where the business model considers viewers as a loss leader, which in turn attracts advertisers. Success or failure in the market for audience contacts is a function of success or failure in the market of content for recipients, and vice versa. A broadcaster or publisher that fails to attract a reasonably large or demographically desirable audience has a relatively unappealing product to sell in the advertising market. The same broadcaster or publisher therefore will not have the financial resources (relative to its competitors) to produce content capable of attracting a larger or more desirable audience since prices for readers or viewers are subsidized (Kaiser and Wright

2006). Thus, the audience and advertising markets are tightly intertwined, even if all revenue is derived from the advertising market.

This dual-product market would not work, though, without well-established and accepted commercial audience research (Ang 1991; Siegert 1993: 15; Ettema and Whitney 1994; Webster et al. 2006; Frey-Vor et al. 2008). Therefore, commercial audience research is discussed as an indispensible market information system (Phalen 1998). It measures, segments, and rates the audience of past programs and provides estimates of the future audience. As a result, it makes the invisible and sometimes unknown audience visible and marketable to advertisers. Ratings are one of the most common examples of commercial audience research and have found their way into popular culture.

2.4 Market failure and regulation

Broadcast media in particular are regarded as a prime example of a public good (see Section 2.1). The characteristics of public goods lead to market failure because, if no one can be excluded from the use of a commodity, people will try to get a free ride and the willingness to pay will converge to zero. If the consumption of a commodity by one person does not restrict availability for others, the commodity is not scarce, and thus, again, it is impossible to discriminate using the price mechanism. In most European countries, legislators introduced public service media to address market failure, which ensured that consumers pay for the media via the license fee or taxes while maximizing the public good to society's benefit (Graham 1999). Commercial broadcasters address the market failure by bringing in the advertising industry as a middle man. In this model, the broadcaster actually does not want to exclude anybody from consumption since the objective is to generate the most attention among recipients.

Technological progress rendered the issue of market failure partly obsolete once it became possible to exclude potential free riders using digital rights management or scrambled signals. Digitization also has increased the available supply and freed the medium from the limits of linearity. However, even in the digital media industry of the twenty-first century, public service media still exist because in addition to the public good character, an even more powerful argument for regulation lies in the merit good character of the media (Ward 2006). Media are said to feature positive externalities in wide areas of society with social benefits clearly exceeding private ones. Governments that identify a merit good with its positive impact on society usually introduce measures that maximize the consumption and supply of the desirable good or service, which is done by subsidies. In the case of broadcasting, the instrument of choice is the introduction of public service media; for newspapers and magazines, common measures include indirect measures, such as a reduced sales tax, and direct measures, such as reduced distribution fees (Fernández Alonso et al. 2006: 2). In the audiovisual sector, almost every developed country offers some form of subsidies in the shape of film funding schemes.

Public service media in small countries gain an outstanding importance. Small countries are characterized by small media markets and a shortage of resources. As a consequence, there are special constraints for small states: dependence and vulnerability (Trappel 1991; Meier and Trappel 1992; Siegert 2006b). Furthermore, small states struggle at times to protect their cultural heritage when confronted with the dominance of international content and content from larger neighboring states. Therefore, regulation in small states tends to interfere more directly with the content while allowing cross-media ownership for national champions (Puppis 2009). Also, public service media in small states are expected to support cultural national identity.

Providing platforms for interpersonal communication usually also involves dealing with regulation. Since network effects are deemed positive for society, regulators demand universal service for everybody and may set a low price for a basic service in order to include every citizen in the communication network. Communication networks often have the character of a natural monopoly which makes regulation even more necessary to prevent excessive tariffs (Meyer et al. 1980).

2.5 Business and revenue models

Business models connect media economics to media management by describing underlying characteristics of the industry sector that enable commerce in the product or service. Thus, media business models are not so much about daily business activities, but a fundamental concept of how the business can operate, what interfaces it offers for other industries, and what trade relations and financial interactions render it potentially successful. They can be described as structural design of the relevant flows of information, services, and, finally, products, and include an account of the necessary business activities and their reciprocal importance (Picard 2002). A business model consists of several submodels: procurement; market (demand, competition); goods and services; service offerings; distribution; and capital (funding, revenue). Additionally, a business model should include a description of the potential benefits of the various business actors and the sources of revenue. This constitutes the revenue model, which addresses questions regarding how revenue can be retrieved and from what sources, as well as what amount is necessary to finance the ongoing operations.

Revenue models can be distinguished by direct and indirect sources of revenue (Zerdick et al. 2000: 25) or by separating the relevant markets in which an organization is engaged (Wirtz 2009: 78). These two typologies can be applied both to mass communication and interpersonal communication platforms.

In the first perspective, direct financing is most often obtained from the users, while indirect financing can be derived from companies (advertising) or the state (subsidies). The other perspective differentiates three markets where revenue can be realized: content markets, audience/user markets, and advertising markets. On content markets, media organizations trade licenses and exploitation rights, and the 'non-rivalrousness' of media use creates secondary markets. A broadcaster can sell the rights to a successful TV show to a different territory, or a publisher can license the concept of a successful magazine to another country. In addition, services and merchandise might be sold. It has nothing in common with interpersonal communication since usually it consists of inputs from two partners who will not bill each other for the words spoken during a conversation. From an economic perspective, issues of interpersonal communication mostly concern how to provide a platform where the communication takes place and then gain profit from operating that platform. Platforms for interpersonal communication do not need to be based on a technological network, but can be a coffee house where people meet for a hot drink and a chat. Overall, if we neglect the content market, interpersonal and mass communication have the same business models on the user and advertising markets. According to the concept of two-sided markets (Rochet and Tirole 2006), both markets are interdependent and connected via the price mechanism. Changes in price on the audience/user market influence the demand on the advertising market, and vice versa.

When looking at mass communication advertising markets, different advertising formats with associated recipient attention or recipient information can be sold. New means of interpersonal communication such as email services, chat rooms, and social networks on the Internet employ the same funding scheme as most mass media: selling attention to advertisers and selling consumer profiles to marketers. However, the quality of contact might be better than in mass media, and targeting of advertisements can be improved as social media networks struggle to capitalize on the attention of users.[3] In the context of interpersonal communication, advertising might be considered even more intrusive than when used as part of mass media content. We see the same tendencies toward ad avoidance on the consumer side, as well as the blending of content and advertising on the side of the platform providers and advertisers.

However, advertising does not constitute the only opportunity to bundle communication with another product or service to realize an indirect means of funding.

---

[3] Recently, a new form of predominantly interpersonal communication (social online networks) has changed marketing since they enable corporations to establish quasi-interpersonal communications with potential consumers. In a social media network, the concept of a brand personality (Aaker 1997) is enlivened because it becomes possible to make friends with a brand and interact and communicate with it as if it were a real person (Burns 2010). In the course, brand communication becomes part of other interpersonal communications, for instance, when individuals pass on funny clips from a viral marketing campaign (Bauer et al. 2008).

In the coffee house example mentioned earlier, the platform for interpersonal communication is funded by the price of a cup of coffee. Another example would be the price of Internet access that includes a personal email address. Because the platform is funded indirectly, though, providers have to make sure that the unpaid part of the bundle is not over used. Thus, Internet service providers introduce email quotas, and the coffee house's host might ask a lingering patron to either order another drink or leave, opening up the table for a new paying customer.

A network or platform operator who enables interpersonal communication can exclude potential users, and thus is able to charge whenever the network is used. This can be based on time or distance, e.g., when a telephone provider charges by the minute or a postal service sets different prices for letters to foreign countries depending on the distance required for delivery. As with newspapers, single payments can be replaced by subscriptions. Telephone providers in most countries now offer flat rates that allow users to use the network more or less without limits. Subscription models require that the average usage time results in costs below the net costs. Flat fees are a means to improve the capacity utilization if network costs are fixed. The same is true in the context of mass communication. Recipients can be charged for access to media or for media use. Again, there are subscription models that make the cash flow more predictable and also single payments for items in high demand that can seek a premium due to a willingness to pay. However, the merit good character of some media implies that the totaled individual willingness to pay cannot cover the production costs. Since the public has an interest in these media offerings, the state is an important fourth source of revenue or cost reduction. The media is considered important and influential for the political and cultural development and cohesion of a society, so in many countries the state supports the media by introducing a license fee to finance a public broadcaster (e.g., UK) or financing it directly through tax money (e.g., Spain). Most countries have reduced tax rates for media products and often the distribution is sponsored through subsidized postal fees. Film producers often enjoy tax breaks or even receive substantial direct financial contributions.

While interpersonal communication is predominantly financed directly through transmission charges, most media companies use mixed financing to spread risks while avoiding dependencies. The respective contribution of each revenue source depends on good characteristics as well as competition (Kind et al. 2009).

2.6 Added value and value chain

The concept of added value is derived from macroeconomic accounting where it is used to measure the contribution of an industry to the GDP. To analyze the performance of the media as an industry sector, market boundaries must be defined (see Section 2.2) and relations to other sectors up- and downstream need to be clarified. We can speak of a division of labor on an industry level, which in microeconomics can be described as value chain. The concept was introduced to business management by Porter (1985) as a succession of discrete activities for a firm operating in a specific industry. The products are taken through each of these activities and gain value every time they conclude a step. The chain of activities lends more added value to the product than the sum of added values of all activities.

The value chain can be used as a means to define markets – all firms on the same level compete with each other. It can also be used to conceptualize business models since it defines the interfaces between different steps in development from idea to reception. Typically the value chain for the media industry cannot use the element of the original concept with inbound logistics, operations, outbound logistics, marketing and sales, and service accompanied by overarching support activities such as infrastructure, human resources, technology, and procurement. With predominantly intangible input factors and output terms of classic inventory management become murky. Furthermore, the duality of the media as content and advertising vehicle complicates the structure (Wirtz 2009).

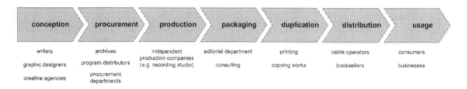

Fig. 1: Generic value chain in the media industry

There used to be distinct value chains for different media technologies with little, if any, overlapping between them. Changes in the technology and in the way the industry is organized have blurred the boundaries between technology-specific value chains and created a more generic multimedia value chain (see Fig. 1). Technological progress allows for disintermediation, or the systematic canceling of certain steps in the value chain. For example, electronic media such as radio and television do not have to be printed and copied, but can be directly distributed. Musicians who sell their recordings directly via the Internet skip procurement and integrate production, and if they use their own web site instead of platforms such as iTunes, they can even leap the packaging step. Convergence (see Section 3.2) has made this research perspective more complicated and less easily applicable.

2.7 Network effects and network externalities

Media content is often produced in networks by combining the expertise of different media workers. It is distributed using transmission networks and consumed by recipients who use media content as conversation subjects in their social networks. Thus, networks matter in media economics. Network goods differ from other goods concerning the value creation because of network externalities; consumers deciding between substitutable goods consider how their decision will affect others and how the decision of others will affect them. The utility that a user derives from the consumption of a network good increases with the number of others consuming the good (Katz and Shapiro 1985).

Generally, we can differentiate between direct and indirect network effects. In the first case, consumption externalities result from a direct physical effect of the number of purchasers on the product quality. A classic example would be a telephone network where the utility that a consumer derives from joining the network by buying access from the operator depends directly on the number of others who have already joined the network. Indirect network effects do not require a physical connection. When more consumers buy a certain kind of hardware, it increases the likelihood that a wide variety of different kinds of compatible software will be available for it. This phenomenon can be observed each time different standards for a new medium compete for user acceptance. For example, when consumers decide between HD-DVD or Blu-ray player disc technology, their individual decisions make one format more attractive than the other, since the home entertainment industry is likely to offer more movies in the more widely adopted format. The utility of a product increases with the greater availability of compatible complementary products.

For media content, an externality lies in the consumer capital for discussing common experiences when recipients have shared the experience of a certain content. But the case in point of network effects is the dual-product marketplace of traditional media (see Section 2.3). For users, network effects can lead to a lock-in due to high switching cost. For instance, a fan of a certain daily soap opera benefits from the fact that a large number of viewers watch the same show, and thus they have a common conversation topic. So this viewer might hesitate to switch to a competing soap airing at the same time because in addition to learning new characters and plotlines, s/he would not be able to talk about the new experience with those still watching the first show. Therefore, media companies can use network effects to tie the customers to their products.

However, network effects wear out as a network enlarges (Leibenstein 1950). The marginal benefit of one new user is much higher in a small network than in a big one. With the penetration of a phone network at almost 100%, the value of that phone network does not further increase with a new installation.

Externalities result in economies of scale on the demand side. Larger companies with larger networks benefit more from externalities, thus their existence is a strong driver of concentration (see Section 3.1). This most often leads to natural monopolies in the case of broadcasting and telecommunication infrastructure (Posner 1969) since new entrants to the market cannot compete with the incumbent operator in terms of cost advantages and utility for users.

3 Fundamental developments in media systems

3.1 Media concentration

Media goods feature several traits that make consolidation and concentration attractive. Since media content is unique, the costs of development are high. Consumers constantly demand novelty and their interests often are hard to predict, so production is risky. This means that being big is attractive in the industry. Economies of scale and scope lead to higher efficiency in larger companies. The advantage of size rests in the possible offset of risk and in the maximization of exploitation of content rights, especially in unit cost savings when first copy costs can be distributed over more copies. Furthermore, size brings about important advantages such as negotiation power with advertisers and improved access to capital. The latter proves important when new markets open up. Since the 1980s, only large companies have had the financial strength to enter the new broadcasting and telecommunication markets introduced when media policy ended a public service monopoly in much of the developed world (Picard 1998).

However, what is considered good from an entrepreneurial perspective might not be in the best interest of the society as a whole. Media concentration is regarded as a possible threat to diversity of ideas, tastes, and opinions. On the contrary, media diversity and media pluralism are considered prerequisites for effective freedom of expression and information (Meier and Trappel 1998). Even if we only consider economic aspects, though, concentration is not in the best interest of consumers. When the level of concentration reduces competition, it leads to higher prices, fewer choices, and poorer service for consumers. Concentration gives dominant firms control over resources that can be used against smaller firms in a competitive marketplace.

Concentration is not a new phenomenon. During the 1950s and 1960s, a consolidation of newspapers in several western European countries triggered extensive research (Aufermann and Heilmann 1970), but the deregulation of the audiovisual sector in Europe since the 1980s has pronounced the issue. Publishers expanded their operations to the TV sector, and thus claimed a bigger share of the media and opinion market as a whole. The professionalization of advertising and the emergence of huge international advertising networks serving brands that expand internationally have increased the pressure among media firms to grow and build market power.

We need to distinguish between different aspects of what is called media concentration:

- Horizontal concentration or mono-media concentration (Meier and Trappel 1998) looks at distinct media markets separated by geography or the means of distribution, e.g., the development of the market shares of British national newspapers. From an economic perspective, only horizontal concentration actually describes a concentration.

- Vertical integration considers the effect of mergers and acquisitions on the concentration of power of one corporation across the value chain (see Section 2.6). If a TV network buys a big production company, this increases concentration neither in the broadcasting market nor in the production market. However, it increases the market power of that corporation and transforms a transparent exchange relationship on the market into internal affairs of that corporation.
- Cross-media or multimedia concentration (Sánchez-Tabernero 1993: 16) considers the media market as a whole where mergers and acquisitions among different media technologies (e.g., newspapers and broadcasters) not only create synergies but also increase market power in the overall 'market' of public opinion.
- Conglomerate concentration may occur when surplus capital from one industry seeks new business opportunities, or when new markets that open require considerable investment. The latter was the case when broadcasting was deregulated in France and Italy and commercial broadcasters were financed by banks or construction companies. For conglomerate concentration, different misgivings emerge. While the level of competition within the media market might not be reduced, chances are that the conglomerate tries to use its media ownership to influence the media content in its own best interest.

For cross-media concentration, the question arises: to what extent are the markets actually separated? Consumers as well as advertisers might use different media as substitutes so that they form a common relevant market. Thus, the concentration of ownership does not always imply less diversity in content. When two newspapers in the same region merge, it is likely that the content of the merged newspaper is less diverse. However, if a newspaper from another region, or if the dominant national TV chain buys a regional newspaper, neither the size of the staff nor the diversity of the content in that market have to change.

In markets for communication infrastructure, there is a tendency toward a natural monopoly. The high costs of setting up a cable infrastructure or of running a satellite distribution system prohibit the building of two competing networks. While there usually is competition between different distribution channels, each channel is run by a regional monopolist. In this context, it is evident that technological progress can at times reduce the potentially harmful effect of concentration. The development of digital subscriber line (DSL) technology enabled telephone operators to compete with cable operators, not only in the new field of data traffic, but also in the market for TV distribution. The Internet has vastly expanded the news sources available to recipients. Citizens living in a region with a monopolist newspaper can read newspapers from other regions online or access firsthand information from other sources within their region. Technology leads to fragmentation, so owning several media outlets does not necessarily lead to concentration, but can be regarded as a means to retain market share. Depending on the market in question, concentration is not always on the rise.

Media concentration policy tries to control the potentially harmful effects of media concentration. Policy instruments differ widely between different countries; however, some measures seem to be prevalent. Either the number of media outlets or the market share that may be controlled by a single company is limited. Often cross-media ownership also is limited, meaning that a dominant player in one media technology may not expand into another to keep competition between the two genres alive.

However, studies about the effect of media concentration policy in general, and press concentration in particular, suggest that the measures are not effective. In some cases, there are even unintended outcomes ultimately favoring big integrated media corporations (Tunstall 1996; Knoche 1997).

3.2 Convergence

Changing technological standards challenge the body of acquired knowledge concerning media markets, value chains, and media business models. They provide the bases for variation and innovation on different levels – mostly analyzed by using the convergence concept. The concept of media convergence has multiple meanings and includes various changes in media's environments and behavior. Across the literature (e.g., overview by Wirth 2006; articles in IJMM 2003, No. 1 or the journal *Convergence*), convergence is seen as a multidimensional process that comprehends:

- Technological convergence (e.g., innovation, digitization, standardization)
- Economic convergence (e.g., merging of formerly divided markets, reconfiguration of value chains)
- Social convergence/convergence in media usage (e.g., consumer preferences and behavior)
- Cultural convergence (e.g., cross-media storytelling and mutual interrelated content)
- Policy convergence (e.g., deregulation, liberalization, convergence of formerly separate regulatory bodies and models)
- Global convergence (e.g., internationalization of strategies and content)

Additionally, the various dimensions should not be regarded as isolated, but rather as co-evolutionary developments (Latzer 1997). Some authors doubted whether consumer preferences and behavior would change (Stipp 1999; Höflich 1999). However, recent research results show that the use of online content increases and affects the use of traditional media and the definition of media markets (Gerhards and Klingler 2007; de Waal et al. 2005; Cole 2004; van Eimeren and Frees 2009).

From the perspective of media companies, convergence appears as reconfiguration of value chains and, following Wirth (2006), searching for synergy, increasing mergers and acquisition activities, and repurposing content on new media platforms. As discussed, value chains of the telecommunication industry, IT industry, and media industry merge into a convergent value chain. Telecom, IT, and media companies develop new business segments and pursue cross-media strategies. They increasingly operate in a common convergent market and have to face new competitors with different backgrounds, as shown in Fig. 2.

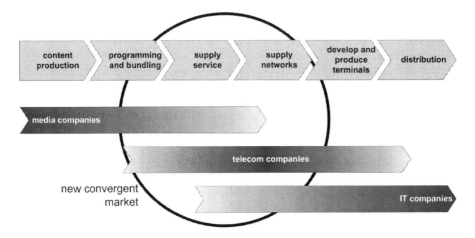

Fig. 2: Convergent value chains and markets

The rise of the Internet in particular has affected the business model of traditional media companies and gave a boost to free content. Although the demand for free content is high, the revenue model unfortunately does not pay off for media companies. Against the background of the last two economic crises (2000/2001: the burst of the so-called dotcom bubble, and 2008/2009: the worldwide financial crisis) media companies continuously complained about their role as producers of high-quality journalism without receiving adequate funding. While traditional media companies have to pay for the immense costs of good media coverage, Apple and Google realize profits with ad search and online advertising.

3.3 Internationalization

In recent decades, the media industry has evolved from clearly separated markets, in which family-owned businesses arranged themselves in a setting of low competition, to an international industry (Smith 1991; Demers 2002). Bertelsmann, for instance, was founded in 1835 as a publisher in North Rhine-Westphalia and now has about 500 newspaper and magazine titles in 30 countries, holds TV and radio stations in ten European countries, and produces TV content in 22 countries and licenses content in 150 countries.

Internationalization is driven by two factors. First, media companies have an interest in expanding across borders; second, media recipients have a certain interest in foreign content (Sánchez-Tabernero 2006). Saturated national markets and barriers to cross-ownership force growing media companies to enter foreign markets. Generally, there are three strategies to enter a foreign market (Hafstrand 1995). The simplest way is to export ready-made media products. While this requires only small investments to achieve economies of scale, it is only feasible when the market entered is nearby and similar in culture and demand structure. This way of internationalization is common between neighboring countries sharing the same language, e.g., French media in Belgium, or German media in Austria and Switzerland. Another option is foreign direct investment, either in the form of joint ventures, mergers and acquisitions, or greenfield, i.e., starting a new operation from scratch (Gershon 2000). Foreign direct investment provides a high degree of control but requires a similarly high level of resources and commitment. The strong cultural component of the media industry renders a greenfield strategy less attractive since it does not allow building from knowledge of the new market. The third strategy is licensing where a firm in the host country is permitted to use a (intangible) property of the licensor such as trademarks, patents, production techniques, or content templates. Licensing requires very little investment, but it does not allow for generating revenue from production and marketing in the host country. Even more important, licensing includes a transfer of know-how that also might be utilized beyond the licensed product, and thus could strengthen possible competitors.

Apart from the upsides in terms of economies of scale and scope and new growth opportunities, internationalization also poses some problems for media companies. Media content is highly dependent on the cultural context. For instance, only a fraction of news content can be reused in other markets since most news broadcasts are relevant only in a certain market and recipients, as well as advertisers, are interested in local, regional or national content (Reid et al. 2005; Aldridge 2003). Entertainment content generally travels more easily, although cultural and linguistic borders exist as well. Supported by powerful global distribution and marketing, Hollywood movies are quite successful in foreign markets, and the very basic storylines of Latin American telenovelas make them universally deployable.

Nevertheless, there is a cultural discount for media content. Since media content distributed in a foreign market does not completely address the cultural framework, it will most likely draw a smaller audience, and thus be less valuable (McFadyen et al. 2000). Non-fiction programming is harder to transfer from one market to another due to its reliance on personalities (show host, celebrity guests, etc.). In this case, the strategy of choice is licensing, rather than exporting content. The emergence of an international trade in TV formats is a visible outcome of this relationship (Moran and Malbon 2006; Altmeppen et al. 2007). Instead of exporting complete shows, trade takes place via show templates that define game concept, the actor setting, and the dramaturgy. A format proven successful in one market offers reduced risk and required time to market in other markets while allowing for adjustments of the concept to local customs. This phenomenon is not limited to TV formats such as 'Who wants to be a Millionaire?' (Freedman 2001), but also happens with print magazines (Hafstrand 1995).

The other driving factor of internationalization is found in the recipients' interests. Cairncross (1997) diagnosed a "death of distance" where space is no longer the determining factor for social, information, and commercial relationships. Distance has become relative and this means the audience market becomes segmented by interests rather than by geographic factors. The "long tail" (Anderson 2006) for cultural goods can only work in a much expanded marketplace. Audience demand that was too obscure in the traditional media market becomes a viable market niche when search engines and recommendation systems allow recipients to find products outside of their geographic area. Of course, cultural and linguistic boundaries still remain, but with reduced cost for logistics, especially for digital products, exporting media content at a global scale is feasible even for specialized content.

4 Outlook

The fundamental importance of communication in modern societies is attended by the public interest in the economic bases of communication and the respective industry. Due to the various characteristics of interpersonal and mass communication, neither markets nor business models work as they do in other industries. The economics and management of media and communication are affected by the public and merit good character; the experience and credence good character of media content, externalities, and network effects; and economies of scale and scope. Furthermore, concentration, convergence, and internationalization tendencies not only challenge the media industry but the respective research and literature. It is an ongoing discussion whether the combination of characteristics makes it impossible for a commercial media system to serve the public interest, or whether there is a way to link quality and profit.

Further reading

Bagdikian, Ben H. 2000. *The Media Monopoly*, 6th edn. Boston, MA: Beacon Press.

Doyle, Gillian. 2002. *Understanding Media Economics*. London: Sage Publications.

Picard, Robert G. 2002. *The Economics and Financing of Media Companies*. New York: Fordham University Press.

Sánchez-Tabernero, Alfonso. 1993. *Media Concentration in Europe: Commercial Enterprise and the Public Interest*. Düsseldorf: European Institute for the Media.

Wirth, Michael O. 2006. Issues in media convergence. In: Alan B. Albarran, Sylvia M. Chan-
Olmsted and Michael O. Wirth (eds.), *Handbook of Media Management and Economics*, 445–
462. Mahwah, NJ: Lawrence Erlbaum Associates.

References

Aaker, Jennifer L. 1997. Dimensions of brand personality. *Journal of Marketing Research* 34 (3).
347–356.

Aldridge, Meryl. 2003. The ties that divide: Regional press campaigns, community and populism.
Media, Culture and Society 25 (4). 491–509.

Altmeppen, Klaus-Dieter, Katja Lantzsch & Andreas Will. 2007. Flowing networks in the
entertainment business: Organizing international TV format trade. *The International Journal
on Media Management* 9 (3). 94–104.

Anderson, Chris. 2006. *The Long Tail: How Endless Choice Is Creating Unlimited Demand. The
New Economics of Culture and Commerce*. London: Random House.

Ang, Ien. 1991. *Desperately Seeking the Audience*. London and New York: Routledge.

ALM (Arbeitsgemeinschaft der Landesmedienanstalten in der Bundesrepublik Deutschland) (ed.).
2010. *Wirtschaftliche Lage des Rundfunks in Deutschland 2008 / 2009*. Berlin: Vistas.

Aufermann, Jörg & Peter Heilmann (eds.). 1970. *Pressekonzentration: Eine kritische
Materialsichtung und -systematisierung*. München: Verlag Dokumentation.

Bagdikian, Ben H. 2000. *The Media Monopoly*. 6th edn. Boston, MA: Beacon Press.

Bauer, Hans H., Thomas E. Haber, Carmen-Maria Albrecht & Tom Laband. 2008. Viral Advertising.
In: Hans H. Bauer, Dirk Große-Leege and Jürgen Rösger (eds.), *Interactive Marketing im Web
2.0+: Konzepte und Anwendungen für ein erfolgreiches Marketingmanagement im Internet*,
2nd edn, 268–282. München: Vahlen.

Baumol, William J. & Alan S. Blinder. 2006. *Microeconomics: Principles and Policy*. Mason, OH:
Thomson/South-Western.

Burns, Kelli. 2010. Brands among friends: An examination of brand friending and engagement on
facebook. Paper presented at the annual meeting of the Association for Education in
Journalism and Mass Communication, Denver, CO, Aug 04, 2010.

Cairncross, Frances. 1997. *The Death of Distance: How the Communications Revolution Will
Change Our Lives*. Boston, MA: Harvard Business School.

Caves, Richard E. 2000. *Creative Industries: Contracts Between Art and Commerce*. Cambridge,
MA: Harvard University Press.

Chan-Olmsted, Sylvia M. 2006. Issues in strategic management. In: Alan B. Albarran, Sylvia M.
Chan-Olmsted and Michael O. Wirth (eds.), *Handbook of Media Management and Economics*,
161–180. Mahwah, NJ: Lawrence Erlbaum Associates.

Cole, Jeffrey I. 2004. *The Digital Future Report. Surveying the Digital Future: Ten Years, Ten
Trends*. Los Angeles: Digital Center.

Croteau, David & William Hoynes. 2001. *The Business of Media: Corporate Media and the Public
Interest*. Thousand Oaks: Pine Forge Press.

Darby, Michael R. & Edi Karni. 1973. Free competition and the optimal amount of fraud. *Journal of
Law and Economics* 16 (1). 67–88.

de Waal, Ester, Klaus Schönbach & Edmund Lauf. 2005. Online newspapers: A substitute or
complement for print newspapers and other information channels? *Communications* 30 (1).
55–72.

Demers, David P. 2002. *Global Media: Menace or Messiah?* 2nd edn. Creskill, NJ: Hampton Press.

Demsetz, Harold. 1970. The private production of public goods. *The Journal of Law and Economics* 13 (2). 293–306.

Doyle, Gillian. 2002. *Understanding Media Economics*. London: Sage Publications.

Ettema, James S. & D. Charles Whitney. 1994. The money arrow: An introduction to audiencemaking. In: James S. Ettema and D. C. Whitney (eds.), *Audiencemaking: How the Media Create the Audience*, 1–18. Thousand Oaks: Sage Publications.

Fernández Alonso, Isabel, Miquel de Moragas, Jose J. Blasco Gil & Nuria Almiron (eds.). 2006. *Press Subsidies in Europe*. Barcelona: Generalitat de Catalunya.

Fishbein, Martin & Icek Ajzen. 1975. *Belief, Attitude, Intention and Behavior: An introduction to theory and research*. Reading, MA: Addison-Wesley.

Fisher, Roger & William Ury. 1981. *Getting to Yes: Negotiating Agreement Without Giving in*. Boston: Houghton Mifflin Company.

Freedman, Des. 2001. Who wants to be a millionaire?: The politics of television exports. *Information, Communication and Society* 6 (1). 24–41.

Frey-Vor, Gerlinde, Gabriele Siegert & Hans-Jörg Stiehler (eds.). 2008. *Mediaforschung*. Konstanz: UVK.

Gandy, Oscar H. 2004. Audiences on demand. In: Andrew Calabrese and Colin Sparks (eds.), *Toward a Political Economy of Culture: Capitalism and Communication in the Twenty-First Century*, 327–341. Lanham, MD: Rowman and Littlefield.

Gerhards, Maria & Walter Klingler. 2007. Mediennutzung in der Zukunft: Eine Trendanalyse auf der Basis heutiger Datenquellen. *Media Perspektiven* 6. 295–309.

Gershon, Richard A. 2000. The transnational media corporation: Environmental scanning and strategy formulation. *Journal of Media Economics* 13 (2). 81–101.

Gershon, Richard A. 2006. Issues in traditional media management. In: Alan B. Albarran, Sylvia M. Chan-Olmsted and Michael O. Wirth (eds.), *Handbook of Media Management and Economics*, 203–228. Mahwah, NJ: Lawrence Erlbaum Associates.

Graham, Andrew (ed.). 1999. *Public Purposes in Broadcasting: Funding the BBC*. Luton: University of Luton Press.

Hafstrand, Helene. 1995. Consumer magazines in transition: A study of approaches to internationalization. *Journal of Media Economics* 8 (1). 1–12.

Hamilton, James T. 2004. *All the News that's Fit to Sell: How the Market Transforms Information into News*. Princeton, NJ: Princeton University Press.

Heinrich, Jürgen. 2010. *Medienökonomie: Band 1: Mediensystem, Zeitung, Zeitschrift, Anzeigenblatt*. 3rd edn. Wiesbaden: VS Verlag.

Heinrich, Jürgen & Frank Lobigs. 2003. Wirtschaftswissenschaftliche Perspektiven IV: Neue Institutionenökonomik. In: Klaus-Dieter Altmeppen and Matthias Karmasin (eds.), *Medien und Ökonomie: Band 1/1: Grundlagen der Medienökonomie: Kommunikations- und Medienwissenschaft, Wirtschaftswissenschaft*, 245–268. Wiesbaden: Westdeutscher Verlag.

Höflich, Joachim R. 1999. Der Mythos vom umfassenden Medium: Anmerkungen zur Konvergenz aus einer Nutzerperspektive. In: Michael Latzer, Ursula Maier-Rabler, Gabriele Siegert and Thomas Steinmaurer (eds.), *Die Zukunft der Kommunikation: Phänomene und Trends in der Informationsgesellschaft*, 43–59. Innsbruck: Studienverlag.

Kaiser, Ulrich & Julian Wright. 2006. Price structure in two-sided markets: Evidence from the magazine industry. *International Journal of Industrial Organization* 24 (1). 1–28.

Katz, Michael L. & Carl Shapiro. 1985. Network externalities, competition, and compatibility. *The American Economic Review* 75 (3). 424–440.

Kiefer, Marie L. 2005. *Medienökonomik: Einführung in eine Ökonomische Theorie der Medien*, 2nd edn. München, Wien: Oldenbourg.

Kind, Hans J., Tore Nilssen & Lars Sorgard. 2009. Business models for media firms: Does competition matter for how they raise revenue? *Marketing Science* 28 (6). 1112–1128.

Knoche, Manfred. 1997. Medienpolitik als Konzentrationsförderungspolitik: Auch Österreich tappt in die Privatisierungsfalle. *Medien Journal* 21 (2). 14–25.

Latzer, Michael. 1997. *Mediamatik: Die Konvergenz von Telekommunikation, Computer und Rundfunk.* Opladen: Westdeutscher Verlag.

Leibenstein, Harvey. 1950. Bandwagon, snob, and veblen effects in the theory of consumers' demand. *The Quarterly Journal of Economics* 64 (2). 183–207.

Lobigs, Frank. 2004. Funktionsfähiger journalistischer Wettbewerb: Institutionenökonomische Herleitung einer fundamentalen publizistischen Institution. In: Gabriele Siegert and Frank Lobigs (eds.), *Zwischen Marktversagen und Medienvielfalt: Medienmärkte im Fokus Neuer medienökonomischer Anwendungen*, 53–68. Baden-Baden: Nomos.

Luhmann, Niklas. 1996. *Die Realität der Massenmedien.* 2nd edn. Opladen: Westdeutscher Verlag.

McFadyen, Stuart M., Colin Hoskins & Adam Finn. 2000. Cultural industries from an economic/ business research perspective. *Canadian Journal of Communication* 25 (1). 127–144.

McManus, John H. 1994. *Market-Driven Journalism: Let the Citizen Beware?* Thousand Oaks: Sage Publications.

McQuail, Denis. 1998. Commercialization and beyond. In: Denis McQuail and Karen Siune (eds.), *Media policy: Convergence, Concentration and Commerce*, 107–127. London: Sage Publications.

Meier, Werner A. & Josef Trappel. 1992. Small states in the shadow of giants. In: Karen Siune and Wolfgang Treutzschler (eds.), *Dynamics of Media Politics: Broadcast and Electronic Media in Western Europe*, 129–142. London: Sage Publications.

Meier, Werner A. & Josef Trappel. 1998. Media concentration and the public interest. In: Denis McQuail and Karen Siune (eds.), *Media Policy: Convergence, Concentration and Commerce*, 38–59. London: Sage Publications.

Meyer, John R., Robert W. Wilson, M. A. Baughcum, Ellen Burton & John R. Meyer. 1980. *The Economics of Competition in the Telecommunications Industry.* Cambridge, MA: Oelgeschlager Gunn and Hain.

Moran, Albert & Justin Malbon. 2006. *Understanding the Global TV Format.* Bristol: Intellect.

Napoli, Philip & Nancy Gillis. 2006. Reassessing the potential contribution of communications research to communications policy: The case of media ownership. *Journal of Broadcasting and Electronic Media* 50 (4). 671–691.

Nelson, Phillip. 1970. Information and consumer behavior. *The Journal of Political Economy* 78 (2). 311–329.

Phalen, Patricia F. 1998. The market information system and personalized exchange: Business practices in the market for television audiences. *Journal of Media Economics* 11 (4). 17–34.

Picard, Robert G. 1989. *Media Economics: Concepts and Issues.* Newbury Park, CA: Sage Publications.

Picard, Robert G. 1998. Media concentration, economics and regulation. In: Doris A. Graber, Denis McQuail, Pippa Norris and Doris Graber (eds.), *The Politics of News: The News of Politics*, 193–217. Washington DC: CQ Press.

Picard, Robert G. 2002. *The Economics and Financing of Media Companies.* New York: Fordham University Press.

Picard, Robert G. 2004. Commercialism and newspaper quality. *Newspaper Research Journal* 25 (1). 54–65.

Picard, Robert G. 2005a. Money, media, and the public interest. In: Geneva Overholser (ed.), *The Press*, 337–350. New York: Oxford University Press.

Picard, Robert G. 2005b. Unique characteristics and business dynamics of media products. *Journal of Media Business Studies* 2 (2). 61–69.

Porter, Michael E. 1985. *Competitive Advantage: Creating and Sustaining Superior Performance.* New York: Free Press.

Posner, Richard A. 1969. Natural monopoly and its regulation. *Stanford Law Review* 21 (3). 548–643.

Puppis, Manuel. 2009. Introduction: Media regulation in small states. *The International Communication Gazette* 71 (7). 7–17.

Reid, Leonard N., Karen Whitehill King, Hugh J. Martin & Hyeonjin Soh. 2005. Local advertising decision makers' perceptions of media effectiveness and substitutability. *Journal of Media Economics* 18 (1). 35–53.

Rochet, Jean-Charles & Jean Tirole. 2006. Two-sided markets: A progress report. *RAND Journal of Economics* 37 (3). 645–667.

Sánchez-Tabernero, Alfonso. 1993. *Media Concentration in Europe: Commercial Enterprise and the Public Interest.* Düsseldorf: European Institute for the Media.

Sánchez-Tabernero, Alfonso. 2006. Issues in media globalization. In: Alan B. Albarran, Sylvia M. Chan-Olmsted and Michael O. Wirth (eds.), *Handbook of Media Management and Economics*, 463–492. Mahwah, NJ: Lawrence Erlbaum Associates.

Scherer, Frederic M. 1980. *Industrial Market Structure and Economic Performance*, 2nd edn. Chicago: Rand McNally.

Siegert, Gabriele. 1993. *Marktmacht Medienforschung: Die Bedeutung der empirischen Medien- und Publikumsforschung im Medienwettbewerbssystem.* München: Reinhard Fischer.

Siegert, Gabriele. 2001a. *Medien Marken Management: Relevanz, Spezifika und Implikationen einer medienökonomischen Profilierungsstrategie.* München: Reinhard Fischer.

Siegert, Gabriele. 2001b. Ökonomisierung der Medien aus systemtheoretischer Perspektive. *Medien und Kommunikationswissenschaft* 49 (2). 167–176.

Siegert, Gabriele. 2003. Im Zentrum des Taifuns: Die Ökonomisierung als treibende Kraft des medialen Wandels? *Medien Journal* 27 (1). 20–30.

Siegert, Gabriele. 2006a. Brands and reputation in principal-agent-relationships in the media industry. Paper presented at the 7th World Media Economics Conference, Beijing, China, May 15–19, 2006.

Siegert, Gabriele. 2006b. The role of small countries in media competition in Europe. In: Jürgen Heinrich and Gerd G. Kopper (eds.), *Media Economics in Europe*, 191–210. Berlin: Vistas.

Siegert, Gabriele, Matthias Gerth & Patrick Rademacher. 2011. Brand identity-driven decision making by journalists and media managers: The MBAC model as a theoretical framework. *The International Journal on Media Management* 13 (1). 53–70.

Siegert, Gabriele, Patrick Rademacher & Frank Lobigs. 2008. Pessimistische Theorie – Optimistische Praxis?: Unterschiedliche Sichtweisen auf die Konsequenzen der Ökonomisierung der Medien für deren seismographische Funktion in der Demokratie. In: Heinz Bonfadelli, Kurt Imhof, Roger Blum and Otfried Jarren (eds.), *Seismographische Funktion von Öffentlichkeit im Wandel*, 210–229. Wiesbaden: VS Verlag.

Siwek, Stephen E. 2004. *The Economic Contribution of Copyright-Based Industries in USA: The 2004 Report.* Washington DC: World Intellectual Property Organization.

Smith, Anthony. 1991. *The Age of Behemoths: The Globalization of Mass Media Firms.* New York: The Century Foundation.

Stipp, Horst. 1999. Convergence now? *The International Journal on Media Management* 1 (1). 10–14.

Trappel, Josef. 1991. Born losers or flexible adjustment?: The media policy dilemma of small states. *European Journal of Communication* 6 (3). 355–371.

Tunstall, Jeremy. 1996. *Newspaper Power: The New National Press in Britain.* Oxford: Clarendon Press.

van Eimeren, Birgit & Beate Frees. 2009. Der Internetnutzer 2009 – multimedial und total vernetzt: Ergebnisse der ARD/ZDF-Onlinestudie 2009. *Media Perspektiven* 7. 334–348.

Ward, David. 2006. Can the market provide?: Public service media, market failure and public goods. In: Christian S. Nissen (ed.), *Making a Difference: Public Service Broadcasting in the European Media Landscape*, 51–64. London: John Libbey.

Webster, James G., Patricia F. Phalen & Lawrence W. Lichty. 2006. *Ratings Analysis: The Theory and Practice of Audience Research*, 3rd edn. Mahwah, NJ: Erlbaum.

Wirth, Michael O. 2006. Issues in media convergence. In: Alan B. Albarran, Sylvia M Chan-Olmsted and Michael O. Wirth (eds.), *Handbook of Media Management and Economics*, 445–462. Mahwah, NJ: Lawrence Erlbaum Associates.

Wirtz, Bernd W. 2009. *Medien- und Internetmanagement*, 6th edn. Wiesbaden: Gabler Verlag.

Zerdick, Axel, Arnold Picot, Klaus Schrape, Alexander Artopé, Klaus Goldhammer, Ulrich T. Lange, Eckart Vierkant, Esteban López-Escobar & Roger Silverstone. 2000. *E-conomics: Strategies for the Digital Marketplace*. Berlin: Springer.

Cees J. Hamelink

8 Normative bases for communication

Abstract: In this chapter the most prominent normative standards for human communication are presented. These are the standards of fairness in speech, freedom of speech, responsibility, confidentiality and truth in communication. The most important sources of normative rules for human communication are listed in the text, described in detail, and their most important provisions quoted.

Keywords: Fair speech, free speech, truth, confidentiality, privacy, international law, professional codes of conduct

1 Norms for communicative action

With the growing complexity of human societies essential standards of behaviour evolved to enable human beings to live together and not destroy each other. Also for the guidance of human communicative action normative standards – that suggest what to do and what not to do – were developed. Very prominent among these were standards based upon the norms of fairness in speech, freedom of speech, responsibility, confidentiality and truth in communication. In discussing these standards that find their origin in codes of morality and law the most important sources of normative rules for human communication will be named, described and quoted.

2 Fair speech

Among the first normative rules were instructions that vizier Ptah Hotep in the fifth Egyptian Dynasty (3580–3536 BC) gave for wise men to convey to their sons. Several of these rules have normative implications for how people should speak with each other. A general norm of human speech is that it be fair. This means people should be humble in speaking and listening, that they should refrain from speaking in an evil way, not use vile words, and not be angry when a debater does not agree with them. They should beware of making enmity by their words and perverting the truth. They should not engage in gossip or extravagant speech, realize that silence is more profitable than abundance of speech and they should speak as true friends. As early as the Bronze Age (the third millennium BC) the rulers that were intent on civilizations living together and not destroying each other engaged in cultural diplomacy. Their emissaries who conveyed messages and brought learning back were instructed by their kings that their communicative behaviour should be guided by modest and respectful speech.

This age-old normative guidance for communication expresses what, more recently in human history, became the key standard in the catalogue of moral values that the international community formulated after the Second World War. In the Universal Declaration of Human Rights (1948) respect for "human dignity" is the basis for human interaction. One way to concretize this essential notion of the Universal Declaration of Human Rights (United Nations 1948) is to define it as the rejection of all forms of human humiliation. Human humiliation would include acts such as:

- de-individualization of people – where people's personal identity is undermined, their sense of personal significance is taken away, they are reduced to numbers, cases, or files, and they are treated as group members and not as individuals;
- discrimination against people, treating them according to judgements about superior versus inferior social positions. This is where 'inferior' people are excluded from the social privileges the 'superior' people enjoy;
- disempowerment of people by denying them 'agency' – where people are treated as if they lack the capacity of independent choice and action;
- degrading of people by forcing them into dependent positions in which they efface their own dignity and exhibit servile behaviour. This is where people are scared in ways that make them lose control over their behaviour (dirtying themselves for example), and make them beg on their knees for approval, blessing or forgiveness.

Since the discourse of international human rights has established that 'all people matter,' no one should be excluded from the maxim by which one must treat other human beings in non-humiliating ways. This implies the moral commandment against modalities of communication that treat people in humiliating ways.

3 Free speech

Early in human history the idea emerged that in order to maximally profit from the human communicative capacity the freedom of the word should be promoted and protected. Since the development of language there was always the idea that without the freedom to speak it would render meaningless the fact that humans are language-using animals. Concern about the freedom of information is reported as early as 350 BC when the Greek statesman and orator Demosthenes said that taking away the freedom of expression is one of the greatest calamities for human beings. Socrates reminded his judges of the great importance of free speech and free reflection. Despite a level of intolerance of free thought, such philosophical schools as the Stoics, the Epicureans and the Sceptics developed and claimed for themselves a large measure of intellectual freedom. Roman historian Tacitus (55–116) complimented the emperor Trajan for the felicitous times when one could freely express whatever one wanted to say.

Throughout the Middle Age the heretics claimed their right to free thought and its expression. Against the secular suppression of the freedom of expression, John Milton published his Areopagitica in 1644. In this famous speech to the Parliament of England on the liberty of unlicensed printing, Milton claimed: "Truth needs no licensing to make her victorious." In 1695, the Regulation of Printing Act against which he spoke was revoked. Interestingly enough, Milton's plea for freedom of printing did not apply to Roman Catholics as he felt one should not extend principles of tolerance to those who are intolerant.

In Sweden in 1766 an Order on the Freedom of the Printing Press was enacted as formal law, including the rights of access to public information. The oldest catalogue of fundamental rights (in the sense of human rights and civil rights that possess a higher legal force) is the Declaration of Rights, preceding the constitution of the state of Virginia, in 1776. Here the freedom of expression was formulated as press freedom, "That the freedom of the Press is one of the greatest bulwarks of liberty, and can never be restrained but by despotic governments." Following the Anglo-Saxon tradition, the French Declaration on human and citizen rights (*Déclaration des droits de l'homme et du citoyen*) was formulated in 1789. This declaration went beyond the Virginia declaration in stating that the unrestrained communication of thoughts or opinions is one of the most precious rights of man; every citizen may speak, write and publish freely, provided he [sic] is responsible for the abuse of this liberty, in the cases determined by law. Then, in 1791, the US Bill of Rights stated in Article I, the famous provision that "Congress shall make no law...abridging the freedom of speech, or of the press." (Hamelink, 1994: 150–151). In nineteenth century legislation on fundamental rights the right to freedom of information emerged in many countries and the freedom of the press, primarily in the form of the prohibition of censorship, became a central issue. This was reflected in many national constitutions.

Until the twentieth century the concern about freedom of information remained almost exclusively a domestic affair. Interestingly enough, when the League of Nations focused on the problems of false news and propaganda in the early twentieth century, it did not address the protection of freedom of expression. The UNESCO Constitution, adopted in 1945, was the first multilateral instrument to reflect the concern for the freedom of information. To promote the implementation of this concern, a special division of 'free flow of information' was established in the secretariat in Paris.

In 1946, the delegation of the Philippines presented to the UN General Assembly a proposal for a resolution on an international conference on issues dealing with the press. This became UNGA Res. 59 (I) which was adopted unanimously in late 1946. According to the resolution the purpose of the conference would be to address the rights, obligations and practices which should be included in the concept of freedom of information. The resolution called freedom of information, "the touchstone of all the freedoms to which the United Nations is consecrated." It described the freedom of information as "the right to gather, transmit and publish news anywhere and everywhere without fetters."

In 1948, the United Nations convened an international conference on the Freedom of Information. Following the conference one of the articles of the Universal Declaration of Human Rights was dedicated to the freedom of expression. This became the well-known Article 19 which states, "Everyone has the right to freedom of opinion and expression; this right includes freedom to hold opinions without interference and to seek, receive and impart information and ideas through any media and regardless of 'frontiers'."

Crucially, the authors of Article 19 constructed freedom of information with reference to five components. The first is the classical defence of the freedom of expression. The second is the freedom to hold opinions. This provision was formulated as protection against brainwashing, against the forced imposition of a political conviction. The third is the freedom to gather information. This reflected the interests of international news agencies to secure freedom for foreign correspondents. The fourth is the freedom of reception. This has to be understood as a response to the prohibition on receiving foreign broadcasts during the war. The fifth is the right to impart information and ideas. This is a recognition of the freedom of distribution in addition to the freedom of expression. The formulation of Article 19 offered important guidance for later international documents that articulated the concern about freedom of information. Important illustrations are the European Convention for the Protection of Human Rights and Fundamental Freedoms (1950) and the International Covenant on Civil and Political Rights (1966). The latter stated the matter as follows:

1. Everyone shall have the right to hold opinions without interference.
2. Everyone shall have the right to freedom of expression; this right shall include freedom to seek, receive and impart information and ideas of all kinds regardless of frontiers, either orally, in writing or in print, in the form of art, or through any other media of his choice.

Other statements of the norm of freedom in communication from the period include the American Convention on Human Rights (1969) and the African Charter on Human and Peoples' Rights (1981). Significantly, the Convention on the Rights of the Child (adopted by the United Nations General Assembly on 20 November, 1989) extended the principle of freedom in communication to young people. In Article 13, it states that

> The child shall have the right to freedom of expression; this right shall include freedom to
> seek, receive and impart information and ideas of all kinds, regardless of frontiers, either

orally, in writing or in print, in the form of art, or through any other media of the child's choice.

There are also a number of freedom of communication provisions in professional codes: the IFJ Declaration of Principles on the Conduct of Journalists (the Bordeaux Code, adopted by 1954 World Congress of the IFJ and amended by the 1986 World Congress), the Resolutions by the Second World Meeting of Journalists, 1960; the Charter for a Free Press, World Press Freedom Committee, 1992. These declarations and these codes, then, from Demosthenes onwards, form the basis of communication according to the norm of free speech.

4 Responsibility

In many societies rulers have been opposed to the norm of free speech. The 'power elites' in various ages exercised censorship to protect their interests as they perceived free thought to be dangerous to their authority. The idea that people should be free to think and speak as they wish and should have access to information and knowledge as they need, was (and is) often seen by authoritative intellectual and political elites as undesirable. The powerful of all ages and societies have tended to prefer the standard of control. Without adequate control the free speech of common people could only mean trouble.

Control over communication was known and widely used in the ancient Egyptian, Sumerian, Greek and Roman societies. In Egypt, the ruling class censored what knowledge could be made available. When the medium of communication in ancient Egypt (2700–2600 BC) shifted from stone to papyrus, the scribe became a highly honoured magistrate and member of a privileged profession. The art of writing was held in high esteem and the scribe "was included in the upper classes of kings, priests, nobles, and, generals..." (Innis, 1972: 16). He became part of the ruling class that monopolized knowledge. In classical Athens Socrates was silenced for exercising free speech. By the time of Socrates's trial, censorship was extensive in Greece. There were charges of blasphemy against the philosophers Anaxagoras and Protagoras. In the Roman empire, emperor Augustus was probably the first political leader to promote a law that prohibited libellous writing.

In early Christianity, the apostle Paul advocated burning the books of adversaries (Acts 19:19). With the adoption of the Christian faith by Emperor Constantine the Great (313), freedom of religious thought began to be violently suppressed. Heretical thought was punished by cruel torturing and death. During the Middle Ages the Christian Church fought a bitter battle against any form of heterodoxy. Heretics – men, women and even children – were hanged and burned. To effectively organize the ruthless suppression of heresy, Pope Gregory IX established a special institution of persecution in 1233, the Inquisition. In 1493, the Inquisition in Venice issued the first list of books banned by the Church. In 1559, the Index Librorum Prohibitorum was made binding for all Roman Catholics and was administered by the Inquisition. The case of Copernicus's (1473–1543) publication, *On the Revolution of the Celestial Spheres*, is a famous one from this period. The book was not published until after his death to avoid persecution by the Church. In 1616, the Church put the book on its index of prohibited books. Galileo Galilei (1564–1642) made his own Copernican worldview public and was made to retract this under the threat of torture. Only in 1967 did the Catholic Church stop its efforts to proscribe texts by authors such as Erasmus, Descartes, Rousseau, Voltaire, Newton, Milton, Kant, Spinoza, Pascal, Comte, Freud and Sartre.

The protagonists of the Reformation were no less interested in control than their Catholic opponents were. In sixteenth century Geneva, heavy censorship was exercised by John Calvin who was famous for his extreme intolerance. Also, theologian Martin Luther had little difficulty with suppressing the freedom of thought. He was quite opposed to liberty of conscience and held that Anabaptists should be put to the sword. Jansen writes:

> As early as 1525 he invoked the assistance of censorship regulations in Saxony and Brandenberg to suppress the 'pernicious doctrines' of the Anabaptists and Zwinglians....Melanchton, Calvin, and Zwingli subsequently enforced censorial controls that were far more restrictive that any instituted by Rome or by Luther. (Jansen 1991: 53)

Secular powers followed these examples and issued forms of regulation to control free expression. Emperor Frederick II (1194–1250) issued legislation in which burning at the stake became the popular way of punishing the heresy of free thinkers. In France, King Henry II (1519–1559) declared printing without official permission punishable by death. The official rationale was greatly inspired by Thomas Hobbes's reflections in his *Leviathan* (1651) where he extended state sovereignty to the opinions and persuasions of the governed. An example of such sovereign control was the English Regulation of Printing Act. This licensing law provided for a system of censorship through licences for printing and publishing.

Nineteenth century regulation of international postal and telegraph traffic introduced among its basic norms and rules the freedom of transit and free passage of messages. In the world's first international communication conventions (the 1874 Treaty of Berne that founded the General Postal Union and the Berne Telegraph Convention of 1858 that founded the International Telegraph Union) the freedom of communication was provided but at the same time also restricted as states reserved the right to interfere with free message passage in case of threats to state security, violations of national laws or danger to public order and morals.

This tension between freedom and interference remained a much debated topic among politicians, regulators, content carriers and users over the years. Since the late nineteenth century, media content has been an issue of international concern. The ambiguity of the freedom of content versus the need to interfere with this freedom posed a challenge for attempts at global governance. On the side of free-dom of content, one finds classical civil and political rights arguments in favour of 'free speech.' On the side of interference, there are arguments about 'national sovereignty' and about the responsibility of speech vis-à-vis the rights and reputa-tions of others. The 'free speech' argument promotes an unhindered flow of messa-ges into and out of countries. The sovereignty argument provides for protective measures against flows of messages that may impede autonomous control over social and cultural development. The 'responsible speech' argument claims the right to protection against the harmful effects of such free flows. Historically, then, the norm of communication based on free speech has always had its obverse: the norm of censorship.

Debates on freedom of information have always had an association with reflec-tions and viewpoints on the social responsibility of the media of mass communica-tion. The key normative provisions on freedom of information permit freedom of expression 'without fetters,' but also bind this to other human rights standards. The clear recognition of the right to freedom of information as a basic human right in the Universal Declaration of Human Rights (UDHR) was positioned in a stand-ard-setting instrument that also asked for the existence of an international order in which the rights of the individual can be fully realized (Article 28 of the UDHR). This implies that the right to freedom of speech is linked with the concern for a responsible use of communication. This linkage laid the basis for a controversy in which one normative position emphasized the free flow principle, whereas another normative position stressed the social responsibility principle. The UNESCO Consti-tution already featured a tension between the two approaches. It accepted the principle of a free exchange of ideas and knowledge, but it also stressed the need to develop and use the means of communication toward a mutual understanding among nations and to create an improved factual knowledge of each other. This could also be seen in the post-war development of the professional field. The Inter-national Federation of Journalists of Allied or Free Countries (IFJAFC) convened a World Congress of Journalists in Copenhagen in June, 1946. This congress was attended by some 165 delegates from 21 countries. In the invitation letter the Execu-tive Committee of the IFJAFC indicated that among the purposes of the congress, was "to discuss methods of assuring the freedom of the press" (Kubka and Norden-streng, 1986: 10). The discussions largely focused on the establishment of a new international professional organization, a provisional constitution was unani-mously adopted and the International Organization of Journalists was created. Spe-cial attention was given to the debate on the liberty of the press and at the end of the Congress a Statement of Principle on the freedom of the press was adopted: "The International Congress of Journalists affirms that freedom of the press is a fundamental principle of democracy and can function only if channels of informa-tion and the means of dissemination of news are made available to all." The State-ment stressed:

the responsibility of every working journalist to assist by every means in his power the development of international friendship and understanding and instructed the Executive Committee to examine the various codes of professional ethics adopted by national bodies, particularly in respect of any journalist deliberately and knowingly spreading – whether by press or radio or news agencies – false information designed to poison the good relations between countries and peoples. (Kubka and Nordenstreng 1986: 10)

This social responsibility dimension was even more forcefully present in the resolution on press and peace that stated that:

this congress considers the cementing of lasting international peace and security the paramount aim of humanity, and calls upon all the 130,000 members of the IOJ to do their utmost in support of the work of international understanding and co-operation entrusted to the United Nations." (Kubka and Nordenstreng 1986: 10)

As the Cold War was already by 1948 a key dimension of world politics, the norm of social responsibility and the free flow principle clashed in the early UN debates largely in line with East/West ideological confrontations. In 1947, the Yugoslav delegation, for example, proposed legislation in the UN General Assembly to "restrict false and tendentious reports calculated to aggravate relations between nations, provoke conflicts and incite to war." This was unacceptable to the Western delegations and eventually a compromise text (proposed by France) was adopted that recommended the study of measures, "to combat, within the limits of constitutional procedures, the publication of false or distorted reports likely to injure friendly relations between states" (UNGA Resolution 127(II)).

The free speech norm is, like other human rights norms far from absolute and its exercise can be subject to limitations. This obviously implies the risk of abuse by those actors (and particularly governments) who are intent on curbing free speech. Limitations could easily erode the significance of a normative standard. For this reason a threefold test has been developed in international law to assess the permissibility of limitations. These must be provided by law. They must serve purposes expressly stated in international agreements and they must be shown to be necessary in a democratic society. The UN Special Rapporteur on freedom of information has expressed concern about the tendency of governments to invoke Article 4 of the International Covenant on Civil and Political Rights in justification of the suspension of free speech. This Article lists the human rights provisions that are non-derogable. This means that under no circumstance, not even in times of war, can they be suspended. The right to freedom of expression is not listed in Article 4. However, the Human Rights Committee, in its General Comment No. 29 (CCPR/C/21/Rev.1/Add.11), has identified the conditions to be met for a State to invoke article 4(1) of the Covenant to limit certain rights enshrined in its provisions, including the right to freedom of opinion and expression. Inter alia, the measures must be strictly limited in time, provided for in a law, necessary for public safety or public order, serve a legitimate purpose, not impair the essence of the right and conform with the principle of proportionality.

Over the years, the international community and individual national governments have repeatedly tried – not very successfully – to establish governance mechanisms (rules and institutions) to deal with the 'freedom versus responsibility' issue. The Broadcasting Convention of 1936 (International Convention Concerning the Use of Broadcasting in the Cause of Peace, signed at Geneva, 23 September 1936) contains the following indicative articles:

Article 1
The High Contracting Parties mutually undertake to prohibit and, if occasion arises, to stop without delay the broadcasting within their respective territories of any transmission which to the detriment of good international understanding is of such a character as to incite the population of any territory to acts incompatible with the internal order or the security of a territory of a High Contracting Party.

Article 2
The High Contracting Parties mutually undertake to ensure that transmissions from stations within their respective territories shall not constitute an incitement either to war against another High Contracting party or to acts likely to lead thereto.

Article 3
The High Contracting parties mutually undertake to prohibit and, if occasion arises, to stop without delay within their respective territories any transmission likely to harm good international understanding by statements the incorrectness of which is or ought to be known to the persons responsible for the broadcast.
They further mutually undertake to ensure that any transmission likely to harm good international understanding by incorrect statements shall be rectified at the earliest possible moment by the most effective means, even if the incorrectness has become apparent only after the broadcast has taken place.

Article 4
The High Contracting Parties mutually undertake to ensure, especially in time of crisis, that stations within their respective territories shall broadcast information concerning international relations the accuracy of which shall have been verified – and that by all means within their power – by the persons responsible for broadcasting the information.

Other provisions have been offered in a similar vein. There are the Resolutions of the United Nations Conference on Freedom of Information, 1948:

Resolution 4
To facilitate the solution of the economic, social and humanitarian problems of the world as a whole through the free interchange of information bearing on such problems;
To help promote respect for human rights and fundamental freedoms without discrimination;
To help maintain international peace and security.

The International Covenant on Civil and Political Rights notes that the exercise of the rights provided for in paragraph 2 of Article 19 (on freedom) carries with it special duties and responsibilities. It may therefore be subject to certain restrictions, but these shall only be such as are provided by law and are necessary:

> For respect of the rights or reputations of others;
> For the protection of national security or of public order *(ordre public)*, or of public health or morals.

Thus

> Any propaganda for war shall be prohibited by law.
> Any advocacy of national, racial or religious hatred that constitutes incitement to discrimination, hostility or violence shall be prohibited by law.

And, again, as rights of freedom are extended to children, so is the norm of responsibility in communication. The Convention on the Rights of the Child states that the exercise of the right to freedom may be subject to certain restrictions, but these shall only be such as are provided by law and are necessary:

> For respect of the rights or reputations of others; or
> For the protection of national security or of public order *(ordre public)*, or of public health or morals.

Furthermore, the issue of responsibility and freedom in communication is broached in terms of colonialism and international conflict. The UNESCO Declaration on Fundamental Principles Concerning the Contribution of International Understanding, to the Promotion of Human Rights and to Countering Racialism, Apartheid and Incitement to War proclaimed by the General Conference of the United Nations Educational Scientific and Cultural Organization at its 20th session, on 28 November 1978 has the following key article:

> Article 3. With a view to the strengthening of peace and international understanding, to promoting human rights and to countering racialism, apartheid and incitement to war, the mass media throughout the world, by reason of their role, contribute to promoting human rights, in particular by giving expression to oppressed peoples who struggle against colonialism, neo-colonialism, foreign occupation and all forms of racial discrimination and oppression and who are unable to make their voices heard within their own territories.

The international community has not managed to develop a satisfactory answer to these questions. Striking a balance between the standard of freedom of information and the standard of responsible speech and national sovereignty turned out to be too difficult a challenge! Again, there are also a number of responsibility-of-communication provisions in professional codes IFJ Declaration of Principles on the Conduct of Journalists, 1954; Resolutions by the Second World Meeting of Journalists, 1960; International Principles of Professional Ethics in Journalism, 1988. The tension in these normative bases of communication is perennial.

5 Confidentiality

This normative basis emerged with the Platonic recognition of a dualism between a visible material body and an invisible immaterial soul. What people think takes place in the soul and is thus hidden from others. Human reason resides in a private sphere and should only be revealed in word or conduct with the person's consent. This private sphere or 'inner life' became, over the ages, a prime target for surveillance by clerical and secular authorities. Against these intrusions John Stuart Mill claimed for the "inward domain of consciousness" an absolute freedom (Mill in Robson 1966: 16).

The experience of a private inner realm was (and continues to be) variegated across cultures and ages but nonetheless possesses – universally – a set of key dimensions. There is a physical dimension (the need of bodily integrity) and a territorial dimension which was well articulated by William Pitt (1776) when he wrote about the cottage of the poorest man: "It may be frail, its roof may shake; the wind may blow through; the storm may enter; the rain may enter; but the King of England may not enter; all his forces dare not cross the threshold of the ruined tenement" (quoted in Barth, 1961: 73). From these core dimensions the notion of a 'private sphere' extended to any space where individuals encountered others. The first legal articulation of the need to protect this sphere came from the American lawyers, Warren and Brandeis in a famous article in the *Harvard Law Review* ('The right to privacy'). They wrote "For years there has been a feeling that the law must afford some remedy for the unauthorized circulation of portraits of private persons; and the evil of the invasion of privacy by the newspapers, has long been keenly felt" (Warren and Brandeis 1890: 195–6). Warren and Brandeis described the right to privacy as "the right to be let alone." This right to privacy includes those communicative acts that take place in the private sphere where participants deem it essential that their exchanges remain confidential. This is particularly clear in encounters between medical, legal or clerical professionals and their patients/clients. Outside the private sphere, the right to privacy operates as informational privacy: the right to the protection of data collected, stored and used in connection with private persons.

Since the nineteenth century the norm of confidentiality in communications has been codified in national and international legislation. In the Universal Declaration of Human Rights (1948) the norm of confidentiality was established in Article 12 that provides that "No one shall be subjected to arbitrary interference with his privacy, family, home or correspondence...." This is affirmed in the International Covenant on Civil and Political Rights (1966) and again extended to children by the Convention on the Rights of the Child (1989). The norm of confidentiality is however constantly challenged by ordinary human curiosity and increasingly, also, by the administrative requirements of modern states (for example, the tax bureaucracy and the law enforcement system), the commercial interest in acquiring and selling personal data and the widespread availability of surveillance technology. Many countries have introduced privacy laws and special rules for the protection of doctor-patient or attorney-client exchanges.

The pledge of confidentiality in communication in the medical profession goes back to the Hippocratic Oath which is often rendered as, "Whatsoever things I see or hear concerning the life of men, in my attendance on the sick or even apart therefrom, which ought not to be noised about, I shall keep silence thereon, counting such things to be as sacred secrets" (around 400 BC). Most recently, the protection of professional confidentiality in journalism has become a challenging issue that was decided by the European Court of Human Rights in favour of the recognition of professional secrecy, albeit under special circumstances (the Goodwin arrest of 27 March 1996). When the first international treaty to deal with global communication was signed (the International Telegraph Convention) in 1985 the confidentiality of correspondence across national borders was secured. At the same time, however, governments reserved the right to interfere with any message they considered dangerous for state security or in violation of national laws, public order or morality. Again, then, the normative bases of communication are double-sided: a similar tension as can be found between freedom and responsibility in communication developed between the right to confidentiality and the right of states to interfere in private communications.

6 Truth

Possibly the oldest source for the standard of truth in communication is found in the Ten Commandments (the Decalogue) that were given through Moses to the Hebrew people. One of these commandments provides that one shall bear no false witness. Although it is contested whether this contains a general prohibition to lie it would seem to refer to an admonition to speak the truth at least in legal matters. A moral rule against lying is certainly very articulate in Old Testament texts such as Psalm 5 that commands that "you destroy those who tell lies" or the book Leviticus (Leviticus 19:11) where God gives Moses the rule that says "Do not lie and Do not deceive one another. " And in the New Testament (in John 8:44) it is written said about Satan "You belong to your father, the devil, and you want to carry out your father's desires. He was a murderer from the beginning, not holding to the truth, for there is no truth in him. When he lies, he speaks his native language, for he is a liar and the father of lies." Also in other religions, like the Islam, we find a strong moral preference for speaking the truth.

These norms of truth sound obvious but they are complicated in the light of the fact that much human interaction is characterized by deception. Lies are important tools in human communication. People lie much of the time throughout history, across cultures, irrespective of social class or education in relations between parents and children, employers and employees and among lovers. Deceptive communication occurs in politics, business and science. Also the modern mass media are often associated with false, biased and disported communications about the world's events. Against this reality various legal and professional instruments have provided the normative guidance that communication should be true. Notably, the Resolutions of the United Nations Conference on Freedom of Information, 1948, UN General Assembly Resolution 127 (II) laid down provisions for the press. Here, the emphasis was on a consensus of professionals to prevent false reporting. The IFJ Declaration of Principles on the Conduct of Journalists (the Bordeaux Code), built upon this professional consensus by highlighting the following articles:

> Article 1.
> Respect for truth and for the right of the public to truth is the first duty of the journalist.
>
> Article 3.
> The journalist shall report only in accordance with facts of which he/she knows the origin. The journalist shall not suppress essential information or falsify documents.

The Second World Meeting of Journalists, 1960 resulted in resolutions concerning professional ethics:

> We believe that the ethics of journalism requires every journalist today to fight against the distortion of the truth and to oppose all attempts at falsification, misinformation and slander.

While the 'Mexico Declaration' adopted by Representatives of International and Regional Organizations of Professional Journalists in 1980 stated as Principle II, 'The journalist's social responsibility':

> The foremost task of the journalist is to serve this right to true and authentic information, information understood as a social need and not commodity, which means that the journalist shares responsibility for the information transmitted and is thus accountable not only to those controlling the media but ultimately to the public at large, including various social interests.

Similar declarations were made on ethics and responsibility in the International Principles of Professional Ethics in Journalism adopted by the Council of the International Catholic Union of the Press, 1988, and the 'Code of Athens.'

Journalism, however, was not the only part of the media where fidelity to truth developed as a normative basis of communication in the modern period. Advertising, especially, has been subject to measures designed to ensure conformity with truth. Most significantly the International Code of Advertising Practice as revised and adopted by the International Chamber of Commerce (ICC) in 1973 declared as one of its basic principles that

> All advertising should be legal, decent, honest and truthful. Every advertisement should be prepared with a due sense of social responsibility and should conform to the principles of fair

competition, as generally accepted in business. No advertisement should be such as to impair public confidence in advertising.

These landmark legal and professional provisions offer a picture of some of the issues that, to varying degrees, have been taken for granted in the modern world but which have often involved considerable human struggle to establish.

7 Conclusion

Throughout history, normative rules have been formulated for human communication. Essential standards of communicative action are that it should be fair, free, responsible and true. The international community has developed instruments both as binding law and as voluntary professional codes to address the standards of freedom, responsibility, confidentiality and truth. The norm of respectful and fair communication has not been articulated in formal laws or codes of conducts. This may be understandable since rules on fair speech cannot be formulated as an enforceable legal instruction and their concrete application is largely dependent upon the pedagogical instructions that wise people convey to their sons and daughters. It may well be, however, that exactly the standard of fair and respectful communication is quintessential to finding an adequate response to the experience of communication in interpersonal interaction and in public media (in news, entertainment and advertising) that treat people in de-individualizing, discriminating, disempowering and degrading ways.

Further reading

Casmir, Fred L. 1997. *Ethics in intercultural and international communication*. Mahwah, NJ: Lawrence Erlbaum Associates.

Christians, Clifford G., John P. Ferré & P. Mark Fackler (eds.). 1993. *Good news. social ethics and the press*. New York and Oxford: Oxford University Press.

Christians, Clifford & Lee Wilkins (eds.). 2009. *The handbook of media ethics*. London: Routledge.

Moore, Roy L. 1999. *Mass communication law and ethics*. Mahwah, NJ: Lawrence Erlbaum Associates.

Pattyn, Bart (ed.). 2000. *Media ethics: opening social dialogue*. Leuven: Peeters Publishers.

References

Barth, Alan. 1961. *The price of liberty*. New York: The Viking Press.

Hamelink, Cees J. 1994. *The politics of world communication*. London: Sage.

Hamelink, Cees J. 2004. *Human rights for communicators*. Cresskill: Hampton Press.

Innis, Harold. A. 1972. *Empire and communications*. Toronto: University of Toronto Press.

Jansen, Sue C. 1991. *Censorship*. Oxford: Oxford University Press.

Kubka, Jiri & Kaarle Nordenstreng. 1986. *Useful recollections*. Part II. Prague: International Organization of Journalists.

Milton, John. 1644. *Aeropagitica*. London: MacMillan (limited edition, 1915).

Robson, John M. (ed.). 1966. *John Stuart Mill: a selection of his works*. Indianapolis: Indiana University Press.

Warren, Samuel D. & Louis D. Brandeis. 1890. The right to privacy. Harvard Law Review. IV: 193–220.

Christopher Tindale

9 Models of communicative efficiency

Abstract: This chapter explores the close relationships between good communication and the traditions of rhetoric and argumentation, from their Aristotelian roots through to contemporary theories of reasoning and dialectics. While this core narrative is concerned primarily with communication in the Greco-Roman tradition and between human agents, the closing section draws on recent scholarship in expanding the discussions to include Asian schools and the impact of artificial intelligence on communication.

Keywords: Argumentation, Asian tradition, dialectics, Greco-Roman tradition, informal logic, rhetoric

1 Introduction

Part of the social nature of human animals involves the practiced ability to communicate in a range of different ways, whether to express needs, issue requests or commands, or attempt to solicit the agreement of others. We cannot avoid such activities and, contrary to what the tradition of the isolated Cartesian ego suggests, they are the foundations from which we emerge as self-conscious agents. Not all communication is effective, however, and beyond the needs of mere expression, to function well in society we need to develop in ourselves the abilities to influence others through the clear articulation of claims and persuasive discourse. To such ends, this chapter is concerned mainly with the traditions of argumentation and rhetoric, principally as these have been developed in Western cultures, but also with some attention to the emerging fields of Asian argumentation and rhetoric.

It may seem strange to link communicative efficiency with argumentation and rhetoric in this way, because arguing is often associated with quarreling and rhetoric tied to the exploitation of audiences. On these terms, clear communication would seem to be the first casualty. But these are narrow conceptions of both argumentation and rhetoric and a moment's consideration should indicate the close relationships between good communication, argumentation, and rhetoric. Of importance to both argumentation and rhetoric is the audience for whom the discourse is intended. When we enter debates, negotiate agreements, investigate hypotheses together, deliberate over choices in deciding how to act, and solicit the assent of others, we use argumentation and rhetoric. And when we use these well, we communicate effectively by achieving such ends of communication in mutually satisfactory ways.

The situations in which argumentation and rhetoric are used, then, are not restricted to those that are characterized by disagreements. They include situations in which ideas are reinforced. Proposals are introduced and reviewed cooperatively, and parties endeavor to achieve understanding even when the starting points from which they each begin are far apart. Communication faces its greatest challenges in these last kinds of cases, particularly when values and terms are not held in common. But the traditions of argumentation theory and rhetoric are rich in ideas and strategies to address even the most intractable problems. And the fact that we can successfully communicate both our common understandings and our disagreements, and operate so well in societies where major values are continuously contested, is testimony to the strengths of the traditions employed and the tools they contain.

The chapter traces the modern traditions of rhetoric and argumentation that exemplify communicative efficiency to their common Aristotelian root. To this end, the Section 2 details Aristotle's account of how humans should proceed in order to communicate effectively. This account, while modified through the ages, is still recognizable in contemporary theories, and we see the truth of this in Section 3 on communication and reasoning. Three dominant models of argumentation reflect the Aristotelian triad of rhetoric, dialectic, and logic. The chapter section considers at least one significant position under each of these headings. The Section 4 expands the discussion to explain ways in which these ideas have been taken up in new technology, particularly work on artificial intelligence, and also considers similar approaches to communicative efficiency that have been recognized in the Asian tradition.

2 Communicative efficiency and the rhetorical tradition

In the West, we are the fortunate inheritors of the Greco-Roman rhetorical tradition, one in which argumentation plays important roles, but which is quite distinct in its own terms and so can be explored first. Recent work on rhetorical theories has pushed beyond the limits of rhetoric's past as it responds to the situations and problems cast up by contemporary society, but all of this is rooted in the history of rhetoric and can only be fully understood on its terms.

Traditionally, rhetoric is understood as the use of language to bring about persuasion. Although there may be as many current definitions as there are theorists, to understand how rhetoric bears on central questions of communication we can stay with this traditional view. Aristotle (384–322 BC) is instrumental in giving substance to this understanding, defining rhetoric as the "ability to see the available means of persuasion" (Aristotle 2007: I,2,1). Important in this statement is the insight that there are both practical and theoretical components to the enterprise.

There is attention to the means of persuading, but also the ability to 'see' these means. This seeing (*theorin*) is related to the terms used for both 'theory' and 'theatre,' and the idea of some spectacle captured in the mind's eye, where it can be reviewed and understood is presented to us. Such theorizing, Aristotle believed, set his account apart from many of his predecessors and contemporaries who produced handbooks on rhetoric (Kennedy 1963) but without the attention to detail for which Aristotle would become so influential. While most aspects of Aristotle's treatment were present in the argumentative and rhetorical practices of his predecessors (Schiappa 1999; Tindale 2010), no one had approached them with Aristotle's philosophical rigor.

Central to Aristotle's account of efficient communication, and all subsequent treatments, is the idea of audience: that body of people that the speaker aims to persuade through her or his discourse. His ideas of audience influenced the way he viewed rhetoric, judging there to be three genres corresponding to three basic audiences: the deliberative, the judicial (or forensic), and the epideictic. Under the first, a speaker encourages an audience to deliberate about the right course of action to pursue. Aristotle here sees audiences as judges about future events, engaging their ideas by drawing examples from their experience. This rhetoric lends itself well to political situations. The second genre expects the audience to judge the past and come to some kinds of truths about it. Different types of evidence must be used here to communicate what the speaker has in mind. The third genre is often judged by commentators to be the grab bag into which everything else is placed (although the twentieth century theorist Chaim Perelman (1982) claimed that this was the most fundamental genre). Epideictic rhetoric is one that conveys and explores values. It is characterized by praise and blame and well illustrated in the funeral speech. This audience is a spectator. But one that in watching and listening learns the values of the community and is encouraged to emulate them and avoid values that conflict with them.

Another important aspect of Aristotle's account which further reflects his appreciation of the importance of audience is his treatment of 'proofs,' again presented as a triad of ideas: *logos, ethos*, and *pathos*. These three can be understood in terms of the three central components of any rhetorical communication: the speaker (*ethos*), the audience (*pathos*), and the discourse that joins them (*logos*). As rhetorical proofs, each of these is involved in the process of bringing about persuasion. The rhetorical *logos* captures the way reasoning is packaged as an argumentative product at the heart of communication. *Logos* best encourages persuasion in the form of the enthymeme or example, which invites the audience's involvement in drawing a conclusion. Something in the background of the audience is drawn on or assumed in the choice of example or construction of the enthymeme. The audience provides that component thus completing the reasoning in a way that personalizes it for them. As contemporary advertisers appreciate when exploiting the deductive principle, a message is far more persuasive if the audience believes they have drawn the conclusion for themselves. Told that bigger burgers are better burgers and that a national chain sells bigger burgers, audiences do not also need to be told that the same chain's burgers are better. They can draw that conclusion for themselves. Something similar is assumed in Aristotle's rhetorical *logos*.

The importance of *ethos* is recognized whenever a message is listened to because of *who* is delivering it. Aristotle tells us that we are more likely to believe fair-minded people, and so speakers are advised to communicate this attitude through what they say. Character, on these terms, is constructed *through* the speech itself, showing something of the power of words to create trust and credibility. Aristotle lays little stress on the effect that prior reputation has, but Cicero later added the importance of a person's achievements and reputation, and we would now naturally include such matters under the label of 'ethos.'

The third 'proof' – *pathos* – builds on the insight that audiences form different judgments about an issue depending on their emotional state. We do not judge the same way when we are angry as when we are calm or feeling pity. Logicians have attempted to drive a wedge between reason and emotion, but Aristotle was not sympathetic to this. Rhetoric aims at the whole person, not some isolated part located in the 'reason.' Thus, an effective speaker must learn the nature of the emotions, and how to stimulate them in an audience. At this point, if not earlier, we might see the specter of exploitation lurking in the background. But Aristotle associates rhetoric with ethics, and believes that a speaker should foster the qualities of good will (*eunoia*), practical wisdom (*phronesis*), and virtue (*arête*), and will be more persuasive if these qualities are active in them.[1] So, the emotional responses that are stimulated in an audience are appropriate to the situation. Feeling pity at the sight of an earthquake victim is an appropriate response and prepares the right kind of judgment for the action that should follow.

A traditional way of viewing rhetoric is in terms of adornment, and perhaps nothing more than this. Certainly, style and arrangement are important to the Aristotelian account. But as he turns to them in the last book of the *Rhetoric*, they are presented in terms of the core ideas. While we do not find a full theory of figuration, for example, that will characterize later accounts, Aristotle sets the groundwork for such theories in his recognition that *how* something is said is as important as *who* says it, *what* is said, and to *whom* it is said. Thus, he takes a *trope* like metaphor and explores ways in which communication is made more effective when words carry a different meaning from one context to another – a semantic change. And he takes a *figure* like the antithesis and notes how it encourages an audience to complete an idea when cola are juxtaposed so that if told 'we trust those we like, and we like ...' we can add 'those we trust.' Here, the feature

---

1 The idea of rhetoric having a fundamental ethical character is central to the thinking of Quintilian for whom rhetoric was the art of a *good* citizen speaking well.

is built on a syntactic structure. Subsequent theories of rhetoric construct considerable lists of rhetorical figures, each designed when used correctly to make ideas *present* to an audience.[2]

Later theories adapt other central components of the Aristotelian account (see Kennedy 1972). Cicero (106–43 BC), for example, recognizes the importance of *logos, ethos,* and *pathos,* while adjusting the focus of the first two and giving particular emphasis to the third. Like Aristotle, Cicero believes a speaker must have a full knowledge of the emotions in order to communicate effectively, and he devotes a lengthy discussion of his mature work on rhetoric – *De Oratore* – to this. In part this is so important because Cicero also values the centrality of the audience, captured in the idea of the *sensus communis*, or sense of community (Cicero 1976: I.iii.12). This is the language of everyday life and the worst mistake a speaker can make is to ignore it. There is much else to recommend Cicero's treatment of rhetoric, both in the early *De Inventione*, written when he was only nineteen, and in the mature work. Perhaps of chief interest are his five divisions of the cannons of oratory: invention, arrangement, expression, memory, and delivery. These cover the full range of rhetorical considerations from the discovery of arguments through to the ways in which the body and voice are controlled in the delivery.

One important feature of Aristotle's account that Cicero adopts and clarifies is his system of argument schemes or *topoi*. Aristotle had been vague on the nature of *topoi*, treating the subject as if his readers readily understood what he meant by the term 'topos.' Thus, Cicero's account is useful both in its own right and in the way it sheds light on its predecessor. For Cicero a *topos* or topic is the region from which an argument is drawn. That is, there are commonplaces both general and specific that are shared by speakers and audiences, and making use of these a speaker might communicate more effectively with her audience because of the ground that they share. Cicero (1949) divides topics between those that are attached to the subject of interest and those that are drawn from outside of it. Of those drawn from within he notes that they are distributed under many heads and lists relations to the subject "either by nature, or by their form, or by their resemblance to one another, or by their differences, or by their contrariety to one another, or by adjuncts, or by their antecedents, or by their consequents, or by what is opposed to each of them, or by causes, or by effects, or by a comparison with what is greater, or equal, or less" (*Topics*, Cicero 1949: 3). Arguments drawn

---

2 The Roman writer Longinus (c. 213–273 AD), gave advice about the use of figures of speech, stressing that a figure is most effective when it goes unnoticed, an idea that would later be echoed by Chaim Perelman. Figures for Longinus are related to the arousing of feelings in an audience (see Vickers 1988: 310). Not until the work of Peter Ramus (1515–1572) and his associates, however, is the prior history of tropes and figures organized in an economical manner (see Conley 1990: 131).

from outside, however, "are deduced chiefly from authority" (*Topics*, Cicero 1949: 4).[3]

While Cicero was the exemplary speaker and theorist of rhetoric, Quintilian (CE 35–100) stands out as its most successful teacher. Together with the anonymous *Rhetorica ad Herennium* they influenced the teaching of rhetoric in Europe up until the time of the American Revolution (Herrick 2001: 92). In *Institutes of Oratory* (1959) Quintilian developed Cicero's topical system for discovering arguments into a means of teaching argumentation. Rather than treating them as mnemonic devices, he associated them with habits of thought that students would develop through constant practice. But in these, as in many of the earlier matters, we see the close connections in the tradition of rhetoric and argumentation.[4]

3 Communication and reasoning: argumentation

While argumentation as a discipline has received the most theoretical attention since several key texts were published in the middle of the last century (Perelman and Olbrechts-Tyteca 1958 [1969]; Toulmin 1958), its roots stretch back to Aristotle's triadic approach that distinguishes the rhetorical, dialectical, and logical. Each of these captures ways in which argumentation promotes communicative efficiency.

Habermas (1984) expressed this triad in terms of process, procedure, and product (see also Wenzel 1979). With the rhetorical, as was suggested in Section 2, attention is paid to the argumentative communications between arguer and audience. Questions are raised about the nature of the audience, along with the character and interests of the arguer and the background circumstances of the argument. These components contribute to a fuller understanding of the argumentative context. The dialectical sense of argument focuses attention on exchanges within a dialogue and the moves involved. Dialogues of interest include the quarrel, the negotiation, the debate, and the inquiry. Theorists who study the dialectical sense of argument uncover and devise rules governing the correct procedures by which such arguments should be conducted. Finally, the logical approach stresses the product of statements expressed in the relationship of premises to conclusions. This sense receives the attention of logicians, both formal and informal. While the structure of arguments is important in this approach, a further component of inter-

---

3 See Rubinelli (2009) for a discussion of the relations between Aristotle's treatment of the *topoi* and that of Cicero.

4 Of course, important developments in the history of rhetoric do not end with the Greek and Roman thinkers. A rich tradition develops through the Renaissance and Enlightenment and into contemporary discussions. But little of this can be covered in this short survey and attention is being given to the foundations on which much else is built. As will be seen, rhetorical questions continue to be relevant in contemporary treatments of argumentation.

est concerns the intention behind arguments, namely to convince others to accept the proposition advanced as the conclusion.

Few approaches to argumentation attempt to integrate all three perspectives. An exception to this is Habermas himself, who insists "[a]t no single one of these analytic levels can the very idea intrinsic to argumentative speech be adequately developed" (Habermas 1984: 26). This forms the basis of his critique of other theories of argument, such as Stephen Toulmin's (that we will consider in Section 3.3), who is challenged for failing to address the levels of procedure and process (1984: 34). Habermas's theory of communicative action, in which his theory of argumentation is embedded, is discussed in Chapter 2, Eadie and Goret and Chapter 3, Craig in this volume. In this section, we will explore models of argumentation that take one of these three approaches as basic, and thus serve to illustrate what is involved in each case.

3.1 Perelman and Olbrechts-Tyteca and the New Rhetoric[5]

The appearance in 1958 of *La Nouvelle Rhétorique* marked an attempt to develop a model of rhetorical argumentation based on Aristotle's ideas. Elsewhere, Perelman explains that the object of the new rhetoric was to amplify and extend Aristotle's work (Perelman 1982: 4). Grounded also on a jurisprudential model, the aim was a "logic of value" that would "show that philosophers cannot do without a rhetorical conception of reason" (Perelman 1979: 42). From the outset Perelman and Olbrechts-Tyteca separate the realm of argumentation from demonstration with its self-evident truths. Unlike demonstration, argumentation deals with what is always open to question – the uncertainties of everyday existence. It is here that problems of communication might most readily arise and so clear means of developing argumentation need to be provided to combat such situations.

As we would expect, this is an audience-centered account, with audience understood as that individual or group who the arguer intends to influence with arguments.[6] No longer is the account restricted to the speeches of orators, but is expanded to include the audiences of written communications. The new rhetoric engages three types of audience: the self-deliberator who is the audience for her or his own arguments; the single hearer who forms the audience in dialogical encounters; and the universal audience that provides some standard of objectivity behind or within each particular audience that is addressed. From the perspective of efficient communication, each of these three basic audiences offers questions, challenges, and insights. The self-deliberator does not seem like any other audi-

---

5 Citations are to the English translation (1969).

6 This is a limitation to the account, since it would seem to overlook audiences for argumentation – like those who engage historical arguments – who could never have been anticipated by the arguer.

ence because it is, in theory, better known, with none of its beliefs and motivations hidden; and the single hearer helps us understand how an argument can be controlled to bring about mutually satisfactory results. But the universal audience seems as vague as the self-deliberator is clear, and stands as Perelman's most difficult idea. It is important to consider carefully what it can contribute to argumentation.

Part of the difficulty commentators have with this concept is the different ways in which it is expressed. Since the other party to a dialogue and the self-deliberator can "never amount to more than floating incarnations of this universal audience" (Perelman and Olbrechts-Tyteca 1958 [1969]: 31), it must provide "a norm for objective argumentation." As such it is "an audience attuned to reason" (Perelman 1979: 57); or "those who are disposed to hear [the philosopher] and are capable of following his argumentation" (Perelman 1982: 17). These statements seem restrictive, and given that "everyone constitutes the universal audience from what he knows of his fellow men" (Perelman and Olbrechts-Tyteca 1958 [1969]: 33), it has led to charges of relativism (van Eemeren and Grootendorst 1995).

What Perelman and Olbrechts-Tyteca do not have in mind is a model of universality traditionally popular with philosophers; one that stands outside of time and place as a constant measure of what is reasonable. Their universal audience is embedded in real audiences, since each 'individual, each culture' has a personal conception of it. It emerges as a standard of what is reasonable that is alive in particular audiences and which is activated as a check against the unreasonable. The assumption here is that the reasonable is not a fixed idea but one that moves and progresses across time and within communities. When we reflect on our own communities we recognize that we no longer accept as reasonable what once was seen as so. In our own time, we have seen attitudes to the environment change in this way. It would be unusual – and judged unreasonable – to see a pedestrian simply drop wastepaper on the ground. Not so long ago such behavior would have been accepted. How such changes in attitude towards the reasonable come about is through argumentation, and this assumes that we must be able to stand aside from our prejudices and special interests and judge things from an 'objective' perspective. And on the basis of such reviews, we change our minds.

For Perelman and Olbrechts-Tyteca argumentation is aimed at inducing or increasing the mind's adherence to theses presented to it for its assent. 'Adherence' is a complex idea here because, as the theory develops, it involves not just the mind but encompasses the entire person. The aim is not purely intellectual adherence, but the inciting of an action or creating a disposition to act (see Tindale 2010b). One set of adherences is the starting point of argumentation and involves the initial communication between arguer and audience predicated on commonalities of meaning or belief. This is the level of agreement of basic premises, those premises which need no further support and can be taken as given. Thus, initially, an arguer employs techniques to recognize adherence, looking for 'tokens' of its presence. Through the process of argumentation, the audience is moved from that initial base of agreement to another set of adherences that is brought to exist.

It may be more difficult to find tokens of this second set of adherence, since this involves the determination of the strength of arguments. On the one hand, it looks as if adherence should be measured by the actions of the audience, as those actions *and* audience are intended by the arguer. Hence, Perelman and Olbrechts-Tyteca (1958 [1969]: 49) speak of ongoing argumentation until the desired action is actually performed. And thus adherence can be measured by how audiences behave: what obstacles they overcome, what sacrifices they make, and so on. But this, as the authors concede, leads to a hazard: since the adherence can always be reinforced, we cannot be sure *when* to measure the effectiveness of the argumentation. If audience uptake is the only criterion, we may be premature in judging the quality of the argumentation or left unable to decide.

Focus on the effectiveness of argumentation as the sole criterion of strength can obscure the full weight of the proposals and lead to the kind of dismissive judgments we see from some of the new rhetoric's critics. Such a focus overlooks the way this issue is brought to the fore in one of the key questions of *The New Rhetoric*: "Is a strong argument an *effective* argument which gains the adherence of the audience, or is it a *valid* argument, which ought to gain it?" (Perelman and Olbrechts-Tyteca 1958 [1969]: 463). Just posing the question in this way puts us outside the chronology of argumentative events where we are left waiting for the tokens of efficacy. Here, we might appraise the argumentation in terms of how well the arguer has mustered the elements that should bring about adherence, given what is known of the audience. Here, Perelman (1979: 58) observes that "the philosopher must argue in such a manner that his discourse can achieve the adhesion of the universal audience." Because the quality of a discourse cannot be judged by its efficacy alone, this more objective standard of reasonableness is important.

The value of adherence can be seen as an extension of the Aristotelian rhetorical account, with its recognition of the importance of understanding audiences and creating in them a disposition to act in certain ways. Other Aristotelian elements appear in the attention given to character considerations and to the importance of *logos*, understood as the use of quasi-logical arguments. These are arguments that assume an understanding of validity found in formal thinking, but apply that understanding to everyday argumentation that lacks the certainty and rigor of the formal. Thus, for example, incompatibility is a type of quasi-logical argument that resembles contradiction but is less rigorous and requires an assessment of the context in which it arises to be identified and evaluated.

Another feature of the new rhetoric project that bears on this as a model of communicative efficiency is the importance given to achieving communion with an audience by making the objects of discourse present to the mind. This is one way in which the project makes use of the tradition of figuration, since many rhetorical figures can be employed to activate and focus ideas in the mind of the audience (Perelman and Olbrechts-Tyteca 1958 [1969]: 171–179).

Perelman provides a comprehensive model of rhetorical argumentation with strong Aristotelian roots, organized around a central concern with the communication between arguers and audiences. Other rhetorical models continue this emphasis, but none captures the range of Perelman's ideas (see Tindale 1999, 2004).[7]

3.2 Grice and the pragma-dialecticians

Dialectical models of argumentation concentrate on the procedures involved, usually presenting them in terms of maxims or rules to govern good practice. Two such approaches offered by the philosopher Paul Grice and the Dutch school of pragma-dialectics illustrate this approach.

Grice (1913–1988) does not present a full model of argumentation but his work on logic and conversation is rooted in dialectics and he was one of the first philosophers to take seriously the business of offering advice – in the form of maxims – for capturing the procedures involved in effective communication.

The Cooperative Principle with its associated sense of implicature, forms the heart of Grice's seminal paper, 'Logic and conversation' (Grice 1989: 22–40). Talking is a goal-oriented activity and so its purposes may be better achieved in some ways than in others, depending on the goal involved. People are advised to make their contributions to a conversation such as is required by the purpose of the conversation, and the stage involved. This is the Cooperative Principle. This Principle, and the primary maxims associated with it, are presented and discussed by Tim Wharton in his chapter on 'Linguistic action theories of communication' in this volume. So the discussion here will focus on further aspects of Grice's pragmatics related to his dialectical model of argumentation and its role in communicative efficiency.

Of the four maxims that Grice introduces (quantity, quality, relation, and manner), the last of these may be judged most important for our purposes because of the way in which Grice supplements it. In the paper 'Presupposition and conversational implicature' (Grice 1989: 269–282), Grice is concerned with the way that some assertions invite a denial of all or part of what has been said. In this respect, he suggests adding to his maxims one which governs such invitations: "Frame whatever you say in the form most suitable for any reply that would be regarded as appropriate"; or "Facilitate in your form of expression the appropriate reply" (1989: 273). This is an important addition on a number of fronts, most particularly because it constitutes an explicit movement toward the audience. What is said is

---

7 Critics also identity a failure to include all Aristotle's insights, such as those regarding *pathos* (Gross and Dearin 2003).

said not just with an audience in mind, but in anticipation of a *response* from that audience. Among other things, this means that a speaker must have quite a clear idea of who that audience is and what range of responses is likely to follow. The maxim does not imagine a passive audience receiving messages, but one actively engaged in the exchange of conversation.

In asking what reasons we have for believing that people cooperate in ways suggested by the Cooperative Principle, Grice falls back onto experiential ground. It is "just a well-recognized empirical fact that people do behave in these ways" (Grice 1989: 29), although he admits he should provide further proof that people not only do follow the principle but that it is *reasonable* for them to do so. Essentially, a later examination of reasons and reasonableness (Grice 2001) meets this requirement: we derive satisfaction or happiness in general from exercising those capacities that allow us to function as widely as possible under human living conditions. In the context of the discussion in (Grice 1989) we can understand that cooperation provides a satisfaction stemming from the exercise of excellences developing in us as rational beings. The actual discussion phrases things a little differently in terms of interests: "anyone who cares about the goals that are central to conversation/communication (such as giving and receiving information, influencing and being influenced by others) must be expected to have an interest, given suitable circumstances, in participation in talk exchanges that will be profitable only on the assumption that they are conducted in general accordance with the Cooperative Principle and maxims" (Grice 1989: 30).

Grice's work did much to clarify the distinction between semantics and pragmatics, but one of its primary influences remains on argumentation theory and the ideas on communication that underlie it (see Kauffeld 1998). Douglas Walton sees in Grice the idea that parameters of reasonable dialogue are unstated conventions in realistic argumentation (Walton 1989: 33n1), and Grice has also been seen as an influence on the development of informal logic (van Eemeren et al. 1996).

A more conscious development of the dialectical approach to argumentation is illustrated in the theory of pragma-dialectics from the Amsterdam School, initiated by Frans van Eemeren and Rob Grootendorst (1984, 1992, 2004), and developed by van Eemeren (2010) alone and with Peter Houtlosser (van Eemeren and Houtlosser 1999, 2000, 2002) and others.

Pragma-dialecticians conceive of all argumentation as part of a critical discussion aimed at resolving differences of opinion. They approach this through the identification and clarification of certain procedural rules, thus conforming to the dialectical perspective's interest in argument as procedure. One rule, for example, requires someone who advances a standpoint to defend it if requested; another requires the correct application of an argumentation scheme before a standpoint can be regarded as conclusively defended. The rules govern four stages of dispute resolution: a confrontation stage, an opening stage, and argumentation stage, and a concluding stage.

Pragma-dialectics is an exemplary model of communicative efficiency. It aims to be normative and disambiguate language so as to facilitate understanding and, hence, agreement. In fact, the rules employed can be seen as 'communication rules' drawing on some of Grice's insights into verbal communication and interaction (van Eemeren 2010: 16). This follows from the observation that argumentation is a "*communicative act complex*" (27). Van Eemeren and Houtlosser (2005) introduce the idea of an "activity type" to describe the different domains of communicative activity in which argumentation operates. These activity types are conventional practices that meet and reflect the needs in specific domains of communication (van Eemeren 2010: 139). So, for example, a domain such as legal communication is characterized by adjudication as the genre of communicative activity, with court proceedings, arbitration and summoning as the corresponding activity types. This organizing of types within domains recalls something of Toulmin's field-approach addressed below.

3.3 Toulmin and informal logic

If we accept something of Perelman's divide between demonstration and argumentation, where demonstration captures the self-evident reasoning of formal logic, then the types of logic that will interest us in the logical approach to argumentation will be informal or ordinary logics.

Pioneers in the development and dissemination of informal logic, Ralph Johnson and J. Anthony Blair describe it as: "the normative study of argument. It is the area of logic which seeks to develop standards, criteria and procedures for the interpretation, evaluation and construction of arguments and argumentation used in natural language" (Blair and Johnson 1987: 148). At the heart of this definition is the product of argumentation – the argument. But rather than a product that has been torn from the ebb and flow of an argumentative exchange, the 'informal' argument is considered within the context of its origin with many features of that context deemed relevant for the analysis and evaluation of the argument. It matters who the parties are and what was trying to be achieved in the argument. Thus, an argument scheme like the *ad hominem* will bring the person essentially into consideration as it is decided whether the attack on the person is relevant given the circumstances involved.

Stephen Toulmin (1922–2009) has an ambiguous relationship with informal logic and commentators are often unsure whether or not to include him. But insofar as he has presented a complete non-formal theory with clear implications for communicative efficiency, and his model is widely adopted by the American Speech and Communication community,[8] then it deserves consideration.

---

8 Douglas Ehninger and Wayne Brockriede (1960) introduced the field of communication to Toulmin's work, popularizing its use as a method for working with public discourse and as a logical model for use in rhetorical situations.

Toulmin asks what makes arguments work and how are their contents communicated effectively? He rejects the idea that argumentation can be evaluated solely using universal norms based on logical form. Instead, he introduces as a technical term the idea of a *field* of argument and explores the norms related to different fields (law would be such a field) and deciding what things about the form and merit of an argument are field-variable and what field-independent (Toulmin 1958: 14–15).

The 'Toulmin model' of argument uses the terms 'claim,' 'data,' 'backing,' and 'warrant' to describe an argument's components. Essentially, this means that the evidence provided for a claim is more varied and complex than in other logical models. The claim is based on a set of data, but the use of that data is justified by a warrant that links the data and claim. In some cases the warrant itself will require some authoritative support, and this is provided by the backing. In this way, Toulmin achieves what had been accomplished in different ways in the rhetorical and dialectical models – he establishes basic 'premises' on which an argument is grounded, a ground that is assumed acceptable by the audience and that requires no further support.[9] This grounds the communication of arguments in a common foundation and this facilitates the introduction of new elements which an audience is being asked to embrace.

4 Conclusion: wider applications and sources for argumentation and rhetoric

As the foregoing indicates, the traditions of argumentation and rhetoric have provided important models of communicative efficiency. These models have essentially been those of the Greco-Roman world brought into contemporary discussion by a range of theoretical approaches. They have also been concerned primarily with communication between human agents. More recent scholarship has challenged the prejudices and limits inherent in these traditions.

Attention has been turned, for example, to different traditions coming out of India and Asia. While Hamblin (1970) paid some attention to Indian logic in his study of fallacies, he overlooked the way that so much Indian philosophy employs narrative as an efficient way to communicate ideas. Western thinkers have also begun to pay more attention to the role of narratives in argumentation, and drawing on this Indian source proposes to enrich and extend that understanding (Stroud 2004).

Asian rhetoric and argumentation also has traditions that are relevant to considerations of communicative efficiency, but that have been largely overlooked in

---

9 For an extended example in which Toulmin employs and illustrates all these terms see Toulmin (1958: 92–99). The full model employs the further terms 'rebuttal' and 'qualifier.'

the West. They are now getting important if limited attention (See Jensen 1987; Wang 2004). This research proceeds with a cautious desire not to impose Western conceptions on Asian rhetoric and argumentation, but much of the current work almost necessarily begins from a Western standpoint and approaches the subject in a comparative manner. Thus, Mary Garrett (1993) explores pathos in light of Chinese rhetoric and the importance of emotion in communicating positions, and Jensen (1992) explains the practices of Asian argumentation in terms understandable to a Western audience. But there is much more to gather from these sources as more scholars turn their attention to the East.

Another growing area of scholarship explores relations between communication, argumentation, and artificial intelligence and ways in which new media like the Internet affect the roles rhetoric and argumentation play in communicative efficiency. The work of informal logician Douglas Walton has been widely embraced by computer scientists looking to use tools like argumentation schemes (Walton et al. 2008) to develop systems that will model natural language argumentation. Walton himself is involved in this work (see Reed and Walton 2005), arguing at one point that the influence of argumentation on artificial intelligence has developed within a framework consistent with pragma-dialectics (Walton and Godden 2006). Overall this innovative work pushes for a model of scheme-based communication reflective of the Aristotelian and Ciceronian use of topics. It is a model that combines the work of computer scientists with advanced understandings in argumentation theory to further effective communication.

A lot of attention has also been devoted to the ways in which new media enhance the communication processes that employ rhetoric and argumentation. Chief among these is the use of the Internet to reach diverse audiences that could never have been imagined by earlier communicators. The Obama presidential campaign of 2008 incorporated new media in communicating its messages and responding quickly to counter-messages. Such speed in communication is one of the key advantages of such media. Balanced by the disadvantage of the loss of a clearly identifiable audience whose responses can be measured and accommodated.

Barbara Warnick's (2007) book is among several innovative treatments of the use of rhetoric online. She addresses the importance of analyzing rhetorical activity on the web, especially as this is expressed through political campaigns. Clearly, this is a field that will and should continue to attract the attention of rhetoric and argumentation theorists interested in these disciplines as models of communicative efficiency.

In many ways, the virtual world, like the traditions of the East, is a realm untested by the standards of Western rhetoric and argumentation, and so its promise for improving communication remains unclear. While these traditions have played a fundamental role in how we have understood ourselves as communicators, they also stand to be reassessed as these new areas of communicative experience are explored. The results will enrich not just our understanding of the powers inherent in rhetoric and argumentation to foster models of communicative efficiency but also of ourselves as social agents negotiating the terms of our encounters.

Further reading

Blair, J. A. 2011. *Groundwork in the Theory of Argumentation*. New York: Springer.

Fahnestock, J. 2011. *Rhetorical Style: The Uses of Language in Persuasion*. Oxford: Oxford University Press.

Mercier, H. & D. Sperber. 2011. Why Do Humans Reason? Arguments for an Argumentative Theory. *Behavioral and Brain Sciences* 34 (2). 57–74.

References

Aristotle. 2007. *On Rhetoric: A Theory of Civic Discourse*, 2nd edn, Kennedy, G. (trans.). Oxford: Oxford University Press.

Blair, J. A. & R. H. Johnson. 1987. The Current State of Informal Logic. *Informal Logic* 9. 147–151.

Cicero. 1949. *On Invention. The Best Kind of Orator. Topics*, Hubbell, H. M. (trans.). Cambridge, MA: Loeb Classical Library.

Cicero. 1976. *De Oratore*, Sutton, E. W. and Rackham, H. (trans.). Cambridge, MA: Loeb Classical Library.

Cicero. 1976. *De Inventione*, Hubbell, H. M. (trans.). Cambridge, MA: Loeb Classical Library.

Conley, T. M. 1990. *Rhetoric in the European Tradition*. Chicago, IL: University of Chicago Press.

Ehninger, D. & W. Brockriede. 1960. Toulmin on Argument: An Interpretation and Application. *Quarterly Journal of Speech* 46. 44–53.

Garrett, M. 1993. Pathos Reconsidered from the Perspective of Classical Chinese Rhetorical Theories. *Quarterly Journal of Speech* 79. 19–39.

Grice, H. P. 1989. *Studies in the Way of Words*. Cambridge, MA: Harvard University Press.

Grice, H. P. 2001. *Aspects of Reason*. Oxford: Clarendon Press.

Gross, A. & R. Dearin. 2003. *Chaim Perelman*. New York: State University of New York Press.

Habermas, J. 1984. *The Theory of Communicative Action: Reason and the Rationalization of Society, Vol. 1*, McCarthy, T. (trans.). Boston: Beacon Press.

Hamblin, C. 1970. *Fallacies*. London: Methuen.

Herrick, J. A. 2001. *The History and Theory of Rhetoric: An Introduction*. Boston: Allyn and Bacon.

Hitchcock, D. & B. Verheij. 2006. *Arguing on the Toulmin Model: New Essays in Argument Analysis and Evaluation*. Berlin: Springer.

Jensen, V. J. 1987. Rhetoric of East Asia – A Bibliography. *Rhetoric Society Quarterly* 17. 213–230.

Jensen, V. J. 1992. Values and Practices in Asian Argumentation. *Argumentation and Advocacy* 28. 153–166.

Kauffeld, F. 1998. Presumption and the Distribution of Argumentative Burdens in Acts of Proposing and Accusing. *Argumentation* 12. 245–266.

Kennedy, G. 1963. *The Art of Persuasion in Greece*. Princeton, NJ: Princeton University Press.

Kennedy, G. 1972. *The Art of Rhetoric in the Roman World*. Princeton, NJ: Princeton University Press.

Perelman, Ch. 1979. *New Rhetoric and the Humanities*. Dordrecht: Reidel.

Perelman, Ch. 1982. *The Realm of Rhetoric,* Kluback, W. (trans.). Notre Dame, IN: University of Notre Dame Press.

Perelman, Ch. & L. Olbrechts-Tyteca. 1958. *La Nouvelle Rhétorique: Traité de l' Argumentation*. Presses Universitaires de France. Wilkinson, J. and Weaver, P. (trans.) 1969 *The New Rhetoric: A Treatise on Argumentation*. Notre Dame, IN: University of Notre Dame Press.

Quintilian. 1959–1963. *Institutio Oratoria*, 4 vols, Butler, H.E. (trans). Cambridge, MA: Loeb Classical Library.

Reed, C. & D. Walton. 2005. Towards a Formal and Implemented Model of Argumentation Schemes in Agent Communication. In: I. Rahwan (ed.), *Argumentation in Multi-Agent Systems: ArgMAS 2004*, 19–30. Berlin: Springer-Verlag

Rubinelli, S. 2009. *Ars Topica*. Berlin: Springer-Verlag.

Schiappa, E. 1999. *The Beginnings of Rhetorical Theory in Classical Greece*. New Haven, CT: Yale University Press.

Stroud, S. R. 2004. Narrative as Argument in Indian Philosophy: The Astavakra Gita as Multivalent Narrative. *Philosophy and Rhetoric* 37. 42–71.

Tindale, C. W. 1999. *Acts of Arguing: A Rhetorical Model of Argument*. Albany, NY: State University of New York Press.

Tindale, C. W. 2004. *Rhetorical Argumentation*. Thousand Oaks, CA: Sage Publications.

Tindale, C. W. 2010. *Reason's Dark Champions: Constructive Strategies of Sophistic Argument*. Columbia, SC: University of South Carolina Press.

Tindale, C. W. 2010b. Ways of Being Reasonable: Perelman and the Philosophers. *Philosophy and Rhetoric* 43. 337–361.

Toulmin, S. 1958. *The Uses of Argument*. Cambridge: Cambridge University Press.

van Eemeren, F. H. 1996. *Fundamentals of Argumentation Theory: A Handbook of Historical Backgrounds and Contemporary Developments*. Mahwah, NJ: Lawrence Erlbaum Associates.

van Eemeren, F. H. 2010. *Strategic Maneuvering in Argumentative Discourse*. Amsterdam: John Benjamins Publishing Company.

van Eemeren, F. H. & R. Grootendorst. 1984. *Speech Acts in Argumentative Discussions*. Dordrecht, NL: Foris.

van Eemeren, F. H. & R. Grootendorst. 1992. *Argumentation, Communication, and Fallacies*. Hillsdale, NJ: Lawrence Erlbaum.

van Eemeren, F. H. & R. Grootendorst. 1995. Perelman and the Fallacies. *Philosophy and Rhetoric* 28. 122–133.

van Eemeren, F. H. & R. Grootendorst. 2004. *A Systematic Theory of Argumentation*. Cambridge: Cambridge University Press.

van Eemeren, F. H. & P. Houtlosser. 1999. Strategic Manoeuvering in Argumentative Discourse. *Discourse Studies* 1. 479–497.

van Eemeren, F. H. & P. Houtlosser. 2000. Rhetorical Analysis within a Pragma-Dialectical Framework: The Case of R.J. Reynolds. *Argumentation* 14. 293–305.

van Eemeren, F. H & P. Houtlosser. 2002. Strategic Manoeuvering with the Burden of Proof. In: F.H. van Eemeren (ed.),
Advances in Pragma-Dialectics, 13–29. Amsterdam: SicSat.

van Eemeren, F. H. & P. Houtlosser. 2005. Theoretical Construction and Argumentative Reality: An Analytic Model of Critical Discussion and Conventional Types of Argumentative Activity. In: D. Hitchcock and D. Farr (eds.), *The Uses of Argument: Proceedings of a Conference at McMaster University, 18–21 May 2005*, 75–84. Hamilton, ON: Ontario Society for the Study of Argumentation.

Vickers, B. 1988. *In Defense of Rhetoric*. Oxford: Oxford University Press.

Walton, D. 1989. *Question-Reply Argumentation*. New York: Greenwood Press.

Walton, D., C. Reed & F. Macagno. 2008. *Argumentation Schemes*. Cambridge: Cambridge University Press.

Walton, D. & D. Godden. 2006. The Impact of Argumentation on Artificial Intelligence. In: P. Houtlosser and A. van Rees (eds.), *Considering Pragma-Dialectics*, 287–299. Mahweh, NJ: Lawrence Erlbaum.

Wang, B. 2004. A Survey of Research in Asian Rhetoric. *Rhetoric Review* 23. 171–181.

Warnick, Barbara. 2007. *Rhetoric Online: Persuasion and Politics on the World Wide Web*. New York: Peter Lang Publishing Company.

Wenzel, J. 1979. Jürgen Habermas and the Dialectical Perspective on Argumentation. *Journal of the American Forensic Association* 16. 83–94.

John O. Greene and Elizabeth Dorrance Hall

10 Cognitive theories of communication

Abstract: Over the last three decades cognitivism has remained among the dominant theoretical perspectives in the field of communication. In point of fact, however, the domain of "cognitive theories of communication" encompasses a variety of only-partially-overlapping approaches to theorizing. In an effort to impose some conceptual order on this broad and diverse set of theories, functionalism/human information processing is employed as a reference point for characterizing other cognitive approaches, including: lay cognitivism, social cognition, and neuroscience. Exemplars of each sort of theory are examined, and promising areas for future theorizing are discussed.

Keywords: Associative networks, cognitivism, embodied cognition, functionalism, human information processing, interpersonal transcendence, social cognition, neuroscience

1 Introduction

The essential warrant underlying the rise of cognitive theories of communication is the simple notion that understanding communication processes can be advanced by examining the nature of the mind (and mental processes). This fundamental assumption might appear to be incontrovertible (particularly at this point in the historical development of the communication discipline), but it is useful at the outset to remind ourselves of the degree to which the realm of the mental interpenetrates that of the social. Indeed, at the risk of belaboring the obvious, without cognition there is no communication. And, regardless of the particular communication domain of interest, be it interpersonal communication, rhetoric, mass communication, or what have you, always at the core one confronts issues of meaning (e.g., significance and sense-making), memory (e.g., information acquisition and skill development), and action (e.g., verbal and nonverbal message behavior, voting and purchase decisions).

It is quite natural, then, that in pursuit of their various research interests, communication scholars would seek the insights afforded by taking into account these foundational mental operations. Indeed, this "cognitive turn" can be seen in the pioneering work of people like Lasswell, Hovland, and their contemporaries whose analyses of mass media influences predate even the emergence of departments of communication in American universities (see Carey 1996; Delia 1987; Schramm 1997). For these early researchers the fact that the mass media did not produce uniform, pervasive effects necessitated a concern with individual information processing reflected in conceptions of attention, attitudes, stereotypes, and the like.[1]

But if there is a sense in which the adoption of a cognitive perspective was early and obvious, there is another in which this move among communication scholars has been a relatively recent development. Indeed, "cognitive science" is itself a relative newcomer to the panoply of social and behavioral sciences. While the field of experimental psychology began to develop in the late nineteenth century, and social and developmental psychology in the early part of the twentieth, George A. Miller put the date of inception of cognitive science as September 11, 1956 (the second day of the Symposium on Information Theory held at the Massachusetts Institute of Technology; see Gardner 1985: 28). To our knowledge, the earliest examinations of cognitive science and human information processing in the field of communication proper can be dated to about 1970 and the years immediately following (see: Craig 1978; Miller 1969, 1976). And it was not until the 1980s that cognitive approaches to various communicative phenomena became commonplace (see Berger 2005; Roskos-Ewoldsen and Monahan 2007). Since that time, however, various stripes of cognitivism have remained among the dominant theoretical perspectives in the field (see Craig 1999; Hamilton and Nowak 2005; Knapp and Daly 2011; Nussbaum and Friedrich 2005; Powers 1995).

2 Mapping the domain

There are numerous ways that one might seek to organize a discussion of cognitive theories of communication (e.g., by communication sub-discipline – theories of interpersonal processes, mass communication processes, etc.; by processing system – attention, working memory, long-term memory, etc.; by conceptions of theoretical formalisms – scripts, production systems, etc.). In point of fact, the domain of "cognitive theories of communication" is tremendously broad and encompasses a variety of only-partially-overlapping approaches to theorizing. One might think of these various theoretical perspectives as "fuzzy sets," with central exemplars, but no clearly defined boundaries. Our approach here, then, is to begin by describing one particular approach to cognitive theorizing – a conceptual lodestar as it were – which can then be used as a reference point for mapping the constellation of other theoretical perspectives.

---

1 It is equally germane that this same time period witnessed the development of the nascent discipline of social psychology which reflected a similar embrace of mental constructs in exploring interpersonal and group dynamics (see Jones 1998).

2.1 Canonical cognitive science: functionalism and human information processing

We take as our point of departure the meta-theoretical stance that is most widely held among cognitive scientists, that of functionalism (see Churchland 1992; Flanagan 1991). Functionalism can be seen as a reaction to the various strands of behaviorism that dominated experimental psychology in the United States during the first half of the twentieth century. The behaviorists, in pursuit of an objective science of psychology, dismissed appeals to mental states and processes in favor of analyses based solely on observables (i.e., stimuli and responses).

In contrast, the essence of functionalism is to posit a model of the mental system that links stimulus inputs to outputs. Beyond a commitment to focusing on, rather than eschewing, mental states and events, a second key feature of the functionalist perspective is that models of the processing system are cast at the level of mind rather than brain. In other words, rather than focusing on underlying neurophysiological processes, the primary concern is with understanding the nature of the *functions* the information processing system must execute in order to perform as it does (e.g., if people are able to retain information over some extended span of time, then the mind must include some sort of long-term memory system capable of carrying out this function).

The philosophical commitments of functionalism are most fully expressed in the human information processing (HIP) approach to research and theory construction. At the heart of the HIP project is the notion of mind as a representational system (or more correctly, as a series of representational subsystems). Simply put, the conception is of: (1) a series of processing stages linking inputs to responses, (2) where at each stage, information, represented in some form, is subjected to the dedicated process(es) characteristic of that subsystem. To illustrate, a general HIP model might include the following subsystems:

- *Sensory registers* – very short-term buffers that hold information in veridical (i.e., uninterpreted) form prior to processing by subsequent systems.
- *Pattern recognition* – a system that draws upon information in both sensory buffers and long-term memory to permit identification of visual (e.g., edges and curves, faces) and auditory patterns (e.g., phonemes, prosodic features).
- *Long-term memory* – a system that retains various sorts of information, in various formats, potentially over spans of years. Among the distinctions commonly drawn between LTM subsystems is that between *declarative* and *procedural* memory, where the former is held to be the repository of *knowledge that*, i.e., the factual knowledge that one has acquired about the world, and the latter, the store of *knowledge how*, i.e., memory representations relevant to skills such as speaking, interaction regulation, and so on. The declarative memory subsystem can be further partitioned into *episodic* and *semantic* stores. Episodic memory is the repository of the events (or episodes) of one's

life (e.g., the first kiss, yesterday's conversation over lunch). Semantic memory, in contrast, is the site of acquired information that has been abstracted from specific episodes – such as the names of one's friends, and most especially, word meanings.
–   *Working memory* – a system that is limited in capacity and/or duration, where information is actively manipulated, and whose contents are typically held to be consciously available. Working memory is the site of message planning and rehearsal, rumination over the events of the day, and reflections on the mass media content one has encountered.
–   *Effector system* – the site of overt response generation. It is here that motor programs for speech and movement are assembled and executed.

Embracing the conception of mind as a representational system brings to the fore two essential features of fully developed functional/HIP models. The first of these, *structure*, involves the question of *how* information is represented in some cognitive stage (or subsystem). To illustrate, information in long-term declarative memory may be represented in a network structure with nodes corresponding to concepts and associative links representing relationships between those concepts (see Section 2.3). Or, to cite other common examples, *schemata* – structures that organize knowledge about categories (e.g., "conservatives," "electric cars") and *scripts* – long-term memory representations of familiar sequences of events (e.g., "passing through airport security," "ordering coffee at Starbucks").

The second component of functional models, *process*, involves specification of the nature and characteristics of the mechanisms by which cognitive content is utilized or transformed. To continue the associative network example, because any specific memory (e.g., memories of one's wedding or the birth of his or her first child) is not always the focus of our consciousness, functional models typically invoke conceptions of an activation process that serves to bring memory content to mind. Similarly, information processing models that invoke conceptions of schemata and scripts usually also incorporate notions of structure activation and "slot filling" – i.e., inserting the specific details of one's present situation into the generalized specifications in long-term memory.

Because functional/HIP theories are cast at the level of mind rather than brain, such theories are not formulated (or tested) by inspection of physical structures and events (e.g., areas of the brain, synaptic firings, etc.). Instead, functional models are formulated via the method of "transcendental inference" (Flanagan 1991). In essence, the aim is to posit a system of structures and processes that can account for observed input-output regularities. For example, it is well established that people have very limited memory for the specific words of a message, but memory for the gist or meaning of messages tends to be quite good. This regularity led to the development of models which hold that information is represented in memory as "propositions" (i.e., meaning units) rather than as words and word orders (e.g., Anderson 1976; Frederiksen 1975).

Because transcendental inference proceeds from analysis of input-output relationships, cognitive science is characterized by experimental methods that are remarkably clever in their efforts to manipulate stimulus features and in identifying and isolating characteristics of the responses to those stimuli. Cataloguing cognitivists' techniques for manipulating stimulus inputs in theoretically meaningful ways may be a nearly impossible project, and certainly it is one beyond the scope of this chapter. On the output side of the system, however, it is possible to identify the most common tools at the theorist's disposal (see Greene 1988, 2008), including verbal reports of thought processes, memory assessments (e.g., recognition and recall), temporal measures (e.g., reaction time, time to task completion), and analysis of performance errors (e.g., speech errors). By their very nature, functional/HIP models are said to be *indeterminate* because it is possible to develop multiple alternative models to account for the same input-output regularities. That is, given one specification of structures, and processes operating over the content represented in those structures, it is possible to develop another (actually, many other) structure-process model(s) that would yield the same predictions.

While the overarching project of functionalism/HIP is to specify the nature of the stages that link inputs to responses, no theorist sets for him- or herself such an ambitious task. Rather, individual theories are developed to explain the operation of an information-processing subsystem, or combination of subsystems, that give rise to the particular behavioral phenomena of interest. Moreover, within the overarching functionalism/HIP framework it is possible to discern two very general approaches to theory building, characterized on one hand by theories that accord explanatory prominence to specifications of cognitive structures, and on the other by theories in which the explanatory "heavy lifting" is located in conceptions of process. At the risk of putting too fine a point on the issue, the distinction hinges on whether the content of the subsystem of interest is thought to be *stored* or *computed*. But again, the issue is one of relative emphasis: fully developed HIP models incorporate specifications of both structure and process; nevertheless it is possible to discern those theories whose primary explanatory power is located in conceptions of what and how information is stored and those where explanatory insights stem from specifications of process(es). To illustrate, let us consider an exemplar of each sort, both pertaining to message production.

Drawing on an earlier model of message behavior developed by Herrmann (1983), O'Keefe and Lambert (1995) propose that message production involves selection of relevant facts from one's long-term store of knowledge. These facts are activated on the basis of one's goals and construal of the situation, and comprise the "propositional base," or intended meaning of an utterance. Some further subset of the propositional base, then, is selected as the "semantic input" to overt message production. Here, then, we find an exemplar of approaches to theorizing that accord emphasis to what is stored rather than to computation: the speaker is assumed to possess preformed ideas, and message production involves winnowing a series of these ideas for overt articulation. (To be fair, both O'Keefe and Lambert and Herrmann do acknowledge that the content of the propositional base may not always consist of established ideational content, and instead, may in some cases be actively constructed, but neither theory offers any insight about the nature of this construction process.)

In contrast to models like that of O'Keefe and Lambert, other HIP theories accord greater explanatory prominence to the processes that operate over those structures. An example of a theory of the latter sort is found in second generation action assembly theory (AAT2; Greene 1997). This theory was developed as a model of the output system that gives rise to covert (i.e., thoughts) and overt (i.e., verbal and nonverbal) behaviors, and in particular, the theory is concerned with the fact that people are able to formulate novel, creative thoughts and actions.

At the foundation of the theory is the conception of a "procedural record" – basically an associative-network structure that preserves relationships between features of action, outcomes, and situations – that, as in most network models, is activated when an individual encounters conditions that correspond to the features represented in that record. AAT2 departs from functional/HIP models that accord a primary role to storage in that activation of action features represented in pro-cedural records, like turning the ignition key of an automobile, only sets in motion the operation of the output system. From the perspective of AAT2, even the sim-plest behavior consists of the integration of a great many action features. As a computation-primacy HIP model, then, AAT2 gives emphasis to specifying the nature of the "assembly" process by which elemental action features are inte-grated – a process characterized as "coalition formation" – to form configurations of thought and action that an individual has never encountered or produced before.

With functionalism/HIP as a reference point, then, let us consider the larger landscape of cognitive theories of communication.

2.2 Lay cognitivism

Just on the horizon from our functionalism vantage point is the scholarly tradition of invoking cognitive terms to ground and make sense of communication processes. This sphere is characterized by appeals to everyday notions of "perception", "com-prehension," "memory," "thought," "belief," "learning," and so on – and where, as is depicted in Fig. 1, the underpinning philosophical foundation is that of "folk psychology" (Churchland 1992). Here we find inquiry grounded, sometimes informed, and in some cases even motivated, by conceptions of terms that are a part of the vernacular. As an exemplar we might point to Plato's *Phaedrus* which centers on the role of memory and (cognitive) deliberation in communicative dis-course. Other examples abound in areas of inquiry as seemingly removed from cognitive science as critical and interpretive theory. Indeed, this stance can be seen to infuse the entire field of communication, and even where authors do not explicitly invoke the terms of lay (latent?) cognitivism, a probing question or two concerning their work will elicit just such terminology.

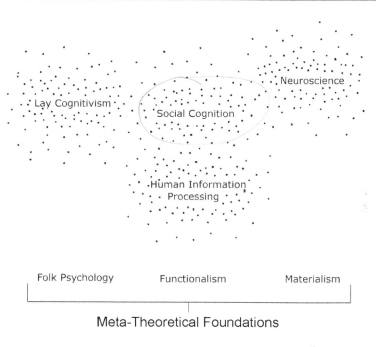

Fig. 1: The constellation of cognitive theories of communication

2.3 Social cognition

Distinct from the tradition of invoking (or assuming) everyday cognitive terms is the broad sweep of scholarly inquiry that falls under the rubric of "social cognition." Most generally, social cognitive theories are concerned with how people make sense of their environment (including their message environment), others, and themselves (see Fiske and Taylor 1991; Jones 1998). This is a very broad set, indeed, and one that, like functionalism/HIP, is comprised of various "fuzzy subsets." For present purposes, however, let us restrict discussion to two general theoretical orientations that fall under the heading of "social cognition" – the first in which the focus and emphasis of theorizing is on explicating various cognitive processes ("process-primacy social cognition"), and the second where theorizing centers on description of structure-process systems ("structure-process social cognition").[2]

Process-primacy social cognition (nearest to the "lay cognition" fuzzy set), includes the constellation of concepts and theories that constitute the historical foundations of social cognition. Here are located the various instantiations of cognitive dissonance theory, social perception and attribution theories, social learning theory, theories of group influence, social comparison theory, and so on (see Jones 1998). The distinction between the exemplars of lay cognitivism and those of theories of this sort is that, in the latter, cognitive concepts take on a primary theoretical or explanatory focus. Thus, lay cognitivists may make reference to "self-concept" or "attitudes," as examples, but in the traditions of social cognition, the nature of the self and attitudes are a central focus of theorizing. As exemplars of the process-primacy fuzzy subset, let us consider three particularly prominent theories, one focused on attitude change, the second on the link between attitudes and behavior, and the last on social perception processes.

The elaboration likelihood model (ELM) is one of a class of theories developed to address seeming anomalies in studies of persuasion and attitude change (see Petty and Wegener 1998). These "dual-process" theories posit that people may engage in effortful scrutiny and analysis of the evidence and arguments in a message, or they may rely on simple heuristics and "rules of thumb." According to the ELM, both types of processing are typically at work, but the relative influence of analytic (or "central") versus heuristic (or "peripheral") processing is determined, in large part, by an individual's *motivation* and *ability* to process a message. Thus, messages that are personally relevant or that pertain to topics one is knowledgeable about are more likely to generate message-relevant thoughts, or "elaborations."

---

2 There is a third, very common, variant of social cognitive theorizing in communication that merits note in this context. In truth, this approach is probably as much a presentational convention as a distinct approach to theory building, so despite its ubiquity, we have opted to relegate it to a footnote, recognizing that specific instantiations of theories of this type may be roughly categorized as either "process-primacy" or "structure-process" models. In the spirit of HIP approaches, "white-boxology" or "box-and-arrow" models specify some sequence of processing stages underlying the cognitive, affective/emotional, or behavioral phenomena of interest (but in almost all cases, rather than a strictly linear ordering, these models incorporate recursive paths that feed back to prior stages). Such models may be more or less elaborate, specifying few or many processing steps (and the detail in specification of processes at each step also varies considerably). A typical example of a more parsimonious formulation is found in Dillard's (2008) presentation of the Goals-Plans-Action (G-P-A) theory of message production which identifies just five processing steps ("goal assessment," "decision to engage," "plan generation," "plan selection," and "tactic implementation,") along with a short-term buffer system, to explicate goal-relevant message behavior. At the other extreme of the elegance/parsimony continuum are models such as those surveyed by Hamilton (2007) in his review of theories of persuasive message processing where some frameworks invoke dozens of cognitive states and processes.

The ELM further posits that attitudes established via central processing are more likely to persist, influence behavior, and to be resistant to counter-persuasion.

A second example of theories in this fuzzy subset grew out of the common empirical observation that attitudes are often only weakly predictive of attitude-relevant behaviors. As an initial attempt to address this issue, Fishbein (e.g., Fishbein and Ajzen 1975) developed the Theory of Reasoned Action (TRA) which, among other contributions, introduced the idea that the link between attitudes about some target and behavior toward that target is mediated by intention to perform the behavior. These intentions, in turn, were held to be a function of attitudes toward the behavior and social normative pressures. The TRA was subsequently extended in Ajzen's (e.g., 1991) Theory of Planned Behavior (TPB). The key move in the TPB was to posit that, in addition to attitudes toward the behavior and subjective social norms, there is a third factor, perceived behavioral control, at work. In essence, perceived behavioral control involves the ease or difficulty of performing the behavior in question. The upshot of the theory, then, is that intentions to perform a behavior will be increased when an individual has a positive attitude toward the behavior, when the person perceives that he or she can successfully execute that behavior, and when the behavior is expected and approved by others.

A third important exemplar of process-primacy theorizing is found in uncertainty reduction theory (URT; Berger and Bradac 1982). This theory proposes that human beings have a fundamental social motivation to reduce uncertainty about themselves and others. This motivation is heightened under certain conditions, including circumstances where people expect continued interaction with another, when others act in unusual ways, and when another has the ability to dispense rewards and punishments. The theory further specifies three broad classes of strategies that people may employ to reduce uncertainty: passive (e.g., simply observing another), active (i.e., taking action to learn about another without actually talking to him or her), and interactive (i.e., communicating with the target person). In later treatments of URT (e.g., Berger 1997), various linguistic devices for dealing with conditions of uncertainty are also specified.

As should be apparent from our exposition of the ELM, TPB, and URT, the focus of social cognitive theories of this sort is on explicating various mental processes, and issues of structure are accorded less (if any) consideration. In contrast, a second constellation of theories in the social cognition fuzzy set, more in the tradition of functionalism/HIP, incorporates both structure and process specifications. Three exemplars illustrate theorizing of this type; two we have selected because they represent the most common approach to structure-process social cognitive theorizing, and the third because it exemplifies other theoretical possibilities.

Communication theorists commonly acknowledge that people produce messages in pursuit of various goals (e.g., to persuade, to build relationships, etc.), but whence come those goals? (see also Chapter 14, Bangerter and Mayor). Wilson's (e.g., 1995) cognitive rules model was developed to address just this question. Wilson posits an associative network, like those mentioned above, where the nodes (or concepts) represent situational features, social roles, properties of interpersonal relationships, desired outcomes, and so on. Also as is typical for associative network models, the theory assumes a spreading activation process such that excitation of one node spreads to other associated nodes. The upshot is that encountering situational and relational conditions that correspond to those represented in a particular network serves to activate a representation of what to do in that situation. The greater the fit between one's current situation and the features represented in some particular structure, the more highly activated that structure will be. When activation exceeds some threshold level, a goal is thought to be triggered. And, finally, as is also common in associative network approaches, the cognitive rules model maintains that the associative links in a network vary in strength, where strength is a function of recency of activation. As a result, some goals may become chronically accessible as the structures in which they are embedded become increasingly stronger.

A second instantiation of associative network theorizing is found in attitude accessibility theory (see Roskos-Ewoldsen 1997). In this theory, concepts represented in memory are linked to various evaluative responses, as, for example, a person associating "Adolf Hitler" with "revulsion." When the associative link between a concept and evaluative response is sufficiently strong, reactions to presentations of that concept are fast and cognitively effortless. Moreover, borrowing from the ELM discussed above, more accessible attitudes are posited to lead to central-route processing and greater attitude – behavior consistency.

Our third example, Berger's (e.g., 1997) work on message planning, illustrates a very different approach to structure-process social cognitive theorizing. Plans are typically thought to consist of a specification of some initial state, a desired end state, and a series of steps or sub-goals linking the two. Berger proposes that plans vary in complexity, where complexity reflects both the level of detail and the number of contingencies represented in the plan. He further specifies factors that will affect plan complexity (e.g., level of motivation to accomplish some goal; extensiveness of a person's knowledge relevant to pursuit of the goal) and behavioral consequences of enacting more and less complex plans. A second important set of ideas put forward by Berger concerns the nature of plan revisions made in response to thwarting. Beginning with the standard conception of plans as hierarchical structures where abstract conceptions at upper levels are specified at successively more concrete levels, he introduces the "hierarchy principle" which posits that, *ceteris paribus*, in the face of initial failure, people will first seek to modify low-level properties of their actions, and only with continued thwarting will they endeavor to alter higher level components of their plans.

2.4 Neuroscience

A fourth fuzzy set in the cognitive constellation involves theories cast at the level of neural structures and processes. In contrast to folk psychology and functionalism, then, the underpinning philosophical stance here is one or another version of materialism (see Churchland 1992). As is true of each of the other approaches we've examined here, the neuroscience fuzzy set is, itself, comprised of various subsets. At the rightmost edges of the set depicted in Fig. 1 are studies of brain function that bear on communication only insofar as they are concerned with deficits stemming from neural disorders and injury (e.g., autism, aphasia). More centrally, there is the sphere of "computational neuroscience," or, more generally, "cognitive neuroscience" (see Schwartz 1990) which, like functionalism/HIP is concerned with issues of information processing (e.g., pattern recognition, memory, etc.), but, in contrast to the latter, seeks to understand these phenomena at the level of brain rather than mind.

Among the projects of cognitive neuroscience that are of greatest relevance to communication theorists is the work on mirror neurons (see Gallese 2009). These are neurons that fire not only when a person performs some motor task, but also when he or she simply observes someone else performing that task. Such neurons may play a role in language acquisition (see Theoret and Pascual-Leone 2002), and empathy, rapport, and interpersonal bonding (see Cappella and Schreiber 2006). A second cluster in the cognitive neuroscience realm consists of studies of adrenal functioning, particularly cortisol, in response to stressful social situations and events (see Dickerson and Kemeny 2004). Yet another emerging research nexus involves examination of brain metabolism in response to message inputs via recourse to functional magnetic resonance imaging (fMRI). Examples of studies of this sort include investigations of responses to mass media content (see Anderson and Murray 2006) and processing facial expressions of emotion (see Phelps 2006). One final fuzzy subset of note here is that of "social neuroscience" (see Cacioppo 2002), where early studies have indicated that social mentation (e.g., deliberating about the actions or motives of others) is associated with patterns of brain activity that are distinct from those associated with other types of thought.

3 Unfinished business

The discussion to this point should make clear that the realm of "cognitive theories of communication" is both extensive and diverse, and this has necessitated that we paint in very broad strokes in attempting to address the topic in a conceptually coherent and meaningful way. Moreover, from all the possible theories we might have chosen to examine, we have been selective in choosing as our exemplars those that are especially illustrative of some point of emphasis or that have been particularly influential in shaping understandings of communication processes. But in so doing we have omitted examination of several important traditions of research and theory, and any chapter purporting to survey the domain ought at least to apprise the reader of what did not find its way into our treatment (and point him or her to some resource for further research). Space permitting, then, the map depicted in Fig. 1 could be augmented with additional fuzzy sets, subsets, and exemplars, including the following: communication-skill acquisition (see Greene 2003), discourse processing (Kintsch 1992), cognitive development and language acquisition (see Clark 2003), decision-making and problem-solving (see Holyoak and Morrison 2005), affect and emotion (see de Houwer and Hermans 2010), and self-concept, self-presentation, and self-regulation (see Baumeister 1998).

Each of these topics, and others we might have as easily included, is a focus of longstanding traditions of research and theorizing. Let us conclude, though, by examining some other perspectives and approaches that have not, to date, had the same degree of impact in theorizing about communication, but that might assume greater prominence in the future.

3.1 Embodied cognition

As described above, HIP and social cognitive approaches to theorizing about communication have traditionally reflected a functionalist foundation in that they eschew physical terms in favor of accounts cast at the level of mind. And, as we've seen, grounded in materialism, neuroscience focuses primarily on brain structures and processes. Embodied cognition extends the materialist project beyond the brain in that bodily states, including sensory systems and muscle movements and configurations, are seen to impact perception, memory, and other aspects of information processing (see Prinz 2002). Thus, studies show, for example, that inducing subjects to nod their heads up and down facilitates positive thoughts and impedes the converse (Wells and Petty 1980), and that people find cartoons funnier when they hold a pencil horizontally in their lips, approximating the muscle configuration of a smile (Strack et al. 1988). Scholars in the field of communication proper have not made extensive inroads in applying the concepts of embodied cognition in their theorizing to this point, but researchers in cognate disciplines have made growing use of this framework in exploring phenomena like persuasive message processing (see Bohner and Dickel 2011) and emotion (see Barrett 2006) that are of central concern to people in the field.

3.2 Conjoint mentation

We noted in the introduction to this chapter that cognitivism has remained among the most influential approaches to theorizing about communication processes for the last 30 years. That said, cognitivism has not been without its critics. Among the earliest (and most often echoed) critiques is that cognitive theorizing is too individualistic – that in focusing on conceptions of individual information processors, cognitivism distorts what are fundamentally social processes (see: Harre 1981; Sampson 1981). As one of your authors has noted elsewhere (Greene and Herbers 2011), arguments on either side of this issue highlight a tension between thinking of people as "cognizers" or "communicators" – as the site of input, memory, and output systems, or as social actors inextricably linked to others. It is certainly true that, historically, cognitive science has given emphasis to analysis of individual information processing, but it need not necessarily be so. Here and there we find attempts to theorize the "cognitive communicator" – to address the socially embedded, interactive nature of thought.

As our final exemplar, then, we would point to Greene and Herbers's (2011) theory of "interpersonal transcendence." In their view, transcendence is a state of maximal interpersonal engagement, characterized by experiences of mutuality, joint discovery, and play. Interactions of this sort are memorable, exhilarating, and seemingly, rare. The thrust of the theory is to explicate the cognitive mechanisms by which one's actions spur the thoughts and actions of his or her interlocutor. Drawing on the action assembly theory (AAT2) discussed in Section 2.1, the theory of interpersonal transcendence locates the foundations of conjoint mentation in properties of activation of long-term memory structures, the assembly of activated information, and the nature of executive processes that keep self-focused ideations at bay.

4 Conclusion

A key component of our attempt to trace the contours of the constellation of "cognitive theories of communication" is the identification of the three underlying meta-theoretical perspectives depicted in Fig. 1. Thus, theorizing about the cognitive bases of message processing and production can be seen to be grounded in the everyday terms and concepts afforded by folk psychology, formulations cast in functional terms, or by recourse to neurophysiological states and processes. At the same time, we have tried to emphasize that the lines between these various stances are blurred, and that, in the realm of science and theory (rather than meta-theory), each blends into the others.

As a final note we would point to a fourth conceptual perspective relevant to the issues at hand. Generative realism (see Greene 1994) is a meta-theoretical framework developed within the broader commitments of transcendental realist conceptions of scientific theory which hold that behavioral phenomena are the result of the complex interplay of various causal mechanisms and that the essential project of science is to describe those mechanisms (see Bhaskar 1978; Manicas and

Secord 1983). A central claim of generative realism, then, is that people are not social beings, nor psychological beings, or even physiological beings. Rather, it is more appropriate to conceive of persons as, simultaneously, all three, and the task of theories of human behavior is to explicate the mechanisms by which the social, psychological, and physiological interact. But, obviously, the project of generative realism would blur even more the distinctions that we have tried to sketch here, and future writers attempting to survey the realm of cognitive theories of communication and impose some meaningful conceptual organization on that body of work may find that task even more complex and daunting than have we.

Further reading

Berger, Charles R. & Nicholas A. Palomares. 2011. Knowledge structures and social interaction. In: Mark L. Knapp and John A. Daly (eds.), *The SAGE Handbook of Interpersonal Communication*, 4th edn, 169–200. Thousand Oaks, CA: Sage.
Greene, John O. 2008. Information processing. In: Wolfgang Donsbach (ed.), *The International Encyclopedia of Communication, Volume 5*, 2238–2249. Malden, MA: Blackwell.
Greene, John O. & Melanie Morgan. 2009. Cognition and information processing. In: William F. Eadie (ed.), *21st Century Communication: A Reference Handbook, Volume 1*, 110–118. Thousand Oaks, CA: Sage.
Roskos-Ewoldsen, David R. & Jennifer L. Monahan (eds.). 2007. *Communication and Social Cognition: Theories and Methods*. Mahwah, NJ: Erlbaum.
Wilson, Steven R., John O. Greene & James Price Dillard (eds.). 2000. Special issue: Message production: Progress, challenges, and prospects. *Communication Theory* 10 (2).

References

Ajzen, Icek. 1991. The theory of planned behavior. *Organizational Behavior and Human Decision Processes* 50. 179–211.
Anderson, Daniel R. & John P. Murray (eds). 2006. Special issue: fMRI in media psychology research. *Media Psychology* 8 (1).
Anderson, John R. 1976. *Language, Memory, and Thought*. Hillsdale, NJ: Erlbaum.
Barrett, Lisa F. 2006. Solving the emotion paradox: Categorization and the experience of emotion. *Personality and Social Psychology Review* 10. 20–46.
Baumeister, Roy F. 1998. The self. In: Daniel T. Gilbert, Susan T. Fiske, and Gardner Lindzey (eds.), *The Handbook of Social Psychology Volume 1*, 4th edn, 680–740. Boston: McGraw-Hill.
Berger, Charles R. 1997. *Planning Strategic Interaction: Attaining Goals Through Communicative Action*. Mahwah, NJ: Erlbaum.
Berger, Charles R. 2005. Interpersonal communication: Theoretical perspectives, future prospects. *Journal of Communication* 55. 415–447.
Berger, Charles R. & James J. Bradac. 1982. *Language and Social Knowledge: Uncertainty in Interpersonal Relationships*. London: Edward Arnold.
Bhaskar, Roy. 1978. *A Realist Theory of Science*. Atlantic Highlands, NJ: Humanities Press.

Bohner, Gerd & Nina Dickel. 2011. Attitudes and attitude change. *Annual Review of Psychology* 62. 391–417.

Cacioppo, John T. 2002. Social neuroscience: Understanding the pieces fosters understanding the whole and vice versa. *American Psychologist* 57. 1019–1028.

Cappella, Joseph N. & Darren M. Schreiber. 2006. The interaction management function of nonverbal cues: Theory and research about mutual behavioral influence in face-to-face settings. In: Valerie Manusov and Miles L. Patterson (eds.), *The SAGE Handbook of Nonverbal Communication*, 361–379. Thousand Oaks, CA: Sage.

Carey, James. 1996. The Chicago School and mass communication research. In: Everette E. Dennis and Ellen Wartella (eds.), *American Communication Research: The Remembered History*, 21–38. Mahwah, NJ: Erlbaum.

Churchland, Paul M. 1992. *Matter and Consciousness*, rev. edn. Cambridge, MA: Bradford.

Clark, Eve V. 2003. *First Language Acquisition*. Cambridge, UK: Cambridge University Press.

Craig, Robert T. 1978. Information systems theory and research: An overview of individual information processing. In: Daniel T. Nimmo (ed.), *Communication Yearbook III*, 99–121. New Brunswick, NJ: Transaction-ICA.

Craig, Robert T. 1999. Communication theory as a field. *Communication Theory 9*. 119–161.

de Houwer, Jan & Dirk Hermans (eds.). 2010. *Cognition and Emotion: Reviews of Current Research and Theories*. Hove, UK: Psychology Press.

Delia, Jesse G. 1987. Communication research: A history. In: Charles R. Berger and Steven H. Chaffee (eds.), *Handbook of Communication Science*, 20–98. Newbury Park, CA: Sage.

Dickerson, Sally S. & Margaret E. Kemeny. 2004. Acute stressors and cortisol responses: A theoretical integration and synthesis of laboratory research. *Psychological Bulletin* 130. 355–391.

Dillard, James Price. 2008. Goals-plans-action theory of message production. In: Leslie A. Baxter and Dawn O. Braithwaite (eds.), *Engaging Theories in Interpersonal Communication: Multiple Perspectives*, 65–76. Los Angeles: Sage.

Fishbein, Martin & Icek Ajzen. 1975. *Belief, Attitude, Intention, and Behavior: An Introduction to Theory and Research*. Reading, MA: Addison-Wesley.

Fiske, Susan T. & Shelley E. Taylor. 1991. *Social Cognition*, 2nd edn. New York: McGraw-Hill.

Flanagan, Owen J., Jr. 1991. *The science of the mind*, 2nd edn. Cambridge, MA: MIT Press.

Frederiksen, Carl H. 1975. Representing logical and semantic structure of knowledge acquired from discourse. *Cognitive Psychology 7*. 371–458.

Gallese, Vittorio. 2009. Mirror neurons. In: Tim Baynes, Axel Cleeremans, and Patrick Wilken (eds.), *The Oxford Companion to Consciousness*, 445–446. Oxford, UK: Oxford University Press.

Gardner, Howard. 1985. *The Mind's New Science: A History of the Cognitive Revolution*. New York: Basic Books.

Greene, John O. 1988. Cognitive processes: Methods for probing the black box. In: Charles H. Tardy (ed.), *Methods and Instruments of Communication Research: A Handbook for the Study of Human Interaction*, 37–66. Norwood, NJ: Ablex.

Greene, John O. 1994. What sort of terms ought theories of human action incorporate? *Communication Studies* 45. 187–211.

Greene, John O. 1997. A second generation action assembly theory. In: John O. Greene (ed.), *Message Production: Advances in Communication Theory*, 151–170. Mahwah, NJ: Erlbaum.

Greene, John O. 2003. Models of adult communication skill acquisition: Practice and the course of performance improvement. In: John O. Greene and Brant R. Burleson (eds.), *Handbook of Communication and Social Interaction Skills*, 51–91. Mahwah, NJ: Erlbaum.

Greene, John O. 2008. Information processing. In: Wolfgang Donsbach (ed.), *The International Encyclopedia of Communication, Volume 5*, 2238–2249. Malden, MA: Blackwell.

Greene, John O. & Lauren E. Herbers. 2011. Conditions of interpersonal transcendence. *International Journal of Listening* 25. 66–84.

Hamilton, Mark A. 2007. Motivation, social context, and cognitive processing as evolving concepts in persuasion theory. In: David R. Roskos-Ewoldsen and Jennifer L. Monahan (eds.), *Communication and Social Cognition: Theories and Methods*, 417–447. Mahwah, NJ: Erlbaum.

Hamilton, Mark A. & Kristine L. Nowak. 2005. Information systems concepts across two decades: An empirical analysis of trends in theory, methods, process, and research domain. *Journal of Communication* 55. 529–553.

Harre, Rom. 1981. Rituals, rhetoric, and social cognition. In: Joseph E. Forgas (ed.), *Social Cognition: Perspectives on Everyday Understanding*, 211–224. London: Academic Press.

Herrmann, Theo. 1983. *Speech and Situation: A Psychological Conception of Situated Speaking*. Berlin: Springer-Verlag.

Holyoak, Keith J. & Robert G. Morrison (eds.). 2005. *The Cambridge Handbook of Thinking and Reasoning*. Cambridge, UK: Cambridge University Press.

Jones, Edward E. 1998. Major developments in five decades of social psychology. In: Daniel T. Gilbert, Susan T. Fiske, and Gardner Lindzey (eds.), *The Handbook of Social Psychology, Volume 1*, 4th edn, 3–57. Boston: McGraw-Hill.

Kintsch, Walter. 1992. A cognitive architecture for comprehension. In: Herbert L. Pick, Paul van den Broek and David C. Knill (eds.), *The study of cognition: Conceptual and methodological issues*, 143–164. Washington, DC: American Psychological Association.

Knapp, Mark L. & John A. Daly. 2011. Background and current trends in the study of interpersonal communication. In: Mark L. Knapp and John A. Daly (eds.), *The Sage Handbook of Interpersonal Communication* 4th edn, 3–22. Los Angeles: Sage.

Manicas, Peter T. & Paul F. Secord. 1983. Implications for psychology of the new philosophy of science. *American Psychologist* 37. 399–413.

Miller, Gerald R. 1969. Human information processing: Some research guidelines. In: Robert J. Kibler and Larry L. Barker (eds.), *Conceptual Frontiers in Speech Communication*, 51–68. New York: Speech Communication Association.

Miller, Gerald R. 1976. The person as actor – Cognitive psychology on the attack. *Quarterly Journal of Speech* 62. 82–87.

Nussbaum, Jon F. & Gustav Friedrich. 2005. Instructional/developmental communication: Current theory, research, and future trends. *Journal of Communication* 55. 578–593.

O'Keefe, Barbara J. & Bruce L. Lambert. 1995. Managing the flow of ideas: A local management approach to message design. In: Brant R. Burleson (ed.), *Communication Yearbook 18*, 54–82. Thousand Oaks, CA: Sage.

Petty, Richard E. & Duane T. Wegener. 1998. Attitude change: Multiple roles for persuasion variables. In: Daniel T. Gilbert, Susan T. Fiske, and Gardner Lindzey (eds.), *The Handbook of Social Psychology, Volume 1*, 4th edn, 323–390. Boston: McGraw-Hill.

Phelps, Elizabeth A. 2006. Emotion and cognition: Insights from studies of the human amygdala. *Annual Review of Psychology* 57. 27–53.

Powers, John H. 1995. On the intellectual structure of the human communication discipline. *Communication Education* 44. 191–222.

Prinz, Jesse J. 2002. *Furnishing the Mind: Concepts and Their Perceptual Basis*. Cambridge, MA: MIT Press.

Roskos-Ewoldsen, David R. 1997. Attitude accessibility and persuasion: Review and a transactive model. In: Brant R. Burleson (ed.), *Communication Yearbook 20*. 185–225. Beverly Hills, CA: Sage.

Roskos-Ewoldsen, David R. & Jennifer L. (eds.) Monahan. 2007. *Communication and Social Cognition: Theories and Methods*. Mahwah, NJ: Erlbaum.

Sampson, Edward E. 1981. Cognitive psychology as ideology. *American Psychologist* 36. 730–743.

Schramm, Wilbur. 1997. *The Beginnings of Communication Study in America: A Personal Memoir* (Chaffee, Steven H. and Rogers, Everett M., eds.). Thousand Oaks, CA: Sage.

Schwartz, Eric L. (ed.). 1990. *Computational Neuroscience*. Cambridge, MA: MIT Press.

Strack, Fritz, Leonard L. Martin & Sabine Stepper. 1988. Inhibiting and facilitating conditions of the human smile: A nonobtrusive test of the facial feedback hypothesis. *Journal of Personality and Social Psychology* 54. 768–777.

Theoret, Hugo & Alvaro Pascual-Leone. 2002. Language acquisition: Do as you hear. *Current Biology* 12.

Wells, Gary L. & Richard E. Petty. 1980. The effects of overt head movement in persuasion: Compatibility and incompatibility of responses. *Basic and Applied Social Psychology* 1. 219–230. R736–R737.

Wilson, Steven R. 1995. Elaborating the cognitive rules model of interaction goals: The problem of accounting for individual differences in goal formation. In: Brant R. Burleson (ed.), *Communication Yearbook 18*, 3–25. Thousand Oaks, CA: Sage.

Jonathan T. Delafield-Butt and Colwyn Trevarthen

11 Theories of the development of human communication

Abstract: We consider evidence for innate motives for sharing rituals and symbols from animal semiotics, developmental neurobiology, physiology of prospective motor control, affective neuroscience and infant communication. Mastery of speech and language depends on polyrhythmic movements in narrative activities of many forms. Infants display intentional activity with feeling and sensitivity for the contingent reactions of other persons. Talk shares many of its generative powers with music and the other 'imitative arts.' Its special adaptations concern the capacity to produce and learn an endless range of sounds to label discrete learned understandings, topics and projects of intended movement.

Keywords: Motives, emotions, creativity, infant development, intersubjectivity, cooperative awareness, narrative, ritual, meaning, musicality

1 Introduction: creating a human self: from intercellular cooperation to the shared imagination of culture

1.1 Making persistent individuals

This paper describes *anticipatory adaptations* of body and brain that create learning of communication, particularly the learning of language. Inborn endowments for expressive movement enable human infants to share intentions, experiences and emotional evaluations, including esthetic and long before they speak, moral feelings about 'self-with-other' experiences. Expressive actions of young children motivate shared experience in conversation and eager cooperation in imaginative projects. These actions will mediate in the transmission of artificial practices, beliefs and techniques between individuals throughout life, and build knowledge and skills between generations.

We seek to give a more natural scientific foundation to abstract speculations in psychology and linguistics about how a child is led to learn words and to understand what they mean – not only what purposes and facts spoken words specify, but also how they 'feel' in live transmission. Prevailing theories of innate cognitive programs for discrimination and generation of the semantic and syntactical functions of text ignore the motivating and affective roots. They do not adequately reflect either the knowledge we have about vocal and postural communication in animals, or the development of unique vocal and gestural communication skills in human beings before they are able to speak. They disregard the capacity these expressive ways of moving have for cultivation into symbolic representations of projects, imaginative ideas and acquired knowledge (Merker 2009a; Trevarthen et al. 2011). They neglect the functional social space of meaning (Halliday and Matthiessen 2004) and the poetic/emotional 'languages within language' (Fónagy 2001), which guide the mastery of communication in early childhood (Bråten 1998, 2009). They regard emotional expression as a manifestation of stresses in regulation of the body and of information processing, not as integral with the causal motivators of adaptive action and experience (cf. Panksepp 1998, 2003; Panksepp and Trevarthen 2009; Trevarthen 2009).

We examine how the organic or biological and psychological foundations of ideas carried in language emerge before birth in the body-with-brain and its feeling-full activities. We look for the antecedent developmental states and tendencies, from conception through gestation, to trace how the first movements and their intentions and affections become shared as imaginative narrative projects and enriched with consciousness of valued meaning (Bruner 1990; Trevarthen and Delafield-Butt 2011). First, however, we are concerned with the nature of self-regulating systems in general, and how developing life forms, as *agents*, demonstrate general evolutionary principles of *creativity* and *cooperation*.

1.2 Self-generated activity, context, and cooperative adaptation in natural phenomena

Scientific description and measurement reveals that any enduring substance or system requires *cooperation*, both between its elements, and with its environment. Adaptive, self-organizing connectedness and rhythmic harmonies of process and form give rise to a unique organization in living organisms (Whitehead 1929; Prigogine and Stengers 1984). The self-sustaining dynamic relationships between its elements, their mutual active values, are also *creative*. They determine the development or 'ontogeny' of that kind of being – how it will interact with different conditions to sustain its individual being. Anticipatory adaptations cope with probable change in circumstances – as Whitehead says, even inorganic 'organisms' "create their own environment" (Whitehead 1929: 138).

A living organism sustains its creative form of organization by processes of growth and activity, challenging its relationship with the environment. From this we infer that the *function of intelligence* in the regulation of the vitality of an animal, including its communication of purposes, feelings, and understandings to other individuals in a shared world for cooperative goals, is to create and propagate its ways of moving to use its accessible world in self-sustaining ways. Regulation of vitality and agency of the body is the adaptive function of the animal's nervous system, in all its parts, and as a whole sensory-motor Self (Sherrington 1906; Merker 2005; Packard 2006; Northoff and Panksepp 2008).

1.3 Ontogenesis of intelligent life forms and their societies

Living organisms grow and survive in epigenetically regulated relations with their surroundings, changing expression of their genes in creative response to circumstances, reproducing bodies and life histories that both 'expect' and 'depend on' environmental opportunities for their vitality (Bateson 1894; Whitehead 1929; Bateson 1980). The molecular ecology within and between living cells can only thrive if the systems and organs of the life form they are within also thrive, function and develop as they are adapted to do. The dynamic neural regulations in an animal organism have inner and outer aspects of 'self-related processing' (Northoff and Panksepp 2008), and a child thrives only if it inspires the human world with a love generated by a powerful desire to meet the child's needs for survival and development (Narváez et al. 2011). There is an inborn collaboration between a supportive ecology *inside* each animal, the 'milieu interne' of Claude Bernard (1865), and an arousal of instincts for behavioral engagements with media and agents *outside* the body. These together, the self-maintenance of vital states and the action in the world, provide the essential adaptive structure for psychobiological development and the success of animals and humans and of their societies. Human societies depend on the impulses of young children to find parental companions, and to inspire affection and playful desires for sharing experiences and making them meaningful. The natural motives in child and parent are complementary 'co-adaptations' for the life of human society (Bateson 1979; Narváez et al. 2011).

In the development of this human child the principle of creative and cooperative vitality is repeated over all the scales of organization of the units of vitality, from beginnings in the fertilized egg, through the tissues and organs of embryo, fetus, and developing child, to participation in the social organization of a culture, drawing on accumulated knowledge and skills (Trevarthen et al. 2006).

1.4 Consciousness is the prospective control of agency, generated for coordination and regulation of movement

Animals as embodied and motivated *agents* are coherent and self-regulated. Their bodies are prepared to move with *prospective control* in an awareness of space and time that is created for integrated guidance of their limbs and senses (von Hofsten 1993; von Hofsten 2004; Lee 2005). They act intelligently, with *affective evaluation* of what they are doing in the immediate present, what they may do in the more distant future, and what they remember having done in the past. This 'life world' in action (von Uexküll 1957) can be elaborated by learning, but it cannot be created by learning – it learns in order to grow. Humans exhibit exceptionally rich 'auto-noesis' or the making of a 'personal life history' (Tulving 2002), as well as cultural 'socionoesis' or the making of a 'habitus' of meaning by 'story-telling' (Bruner 1990, 2003; Trevarthen 2011a).

The brain is formed to be the generator of an intentional and feeling-full consciousness in an individual. Its spontaneous activity 'knows' ahead in time what any of its movement will do or lead to, 'expects' the effects of stimuli in a 'body-centered world,' and can 'project' or 'associate' its experience of vital physiological arousal and need onto items of experience to give situations and objects affecting qualities or feelings (Sherrington 1906; Lashley 1951; Sperry 1952; von Holst and von St. Paul 1960; Gibson 1966; Bernstein 1967; Damásio 2010). The evidence from embryogenesis confirms that the integrative neural mechanism is mapped early in development to excite prospective movement in integrated command of the form and functions of the body, with its environment-directed effectors and receptors and internal felt needs. In this *behavior field*, different innate adaptive *modes of activity and awareness* (Trevarthen 1986a), different 'arousals' of awareness with feeling (Pfaff 2006; Stern 2010), guide complementary functions between perceptions – of objects and agents in the environment, of body movement, and of internal vital physiological need – to give 'self-related processing' (Sherrington 1906; Northoff and Panksepp 2008; Panksepp and Northoff 2009).

The actions of the animal sustain physiological wellbeing by guiding locomotion through the media of the surrounding world with selective attention to local objects identified for their life-giving potencies as *good* (i.e., to be sought for and taken up), *bad* (i.e., dangerous, to be avoided) or *neutral* (i.e., safe to ignore). These embodied principles of evaluation can be transmitted as signals to other individuals if they are endowed with the same sensory capacities enabling a sympathetic 'mirroring' of rhythmic patterns of body movement and inner regulatory dynamics (von Uexküll 1957; Trevarthen 1986b; Bråten 2009).

A child's movements powerfully communicate to other human beings the inborn regulatory process of the human mind and their acquired modifications (Aitken and Trevarthen 1997; Bråten and Trevarthen 2007; Panksepp and Trevarthen 2009). They display the 'motor images' which assist the planning of their efficient mastery of the mechanics of a heavy moving body with complex limbs (Bernstein 1967), the spontaneous 'serial ordering' of their movements in body-related space and time (Lashley 1951) and the 'prospective control' of the reach and force of their individual actions in this space-time field (Lee 2005, 2009). When we move with grace and purpose we assimilate sensory input to guide output of our nervous system by a process that aims to control the future experience of our behavior. This process becomes communicative by transfer of action-related information between intra- and inter-subjective realms (Trevarthen 1986b; Gallese

2001; Sinigaglia and Rizzolatti 2011; Trevarthen et al. 2011). Learned complexes of gesture become habits of individual action and of cooperation in shared, cultural experience, including the imitative arts of music, theatre, and dance, which, with poetry and song, bring the referential communication of language back to its interpersonal and self-sensing foundations (Fónagy 2001; Malloch and Trevarthen 2009).

1.5 Communication in the making of animal society, human culture, and language

The principles of animal semiosis, or social signalling, elucidated by Jacob von Uexküll (von Uexküll, 1926) were developed by Sebeok (1977: 1994) as a science of 'semiotics.' They affirm an evolutionary theory of human symbolic communication and the social foundations of language (Halliday 1978; Rommetveit 1998), and they elucidate how the special human aptitudes for invention of art and technology grow from the creative and cooperative abilities of expression and response which infants show (Stern et al. 1985; Trevarthen and Logotheti 1987; Trevarthen 1990; Reddy 2008; Stern 2010). Human beings transform their environment by projects and structures they invent: "The tool kit of any culture can be described as a set of prosthetic devices by which human beings can exceed or even redefine the 'natural limits' of human functioning" (Bruner 1990). Infants and children are ready for this cultural creativity (Trevarthen 2011a). They share an imaginative and highly emotional life in intimate and playful attachments with parents, peers, and neighbours. Language amplifies and extends the intrinsic impulses and feelings for co-operative functioning, and becomes an historically elaborated descriptive and informative 'tool' for making shared projects more effective by describing flexible inventive forms of social coordination, perspective-taking and joint action (Tylén et al. 2010).

Cooperative rituals of art and technique support group mastery of the environment by expanding shared imagination as a history (Turner 1982; Turner and Bruner 1986; Donald 2001). The building of cultural knowledge is aided by carrying messages through many generations in symbolic activities, products, and language, transforming intelligence about the uses and qualities of the world and how individuals perceive one another and share purposes and feelings (Darwin 1872; Vygotsky 1978; Bruner 1990; Bråten 1998, 2009). Speech and language depend on new motor skills and a special human enthusiasm for elaborate ritual and vocal learning (Merker 2009a, b, 2012; MacNeilage 2008; MacNeilage 2011), and on emotional communication in the 'musicality' of gesture and vocalization (Bloom 2002; Lüdtke 2011). In art, technology and language, these adaptations expand the capacity for communication of experiences and inventions through different 'loci of concern,' from the immediate present realm of space and time, to future events, to remembered pasts, and to imagined, mythical or theoretical times and places (Donaldson 1992).

2 Cooperative vitality in the creation and nurture of a human communicative self before birth: The first 60 days: cells cooperate to build tissues and organs of an embryo human being

A human life begins with the creative act of two individuals coming together in intimacy, disengaged from practical concerns, with eagerness for life and joy in the risk of shared bodies, in impulsive activity that sends the sperms of the male toward the ova inside the female. Their hormonal mechanisms and physiological arousal systems are powerfully engaged (Pfaff 2006). The fertilized human egg joins with a mother's body that is adapted to protect and aid the formations of the body and brain of a new form of primate. The creation of a new human life shows cooperation at all the levels of biological organization (Trevarthen et al. 2006).

Cells produced by division of the fertilized egg regulate their gene activity by reciprocal, cooperative systems that govern how their populations will divide, migrate, and differentiate (Waddington 1940). 'Sense data' appropriated between neighbouring cells through diffusible bio-molecules, surface-surface contact, and mechanical tensions activate patterns of genes, which determine how cells will aggregate to form tissues and organs with different functions (Edelman 1988). The polarized body is formed with sensitive head end and active posterior, and nervous and humoral regulations of a variety of arousals for world-related action and preservation of internal vitality, and their timing (Trevarthen et al. 2006). The central nervous system is integrated as the coordinator of a being that, though still immobile and insensitive, is formed for the joys and fears of a future mobile life in intelligent engagement with the environment (Beddington and Robertson 1999).

Collaboration between the germ layers of the embryo begins early in embryogenesis, as each tissue "needs the help of its sister travellers..." (Pander 1817). The endoderm forms the digestive tract that appropriates and digests food; the mesoderm becomes the visceral organs, muscles, and bone that make up the bulk of the body with its transformative and life-sustaining functions; and the ectoderm forms both the skin and all of the nervous tissue of the sense organs, brain, and peripheral nervous system with its sensory and motor components, somatic and visceral (Hamilton et al. 1962). Both brain and skin are adapted for selective engagement with the outside world and for protecting and regulating the energy balance of vitality inside.

3 The fetus develops organs for life in an imaginative cultural world

3.1 Growth of centrencephalic systems for intentions, emotions and conscious agency

According to the 'centrencephalic' theory of consciousness, first presented by Penfield and Jasper (1954), the midbrain, though *anatomically sub-cortical,* is *functionally supra-cortical.* The sub-cortical upper brain stem and midbrain territories between the hypothalamus and superior colliculi are responsible for emotionally charged states of our core, embodied 'anoetic' conscious agency (Vandekerckhove and Panksepp 2011), which serve basic generation of action, orientations to experience and emotional appraisals. These primary mental functions ontogenetically and functionally precede cortically-mediated cognitive ones. Cognition may enhance and assist with additional 'tools' for use by this core control system and its expansion in learning adaptation to external realities, but the primary motives and evaluations remain sub-cortically-mediated. Expression of this core consciousness makes intersubjective engagements of action and awareness possible (Watt 2004).

The centrencephalic theory is confirmed by studies of the growth of intelligent activity and 'self-related processing' in the human embryo. The first integrative pathways of the brain are in the core of the brain stem and midbrain (Windle 1970), and the earliest whole body movements, though undifferentiated in their goals, are coherent and rhythmic in time (Lecanuet et al. 1995). When sensory input develops, there is evidence, not just of reflex *response* to stimuli, but of the *intrinsic generation of prospective control* of more individuated actions, before the neocortex is functional. In the third trimester of gestation, when the cerebral neocortex is beginning formation of functional networks, movements show guidance by touch, by taste and by responses to the sounds of the mother's voice, with learning.

After birth the infant's conscious activity soon exhibits what Sherrington (1906) called 'projicience' of sight and hearing to anticipate the location and properties of objects external to the body, and evaluation or 'affective appraisal' of those properties in relation to vital processes. The former are dependent on neocortex, but the latter are created in subcortical systems. A newborn infant has well-developed coordination of the body, expression of vital needs, and means for selective communication with the affectionate attentions of the mother and by engaging with her complementary adaptations for affectionate response to the infant's needs (Als 1995). The role of the cerebral cortex, in imaginative identification and memorizing of features of the environment and of objects, and for refined sensory control of complex movements of manipulation and articulation of vocalizations, is critical for adaptation of practical activities and for communication by language learned in the years after birth. But the prenatal development of subjective and intersubjective motives demonstrates that the 'intentional core' and 'seat of consciousness,' with emotional regulation of purposeful action and its communication, should not be identified with a learned 'executive' function of the cerebral cortices, as cognitive science proposes. Specifications for a body-centered neural field for perceptual guidance of whole-body action forms a scaffold for higher mental processes and more complex patterns of action, which are laid down in the fetal period by growth of additional structures of body and brain for sensory regulation of movements in an unstimulating, highly-controlled intrauterine environment (Trevarthen 1985). The first motor, sensory, and interneuronal connections in humans at 35 to 40 days form a basic nerve network in advance of any receptor excitation.

3.2 Fetal syntax: signs of self-generated feelings and imaginative intentions in the first and second trimesters of gestation

After two months gestation the developing child already has body parts adapted for forms of action, awareness, and communication characteristic of the human species (Hamilton et al. 1962; Trevarthen 1985). Organs of selective awareness and communicative expression – mobile head, eyes, face, and vocal system – are differentiated and approximate to their adult forms. The first spontaneous body movements occur at this time (de Vries et al. 1982; Prechtl 1986). Cycles and rhythmical or pulsating bursts of movement of the early fetus indicate autogenous, i.e. 'self-generated,' pacemaker systems that will animate perception of time and give tempo to later acts of communication (Wolff 1966; Osborne 2009; Trevarthen 2009).

After three months, information from eyes, ears, nose, and mouth is carried in an impulse code and mapped out in central nerve circuits specified to relate movements in one body-related behavior field (Trevarthen 1985). The precocious appearance of adaptively organized reaching and touching movements with postural control and accompanied by compensatory eye movements, indicates that the first organized efferent-afferent neural feedback loops, carrying signals from the brain to excite the peripheral motor effect and reflecting back sensations, are those representing a whole-Self-sensing system that controls the coordinated displacement of many body parts. Organized whole-body or body-part movements of the early fetus include 'bicycling' of the legs, turning the body in the womb, reaching to touch the placental and umbilical cord, and reaching to parts of the fetus's own body or a twin fetus (de Vries et al. 1982; Piontelli 1992, 2010). All confirm that the fetal motor actions are enacted with prospective, Self-sensing control.

It is particularly important in relation to conversational skills that fetal arm movements may be aimed so the hands can feel the face and head (Piontelli 2010). Studies of fetal behavior using real-time ultrasonography demonstrate exploratory sensation-testing movements from as early as ten weeks, when innervated areas –

lips, cheeks, ears, and parietal bone – are frequently touched by the hands, the fingers of which are themselves richly innervated with sensory fibers. These touches create autostimulatory feed-back; the action creates contact between the fingers and head, giving simultaneously a proprioceptive response, sensation of touch in the fingers, and sensation of touch in the innervated region. This action-generated loop may be considered as the precursor of intersubjective 'self-other' regulatory processes from which communication of mental states develops. Fetuses explore the boundary of the innervated and uninnervated regions at the anterior fontanel of the forehead, testing the differences in feed-back either side of the boundary (Piontelli 2010: 61–67).

Later in fetal development, other explorations of self and environment can be observed as the hands touch the eyes, the mouth, the uterine wall, and so on. And individual 'habits' appear, such as a propensity to fondle the umbilical cord, scratch at the placenta, or to make twin-directed movements (Piontelli 1992, 2002; Jakobovits 2009). Self-touching actions continue throughout life as restless gestural 'self adaptors' (Ekman and Friesen 1969), also very evident in animated face-to-face conversation (Kendon 1980). They express a dynamic sense of self that communicates changing states of mind.

At two months of gestation the cortex has no neural cells and thalamo-cortical projections are just starting to grow (Larroche 1981; Hevner 2000), but there is sufficient sensory and motor nervous connectivity for dynamic proprioceptive motor control (Okado 1980). At $3\frac{1}{2}$ months, quantified kinematic analyses indicate that fine movements of hands and fingers guided by sensitive touch, show a sequential patterning with modulation of arousal state that may give a grounding for 'narrative imagination,' and ultrasound recordings of twin fetuses at $4\frac{1}{2}$ months show regulations that distinguish movements of self-exploration from those directed to a twin, and this is taken to confirm a primary 'social awareness' (Castiello et al. 2010). Certainly, by $5\frac{1}{2}$ months the kinematic form of the arm movements of single fetuses confirms that 'imaginative' and 'self-aware' motor planning is operative (Zoia et al. 2007). This natural history of human movement appears to confirm the suggestion by Lashley (1951: 122) that propositional thought may depend on the spontaneous syntactic ordering of movements.

Movements are not only directed to engage with the external inanimate world or the body of the Self. Facial expressions in fetuses and movements of distress and curious exploration give evidence of emotions of discomfort or pleasure that may be adapted for communicating feelings. In the third trimester, separate movements of the facial muscles visualized by 4D ultrasound develop into complexes that define a 'cry face gestalt' or a 'laughter gestalt,' expressing emotions that will communicate powerfully after birth in the regulation of parental care (Reissland et al. 2011). Maternal hunger with depletion of energy supply to the fetus drives 'anxious' patterns of fetal movement. There is consensus in modern pediatrics that by 24 weeks the fetus should be considered a conscious agent deserving the same standard of medical care as adults (Royal College of Obstetricians and Gynaecologists 2010). The mid-term human fetus has the foundations for the space-time defining functions of intention in action, and for the emotional regulation of esthetic relations with the objective world and moral relations with other persons.

When considering the emergence of consciousness, it is important to note, however, that the special sense organs, having attained their basic function-specific form in the late embryo, are cut off from stimulation by morphological changes in the early fetal period (Hamilton et al. 1962; Trevarthen 1985). While a self-regulating mobility is clearly functioning, the organs that will explore the rich variety of experiences after birth have no function. The eyelids grow over the cornea to fuse at 7½ weeks. They reopen at six months. The ear ossicles develop within a spongy mesoderm that remains to block transmission until the last fetal months, when a cavity forms around the ossicles. The tympanic cavity remains obliterated by endodermal thickening and swelling and is excavated shortly after birth in association with changes that accompany the onset of pulmonary respiration. Auditory discrimination appears possible only in the last trimester. From the second to sixth gestational months the nostrils are closed by epithelial plugs.

At six months, the fetus awakens to a sensible world and the neurological and metabolic processes are sufficiently advanced for survival in an incubator, or with vital support from ventro-ventral contact with a parent's body in 'kangarooing.' The change to this level of competence is a sudden one, the six-month-old fetus having achieved a characteristic state of sensori-motor readiness, including the fundamental controls for seeing. During the eighth and ninth lunar months, the infant develops muscle tone from lower to upper limbs and assumes a comfortable rest posture, but mobility is less than at early stages of prematurity. This is when the developing child takes the first steps to cooperate purposefully with another human being in regulation of arousal and appraisal of experiences.

Neuroblast production to establish the neocortex is maximum at 20 weeks, mid-gestation (Trevarthen 2004). Sensory, motor and motivational representations in the cortex, and that will carry cognitive advancements, are mapped out, and its cells impregnated with affinities for connection with their complementary subcortical systems. It is important that the first developing regions – in the parietal, temporal and frontal cortices – are the same ones that will undergo massive elaboration throughout life. Just these are uniquely enlarged in *Homo sapiens sapiens*, compared to earlier evolved *Homo* (Bruner 2010). They are the tissues for cultural learning, and they include areas for language learning.

3.3. Fetal sensitivity: rapid brain and muscle development for cultural learning and preparation for engagement in the third trimester of gestation

Between 24 and 40 weeks gestation the human head grows more than the body as the delicately layered neocortical sheet expands. The positions and interconnections of its neurons depend not only upon input from the sensory relay nuclei of the thalamus, but especially from the motivation systems of the core Self already developed (Northoff and Panksepp 2008). Cortical dendrites proliferate with the support of abundant interneuronal glia cells. These multiply at an accelerating rate toward a climax two weeks after term, accompanying the proliferation of dendrites and the development of synaptic fields (Trevarthen 2004).

The cortex develops its characteristic folds in the final ten weeks before birth and the patterning of gyri shows differences between the hemispheres characteristic of humans, which reflect asymmetries in sub-cortical self-regulating systems, the right side of the brain being more self-related or proprioceptive and the left being more discriminatory of environmental affordances and eventually directed to learn adaptive articulations of the hands and of vocal activity (Trevarthen 1996). Importantly, areas later to be essential for perceiving and producing sounds of words are evident in the left hemisphere at 30 weeks. Complementary enlargements in the right hemisphere are adapted for both visual and auditory evaluations of other persons' expressions and identity.

The late fetus is in a quiescent state, but can be awakened and can learn. At seven months it shows cardiac accelerations and startles to sounds. While general body movements decrease, respiratory movements increase, as do face, tongue movements, smiling, eye movements, and hand gestures. All these are forms of action that will serve not only in self-regulation, but in expression of self-related states for intimate communication and for learning language. Fetuses interact with the mother's movements and uterine contractures and, after 25 weeks, can learn her voice, a process that engages the right cerebral hemisphere (DeCasper and Prescott 2009). There are also motor reactions to rhythmic sounds, such as the bass pulse of dance music, and melodies that the mother attends to frequently or performs on a musical instrument can be learned.

The last trimester is critical for elaboration of asymmetries of cerebral function adapted for cultural learning. First it will be necessary to form an intimate attachment with a caregiver, normally the mother, whose hormonal changes support special affectionate ways of acting that match the newborn's needs. The right hemisphere orbito-frontal system motivates affective communication with the musical prosody of infant-directed parental speech (Schore 2011), and the left orbito-frontal cortex has a complementary adaptation for generation of affective signals by the infant (Trevarthen 1996).

Beneath the cerebral cortex the brain generates fundamental rhythms for self-synchrony of movements of body parts and inter-synchrony in exchanges of signals of motives and emotions from other humans (Buzsáki 2006), including the faster components that become essential for the learning of manipulative skills and the rapidly articulated movements of language or gestural signing (Condon and Sander 1974; Trevarthen et al. 2011). Brain rhythms enable the fetus to move in coordination with the sounds of music and to learn certain melodies or musical narrations

(Malloch 1999; Gratier and Trevarthen 2008). They also favor a selective sensitivity to expressive features that identify the mother's voice, which is mediated by the right hemisphere (Panksepp and Trevarthen 2009; Turner and Ioannides 2009). Respiratory movements and amniotic breathing appear several weeks before birth, and heart rate changes have been coordinated with phases of motor activity from 24 weeks (James et al. 1995). This is indicative of the formation of a prospective control of autonomic state coupled to readiness for muscular activity on the environment, a feature of brain function, which Jeannerod (Jeannerod 1994) has cited as evidence for the formation of cerebral 'motor images' underlying conscious awareness and purposeful movement.

3.4 Proof of human impulses for self-expression and communication from the development of premature infants

Infants born four months before term can develop well if given ventro-ventral, skin-to skin contact in 'kangarooing,' which compensates for the loss of the intimate amphoteronomic support provided within the mother's body (Als 1995). Comparisons with traditional artificial intensive care confirm that kangaroo care benefits both infant and mother for intimacy of interaction and maternal feeding, reduces maternal distress, and leads to better development of communication through infancy (Tallandini and Scalembra 2006). A recording made of a prematurely born infant in intimate body contact of 'kangarooing' with the father's body demonstrates that vocal expression and exchange by simple 'coo' sounds is possible at 32 weeks, and the timing of the alternating sounds of infant and father matches that of normal syllables and phrases in fully articulate speech (Trevarthen 1999).

From the eighth month and through the first six weeks after full term birth, the neonate's mind is in a quiescent state, well-coordinated but mostly in a deep sleep, able to cooperate with support, comforting and breast feeding, but with limited curiosity for the new much richer environment.

4 The infant's initiative toward cultural learning and language

4.1 Infant intentional communication as groundwork for the interpersonal and practical functions of language

Immediately after birth, a healthy full-term infant may be attractively active, alert, and responsive – orienting to the mother's voice, showing interest and affection with well-directed movements of the whole body, of the eyes and face and of the gesturing hands. The baby may imitate expressions of head and eyes, face and mouth, voice or hands, and become involved in a dialogue with an attentive and affectionate parent, actively seeking a gently regulated imitative exchange with a responsive partner (Nagy and Molnar 2004; Nagy 2011). Accurate observations prove that the infant has innate prospective awareness and curiosity as a coherent self, and special intuitions for sharing activities and experiences. Human beings are born with both 'subjectivity' and 'intersubjectivity' (Trevarthen 1979, 1998; Nagy 2008). Demonstration of the capacity for active interest and communication has transformed neonatal care (Brazelton 1979). The increased activity in response to approach by a parent who offers eye-contact, gentle touching and the modulated vocalizations of motherese, the seeking of communication and imitative responses between them, confirm that the human brain is innately convivial and adapted for learning language (Papoušek 1994). Cyclic sequences of movement become orchestrated to make 'narratives' that express internal regulations of vitality with an innate time sense (Wittmann 2009).

Within a few weeks the 'protoconversational' behavior is more quickly regulated by improvements in visual and auditory awareness and, in interaction with the adult behaviors this development attracts, the infant can take a precisely regulated part in a rhythmic exchange of visible and audible signals of vitality and relational emotions. The capacity for this sustained communication has been called 'primary intersubjectivity' (Bateson 1979, Trevarthen 1979). By three months an intimate attachment with the mother is consolidated by increased playfulness with body movements and sounds, and games with the infant become attractive to the father and other family members as well. The play takes increasingly ritual forms in body games and song that attract interest and attuned response from the infant. A 'proto-habitus' of performances develops through the first semester, and the infant starts to adapt to the particular cultural forms of body expression and voice, learning to reproduce 'performances' for appreciation by others (Gratier 2003; Gratier and Trevarthen 2008). The baby becomes increasingly demonstrative, seductive and self-conscious as 'self-other' awareness grows (Reddy 2008). This is a development of an 'anoetic' emotional consciousness of self and of other persons that requires no rational or articulate 'theory of mind,' the later development of which is artificial and optional (Panksepp and Northoff 2009).

By seven months more vigorous and more rapid rhythmic movements begin – banging with the hands, but also syllabic babbling, which appears to be the innate repetitive motor function that made learning of speech possible, as Darwin proposed (Darwin 1872; MacNeilage 2008, 2011). The infant is also demonstrating a more intense awareness of the quality of response from a partner who seeks intimate communication, showing wary attention or distress and withdrawal if approached too directly by a stranger who 'does not know the game' (Trevarthen 2005; Reddy 2008). This manifestation of heightened temperament in sociability appears just before a striking change at nine months in the infant's willingness to share a task that requires shared actions on objects in cooperative work (Trevarthen and Hubley 1978; Hubley and Trevarthen 1979). In preceding weeks, eagerness to look for, grasp, and manipulate has been incorporated in person-person-object games with 'toys.' The infant's capacities to express shifting interests with movements of head, eyes and hands being recruited in intersubjectively created rituals of narration (Merker 2009b). This joint performance has clear foundations in the spontaneous indicative and narrating movements of pointing with eyes and hands evident from birth (Trevarthen et al. 2011).

Throughout early development, a matching hierarchical set of rhythms of movement facilitates coordination of motives and actions between infant and adult. Perturbation tests prove that the infant is sensitive to both the affective quality of a parent's expressions and to their contingent timing (Murray and Trevarthen 1985). The spontaneous movements of the infant demonstrate self-synchrony between body parts, and in communication infant and parent show precise intersynchrony (Condon and Sander 1974). Musical acoustic analysis of vocal exchanges in proto-conversations and singing play has demonstrated that the rhythmic and melodic patterns of music originate in an innate 'communicative musicality' that makes possible the close cooperation of human companionship (Merker 2009b). Difficulties due to abnormal development of motive processes in the infant, or to emotional disorder in the mother, are marked by loss of responsive musicality (Cooper and Murray 1998; Field 2010), and the principles of this fundamental patterning of human sound making by body movement are applied with benefit in therapy and teaching (Malloch and Trevarthen 2009). Musical forms of communication support language learning at later stages of life as well (Ludke 2009).

4.2 Proto-language as a social/emotional advance, animated by development of left hemisphere skills for discretization and serial ordering of learned vocal sounds and gestures of narration

Infants begin to combine learned vocalizations and gestures after the first birthday to make utterances that imitate simplified adult speech. A normally developing child soon names persons, objects, and actions, and responds to words, especially to their own name and the name of familiar persons and pets. By the end of the second year a rapid accumulation of a vocabulary begins and the child begins to use serial combinations of words. From this point one can study the development of true language (McNeill 1970; Locke 1993). Clearly it depends on the biological adaptations of the human body and brain for narrating the purposeful and emotionally valued experiences and achievements of life with other speaking human beings (Lenneberg 1967; Bruner 1983). It shows systematic distortion in developmental disorders such as autism, which offer additional evidence of an age related process governing the growth and differentiation of intersubjective awareness and shared agency (Trevarthen and Aitken 2003; Trevarthen et al. 2006; Saint-Georges et al. 2010). The linguist Michael Halliday (1975) developed a socio-linguistic theory sensitive to the expressiveness of nonverbal vocalizations and gestures to chart the progress of his son to fluent use of words through the first two years. He identified these developmental phases:

Birth to 9 months, 'protoconversation,' changing to 'conversation'
- 10 to 15 months, 'proto-language,' changing to 'language'
- 15 to 20 months, 'proto-narrative and dialogue' changing to 'narrative and dialogue,'
- and, after 20 months, 'proto-discourse.'

Similar transitions in representations leading to language, with varied interpretations, usually led by cognitive or linguistic theory, have been charted by Bates (1979) and Nelson (1996). Bruner (1990) and Rogoff (2003), who are interested in the interpersonal context of story-making and the learning of meaning, note that the purposes and procedures in narrating with young children may vary greatly across cultures. Gestures add metaphorical richness to conversational speech at all ages (Goldin-Meadow and McNeill 1999) constituting a component of all languages, complementary to speech (McNeill 2005). A deaf baby may substitute learning of contrived hand movements for spoken words, mastering hand sign language through comparable ages (Volterra 1981; Petitto and Marentette 1991). Donaldson (1992) gives an account of the growth of modes of narrative and explanation by expansion of the imagination and purposefulness or 'locus of concern' in late infancy and pre-school years, which development is reflected in the utterances of children before they develop what she calls the 'construct mode' of mind around three or four years. Hobson (2002) describes in similar terms how the foundations of thought are built in the affective communications of infancy, and Lüdtke (2011) reviews the evidence that relational emotions play a key role at all stages of semiotic and linguistic development and in language learning and language therapy.

The change from intuitive sharing of actions and feelings in intimate affectionate attachment to family and friends to mastery of the skills of a culture and its speaking is animated by growth of the brain with development of regulation of intentions and awareness in the left cerebral cortex. For several years the creative and cooperative imagination of the child, which was apparent at birth, remains the primary motivator for cultural learning, before formal teaching in the tools of culture and its social institutions can be accepted and effective (Halliday and Matthiessen 2004; Bateman et al. 2010; Trevarthen 2011b). At no point is development of mastery of language independent of the emotional regulation of human initiative and its sharing. Natural language is an artful tool for extending the innate motives for cooperative awareness and cultural learning, not just an abstract technical system of symbols for artificial representation and logical explanation (Reid 1764).

5 Conclusion

To understand how language can share intentions, experiences, and feelings, and how it must be represented widely in the brain, we recognize that the sense of words is transmitted to a child initially by rhythmically patterned movement of the whole body, and is taken up by perceptive response to other persons' self-related feelings for their experiences and prospects of action. Language is a function of intersubjective resonance of conscious embodied agency and esthetic and moral emotions. All these requirements have manifestations in a newborn infant, and they can be traced back to species-specific organic and psychological capacities emerging in the human embryo and fetus. We are made for sympathetic cooperative creativity, and we learn words to define its purposes.

A new research field of research focusing on the actions of emotional, embodied communication and their development is challenging developmental psychologists, psychiatrists, cognitive neuroscientists, sociologists, anthropologists, and philosophers, as well as language scientists, to combine their knowledge and methods to discover, in detail, how gesture and voice become discretized as syllables, words, and phrases, and how they are serially ordered to make meaningful propositional narrations. We will need to study more closely how movements are made and sensed in affective company for joint meaning-making, and to follow them through all the stages by which language is prepared for, mastered and elaborated. This work promises a new understanding of how language evolved, taking into account its rich embodied origins in the feeling and sharing of states of mind in rhythmic musicality of agency in the human brain and body.

Further reading

Bråten, Stein. 2009. *The Intersubjective Mirror in Infant Learning and Evolution of Speech*. Amsterdam/Philadelphia: John Benjamins.

Bruner, Jerome S. 1990. *Acts of Meaning*. Cambridge, MA: Harvard University Press.

Malloch, Stephen & Colwyn Trevarthen (eds.). 2009. *Communicative Musicality: Exploring the Basis of Human Companionship*. Oxford: Oxford University Press.

Reddy, Vasudevi. 2008. *How Infants Know Minds*. Cambridge, MA: Harvard University Press.

Stern, Daniel N. 2010. *Forms of Vitality: Exploring Dynamic Experience in Psychology, the Arts, Psychotherapy and Development*. Oxford: Oxford University Press.

References

Aitken, Kenneth J. & Colwyn Trevarthen. 1997. Self-Other Organization in Human Psychological Development. *Development and Psychopathology* 9. 651–675.

Als, Heidelise. 1995. The Preterm Infant: A Model for the Study of Fetal Brain Expectation. In: J.-P. Lecanuet, W. P. Fifer, N. A. Krasnegor and W. P. Smotherman (eds.), *Fetal Development: A Psychobiological Perspective*, 439–471. Hillsdale, NJ: Erlbaum.

Bateman, John A., Joana Hois, Robert Ross & Thora Tenbrink. 2010. A Linguistic Ontology of Space for Natural Language Processing. *Artificial Intelligence* 174 (14). 1027–1071.

Bates, Elizabeth. 1979. *The Emergence of Symbols: Cognition and Communication in Infancy.* New York: Academic Press.

Bateson, Gregory. 1980. *Mind in Nature: A Necessary Unity.* Toronto: Bantam Books.

Bateson, Mary Catherine. 1979. The epigenesis of conversational interaction: A personal account of research development. In: M. Bullowa (ed.), Before Speech: The Beginning of Human Communication, 63–77. London: Cambridge University Press.

Bateson, William. 1894. *Materials for the Study of Variation Treated with Especial Regard to Discontinuity in the Origin of Species.* Baltimore and London: Johns Hopkins University Press.

Beddington, Rosa S. P. & Elizabeth J. Robertson. 1999. Axis Development and Early Asymmetry in Mammals. *Cell* 96. 195–209.

Bernard, Claude. 1865. *Introduction À la Médecine Expérimentale.* Paris: Bordas.

Bernstein, Nikolai A. 1967. *The Co-Ordination and Regulation of Movements.* Oxford: Pergamon Press.

Bloom, Lois. 2002. *The Transition From Infancy to Language: Acquiring the Power of Expression.* Cambridge: Cambridge University Press.

Bråten, Stein (ed.). 1998. *Intersubjective Communication and Emotion in Early Ontogeny.* Cambridge: Cambridge University Press.

Bråten, Stein. 2009. *The Intersubjective Mirror in Infant Learning and Evolution of Speech.* Amsterdam/Philadelphia: John Benjamins.

Bråten, Stein & Colwyn Trevarthen. 2007. Prologue: From Infant Intersubjectivity and Participant Movements to Simulations and Conversations in Cultural Common Sense. In: *On Being Moved: From Mirror Neurons to Empathy.* Amsterdam/Philadelphia: John Benjamins.

Brazelton, T. Berry. 1979. Evidence of Communication During Neonatal Behavioural Assessment. In: *Before Speech: The Beginning of Human Communication*, 79–88. London: Cambridge University Press.

Bruner, Emiliano. 2010. Morphological Differences in the Parietal Lobes Within the Human Genus: A Neurofunctional Perspective. *Current Anthropology* 51.

Bruner, Jerome S. 1983. *Child's Talk: Learning to Use Language.* New York: Norton.

Bruner, Jerome S. 1990. *Acts of Meaning.* Cambridge, MA: Harvard University Press.

Bruner, Jerome S. 2003. *Making Stories: Law, Literature, and Life.* New York: Farrar, Strauss, and Giroux.

Buzsáki, Gyoergy. 2006. *Rhythms of the Brain.* Oxford: Oxford University Press.

Castiello, Umberto, Cristina Becchio, Stefania Zoia, Cristian Nelini, Luisa Sartori, Laura Blason, Giuseppina D'Ottavio, Maria Bulgheroni & Vittorio Gallese. 2010. Wired to be social: The ontogeny of human interaction. *PLoS ONE* 5 (10).

Condon, William S. & Louis W. Sander. 1974. Neonate movement is synchronized with adult speech: Interactional participation and language acquisition. *Science* 183. 99–101.

Cooper, Peter J. & Lynne Murray. 1998. Fortnightly review: Postnatal depression. *British Medical Journal* 316. 1884–1886.

Damásio, António. 2010. *Self Comes to Mind: Constructing the Conscious Brain*. New York: Pantheon Books.

Darwin, Charles. 1872. *The Expressions of Emotion in Man and Animals*. London: Methuen.

de Vries, J. I. P. (Hanneke), G. H. A. Visser & Heinz. F. R. Prechtl. 1982. The emergence of fetal behavior, I. Qualitative aspects. *Early Human Development* 7. 301–322.

DeCasper, Anthony J. & Phyllis Prescott. 2009. Lateralized processes constrain auditory reinforcement in human newborns. *Hearing Research* 255. 135–141.

Donald, Merlin. 2001. *A Mind So Rare: The Evolution of Human Consciousness*. London and New York: Norton.

Donaldson, Margaret. 1992. *Human Minds: An Exploration*. London: Allen Lane.

Edelman, Gerald M. 1988. *Topobiology: An Introduction to Molecular Embryology*. New York: Basic Books.

Ekman, Paul & Wallace V. Friesen. 1969. The Repertoire of Nonverbal Behavior: Categories, Origins, Usage, and Coding. *Semiotica* 22. 353–374.

Field, Tiffany. 2010. Postpartum Depression Effects on Early Interactions, Parenting, and Safety Practices: A Review. *Infant Behavior and Development* 33. 1–6.

Fónagy, Iván. 2001. *Languages Within Language: An Evolutive Approach*. (13). Amsterdam/ Philadelphia: John Benjamins.

Gallese, Vittorio. 2001. The 'Shared Manifold' Hypothesis: From Mirror Neurons to Empathy. *Journal of Conciousness Studies* 8 (5–7). 33–50.

Gibson, James J. 1966. *The Senses Considered as Perceptual Systems*. Boston: Houghton Mifflin.

Goldin-Meadow, Susan & David McNeill. 1999. The role of gesture and mimetic representation in making language. In: M. C. Corballis and E. G. Lea (eds.), *The Descent of Mind: Psychological Perspectives on Hominid Evolution*, 155–172. Oxford: Oxford University Press.

Gratier, Maya. 2003. Expressive timing and interactional synchrony between mothers and infants: Cultural similarities, cultural differences, and the immigration experience. *Cognitive Development* 18: 533–554.

Gratier, Maya & Colwyn Trevarthen. 2008. Musical narratives and motives for culture in mother-infant vocal interaction. *Journal of Consciousness Studies* 15. 122–158.

Halliday, Michael A. K. & Christian M. I. M. Matthiessen. 2004. *An Introduction to Functional Grammar, 3rd edn*. London: Arnold.

Halliday, Michael A. K. 1975. *Learning How to Mean: Explorations in the Development of Language*. London: Edward Arnold.

Halliday, Michael A. K. 1978. *Language as Social Semiotic: The Social Interpretation of Language and Meaning*. London: Edward Arnold.

Hamilton, William J., James D. Boyd & Harland W. Mossman. 1962. *Human Embryology: Prenatal Development of Form and Function*. Cambridge: Heffer and Sons.

Hevner, Robert F. 2000. Development of connections in the human visual system during fetal mid-gestation: A dil-tracing study. *Journal of Neuropathology and Experimental Neurology* 59: 385–392.

Hobson, Peter. 2002. *The Cradle of Thought: Exploring the Origins of Thinking*. Oxford: Macmillan.

Hubley, Penelope & Colwyn Trevarthen. 1979. Sharing a task in infancy. In: I. Uzgiris (ed.), *Social Interaction During Infancy*, 57–80. San Francisco: Jossey-Bass.

Jakobovits, Akos A. 2009. Grasping activity in utero: A significant indicator of fetal behavior. *Journal of Perinatal Medicine* 37. 571–572.

James, David, Mary Pillai & John Smoleniec. 1995. Neurobehavioral development of the human fetus. In: J.-P. Lecanuet, W. P. Fifer, N. A. Krasnegor and W. P. Smotherman (eds.), *Fetal Development: A Psychobiological Perspective*, 101–128. Hillsdale, NJ: Erlbaum.

Jeannerod, Marc. 1994. The representing brain: Neural correlates of motor intention and imagery. *Behavioral and Brain Sciences* 17. 187–245.

Kendon, Adam. 1980. Gesticulation and speech: Two aspects of the process of utterance. In: M. R. Key (ed.), *The Relationship of Verbal and Nonverbal Communication*. The Hague: Mouton.

Larroche, Jeanne-Claudie. 1981. The marginal layer in the neocortex of a 7 week-old human embryo: A light and electron microscopy study. *Anatomy and Embryology* 162. 301–312.

Lashley, Karl S. 1951. The problem of serial order in behavior. In: L. A. Jeffress (ed.), *Cerebral Mechanisms in Behavior*, 112–136. New York: Wiley.

Lecanuet, Jean-Pierre, William P. Fifer, Norman A. Krasnegor & William P. Smotherman (eds.). 1995. *Fetal Development: A Psychobiological Perspective*. Hillsdale, NJ: Erlbaum.

Lee, David N. 2005. Tau in action in development. In: J. J. Rieser, J. J. Lockman and C. A. Nelson (eds.), *Action as an Organiser of Learning*. Hillsdale, New Jersey: Erlbaum.

Lee, David N. 2009. General tau theory: Evolution to date. *Perception* 38. 837–858.

Lenneberg, Eric H. 1967. *Biological Foundations of Language*. New York: John Wiley and Sons.

Locke, John L. 1993. *The Child's Path to Spoken Language*. Cambridge, MA: Harvard University Press.

Ludke, Karen. 2009. Teaching foreign languages through songs. In: *Practical Educational Workbook for Teachers to Use Songs in the Modern Language Classroom*, 1–40. Edinburgh: University of Edinburgh.

Lüdtke, Ulrike. 2011. Relational emotions in semiotic and linguistic development: Towards an intersubjective theory of language learning and language therapy. In: J. Zlatev, T. Racine, U. Lüdtke and A. Foolen (eds.), *Moving Ourselves, Moving Others: Motion and Emotion in Consciousness, Intersubjectivity and Language*. Amsterdam: John Benjamins.

MacNeilage, Peter F. 2008. *The Origin of Speech*. Oxford: Oxford University Press.

MacNeilage, Peter F. 2011. Lashley's serial order problem and the acquisition/evolution of speech. *Cognitive Critique 3*, 49–83. University of Minnesota: Center for Cognitive Sciences.

Malloch, Stephen. 1999. Mothers and infants and communicative musicality. *Musicae Scientiae*. Special Issue: Rhythms, Musical Narrative, and the Origins of Human Communication. 29–57.

Malloch, Stephen & Colwyn Trevarthen (eds.). 2009. *Communicative Musicality*. Oxford: Oxford University Press.

McNeill, David. 1970. *The Acquisition of Language: The Study of Developmental Psycholinguistics*. New York: Harper and Row.

McNeill, David. 2005. *Gesture and Thought*. Chicago: University of Chicago Press.

Merker, Bjørn. 2009a. Returning language to culture by way of biology. *Behavioral and Brain Sciences* 32 (5): 460.

Merker, Bjørn. 2009b. Ritual foundations of human uniqueness. In: S. Malloch and C. Trevarthen (eds.), *Communicative Musicality: Exploring the Basis of Human Companionship*, 45–60. Oxford: Oxford University Press.

Merker, Bjørn. 2012. The vocal learning constellation: Imitation, ritual culture, encephalization. In: Nicholas Bannan, (ed). *Music, Language, and Human Evolution*. Oxford: Oxford University Press.

Merker, Bjørn. 2005. The liabilities of mobility: A selection pressure for the transition to consciousness in animal evolution. *Consciousness and Cognition* 14. 89–114.

Murray, Lynne & Colwyn Trevarthen. 1985. Emotional regulation of interactions between two-month-olds and their mothers. In: *Social Perception in Infants*, 177–197. Norwood, NJ: Ablex.

Nagy, Emese. 2011. The newborn infant: A missing stage in developmental psychology. *Infant and Child Development* 20 (1): 3–19.

Nagy, Emese. 2008. Innate intersubjectivity: Newborns' sensitivity to communication disturbance. *Developmental Psychology* 44 (6). 1779–1784.

Nagy, Emese & Peter Molnar. 2004. Homo imitans or *Homo provocans*? Human imprinting model of neonatal imitiation. *Infant Behavior and Development* 27. 54–63.

Narváez, Darcia, Jaak Panksepp, Alan N. Schore & Tracy Gleason (eds.). 2011. *Human Nature, Early Experience, and the Environment of Evolutionary Adaptedness*. New York: Oxford University Press.

Nelson, Katherine. 1996. *Language in Cognitive Development: Emergence of the Mediated Mind*. New York: Cambridge University Press.

Northoff, Georg & Jaak Panksepp. 2008. The trans-species concept of self and the subcortical-cortical midline system. *Trends in Cognitive Sciences* 12. 259–264.

Okado, Nobuo. 1980. Development of the human cervical spinal cord with reference to synapse formation in the motor nucleus. *The Journal of Comparative Neurology* 191. 495–513.

Osborne, Nigel. 2009. Towards a chronobiology of musical rhythm. In: S. Malloch and C. Trevarthen (eds.), *Communicative Musicality: Exploring the Basis of Human Companionship*, 545–564. Oxford: Oxford University Press.

Packard, Andrew. 2006. Contribution to the whole (H). Can squids show us anything that we did not already know? *Biology and Philosophy* 21. 189–211.

Pander, Christian Heinrich. 1817. *Beiträge zur Entwicklungsgeschichte des Hühnchens im Eye*. Würzburg: Brönner.

Panksepp, Jaak. 1998. *Affective Neuroscience: The Foundations of Human and Animal Emotions*. New York: Oxford University Press.

Panksepp, Jaak & Georg Northoff. 2009. The trans-species core self: The emergence of active cultural and neuro-ecological agents through self-related processing within subcortical-cortical midline networks. *Consciousness and Cognition* 18. 193–215.

Panksepp, Jaak & Colwyn Trevarthen. 2009. The neuroscience of emotion in music. In: S. Malloch and C. Trevarthen (eds.), *Communicative Musicality: Exploring the Basis of Human Companionship*, 105–146. Oxford: Oxford University Press.

Papoušek, Mechthild. 1994. Melodies in caregivers' speech: A species specific guidance towards language. *Early Development and Parenting* 3. 5–17.

Penfield, Wilder & Herbert H. Jasper. 1954. *Epilepsy and the Functional Anatomy of the Human Brain*. London: Little, Brown, and Co.

Petitto, Laura A. & Paula F. Marentette. 1991. Babbling in the manual mode: Evidence for the ontogeny of language. *Science* 251. 1493–1496.

Pfaff, Donald W. 2006. *Brain Arousal and Information Theory: Neural and Genetic Mechanisms*. Cambridge, MA: Harvard University Press.

Piontelli, Alessandra. 2010. *Development of Normal Fetal Movements: The First 25 Weeks of Gestation*. Wien and New York: Springer-Verlag.

Piontelli, Alessandra. 1992. *From Fetus to Child*. London: Routledge.

Piontelli, Alessandra. 2002. *Twins: From Fetus to Child*. London: Routledge.

Prechtl, Heinz F. R. 1986. Prenatal motor behaviour. In: M. Wade and H. T. A. Whiting (eds.), *Motor Development in Children: Aspects of Coordination and Control*, 53–64. Amsterdam: Elsevier, North-Holland.

Prigogine, Ilya & Isabelle Stengers. 1984. *Order Out of Chaos: Man's New Dialogue With Nature*. London: Flamingo.

Reddy, Vasudevi. 2008. *How Infants Know Minds*. Cambridge, MA: Harvard University Press.

Reid, Thomas. 1764. *An Inquiry Into the Human Mind on the Principles of Common Sense*. Edinburgh: A. Kinkaid and J. Bell.

Reissland, Nadja, Brian Francis, James Mason & Karen Lincoln. 2011. Do Facial expressions develop before birth? *PLoS ONE* 6 (8). 1–7.

Rogoff, Barbara. 2003. *The Cultural Nature of Human Development*. Oxford: Oxford University Press.

Rommetveit, Ragnar. 1998. Intersubjective attunement and linguistically mediated meaning in discourse. In: S. Bråten (ed.), *Intersubjective Communication and Emotion in Early Ontogeny*, 354–371. Cambridge: Cambridge University Press.

Royal College of Obstetricians and Gynaecologists. 2010. *Fetal Awareness: Review of Research and Recommendations for Practice*. London: Royal College of Obstetricians and Gynaecologists.

Saint-Georges, Catherine, Ammar Mahdhaoui, Mohamed Chetaoani, Raquel S. Cassel, Marie-Christine Laznik, Fabio Apicella, Pietro Muratori, Sandra Maestro, Filippo Muratori & David Cohen. 2010. Do parents recognize autistic deviant behavior long before diagnosis? Taking into account interaction using computational methods. *PLoS ONE* 6 (78).

Schore, Alan N. 2011. Bowlby's environment of evolutionary adaptedness: Recent studies on the interpersonal neurobiology of attachment and emotional development. In: D. Narváez, J. Panksepp, A. Schore and T. Gleason (eds.), *Human Nature, Early Experience, and the Environment of Evolutionary Adaptedness*. New York: Oxford University Press.

Sebeok, Thomas A. 1977. *How Animals Communicate*. Bloomington: Indiana University Press.

Sebeok, Thomas A. 1994. *Signs: An Introduction to Semiotics*. Toronto: University of Toronto Press Inc.

Sherrington, Charles. 1906. *The Integrative Action of the Nervous System*. New Haven, CT: Yale University Press.

Sinigaglia, Corrado & Giacomo Rizzolatti. 2011. Through the looking glass: Self and others. *Consciousness and Cognition* 20. 64–74.

Sperry, Roger W. 1952. Neurology and the mind-brain problem. *American Scientist* 40. 291–312.

Stern, Daniel N. 2000. *The Interpersonal World of the Infant,* 2nd edn. New York: Basic Books.

Stern, Daniel N. 2010. *Forms of Vitality*. Oxford: Oxford University Press.

Tallandini, Maria A. & Chiara Scalembra. 2006. Kangaroo mother care and mother-premature infant dyadic interaction. *Infant Mental Health Journal* 27 (3). 251–275.

Trevarthen, Colwyn. 1979. Communication and cooperation in early infancy: A description of primary intersubjectivity. In: M. Bullowa (ed.), *Before Speech: The Beginning of Human Communication*, 321–347. London: Cambridge University Press.

Trevarthen, Colwyn. 1985. Neuroembryology and the development of perceptual mechanisms. In: F. Falkner and J. M. Tanner (eds.), *Human Growth*, 2nd edn, 301–383. New York: Plenum.

Trevarthen, Colwyn. 1986a. Development of intersubjective motor control in infants. In: M. G. Wade and H. T. A. Whiting (eds.), *Motor Development in Children: Aspects of Coordination and Control*, 209–261. Dordrecht: Martinus Nijhoff.

Trevarthen, Colwyn. 1986b. Form, significance, and psychological potential of hand gestures in infants. In: J-L. Nespoulous, P. Perron and A. R. Lecours (eds.), *The Biological Foundation of Gestures: Motor and Semiotic Aspects*, 149–202. Hillsdale, NJ: Erlbaum.

Trevarthen, Colwyn. 1990. Signs before speech. In: T. A. Sebeok and J. Umiker-Sebeok (eds.), *The Semiotic Web 1989*, 689–755. Berlin: Mouton de Gruyter.

Trevarthen, Colwyn. 1996. Lateral asymmetries in infancy: Implications for the development of the hemispheres. *Neuroscience and Biobehavioral Reviews* 20 (4). 571–586.

Trevarthen, Colwyn. 1999. Musicality and the Intrinsic Motive Pulse: Evidence from human psychobiology and infant communication. *Musicae Scientiae*. Special Issue Rhythms, Musical Narrative, and the Origins of Human Communication: 157–213.

Trevarthen, Colwyn. 2004. Brain development. In: R. L. Gregory (ed.), *Oxford Companion to the Mind*, 116–127. Oxford and New York: Oxford University Press.

Trevarthen, Colwyn. 2005. Stepping away from the mirror: Pride and shame in adventures of companionship and refelections on the nature and emotional needs of infant intersubjectivity. In: C. S. Carter, L. Ahnert, K. E. Grossman, S. B. Hrdy, M. E. Lamb, S. W. Porges and N. Sachser (eds.), *Attachment and Bonding: A New Synthesis*, 55–84. Cambridge, MA: The MIT Press.

Trevarthen, Colwyn. 2011a. Born for art, and the joyful companionship of fiction. In: D. Narváez, J. Panksepp, A. Schore and T. Gleason (eds.), *Human Nature, Early Experience and the Environment of Evolutionary Adaptedness*. New York: Oxford University Press.

Trevarthen, Colwyn. 2011b. What young children give to their learning, making education work to sustain a community and its culture. *European Early Childhood Education Research Journal* 19 (2). 173–193.

Trevarthen, Colwyn. 1998. The concept and foundations of intersubjectivity. In: S. Braten (ed.), *Intersubjective Communication and Emotion in Early Ontogeny*, 15–46. Cambridge: Cambridge University Press.

Trevarthen, Colwyn. 2009. Human biochronology: On the source and functions of 'musicality'. In: R. Hass and V. Brandes (eds.), *Music That Works*. Wien and New York: Springer.

Trevarthen, Colwyn & Kenneth J. Aitken. 2003. Regulation of brain development and age-related changes in infants' motives: The developmental function of regressive periods. In: M. Heimann (ed.), *Regression Periods in Infancy*, 107–184. Mahwah, NJ: Erlbaum.

Trevarthen, Colwyn, Kenneth J. Aitken, Emese Nagy, Jonathan T. Delafield-Butt & Marie Vandekerckhove. 2006. Collaborative regulations of vitality in early childhood: Stress in intimate relationships and postnatal psychopathology. In: D. Cicchetti and D. J. Cohen (eds.), *Developmental Psychopathology*, 65–126. New York: John Wiley and Sons.

Trevarthen, Colwyn & Jonathan T. Delafield-Butt. 2011. Biology of shared meaning and language development: Regulating the life of narratives. In: M. Legerstee, D. Haley and M. Bornstein (eds.), *The Developing Infant Mind: Integrating Biology And Experience*. New York: Guildford Press.

Trevarthen, Colwyn, Jonathan T. Delafield-Butt & Benjamin Schögler. 2011. Psychobiology of musical gesture: Innate rhythm, harmony and melody in movements of narration. In: A. Gritten and E. King (eds.), *Music and Gesture Ii*. Aldershot: Ashgate.

Trevarthen, Colwyn & Penelope Hubley. 1978. Secondary intersubjectivity: Confidence, confiding and acts of meaning in the first year. In: A. Lock (ed.), *Action, Gesture and Symbol*, 183–229. London: Academic Press.

Trevarthen, Colwyn & Katerina Logotheti. 1987. First symbols and the nature of human knowledge. In: J. Montangero, A. Tryphon and S. Dionnet (eds.), *Symbolisme Et Connaissance/Symbolism and Knowledge*, 65–92. Geneva: Jean Piaget Archives Foundation.

Tulving, Endel. 2002. Episodic memory: From mind to brain. *Annual Review of Psychology* 53: 1–25.

Turner, Robert & Andreas A. Ioannides. 2009. Brain, music, and musicality: Inferences from neuroimaging. In: S. Malloch and C. Trevarthen (eds.), *Communicative Musicality: Exploring the Basis of Human Companionship*, 147–184. Oxford: Oxford University Press.

Turner, Victor W. 1982. *From Ritual to Theatre: The Human Seriousness of Play*. New York: Performing Arts Journal Publications.

Turner, Victor W. & Edward M. Bruner (eds.). 1986. *The Anthropology of Experience*. Urbana: University of Illinois Press.

Tylén, Kristian, Ethan Weed, Mikkel Wallentin, Andreas Roepstorff & Chris D. Frith. 2010. Language as a tool for interacting minds. *Mind and Language* 25. 3–29.

Vandekerckhove, Marie & Jaak Panksepp. 2011. A neurocognitive theory of higher mental emergence: From anoetic affective experiences to noetic knowledge and autonoetic awareness. *Neuroscience and Biobehavioral Reviews* 35 (9). 2017–2025.

Volterra, Virginia. 1981. Gestures, signs and words at two years: When does communication become language? *Sign Language Studies* 33. 351–362.

von Hofsten, Claes. 1993. Prospective control – a basic aspect of action development. *Human Development* 36. 253–270.

von Hofsten, Claes. 2004. An action perspective on motor development. *Trends in Cognitive Sciences* 8. 266–272.

von Holst, Erich & Ursula von St. Paul. 1960. Vom Wirkungsgefüge der Triebe. *Die Naturwissenschaften* 47. 409–422.

von Uexküll, Jakob. 1926. *Theoretical Biology.* London: Kegan Paul, Trench, Trubner, and Co.

von Uexküll, Jakob. 1957. A stroll through the worlds of animals and men. In: C. H. Schiller (ed.), *Instinctive Behavior: The Development of a Modern Concept*, 5–80. New York: International Universities Press.

Vygotsky, Lev. 1978. *Mind in Society.* Cambridge, MA: Harvard University Press.

Waddington, Conrad Hal. 1940. *Organisers and Genes.* Cambridge: Cambridge University Press.

Watt, Douglas F. 2004. Review of Beauregard, M. (ed.) 2004. "Consciousness, Emotional Self-Regulation, and The Brain". *Journal of Consciousness Studies* 11 (9). 77–82.

Whitehead, Alfred North. 1929. *Process and Reality.* New York: Macmillan.

Windle, William F. 1970. Development of neural elements in human embryos of four to seven weeks of gestation. *Experimental Neurology* 5 (Supplement). 44–83.

Wittmann, Marc. 2009. The inner experience of time. *Philosophical Transactions of the Royal Society B – Biological Sciences* 364. 1955–1967.

Wolff, Peter H. 1966. The causes, controls, and organization of behavior in the neonate. *Psychological Issues* 5 (Monograph 17). 1–19.

Zoia, Stefania, Laura Blason, Giuseppina D'Ottavio, Maria Bulgheroni, Eva Pezzetta, Aldo Scabar & Umberto Castiello. 2007. Evidence of early development of action planning in the human foetus: A kinematic study. *Experimental Brain Research* 176. 217–226.

Paul Cobley

12 Semiotic models of communication

Abstract: This chapter outlines the way semiotics has offered models that have made a contribution to defining communication science. Broadly, it identifies a period in twentieth-century sign study in which semiology provided a model for understanding communication. Two of the central features of this model were the notion of a fixed (linguistic) 'code' and the concept of the 'text.' The chapter goes on to discuss how the fixed 'code' was loosened and superseded by a model of communication which focused on communication of all kinds (verbal and non-verbal). The chapter suggests some consequences of semiotic models for communication research.

Keywords: Semiology, semiotics, code, myth, text, cultural anthropology, interpretant, encoding/decoding, nonverbal communication, biosemiotics

1 Introduction

Semiotic models of communication have endured a curious history of centrality and marginality. This is the case even in the last century in which communication science – as a largely institutionalized discipline – and semiotics – as a barely institutionalized one – have come to the fore. A number of the contributions to the present volume attest to the influence of semiotically-orientated thinking about communication. Yet, at the same time, semiotic models are also a chimera, drifting into ill-defined view and then out into the wilderness. One reason for this, paradoxically, is that semiotics, in the guise of a glottocentric semiology, became fashionable in a number of academic fields in the West in the late 1960s and mid-1970s. As such, semiotics was always vulnerable to falling *out* of fashion and being blamed for all sorts of ills in communication study (particularly in textual and cultural analysis) of which semiotics as a whole was not actually guilty (for example, bracketing audiences, reception and political economy). The initial success of semiotics in communication science fixed a limited view of what semiotic models actually offer, often promoting, instead, a linguistic version of 'codes' plus the task of unravelling them to reveal ideology (see also Chapter 18, Schrøder).

2 Semiotics, linguistics, communication

Although a great deal of contemporary communication science is closely related to mass communications and media and these are the areas that have most often spawned the kind of models that are defined and outlined in the current volume, both semiotics and communication science have had close relations to linguistics. Indeed, they have relations to a specific strand of linguistics: not the tradition of American linguistics from Whitney through the anthropological linguists (Boas, Sapir, Whorf), behaviourists (Bloomfield), American structuralists (Harris) to Chomsky and the post-Chomskyans, but the Saussurean, and sometimes code-orientated, linguistics that, arguably, remains current today in the form of Critical Discourse Analysis and systemic functional linguistics (see Chapter 18, Schrøder). This latter has been of comparable importance to some kinds of communication theory as, for example, the pragmatics approach that takes its inspiration from Austin and Grice (see Chapter 13, Wharton and Chapter 14, Bangerter and Mayor). The key name associated with code-orientated linguistics, particularly during the fashionable days of semiology, is that of the Swiss linguist, Ferdinand de Saussure (1857–1913).

Saussure's contribution to communication theory is principally to be found in his *Cours de linguistique générale* (*Course in General Linguistics* 1916; translated into English in 1959 and 1983), although since the discovery of Saussure's original notes for his course at the University of Geneva, his entire *oeuvre* has undergone positive reassessment (see Bouissac 2010; Sanders 2004; Harris 2006). The original book of Saussure's *Cours*, based on the notes of his students, projects 'semiology,' "a science *which studies the role of signs as part of social life*" (1983: 15). This entails a study of signs which, rather than just tracking the ways in which they have been used to refer to objects from one epoch to the next, institutes a 'synchronic' interrogation of the very conditions upon which signs operate. From the beginning, despite the call for a general sign science, Saussure focused on the linguistic sign. This feature of communication he sees as a "two-sided psychological entity" and not as a "link between a thing and a name, but between a concept and a sound pattern" (1983: 66). Referring to the sound pattern as the *signifiant* and the concept as the *signifié*, Saussure insisted that there was a *signifié* bound to each *signifiant* but that the reasons for their binding was not natural or pre-ordained. This is, for him, the most fundamental characteristic of the sign: that the relation in it is *arbitrary*.

Saussure's concomitant emphasis on the language system (*langue*) underlying sign use derives precisely from the principle of arbitrariness. What binds this system is the sum of differences that occur between linguistic signs, none of which can rely on a natural process of 'meaning' but, rather, consist of the 'values' generated by each other's arbitrary relation between sound pattern and concept. As such, instances of linguistic communication – *parole* – in all their richness and variegation, are not to be analyzed simply in terms of a semantic link that it might be assumed their individual signs enjoy with the objects to which they refer but, rather, within the frame of a relationship of difference to all the other linguistic signs in *langue*. Saussurean semiology is not principally concerned with how signs indicate or communicate about specific objects; instead, its focus is how regimes of communication, somewhat removed from specific objects, are sustained and perpetuated.

The consequences of the Saussurean perspective were initially felt most strongly in linguistics (Harris 2001: 118) through the work of Karcevskij, Jakobson, Bühler, and Vološinov, extended by Louis Hjelmslev and the Copenhagen School of linguistics, for whom the Saussurean dictum that "*langue* is a form and not a substance" was to be taken to its logical conclusion (Hjelmslev 1970), and technically developed into a more systematic semiology (Buyssens 1967, Prieto 1968). It was from these developments that Saussure's linguistics started to find applications outside the field of spoken discourse. The early work of Roland Barthes marks him, perhaps, as heir to Hjelmslev as much as to Saussure. This is particularly clear in some of Barthes's formulations such as 'denotation,' 'connotation' and 'metalanguage,' although Barthes ultimately saw himself initiating Saussure's vaunted project of a semiology.

In *Elements of Semiology* (1964, translated into English 1967), Barthes presented an amalgam of his own work on fashion plus a primer of Saussurean linguistics. Barthes's earlier volume *Mythologies* (1957, translated into English 1973), had grafted a Saussurean theory onto a series of articles on popular culture that Barthes had penned for mainstream magazines in the mid-1950s. Each essay in the volume dealt with a 'mythology' of French life – wrestling, the haircuts of the Roman characters in Mankiewicz's film of *Julius Caesar*, the face of Garbo, *steack frites*, striptease, the New Citroën and the brain of Einstein – providing evidence for Barthes that "myth is a language" (Barthes 1973: 11). In a loose way, the topics of the essays, individual mythologies, were presented as instances of *parole* emanating from a basis in a general 'myth' or *langue*. Yet, as a conclusion to the articles which comprised the body of the book, *Mythologies* also contained an essay at the end called 'Myth today.' Here, it was suggested that the myth that creates specific mythologies produces a further two levels of signification. The first level of this system Barthes called the *language-object*: "it is the language which myth gets hold of in order to build its own system" (1973: 115). This level is the domain of the *signifiant* (sound pattern) and *signifié* (mental concept). For Barthes, this level is where straightforward indicating takes place: denotation. The second level, on the other hand, is *metalanguage*: a language that speaks about the first level. The level of metalanguage is constituted by connotation and Barthes suggests that it is *cynical* because it relies on the level of denotation to naturalize any ideological proposition which it embodies. As such, a communication of a black soldier saluting the French flag in the 1950s, for example, is suffused by connotative potential which immediately strikes the viewer as an image of the loyalty of the colonial subject; but the flagrantly mendacious nature of this ideological communication is tempered by the 'reasonable' denotation which depicts the scene 'as it happened.'

So influential was this early incarnation of semiology that it almost made Saussurean sign theory synonymous with the analysis of everyday phenomena. *Mythol-*

ogies can be said to have achieved two things for this area of communication theory. Firstly, it provided a Saussurean/Hjelmslevean model for the analysis of manifold nonverbal, rather than just verbal, communication. Secondly, it transformed unconsidered trifles of daily life into complex *texts* to be read by competent readers. In his writings on photography from the 1960s (see Barthes 1977a), Barthes also made a significant contribution to communication study by showing how various features of the photographic repertoire were not so much instruments of the process of denotation but, instead, a means of promoting connotations. As in 'Myth today,' he exposed, with the help of Hjelmslev, the way in which an 'expression plane' and 'content plane' of signs can combine to form a new 'expression plane'; or, put another way, how one sign repertoire transforms into another one. This indicated a feature of the reading process which had been seldom theorized hitherto: that readers, viewers, audiences were likely to alight on the connotations of some communications 'prior to' considering denotations. In consuming an advertisement, for example, the full connotative power of the text would be to the fore whilst the denotative sign system (or 'expression' and 'content' planes) beneath might be given only scant regard or disregarded altogether by the audience.

As with the 'mythologies' in Barthes's earlier essays, the denotative sign's role is not merely a 'secondary' one. Indeed, it is essential to the photographic message especially. In photography, it enacts a motivated relationship – where there is a strong connection between the sign and what it signifies through, for example, resemblance – often as if photography's denotative power is in the service of 'validating' the injustice of the connotative sign, establishing the latter's literalness and helping to *ground* ideology. If it was not clear from the analysis of 'myth' offered by Barthes in *Mythologies*, then *Elements of Semiology* makes it apparent that central to his theory of the sign is the way that the sign can be not simply an ideological *vehicle* but is, in fact, ideological through and through. In general, the procedure to expose this action of cultural signs is probably what most characterized semiotic models of communication when semiotics in general was a fashion. In short, semiotic models promoted the scrutiny of surface phenomena in order to reveal deeper, hidden agendas or, drawing on information theories (see Chapter 4, Lanigan), to reveal the 'code' beneath the manifest 'message.'

3 Semiotics as a code model of communication

Yet, the revealing of a semiotic code was more complicated than even Barthes had allowed. Eco elaborated on the matter in the influential volume translated into English in 1976 as *A Theory of Semiotics*. In a curious synthesis of emerging currents on communication which looks almost untenable today, *A Theory of Semiotics* suggested a semiotic model of communication based on a theory of codes and a theory of sign production. Along the way, it discussed technical semiotic issues –

the status of the referent (from Ogden and Richards), the icon-index-symbol triad (from Peirce but largely established by Jakobson), the translation of 'expression' and 'content' planes (Hjelmslev), denotation and connotation (Hjelmslev again) and 'unlimited semiosis' (derived from Peirce) – that were to become standard in the teaching of communications and media in English-speaking universities in the ensuing decades (see Fiske 1990; Bignell 1997; Dyer 1982; Hartley 1982; etc.). Most importantly, it explicitly addressed and opened up aspects of the theory of codes which, in communication science in general, had been unspoken or neglected. Eco begins his discussion of codes with the example of an engineer in charge of a water gate between two mountains who needs to know when the water level behind the gate is becoming dangerously high. The engineer places a buoy in the watershed; when the water rises to danger level, this activates a transmitter which emits an electrical signal through a channel which reaches a receiver downriver; the receiver then converts the signal into a readable message for a destination apparatus. This allows Eco (1976: 36–7) to demonstrate that, under the designation 'code,' the engineer has four different phenomena to consider:

(a) a set of *signals* ruled by combinatory laws (bearing in mind that these laws are not naturally or determinately connected to states of water – the engineer could use such laws to send signals down the channel to express passion to a lover);

(b) a set of states (of the water); these could have been conveyed by almost any kind of signal provided they reach the destination in a form which becomes intelligible;

(c) a set of behavioural responses at the destination (these can be independent of how a) and b) are composed);

(d) a rule coupling some items from the a) system with some from b) and c) (this rule establishes that an array of specific signals refers to specific states of water or, put another way, a syntactic arrangement refers to a semantic configuration; alternatively, it may be the case that the array of signals corresponds to a specific response without the need to explicitly consider the semantic configuration.

For Eco, only the rule in (d) can really be called a code. However, he points out that combinatory principles that feature in (a), (b), and (c) are often taken for codes. This is consistently the case when such phrases as 'the legal code,' 'code of practice,' 'behavioural code' are in such wide circulation. Yet, what Eco's semiotics makes clear for the study of communication is that 'code' should strictly be taken as a 'holistic' phenomenon in which a rule binds not just the sign-vehicle to the object to which it refers but also binds it to any response that might arise irrespective of the reference to the object becoming explicit. At most, (a), (b) and (c) are to be taken as 's-codes' – systems or 'structures' that subsist independently of any communicative purpose. They can be studied by information theory (see

Chapter 4, Lanigan and Chapter 5, Baecker); but they only command attention from communication science when they exist within a communicative rule or code, (d) (Eco 1976: 38–46).

The other basis of Eco's theory of codes for semiotics concerns the character of codes (and s-codes) in interaction or 'sign-functions.' Rather than the 'referential function' by which a sign refers in a more or less direct way to an object in the world, in a synthesis of Saussurean and information theory perspectives Eco stresses the way in which signs refer to other signs or 'cultural units': "*Every attempt to establish what the referent of a sign is forces us to define the referent in terms of an abstract entity which moreover is only a cultural convention*" (Eco 1976: 66; emphasis in the original). Saussure's *signifié* was always a 'mental concept' rather than an object in the world and its relation with the *signifiant* always arbitrary. Thus, the 'meaning' of a term for Eco can only ever be a 'cultural unit' (1976: 67) or, at most, a psychological one. Moreover, this movement from one sign or cultural unit to another entails that signs are seen to work, along with communication, in a chain, a phenomenon that Eco discusses in terms of Peirce's conception of the *interpretant* (1976: 68–72). Most importantly, Eco casts semiotics as a "substitute for cultural anthropology" (1976: 27), bequeathing to communication science a model of communication which is orientated to the vicissitudes of culture rather than fixated on the possibility of referentiality. This bequest is critically revisited in Section 6, 'After coding.'

4 Text and textuality

If semiotics' concept of code is considered to be one contribution to communication science, then this is tempered somewhat by the fact that associated or prototype uses of code already existed in information theory or in communication theory after Shannon and Weaver (see Chapter 5, Baecker) and, earlier, in the field of cryptography. The most enduring contribution of semiotics to communication science is its general model of textuality or, in short, its concept of the 'text.' Eco (1976: 57) indicates the centrality of text when he states that "a single sign-vehicle conveys many intertwined contents and therefore what is commonly called a 'message' is in fact a *text* whose content is multileveled *discourse*". This statement offers a sense of the way in which the semiotic notion of text stands between two polarities. On the one hand, there is the conception of 'message' in information theory which is concerned with the process of transmission and for which any meaning that accrues is of no real consequence (see, for example, Shannon and Weaver 1949). On the other hand, there is the belief in the 'work' or the opus which suffused the humanities and framed messages in terms of authorial intent, richness of allusion and, often, the possibility of full transmission or pure communication.

Initially, the notion of text was not necessarily seen in relation to overcoded communications and undercoded messages. Barthes's 1971 essay, 'From work to text' (translated into English in 1977), is often taken as programmatic, yet it is principally associated with the working through of the notion of text as a support to the 'radical' writing practices of the *Tel Quel* group. The idea of the text actually has a slightly older provenance in the synchronic perspective that developed, alongside the spread of Saussure's thought, in the first half of the twentieth century. It can be found in Propp's (1968 [1927]) *The Morphology of the Folktale*, then later in the work of the structural anthropologist, Lévi-Strauss. Famously, Propp analyzed 100 Russian folk stories, examining their underlying commonalities and identifying 31 functions characterizing the tales. Lévi-Strauss (for example, 1977) analyzed the 'structure' of myth, re-casting narratives as structural groupings. Through the work of these, as well as a number of other analysts of literature and myth who sought to uncover synchronic textual principles – Greimas, Bremond, Todorov, and the field that became known as narratology (Cobley 2004) – the possibility of a disinterested analysis of literary and other works developed. Barthes summed up this position in his 1966 essay, 'Introduction to the structural analysis of narratives,' as akin to that of Saussure "seeking to extract a principle of classification and a central focus" (Barthes 1977c: 80) amidst bewildering heterogeneity. Certainly, the key issue for these theorists was, as it was for Eco, the problem of analyzing chains of signs. Often concerned with literature, but from a linguistic perspective, inevitably these theorists developed "the notion of text, a discursive unit higher than or interior to the sentence, yet still structurally different from it" (Barthes 1981: 34). Text, then, could be summed up simply as 'a string of signs.' It can be concluded that the concept effectively neutralized the overcoded, value-centric confection of the literary work as well as, perhaps, the idea of a full, intentional 'communication.' Yet, the notion of text amounted to more than this because it did not simply revert to the mechanical concept, central to information theory, of an undercoded transmitted message.

Another semiotician and inaugurator of the concept of text, Juri Lotman (1982), stressed that, as an entity, the text is, in its very nature, *for someone* and can *become for someone* by inviting, in its very fabric, specific modes of reading. Lotman, conducting analyses in the environment of Soviet academia which demanded focus on the national literature, nevertheless implied that the principles of textual orientation to readership in the works of Pushkin and others are applicable across the board in the service of a neutral demystification of literary texts. This, of course, is not to say that a text is always successful because it is always accurately targeted and coded according to a consensus, for "Non-understanding, incomplete understanding, or misunderstanding are not side-products of the exchange of communication but its very essence" (Lotman 1974: 302). The text is thus a part of a translation, a re-encoding. As Barthes (1981: 42) was to put it, with slightly more of a literary slant,

If the theory of the text tends to abolish the separation of genres and arts, this is because it no longer considers works as mere 'messages', or even as 'statements' (that is, finished products, whose destiny would be sealed as soon as they are uttered), but as perpetual productions, enunciations, through which the subject continues to struggle; this subject is no doubt that of the author, but also that of the reader. The theory of the text brings with it, then, the promotion of a new epistemological object: the reading (an object virtually disdained by the whole of classical criticism, which was essentially interested either in the person of the author, or in the rules of manufacture of the work, and which never had any but the most meagre conception of the reader, whose relation to the work was thought to be one of mere projection).

This 'birth of the reader' from the 'text' provided a further semiotic model for communication and, especially, the study of the media.

5 Texts, encoding, decoding and the reader

The semiotic model of 'text/reader' in communications is perhaps best exemplified by the 'encoding/decoding' approach devised by Stuart Hall. Growing out of 'British cultural studies' (see Chapter 18, Schrøder, for a fuller account), it is unsurprising that 'encoding/decoding' derives from Umberto Eco's formulations regarding codes – which, as Eco stated, equate semiotics with cultural anthropology – as well as his commentaries on popular culture. What Hall did with sign study consisted of a furthering of its bearing on political critique as adumbrated in Barthes's work. Hall's essay, 'Encoding and decoding in the television discourse' (1973; often reprinted in truncated form – for example, Hall et al. 1981) produced a fecund synthesis of Barthesian semiology, Gramsci's hegemony theory, a concept of state apparatuses derived from Althusser, plus themes in the sociology of Frank Parkin, to effect a powerful argument about violence on television. The co-opting of Parkin's sociology, in particular, is interesting because it figured semiotics' birth of the reader in sociological terms as 'dominant,' 'negotiated' or 'oppositional' – that is, a reading position that accepts the instilled codes that dominate the media text, one that accepts some of the codes but rejects or is unsure of others, or one that strenuously rejects them. This model is an echo, of course, of Lotman's "Non-understanding, incomplete understanding, or misunderstanding," taking into account that Lotman's situation meant he was compelled to accentuate communicative efficiency (see also Chapter 9, Tindale) rather than resistance. Yet Hall's model was to influence a generation of researchers into 'cultural codes,' forging an orthodoxy for culturally-orientated communications and media studies which has lasted decades, and to play a major part in directing media studies towards audience analysis.

The research of David Morley on the reception of television programmes (1980) explicitly implemented the dominant/negotiated/oppositional trichotomy, sometimes in a fashion that recapitulated the lessons of 'uses and gratifications' approaches of earlier communication theory, but often in a more politically informed manner. Subsequent studies tended to naturalize the text/reader or encoding/decoding model to the extent that it was presented as simultaneously groundbreaking and common wisdom. Hobson's (1982) qualitative study of UK soap opera viewers grew out of work with Hall at the Birmingham Centre for Contemporary Cultural Studies and led a pack of contemporary media audience studies that included Morley (1986, 1992), Ang (1984, 1991, 1996), Radway (1984) Seiter et al. (1989), Lull (1990), Gray (1992), Gillespie (1995), Hermes (1996), Nightingale (1996) plus a revivified part-Uses and Gratifications cross-cultural study of *Dallas* viewers by Liebes and Katz (1993).

Crucial to many of these studies of readers were methods and perspectives borrowed from semiotically-informed anthropology. These aimed to procure greater depth in the understandings of audience responses to texts or, put another way, a 'thicker' description (Geertz 1993). Semiotic models of textuality had also, predictably, influenced literary theory which was, by the early 1980s, attempting to take into account 'reader response' and feeding back into general communication theory (for example, Fish's 1980 formulation of 'interpretive communities'). As one of the key progenitors of the conception of text, literary study was also one of its beneficiaries. Yet, the model that literature had provided for the text/reader relationship, and the encoding/decoding approach to such communications as those offered by television programmes, was rapidly coming into question with the advent of post-internet media in the early twenty-first century, especially Web 2.0. These latter putatively entail more *demonstrable* activity (interactivity, for example) which suggest that the text/audience relationship can once more be measured in terms of *use* (click-throughs, favourites folders, history, for example – see Livingstone 2004) and, arguably, involve a greater concealment of affective or emotional dispositions in communication.

6 After coding

Decades before the influence of the 'encoding/decoding' model had started to wane in communication science, semiotics had moved on from the belief in fixed codes as an explanatory principle in communication. The fashionable moment of semiology was superseded by a broader tradition of semiotics which was made manifest, above all, by the work of the Hungarian polymath, Thomas A. Sebeok (1920–2001) who was instrumental, too, in placing the work of the American logician, scientist and philosopher Charles Sanders Peirce (1839–1914) at the centre of sign study. The fate of the concept of code in particular in post-Sebeokean semiotics is instructive when considering the importance of semiotic models for communication science. In his final book, Sebeok (2001) repeatedly made reference to the five major codes: the immune code, the genetic code, the metabolic code, the neural code and, of course, the verbal code – the first four being precisely the codes that Eco (1976: 21) had declared to be outside the remit of semiotics. Sebeok's use of the term 'code' had undergone evolution, with the decisive moment – both for semiotics and for communication study – coinciding with Sebeok's increasing attention to non-human communication as he developed 'zoosemiotics' (see Cobley in press). Despite his close involvement in the development of post-war communication and information theory, Sebeok initially proceeded in zoosemiotics not with a concept of code drawn directly from those influences but from an information theory-inflected post-Saussurean linguistics. He figured code as a set of 'transformation rules' (Sebeok 1965) known *a priori* by the addresser and addressee (Sebeok 1960), made up of "the atomic particles," the "universal building blocks of language ... 'distinctive features'" (Sebeok 1972: 86). Distinctive features were Jakobson's base units of language, sounds in speech more fundamental than Saussure's phonemes and irreducible beyond their binary status (Fant et al. 1952; Jakobson 1976).

Yet Jakobson, and by association Sebeok, were guilty of what Roy Harris has, from 1978 onwards, called the "fixed code fallacy" (see, for example, Harris 2003: 96). Like the majority of perspectives in the history of linguistics, the fallacy fixated on 'language' rather than the study of 'communication.' Put in more informational terms, this perspective insists that a message is ineluctably dependent on the code rather than the panoply of contextual factors impinging on communication at any one moment. As Sebeok continued his work on non-human communication, he moved away from 'fixed' codes towards a flexible version of coding. In his later writings Sebeok referred to a proliferation of 'cultural' and 'natural' codes – from those in specific film genres to those in the social world of cats. *Contra* Eco once more, Sebeok started to give more attention to the s-codes that Eco had discussed. As early as 1970, Sebeok described different kinds of coding, (not unproblematically) considering Mozart's *Don Giovanni* to consist of a primary code – "natural language"; a secondary code – libretto; a tertiary code – score; and then the performance (see also Sebeok 1972: 164). He noted that the "need for different kinds of theory at different levels of 'coding' appears to be a pressing task" (1972: 112); and, in 1972, he posed a key question for current investigation, "what is a sign, how does the environment and its turbulences impinge upon it, how did it come about?" (1972: 4).

Although this question is not inapplicable to linguistic signs, it is clear that in the development of semiotics it is associated with the move towards an understanding of semiosis that is not restricted to linguistic models. In particular, this understanding is associated with the (re)discovery of the sign theory of Peirce. As is well known, the most striking difference between the sign in Saussure and that in Peirce is that the latter envisages a trichotomy consisting of a Sign or 'Representamen,' an Object and an 'Interpretant.' While this distinction is obvious, it is nevertheless significant because it derives from a tradition of thinking much different from that of the relatively recently developed linguistics and, indeed, the history of thought as conceived since the Enlightenment. That a Representamen (a sign-vehicle) can stand for an Object (something in the mind or something in the world) is no more illuminating than a *signifiant* being tied to a *signifié* in the mind. What is frequently considered the sign – the 'relation' between some ground and some terminus – had already been discovered to be false by Latin thinkers.

The advance inherent in the triadic sign is that the Interpretant does two jobs. Firstly, it sets up the sign relation: it is the establishment of a sign configuration involving Representamen and Object. When a finger (Representamen) points at something (Object), this is only a sign configuration if somebody else makes the link between the pointing digit and the something that is 'pointed to.' This making of the link is the Interpretant. If the finger pointed but was placed behind its owner's back, concealed from anyone else in that space, then there is no sign configuration however much the finger points. Put another way, no Interpretant is produced. The second feature of the Intrepretant consists in the way that any person looking at what the finger points to is bound to produce another sign (e.g. the finger points at the painting on the wall and the onlooker says: "Brueghel the Elder"). So the Interpretant is another Representamen, "an equivalent sign, or perhaps a more developed sign" (*CP* 2.228). The fact that the Interpretant becomes in itself a sign or Representamen amounts to a sequence of an "interpretant becoming in turn a sign, and so on ad infinitum" (*CP* 2.303). As has been seen, Eco concluded from this that the sign is constituted by a chain; equally, it could be said that the sign thus exists in a *network* of Interpretants (*CP* 1.339) whose bearing is determined by prevailing circumstances. For the Latins, and then Peirce, the sign is constituted by the *relation* of all three of its elements. As such, the sign is not so much suprasubjective, like a coded entity; rather, it is constituted in a fashion which renders it wholly susceptible to contextual factors. For the Latins, in one set of circumstances the relation in a sign could be of the order of *ens reale* (independent of mind for its existence), in another set it could be of *ens rationis* (dependent on mind for its existence – see Deely 2001: 729).

The Peircean version of the sign, and the orientation in this tradition towards forms of communication which were not just linguistic, produced an emergent model for communication science and a number of ramifications. Firstly, the fixity and rule-bound conception of code was loosened. Indeed, Sebeok's later work treated the term 'code' merely as a synonym for 'interpretant' (see, for example, Sebeok 2001: 80 and 191 n. 13) as part of a pluralistic conception of codes which was coupled with an as yet unspecified determining role of the genetic master code. With the loosening of 'code' from its mooring in linguistics and human communication, plus the realization that the overwhelming amount of communication in the world is nonverbal, as opposed to a relatively minuscule amount of verbal communication, Sebeok identified "terminological chaos in the sciences of communication, which is manifoldly compounded when the multifarious message systems employed by millions of species of languageless creatures, as well as the communicative processes inside organisms, are additionally taken into account" (1991: 23). From his zoosemiotic period onwards, Sebeok continually attempted to draw the attention of glottocentric communication theorists to the larger framework in which human verbal communication is embedded. Peirce's triadic version of the sign, his typologies of sign functioning and the design of his sign theory to cover all domains, provided the groundwork for Sebeok to make his work amount to an outline of the way that semiosis is the criterial attribute of life (see Sebeok 2001; cf. Petrilli and Ponzio 2001). Semiotics, in this formulation, was not just a method for understanding some artefacts of interest to arts and the humanities. Rather, it evolved as the human means to think of signs *as* signs, whether they be part of communication in films or novels, the aggressive expressions of animals or the messages that pass between organisms as lowly as the humble cell. As Sebeok (1997) demonstrates, when one starts to conceive of communication in these places then the sheer number of transmissions of messages (between components in any animal's body, for example) becomes almost ineffable. This amounts to a major re-orientation for communication. To be sure, the communication that takes place in the sociopolitical sphere is of utmost importance: the future of this planet currently depends on it. However, the model of communication put forth by contemporary semiotics insists on the understanding that human affairs are only a small part of what communication science's proper object is.

The fast-growing field of 'biosemiotics' (Sebeok and Umiker-Sebeok 1992; Hoffmeyer 1996, 2008; Kull 2001; Barbieri 2007) is now making it ever more apparent that the objects of biology are absolutely traversed by communicative processes and, in turn, that communication theory can no longer eschew biological principles. One of the planks of biosemiotics in its investigation of semiosis across all life is the concept of code duality (Hoffmeyer and Emmeche 2007: 27). Put briefly, it indicates that there is a code for action and a code for memory in life. Because organisms do not survive forever, they pass on signs as 'versions' of themselves, making heredity into a matter of "semiotic survival" (Hoffmeyer and Emmeche 2007: 24). Action in a lifespan is dominated by analogue signs, changeable and interpretable to different degrees; whereas "genetic memory works as read-only" (Kull 2007: 8). The broader point that code duality seems to underline is that digital codes (e.g. the notion of the 'selfish gene') have been imputed with an autonomous character when, in fact, their sphere of efficacy is limited. Conversely, analogue coding has acquired a reputation for independence and individualism when, in fact, individuals are subject to species history, mortality and the need to sexually reproduce (Hoffmeyer and Emmeche 2007: 51).

In his idea of 'semiotic freedom' Hoffmeyer (1996, 1998, 1999, 2008; Hoffmeyer and Emmeche 2007) also indicates the capacity of a cell, organism, species to distinguish parameters in its surroundings or its own interior and use them in regard to significance. Such 'freedom' is very low at primitive levels and it is a species property and not an organismic property (Hoffmeyer 2009: 35); yet, biosemioticians would argue strenuously that it is still a matter of behavioural and communicative change of a kind experienced by all organisms, including the human.

Initially, driven by Sebeok, another key theory in biosemiotics which facilitates an understanding of continuity across species concerns the organism's *Umwelt*: the 'world' of species according to their specific modelling devices, sensorium, or semiotic capacity to apprehend things (von Uexküll 2001a, 2001b). The theory posits that different species effectively inhabit 'different worlds' because the character of the 'world' they apprehend is determined by the semiotic resources that are available to them through their sensoria. A dog can apprehend sweetness in a bowl of sugar, but it cannot measure the amount of sugar, gain a knowledge of the history of sugar production or use the sugar in different recipes; a human can do all of these and also listen to stories about sugar, but it cannot hear very high pitched sounds like the dog can. The human inhabits an *Umwelt* characterized by nonverbal and verbal communication according to the senses it possesses. Those senses, of course, as the example of the dog's 'superior' hearing demonstrates, are not unlimited but, rather, specifically geared for the exigencies of survival.

The leading contemporary semiotic model of communication, then, is one which, among other things,

– embeds human communication in the wider context of non-human (nonverbal) communication;
– sees communication not so much restricted by its fixed code-based nature but rather in the potentialities of a network of interpretants;
– figures the 'openness' of analogue codes in relation to the restrictions of digital ones (such as the genetic code) and the restrictions of digital codes as vitiated by the capacity to enjoy differing degrees of 'freedom' within different *Umwelten*.

The first of these, to some extent, goes hand-in-hand with the massive growth of study of nonverbal communication since the 1960s (see, for example, Weitz 1974, Knapp 1978, Kendon 1981, Poyatos 1983; Hall 1990; Beattie 2003; the *Journal of Nonverbal Behavior*, 1976-present) and also the broad interest in the status of the animal and its forms of communication which has developed in the last decade, particularly in relation to posthumanism (see, for example, Baker 2000; Wolfe 2003; Fudge 2004; Wolfe 2010). The second has affinities with the influential notion that contemporary communication exists within a network society in which the self is at once plugged into a potentially global system of communications yet, in the instrumentality of much communication, is rendered isolated or restricted in developing global collectivity (see, for example, Castells 2005, 2009; van Dijk 2012). Such a situation – one of many potential situations for communication in the present – arises from the loosening of codes in communications and a techno-logical facilitation of the full force of the sign's constitution in 'relation' and its susceptibility to contextualization. The third provides a model of communication which concerns both of these issues, such that communication is to be conceived in terms of its 'analogue' code in which there are clear degrees of freedom, but must also be conceived at the level of the species, governing which forms of com-munication will benefit the project of survival.

7 Conclusion

One final observation should be offered in respect of the contemporary semiotic model's implications for research in communication. In semiology, in Barthes's interrogation of 'mythologies' and, explicitly, in Eco's account of semiotics, there is the alignment of semiotics with cultural anthropology. Indeed, in semiotics as it emerged from the work of Sebeok and others, anthropology maintained a promi-nent position, with numerous contributors from anthropology, the inaugural vol-ume of the disciplinary field being a publication with a strong anthropological bent (Sebeok et al. 1965) and Sebeok himself having spent many years pursuing anthropological linguistics in the American tradition (see, for example, Sebeok and Ingemann 1956). Yet, this seems to be at odds with the flavour of the work that contemporary semiotics values. Taking its cue from Peirce's focus on science as the possibility of projection and the predictive capability of laws, along with his theory of the potential engendered by the interpretant, the contemporary semiotic model tries to incorporate a *vis a prospecto*, anticipating future developments and considering even those potentialities that remain hidden. By contrast, anthropolog-ical approaches are concerned with what peoples can be seen to do (or seen to have done – with communication or anything else). The 'encoding/decoding' model harboured a predictive element in that it suggested ways in which certain groups would deal with certain communications. However, the research that Hall and his colleagues carried out was fixated on such phenomena as the spectacular codes of subcultures, reporting their displays and what members of subcultures said about themselves, but seldom venturing into private spaces or daring to pre-dict how subculture participants' communications would develop. For researchers in the present, the discernment of the 'uses' of communications, and indeed the study of subcultures, is a much more fraught affair punctuated by numerous obsta-cles to procuring reliable data. So, one lesson for communication science that semiotic models may hold is that not only do today's communications require that more research is conducted in the private space of communication (e.g. Livingstone 2009), but that research may be geared to anticipating the new contexts of the network society and new forms of communication.

Further reading

Cobley, Paul (ed.). 2010. *The Routledge companion to semiotics*. London: Routledge.

Craig, Robert T. 2008. Code. In: Wolfgang Donsbach (ed.), *International encyclopedia of communication, Volume 2*, 529–532. Oxford and Malden, MA: Wiley-Blackwell.

Deely, John. 2010. *Semiotics seen synchronically*. New York: Legas.

Krampen, Martin. 1997. Communication models and semiosis. In: Roland Posner, Klaus Robering and Thomas A. Sebeok (eds.) *Ein Handbuch zu den zeichentheoretischen Grundlagen von Natur und Kultur, Volume 1*: 247–287. 4 vols. Berlin: de Gruyter.

Sebeok, Thomas A. 1991. Communication. In: *A Sign is Just a Sign*, 22–35 Bloomington: Indiana University Press.

References

Ang, Ien. 1984. *Watching* Dallas: *soap opera and the melodramatic imagination*. London: Routledge.

Ang, Ien. 1991. *Desperately seeking the audience*. London: Routledge.

Ang, Ien. 1996. *Living room wars: rethinking media audiences for a postmodern world*. London: Routledge.

Baker, Steve. 2000. *The postmodern animal*. London: Reaktion.

Barbieri, Marcello (ed). 2007. *Introduction to biosemiotics: the new biological synthesis*. Dordrecht: Springer.

Barbieri, Marcello. 2003. *The organic codes: an introduction to semantic biology*. Cambridge: Cambridge University Press.

Barthes, Roland. 1967. [1964]. *Elements of semiology*. Lavers, Annette and Smith, Colin (trans.) London: Cape.

Barthes, Roland. 1973. *Mythologies*. Lavers, Annette (trans.). London: Paladin.

Barthes, Roland. 1977a. *Image – Music – Text*. In: Stephen Heath (ed. and trans.). London: Fontana.

Barthes, Roland. 1977b. From 'work' to 'text'. In: Stephen Heath (ed. and trans.), *Image – Music – Text*. London: Fontana.

Barthes, Roland. 1977c. Introduction to the structural analysis of narratives. In: Stephen Heath (ed. and trans.), *Image – Music – Text*. London: Fontana.

Barthes, Roland. 1981. Theory of the text. In: Robert Young (ed.), *Untying the text: a poststructuralist reader*. London: Routledge.

Beattie, Geoffrey. 2003. *Visible thought: the new psychology of body language*. London: Routledge.

Bignell, Jonathan. 1997. *Media semiotics: an introduction*. Manchester: Manchester University Press.

Bouissac, Paul. 2010. *Saussure: A Guide for the Perplexed*. London: Continuum.

Buyssens, Eric. 1967. *La communication et l'articulation linguistique*. Brussels: Presses Universitaires.

Castells, Manuel. 2009. *The rise of the network society*, 2nd edn. New York: WileyBlackwell.

Castells, Manuel (ed.). 2005. *The network society: a cross-cultural perspective*. London: Edward Elgar.

Cobley, Paul. 2004. Narratology. In: Michael Groden (eds.), *The Johns Hopkins guide to literary theory and criticism*, 677–682. Baltimore and London: Johns Hopkins University Press.

Cobley, Paul. in press. Codes and coding: Sebeok's zoosemiotics and the dismantling of the fixed-code fallacy. *Semiotica*.

de Saussure, Ferdinand. 1959. [1916]. *Course in General Linguistics*. Baskin, Wade (trans.). New York: McGraw-Hill.

de Saussure, Ferdinand. 1983. [1916]. *Course in General Linguistics*. Harris, Roy (trans.). London: Duckworth.

Deely, John. 2001. *The four ages of understanding: the first postmodern survey of philosophy from ancient times to the turn of the twenty-first century*. Toronto: University of Toronto Press.

Dyer, Gillian. 1982. *Advertising as communication*. London: Routledge.

Eco, Umberto. 1976. *A theory of semiotics*. Bloomington: Indiana University Press.

Fant, Gunner C., Morris Halle & Roman Jakobson. 1952. *Preliminaries to speech analysis*. Cambridge, MA: MIT Press.

Fish, Stanley E. 1980. *Is there a text in this class? The authority of interpretive communities*. Cambridge, MA: Harvard University Press.

Fiske, John. 1990. *Introduction to communication studies*, 2nd edn. London: Routledge.

Fudge, Erica. 2004. *Renaissance beasts: of animals, humans, and other wonderful creatures*. Urbana: University of Illinois Press.

Geertz, Clifford. 1993. Thick description: toward an interpretive theory of culture. In: *The interpretation of cultures: selected essays*. London: Fontana.

Gillespie, Marie. 1995. *Television Ethnicity and Cultural Change*. London: Routledge.

Gray, Ann. 1992. *Video playtime: the gendering of a leisure technology*. London: Routledge.

Hall, Judith A. 1990. *Nonverbal sex differences: communication accuracy and expressive style*. Baltimore and London: Johns Hopkins University Press.

Hall, Stuart. 1973. *Encoding and decoding in the television discourse, Occasional Paper No. 7*, 1–12. Birmingham: Centre for Contemporary Cultural Studies.

Hall, Stuart (eds.). 1981. *Culture, media, language*. London: Hutchinson.

Harris, Roy. 1978. *The language myth*. London: Duckworth.

Harris, Roy. 2001. Linguistics after Saussure. In: Paul Cobley (ed.), *The Routledge companion to semiotics and linguistics*. London: Routledge.

Harris, Roy. 2003. *Saussure and his interpreters*, 2nd edn. Edinburgh: Edinburgh University Press.

Harris, Roy. 2006. Was Saussure an integrationist? In: Louis de Saussure (ed.), *Nouveaux regards sur Saussure: mélange offerts á René Amacker*. Geneva: Librairie Droz.

Hartley, John. 1982. *Understanding News*. London: Routledge.

Hermes, Joke. 1996. *Reading Womens Magazines: An Analysis of Everyday Media Use*. Oxford: Polity.

Hjelmslev, Louis. 1970. *Prolegomena to a theory of language*. Whitfield, Frank J. (trans.). Madison and London: University of Wisconsin Press.

Hobson, Dorothy. 1982. *Crossroads: The drama of a soap opera*. London: Methuen.

Hoffmeyer, Jesper. 1996. *Signs of meaning in the universe*. Haveland, Barbara J. (trans.) Bloomington: Indiana University Press.

Hoffmeyer, Jesper. 1998. Surfaces inside surfaces. On the origin of agency and life. *Cybernetics and Human Knowing* 5. 33–42.

Hoffmeyer, Jesper. 1999. Order out of indeterminacy. *Semiotica* 127 (1–4). 321–344.

Hoffmeyer, Jesper. 2008. *Biosemiotics. an examination into the signs of life and the life of signs*. Scranton: Scranton University Press.

Hoffmeyer, Jesper. 2009. Semiotics of nature. In: P. Cobley (ed), *The Routledge companion to semiotics*. London: Routledge.

Hoffmeyer, Jesper & Claus Emmeche. 2007. Code-duality and the semiotics of nature. Revised version. In: Marcello Barbieri (ed.), *Biosemiotics: information, codes and signs in living systems*. New York: Nova.

Jakobson, Roman. 1976. *Six lectures on sound and meaning*. Hassocks: Harvester.

Kendon, Adam. 1981. *Nonverbal communication: interaction and gesture*. Berlin: Mouton.

Knapp, Mark L. 1978. *Nonverbal communication in human interaction*. London: Thomson.

Krampen, Martin. 2010. Code. In: Marcel Danesi and Thomas A. Sebeok (eds.), *Encyclopedic Dictionary of Semiotics*. Berlin: de Gruyter Mouton.

Kull, Kalevi (ed.). 2001. *Jakob von Uexküll*. [Special issue]. *Semiotica* 134 (1/4).

Kull, Kalevi. 2007. A brief history of biosemiotics. In: Marcello Barbieri (ed.), *Biosemiotics: Information, codes and signs in living systems*. New York: Nova.

Lévi-Strauss, Claude. 1977. The structural study of myth. In: Claire Jacobson and Brooke Grundfest Schoepf, *Structural Anthropology Volume 1*. (trans.). Harmondsworth: Penguin.

Liebes, Tamar & Elihu Katz. 1993. *The export of meaning: cross-cultural readings of* Dallas, 2nd edn. Oxford: Polity.

Livingstone, Sonia. 2004. The challenge of changing audiences. Or, what is the audience researcher to do in the age of the internet? *European Journal of Communication*. 19 (1). 75–86.

Livingstone, Sonia. 2009. *Children and the internet*. Cambridge: Polity.

Lotman, Juri. 1974. The sign mechanism of culture. *Semiotica*. 12 (4). 301–305.

Lotman, Juri. 1982. The text and the structure of its audience. *New Literary History*. 14 (1). 81–87.

Lull, James. 1990. *Inside family viewing: ethnographic research on television's audience*. London: Routledge.

Morley, David. 1980. *The* Nationwide *audience*. London: B.F.I.

Morley, David. 1986. *Family television* London: Comedia.

Morley, David. 1992. *Television, audiences and cultural studies*. London: Routledge.

Nightingale, Virginia. 1996. *Studying audiences: the shock of the real*. London: Routledge.

Peirce, Charles Sanders. 1931–58. *The collected papers of Charles Sanders Peirce. Vols. I-VI*, Hartshorne, Charles and Weiss, Paul (eds.), *Vols. VII–VIII*, Burks, Arthur W. (ed.) Cambridge, MA: Harvard University Press.

Petrilli, Susan & Augusto Ponzio. 2001. *Thomas A. Sebeok and the Signs of Life*. Cambridge: Icon.

Poyatos, Fernando. 1983. *New perspectives in nonverbal communication*. Oxford: Pergamon.

Prieto, Luis J. 1968. La sémiologie. In: André Martinet (ed.), *Le langage*, 93–114. Paris: Gallimard.

Propp, Vladimir. 1968. , [1927]. *Morphology of the Folktale*. Scott, Laurence (trans.). Austin: University of Texas Press.

Radway, Janice A. 1984. *Reading the romance: women, patriarchy and popular culture*. Chapel Hill and London: University of North Carolina Press.

Sanders, Carol (ed.). 2004. *The Cambridge Companion to Saussure*. Cambridge: Cambridge University Press.

Saussure, Ferdinand de. 1959. *Course in General Linguistics,* Baskin, Wade (trans). New York: Philosophical Library.

Saussure, Ferdinand de. 1983. *Course in General Linguistics,* Harris, Roy (trans). London: Duckworth.

Sebeok, Thomas A. 1960. Coding in the evolution of signalling behavior. Paper delivered at the symposium on Comparative aspects of animal communication, Wenner-Gren Foundation, Burg Wartenstein, September 4–10.

Sebeok, Thomas A. 1965. Animal communication. *Science*. 147. 1006–1014.

Sebeok, Thomas A. 1970. Zoosemiotic structures and social organization. In: *Linguaggi nella societá e nella tecnica: Convegno promosso dalla Ing. C. Olivetti and C., S.p.A. per il centenario della nascita di Camillo Olivetti*, 113–128. Milan: Edizioni di Communitá.

Sebeok, Thomas A. 1972. *Perspectives in zoosemiotics*. The Hague: Mouton.

Sebeok, Thomas A. 1991. Communication. In: *A Sign is Just a Sign*, 22–35. Bloomington: Indiana University Press.

Sebeok, Thomas A. 1997. The evolution of semiosis. In: Roland Posner (eds.), *Semiotics: A Handbook on the Sign-Theoretic Foundations of Nature and Culture*, 436–446. Berlin: de Gruyter.

Sebeok, Thomas A. 2001. *Global Semiotics*. Bloomington: Indiana University Press.

Sebeok, Thomas A. & Frances J. Ingemann. 1956. *Studies in Cheremis: The Supernatural*. New York: Wenner-Gren.

Sebeok, Thomas A., Alfred S. Hayes & Mary Catherine Bateson (eds.). 1965. *Approaches to Semiotics*. The Hague: Mouton and Co.

Sebeok, Thomas A. & Jean Umiker-Sebeok (eds.). 1992. *Biosemiotics: the semiotic web 1991*. Berlin: Mouton de Gruyter.

Seiter, Ellen. 1989. *Remote control: television, audiences and cultural power*. London: Routledge.

Shannon, Claude E. & Warren Weaver. 1949. *The mathematical theory of communication*. Urbana: University of Illinois Press.

van Dijk, Jan A. G. M. 2012. *The network society. The social aspects of new media*, 3rd edn. London and Thousand Oaks: Sage.

von Uexküll, Jakob. 2001a. An Introduction to Umwelt. *Semiotica*. 134 (1/4). 107–110.

von Uexküll, Jakob. 2001b. The new concept of Umwelt: A link between science and the humanities. *Semiotica*. 134 (1/4): 111–123.

Weitz, Shirley (ed.). 1974. *Nonverbal communication: readings with commentary*. Oxford: Oxford University Press.

Wolfe, Cary. 2010. *What is posthumanism?* Minneapolis: University of Minnesota Press.

Wolfe, Cary (ed.). 2003. *Zoontologies: the question of the animal*. Minneapolis: University of Minnesota Press.

Tim Wharton

13 Linguistic action theories of communication

Abstract: Early work on the philosophy of language was unconcerned with language as a tool for communication: the pioneers of 'ideal' language philosophy were interested in how insights from logical languages might be applied to the study of 'language' in a very general sense. This chapter traces the development of a less formalized approach to meaning and communication based around linguistic action. It discusses Austin's speech act theory and Grice's theories of conversation and meaning and shows how this work laid the foundations not only for a more action-oriented account of communication but also a more psychological view of pragmatics.

Keywords: Action, speech act, Grice, conversation, maxims, implicature, relevance theory, pragmatics

1 Introduction

> The reason for concentrating on the study of speech acts is simply this: all linguistic communication involves linguistic acts (Searle 1969: 16).

Early work on the philosophy of language in the modern era was unconcerned with language as a tool for communication: the pioneers of 'ideal' language philosophy such as Frege, Russell, and Tarski were logicians, interested in how insights from logical languages might be applied to the study of 'language' in a very general sense. Carnap's logical positivists took the approach to surprising extremes. They suggested that a sentence that was incapable of being proven true or false, was in essence meaningless. Much work in logical positivism thereafter consisted in attempts to purify the philosophy of language by ridding it of unverifiable elements.

In the 1940s and 50s a group of Oxford philosophers began to question this approach, arguing that it obscured the crucial features of language rather than shed any light on them. They maintained that the truth-conditions of sentences exist only in virtue of the linguistic act, or *speech act*,[1] the sentence is used to

---

1 Though Austin and his colleagues are generally credited with laying the foundations of speech act theory (and Searle 1969 with building on these foundations), the term 'speech act' pre-dated 1940s Oxford. See Schumann and Smith (1990) for analysis of the pre-history of speech act theory, dating back to the work of Thomas Reid.

perform. The group became known as the 'ordinary' language philosophers and among them we can single out J. Austin, P. Strawson, and H. P. Grice.

The aim of this chapter is to trace the development of a less formalized approach based around linguistic action. Section 2 provides an outline of speech act theory and shows how while it was originally considered to be an alternative to the formal approach, the two approaches now happily co-exist. Section 3 shows how Grice's theories of conversation and meaning have laid the foundations not only for a more action-oriented account but also a more psychological view of pragmatics. Section 4 introduces relevance theory (Sperber and Wilson 1986/1995), a cognitive theory of utterance interpretation inspired by Grice's work and based around the notion of ostensive linguistic (and non-linguistic) acts. The chapter closes in Section 5 with some remarks on how a theory based on ostensive communicative acts might shed light on both the psychological and social domains – linguistic action, after all, is what makes the psychological social – and how the speech act conception of language as action spawned a whole range of other disciplines.

2 Speech act theory

The central idea behind speech act theory is that while ideal language philosophy can tell you all sorts of things about sentence meaning, it misses the fact that when we speak, we are performing actions. Austin's response to the logical positivists was that you can't reduce meaning to truth because many sentences both in the language of philosophy and in everyday language aren't intended to be true or false: approaching them from the perspective of truth is to misunderstand completely what they're doing. The most developed and sustained work in speech act theory is Searle (1969). Since linguistic acts are understood in virtue of the intentions behind them, a theory of language (and language use) – according to him – should form part of a larger theory of action.

Some sentences are obvious candidates for the kind of thing speech act theorists had in mind. Consider **(1)** and **(2)**. Intuitively, neither of these can be said to be true or false:

(1)   Shall we dance?

(2)   Leave me alone!

However, Austin identified a whole range of other sentences that don't lend themselves to being analyzed in terms of truth and falsity. Examples **(3)–(6)** are taken from Austin (1962: 5):

(3) 'I do² (take this woman to be my lawful wedded wife)' – as uttered in the course of the marriage ceremony.

(4) 'I name this ship the Queen Elizabeth' – as uttered when smashing the bottle against the stern.

(5) 'I give and bequeath my watch to my brother' – as occurring in a will.

(6) 'I bet you sixpence it will rain tomorrow.'

Austin dubbed sentences such as those in **(3)–(6)** *performative* utterances. These he contrasted with sentences/utterances that describe states of affairs in the world: *constatives*. Consider **(7)** and **(8)** below:

(7) I bequeathed my watch to my brother.

(8) I bet him sixpence that it was going to rain today.

Example **(7)** describes or reports a particular state of affairs (the state of affairs that at a particular time a certain individual bequeathed a watch to his brother, presumably whilst drawing up a will). This can be sharply contrasted with **(5)**, which doesn't describe the act of bequeathing at all. Rather, it *is* the act of bequeathing. Example **(8)** describes the state of affairs in which the individual in question made a bet concerning the weather with a particular person. This can be contrasted with **(6)**, which doesn't describe an act of betting but *is* an act of betting. The acts in question Austin called speech acts, hence 'speech act theory' and speech act types.

The first two thirds of Austin's book examines ways in which his constative/ performative distinction might be maintained. Might there be, for example, grammatical or syntactic criteria by which performatives can be identified? He concluded there were not and looked for an explanation as to why. But as anyone who has read *How to Do Things with Words* knows, the book has a twist in the tale. Beneath the surface there is consideable guile and towards the end of the book the argument takes a seismic shift. Having introduced the constative/performative distinction, and having used the latter as an argument against ideal language philosophy, Austin decides that actually there is *no* systematic way to maintain it. Moreover, he suggests that the distinction should be dropped! Once the distinction is dropped, however, it becomes clear that Austin's real claim is that *all* utterances, not just the ones that he has called performatives, are used to perform speech acts.

He distinguished three main types of speech act that are performed when someone says something: the first of these is the *locutionary act*, the act of saying

---

2 J. Urmson, who wrote the preface to the first edition, points out in a footnote that Austin's mistake, i.e. that the phrase 'I do' is not used in the wedding ceremony, was realized.

something; the second is the *illocutionary act*, the act performed *in* saying something: so in saying **(10)** I might be warning you (asserting, complaining, apologizing, commanding, requesting etc.); the third is the *perlocutionary act*, the one that results in an actual effect on the hearer.

Speech act theory enabled philosophers to ask new questions. According to one radical interpretation the study of meaning cannot be divorced from the study of language use. Construed in this way speech act theory is an *alternative* to the kind of formal approach advocated by ideal language philosophers. Austin (1962) used the terms sentence and utterance interchangeably: this was because at the time he wrote those words the modern distinction between sentences and utterances – or semantics and pragmatics – did not exist.

A more moderate interpretation would be that speech act theory could supplement formal semantics. Put differently, while Austin's intention was to say that the study of semantics was, in effect, better construed as the study of pragmatics, the real contribution of speech act theory was to confirm that when it comes to the study of meaning, there are different levels to consider. In the late 60s, the work of Paul Grice, himself one kind of ordinary language philosopher, suggested ways in which the work of the formalists and the speech act theorists might finally be reconciled.

3 Gricean pragmatics

3.1 Meaning

We may owe the term 'pragmatics' to Charles Morris (1938), but it is Paul Grice who laid the foundations upon which modern pragmatic theories are built. His work is generally regarded as being based around two theories: of *meaning* and *conversation*. But the theories are far from distinct and it could be argued that the latter is a component of the former (Neale 1992). Indeed, both theories formed part of much a larger programme on reasons, reasoning and rationality (Grice 2001). There has been little discussion of how Grice's theories of conversation and meaning fit into his larger programme (though see Chapman 2005 and Allott 2007), largely – perhaps – due to the fact that this dimension of Grice's work was only published in 2001. His later work, however, can certainly be interpreted as a continuation of his exploration into earlier themes. Grice was committed to seeing humans as rational beings. We have reasons for our attitudes – and hence our linguistic actions – and have evolved to interpret the behaviour of others in terms of the reasons behind it. Moreover, the way we interpret the actions and utterances of others constitutes in itself a form of reasoning. Thanks in no small part to Grice's work it is now increasingly recognized that verbal communication is more than a simple coding-decoding process.

For Grice meaning was to be understood in terms of propositional-attitude psychology. Ultimately, the meaning of words reduced to the beliefs, desires and intentions of communicators who uttered them. He began his 1957 paper 'Meaning' by distinguishing two types of meaning: natural meaning – see **(9)** below – and non-natural meaning (meaning$_{NN}$) – **(10)**:

(9)   Those spots mean measles.

(10)   That remark means he has measles.

Grice's principal concern was meaning$_{NN}$, and in particular, how the kind of meaning exemplified in **(10)** might be characterized in terms of the expression and recognition of intentions. He moved through a series of carefully constructed examples in order to identify the kind of intentions are required. Having dismissed those examples in which a person has an intention to inform someone of something, but keeps that intention secret (the intention can therefore play no role), Grice turned to a series of further examples, where the 'communicator' provides overt evidence of their informative intention:

> Clearly we must at least add that, for x to have meant$_{NN}$ anything, not merely must it have been "uttered" with the intention of inducing a certain belief but also the utterer must have intended the "audience" to recognize the intention behind the utterance. [...]
>
> (1)   Herod presents Salome with the head of St. John the Baptist on a charger.
>
> (2)   Feeling faint, a child lets its mother see how pale it is (hoping that she may draw her own conclusions and help).
>
> (3)   I leave the china my daughter has broken lying around for my wife to see. (1989: 218)

For Grice, however, a problem remained. There is still a sense in the above examples in which the communicator's intentions are incidental to the audience's intended response. In **(1)**, for example, Salome can infer that St. John the Baptist is dead on the strength of the evidence presented and independently of any intentions Herod has. Grice wanted to distinguish between drawing someone's attention to a particular object or a certain type of behaviour overtly – 'showing,' which in his view did not amount to the object or behaviour meaning$_{NN}$ anything – and something being meant$_{NN}$ by the object or behaviour in question, or by the person responsible for using the object or behaviour in a certain meaningful$_{NN}$ manner.

In any act carried out in which evidence is provided of an intention to convey information there are two layers to be retrieved by the audience. First, there is the information being pointed out, in Grice's example **(2)**, the fact that John the Baptist is dead. Second, there is the information that this first layer is being pointed out intentionally. Notice that in example **(1)** while Herod does indeed provide overt evidence of an intention to inform, the first layer of information is derivable *entirely without reference to this intention*. **(2)** and **(3)** work in the same way. Grice proposed that for a case to count as one of meaning$_{NN}$ the first layer should *not* be entirely derivable without reference to the second layer. Grice's famous definition of meaning is provided below (see Grice 1989: 92):

"*U* meant something by uttering *x*" is true if, for some audience *A*, *U* uttered *x* intending:

(1)   *A* to produce a particular response *r*

(2)   *A* to think (recognize) that *U* intends (1)

(3)   *A* to fulfil (1) on the basis of his fulfilment of (2).

3.2 Conversation

It is probably true that when most people hear Grice's name it is his work on the Cooperative Principle and Maxims that comes to mind. By drawing a distinction between the levels of *what is said* and *implicature*, Grice aimed to suggest ways in which the essential differences between the ideal and ordinary philosophy movements may be reconciled. In effect, he proposed a distinction between semantics, the study of linguistic meaning, and pragmatics, the study of language use, a distinction that allowed ideal and ordinary language philosophy to coexist.

Consider the exchange in **(11)** below. Bob, Karen and Mary work in the same building:

(11)   Bob: Is Mary still here?
        Karen: Well, her door is open.

Karen's response to Bob's question is at best indirect. He has asked her a specific question and rather than answer him directly she has responded with information about a door. However, it is not hard to imagine a context in which Bob would infer that Karen has implied – or 'implicated' – that Mary is still here. Grice wanted to explain how it is that such inferences are so easily arrived at by hearers. His idea was that communication is a cooperative activity, and when two or more people are communicating, it is in both their interests to make the communication go as smoothly as possible in order to achieve their mutual aim. Because communication is cooperative, speakers behave in certain predictable ways. In general, for instance, a speaker is not going to say something that is totally irrelevant, or that will not tell the hearer what he wants to know.

But Grice's insight raises as many questions as it answers. What are these predictable ways in which cooperative speakers behave? What counts as being cooperative? Grice's answer to this question was that the cooperative principle can be broken down into a number of different maxims of conversation – *Quantity, Quality, Relation* and *Manner*. His idea was that speakers will, on the whole, make sure that their conversational contributions comply with these maxims and, hence, the Cooperative Principle. Grice presented the Cooperative Principle and maxims as follows:

Cooperative Principle
Make your contribution such as is required, at the stage at which it occurs, by the accepted purpose or direction of the talk exchange in which you are engaged.

Quantity maxims
1. Make your contribution as informative as is required (for the current purposes of the exchange).
2. Do not make your contribution more informative than is required.

Quality maxims
Supermaxim: Try to make your contribution one that is true.
1. Do not say what you believe to be false.
2. Do not say that for which you lack adequate evidence.

Maxim of Relation
Be relevant.

Manner maxims
Supermaxim: Be perspicuous
1. Avoid obscurity of expression.
2. Avoid ambiguity.
3. Be brief (avoid unnecessary prolixity)
4. Be orderly (Grice 1989: 26–27).

Grice's framework showed how hearers actually put the linguistic meaning of what has been said together with the assumption that the speaker is being cooperative (and therefore complying with the maxims), and any other necessary world knowledge, in order to finally arrive at the intended interpretation of the utterance in question.

Bob might, for example, wonder whether all Karen wants to communicate to him is that the Mary's door is still open. However, he will justifiably conclude that this is not the case, on the grounds that if that was all she wanted to communicate, it would not satisfy the maxims (and hence would fail to satisfy the Cooperative Principle). For example, Karen's utterance would fail to satisfy the Quantity maxim, since it would not be as informative as is required for the current purposes of the exchange. Nor would it satisfy the maxim of Relation, since her contribution would not be relevant in the context of the exchange.

Bob assumes that Karen *is* obeying the cooperative principle and maxims, and hence he will look for a way of interpreting her utterance such that these apparent violations can be removed. If Karen is being cooperative, then she must think that the fact that Mary's door is open is informative and relevant in some way as a response to Bob's question. Bob knows that Mary closes her door before she leaves work. Moreover, he knows (or at least presumes) that Karen is also aware of these facts. He infers, then, that what she intended to communicate is that because the door is open, Mary has still not left. This is the only way that Karen's utterance can be interpreted on the assumption that she is observing the cooperative principle and maxims. Only in this way is her response both informative and relevant.

It is important not to confuse Grice's claims about conversation with the much stronger claim (which Grice certainly did *not* endorse) that *all* conversations are cooperative, and that the maxims are *always* obeyed. Indeed, Grice listed four ways in which the maxims may fail to be fulfilled. Perhaps the most well known of these are cases in which rather than a maxim or maxims being apparently violated (as in **(10).**), maxims are *overtly* violated. Consider **(15).**. Bob is talking to Karen about their colleague Mary, who has been bad-mouthing them to others:

(15)   Bob: She's an absolute joy to work with.

It is perfectly obvious to Karen that Bob has said something he does not believe, and Bob is well aware of this (and Karen is aware that Bob is aware of it). However, he has done so overtly, and whilst he is clearly violating the first Quality maxim, Karen will infer that he is at least still obeying the Cooperative Principle. Karen will therefore search for another proposition related to the one Bob is expressing. For Grice, the most obvious candidate in this case would be the opposite proposition to the one he has expressed, i.e. that Mary is impossible to work with. This example involves the figurative interpretation of a case of irony. Other figures of speech Grice characterized as relying on the flouting of maxims include metaphor, hyperbole and meiosis (or understatement).

Grice's work on conversation has been hugely influential. For many, the Cooperative Principle and maxims represent the dawn of modern pragmatics. Most people working within pragmatics accept that hearers are guided in the interpretive process by some sort of expectation that a speaker is meeting certain standards. From this it follows that speakers behave in predictable ways and hearers can therefore recognize the best hypothesis about the speaker's meaning by arriving at an interpretation that satisfies those expectations the speaker is aiming at, or standards he or she is trying to meet. Neo-Gricean pragmatists view these standards in a way that remains quite faithful to Grice's framework (Atlas 2005; Bach 1994, 1999, 2001; Gazdar 1979; Horn 1984, 1996, 2005; Levinson 1983, 2000). Whilst doing away with Gricean maxims, Relevance Theory (Sperber and Wilson 1986/ 1995) remains true to Grice's original insights that communication is an inferential activity, and that central to the process of utterance interpretation is the fact an overt act of communication raises certain expectations in its audience.

4 Relevance theory

Relevance theory (Sperber and Wilson 1986/1995, Blakemore 2002, Wilson and Sperber 2004) combines aspects of a Gricean pragmatics with modern psychological research and cognitive science to provide a cognitive-inferential pragmatic framework. It takes as its domain a carefully defined sub-set of those cases that might be referred to as instances of communication. 'Communication' itself is a broad notion. Sebeok (1972: 39) remarks that "...all organic alliances presuppose a measure of communication: Protozoa interchange signals; an aggregate of cells becomes an organism by virtue of the fact that the component cells can influence one another". Construed in this way, a theory of pragmatics would indeed have to be what Chomsky (2000) has termed a 'theory of everything,' and would need to encompass every facet of human interaction definable as 'communicative': from socio-cultural right down to sub-personal phenomena.

But relevance theory has a carefully delimited domain. It is not a 'theory of everything.' In fact is not even a theory of communication *per se*, focusing as it does on a sub-type of human communicative action: action by which a communicator provides evidence that they intend to communicate something.[3] Natural language is seen as governed by a code, itself governed by an autonomous mental grammar. Utterance interpretation, on the other hand, is a two-stage process. The linguistically encoded logical form, which is the output of the mental grammar, is simply a starting point for rich inferential processes guided by the expectation that speakers conform to certain standards or expectations: that in (highly) intuitive terms, an audience knows that a communicator has a good reason for providing the stimulus which attracts attention to their intention to communicate, and that that reason is a good enough one for an audience to attend to it. In contrast with conscious, reflective reasoning, it is proposed that these inferential processes are unconscious and fast, under-pinned by 'fast and frugal heuristics' of the kind currently gaining much currency in cognitive science (Gigerenzer et al. 1999).

Relevance theory is based on a definition of relevance and two general principles: a Cognitive and a Communicative Principle of Relevance (for a recent account see Wilson and Sperber 2004). Relevance is characterized in cost-benefit terms, as a property of inputs to cognitive processes, the benefits being positive cognitive effects, and the cost the processing effort needed to achieve these effects. Other things being equal, the greater the positive cognitive effects achieved by processing an input in a context of available assumptions, and the smaller the processing effort required, the greater the relevance of the input to the individual who processes it. The human disposition to search for relevance is seen as an evolved consequence of the tendency toward greater efficiency in cognition. As Gigerenzer et al.

---

3 For discussion of the crucial differences between relevance-theoretic and Gricean intentions see Wharton (2008).

(1999: 21) put it: "There is a point where too much information and too much information processing can hurt. Cognition is the art of focusing on the relevant and deliberately ignoring the rest." And this disposition is one that is routinely exploited in human communication. Speakers know that listeners pay attention only to ostensive acts that are relevant enough, and so in order to attract and hold an audience's attention they should make their linguistic or non-linguistic acts appear at least relevant enough to be worth processing. More precisely, the Communicative Principle of Relevance claims that by overtly displaying an intention to inform – producing an utterance or other ostensive stimulus – a communicator creates a presumption that the stimulus is at least relevant enough to be worth processing, and moreover, the most relevant one compatible with her own abilities and preferences.

In contrast with Grice, relevance theory aims at providing a characterization of human overt intentional communication generally. Utterances, after all, are not the only kind of ostensive actions, and a communicator might provide evidence of her intention to inform by means of a look, a gesture, or even a natural sign such as a facial expression. Ostensive actions are often a mixture of what Grice would have called natural *and* non-natural meaning, and this is one of the reasons that relevance theory does not attempt to draw the line that Grice wanted to between deliberately and openly letting someone know and telling. There's much more to human communication than language.

Wharton (2009) provides an account of some of the implications redrawing the domain of pragmatics in this way has. One of the most obvious is that focusing on meaning$_{NN}$ has had the effect of excluding from pragmatics the overt showing of spontaneously produced natural behaviours. But there seem to be clear cases where the open showing of spontaneously produced natural signs and signals makes a difference to the speaker's meaning. Take, for example, an utterance of **(12)**:

(12)   Peter is late.

If the utterer of (16) makes no attempt to conceal the spontaneous anger in her facial expression and tone of voice, and hence 'deliberately and openly shows' it, she would naturally be understood as meaning not only that Peter was late but that she was angry that he was late. Grice's framework appears to exclude such spontaneous expressions of emotion from contributing to a speaker's meaning.

Or consider the exchange in **(13)**, uttered on the terrace of a restaurant:

(13)   Jack: Shall we sit out here?
        Lily (shivering ostensively): I'm cold.

Lily's ostensive shiver accompanying her utterance of 'I'm cold' should be salient enough to be picked out by Jack and used in his interpretation of the degree term 'cold.' How much she is shivering will be treated as an indication of how cold she feels, and, in effect, will calibrate the degree of coldness Jack understands her to feel and to be expressing as part of her meaning. The fact that Lily has shivered ostensively – shown, as well as told him she is cold – will motivate Jack's search for the 'extra' meaning Lily intends to convey in return for the extra processing effort required. In this case, Jack would be entitled to understand Lily as implicating that she is definitely cold enough to want to go inside. In a parallel example, Lily's ostensive shiver accompanying her utterance of 'It's lovely on the terrace, isn't it?' might provide Jack with a clue that she is being ironic, that actually she hates it on the terrace and would prefer to go inside. In both cases, openly shown natural behaviours affect the outcome of the interpretive process, guiding the hearer to a certain range or type of conclusions.

It is worth underlining here that these natural behaviours not only help Jack establish the implicit content of Lily's utterance, but also contribute to the truth-conditional content of the proposition he takes Lily to be expressing. The truth conditions of her utterance of 'I'm cold' will vary according to the type or degree of coldness she intends to communicate, which are indicated in her openly shown natural behaviour.

Recall the characterization in the previous section. In any act carried out with the intention of revealing an informative intention, there are two layers of information to be retrieved. The first, basic layer is the information being pointed out, and the second is the information that the first layer is being pointed out intentionally. What makes an individual ostensive act a case of either 'showing' or meaning$_{NN}$ is the precise nature of the evidence provided for the first layer. In cases of showing, the evidence provided is relatively direct – Lily's shiver, for example. In cases of meaning$_{NN}$, the evidence provided is relatively indirect – a linguistic utterance, for example.

Most cases of showing, cases in which the evidence provided of the first layer of information is fairly direct, still require an extra layer of inference before the communicator's full informative intention is recognized, and the extent to which an audience is required to make this extra inference is a question of degree. Not only can what is meant$_{NN}$ be regarded as a sub-set of what is intentionally communicated, but rather than the dichotomy Grice envisaged in his 1957 paper, there is a continuum of cases between showing and meaning$_{NN}$.

The continuum between showing and meaning$_{NN}$ has a variety of applications. At various points along it, we can see the varying extents to which hearers are required to consider speakers' intentions in order to get from the evidence they provide to the first, basic layer of information they are communicating. It therefore provides a 'snapshot' of the types of evidence used in intentional communicative acts and the role inference plays in them. At one extreme of the continuum lie clear cases of spontaneous, natural display. At the other lie clear cases of linguistic coding, where all the evidence provided for the first, basic layer is indirect. In between lie a range of cases in which more or less direct 'natural' evidence and more or less *in*direct coded evidence mix to various degrees: for example, in pointing and stylized expressions of emotion. Equally importantly, the continuum provides a theoretical tool which allows us to conceptualize more clearly the observation made above that ostensive stimuli are often highly complex *composites* of different, inter-related behaviours which fall at various points between 'showing' and 'meaning$_{NN}$.' In Wilson and Wharton (2006) these observations are brought to bear on the analysis of prosody. Wharton (2009) applies them to nonverbal behaviours in general.[4]

I have also argued (Wharton 2003, 2009) that the continuum has diachronic implications. When an interjection such as 'yugh,' for example, moves far enough along the continuum, it may become linguistically productive ('yucky,' 'yuckier,' 'yuckiest'), and some of its uses may be properly linguistic. In many historical linguistic accounts (Aitchison 1991, Lightfoot 1991) children are seen as converging on the simplest grammar that reflects the practice of the speech community to which they are exposed. The continuum could allow us to explore the idea that pragmatic factors may affect this convergence, and to see language change in terms of the micro-processes involved in the emergence of new encoded meanings. Language change might then be characterized in terms of population-scale macro-processes resulting from an accumulation of those micro-processes, leading to the stabilization of new senses.

5 The psychological and the social

Much current work in evolutionary psychology conceives of the mind as an adaptive toolbox, a set of dedicated cognitive mechanisms that evolved in small incremental steps to meet problems in the environment (Barkow et al. 1995; Sperber 2002). One way in which such mechanisms might improve overall cognitive efficiency is by providing what Gigerenzer et al. (1999) call 'fast and frugal heuristics,' which apply to a particular domain, and yield reliable conclusions when applied to input from this domain. As Gigerenzer and Selten (2002: 7) put it: "Heuristics are middle-ranged, that is, they work in a class of situations... What we call the adaptive toolbox contains a number of these "middle-range" tools, not a single hammer for all purposes." On the face of it, having to trust heuristics may seem disadvantageous, especially since they are not foolproof. Gigerenzer and Selten (2002) suggest not. They ask us to consider a thought experiment in which two teams are set the task of designing a robot that can catch a ball. One team adopts an omniscientific approach and

---

4 In that book I also make a further distinction in cases of natural meaning between what I call natural signs and natural signals.

programmes a robot with knowledge of all the projected parabolas a ball might follow, as well as a range of instruments to perform the calculations that will get the robot to the right place to wait and catch the ball. The other team study what baseball players actually do (the first team dismiss this idea because, since sportsmen aren't conscious of the measurements and calculations they are using when they catch a ball). On the basis of this they programme the robot to follow what has been called the *gaze heuristic*. A robot programmed with such a heuristic does not move immediately the ball is airborne. Instead, it makes a rough estimate of whether the ball is going to land in front of it or behind it and then starts running in an appropriate direction whilst fixing its gaze on the ball. From here it adjusts its running speed so that the angle between the eye and the ball remains the same. Using this method, the robot does not need to calculate where the ball will land. Provided it can move quickly enough, it will catch the ball whilst it is running.

Many such heuristics have been identified: the *recognition heuristic*, by which we tend to assign higher value to objects with which we are familiar; the *contagion heuristic*, by which we tend to avoid contact with objects that have come into contact with other objects we regard as contaminated. Emotions may be heuristics. Faced with a dangerous animal, fear puts our body into the state it needs to be in to either fight or run away: we don't need to reason ourselves into feeling frightened, although we sometimes try to reason our way out of it.

There are clear implications for pragmatics. After all, the central question is how it is that hearers accurately and seemingly effortlessly infer speaker meaning. Heuristics would seem an appropriate choice. Levinson (2000) makes use of what he calls an 'I'-heuristic, which yields default inferences in the form of conclusions that are automatically drawn but may be overruled by contextual information. Relevance theory's approach sees cognition and communication as relying heavily on a comprehension heuristic, which make it possible to pick out potentially relevant inputs to cognitive processes and process them in a way that enhances their relevance. So in example **(13)** it is Jack's relevance-based comprehension heuristic that picks out Lily's salient behaviour.

A unique feature of, for example, Grice's legacy is that it continues to reverberate throughout a whole range of disciplines. During a presentation at Oxford in September 2000, psychologist Alan Leslie remarked it was Grice's paper 'Meaning' that was largely responsible for awakening his interest in Theory of Mind and social cognition. But Grice gets credit within the social as well as the psychological sphere. Sociolinguist John Gumperz (2001: 216) has gone on record as remarking it is Grice "who lays the foundation of a truly social perspective on speaking". Opportunities for bridge building between the social and psychological sciences are rare, but they should be embraced (though I have found they are often resisted). Sperber and Wilson (1997: 145) are surely right when they say: "It is not enough to define sociology as what sociologists usually do and psychology as what psychologists usually do: such definitions show too much respect for institutional boundaries." With the exceptions of Brown and Levinson (1979, 1987), Enfield (2003), Enfield and Levinson (2006a,b) researchers who adopt a sociolinguistic or anthropological view have not so far been very interested in building on the foundations of a 'truly social perspective' that Grice laid. How might such bridges be built?

Earlier in this chapter, when I discussed possible implications of the showing-meaning$_{NN}$ continuum for the analysis of language change, I noted that the stabilization of new lexical senses might be characterized in terms of population-scale macro-processes resulting from the accumulation of individual micro-processes. Just as much work in historical linguistics is largely concerned with the patterns of linguistic change themselves (though see Hopper and Traugott [1993] 2003), so work in discourse analysis and sociolinguistics often centres on social notions such as power relations and inequality, and examines how they are manifested, reinforced and even *constructed* by discourse. As Cameron (1997: 57) puts it: "Many sociolinguistic accounts offered within the traditional quantitative paradigm presuppose that ...there exist social categories, structures, divisions, attitudes and identities which are marked, encoded or expressed in language use." But – to paraphrase Harold Garfinkel – people are not 'cultural dopes,' passively and mindlessly producing utterances predetermined by such categories or structures, or their ethnicity, age, sex or social class membership. We are intelligent social beings, capable of making strategic use of language to confirm or contest such categories, structures, divisions etc. What Franks (2011) calls 'the circularity problem,' that just as minds are fundamental to culture, so to is culture fundamental to mind, will not go away, but beginning to adopt ways in which we can approach the sociolinguistic domain from a different perspective – starting with the minds of the individuals who create the discourse, and treating macro-level sociolinguistic phenomena as resulting from an accumulation of individual micro-level acts – might yield interesting and worthwhile results. It may even be a small step to providing the social sciences with a naturalistic ontology.

As for the legacy of Austin, Searle and other true speech act theorists, the broader consequence of their work has been to legitimize the study of language or discourse *as-action*. By analyzing the meaning of utterances in terms of the acts they perform, speech act theory spawned a variety of approaches – including discourse analysis, variationist linguistics and conversation analysis – all of which assume not only that these units of discourse have communicative functions, but also that these functions can be meaningfully identified and labeled. As we have seen, Austin's motives were entirely philosophical, but he unwittingly laid the foundations for a range of disciplines, many of which are discussed at more length in other chapters within this volume.

Further reading

Austin, John. 1962. *How to Do Things with Words*. Oxford: Clarendon Press.

Grice, H. Paul. 1989. *Studies in the Way of Words*. Cambridge, MA: Harvard University Press.

Neale, Stephen. 1992. Paul Grice and the philosophy of language. *Linguistics and Philosophy* 15. 509–559.

Sperber, Dan & Deirdre Wilson. 1986/1995. *Relevance: Communication and Cognition*. Oxford: Blackwell.

Wharton, Tim. 2009. *Pragmatics and Non-Verbal Communication*. Cambridge: Cambridge University Press.

References

Aitchison, Jean. 1991. *Language change: Progress or decay?* 2nd edn. New York: Cambridge University Press.

Allott, Nicholas. 2007. *Relevance and rationality*, unpublished thesis. University College London.

Atlas, Jay. 2005. *Logic, Meaning, and Conversation: Semantical Underdeterminacy, Implicature and their Interface*. Oxford: Oxford University Press.

Austin, John. 1962. *How to Do Things with Words*. Oxford: Clarendon Press.

Bach, Kent. 1994. Conversational impliciture. *Mind and Language* 9. 124–162.

Bach, Kent. 1999. The myth of conventional implicature. *Linguistics and Philosophy* 22: 327–366.

Bach, Kent. 2001. You don't say? *Synthese* 127. 11–31.

Barkow, Jerome, Leda Cosmides & John Tooby. 1995. *The Adapted Mind: Evolutionary Psychology and the Generation of Culture*. Oxford: Oxford University Press.

Blakemore, Diane. 2002. *Relevance and Linguistic Meaning: The Semantics and Pragmartics of Discourse Markers*. Cambridge: Cambridge University Press.

Brown, P. & S. Levinson. 1979. Social structure, groups, and interaction. In: K. R. Scherer and H. Giles (eds.), *Social markers in speech*, 291–341. Cambridge: Cambridge University Press.

Brown, P. & S. Levinson. 1987. *Politeness*. Cambridge: Cambridge University Press.

Cameron, Deborah. 1997. Demythologizing sociolinguistics. In: Nik Coupland and Adam Jaworski (eds.), *Sociolinguistics: A Reader and Coursebook*. London: Macmillan Press Ltd.

Carston, Robyn. 2002. *Thoughts and Utterances: The Pragmatics of Explicit Communication*. Oxford: Blackwell.

Chapman, Siobhan. 2005. *Paul Grice, Philosopher and Linguist*. Basingstoke: Palgrave Macmillan.

Chomsky, Noam. 2000. *New Horizons in the Study of Language and Mind*. Cambridge: Cambridge University Press.

Enfield, N. 2003. *Linguistic Epidemiology: Semantics and Grammar of Language Contact in Mainland South East Asia*. London: Routledge.

Enfield, N. & S. Levinson (eds.). 2006a. *Roots of Human Sociality: Culture, Cognition and Interaction*. New York: Berg Publishers.

Enfield, N. & S. Levinson. 2006b. Introduction: human sociality as a new interdisciplinary field. In: N. Enfield and S. Levinson (eds.), *Roots of Human Sociality*, 1–35. New York: Berg Publishers.

Franks, Bradley. 2011. *Cognition and Culture: an Evolutionary Perspective*. Basingstoke: Palgrave Macmillan.

Gazdar, Gerald. 1979. *Pragmatics: Implicature, Presupposition and Logical Form*. London: Academic Press.

Gigerenzer, Gerd & Reinhard Selten (eds.). 2002. *Bounded Rationality: The Adaptive Toolbox*. Cambridge, MA: MIT Press.

Gigerenzer, Gerd, Peter Todd and the ABC Research Group. 1999. *Simple Heuristics that Make us Smart*. Oxford: Oxford University Press.

Grice, H. Paul. 1957. Meaning. *Philosophical Review* 66. 377–388.

Grice, H. Paul. 1989. *Studies in the Way of Words*. Cambridge, MA: Harvard University Press.

Grice, H. Paul & Richard Warner (ed.). 2001. *Aspects of Reason*. Oxford: Clarendon Press.

Grice, P. 2001. *Aspects of Reason*. Oxford: Clarendon Press.

Gumperz, John J. 2001. Interactional sociolinguistics: A personal perspective. In: D. Schiffrin, D. Tannen and H. E. Hamilton (eds.), *Handbook of Discourse Analysis*. Malden, MA: Blackwell.

Hopper, Paul & Elisabeth Traugott. 1993. [2003]. *Grammaticalization*. Cambridge: Cambridge University Press.

Horn, Laurence. 1984. Towards a new taxonomy for pragmatic inference: Q- and R-based implicature. In: D. Schiffrin (ed.), *Meaning, Form, and Use in Context: Linguistic Applications*. Washington, DC: Georgetown University Press.

Horn, Laurence. 1996. Presupposition and implicature. In: S. Lappin (ed.), *The Handbook of Contemporary Semantic Theory*. Oxford: Blackwell.

Horn, Laurence. 2005. The border wars: a neo-Gricean perspective. In: K. von Heusinger and Ken Turner (eds.), *Where Semantics Meets Pragmatics*. Amsterdam: Elsevier.

Levinson, Steven. 1983. *Pragmatics*. Cambridge: Cambridge University Press.

Levinson, Steven. 2000. *Presumptive Meanings: The Theory of Generalized Conversational Implicature*. Cambridge, MA: MIT Press.

Lightfoot, David. 1991. *How to Set Parameters: Arguments from Language Change*. Cambridge, MA: MIT Press.

Morris, Charles. 1938. Foundations of the theory of signs. In: O. Neurath (ed.), *International Encyclopedia of Unified Science, volume 1, number 2*. Chicago: University of Chicago Press; reprinted in *Writings on the General Theory of Signs* [1971]. The Hague: Mouton.

Neale, Stephen. 1992. Paul Grice and the philosophy of language. *Linguistics and Philosophy*, 15. 509–559.

Schumann, Karl & Barry Smith. 1990. Elements of speech act theory in the work of Thomas Reid. *History of Philosophy Quarterly* 7. 40–66

Searle, John. 1969. *Speech Acts*. Cambridge: Cambridge University Press.

Sebeok, Thomas. 1972. *Perspectives in Zoosemiotics*. The Hague: Mouton.

Sperber, Dan. 2002. In defense of massive modularity. In: Emmanuel Dupoux (ed.), *Language, Brain and Cognitive Development: Essays in Honor of Jacques Mehler*. Cambridge MA: MIT Press.

Sperber, Dan & Deirdre Wilson. 1986. /1995. *Relevance: Communication and Cognition*. Oxford: Blackwell.

Sperber, Dan & Deirdre Wilson. 1997. Remarks on relevance theory and the social sciences. *Multilingua* 16. 145–151.

Wharton, Tim. 2003. Interjections, language and the 'showing'/'saying' continuum. *Pragmatics and Cognition* 11 (1). 39–91.

Wharton, Tim. 2008. Meaning and showing: Gricean intentions and relevance- theoretic intentions. *Intercultural Pragmatics* 5 (2). 131–152.

Wharton, Tim. 2009. *Pragmatics and Non-Verbal Communication*. Cambridge: Cambridge University Press.

Wilson, Deirdre & Dan Sperber. 2004. Relevance Theory. In: Laurence Horn and Greg Ward (eds.), *The Handbook of Pragmatics*. Oxford: Blackwell.

Wilson, Deirdre & Tim Wharton. 2006. Relevance and prosody. *Journal of Pragmatics* 38. 1559–1579.

Adrian Bangerter and Eric Mayor

14 Interactional theories of communication

Abstract: Conversational interaction is the primary means of communication in everyday life. It serves to coordinate joint activities among individuals. But conversation is itself a species of joint activity that gets coordinated in an ongoing, emergent manner by participants. Participants coordinate on who participates in an interaction, what roles participants will enact, actions to be performed, and their timing and location. They achieve mutual understanding, or common ground, on these aspects by signaling to each other their beliefs about the state of the conversation on a moment-by-moment basis. We discuss examples of the myriad ways in which various aspects of joint activities get coordinated.

Keywords: Conversation, social interaction, mutual understanding, common ground, grounding, joint action, coordination

In this chapter, we describe a body of work developed in cognitive psychology and related fields that systematically investigates the cognitive and social processes involved in how people use language to communicate. This work builds on earlier research in the philosophy of language (speech act theory; Austin 1962; Searle 1969), in pragmatics (Grice, 1975), in ethnomethodology and the microsociology of interaction (Goffman 1967; Sacks et al. 1974), and in psycholinguistics (Clark and Clark 1977). We draw in particular on Clark's (1996) theory of language use. This theory specifies the cognitive underpinnings of communication and describes in detail the linguistic acts by which it is accomplished. By focusing on cognition and communication, it is related to, but distinct from, other cognitive science approaches such as cognitive linguistics, which investigate conceptual aspects of language production and understanding as a cognitive process without looking at actual communication (for example, how concepts like metaphors affect thought and understanding; Lakoff and Johnson, 1980).

The research we describe is derived from detailed experimental and field studies (Clark and Bangerter 2004) of everyday conversation, especially in face-to-face settings, but it has also been largely applied to other communicative media (Clark and Brennan 1991). Interactive face-to-face conversation is the fundamental setting in which humans communicate (Clark 1996), and thus is the paradigm case for garnering important insights into the nature of communication.

A fundamental message is that conversation is primarily used to coordinate joint activities among individuals. Another is that conversation is itself a species of joint activity that gets coordinated on a moment-by-moment basis (Holtgraves 2002). We thus first describe the functions of communication (why we communicate) followed by a broad discussion of mutual knowledge, or *common ground*, which is the cognitive foundation of communication. We then discuss examples of the myriad of ways we coordinate various aspects of conversations before concluding.

1 Why we communicate: coordinating joint action

Communication primarily serves to solve problems of cooperation, in other words coordinating joint action. This is true for modern-day humans and is as well the reason why language evolved. Indeed, human social life recurrently involves cooperating to reach goals that a group can achieve better than an individual. Compare the outcomes attainable by a symphonic orchestra, a surgical team, or a group of prehistoric hunters relative to those attainable by a single individual in each of these domains. At the same time, cooperative enterprises pose the so-called *dilemma of cooperation* (Smith 2010): individuals want to cooperate, but run the risk of being deceived or exploited by their partners. Also, even if cooperation partners are motivated by mutually benevolent intentions, they still need to figure out how to coordinate their collaborative endeavor. The dilemma of cooperation, then, poses two problems for would-be cooperators: a *commitment* problem (ensuring all do their part) and a *coordination* problem (putting together individual efforts in a sensible and efficient way). The human capacity for language use is a key factor that facilitates the resolution of these two problems (Smith 2010). In general, then, the selection pressures that have led to the evolution of language stem from the intense sociality of human everyday life (Levinson 2006a), which naturally predisposes humans towards cooperation, be it in sharing goods or information, or in pooling efforts towards a common goal.

A prominent and dynamic field of research is how interactional ability develops during *ontogenesis*, as evidenced by research in child development, and *phylogenesis*, as evidenced by research in comparative psychology. The tendency to cooperate, expressed in altruistic behavior from infancy onwards, is probably part of our genetic makeup (Tomasello 2009). Unlike many other species, human interaction crucially involves interpreting the *intentions* behind another organism's behavior (rather than the behavior itself), as shown by humans' ability to use information from pointing gestures from the age of two years onwards (Povinelli et al. 1997). Interpreting other basic signals of conspecifics' intentions like gaze also emerges early on in development. Children aged three to four interpret gaze direction of others as evidence of cognitive states (Baron-Cohen and Cross 1992). Interestingly, human morphological characteristics have likely evolved to reliably signal gaze information. For example, the sclera (the 'white' of the eye) is a conspicuously unique characteristic of the human eye; many other species do not have exposed sclera (Kobayashi and Kohshima 2001). This characteristic enhances gaze tracking and therefore plausibly evolved to facilitate detection of other humans' intentions (as mediated by their gaze) during interaction. More generally, humans interpret others' behavior by treating them as if they were animated by intentions, in other words, they have a *theory of mind* about other conspecifics (Astington et al. 1988). Not only that, but cooperative action implies that participants reciprocally try to display, recognize and act on each other's intentions, giving rise to shared or collective intentionality (Bratman 1992; Searle 1995; Tomasello and Carpenter 2007).

The structure of human interaction is inextricably linked to this complex cognitive processing of intentions. There is evidence for a basic structure to human interaction that is relatively independent of cultural differences (Levinson 2006b). Recently, Stivers et al. (2009) demonstrated a universal structure of turn-taking in conversation, with a tendency to avoid both overlapping speech and silence. Moreover, human action consists of hierarchically embedded chains of action organized in complex means-ends relationships (Miller et al. 1960; von Cranach et al. 1982). The focus of this chapter will be to describe the link between these two aspects of shared intentionality and joint activity. We do this in two main sections. We first examine how participants solve the fundamental problems involved in coordinating joint activity, before describing how they coordinate specific aspects of joint activities.

2 Solving the problem of coordinating joint activity

2.1 What is a joint activity?

A joint activity is composed of individual actions. For example, to perform a handshake, Horatio and PJ each need to extend their own hand and grasp their partner's hand. Each extension and grasping movement is an individual action. But a joint action is more than the sum of these two individual actions (Clark 1996). Horatio and PJ need to coordinate the timing of their individual movements as well as their extension so that their hands actually meet. Before even launching their arms, they need to position their bodies facing each other. That is, when Horatio and PJ perform their individual actions as part of a joint activity, they are responsive to each other's behavior, actively cooperating in signaling their intentions and commitments in order to further the activity (Bratman 1992). In any joint activity, participants need to solve at least five issues (Clark 2006: 135): who participates, what roles they will enact, the actions to be performed, their timing and location. In doing so, participants orient to two kinds of imperatives (Enfield 2006): an informational or cognitive imperative and a social or affiliational imperative. The cognitive imperative requires participants to keep track of their shared assumptions about the state of the conversation. The affiliational imperative requires participants to perpetually maintain and display their relationship in the course of the conversation. In particular, this entails avoiding conversational situations that may threaten the face of one's partner (Brown and Levinson 1987; Goffman 1955, 1967).

The handshake example illustrates the intense coordination of behavior that makes joint activities possible. Thus, the *basic actions* of the handshake (the arm movements and grasping) are themselves coordinated by a number of *coordinating actions* (e.g., minute, split-second adaptations in trajectory and posture based on visual feedback) (Clark 2006). Of course, a handshake is a trivial activity that even inept individuals like Horatio and PJ can accomplish with ease in everyday life. But how does a handshake relate to verbal conversation? A handshake is itself typically a component part of a larger joint activity, namely greeting someone, which is in turn a component part of a yet larger joint activity, namely a social encounter. And, conversation is itself a form of joint activity. The twin cognitive and social imperatives of coordinating intentions and relations that need to be oriented to remain the same in a handshake and in a conversation, it is only the means used to do so that may be different.

2.2 Common ground and grounding

Early theorists like Heider recognized the dynamic interplay or 'give-and-take' between participants in a conversation (Heider 1958: 34). Merleau-Ponty (1945: 407) described the phenomenological experience of conversational intersubjectivity:

> In the experience of a conversation, a common ground constitutes itself between the other one and myself, my words and his are called out by the phase of the discussion, they insert themselves in a common operation of which neither one of us is the sole creator. (...) Our perspectives glide one into the other, we coexist within the same world.

Modern research in cognitive science and psycholinguistics has developed these insights, nourished by field data from conversation analysis and philosophical analysis of language. The concept that captures how conversational intersubjectivity is accomplished is *common ground*, or mutual knowledge (Clark 1996).

Technically, common ground is the sum total of beliefs that participants in a conversation hold and also believe their partners to hold (Clark 1996). Krauss and Fussell (1990: 112) define mutual knowledge as "knowledge that the communicating parties both share and know they share." As such, common ground is different from related concepts of shared knowledge in the social sciences like social representations (Moscovici 1984) or widespread beliefs (Jaspars and Fraser 1984), because shared knowledge is not necessarily known to be shared by communicators.

Common ground gets built up by participants during conversation – a process called *grounding*. How this is done is the object of a model proposed by Clark and Schaefer (1989). They argued that participants need to arrive at the shared understanding that each new utterance they produce has been understood as intended. There is a basic division of labor in this undertaking. Speakers try be clear in expressing their intentions. Recipients (or addressees) try to display their understanding of the speaker's intent. Thus, both speaker and recipient work together to arrive at the mutual belief that the recipient has understood what the speaker has said. Clark and Schaefer (1989) proposed that common ground accumulates by a unit called a contribution. Contributing to a conversation involves two phases, a presentation and an acceptance phase. Excerpt (1) illustrates a contribution that clearly features these phases (1989: 266):

(1)   Presentation Phase:
       A. is it . how much does Norman get off –
       Acceptance Phase:
       B. pardon
       A. how much does Norman get off
       B. oh, only Friday and Monday

This excerpt illustrates A asking B a question (A is male and B is female). Successfully asking a question is not something that A can do by himself. This is shown by A's initial attempt to ask a question (which constitutes the presentation phase) which is unsuccessful, as evidenced by B's display of lack of understanding (*pardon*). This display is the beginning of the acceptance phase. In response to B's request, A repeats the question. B then utters *oh*. This is a sign she has understood the question and constitutes the end of the acceptance phase: both A and B now mutually believe A is asking a question and that they understand its content.

Excerpt 1 shows how contributing to a conversation can run into problems. B's *pardon* is an example of negative evidence, or evidence that she has not understood A. But participants do not only react to signs of problems, but exchange various kinds of positive evidence about their interpretations of their partners' utterances. Depending on the costs associated with misunderstanding, this evidence is more or less explicit. Clark and Schaefer (1989) describe five levels of positive evidence, from least to most explicit. First, B can simply remain attentive to A. Second, B can initiate the next relevant contribution, for example *only Monday and Friday* in Excerpt (1). Third, B can acknowledge A's utterance, e.g., by *yeah* or *uh huh* or *oh* in Excerpt (1). Fourth, B can demonstrate that she has understood A's utterance, for example by paraphrasing it (*so you mean that...*). Fifth, and most explicitly, B can repeat verbatim part or all of the utterance, as in repeating a telephone number. These different kinds of positive evidence are ubiquitous in conversation and illustrate how both speaker and addressee strive, moment-by-moment, to communicate their construals of each other's actions to each other (for more on addressees, see Bavelas et al. 2000; Schober and Brennan 2003). Their resulting common ground is the outcome of this activity.

3 Coordinating specific aspects of conversation

Grounding is a general process that is accomplished in conversation. In this section, we describe how participants coordinate specific aspects of conversation, focusing on how they refer to objects (audience design), how they coordinate turns at talk, how they coordinate transitions within and between parts of activities, and how they coordinate entering into and exiting from the conversation. All of these aspects require moment-by-moment updating of common ground.

3.1 Coordinating reference: audience design

Common ground has implications for how participants in a joint activity speak with each other. A recurrent observation is that participants systematically design their messages to reflect what their addressees know. This phenomenon is called *recipient design* (Garfinkel 1967) or *audience design* (Clark and Carlson 1982). It is related to the classic sociolinguistic phenomenon of accommodation, for example when participants adapt their accent in conversing with a co-member of a linguistic community or when they adapt their lexical choices when addressing a child (Giles and Coupland 1991).

Many studies have explored audience design, and they often focus on how referring expressions are constructed. There are manifold ways to refer to any particular object. For example, the same pair of objects can be referred to as *shoes*, *brogue boots*, or *Doc Martens*. The question is whether and how participants adapt their choice of referring expressions to their partners. Research on audience design in referring expressions relies heavily on an experimental paradigm called the matching task (Krauss and Weinheimer 1964; Clark and Wilkes-Gibbs 1986). In this task, two people (a director and a matcher) each have a set of identical cards. The director's cards are ordered in a particular sequence and the matcher's cards are ordered randomly. Director and matcher need to collaborate to get their cards in the same order. Neither partner can see the other (e.g., they are separated by a screen or do the task in different rooms), but can both talk freely. To complete the task, they need to identify the cards according to figures depicted on them. The figures are typically ambiguous, and thus, director and matcher have to describe them to each other until they are sure they are talking about the same figure. The task is typically repeated several times (e.g., between four and six times). With increasing repetitions, partners require less and less verbal effort (i.e., less words, less turns) to complete the task. This is due to a phenomenon called lexical entrainment, by which director and matcher come to reuse the same expressions. Excerpt (2) illustrates an example of referring expressions produced by a director from six successive trials (Clark and Wilkes-Gibbs 1986: 12).

(2) 1. All right, the next one looks like a person who's ice skating, except they're
 sticking two arms out in front.
 2. Um, the next one's the person ice skating that has two arms?
 3. The fourth one is the person ice skating, with two arms.
 4. The next one's the ice skater.
 5. The fourth one's the ice skater.
 6. The ice skater.

This example is simplified relative to real dialogue in the matching task (for example, the matcher's contributions are not shown). The simplification makes it easier
to show several typical phenomena. First, participants progressively move from
describing figures to *naming* them. In describing a figure, participants refer to its
component parts (e.g., arms, legs) or to spatial perspectives (e.g., *out in front*).
They also use indefinite reference (*a person* rather than *the person*). Naming
involves definite reference and a label (*the ice skater*). Second, initial trials typically
involve multiple descriptions, often requiring several turns of presentation and
acceptance. Third, they also feature more disfluencies and filled pauses (words
like *uh* or *um*). Fourth, partners also tend to explicitly mark the uncertainty in their
descriptions using hedges (*sort of, purplish*) or use interrogative form (as in Trial
2). Fifth, matchers initially tend to ask more questions and produce more explicit
acknowledgments (Clark and Wilkes-Gibbs 1986).

These phenomena suggest that, in the course of repeatedly referring to the
same object, directors and matchers come to use a reduced set of terms to describe
that object. This in turn suggests that they become increasingly certain that terms
used (e.g., *the ice skater*) mean the same thing to both of them. In other words,
the term becomes part of their common ground, and this is reflected in the way
they design their utterances for each other. Subsequent studies have featured
manipulations where partners are changed mid-task. These studies make the key
demonstration that directors adapt their message formulation to specific addressees and thus change their formulations when the addressee changes. Thus, participants create partner-specific *conceptual pacts* about how to refer to objects (Hupet
and Chantraine 1992; Brennan and Clark 1996). Schober and Clark (1989) further
demonstrated that participating in the grounding process is crucial. They performed a variation on the matching task featuring two matchers. One completed
the task together with a director, whereas the other (an overhearer) completed the
task later by listening to a tape recording of the other participants' conversation.
The overhearer had substantial difficulties and made significantly more errors.

In sum, then, the common ground elaborated by participants who repeatedly
refer to the same objects affects their communication. Through the phenomena of
audience design and lexical entrainment, they accomplish referring in a much
more economical way. Common ground thus facilitates the coordination of understanding in conversation.

3.2 Coordinating turn-taking

A particularly well-studied problem in conversation is how participants coordinate turns at talk. In their influential model of turn-taking, Sacks et al. (1974) proposed a set of rules by which participants ostensibly abide in this endeavor, famously distinguishing between two types of turn-allocation components: the current speaker can either select the next speaker (e.g., by asking him or her a question), or, if the current speaker relinquishes that prerogative, the next speaker can self-select. Turn allocation is facilitated by the use of adjacency pairs, which are two successive turns at talk, whereby the first one projects or constrains the second one, for example, a greeting followed by another greeting, a question followed by an answer, or an offer followed by acceptance.

Like so many conversational phenomena, the turn-taking problem is fascinating because it is apparently trivial but in reality complex. It can be defined as avoiding two extremes. On the one hand, it is desirable to avoid long stretches of silence in a conversation (Jefferson 1989). The next speaker should start speaking as soon as possible after the previous speaker has stopped speaking. On the other hand, it is also desirable to avoid overlapping speech. The next speaker should not start speaking too soon. In a study of speaker transitions, De Ruiter et al. (2006), found that 85% of the time, there was less than 750 milliseconds of either silence or overlap, suggesting that people are very good at solving this problem in everyday conversation. How do participants decide that the current speaker has finished talking and therefore that the floor is available? Given that people are so good at coordinating transitions, it seems impossible that they simply wait for the current speaker to stop speaking. Rather, they try to predict when the current speaker's turn will end. The question then arises what sort of information they use to make this prediction. Candidate sources of information in the verbal and para-verbal modality include syntax (i.e., an upcoming syntactic completion point), lexical information, or intonation. In their study, De Ruiter et al. (2006) experimentally modified speech recordings to either remove lexical and syntactic information, keeping intonation intact, or intonational information, keeping lexical and syntactic information intact. Participants then listened to the recordings and predicted when speakers' turns would end. Participants were worse in the condition where lexical and syntactic information had been removed, suggesting that this information is important to listeners in predicting turn endings.

Participants also may use particular words to signal their wish to take the floor or to keep it. People in the role of the listener often produce acknowledgment tokens, words like *uh-huh*, *yeah*, *right*, and the like, as well as other expressions (e.g., *oh really?*, *wow*) that react to particular aspects of the speaker's turn at talk, but without in themselves constituting a turn. But these words are not equivalent. Jefferson (1984) observed that while *uh-huh* was used in this function, *yeah* often was followed by a bid for the floor (Drummond and Hopper 1993). Speakers, orienting to the affiliational imperative described above, are accountable to their partners for taking the floor. As such, they need to keep speaking or relinquish the floor. Often, however, they may need to interrupt themselves because they have not yet sufficiently planned what they want to say (Clark and Wasow 1998). This creates potential confusion: are they temporarily suspending their speech or relinquishing the floor? Clark and Fox Tree (2002) found that filler words like *uh* and *um* that often precede speech suspensions reliably signal delays in speaking: *uh* signals a minor pause, and *um* signals a major pause. Speakers can introduce additional subtleties into this signal by elongating either *uh* or *um*. For example, *uhhh* signals a longer pause than *uh*. Not only do speakers use these words differently, it also seems they aid comprehension by listeners. Brennan and Schober (2001) tested comprehension of disfluent verbal instructions with fillers (*Move to the yel- uh, purple square*) or without them (*Move to the yel- purple square*) and found they helped listeners cancel the incorrect instruction, speeding up their comprehension.

3.3 Coordinating transitions within and between parts of joint activities

Like any joint activity, conversations are composed of joint actions (Clark 1996). For example, an adjacency pair is a minimal structural unit, or 'building block' of a conversation. But participants do not just accumulate adjacency pairs in conversing. They try to accomplish joint activities, and in doing so, they have to coordinate transitions between parts of the joint activity (e.g., they have to maintain a shared understanding of where they are in the task). Bangerter and Clark (2003) distinguished two basic kinds of transitions in joint activities. First, there are vertical transitions, corresponding to entering (or starting) and exiting (or stopping) a part of an activity. Second, there are horizontal transitions, corresponding to continuing a next step within a particular activity. Participants can be explicit about which part of the activity they propose to enter or exit (e.g., *let's move on to Point 3*). They may also use specialized acknowledgment tokens to coordinate these transitions in a less explicit way. Bangerter and Clark (2003) investigated how people differentially use such tokens to coordinate mutual understanding of progress within a task, proposing that *okay* and *all right* are specialized for marking vertical transitions and *uh-huh* or *yeah* (or *right*) are specialized for marking horizontal transitions. Their propositions were supported across a variety of task settings. Excerpt (3) Bangerter and Clark (2003: 213–214) illustrate the differential use of *okay* and *uh-huh* for vertical and horizontal transitions respectively. Participants coordinated the joint activity of building models made of Lego blocks. One participant, the director (D, female), has to instruct the other, the builder (B, male) to construct a model from another model only D can see (Clark and Krych 2004). D also cannot see what B is doing.

(3)	1	D	*okay*, take a blue two by four,
	2	B	*uh-huh* [takes block],
	3	D	put it on the red,
	4	B	*uh-huh* [gets ready to attach block at a location],
	5	D	so that it's hanging over towards you by two.
	6	B	*okay* [attaches block at the location],
	7	D	*okay*, now take a [proceeds to describe next block].

In 1, D starts describing how to add a blue two by four to the model. This is a vertical transition (i.e., starting a new part of the task). She prefaces this transition using *okay*. In 2, B takes the block, and acknowledges this step with *uh-huh* (a horizontal transition, i.e., continuing with the activity of adding this particular block). In 3, D explains where to add the block – another horizontal transition within this activity, which B acknowledges in 4 using *uh-huh*. Then, in 5, D describes how to position the block. This is all the information B needs to complete placement. He attaches the block in 6 and produces a vertical transition marker, *okay*, displaying his understanding that fixing this particular block is completed, and thereby exiting that part of the task. In 7, D enters the next part of the task – another vertical transition, and again uses *okay* to preface this transition.

3.4 Coordinating transitions into and out of joint activities

Any joint activity can be analyzed into three distinct phases: an entry, a body, and an exit phase (Clark 1996). Each phase arises out of participants' efforts at coordinating transitions into and out of joint activities (similarly to coordinating transitions between parts of an activity as described above). The entry phase is constituted by participants' efforts to coordinate the possibility of the interaction and its general purpose; it involves defining the relevant social identities for the interaction and re-establishes continuity retrospectively towards any past interactions the participants might have accomplished together. Once participants have agreed on these elements, they can transit to the body, where they accomplish the main business of the joint activity. Once this is done, participants need to coordinate getting out of the joint activity; this constitutes the exit phase (Bangerter et al. 2004). In this section, we discuss the coordination of entry and exit phases.

To enter a conversation, would-be participants first need to issue and respond to a summons; this can be constituted by adjacency pairs or their nonverbal equivalents, e.g., A dials B's phone number and B picks up the phone to answer, or A says *excuse me* and B says *yes?* They then need to define the relevant social identities and relations for the encounter. Defining oneself as PJ has other implications for the construal of the encounter than defining oneself as Professor De Ruiter. If participants know each other, they may re-establish some kind of continuity with past encounters, e.g., *how's things?* or *whassup?* They then need to define the business of the encounter. This usually entails a transition into the body of the conversation (*I'm calling about Horatio*).

To end a conversation, participants first need to arrive at the mutual understanding that they are both ready to end the conversation (Schegloff and Sacks 1973). Arriving at this mutual understanding is not trivial. Indeed, a potential ending entails recurring opportunities to discuss topics that have not yet been the object of conversation, for instance because participants didn't want to give them the status of main topic. A solution to this dilemma is to signal one's readiness to end with pre-closings, as when one participant says *okay* and the other replies *okay* (note that moving from the body to the exit phase is also a vertical transition). Once the mutual understanding of readiness to end is established, participants typically move through a set of ritualized actions. Endings are a point where a relationship is vulnerable because they inaugurate an upcoming separation (Albert and Kessler 1976). Participant typically justify the ending with reasons that are external, i.e., over which they have no control (Albert and Kessler 1976), e.g., *I gotta go*. This is done to protect the face (Brown and Levinson 1987) of the partner and orient to the affiliational imperative described above. When ending conversations, participants often project continuity of the relationship into the future (e.g., *Talk to you soon*), and extend good wishes to each other, e.g., *goodbye, bye, ciao, auf Wiedersehen, au revoir* and the like, in order to reaffirm ther social bonds (Albert and Kessler 1978; Clark and French 1981). Excerpt (4) shows the ending of a telephone conversation to illustrate the exit phase. It is taken from the Switchboard corpus (Godfrey et al. 1992), a large set of telephone conversations.

(4) 1 B So those were things we liked.
     2 A Well, sounds good.
     3 B Okay. You have anything else to say?
     4 A No, I think we covered everything.
     5 B [Laughter] Okay, well thanks a lot.
     6 A Well, thank you for being home [laughter].
     7 B [Laughter] Okay.
     8 A Okay, bye-bye.
     9 B Bye-bye.

In 1 and 2, A and B are still engaged in topical talk. In 3 and 4, they jointly establish their readiness to end the conversation. In 5 and 6, they thank each other. In 7 and 8, they use *okay* to mark the transition to the final step in the conversation, an exchange of *bye-bye* (8 and 9). Just like a well-executed handshake, a nicely coordinated exit phase will typically result in both participants hanging up at roughly the same time.

4 Conclusion

In this chapter, we have explored the shared cognitive foundations of communication. We have treated communication, particularly its paradigm case, conversation, as a joint activity. That is, conversation is both used to coordinate joint activity and is itself a highly coordinated form of joint activity. We have started by examining the cooperative nature of human social life and the demands it places on communication. Human communication is fundamentally about displaying, detecting, and coordinating intentions in the context of joint activities and is oriented to two imperatives; an informational and an affiliational imperative. We have described the notion of common ground, or mutual understanding, and how it accumulates in conversation and is used to facilitate subsequent conversations. We also have explored audience design and how various aspects of conversation including referring, turn-taking, transitions and entries and exits are coordinated.

Clark's (1996) theory of language use is unique in linking the cognitive underpinnings of communication with a fine-grained analysis of the linguistic and nonverbal behaviors by which participants coordinate joint activities. Such an approach contributes to communication science in several ways. First, it bridges work on language use seen as a purely cognitive process and work on language use as a purely social process. Second, by focusing on the linguistic means by which communication is accomplished, it offers a more detailed explication of key notions that have all too often remained a 'black box' in the study of communication (e.g., 'sender,' 'receiver,' 'understanding'). These contributions have made Clark's theory relevant and useful for many specific communicative domains, and indeed, beyond the introductory notions and basic research we have reviewed here, Clark's theory has been widely applied to domains including survey methodology (Schober and Conrad 2008), mediated communication (Clark and Brennan 1991; Hancock and Dunham 2001) tutoring in education (Graesser et al. 1995), air-traffic control communication (Morrow et al. 1994), and doctor-patient communication (Bromme et al. 2005), to name but a few.

Further reading

Bangerter, Adrian & Herbert H. Clark. 2003. Navigating joint projects with dialogue. *Cognitive Science* 27. 195–225.

Clark, Herbert H. 1996. *Using Language*. Cambridge: Cambridge University Press.

Clark, Herbert H. 1999. On the origins of conversation. *Verbum* 21. 147–161.

Holtgraves, Thomas M. 2002. *Language as Social Action: Social Psychology and Language Use.* Mahwah, NJ: Erlbaum.

Levinson, Stephen C. 2006. Cognition at the heart of human interaction. *Discourse Studies* 8. 85–93.

References

Albert, Stuart & Suzanne Kessler. 1976. Processes for ending social encounters: The conceptual archaeology of a temporal place. *Journal for the Theory of Social Behaviour* 6. 147–170.

Albert, Stuart & Suzanne Kessler. 1978. Ending social encounters. *Journal of Experimental Social Psychology* 14. 541–553.

Astington, Janet W., Paul L. Harris & David R. Olson (eds.). 1988. *Developing Theories of Mind*. Cambridge: Cambridge University Press.

Austin, John L. 1962. *How to do things with words*. Oxford: Oxford University Press.

Bangerter, Adrian & Herbert H. Clark. 2003. Navigating joint projects with dialogue. *Cognitive Science* 27. 195–225.

Bangerter, Adrian, Herbert H. Clark & Anna R. Katz. 2004. Navigating joint projects in telephone conversations. *Discourse Processes* 37. 1–23.

Baron-Cohen, Simon & Pippa Cross. 1992. Reading the eyes: evidence for the role of perception in the development of a theory of mind. *Mind and Language* 6. 173–186.

Bavelas, Janet B., Linda Coates & Trudy Johnson. 2000. Listeners as co-narrators. *Journal of Personality and Social Psychology* 79. 941–952.

Bratman, Michael E. 1992. Shared cooperative activity. *The Philosophical Review* 101. 327–342.

Brennan, Susan E. & Herbert H. Clark. 1996. Conceptual pacts and lexical choice in conversation. *Journal of Experimental Psychology: Learning, Memory, and Cognition* 22. 1482–1493.

Brennan, Susan E. & Michael F. Schober. 2001. How listeners compensate for disfluencies in spontaneous speech. *Journal of Memory and Language* 44. 274–296.

Bromme, Rainer, Regina Jucks & Thomas Wagner. 2005. How to refer to 'diabetes'? Language in online health advice. *Applied Cognitive Psychology* 19. 569–586.

Brown, Penelope & Stephen C. Levinson. 1987. *Politeness: Some Universals in Language Use*. Cambridge: Cambridge University Press.

Clark, Herbert H. 1996. *Using Language*. Cambridge: Cambridge University Press.

Clark, Herbert H. 1999. On the origins of conversation. *Verbum* 21. 147–161.

Clark, Herbert H. 2006. Social actions, social commitments. In: Nicholas J. Enfield and Stephen C. Levinson (eds.), *Roots of Human Sociality: Culture, Cognition, and Human Interaction*, 126–150. Oxford: Berg Press.

Clark, Herbert H. & Adrian Bangerter. 2004. Changing conceptions of reference. In: Ira A. Noveck and Dan Sperber (eds.), *Experimental Pragmatics*, 25–49. Basingstoke, England: Palgrave Macmillan.

Clark, Herbert H. & Susan E. Brennan. 1991. Grounding in communication. In: Lauren B. Resnick, John M. Levine and Stephanie D. Teasley (eds.), *Perspectives on Socially Shared Cognition*, 127–149. Washington, DC: APA.

Clark, Herbert. H. & Thomas B. Carlson. 1982. Hearers and speech acts. *Language* 58. 332–373.

Clark, Herbert H. & Eve V. Clark. 1977. *Psychology and Language: An Introduction to Psycholinguistics*. New York: Harcourt Brace Jovanovich.

Clark, Herbert. H. & Jean E. Fox Tree. 2002. Using *uh* and *um* in spontaneous speech. *Cognition* 84: 73–111

Clark, Herbert. H. & J. Wade French. 1981. Telephone goodbyes. *Language in Society* 10. 1–19.

Clark, Herbert. H. & Meredyth. A. Krych. 2004. Speaking while monitoring addressees for understanding. *Journal of Memory and Language* 50: 62–81.

Clark, H. H. & Edward F. Schaefer. 1989. Contributing to discourse. *Cognitive Science* 13. 259–294.

Clark, Herbert. H. & Thomas Wasow. 1998. Repeating words in spontaneous speech. *Cognitive Psychology* 37. 201–242.

Clark, Herbert H. & Deanna Wilkes-Gibbs. 1986. Referring as a collaborative process. *Cognition* 22. 1–39.

De Ruiter, Jan-Peter, Holger Mitterer & Nicholas J. Enfield. 2006. Projecting the end of a speaker's turn; a cognitive cornerstone of conversation. *Language* 82. 515–535.

Drummond, Kent & Robert Hopper. 1993. Back channels revisited: Acknowledgment tokens and speakership incipiency. *Research on Language and Social Interaction* 26: 157–177.

Enfield, Nicholas J. 2006. Social consequences of common ground. In: Nicholas J. Enfield and Stephen C. Levinson (eds.), *Roots of Human Sociality: Culture, Cognition, and Human Interaction*, 399–430. Oxford: Berg Press.

Garfinkel, Harold. 1967. *Studies in Ethnomethodology*. Englewood Cliffs, NJ: Prentice Hall.

Giles, Howard & Nikolas Coupland. 1991. *Language: Contexts and Consequences*. Keynes: Open University Press.

Godfrey, John J., Edward G. Holliman & Jane McDaniel. 1992. *SWITCHBOARD: Telephone speech corpus for research and development. Proceedings of the IEEE conference on acoustics, speech, and signal processing*. San Francisco: IEEE.

Goffman, Erving. 1955. On face-work: An analysis of ritual elements in social interaction. *Psychiatry: Journal for the Study of Interpersonal Processes* 18. 213–231.

Goffman, Erving. 1967. *Interaction ritual*. New York: Anchor Books.

Graesser, Art C., Natalie K. Person & Joseph P. Magliano. 1995. Collaborative dialogue patterns in naturalistic one-to-one tutoring. *Applied Cognitive Psychology* 9. 495–522.

Grice, Herbert P. 1975. Logic and conversation. In: Peter Cole and Jerry L. Morgan (eds.), *Syntax and Semantics, Volume 3*, 41–58. New York: Academic Press.

Hancock, Jeff & Philip J. Dunham. 2001. Language use in computer-mediated communication: The role of coordination devices. *Discourse Processes* 31. 91–110.

Heider, Fritz. 1958. *The Psychology of Interpersonal Relations*. New York: John Wiley and Sons.

Holtgraves, Thomas M. 2002. *Language as Social Action: Social Psychology and Language Use*. Mahwah, NJ: Erlbaum.

Hupet, Michel & Yves Chantraine. 1992. Changes in repeated references: Collaboration or repetition effects? *Journal of Psycholinguistic Research* 21. 485–496.

Jaspars, Jos M. F. & Colin Fraser. 1984. Attitudes and social representations. In: Robert M. Farr and Serge Moscovici (eds.), *Social Representations*, 101–123. Cambridge: Cambridge University Press.

Jefferson, Gail. 1984. Notes on a systematic deployment of the acknowledgment tokens 'yeah' and 'mm hm'. *Papers in Linguistics* 17. 197–216.

Jefferson, Gail. 1989. Notes on a possible metric for a 'standard maximum' silence of approximately one second in conversation. In: Derek Roger and Peter Bull (eds.), *Conversation: an Interdisciplinary Perspective*, 166–196. Philadelphia: Multilingual Matters.

Kobayashi, Hiromi & Shiro Kohshima. 2001. Evolution of the human eye as a device for communication. In: Tetsuro Matsuzawa (ed.), *Primate Origins of Human Communication and Behaviour*, 383–401. Tokyo: Springer.

Krauss, Robert M. & Susan R. Fussell. 1990. Mutual knowledge and communicative effectiveness. In: Jolene Galegher, Robert E. Kraut and Carmen Egido (eds.), *Intellectual Teamwork: Social and Technological Foundations of Cooperative Work*. Hillsdale, NJ: Erlbaum.

Krauss, Robert M. & Sidney Weinheimer. 1964. Changes in reference phrases as a function of frequency of usage in social interaction: A preliminary study. *Psychonomic Science* 1. 113–114.

Lakoff, George & Mark Johnson. 1980. *Metaphors We Live By*. Chicago: University of Chicago Press.

Levinson, Stephen C. 2006a. On the human 'interaction engine'. In: Nicholas J. Enfield and Stephen C. Levinson (eds.), *Roots of Human Sociality: Culture, Cognition, and Human Interaction*, 39–69. Oxford: Berg Press.

Levinson, Stephen C. 2006b. Cognition at the heart of human interaction. *Discourse Studies* 8: 85–93.

Merleau-Ponty, Maurice. 1945. *Phénoménologie de la Perception* Paris: Gallimard.

Miller, George, Eugene Galanter & Karl Pribram. 1960. *Plans and the Structure of Behavior.* New York: Holt, Rinehart and Winston.

Morrow, Daniel G., Michelle Rodvold & Alfred Lee. 1994. Nonroutine transactions in controller-pilot communication. *Discourse Processes* 17. 235–258.

Moscovici, Serge. 1984. The phenomenon of social representations. In: Robert M. Farr and Serge Moscovici (eds.), *Social Representations,* 3–70. Cambridge, England: Cambridge University Press.

Povinelli, Daniel J., James E. Reaux, Donna T. Bierschwale, Ashley D. Allain & Bridgett B. Simon. 1997. Exploitation of pointing as a referential gesture in young children, but not adolescent chimpanzees. *Cognitive Development* 12. 327–365.

Sacks, Harvey, Emmanuel A. Schegloff & Gail Jefferson. 1974. A simplest systematics for the organization of turn-taking in conversation. *Language* 50. 696–735.

Schegloff, Emmanuel A. & Harvey Sacks. 1973. Opening up closings. *Semiotica* 8. 289–327.

Schober, Michael F. & Herbert H. Clark. 1989. Understanding by addressees and overhearers. *Cognitive Psychology* 21. 211–232.

Schober, Michael F. & Susan E. Brennan. 2003. Processes of interactive spoken discourse: The role of the partner. In: Arthur C. Graesser, Morton. A. Gernsbacher and Susan R. Goldman (eds.), *Handbook of Discourse Processes*, 123–164. Hillsdale, NJ: Lawrence Erlbaum.

Schober, Michael F. & Frederick G. Conrad. 2008. Survey interviews and new communication technologies. In: Frederick G. Conrad and Michael F. Schober (eds.), *Envisioning the Survey Interview of the Future*, 1–30. New York: Wiley.

Searle, John R. 1969. *Speech Acts*. Cambridge: Cambridge University Press.

Searle, John R. 1995. *The Construction of Social Reality*. New York: Free Press.

Smith, Eric A. 2010. Communication and collective action: language and the evolution of human cooperation. *Evolution and Human Behavior* 31. 231–245.

Stivers, Tanya, Nicholas J. Enfield, Penelope Brown, Christina Englert, Makoto Hayashi, Trine Heinemann, Gertie Hoymann, Federico Rossano, Jan Peter de Ruiter, Kyung-Eun Yoon & Stephen C. Levinson. 2009. Universals and cultural variation in turn-taking in conversation. *Proceedings of the National Academy of Sciences of the United States of America* 106. 10587–10592.

Tomasello, Michael. 2009. *Why We Cooperate*. Cambridge, MA: MIT Press.

Tomasello, Michael & Malinda Carpenter. 2007. Shared intentionality. *Developmental Science* 10. 121–125.

von Cranach, Mario, Kalbermatten Urs, Katrin Indermühle & Beat Gugler. 1982. *Goal-directed Action*. London: Academic Press.

Lijiang Shen

15 Communication as persuasion

Abstract: This chapter reviews persuasion as a form of communication, and focuses on the social scientific study of persuasion since the mid-twentieth century. The chapter provides an overview of some key theories and models of persuasion that focuses on the process of persuasion, including cognitively-oriented theories (cognitive dissonance, balance, congruity, computational theories, and dual process models), and affectively-oriented theories (the drive model, parallel process models, and discrete emotions models). This chapter also calls for a synergy of cognition and affect in persuasion research.

Keywords: Persuasion, process, cognitive dissonance, balance, congruity, computational, dual process, cognition, emotion

1 Communication as persuasion

Persuasion is a ubiquitous form of human communication (O'Keefe 2009). Persuasion can be defined as communicative activity that is intended to shape, reinforce, or change the responses of another, or others, in a given communication context (Miller 1980/2002). Some scholars argue that core cases of persuasion are defined by five elements: (a) persuasion occurs interpersonally rather than intra-personally, (b) persuasion is intentional, (c) persuasion is symbolic, (d) persuasion is non-coercive, and (e) there should be effects. Communication activity that might miss some of these elements are considered as borderline cases of persuasion (Gass and Seiter 2011). Persuasion can occur in different contexts depending on the number of communicators involved, synchronous or asynchronous, modality, mediation, and goals of participants: face-to-face persuasion, public persuasion, and mass media persuasion.

The basic purpose of persuasion lies in "controlling the environment so as to realize certain physical, economic, or social rewards from it." (Miller and Steinberg 1975). Specifically, the function of persuasion can be: (a) acquisition of rewards and benefits, where the desired and obtained outcomes correspond exactly; (b) reality construction, where the purpose of persuasion is to define certain issues, which in turn influences interpretations and evaluations, for example, the debate on gay marriage largely depends on how marriage is defined; (c) impression management, which can take place at the interpersonal level (i.e., social relationships) or at the organization level (i.e., public relationships), and (d) conflict resolution, where the desired and obtained outcomes reflect compromise of the original desires of the involved parties.

Regardless of these features (response shaping, reinforcement or change, core vs. borderline cases, context and function of persuasion), the nature of persuasion can be better understood by examining the key theories and models of persuasion. These theories and models not only specify the process of persuasion, but also clarify how persuasion can work or fail, and provide guidance for effective message design. The study of persuasion dates back to ancient Greece during the fifth century BC, to classics of Plato and Aristotle (see, also, Chapter 9, Tindale). Aristotle provided the first comprehensive theory of persuasion: effective persuasion should be grounded in logos (logic), pathos (emotion), and ethos (source characteristics). Aristotle's perspective on persuasion had long-lasting impact on the study of persuasion throughout history (Pfau and Parrott 1993). However, social scientific studies of persuasion did not get started until the middle of the twentieth century. Although one of the most exciting areas of persuasion research lies in examining the impact of message style, structure, and content (Dillard and Pfau 2002), by taking persuasion research seriously, one should study persuasion *per se*, that is, the persuasion process (Burleson 1992). This chapter provides an overview of some key theories and models in persuasion that focus on the process of persuasion. It is not the goal of this chapter to offer a comprehensive review or update of persuasion theories and models. More comprehensive and detailed review of advances in theory and research are available in monographs and edited volumes of persuasion literature (e.g., Dillard and Pfau 2002; O'Keefe 2002; Perloff 2010). Ever since the persuasion research conducted by the Yale School in the 1950s (e.g., Hovland et al. 1953), a variety of theories and models have been developed in persuasion studies. Generally speaking, these theories and models can be viewed as cognitively or affectively oriented. Within cognitive theories (see also Chapter 10, Greene and Dorrance Hall), computational theories assume that individuals are rational in their thinking, while the dual process models do not share those assumptions. Within affective theories some view affect as dysfunctional; while others disagree.

2 Early cognitive theories of persuasion

The earliest social scientific research in persuasion was conducted by a group of scholars at Yale University in the early 1950s, who looked at both cognition and affect. Among the early cognitive theories of persuasion were the consistency theories. All of such theories are concerned with the relationship of cognitions in a person's mind. The basic assumption is that individuals prefer and strive to maintain/achieve consistency and harmony in their cognition. Inconsistency in cognition motivates individuals to change their beliefs, attitudes, and behaviors to restore consistency. Three such theories will be reviewed in this chapter: cognitive dissonance theory, balance theory, and congruity theory.

2.1 Cognitive dissonance theory

One of the cognitive theories from the Yale group was Cognitive Dissonance Theory (Festinger 1957). Cognitive dissonance is defined as a uncomfortable psychological state caused by holding dissonant cognitions simultaneously. The original theory proposes that the presence of cognitive inconsistency will evoke dissonance, the magnitude of which is a positive function of the number and importance of dissonant cognitions, and a negative function of consonant cognitions. It is assumed that reduction of cognitive dissonance is rewarding and satisfying. Hence, individuals are motivated to reduce or eliminate cognitive dissonance. Dissonance reduction will be altering the cognition that is least resistant to change, which has implications for ways of creating lasting attitude, belief, and behavior change (see Cooper 2005, Harmon-Jones 2002 for revisions and updates for the theory).

There are four major paradigms in research on cognitive dissonance. First, the *free choice* paradigm (Brehm 1956). It is proposed that once a decision is made, dissonance will be aroused. Difficult decisions lead to more dissonance than easier ones because there is a greater proportion of dissonant cognition than consonant cognition. Dissonance can be reduced by reducing dissonant cognition or adding consonant cognition. Second, the *induced compliance* paradigm (Festinger and Carlsmith 1959). This paradigm proposes that dissonance is aroused when an individual does or says something that is inconsistent with an existing belief or attitude. The pre-existing attitude and beliefs are dissonant with the behavior; while the (promised) rewards and (threats of) punishments used to induce the compliance are consonant with the behavior and function as external justifications. The magnitude of dissonance is a negative function of external justification. To reduce the dissonance, individuals tend to change the beliefs and attitudes such that they will be consonant with the behavior (out of the induced compliance). Third, the *belief disconfirmation* paradigm. In this paradigm (Festinger 1957), dissonance is aroused when people are confronted with information that is inconsistent with their beliefs. If the dissonance is not reduced by changing one's belief, the dissonance can result in misperception or rejection or refutation of the information, seeking support from others who share the beliefs, and attempting to persuade others to restore consonance. Fourth, the *hypocrisy* paradigm (Aronson et al. 1991). In this paradigm, individuals are induced to make a public statement that is attitudinally consistent, then reminded of the fact that their past behavior was not consistent with the statement. To reduce dissonance, individuals will either act in accord with their statement, or change their attitude to be more consistent with their past behavior.

2.2 Balance theory

Perception theories offer an alternative explanation to cognitive dissonance theory. Such theories proposed that instead of resulting from dissonance reduction, individuals change their attitudes by observing their own as well as others' behavior and concluding what attitude must have caused them (i.e., attribution). Heider's (1958) balance theory is one member of such perception theories. Balance theory assumes that individuals strive to maintain consistency in patterns of their liking or disliking of objects. When liking and disliking are balanced, structures are stable; when they are imbalanced, structures are unstable and there is pressure to change such that balance will be retained. Specifically, the patterns of perceived relationships (liking or disliking) among three entities, person (P), another person (O), and an object (X), could be either balanced or imbalanced. Imbalance may be resolved by distancing oneself from the situation, or by changing one of the relationships to achieve balance. For example, a person (P) who likes another person (O) will be balanced by an attitude of the same valence toward an object (X). On the other hand, there is imbalance when P like O, O likes X, but P dislikes X. To reduce imbalance and achieve balance, P might distance himself/herself from the situation, or change her/his own attitude toward X (i.e., becomes more positive), or change her/his liking toward O (i.e., O is not that great after all).

2.3 Congruity theory

Congruity theory (Osgood and Tannenbaum 1955) is one of the consistency theories and was developed as an extension to Heider's balance theory. Osgood and Tannenbaum's extension of the balance theory lies in that congruity theory is explicitly oriented toward communication and persuasion. The other person (O) in balance theory becomes a message source. The attitude object (X) is now a concept, and the P is essentially the recipient of a persuasive message. Thus, the theory concerns situations in which a Source makes an assertion about a Concept, and the audience has attitudes toward the Source and the Concept. The only relationship that remains the same is that the assertion of the Source about the Concept is either positive (associative) or negative (disassociative). This theory holds that incongruity (like imbalance) is unpleasant and motivates audiences to change their attitudes. The congruity theory is also more specific regarding the direction and amount of attitude change based on the audience's attitude toward the concept and toward the message source.

3 More recent developments in cognitive theories of persuasion

Corresponding to trends in psychology, persuasion theories and models developed in the 1960s and 1970s were cognitive in nature. The cognitive response theory of persuasion (Greenwald 1968) attempts to understand how attitudes are formed and changed in response to persuasive communication. The general premise of the theory is that messages do not persuade, cognitive responses do. A cognitive response is a thought generated in response to a persuasive message. The way cognitive responses affect persuasion outcomes has to do with the way receivers of the persuasive messages elaborate and integrate the information presented in the message. Cognitive responses can be favorable (e.g., positive evaluation of the message source, content, and advocacy), neutral (e.g., non-evaluative responses), or unfavorable (e.g., counterarguments) toward the persuasive message. Dominant cognitive response indexes the difference between favorable and unfavorable cognitive responses a receiver generates toward a persuasive message. The cognitive response theory posits that dominant cognition is the best predictor of attitude change (Eagly and Chaiken 1993).

Other cognitive theories of persuasion share the general premise that individuals' cognition determines attitude formation and change. However, there are also substantial differences. The computational theories (Fishbein and Ajzen 1975, 2010; Ajzen 1991) assume that individuals engage in some fairly intensive mental arithmetic to arrive at their attitudes or behaviors. Individuals are thus seen to function like computers and to be quite rational: they scan all relevant or available information and combine them and attitude and behaviors are certain functions of these information. On the other hand, the dual process models (Petty et al. 1986; Chaiken et al. 1989) posit that there exist two modes of message processing, one effortful and the other superficial; and that the type and amount of thinking in response to the persuasive messages that determine persuasion that follows. The following sections review these more recent cognitive theories.

3.1 Theory of reasoned action

The theory of reasoned action (TRA; Fishbein and Ajzen, 1975, 2010) begins with the observation that the best single predictor of a person's voluntary action is behavioral intention (Kim and Hunter 1993). In turn, TRA posits that behavioral intentions are determined by two factors: attitude and subjective norms. Attitude is a person's evaluation of the action under consideration. Subjective norm is a person's beliefs about behavioral prescription held by another person in regard the target person. Attitude is a function of two factors: beliefs (the likelihood of a consequence happening), which is weighted by evaluations (the desirability of that consequence). Subjective norms is a function of two factors as well: normative belief (what the other person thinks the target person should or should not do), which is weighted by motivation to comply (the extent to which the target person wants to conform with the opinion of the particular person). Attitude and subjective norm can vary in their relative impact on intention – and this relative impact may vary from behavior to behavior and from person to person. For a given behavior or audience, attitudinal considerations may weigh more heavily than normative ones, but for a different behavior or audience, the reverse may be the case.

3.2 Theory of planned behavior

The theory of planned behavior (TPB; Ajzen, 1991) is an extension to the TRA; the TPB adds a third predictor of behavioral intentions, perceived behavioral control, which is defined as individuals' perception of their ability to perform a given behavior. Perceived behavioral control, in turn, is determined by the total set of control beliefs (i.e., beliefs about the presence of factors that may facilitate or impede the behavior under consideration), weighted by the perceived power of the control factor. In addition, perceived behavioral control may also have a direct impact on behavior. Fig. 1 presents the factors and their relationships in TRA and TPB.

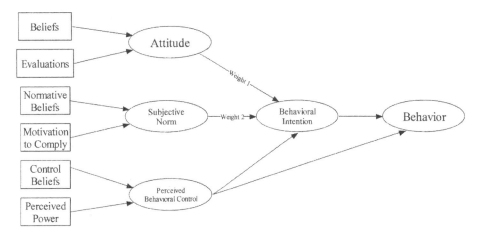

Figure 1: Theory of Reasoned Action and Theory of Planned Behavior

Over 30 years of research on the computational theories have accumulated substantial evidence for the theories. Meta-analytic studies have consistently yielded support for the relationship between behavioral intention and behavior, the combined impact of attitude and subjective norms on behavioral intentions, and the impact of perceived behavioral control on intention (see Hale et al. 2002 for a summary of these meta-analytic findings). However, these findings are based on multiple regression methods, which might not be optimal (Hankins et al. 2000) and they only tested parts of the theories, instead of in their entirety. Albarracin et al. (2001) adopted the structural equation modeling approach in their meta analysis and provided further evidence for the two theories; while testing the two theories in their entirety. However, when past behavior was entered in the model as an exogenous variable, many of the paths became substantially smaller. The impact of past behavior, as well as the impact of non-reasoned variables on behavioral intention and behavior (e.g., moral obligations, self-identity, and affect, see Hale et al. 2002 for a summary) suggest that TRA and TPB have limitations in their scope. More recently, Fishbein (Fishbein and Cappella 2006; Fishbein and Yzer 2003) proposed an integrated model as an extension of TRA and TPB that incorporated factors not included in the original framework.

3.3 The dual process models

The dual process models (Petty and Cacioppo 1986; Chaiken et al. 1989) posit that individuals do not always engage in intensive cognitive thinking in response to persuasive communications. Both the elaboration likelihood model (ELM, Petty and Cacioppo 1986) and the heuristic systematic model (HSM, Chaiken et al. 1989) propose that there are two fundamentally different modes in which persuasion takes place. Despite the obvious similarities, ELM and HSM are also substantially distinctive from each other.

As a derivative of cognitive response theory, the elaboration likelihood model (ELM) assumes that type and amount of cognitive response determine the type and amount of persuasion that follow. ELM posits that elaboration likelihood determines the mode of persuasion. Elaboration likelihood refers to the probability that a persuasive message will be cognitively elaborated. Elaboration likelihood forms a continuum: when elaboration likelihood is high, persuasion occurs via the central route, which is characterized by careful consideration of the message content and argument strength. Individuals tend to scrutinize the argument carefully, analyze the logic in the message, weigh the evidence presented in the message, and carefully evaluate the message advocacy. Persuasion that occurs via the central route leads to strong and durable attitudes. When the elaboration likelihood is low, persuasion takes places via the peripheral route, which is characterized by hasty and superficial processing of cues from the message. Individuals tends to pay attention to the message source or contextual cues. Persuasion via the peripheral route tends to produce flimsy and easily-changed attitudes.

Elaboration likelihood is a joint function of ability and motivation. Ability can be dispositional (e.g., intelligence and prior background knowledge) or situational (e.g., the presence of distraction). Motivation can also be dispositional (e.g., need for cognition) or situational (e.g., receiver involvement, that is, the personal relevance of the topic). For elaboration likelihood to be high and persuasion to occur via central route, both ability and motivation to process the message have to be high. When either ability or motivation is low, elaboration likelihood will be low and persuasion takes places via the peripheral route.

Compared to ELM, the heuristic systematic model (HSM) has specific assumptions: first, individuals are motivated to hold 'correct' attitudes that are useful in a specific context. Second, cognitive thinking is effortful. Third, individuals have limited cognitive capacity that can be allocated for message processing. HSM also proposes two modes in which persuasion takes place. Systematic processing is very similar to central route in ELM: it is data-driven and effortful; it requires high cognitive capacity. On the other hand, heuristic processing is theory-driven and effortless, which means it does not require much cognitive capacity. Heuristics are simple knowledge structures, or implicit theories stored in one's memory. Their utilization in the persuasion process is a function of their availability (i.e., if the knowledge structure is present), accessibility (i.e., readiness and easiness for retrieval), and applicability (i.e., relevance of the knowledge structure) (Todorov et al. 2002). Defined as such, heuristic processing and systematic processing are qualitatively different; while the peripheral route and central route are quantitatively different (i.e., low vs. high elaboration).

Similar to ELM, HSM posits that systematic processing requires both high motivation and ability. However, systematic processing and heuristic processing can co-occur; while in ELM, central route and peripheral route seem to be mutually exclusive, since elaboration cannot be high and low at the same time. The relationship between systematic processing and heuristic processing can be additive (i.e., the two modes add to each other), attenuation (i.e., the impact of the two modes are opposite in direction), or interactive (i.e., when the influence of heuristics causes biased systematic processing). The mode of message processing is a function of two principles: (a) the least effort principle, that is, individuals are cognitive misers; and (b) the sufficiency principle, that is, individuals will exert whatever level of effort is required to attain a sufficient degree of judgmental confidence that they have accomplished their processing goals.

HSM suggests that message processing can be (a) accuracy-motivated, when the processing goal is to achieve valid attitudes that are consistent with reality; (b) defense-motivated, when the processing goal is to reinforce beliefs congruent with one's self-interest and self-definition; and (c) impression-motivated, when the processing objective is to assess the social acceptance of alternative positions, and/or to satisfy current social and interpersonal goals. Types of motivation is conceptually independent of mode of processing. These goals can be attained via either systematic processing or heuristic processing, or co-occurrence of the two. In an effort to extend the ELM, Slater (2002) argued that there exist other types of processing goals and modes of processing: value-protective and value-affirmative processing, which is similar to defense motivated processing in HSM; didactic processing and information scanning, which is for knowledge acquisition; and hedonic processing, which is for the purpose of entertainment. However, the latter two are less relevant to persuasion, as defined earlier in the chapter.

4 Affective theories of persuasion

Affective theories of persuasion argue that in addition to cognitive responses, recipients of persuasive communication also react affectively. These affective responses can be the bases for persuasion. Such affect can be aroused by verbal content, and/or by ancillary, stylistic material. As a more general term, affect subsumes both emotion and mood (see Batson et al. 1992). It can be defined as the irreducible non-cognitive aspect of feeling states (Frijda 1993), and the elemental process of pleasure and activation (Russell and Feldman Barrett 1999). Moods can be defined as affective states without a specific object and with a simple bipolar positive/negative structure (Frijda 1993; Russell 2003). It is lasting, diffuse, and backgrounded. On the other hand, emotions are fleeting, intense, and foregrounded. They are more complex, and can be best understood in terms of *prototypical emotional episodes* that unfold over time, involving (a) cognitive appraisal of the environmental situation, (b) the physiological component of arousal, (c) motor expression, and (d) a motivational component, including behavioral readiness and response. The physiological component, core affect, consists of valence and activation, which form the two orthogonal dimensions of a circumplex (Russell and Feldman Barrett 1999). Fear is the most studied emotion in persuasion research. One camp of theories views fear as obstacle to persuasion and has to be reduced for persuasion to occur: the drive model and the parallel response models. The other camp takes the opposite view and posts that fear is conducive to persuasion.

4.1 The drive model

The basic assumption of the drive model is that fear is a drive that motivates people to follow the recommendation in the persuasive message, either to adopt a certain behavior so that potential threat can be avoided, or to stop certain behavior that is harmful to one's well-being. The drive model claims that the reduction of fear is rewarding – it reinforces the learning and adoption of the recommended behavior. According to the drive model, when fear is aroused the recipient will become motivated to find a response to alleviate the negative emotion, just like people will be motivated to get something to drink when they are thirsty and something to eat when they are hungry. If the recipient perceives the recommendation in the message as reassuring and capable of reducing the fear, it is more likely that s/he will follow the recommendation. In return, the reduction of fear reinforces the adoption of the recommendation. On the other hand, if the recipient does not perceive the recommendation as reassuring and the message cannot successfully reduce the aroused fear, that is when there is residual fear, the recipient will engage in some sort of defensive reaction including denial of the threat or avoidance of the persuasive message (Hovland et al. 1953, Miller 1963).

Janis (1967) extended the drive model. He argued that there is an optimal level of fear arousal and the association between fear and persuasion is quadratic: a persuasive message will have little effect if it does not arouse enough emotion of fear. But excessive fear will lead to hypervigilance and hinder reception of the message, which results in less persuasion, and even a backfire effect. And moderate level of fear will bring about optimal persuasion in the recipients. Janis points out that the optimal level of fear is not a fixed point on the continuum, and proposes a family of curves to illustrate the fear-persuasion association.

4.2 The parallel response models

The parallel response model (PRM, Leventhal 1970) posits that there should be both cognitive and emotional processes in response to persuasive communication. The model claims that fear appeals will activate two primary processes in the recipient: danger control and fear control. Danger control is "a problem-solving process" (Leventhal 1970: 126) where (external) threat-relevant information in the fear appeal message and (internal) coping behaviors and the effectiveness of these coping behaviors are processed. The consequence of danger control can be instrumental – actions to avert the threat, and cognitive – attitude change and/or behavioral intention. Fear control is an emotional process in which the recipient focuses on internal emotional response (fear arousal) and strives to reduce the unpleasant affect. The consequences of fear control include "avoidance reaction" and acts that can "quiet internal signals" and "dull awareness of external danger," which interferes with the acceptance of the persuasive message (1970: 126). Leventhal asserts that danger control and fear control are separate and independent of, but can also compete and interfere with each other. The effectiveness of a fear-arousing persuasive communication depends on whether danger control or fear control dominates the other: when danger control dominates, the message is persuasive; when fear control dominates, persuasion fails.

Witte (1992) extended Leventhal's work in her Expanded Parallel Process Model (EPPM). The key extension by Witte lies in that she strives to explicitly predict when danger control and fear control will take place. The EPPM also suggests that the cognitive evaluation of a fear-arousing message is a two-stage process. The two-stage appraisal can lead to three different results depending on the perception of the threat, fear arousal and perception of the efficacy of the recommendation, which helps to explain the success and failure of fear appeal. The EPPM model suggests that both cognitive and emotional variables have direct impact upon persuasion. The recipient first perceives and evaluates the threat in the fear appeal message. If the recipient perceives the threat as not serious and/or they are not susceptible to the threat, the evaluation and appraisal of the message will stop here. The recipient will not be motivated to continue processing the fear appeal message; the message will be ignored and there will be little or no persuasion. When the threat is perceived as severe and susceptible, the recipient will become scared. The consequent fear arousal motivates the recipient to take some kind of action to reduce the fear, which depends on the perception of the recommendation efficacy (both response efficacy and self-efficacy). If both response efficacy and self-efficacy are high, the recipient will start the danger control process – follow the recommendation to cope the threat and/or seek more information about the threat and coping behavior. If either response efficacy or self-efficacy or both of them are low, the recipient will start the fear control process. The recipient will strive to reduce their fear through denial, defensive avoidance, or psychological reactance.

Although Witte's EPPM is more specific and explicated, the essential view on the impact of fear on persuasion is similar to the drive model. That is, fear needs to be reduced to be persuasive and the optimal level is moderate. Available empirical evidence from meta analyses (Boster and Mongeau 1984; Mongeau 1998; Witte and Allen 2000); however, did not provide support for such a view: The association between fear and persuasion has been linear and positive in these meta analytic studies. Dillard and Anderson (2004) directly tested the four possible ways in which fear could influence persuasion: (a) the proclivity to experience fear, (b) the rise from baseline to peak, (c) peak intensity, and (d) the decline from peak to post-message fear. They found that both rise and peak measures of fear predicted persuasion, but decline in fear had no impact. The EPPM also predicts an interaction between threat components and efficacy components, which has not received empirical evidence either: Witte and Allen (2000) concluded in their meta-analysis that there were only main effects of the threat and efficacy components and that additive model has received the strongest support.

4.3 Model of discrete emotions

The discrete emotions model is based on two premises: (a) a persuasive message oftentimes arouses more than one emotions (Dillard and Peck 2000; Dillard et al. 1996) and (b) these distinctive emotions have differential impact on persuasion based on their respective functions. Cognitive appraisal theories of emotions (Scherer et al. 2001) suggest that individual's emotions can be best understood in terms of three features: function, action tendency, and valence.

First, given a particular appraisal of the person-environment relationship, an emotion is the process of recruiting resources from various physiological, motivational, and cognitive subsystems such that they shift the organism into a state of being designed to address the person-environment relationship (Lazarus 1991; Oatley 1992). For example, the *function* of fear is to instigate efforts at self-protection, whereas anger provides the motivational basis for subduing the offending stimulus. Each emotion has associated with it an *action tendency* of a specific form that aligns with the function of that emotion. Although all action tendencies are some forms of approach/engagement or inhibition/withdrawal, particular emotions produce particular variations on these two broad themes. Happiness and anger, for instance, promote quite different types of engagement. And, although sadness and fear may both be considered withdrawal emotions, their behavioral manifestations are notably distinct: sadness is characterized by lethargy while tension is typical of fear. Emotions may also be characterized in terms of valence. According to contemporary theories of emotion, negative emotions arise from the perception of that the environment is in an incongruent relationship with the individual's goals. In contrast, when an individual judges that the current environment is likely to facilitate his or her goals, positive emotions result (Scherer et al. 2001; Lazarus 1991). The discrete emotions model in persuasion posits that the persuasive impact of each emotion is determined by its function and action tendency, rather than valence. Dillard's work (Dillard and Peck 2000, 2001; Shen and Dillard 2007) have verified that discrete emotions have variable impact on persuasion: specifically, the impact of fear, sadness, guilt and happiness are positive on persuasion; while anger and contentment have a negative impact. The effectiveness of a persuasive message, therefore, is a combined function of the multiple affective states it might elicit, rather than based on a single emotion.

Discrete (message-irrelevant) emotions can also influence message processing. Nabi's (1999, 2002) cognitive functional model posits that the action tendencies of emotions (i.e., approach vs. avoidance) might determine individuals' attention to persuasive messages and the depth of subsequent message processing. Such preexisting discrete emotions can also function as psychological frames (Nabi 2003) such that they privilege information consistent with the action tendencies of emotions in terms of accessibility; in turn, they exert influence on subsequent information seeking and decision making.

5 A synergy of cognition and affect in persuasion

It should be noted that the more recent development in cognitive and affective models of persuasion no longer considers just one type of influence while disregarding the other. As the latest extension to the computational theories, the integrated model included affect as an exogenous factor that could exert influence to the TRA and TPB variables. In the dual process model tradition, affect is considered as a peripheral cue or a heuristic. On the other hand, cognitive processing of the threat and recommendation information was considered as a precedent of fear and danger control processes in the parallel responses model. The discrete emotions model conceptualizes and tests the persuasive impact of emotions above and beyond that of dominant cognition, which is considered as the best predictor of persuasion in the cognitive response tradition. The cognitive-functional model suggests that the impact of pre-existing emotions on persuasion is mediated by cognitive processes. Put simply, these recent developments suggest that cognition and affect interact with each other in the mechanism that underlie persuasion (see also Kuhl 1986).

Communication researchers have realized that it is not sufficient to consider either cognition or affect alone in the study of persuasion. Efforts have been made in recent developments in communication research to investigate the joint force of both cognitive and affective processes that precede persuasion (e.g., Stephenson 2003) and resistance to persuasion (e.g., Pfau et al. 2001). This effort is most salient in recent developments in psychological reactance research. Psychological reactance is often considered as the driving force behind the boomerang effect and failure of persuasion. A series of recent studies on conceptualization and operationalization of psychological reactance have demonstrated considerable evidence that the construct can be modeled as an amalgam of anger and negative cognition (Dillard and Shen 2005; Quick and Stephenson 2007; Rains and Turner 2007). There has been evidence that empathy, a mechanism that reduces psychological reactance is also both cognitive and affective (Shen 2010). However, cognitive and affect are phenomena that change rapidly (van Turennout et al. 1998), at a pace that is beyond traditional measures of cognition and affect in communication research. Better understanding of how cognition and affect interact to produce persuasion outcomes would need further conceptualization and theorization, and better empirical testing.

Further reading

Albarracin, Dolores, Blair T. Johnson & Mark P. Zanna (eds.). 2005. *The handbook of attitudes.* Mahwah, NJ: LEA.

Aronson, Elliot, Carrie Fried & Jeff Stone. 1991. Overcoming denial and increasing the intention to use condoms through the induction of hypocrisy. *American Journal of Public Health* 81 (12). 1636–1638.

Crano, William D. & Radmilla Prislin. 2005. Attitudes and Persuasion. *Annual review of psychology* 57. 345–374.

Dillard, James P. & Lijang Shen. in press. *Handbook of persuasion: Developments in theory and practice*, 2nd edn. Thousand Oaks, CA: Sage.

Eagly, Alice H. & Shelly Chaiken. 1993. *The psychology of attitudes*. Fort Worth, TX: Harcourt Brace Jovanovich Publishers.

References

Albarracin, Dolores, Blair. T. Johnson, Martin Fishbein & Paige. A. Muellerleile. 2001. Theories of reasoned action and planned behavior as models of condom use: A meta-analysis. *Psychological Bulletin* 127. 142–161.

Ajzen, Icek. 1991. The theory of planned behavior. *Organizational Behavior and Human Decision Processes* 50. 179–211.

Batson, C. Daniel, Laura. L. Shaw & Kathryn. C. Oleson. 1992. Differentiating affect, mood, and emotion: Toward functionally based conceptual definitions. In: M. S. Clark (ed.), *Review of Personality and Social Psychology: Emotion*, 294–326. Newbury Park, CA: Sage.

Boster, F. J. & P. Mongeau. 1984. Fear-arousing persuasive messages. In: R. N. Bostrom and B. H. Westley (eds.), *Communication yearbook 8*, 330–375. Newbury Park, CA: Sage.

Brehm, Jack W. 1956. Post decision changes in desirability of alternatives. *Journal of Abnormal and Social Psychology* 52. 382–389.

Burleson, Brant R. 1992. Taking Communication Seriously. *Communication Monographs* 59. 79–86.

Chaiken, Shelly, Akiva Liberman & Alice H. Eagly. 1989. Heuristic and systematic processing within and beyond the persuasion context. In: J. S. Uleman and J. A. Bargh (eds.), *Unintended thought*, 212–252. New York, NY: Guilford Press.

Cooper, Joel. 2005. Dissonance theory: History and progress. In: Rex A. Wright, Jeff Greenberg and Sharon S. Brehm (eds.), *Motivational analysis of social behavior: Building on Jack Brehm's contribution to psychology*, 19–37. Mahwah, NJ: Lawrence Erlbaum Associates.

Dillard, James P. & Jason W. Anderson. 2004. The Role of Fear in Persuasion. *Psychology and Marketing* 21. 909–926.

Dillard, James P. & Eugene Peck. 2000. Affect and persuasion: Emotional responses to public service announcements. *Communication Research* 27. 461–495.

Dillard, James P. & Eugene Peck. 2001. Persuasion and the structure of affect: Dual systems and discrete emotions as complementary models. *Human Communication Research* 27. 38–68.

Dillard, James P. & Michael Pfau (eds.). 2002. *The persuasion handbook: Developments in theory and practice*, 3–16. Thousand Oaks, CA: Sage.

Dillard, James P. & Lijiang Shen. 2005. On the nature of reactance and its role in persuasion. *Communication Monographs* 72. 144–168.

Dillard, James P., C. A. Plotnick, Linda C. Godbold, Vicki S. Freimuth & Timothy Edgar. 1996. The multiple affective consequences of AIDS PSAs: Fear appeals do more than scare people. *Communication Research* 23. 44–72.

Eagly, Alice H. & Shelly Chaiken. 1993. *The Psychology of Attitudes*. Fort Worth, TX: Harcourt Brace Jovanovich Publishers.

Fishbein, Martin & Icek Ajzen. 1975. *Belief, attitude, intention, and behavior*. Reading, MA: Addison-Wesley.

Fishbein, Martin & Icek Ajzen. 2010. *Predicting and Changing Behavior: The Reasoned Action Approach*. New York: Psychology Press.

Fishbein, Martin & Joseph N. Cappella. 2006. The Role of Theory in Developing Effective Health Communications. *Journal of Communication* 56.

Fishbein, Martin & Marco C. Yzer . 2003. Using theory to design effective health behavior interventions. *Communication Theory* 13. 164–183.

Festinger, Leon. 1957. *A theory of cognitive dissonance*. Stanford, CA: Stanford University Press.

Festinger, Leon & Merrill J. Carlsmith. 1959. Cognitive consequences of forced compliance. *Journal of Abnormal and Social Psychology* 58. 203–210.

Frijda, Nico. H. 1993. Moods, emotion episodes, and emotions. In: M. Lewis and J. M. Haviland (eds.), *Handbook of emotions*, 381–403. New York: Guilford.

Gass, Robert H. & John S. Seiter. 2011. *Persuasion: Social Influence and Compliance Gaining.* Boston, MA: Allyn and Bacon.

Godin, Gaston & Gerjo Kok. 1996. The theory of planned behavior: A review of its applications to health-related behaviors. *American Journal of Health Promotion* 11. 87–98.

Greenwald, Anthony G. 1968. On Defining Attitude and Attitude Theory. In: Anthony G. Greenwald, Timothy C. Brock and Thomas M. Ostrom (eds.), *Psychological Foundation of Attitude*, 147–170. New York: Academic Press.

Hale, Jerry L., Brian J. Householder & Kathryn L. Greene. 2002. The Theory of Reasoned Action. In: James P. Dillard and Michael Pfau (eds.), *The persuasion handbook: Developments in theory and practice*, 259–286. Thousand Oaks, CA: Sage.

Hankins, Matthew, French David & Horne Rob. 2000. Statistical Guidelines for Studies of the Theory of Reasoned Action and the Theory of Planned Behavior. *Psychology and Health* 15. 151–161.

Harmon-Jones, Eddie. 2002. A cognitive dissonance theory perspective on persuasion. In: James P. Dillard and Michael Pfau (eds.) *The persuasion handbook: Developments in theory and practice*, 99–116. Thousand Oaks, CA: Sage.

Heider, Fritz. 1958. *The psychology of interpersonal relation.* Hillsdale, NJ: Lawrence Erlbaum Associates.

Hovland, Carl I., Irving. L. Janis & Harold. H. Kelley. 1953. *Communication and persuasion: Psychological studies of opinion change.* New Haven: Yale University Press.

Janis, Irving. L. 1967. Effects of fear arousal on attitude change: Recent developments in theory and experimental research. In: L. Berkowitz (ed.), *Advances in experimental social psychology Volume 3*, 166–224. New York: Academic Press.

Kim, Min-Sun & John. E. Hunter. 1993. Relationships among attitudes, behavioral intentions, and behavior: A meta-analysis of past research, part 2. *Communication Research* 20. 331–364.

Kuhl, J. 1986. Motivation and information processing: A new look at decision making, dynamic change, and action control. In: R. M. Sorrentio and E. T. Higgins (eds.), *Handbook of motivation and cognition: Foundation of social behavior*, 404–434. New York: John Wiley and Sons.

Lazarus, Richard S. 1991. *Emotion and adaptation.* New York: Oxford University Press.

Leventhal, Howard. 1970. Findings and theory in the study of fear communications. In: L. Berkowitz (ed.), *Advances in Experimental Social Psychology Volume 5*, 119–186. New York: Academic Press

Miller, Gerald R. 1963. Studies on the use of fear appeals: A summary and analysis. *Central States Speech Journal* 14. 117–125.

Miller, Gerald R. 1980. /2002. On Being Persuaded: Some Basic Distinctions. In: James. P. Dillard and Michael Pfau (eds.), *The persuasion handbook: Developments in theory and practice*, 3–16. Thousand Oaks, CA: Sage.

Miller, Gerald R. & Mark Steinberg. 1975. *A New Analysis of Interpersonal Communication.* Chicago: Science Research Associates.

Mongeau, P. A. 1998. Another look at fear-arousing persuasive appeals. In M. Allen and R. W. Preiss (eds.), *Persuasion: Advances through meta-analysis*, 53–68. Cresskill, NJ: Hampton Press.

Nabi, Robin. 1999. A cognitive-functional model for the effects of discrete negative emotions on information processing, attitude change, and recall. *Communication Theory* 9. 292–320.

Nabi, Robin. 2002. Anger, Fear, uncertainty, and attitude: A test of the cognitive-functional model. *Communication Monographs* 69. 204–216.

Nabi, Robin. 2003. Exploring the framing effects of emotion: Do discrete emotions differentially influence information accessibility, information-seeking, and policy preference? *Communication Research* 30. 224–247.

Oatley, Keith. 1992. *Best laid schemes: The psychology of emotions.* New York: Cambridge University Press.

O'Keefe, Daniel J. 2002. *Persuasion: Theory and Research*, 2nd edn. Thousand Oaks, CA: Sage.

O'Keefe, Daniel J. 2009. Theories of Persuasion. In: Robin Nabi and Mary Beth Oliver (eds.), *Handbook of Media Processes and Effects*, 269–282. Thousand Oaks, CA: Sage.

Osgood, Charles. E. & Percy H. Tannenbaum. 1955. The principle of congruity in the prediction of attitude change. *Psychological Review* 62. 42–55.

Petty, Richard. E. & John T. Cacioppo. 1986. The elaboration likelihood model of persuasion. In: Leonard Berkowitz (ed.), *Advances in experimental social psychology, Volume 19*, 123–205. San Diego, CA: Academic Press.

Pfau, Michael & Roxanne Parrott. 1993. *Persuasive Communication Campaigns.* Boston, MA: Allyn and Bacon.

Pfau, Michael, A. Szabo, J. Anderson, J. Morrill, J. Zubric & H. Wan. 2001. The role and impact of affect in the process of resistance to persuasion. *Human Communication Research* 27. 216–252.

Perloff, Richard M. 2010. *The Dynamics of Persuasion: Communication and Attitudes in the 21st Century* (4th edn) New York: Routledge.

Quick, Brian L. & Michael T. Stephenson. 2007. Further evidence that psychological reactance can be modeled as a combination of anger and negative cognitions. *Communication Research* 34. 255–276.

Rains, Steve & Monique M. Turner. 2007. Psychological reactance and persuasive health communication. *Human Communication Research* 33. 241–269.

Russell, James. A. 2003. Core affect and the psychological construction of emotion. *Psychological Reports* 110. 145–172.

Russell, James. A. & Lisa Feldman Barrett. 1999. Core affect, prototypical emotional episodes, and other things called emotion: Dissecting the elephant. *Journal of Personality and Social Psychology* 76. 805–819.

Scherer, Klaus. R., Angela Schorr & Tom Johnstone (eds.). 2001. *Appraisal processes in emotion: Theory, Methods, Research.* New York: Oxford University Press.

Shen, Lijiang. 2010. Mitigating psychological reactance: The role of message-induced empathy in persuasion. *Human Communication Research* 36. 397–422.

Shen, Lijiang & James P. Dillard. 2007. The influence of BIS/BAS and message framing on the processing of persuasive health messages. *Communication Research* 34. 433–467.

Slater, Michael. 2002. Involvement as Goal-directed Strategic Processing. In: James. P. Dillard and Michael Pfau (eds.), *The persuasion handbook: Developments in theory and practice*, 175–210. Thousand Oaks, CA: Sage.

Stephenson, M. T. 2003. Examining adolescents' responses to antimarijuana PSAs. *Human Communication Research* 29. 343–369.

Todorov, Alexander, Shelly Chaiken & Marlone, D. Henderson. 2002. The Heuristic-Systematic Model of Social Information Processing. In: James. P. Dillard and Michael Pfau (eds.), *The persuasion handbook: Developments in theory and practice*, 195–211. Thousand Oaks, CA: Sage.

van Turennout, M., P. Hagoort & C.M. Brown. 1998. Brain activity during speaking: From syntax to phonology in 40 milliseconds. *Science* 280. 572–574.

Webb, Thomas L. & Paschal Sheeran. 2006. Does Changing Behavioral Intentions Engender Behavior Change? A meta-analysis of the Experimental Evidence. *Psychological Bulletin* 132. 249–268.

Witte, K. 1992. Putting the fear back into fear appeals: The extended parallel process model. *Communication Monographs* 59. 329–349.

Witte, Kim & Mike Allen. 2000. A meta-analysis of fear appeals: Implications for effective public health campaigns. *Health Education and Behavior* 27. 591–615.

Patricia Moy and Brandon J. Bosch

16 Theories of public opinion

Abstract: While the issue of citizen competency has vexed scholars throughout history, the modern concepts of a mass public and mass media are relatively new. Beginning with the seminal works of Lippmann and Dewey, we chart the evolving theories of public opinion, from the "hypodermic needle" model of the early twentieth century to the more psychologically oriented approach to media effects of today. We argue that in addition to understanding how audiences process media content, theories of public opinion must account for how media content is constructed and disseminated, which is complicated by the ever-changing nature of our media landscape.

Keywords: Public opinion, mass media, gatekeeping, media effects

1 Introduction

Popular discourse about public opinion tends to revolve around key issues of the day. Citizens bemusedly ask themselves how the public comes to hold a particular view on a given issue. Voters anticipate how political candidates will strategize and frame an issue to garner the most support possible. And individuals consume news stories and read blogs on the internet, later taking advantage of comment boxes to share their perspectives.

Academic endeavors related to public opinion focus on the same issues. They examine the process by which information gets presented, how citizens learn about issues, and the effects of this information on attitudes, thoughts, and behaviors. However, scholarship on public opinion is not only empirical in nature: research in this area is undergirded by a strong set of normative assumptions. For example, who constitutes the public? What should the members of an ideal citizenry know about politics and how engaged should they be in the political process? Should an opinion grounded in emotion carry as much weight as an opinion based on information?

In studying the aforementioned processes, public opinion scholars inextricably link public opinion to the functioning of democratic society.[1] Given this view of public

---

[1] Theorists have noted that public opinion plays a major force regardless of the political system in which one finds oneself. Invoking John Locke's law of opinion, reputation, and fashion, Noelle-Neumann (1995) specified how public opinion plays a critical role in promoting social integration. This view of public opinion as a form of social control has allowed researchers to study public opinion in small-group settings and other venues that are not ostensibly political in nature.

opinion as instrumental for democratic processes, the theories covered in this chapter encompass decades of scholarship that are based on distinctly different assumptions of the public as members of a democratic system. In addition, particularly as studied vis-à-vis communication, these theories focus on different outcomes, and as our media landscape continues to evolve, the field must reconsider the impact of each. Although the term "public opinion" was not coined until the mid-1700s (see Peters 1995 for a review), our point of departure is the early twentieth-century intellectual debate between Walter Lippmann and John Dewey, whose differences in perspective reflected longstanding debates and would trickle down through the decades to create a rich corpus of literature. The Lippmann-Dewey debate is critical as its key concerns are reflected in the various theories of public opinion, all of which involve media effects. We review the key perspectives on media effects and public opinion theories over the past century, and end with a discussion of how these theories need to be revisited in light of an increasingly technologically oriented media environment.

2 Early twentieth-century perspectives

2.1 Views of the public: Lippmann vs. Dewey

From ancient Greece onward, citizen competence has been at the heart of many debates about the public. Questions about whether citizens were sufficiently knowledgeable to rule or whether governance should be left to Plato's philosopher kings have emerged consistently over the years. Indeed, this remained the crux of how public intellectual Walter Lippmann and theorist John Dewey saw the public in the early 1900s.

Lippmann, in his oft-cited books *Public Opinion* (1922) and *The Phantom Public* (1925), painted a pejorative portrait of the public – one that was unable to process information deeply or to behave rationally. In *Public Opinion*, Lippmann relied on the allegory of the cave, from Book VII of Plato's *The Republic*. In this story, a group of men has been chained together in a cave since childhood. The chains prevent them from moving their legs or turning their heads; consequently, they are able to see only that which passes before them. And because a fire as well as the mouth of the cave are behind them, the chained men see nothing but the shadows cast upon the wall of the cave as others might walk by. The allegory ends, "And if they were able to talk with one another, would they not suppose that they were naming what was actually before them?"

Lippmann presented another allegory in *Public Opinion*, one set in 1914 at the onset of the Great War. Englishmen, Frenchmen, and Germans lived on an island, sufficiently remote that it received mail once every two months. When the mail arrived in mid-September 1914, they learned how their respective countries had been engaged in hostilities. "For six strange weeks they had acted as if they were friends, when in fact they were enemies" (Lippmann 1922: 3). Lippmann used these two examples to illustrate how indirectly citizens know the environment in which they live. Acknowledging how "the real environment is altogether too big, too complex, and too fleeting for direct acquaintance," he contended that citizens were "not equipped to deal with so much subtlety, so much variety, so many permutations and combinations" (16). As a result, citizens are forced to rely on what they can to create for themselves trustworthy pictures of the world beyond their reach. Naturally, the mass media play a critical role in the construction of these pictures.

As much as citizens can use the media to learn about their unseen lifespace, they inherently cannot process mediated information fully. Lippmann (1922: 30) identified several factors as limiting access to the facts:

> They are the artificial censorships, the limitations of social contact, the comparatively meager time available in each day for paying attention to public affairs, the distortion arising because events have to be compressed into very short messages, the difficulty of making a small vocabulary express a complicated world, and finally the fear of facing those facts which would seem to threaten the established routine of men's lives.

Hence, his skepticism that citizens were able to contribute significantly to democratic processes.

Just as Aristotle's view of the public was antithetical to Plato's, Lippmann's perspective generated much response, most notably from philosopher and education reformer John Dewey, who expressed considerably greater optimism regarding the populace. Like Lippmann, he recognized that citizens were imperfect, but his Aristotelean perspective emphasized the supremacy of public opinion as the best safeguard to democracy (Bullert 1983). Is there potential to strengthen our citizenry, and if so, how? Dewey, in his seminal work *The Public and its Problems* (1927), argued that to help an entity "largely inchoate and unorganized" (109), structural changes were needed: "The essential need... is the improvement of the methods and conditions of debate, discussion and persuasion. That is *the* problem of the public" (208). Indeed, for Dewey, it was necessary to foster "conditions under which the Great Society may become the Great Community" (147).

Dewey's thinking reflected a profound concern with improving how citizens learned and how they could reach their fullest potential. In his works (e.g., *The Logic of Inquiry*, 1938), he advocated the use of logic, supported application of the scientific method, and argued that the use of reasoning should be linked to policy and social concerns.

Though most reviews of Lippmann and Dewey tend to juxtapose them as almost diametrically opposite in thought, the two strands of thinking are aligned with each other. As Sproule (1997: 97) noted, "Their ideas fed a view that the weakminded and dangerously neurotic public could not be trusted to take intelligent political action without formal training, supported by quantitative assessment, in how to think." Nonetheless, this debate would transcend time and implicate the views of how researchers saw citizens being influenced by messages they received.

2.2 Media influences on public opinion

Studies that assess the extent to which messages shaped public opinion go lock-step with studies of media effects in general. The earliest conceptions of media effects were of powerful media exerting great impact on relatively passive audiences, driven by both scholarship and the applied communication studies from which the communication discipline was born. In this section, we discuss perspectives that took hold in the first half of the twentieth century.

2.2.1 All-powerful media and propaganda effects

The earliest conceptions of media effects – as having direct, powerful effects – emerged from a confluence of events. In the United States, the publication of Upton Sinclair's *The Jungle* in 1906 elicited a hue and cry from the mass American public that led to the passage of federal acts and an oversight agency that ultimately would become the Food and Drug Administration. Over two decades later, in 1929, US researchers began to examine the effects of motion pictures on children and youth. These Payne Fund studies, named after the sponsoring foundation, found that young viewers emulated what they witnessed in these films (see Lowery and DeFleur 1995). And in 1938, the radio broadcast of H. G. Wells' *War of the Worlds*, telling the story of Martians landing on Earth, produced panic as many listeners believed the broadcast to reflect real-time reality (Cantril 1940).

Alongside these developments existed a growing body of research on propaganda, particularly in the context of World War I. Harold Lasswell (1927: 214), in his dissertation examining propaganda techniques used by all sides during this global struggle, contended that modern war is fought not only on military and economic fronts, but also on the propaganda front. After all, the countries at war were motivated to rouse patriotic fervor, increase citizens' commitment to the war, and portray their enemies in a negative light and demoralize them.

Lasswell's focus on propaganda highlighted as its primary goal the influencing of opinion (see Welch 2003 for a range of definitions). Indeed, both propaganda and public opinion involve phases of human behavior, with the former evoking negative connotations. Doob's (1948: 240) definition of propaganda considers it "the attempt to affect the personalities and to control the behavior of individuals toward ends considered unscientific or of doubtful value in a society at a particular time." Citing numerous channels through which propaganda can be transmitted – newspapers, radio, books, plays – Doob illustrates that it is more than just a tool for deployment in international conflicts.

Against this backdrop, it is no surprise that scholars began to gravitate toward a view of the media as omnipotent. Contemporary academic discourse tends to use different terms to describe the media power of this era – the "magic bullet" theory or the "hypodermic needle" model, the latter of which some scholars claim derived from the notion of immunizing an audience against propaganda (Chaffee and Hochheimer 1985).

2.2.2 Two-step flow

The view of media as all-powerful lost traction as Klapper (1960: 8) summarized two decades of research, concluding that "mass communication *ordinarily* does not serve as a necessary and sufficient cause of audience effects, but rather functions among and through a nexus of mediating factors and influences." Resonating with this view is the work of Paul Lazarsfeld and his colleagues at Columbia University's Bureau of Applied Social Research, whose studies of various communities revealed that mass media did not influence citizens' behaviors directly, as would be posited by the hypodermic needle or magic bullet models. Rather, media exerted their influence on individuals by virtue of influencing key members of the public identified as opinion leaders, people viewed by others to be influential.

This two-step flow of communication emerged across a number of settings. In the political realm, as shown in Lazarsfeld et al.'s (1948) seminal study of citizens in Erie County, Ohio, during the 1940 election, voters who changed their minds during an election campaign or made up their minds late in the campaign were more likely to mention being influenced by others. Citizens also reported greater exposure to interpersonal discussion of politics than mediated coverage of politics. In addition, those individuals identified as opinion leaders reported greater exposure to the mass media than did their followers. Another community study based on residents of Elmira, New York during the 1948 election season led researchers to conclude that one's social system mattered in decision-making (Berelson et al. 1954). This view would later be dubbed the "Columbia model" or sociological model of voting.

Katz and Lazarsfeld (1955) built on the conclusions that emerged from these two community studies, focusing on how personal influence worked in non-political domains. They examined the process of influence in marketing, movie-going, and fashion decisions as well as in the domain of public affairs. However, instead of looking only at self-reports generated by disparate individuals, Katz and Lazarsfeld also studied the individuals whom opinion leaders considered *their* opinion leaders and the sociodemographic and personality traits they possessed. In the end, this study investigated the diffusion of an idea over time through the social structure of an entire community (Katz 1957). Other early studies of opinion leadership adopted innovative ways of shedding light on this concept: Merton (1949) identified as opinion leaders those individuals whom a minimum of four people had listed as shaping their opinions, and in their study of doctors, Menzel and Katz (1955) found that the diffusion of a new drug could be traced through the social structure of the medical community.

In reviewing these initial studies, Katz (1957: 72) noted that people may be more influential than the media in changing opinions as personal influence is generally non-purposive, flexible, and trustworthy. These studies set the stage for media and interpersonal communication to be viewed as competitive channels, which others would later show to be more complementary than competitive (Chaffee 1982; Rogers 1983).

3 Contemporary theories of public opinion

Coinciding with the cognitive turn in the social sciences in the 1970s, media scholarship moved away from the so-called "minimal effects" paradigm associated with critiques made by Klapper (1960). With the advance of several new communication theories and phenomena, scholars began to gravitate toward a return to all-powerful media (primarily as individuals turned to the media to help themselves define social reality). Only later would they acknowledge the presence of contingent media effects – that powerful media effects occurred some of the time for some individuals. This section presents the key contemporary theories of media effects on public opinion.

3.1 Agenda-setting

Entirely bypassed by the earlier scholarly focus on media persuasion (Kosicki 1993: 231), agenda-setting came to light in a landmark study by McCombs and Shaw (1972), who found that the issues considered most important to Chapel Hill, North Carolina, voters were also the same issues covered by news media in Chapel Hill. Referencing the now-famous words of Bernard Cohen (1963: 13) that "the press may not be successful all the time in telling people what to think, but it is stunningly successful in telling its readers what to think about," McCombs and Shaw (1972) concluded that news media are capable of influencing the political agenda of the public.

The several hundred studies of agenda-setting conducted in the four decades since the Chapel Hill study indicate considerable robustness of the phenomenon. Although studies tend to operationalize media coverage by analyzing easily accessible newspaper coverage and correlating that coverage with survey data, experimental research has shown that agenda-setting effects exist for televised content as well (Iyengar and Kinder 1987). Researchers have investigated agenda-setting effects for short-term issues as well as long-term national concerns such as the 1980s War on Drugs (Gonzenbach 1996); for news processed in hard-copy format and online (Althaus and Tewksbury 2002; Schoenbach et al. 2005); for local and non-local issues (Palmgreen and Clarke 1977); for entertainment content (Holbrook and Hill 2005); for visual content (Coleman and Banning 2006); and across a wide array of individual countries as well as comparatively (Peter 2003).

Despite the general robustness of agenda-setting effects, research has identified a number of factors that mitigate or enhance their magnitude. Some of these factors have generated mixed findings, while others appear more consistently in the literature. For instance, interpersonal discussion can enhance agenda-setting effects (McLeod et al. 1974), dampen them (Atwater et al. 1985), or both (Wanta and Wu 1992).

Level of issue obtrusiveness, however, has over the years emerged as a generally consistent and significant moderator of the media's agenda-setting effects. Namely, media coverage of unobtrusive issues – those issues with which individuals have little or no direct experience – will have stronger agenda-setting effects as the public will need to rely more on the media for information about those issues (Zucker 1978).

Related to the level of issue obtrusiveness, agenda-setting effects can be moderated by one's need for orientation (Weaver 1977), or the extent to which individuals are driven to situate and more fully understand an issue. Need for orientation comprises two dimensions – relevance and uncertainty, with the former serving as the initial necessary condition: people who do not perceive an issue to be relevant will not need to orient themselves on this topic. However, among those who perceive an issue to be relevant to them, there is variance in their levels of uncertainty about that issue. Individuals who have all the information they need on a relevant issue (or are low in uncertainty) will be lower in their need for orientation than individuals who perceive an issue to be highly relevant yet have insufficient information (see McCombs and Reynolds 2009 for a review). These patterns do not elide the fact that even incidental exposure to media messages can have significant consequences. As McCombs (2004) illustrates, the strength of agenda-setting effects is not monotonic, increasing as media exposure increases; rather, it approaches asymptote after a certain level of exposure.

Matthes (2006) called for the study of need for orientation toward not only issues, but also facts (e.g., "I want to know many different sides about that topic") and journalistic evaluations (e.g., "I attach great importance to commentaries on this issue"). The latter resonates with findings showing that audience members' perceptions of media credibility and knowledge can moderate agenda-setting effects (Miller and Krosnick 2000; Tsfati 2003; Wanta 1997).

3.2 Priming

Although the theory of agenda-setting specifies a relationship between media salience of an issue and public salience of that same issue, it says very little about what individuals do with the media content to which they have been exposed. Borrowing from psychologists, who define priming as "the fact that recently and frequently activated ideas come to mind more easily than ideas that have not been activated" (Fiske and Taylor 1984: 231), communication scholars view this concept as an extension of agenda-setting, referring to the power of media to effect "changes in the standards that people use to make [political] evaluations" (Iyengar and Kinder 1987: 63; brackets added).

Like agenda-setting, priming works because individuals tend to rely on memory-based processing of information. Rather than forming attitudes based on impressions (sometimes called on-line processing, McGraw et al. 1990), individuals tend to retrieve information that is more salient (Hastie and Park 1986). Scheufele and Tewksbury (2007: 11) succinctly juxtaposed agenda-setting and framing: "By making some issues more salient in people's mind (agenda setting), mass media can also shape the considerations that people take into account when making judgments about political candidates or issues (priming)."

Studies of priming on topics not ostensibly related to public opinion have found fertile ground in assessing media violence, sexual content in the media, racial representations, and advertisements (Carpentier 2011). However, such content has strong implications for attitudes toward censorship, stereotyping, and consumer purchase behaviors. In the public opinion domain, however, the criterion variable of interest has tended to be judgments of politicians. In their seminal study of the agenda-setting and priming effects of US television, Iyengar and Kinder (1987) found that the more attention paid to a specific problem, the more likely that viewers incorporated what they knew about that problem when assessing the President (see also Pan and Kosicki 1997, and for similar findings related to the governor of Hong Kong, Willnat and Zhu 1996). Looking at evaluations of presidential performance, research has found that media coverage of an issue does increase the ease with which related beliefs are accessed, but do not find priming effects. Rather, politically knowledgeable citizens in the US who trust the media more infer news coverage of that issue to reflect greater importance of that issue and therefore tend to use that issue as a standard for evaluating the President (Miller and Krosnick 2000).

The literature on priming offers many nuanced findings. For instance, unlike in studies of presidential evaluations, priming effects have not been found for interest groups (McGraw and Ling 2003). And although many priming studies assume that audiences use the dominant news agenda in their evaluations, research shows that "big-message" effects are just one part of the story: recent exposure to relevant content can generate priming effects, but *cumulative exposure* plays a greater role (Althaus and Kim 2006).

With few exceptions, such as those examining public support for military conflicts (Althaus and Coe 2011), priming research today remains focused on formal political actors, but has moved to other sites of political news. This shift is particularly important, given that political news can appear in many forms (e.g., Entman 2005). In the United States, late-night comedies such as *The Late Show with David Letterman* are found to influence which traits audiences use to evaluate presidential candidates (Moy et al. 2005), with documentaries (e.g., *Fahrenheit 9–11*, Holbert and Hansen 2006) and fictional programming such as *The West Wing* (Holbert et al. 2003) and *NYPD Blue* (Holbrook and Hill 2005) also able to shift the basis of evaluations of presidents. These findings, however, are contingent on many individual-level factors, including political ideology and political interest.

3.3 Framing

Often discussed in tandem with agenda-setting and priming, framing refers to media influences based on what media coverage of an issue includes. Despite being characterized as a "fractured paradigm" with "scattered conceptualization" (Entman 1993: 51), framing enjoys generally consistent definitions. According to Entman (1993: 52), framing highlights certain aspects of the world in a text "as to promote a particular problem definition, causal interpretation, moral evaluation, and/or treatment recommendation." Similarly, Gamson and Modigliani (1987: 143) define a frame as "a central organizing idea or story line that provides meaning to an unfolding strip of events....The frame suggests what the controversy is about, the essence of the issue." Likewise, Reese (2001: 11) sees frames as "organizing principles that are socially shared and persist over time, that work symbolically to meaningfully structure the social world." In short, scholars view frames as providing meaning about social phenomena through the highlighting and packaging of information.

The bulk of research on framing effects has either identified types of frames that exist or tested their effects. On the former front, one common dichotomization involves episodic vs. thematic frames. Whereas episodic frames adopt a case-study perspective on an issue or portray just one incident, thematic frames provide greater contextualization and background, linking that particular incident to larger concerns. Not surprisingly, individuals exposed to these frames differ in their attribution of responsibility on political issues (Iyengar 1991): episodic frames lead audience members to attribute responsibility of an issue to the individual involved, while thematic frames increase the likelihood of blaming the government or society at large.

Policy vs. strategy frames constitute another common way to differentiate news frames. Usually appearing in the context of election coverage, policy frames focus on substantive issues as well as issue-based information from candidates or parties (Patterson 1993). Strategy frames, on the other hand, emphasize the sport of electoral politics (Farnsworth and Lichter 2007). Often termed "horse-race coverage" – which focuses on which candidate is winning or losing, and by how much – strategy frames are charged with undermining the electoral process by diverting citizens' attention away from the issues that really matter (Cappella and Jamieson 1997; Patterson 1993), though others claim that the drama of horse-race coverage makes news coverage more memorable and can generate interest in a campaign (Bartels 1988).

Because framing is inherent in media coverage, the range of studies in this area is considerable (see, for example, the case studies in Reese et al. [2001] which include examinations of media frames of political correctness and those of a murder trial). Studies of individual-level framing effects, however, have examined gains vs. losses (Tversky and Kahneman 1981) and ethical vs. material frames (Domke et al. 1998); compared human interest, conflict, and personal consequence frames (Price et al. 1997); and looked at similar frames including those emphasizing attribution of responsibility or economics (Valkenburg et al. 1999). While these aforementioned experimental studies highlight the effects of a particular type of frame, other experiments test for the effects of framing of a specific incident. Notable studies include framing a Ku Klux Klan rally as a free-speech issue vs. a disruption of public order (Nelson et al. 1997) and framing the Supreme Court ruling of the 2000 U.S. presidential election as partisan and "stealing the election" vs. a principled vote based on legal considerations (Nicholson and Howard 2003). Findings show that respective levels of support for the Ku Klux Klan and Supreme Court differed depending on the frame to which study participants were exposed.

Framing influences how people understand issues, but their effects are contingent on many individual-level factors. After all, in making sense of media messages, audience members not only consider to varying degrees media content, but they also engage with each other interpersonally (Druckman and Nelson 2003; Walsh 2004) and draw on their experiential knowledge (Gamson 1996).

Beyond the *cognitive* frames that affect citizens' understanding of the specific issue at hand (Iyengar 1991; Tversky and Kahneman 1981), the media can shape audience members' understanding of related concerns by adopting *cultural* frames – frames that "don't stop with organizing one story, but invite us to...[go] beyond the immediate information" (Reese 2001: 12–13). One exemplar of a cultural frame is the "war on terrorism" frame, which "offered a way...to construct a narrative to make sense of a range of diverse stories about international security, civil wars, and global conflict" (Norris et al. 2003: 15).

Although scholars differentiate framing from agenda-setting in that they see the former as concerned with the quality and content of media coverage of an issue and the latter as concerned with only the amount of coverage, some argue that framing can be understood as another type of agenda-setting effect. In other words, agenda setting can influence the public's perception of salience of an issue as well as how it understands that issue (McCombs 2004). Whether or not framing is its own concern or another extension of agenda-setting seems to hinge on the theoretical mechanisms. Some scholars stress that agenda-setting and priming operate via accessibility, noting how exposure to media coverage about an issue increases its accessibility in one's mind, while framing effects are markedly different, relying instead on applicability effects (e.g., Price and Tewksbury 1997). In other words, when an issue is framed in terms of meaning, cause, solution, and responsibility, "the primary effect of [that] frame is to render specific information, images, or ideas *applicable* to [that] issue" (Tewksbury and Scheufele 2009: 21).

4 Conclusions

This chapter focused on key theories of public opinion as they implicate individual-level effects on citizens' attitudes, behaviors, and cognitions. Viewing these theories through this lens suggests a singularity or simplicity that simply does not exist. Agenda-setting research has looked at how media agendas can set policy agendas (Rogers et al. 1993) or other media's agendas (Atwater et al. 1987), and framing research has differentiated between frame-setting and frame-building (Scheufele 1999). Indeed, to truly understand public opinion, we must not only understand the nature of the public and the assumptions that undergird research efforts, but also the nature of mass media. This point was recognized early by Lippmann (1922), whose views on the individual and news media led him to reject the possibility of an informed mass public. Toward this end, we briefly review the literature on key factors that feed into the construction of news, recognizing that, as Shoemaker and Reese (1996: 251) noted, "mass media content is a socially created product, not a reflection of an objective reality" (see also Tuchman 1978).

4.1 A key caveat: the construction of media content

To begin, who determines what is news? What forces within the news media serve as gatekeepers (White 1950) and what forces will shape how content gets presented? At the most micro level, journalists who create news stories and their editors may unknowingly shape content. Their sociodemographics as well as political views and training, and their perceptions of norms all have some bearing on what and how content gets presented. For instance, newspapers with male managing editors produce more coverage of politics and national security over time, while female-led newsrooms produce more indirect leads, a practice common in the crafting of features or news features stories (Beam and DiCicco 2010). Similarly, the relationship between journalists' partisanship and their news decisions appears not only in the United States, but also in Western Europe (Donsbach and Patterson 2004). Differences exist across countries as well, particularly in terms of professional norms: compared to British, Italian, Swedish, and German journalists, American journalists most strongly advocate for a free press, and are more likely to rely on interviews with newsmakers and citizens than on wire-service copy to cover stories (Donsbach and Patterson 2004).

Perhaps most salient as a professional norm of journalism (at least in the United States) is that of objectivity, which holds that journalists should report facts rather than values and present multiple perspectives on a story (Schudson 2001: 150). Paradoxically, this norm tends to introduce its own bias – an overreliance on officials and, coupled with a need for newsworthy sources, encourages *indexing*. Indexing occurs when the types of viewpoints presented in news media tend to be calibrated to "the range of views expressed in mainstream government debate about a given topic" (Bennett 1990: 106). The indexing hypothesis has received empirical support (e.g., Livingston and Bennett 2003; Zaller and Chiu 1996), but has also been refined to account for the ability of presidential administrations to influence media coverage more than members of Congress (Entman 2004). However, other scholarship suggests that journalists are often relatively autonomous in their reporting (Althaus 2003; Patterson 1993). Notably, journalists appear to reject frames from elite politicians and interest groups in favor of framing that heightens the dramatic elements of a news story (Callaghan and Schnell 2001), highlighting the importance of ratings and economics in news production.

Indeed, economic factors need to be taken into account when considering how media content is created (Sparrow 1999). For example, the division of labor associated with the newsbeat system maximizes the efficiency of news collection, though this "news net" is typically cast around "big fish" such as prominent officials and political leaders (Tuchman 1978). To avoid costly original research, journalists rely on credible institutions and elite officials for information (Gans 1979; Sigal 1973). Put differently, the "free" information provided by elite officials and institutions essentially amounts to a subsidy to the news industry (Cook 2005; Fishman 1980). Thus in the same way that news media are dependent upon advertising for revenue, so are journalists dependent on credible sources.

Scholars have also pointed to the effects of media ownership and economics in the production of media content. The study of the political economy of news media is presaged by Marx and Engels' (1845/2004: 64) comment that "the class which has the means of material production at its disposal, has control at the same time over the means of mental production." Some scholars argue that since news media organizations are owned not only by wealthy individuals, but also by corporate conglomerates and dependent upon corporate advertising, news media content will tend to have a pro-corporate capitalism bias (Herman and Chomsky 1994; McChesney 2004; Parenti 1992). However, much of the evidence in support of this claim is anecdotal in nature. Moreover, a content analysis found only limited support of news media synergy bias, which occurs when news media outlets provide more favorable coverage of products and businesses owned by the parent company (Williams 2002).

In fact, outside the realm of news media, many unfavorable depictions of corporations exist in popular media. Lichter et al. (1997) find that business characters were depicted negatively more often (55%) than non-business characters (31%) on television. Whether it be linking capitalism with the murderous creature in *Alien*

(1979) and consumerism with mindless zombies in *Dawn of the Dead* (1978) (Ryan and Kellner 1988), or simply depicting the mundane corporate workplace as a threat to masculinity (Hunter 2003), capitalism often is shown in a threatening light on film. Given the consistently negative depictions of labor unions in film (Christensen and Haas 2005; Puette 1992), it makes more sense to think of mass media as an arena of competing themes, rather than as articulating a single ideology (Ryan and Kellner 1988).

Although cited as a potential motivation of corporate bias, the need for profits can work to produce media critiques of capitalism. According to Kellner (1981: 40), the profit motive can trump class ideology; for instance, "the short-term economic interests of a network may lead them to broadcast news which puts in question aspects of the socioeconomic order, thus jeopardizing their long-range economic interests." Focusing on the economic pressures facing news organizations, Hamilton (2004) argues that network news programming has more "soft" news coverage (focusing less on politics) and is liberal on social issues in order to appeal to 18–34 year-old females, who are a prime demographic for advertisers.

At the most macro level, the construction of news and media content in general can be influenced by broader cultural forces. Entman (1993: 52) notes that along with the communicator, text, and receiver, frames reside in culture. Similarly, Van Gorp (2007) speaks of a "cultural stock of frames" from which both journalists and audiences draw upon to make sense of the world. However, different views exist regarding the actual influence of culture on news coverage: Hallin (1986) argues that coverage is influenced by the cultural consensus surrounding that issue, while Gans (1979) finds news content to be characterized by "enduring values" such as ethnocentrism, individualism, small-town pastoralism, and responsible capitalism. By referring to something resident in the surrounding culture, media frames have "implicit cultural roots" (Tewksbury and Scheufele 2009: 23) and can resonate with audience members (Gamson and Modigliani 1989).

4.2 Some final words about the changing face of public opinion

Conceptualizations of agenda-setting, priming, and framing as media effects on public opinion emerged in an era that was relatively simple compared to today's environment. But as citizens have turned increasingly to social media and other online tools, the field has begun to question the extent to which one can separate mass from interpersonal influences (Mutz and Young 2011) or even the directionality of effects. Agenda-building, which identifies how specific entities can shape the media's agenda, now needs to explicitly include citizens as active newsmakers. If media content is being crafted by the individuals that previously were being told by the media what issues to think about, perhaps the theoretical premises of agenda-setting should be refined. Similarly, groups and individuals that previously had difficulty finding voice through traditional media outlets now have the opportunity to create their own frames and bypass journalistic filters. If frame sponsorship no longer belongs only to elites, and if citizens are setting frames for the media, scholars should reconsider the extent to which hypothesizing about traditional (media-to-audience) framing effects is useful.

As our media landscape becomes more balkanized and fragmented, society has witnessed an increase in selective exposure and a shift toward what Bennett and Iyengar (2008) term "a new era of minimal effects." Indeed, the long-held stages of media effects described here are being questioned: Neuman and Guggenheim (2011) eschew categorizing effects in terms of their power on audience members, proffering instead a six-stage model of media effects that turns on clusters of theories. According to their typology, we have been operating, since 1996, under a "new media theories" framework.

But what are new media? Today's latest technology will likely lose novelty with the appearance of the next one, but not before it has become fully integrated into everyday politics. Information will continue to be sent for the sake of information; messages will continue to be sent to mobilize others to take action; and non-elites will continue using these technologies to join the swelling ranks of citizen-journalists (Cooper 2010). Taken together, these acts of engagement signal how the dichotomies of yore no longer hold. Social media have flattened hierarchies, and media consumers have become producers. With this increased engagement in the media, citizens can find virtually unlimited information on an issue. Unfortunately, this proliferation of media can kindle distrust in sources that espouse dissonant views from one's own. These tensions call for a re-examination of how communication is defined. They also force a reconsideration of who is the source and who is the receiver, and more importantly, how these new communication processes will shape public opinion in a democracy.

Further reading

Bennett, W. Lance & Shanto Iyengar. 2008. A new era of minimal effects? The changing foundations of political communication. *Journal of Communication* 58. 707–731.

Holbert, R. Lance, R. Kelly Garrett & Laurel S. Gleason. 2010. A new era of minimal effects? A response to Bennett and Iyengar. *Journal of Communication* 60. 15–34.

Mutz, Diana C. & Lori Young. 2011. Communication and public opinion: Plus ça change? *Public Opinion Quarterly* 75. 1018–1044.

Price, Vincent. 2011. Public opinion research in the new century: Reflections from a former POQ editor. *Public Opinion Quarterly* 75. 846–853.

Shoemaker, Pamela J. & Stephen D. Reese. 1996. *Mediating the Message: Theories of Influence on Mass Media Content*, 2nd edn. New York, NY: Longman.

References

Althaus, Scott L. 2003. When news norms collide, follow the lead: New evidence for press independence. *Political Communication* 20. 381–414.

Althaus, Scott L. & Kevin Coe. 2011. Social identity processes and the dynamics of public support for war. *Public Opinion Quarterly* 75. 65–88.

Althaus, Scott & David Tewksbury. 2002. Agenda setting and the 'new' news: Patterns of issue importance among readers of the paper and online versions of the New York Times. *Communication Research* 29. 180–207.

Althaus, Scott L & Young Mie Kim. 2006. Priming effects in complex information environments: Reassessing the impact of news discourse on presidential approval. *Journal of Politics* 68. 960–976.

Atwater, Tony, Frederick Fico & Gary Pizante. 1987. Reporting on the state legislature: A case of inter-media agenda setting. *Newspaper Research Journal* 8. 52–61.

Atwater, Tony, Michael B. Salwen & Ronald B. Anderson. 1985. Interpersonal discussion as a potential barrier to agenda-setting. *Newspaper Research Journal* 6. 37–43.

Bartels, Larry M. 1988. *Presidential Primaries and the Dynamics of Public Choice*. Princeton, NJ: Princeton University Press.

Beam, Randal A. & Damon Di Cicco. 2010. When women run the newsroom: Management change, gender, and the news. *Journalism & Mass Communication Quarterly* 87. 393–411.

Bennett, W. Lance. 1990. Toward a theory of press-state relations in the United States. *Journal of Communication* 40. 103–127.

Bennett, W. Lance & Shanto Iyengar. 2008. A new era of minimal effects? The changing foundations of political communication. *Journal of Communication* 58. 707–731.

Berelson, Bernard R., Paul F. Lazarsfeld & William N. McPhee. 1954. *Voting: A Study of Opinion Formation in a Presidential Campaign*. Chicago, IL: University of Chicago Press.

Bullert, Gary. 1983. *The Politics of John Dewey*. Buffalo, NY: Prometheus Books.

Callaghan, Karen & Frauke Schnell. 2001. Assessing the democratic debate: How the news media frame elite policy discourse. *Political Communication* 18. 183–212.

Cantril, Hadley. 1940. *The Invasion from Mars: A Study in the Psychology of Panic*. Princeton, NJ: Princeton University Press.

Cappella, Joseph N. & Kathleen Hall Jamieson. 1997. *Spiral of Cynicism: The Press and the Public Good*. New York, NY: Oxford University Press.

Carpentier, Francesca Dillman. 2011. Priming. In: Patricia Moy (ed.), *Oxford Bibliographies: Communication*. www.aboutobo.com/communication.

Chaffee, Steven H. 1982. Mass media and interpersonal channels: Competitive, convergent, or complementary? In: Gary Gumpert and Robert Cathcart (eds.), *Inter/Media: Interpersonal Communication in a Media World*, 2nd edn, 57–77. New York, NY: Oxford University Press.

Chaffee, Steven H. & John L. Hochheimer. 1985. The beginnings of political communication research in the United States: Origins of the "limited effects" model. In: Everett M. Rogers and Francis Balle (eds.), *The Media Revolution in America and in Western Europe*, 267–296. Norwood, NJ: Ablex Publishing Corporation.

Christensen, Terry & Peter J. Haas. 2005. *Projecting Politics: Political Messages in American Films*. Armonk, NY: M.E. Sharp.

Coleman, Renita & Stephen Banning. 2006. Network TV news' affective framing of the presidential candidates. *Journalism & Mass Communication Quarterly* 83. 313–328.

Cohen, Bernard C. 1963. *The Press and Foreign Policy*. Princeton, NJ: Princeton University Press.

Cook, Timothy E. 2005. *Governing with the News: The News Media as a Political Institution*. Chicago, IL: University of Chicago Press.

Cooper, Stephen D. 2010. The oppositional framing of bloggers. In: Paul D'Angelo and Jim A. Kuypers (eds.), *Doing News Framing Analysis: Empirical and Theoretical Perspectives*, 135–155. New York: Routledge.

Dewey, John. 1927. *The Public and Its Problems*. New York, NY: Henry Holt and Company.

Dewey, John. 1938. *The Logic of Inquiry*. New York, NY: Holt, Rinehart and Winston.

Domke, David, Dhavan V. Shah & Daniel B. Wackman. 1998. Media priming effects: Accessibility, association, and activation. *International Journal of Public Opinion Research* 10. 51–74.

Donsbach, Wolfgang & Thomas E. Patterson. 2004. Political news journalists: Partisanship, professionalism, and political roles in five countries. In: Frank Esser and Barbara Pfetsch (eds.), *Comparing Political Communication: Theories, Cases, and Challenges*, 251–270. New York, NY: Cambridge University Press.

Doob, Leonard W. 1948. *Public Opinion and Propaganda*. New York, NY: Henry Holt and Company.

Druckman, James N. & Kjersten R. Nelson. 2003. Framing and deliberation: How citizens' conversations limit elite influence. *American Journal of Political Science* 47. 729–745.

Entman, Robert M. 1993. Framing: Toward clarification of a fractured paradigm. *Journal of Communication* 43. 51–58.

Entman, Robert M. 2004. *Projections of Power: Framing News, Public Opinion, and U.S. Foreign Policy*. Chicago, IL: University of Chicago Press.

Entman, Robert M. 2005. The nature and sources of news. In: Kathleen H. Jamieson and Geneva Overholser (eds.), *The Press*, 48–65. New York, NY: Oxford University Press.

Farnsworth, Stephen J. & S. Robert Lichter. 2007. *The Nightly News Nightmare: Television Coverage of U.S. Presidential Elections, 1988–2004*, 2nd edn. Lanham, MD: Rowman & Littlefield Publishers.

Fishman, Mark. 1980. *Manufacturing the News*. Austin, TX: University of Texas Press.

Fiske, Susan T. & Shelley E. Taylor. 1984. *Social Cognition*. Reading, MA: Addison-Wesley Pub. Co.

Gamson, William A. 1996. Media discourse as a framing resource. In: Ann N. Crigler (ed.), *The Psychology of Political Communication*, 111–132. Ann Arbor, MI: The University of Michigan Press.

Gamson, William A. & Andre Modigliani. 1987. The changing culture of affirmative action. In: Richard. G. Braungart (ed.), *Research in Political Sociology 13*, 137–177. Greenwich, CT: JAI Press.

Gans, Herbert J. 1979. *Deciding What's News: A Study of CBS Evening News, NBC Nightly News, Newsweek, and Time*. New York, NY: Pantheon Books.

Gonzenbach, William J. 1996. *The Media, the President, and Public Opinion: A Longitudinal Analysis of the Drug Issue, 1984–1991*. Mahwah, NJ: Lawrence Erlbaum Associates, Inc.

Hallin, Daniel C. 1986. *The "Uncensored War": The Media and Vietnam*. New York, NY: Oxford University Press.

Hamilton, James T. 2004. *All The News That's Fit To Sell: How The Market Transforms Information Into News*. Princeton, NJ: Princeton University Press.

Hastie, Reid & Bernadette Park. 1986. The relationship between memory and judgment depends on whether the judgment task is memory-based or on-line. *Psychological Review* 93. 258–268.

Herman, Edward S. & Noam Chomsky. 1994. *Manufacturing Consent: The Political Economy of the Mass Media*. New York, NY: Pantheon Books.

Holbert, R. Lance & Glenn J. Hansen. 2006. Fahrenheit 9–11, need for closure and the priming of affective ambivalence: An assessment of intra-affective structures by party identification. *Human Communication Research* 32. 109–129.

Holbert, R. Lance, Owen Pillion, David A. Tschida, Greg G. Armfield, Kelly Kinder, Kristin L. Cherry & Amy R. Daulton. 2003. *The West Wing* as endorsement of the U.S. presidency: Expanding the bounds of priming in political communication. *Journal of Communication* 53. 427–443.

Holbrook, R. Andrew & Timothy G. Hill. 2005. Agenda-setting and priming in prime time television: Crime dramas as political cues. *Political Communication* 22. 277–295.

Hunter, Latham. 2003. The celluloid cubicle: Regressive constructions of masculinity in 1990s office movies. *The Journal of Popular American Culture* 26. 71–86.

Iyengar, Shanto. 1991. *Is Anyone Responsible?: How Television Frames Political Issues*. Chicago, IL: University of Chicago Press.

Iyengar, Shanto & Donald R. Kinder. 1987. *News that Matters: Television and American Opinion*. Chicago, IL: University of Chicago Press.

Katz, Elihu. 1957. The two-step flow of communication: An up-to-date report on an hypothesis. *Public Opinion Quarterly* 21. 61–78.

Katz, Elihu & Paul Lazarsfeld. 1955. *Personal Influence: The Part Played by People in the Flow of Mass Communications*. Glencoe, IL: The Free Press.

Kellner, Douglas. 1981. Network television and American society: Introduction to a critical theory of television. *Theory & Society* 10. 31–62.

Klapper, Joseph T. 1960. *The Effects of Mass Communication*. New York, NY: Free Press.

Kosicki, Gerald M. 1993. Problems and opportunities in agenda-setting research. *Journal of Communication* 43. 100–127.

Lasswell, Harold D. 1927. *Propaganda Technique in World War I*. Cambridge, MA/London: The M.I.T. Press.

Lazarsfeld, Paul F., Bernard Berelson & Hazel Gaudet. 1948. *The People's Choice*. New York, NY: Columbia University Press.

Lichter, Robert S., Linda S. Lichter & Daniel Amundson. 1997. Does Hollywood hate business or money? *Journal of Communication* 47 (1). 68–84.

Lippmann, Walter. 1922. *Public Opinion*. New York, NY: Macmillan.

Lippmann, Walter. 1925. *The Phantom Public*. New York, NY: Harcourt, Brace and Company.

Livingston, Steven & W. Lance Bennett. 2003. Gatekeeping, indexing, and live-event news: Is technology altering the construction of news? *Political Communication* 20. 363–380.

Lowery, Shearon A. & Melvin L. DeFleur. 1995. *Milestones in Mass Communication Research: Media Effects*, 3rd edn. White Plains, NY: Longman.

Marx, Karl & Friedrich Engels. 1845. /2004. *The German Ideology: Part One, with selections from parts Two and Three, together with Marx's 'Introduction to a Critique of Political Economy'*. London: Lawrence & Wishart.

Matthes, Joerg. 2006. The need for orientation towards news media: Revising and validating a classic concept. *International Journal of Public Opinion Research* 18. 422–444.

McChesney, Robert. 2004. *The Problem of the Media: US Communication Politics in the 21st Century*. New York, NY: Monthly Review Press.

McCombs, Maxwell E. 2004. *Setting the Agenda: The Mass Media and Public Opinion*. Cambridge, UK: Polity Press.

McCombs, Maxwell E. & Salma I. Ghanem. 2001. The convergence of agenda setting and framing. In: Stephen D. Reese, Oscar H. Gandy, Jr. and August E. Grant (eds.), *Framing Public Life: Perspectives on Media and Our Understanding of the Social World*, 67–81. Mahwah, NJ: Lawrence Erlbaum Associates.

McCombs, Maxwell & Amy Reynolds. 2009. How the news shapes our civic agenda. In: Jennings Bryant and Mary Beth Oliver (eds.), *Media Effects: Advances in Theory and Research*, 3rd edn, 1–16. New York, NY: Routledge.

McCombs, Maxwell E. & Donald L. Shaw. 1972. The agenda-setting function of mass media. *Public Opinion Quarterly* 36. 176–187.

McGraw, Kathleen M. & Cristina Ling. 2003. Media priming of presidential and group evaluations. *Political Communication* 20. 23–40.

McGraw, Kathleen M., Milton Lodge & Patrick Stroh. 1990. On-line processing in candidate evaluation: The effects of issue order, issue importance, and sophistication. *Political Behavior* 12. 41–58.

McLeod, Jack M., Lee B. Becker & James E. Byrnes. 1974. Another look at the agenda-setting function of the press. *Communication Research* 1. 131–166.

Merton, Robert K. 1949. Patterns of influence: A study of interpersonal influence and communications behaviors in a local community. In: Paul F. Lazarsfeld and Frank N. Stanton (eds.), *Communications Research, 1948–9*, 180–219. New York, NY: Harper and Brothers.

Menzel, Herbert & Elihu Katz. 1955. Social relations and innovation in the medical profession. *Public Opinion Quarterly* 19. 337–352.

Miller, Joanne M. & Jon A. Krosnick. 2000. News media impact on the ingredients of presidential evaluations: Politically knowledgeable citizens are guided by a trusted source. *American Journal of Political Science* 44. 301–315.

Moy, Patricia, Michael Xenos & Verena K. Hess. 2006. Priming effects of late-night comedy. *International Journal of Public Opinion Research* 18. 198–210.

Mutz, Diana C. & Lori Young. 2011. Communication and public opinion: Plus ça change? *Public Opinion Quarterly* 75. 1018–1044.

Nelson, Thomas E., Rosalee A. Clawson & Zoe M. Oxley. 1997. Media framing of a civil liberties conflict and its effect on tolerance. *The American Political Science Review* 91. 567–583.

Nicholson, Stephen P. & Robert M. Howard. 2003. Framing Support for the Supreme Court in the Aftermath of Bush v. Gore. *Journal of Politics* 65. 676–695. DOI: 10.1111/1468-2508.00207.

Neuman, W. Russell & Lauren Guggenheim. 2011. The evolution of media effects theory: A six-stage model of cumulative research. *Communication Theory* 21. 169–196.

Noelle-Neumann, Elisabeth. 1995. Public opinion and rationality. In: Theodore L. Glasser and Charles T. Salmon (eds.), *Public Opinion and the Communication of Consent*, 33–54. New York, NY: Guilford Press.

Norris, Pippa, Montague Kern & Marion R. Just. 2003. *Framing Terrorism: The News Media, the Government, and the Public*. New York, NY: Routledge.

Palmgreen, Philip & Peter Clarke. 1977. Agenda-setting with local and national issues. *Communication Research* 4. 435–452.

Pan, Zhongdang & Gerald M. Kosicki. 1993. Framing analysis: An approach to news discourse. *Political Communication* 10. 55–75.

Parenti, Michael. 1993. *Inventing Reality: The Politics of Mass Media*. New York, NY: St. Martin's Press.

Patterson, Thomas E. 1993. *Out of Order*. New York, NY: Knopf.

Peter, Jochen. 2003. Country characteristics as contingent conditions of agenda setting: The moderating influence of polarized elite opinion. *Communication Research* 30. 683–712.

Peters, John Durham. 1995. Historical tensions in the concept of public opinion. In: Theodore L. Glasser and Charles T. Salmon (eds.), *Public Opinion and the Communication of Consent*, 3–32. New York, NY: Guilford Press.

Price, Vincent & David Tewksbury. 1997. News values and public opinion: A theoretical account of media priming and framing. In: George A. Barnett and Franklin J. Boster (eds.), *Progress in the Communication Sciences: Advances in Persuasion, Vol. 13*, 173–212. Greenwitch, CT: Ablex.

Price, Vincent, David Tewksbury & Elizabeth Powers. 1997. Switching trains of thought: The impact of news frames on readers' cognitive responses. *Communication Research* 24. 481–506.

Puette, William J. 1992. *Through Jaundiced Eyes: How the Media View Organized Labor*. Ithaca, NY: ILR Press

Reese, Stephen D. 2001. Framing public life: A bridging model for media research. In: Stephen D. Reese, Oscar H. Gandy, Jr. and August E. Grant (eds.), *Framing Public Life: Perspectives on*

Media and Our Understanding of the Social World, 7–31. Mahwah, NJ: Lawrence Erlbaum Associates.

Reese, Stephen D., Oscar H. Gandy Jr. & August E. Grant. 2001. *Framing Public Life: Perspectives on Media and Our Understanding of the Social World*. Mahwah, NJ: Lawrence Erlbaum Associates.

Rogers, Everett M. 1983. *Diffusion of Innovations*, 3rd edn. New York, NY: The Free Press.

Rogers, Everett M., James W. Dearing & Dorine Bregman. 1993. The anatomy of agenda-setting research. *Journal of Communication* 43. 68–84.

Ryan, Michael & Douglas Kellner. 1988. *Camera Politica: The Politics and Ideology of Contemporary Hollywood Film*. Bloomington, IN: Indiana University Press.

Scheufele, Dietram A. 1999. Framing as a theory of media effects. *Journal of Communication* 49. 103–122.

Scheufele, Dietram A. & David Tewksbury. 2007. Framing, agenda setting, and priming: The evolution of three media effects models. *Journal of Communication* 57. 9–20.

Schoenbach, Klaus, Ester de Waal & Edmund Lauf. 2005. Online and print newspapers: Their impact on the extent of the perceived public agenda. *European Journal of Communication* 2. 245–258.

Schudson, Michael. 2001. The objectivity norm in American journalism. *Journalism* 2. 149–170.

Shoemaker, Pamela J. & Stephen D. Reese. 1996. *Mediating the Message: Theories of Influence on Mass Media Content*, 2nd edn. New York, NY: Longman.

Sigal, Leon, V. 1973. *Reporters and Officials: The Organization and Politics of Newsmaking*. Lexington, MA: D.C. Heath.

Sparrow, Bartholomew H. 1999. *Uncertain Guardians: The News Media as a Political Institution*. Baltimore, MD: Johns Hopkins University Press.

Sproule, J. Michael. 1997. *Propaganda and Democracy: The American Experience of Media and Mass Persuasion*. New York, NY: Cambridge University Press.

Tewksbury, David & Dietram A. Scheufele. 2009. News framing theory and research. In: Jennings Bryant and Mary Beth Oliver (eds.), *Media Effects: Advances in Theory and Research*, 3rd edn, 17–33. New York, NY: Routledge.

Tsfati, Yariv. 2003. Does audience skepticism of the media matter in agenda setting? *Journal of Broadcasting & Electronic Media* 47. 157–176.

Tuchman, Gaye. 1978. *Making News: A Study in the Construction of Reality*. New York, NY: Free Press.

Tversky, Amos & Daniel Kahneman. 1981. The framing of decisions and the psychology of choice. *Science* 211. 453–438.

Valkenburg, Patti M., Holli A. Semetko & Claes H. De Vreese. 1999. The effects of news frames on readers' thoughts and recall. *Communication Research* 26. 550–569.

Van Gorp, Baldwin. 2007. The constructionist approach to framing: Bringing culture back in. *Journal of Communication* 57. 60–78.

Walsh, Katherine C. 2004. *Talking about Politics: Informal Groups and Social Identity in America*. Chicago, IL: University of Chicago Press.

Wanta, Wayne. 1997. *The Public and the National Agenda: How People Learn about Important Issues*. Mahwah, NJ: Lawrence Erlbaum.

Wanta, Wayne & Yi-Chen Wu. 1992. Interpersonal communication and the agenda-setting process. *Journalism & Mass Communication Quarterly* 69. 847–855.

Weaver, David H. 1977. Political issues and voter need for orientation. In: Donald L. Shaw and Maxwell E. McCombs (eds.), *The Emergence of American Political Issues*, 107–119. St. Paul, MN: West.

Welch, David. 2003. Definitions of propaganda. In: Nicholas J. Cull, David Culbert and David Welch (eds.), *Propaganda and Mass Persuasion: A Historical Encyclopedia, 1500 to the Present*, 317–323. Santa Barbara, CA: ABC-CLIO.

White, David Manning. 1950. The "gate keeper": A case study in the selection of news. *Journalism Quarterly* 27. 383–390.

Williams, Dmitri. 2002. Synergy bias: Conglomerates and promotion in the news. *Journal of Broadcasting & Electronic Media* 46. 453–472.

Willnat, Lars & Jian-Hua Zhu. 1996. Newspaper coverage and public opinion in Hong Kong: A time-series analysis of media priming. *Political Communication* 13. 231–246.

Zaller, John & Dennis Chiu. 1996. Government's little helper: U.S. press coverage of foreign policy crises, 1945–1991. *Political Communication* 13. 385–405.

Zucker, Harold G. 1978. The variable nature of news media influence. In: Brent D. Ruben (ed.), *Communication Yearbook 2*, 225–240. New Brunswick, NJ: Transaction Books.

David Crowley
17 Mediation theory

Abstract: The medium concept, initially proposed in the work of Harold Innis and Marshall McLuhan, has led to on-going efforts to account for the historical shifts in media and to assess their impact on the mediation of experience and the channeling of behavior. This chapter follows the medium concept through the latter half of the twentieth century as it amalgamated aspects of social history and social theory and more recently the cultural turn. Today changes and developments in the post-mass media environment associated with the rise of a global internet have rekindled interest in the medium concept and in mediation theory as a useful orienting framework for understanding the emergence of new electronic embodiments of symbolic exchange and interaction.

Keywords: Mediated information, medium concept, mediators, conditional embodiments, recursiveness, social feedback, temporality, electronic mediations

Today's information environment poses a challenge to all those disciplines that take some account of media, namely how to orient ourselves to a communicational world in play. In recent decades we have witnessed the falling away of much of our central media into something like a post-mass media condition. Overlapping this and increasingly implicated in its fate has been the growth and intensification of alternative electronic platforms for symbolic exchange and the continued blurring at the interfaces of formerly discrete domains of production, dissemination, and reception. Within the field of communication and media studies, as in areas of related scholarship and in public policy forums, there is a felt need for approaches that speak to these historic events in ways that inform our understanding of these changes. This question – of how we account for historical shifts in media and their impact on the mediation of experience and the channeling of behavior – has long been at the core of a mediationist approach.

Mediation as a theme has figured in several areas of communication and media studies. Whether we approach this thematic from some aspect of media ecology, as communication history, in terms of media archeology, or even via science studies' attention to the devices of observation, representation and transmission, there is some defining common ground. To an extent all these approaches focus attention on the distinctive technical modes of communication and take account of their material embodiments as well as their uses and the broader social and institutional consequences of their uptake.[1] Accounting for the specificity of the medium is seen

---

1 I mean here material cultural embodiments. In social informatics and in fact since early cybernetics we have worked with a 'mix' of electronic and non-electronic sources for information

as a necessary step for getting at how we as individuals and societies become enmeshed in systematic webs of signification – those ubiquitous theaters of visual and auditory expression that feed and drive so much of private and public experience and behavior – where they come from, what they do, how we participate, and why it matters. This way of characterizing the organization of media as flowing around and through a mix of informational and material technics is meant to draw attention to the 'message' of the medium of communication itself. According to mediationists, problematizing the medium in this way fills a gap – perhaps a blind spot – in research strategies in the humanities and social sciences that prefer to bracket questions about the medium entirely and to make do with assumptions about the neutrality of technologies. It is also of course what that arch-student of aphorisms and advocate for a mediation perspective, Marshall McLuhan (1964), meant by "the medium is the message."[2]

By focusing on the status of the medium, the mediation approach initially at least offsets itself from other research strategies that prefer to bracket questions of technology – and even technics more generally – within assumptions about the neutrality of tools. In communication and media studies this bracketing establishes a kind of technological neutral zone – usually linked in some way to the critique of technological determinism – and as such it has had practical efficacy. It has allowed practitioners to address the appeal and meaning of media products and media institutions by focusing directly on the content of symbolic exchange, at the role of information in the reproduction of behaviors and beliefs and at the self-limiting context of actual readers, listeners, and viewers in assessing media's effects.[3] Mediation theory by contrast brackets these questions in order to take fuller account of the inscriptive context itself, at the assemblages of codes, conventions, and practices around these inscriptive devices; and at how they emerge in the first place, why they do or do not persist and with what consequences.[4] This places the mediationist approach between those scholarly preoccupations with media messages and those scholarly preoccupations with what subjects do with

---

and their shifting balance. See Stanley N. Salthe (2011), *Naturalizing Information*. Information 2(3). 417–425. Special thanks to Maria Merkling Havens for advice and edits.

2 I am aware that there are other ways in which mediation has been proposed and explored in relation to media. Some of these are noted below, but in this essay I wish to demonstrate that there has been a sustaining theme in communication and media studies that begins with a recognition and problematizing of the medium.

3 The classic statement in this regard is Wilbur Schramm et al. (1961) *Television in the Lives of Our Children*. Schramm explicitly sets up print as reality-based and proposes to examine the contrasting tendency of image-based televisual fare toward fantasy. It was this unexamined claim to reality-based status for print that McLuhan singled out for criticism in *The Gutenberg Galaxy*.

4 In using terms such as "assemblages" I am following contemporary usage in the socio-technical literature. See for instance Bruno Latour (1994), "On Technological Mediation." Thanks to Marco Adria for this reference.

them. As a theory of media, the focus is on control mechanisms as structured agency, or, if that is too hard-edged, then directed interaction.

The appeal of the mediationist perspective in other disciplines has always stirred controversy, especially the stronger versions emphasizing media's enabling and constraining 'bias.' However, the renewed scholarly engagement with examining the drivers of the modern and its continuing consequences – postmodern, globalizing, electronic – attaches new urgency to accounting for the role of media and its informational technics in this way. No less a social theorist than Anthony Giddens, both in his writing on the theme of modernity and through talks delivered at conferences of communication scholars, helped underscore that "(m)echanized technologies of communication have dramatically influenced all aspects of globalization...(and) form an essential element of the reflexivity of modernity and of the discontinuities which have torn the modern away from the traditional" (Giddens, 1990).

Methodological issues have encouraged engagement with the theme of mediation as well. Robert Darnton has long called for historians to take greater account of the backstage machinery of textual production and dissemination as part of the task of vetting the status of textual information. As president of the American Historical Association, Darnton (2000) was concerned about the reluctance of some historians to look behind the historical documents at the information circuitry that gave rise to these documents in the first place. Along with other colleagues, many identified with histories of reading and histories of the book, he laid out ambitious alternatives for dealing with the information context that is attentive both to the interplay of communication modes – oral, written, and print for instance – and to the embodiments of those modes – everything from characteristics of paper manufacture, bindings, and layout to the tracking of buying, selling, circulation, and readership – as well as the genealogy of the surviving historical documents themselves through attention to the processes of collection, storage and archiving. All of which follows the mediation theme in calling attention less to the *what* of information construal and more to the *how* of its making, movement and access.

This is not to say that attention to a medium concept is only of recent vintage. As a theme, it has been present since the eighteenth century, if not earlier. Plato is regularly cited as acknowledging and indeed lamenting how the new mode of writing was impacting and undermining the central strengths of Greek oral culture. In *Phaedrus* and *The Seventh Letter* he explored the trade-offs when we move our primary orientation from one modality to another. Plato may have sided rhetorically with the oral tradition and the efficacies of bio-social memory as the embodiment of choice, but he also grasps the autonomous embodiments of these modes and gives us some early appreciation of writing as an inscriptive system with its ability to fix oral expression, to disseminate captured speech, and to archive or store it as content for future reference.

In a similar vein, Jean-Jacques Rousseau frequently mused about the organizing powers of language, the multiple ways in which oral and the literate forms acted as containers to attract and to channel social interactions. From his eighteenth century perspective, Rousseau witnessed the enduring vibrancy of the theatre, the rise of the novel, and the raging popularity of the new board games, all demonstrating the power of such containers as vehicles for organizing social interaction and focusing behavior. By the nineteenth century, writing in the shadow of Darwin's inversion of the idea of human descent, the anthropologist Edward Burnet Tylor (1964) could take a deep look back at earlier non-western societies and examine the choice of scripts and other notational tools as a source of insight into past practices and beliefs.

By the early decades of the twentieth century, at least three broad themes can be seen forming around the intellectual challenges posed by the new technologies and realities of symbolic exchange. It was a time of vertiginous change – the rapid spread of electrical signaling systems from nineteenth century beginnings and parallel developments in optical and acoustic machinery for the capture and reproduction of image and sound, followed in short order by the knitting together of audiovisual formats first in cinema, then television. In the first of these thematic responses, an urgency grew around the perceived loss of community in the face of industrialization, urbanization, and the growth of mass communication. Where some, such as Walter Lippmann, feared for the future of democratic politics as it shifted toward a national stage and its mass media machinery (the concept of persuasion as an organizing metaphor for media studies dates from this period) others called for new approaches that would help tame these same challenges. The philosophically informed pragmatism of the Chicago School exemplifies the latter. In the decades after World War I, through the work of Robert Park and John Dewey, coming to grips with the role of media in contemporary society became an accepted idea in the academic landscape and in public debate. Park emphasized the cognitive and institutional resources that media such as the newspaper provisionally afforded a populace confronted by social change; and Dewey explicitly saw eduction, including a nascent role for media literacy, as a counter-balance to the wrenching dislocations of the modern.

A second theme turned attention toward the new material culture. The Frankfurt School, displaced by the rise of Nazism from Germany to America in the 1930s, provided an early concept of the emerging 'cultural industries' as they labeled the organizational nexus of mass entertainment and its construction of the star system and commercialized popular culture. While neither of these 'schools' would deal directly with mediation or develop a concept of the medium, both did direct attention to the sea-change in the modes of communication and information. And one scholarly associate, Walter Benjamin (2008), in a famous work first published in 1936, came suggestively close to formulating the mediating function in comparing painting versus photography and theatre versus film.

A third theme, trans-Atlantic in articulation, developed from the growing pre-occupations with material culture, added a stronger sense of culture as technology. Today this theme can be identified with the origins of an ecological perspective in the social sciences, including post-war communication studies (Strade and Lum 2000). Three figures are often mentioned as emblematic: Patrick Geddes, Lewis Mumford, and Siegfried Giedion. All three advanced an understanding of the role of communication/information in human settlement, how it is pooled and punctuated and how it circulates in and through the social environment. Geddes was among the first urban sociologists. He was a traveler and explorer of the great American and European cities, and, for the last decade of his life, the urban areas of India. Geddes grasped Dewey's dilemma of the slipping away of forms of life rooted in community and put forward a matching strategy. The city for him was modernity's grand experiment, conducted on a global scale, a laboratory of interactions and information flows, where the self-organizing characteristics of neighborhoods, associational relations and local organizations were the fruitful building blocks of development, properly understood and supported. Like Dewey he advocated for more access to life-long skills development. Geddes passionately dissented from the prevailing wisdom of the day that argued that the circuitry of urban worlds was best modernized by attending to and facilitating traffic flows. For Geddes such results were especially disruptive of the human resources of cities when, as urban planners or developers, we opted for a transportation rather than a communications optic to inform our interventions in social and economic life.

To Geddes's portrait of the interaction orders that punctuated urban space, Lewis Mumford contributed the idea of punctuated time. In *Civilization and Technics* (Mumford 1934), he built directly on Geddes's spatial organizing insights, arguing that clock time, the result of the introduction of mechanical timekeeping into medieval Europe, refigured the temporal rhythms of everyday life, especially as religious and economic life assimilated their schedules to the force field of mechanical time. Mumford saw this as a large scale instance of the technics of 'autonomous technology,' as daily life took on the directed interactions of a new time regime. Mumford would later credit the printing press with an equivalent effect, as the technics of printing became the primary vehicle and container for the pooling and circulation of information of all kinds. These autonomous technics became the machinery within Geddes' grand urban experiment.

Siegfried Giedion pushed further. Resident in America during World War II, Giedion set himself the task of documenting the deepening commitment he saw in modern culture to objectified forms of subjectivity. In *Mechanization Takes Command* (Giedion 1948), seen as a founding work in the history of technology, Giedion compiled a dense genealogy of technology's absorption into the everyday. His search was for the modern equivalent of earlier civilization's screws, wheels, and pulleys, transformed as he saw it into the technics of bathrooms, lit interiors, parlors, kitchens, and eating areas of domestic space. These end-use spaces were made possible by complex support systems: everything from the fabricating facilities for the in-home infrastructure, to the assembly lines for the disassembly of livestock carcasses for domestic food supply, to the optical and acoustic devices that made the products for leisure-time use and so on – a vast compendium of the domestic world as mediating objects. This was backstage accounting for the modern world's at times awkward embrace of human-machine relationships, which was transmuting the techno-scientific into the techno-cultural, for better or for worse. The influences, however, ran in both directions; for Giedion the appeal and rationalization of nineteenth century mechanization moved forward as it did because the culture provided openings for, or resisted, its amalgamation. The context mattered deeply. With this simple formula, Giedion sketched an approach for examining how much the technologies of the everyday were the product of social responses and how much the result of imposition. The communication flows that ran between technology and culture and vice versa were structured and given the force of agency by the assemblages of human technics arrayed around both their building and their use. *Mechanization Takes Command* advanced an optimistic thesis that might well have alarmed Geddes and Mumford. It did nonetheless help clarify the status of technologies as mutable and responsive to use: because following the logic flow of Giedion's argument the "mechanistic conception of the world" should in principle be routinely undermined by how machines, developing in active interplay with the social world, are nudged in the direction of becoming increasingly mimetic instruments of human interaction.[5]

Evident in all of these works from the first half of the twentieth century is growing appreciation of the backstage machinery of modern culture and society. Absent is a robust sense of the scope and scale of the actual machinery of symbolic mediation and its implications. Two unrelated projects, both incubated during World War II and published by the early 1950s, provided a sense of that linkage: firstly, a systematic concept of the medium of communication advanced by Harold Innis and worked out by members of the Toronto School; and secondly, a concept of information proposed initially by Claude Shannon and elaborated through the work of the cybernetics group.[6]

Innis provided the first systematic work on the role of the medium and a provisional account of media as information control. The concept of medium fell out of his struggles to articulate it. Around him in the late 1940s were multiple if uncon-

---

5 Giedion's work is enjoying something of a revival today. See the excellent classics revisited essay by Arthur P. Molella (2002), Science moderne: Siegfried Giedion's *Space, Time and Architecture* and *Mechanization Takes Command*.

6 I do not deal with the work on information in this essay, except to note that both the medium concept and the information concept can be seen as complementary developments in a theory of mediation. Both deal with conditional embodiments of information, and both are articulated as second order theories that propose ways to step back from the mangle of information content/ meaning issues while attending to the role of mediatory environments.

nected clues: archeologists looking at how inscriptive systems had organized ancient worlds, classicists assessing the effects of the intrusion of alphabetic writing into the oral cultures of Western civilization, anthropologists and linguists speculating about the differential cognitive effects of speech and writing, historical sociologists sketching the interaction orders in human groups and settlements. The medium concept was something as basic as the machinery of inscription and at the same time more complex, as a way of looking at information conveyance that placed the organizing effects well beyond the meaning of the messages themselves.

Innis proposed three ways to think about the medium concept: firstly, by taking account of the ease of inscription and allied to this the cost and the availability of its raw materials (in the case of writing the use of clay, papyrus, parchment, paper). Secondly, by accounting for the speed of circulation and for portability, because all successful states and expansive empires, he argued, had needed to efficiently move information around. And thirdly, in terms of persistence, the capacity for information to endure in time and space. With each medium chosen there would be trade-offs for inscription, dissemination, and persistence. The success of statecraft, he believed, in no small measure rested upon how these variables were managed.

The medium concept then, with its material embodiments, the specificities of its assemblages of actors, skills, tools, and practices, formed the underpinnings of a theory of mediation which Innis applied to historical social change. In key works all published at mid-century – *Empire and Communication* (Innis [1950] 1975), *The Bias of Communication* (Innis [1951] 1995), and *The Changing Concept of Time* (Innis [1952] 2003) – he outlined how major shifts in history roughly corresponded to changes in the medium and technics of communication. The first of these shifts was the deployment of viable systems of writing from ancient regimes through early western societies. Then came the long period of mechanization of writing via printing technologies, beginning in the fifteenth century. The third shift started in the nineteenth century, when print was superseded by real time communication at increasing distances through electro-mechanical signaling networks and their subsequent integration with other devices for inscription and reproduction of acoustic and optical content.

In the first two developments the movement of information is entwined with transportation infrastructures for moving other types of goods. In the third, telegraphy breaks the relationship with transport, realigning information flows to new conditions of simultaneity and co-location, in the process opening society to new forms of access to and accountability for its relations in time and space. These intellective tools and their material means of conveyance underpinned the efforts of states and civilizations – and in fact all subsequent forms of modern organization – to extend their activities in time and space. The tools provided stability – the raw power of recorded data, systematic surveillance, schedules, and contracts – and also introduced potential conditions of instability that became apparent to Innis as he put together portraits of the relations of geographic peripheries and centers, where the further one moved from the center, the more uncertain the scope of compliance, the more influenced matters became by the contingencies of the local, and the more the characteristics of the medium itself came into play, as factors of distance, time, and the limitations of conveyance entered the equation. The embodiments always mattered. Light/portable/fragile creates an information situation different from that of heavy/fixed/durable. In the long view of human settlement and civilization, the choice of a primary medium acquired an assemblage of practices appropriate to it. This then was the beginning of an impious theory, namely, that the intellective technics by which we communicate are themselves enabled and constrained by their embodiments, never just by how they are used.

Innis's theory finished much as it had begun, as a kind of bricolage of evidence from a clutch of disciplines and scholarly informants that piece together provisionally an idea of communication as modalities, potentially autonomous, whose specificities as codes and material enabled and constrained the shape of the information environment. To understand trade and commerce, to understand statecraft, to understand the arts and culture, you needed to come to grips with the technics of how these systems of signification were organized and deployed.[7]

His research was completed in the shadow of the Cold War, which he believed would be largely informational in character; he died before he could tackle the implications of this. After Innis, research on mediation via theorizing the medium and mediality more generally has gone through significant phases: initially by extending the concepts of medium and technics; followed by a turn to social theory and history with lessons about how systems emerge, and finally a new cultural turn with a timely opening towards conceptualizing new media.

Since subsequent scholarship deserves to be considered in itself and since much of it, moreover, can only be indirectly linked to Innis's earlier project, I will briefly suggest three ways in which our contemporary understanding of the theme of mediation has been informed and elaborated by these diverse efforts: firstly, in showing how a medium concept brings back a sense of technics into our analysis of symbolic systems; secondly, in alerting us to the constitutive power of the social in accounting for how media systems come to have the shape they do and why this changes; and finally, through noting new conceptual work on electronic media and their suggestions for a concept of intermediation in communication. An essay is not the space to do justice to these matters, so what follows should be seen as prologue.

---

7 A useful introductions to Innis' communications work is James Carey's (1989) *Communication as Culture*. For a comprehensive recent treatment, see Paul Heyer (2003), *Harold Innis*.

1 The medium turn

The publication of this handbook volume and handbook series marks the 50th anniversary of a seminal event in mediation theory. 1962/63 saw the publication of three works which established a forceful version of the medium and technics thesis: Eric Havelock's (1963) *Preface to Plato*, Marshall McLuhan's *The Gutenberg Galaxy* (1962), and Jack Goody and Ian Watt's (1963) seminal essay on 'The consequences of literacy.' These were important benchmarks, nothing less than an effort to unpack the mechanics of literacy and to outline the cognitive and cultural impacts of its long historical development. Havelock, McLuhan, and Goody are all linked to the work of the Toronto School and all embraced an idea of 'mediacy' in accounting for communication and historical shifts in the organization of expression and experience.

Havelock provided a key concept. He proposed proto-literate periods to account for how the technics of literacy were assembled, changed, and adapted in response to social context. As subsequent scholarship has confirmed, he showed how early Greek writing was done, largely without punctuation, as an unbroken stream of words. Reading, by contrast, was initially a public activity in which the text was read aloud to listeners. For a substantial period most early writing was accessed as spoken text, interpreted through performance by those with special skills to involve listeners as active participants. These transitional oral readers could be seen as speaking devices, mediating the author-text-reader relationship until more autonomous forms of reading arose. Silent reading is one such development, which encloses the reading act within personal space; theater is another, where actors take on the impersonation of characters from the text. In both cases, the transitional figure of the oral reader is effaced and the subsequent assemblage demonstrates how changes in the mediation of experience arise as an interplay of technologies and social context. This way of constructing the medium concept strongly suggested that media should seen as facilitating behavior whose emergence was closely tied to societal engagement.[8]

In 'The consequences of literacy' Jack Goody and Ian Watt outlined a model for how an emerging technics around literacy could over time fashion writing into types of autonomous language, separate from its oral forms. While 'Consequences' focused on the technics of the early Greek alphabet, Goody's subsequent case studies, ranging from writing in ancient civilizations to literacy in contemporary Africa, would go on to show how the acquisition of everyday literate devices, such as lists and tables, institutionalized broad-based metalinguistic skill sets for activities such as recording, counting, and organizing. These skill sets, Goody maintained, once widely accepted into everyday use, worked to bring about new forms

---

8 See Oswyn Murray (1980), *Early Greece* and Bruno Gentili (1988), *Poetry and its Public in Ancient Greece*. I am drawing on Murray's interpretation and extension of Havelock's ideas.

of practice, distinct from those of oral culture. This in turn had implications for how the social world was organized and for how information functioned.

It has been said that Marshall McLuhan's two seminal works, *The Gutenberg Galaxy* (1962) and *Understanding Media* (1964), helped put the historical machinery of communication on display, providing us with a preliminary toolkit for theorizing the effects of this backstage machinery on social change. These works also drew attention to the processes through which the media of a given age and in a given context achieved conditions of relative autonomy – that is, how the dominant medium came to be experienced as a naturalized part of human culture.

In retrospect, his enduring contribution lay in drawing our attention to media's historical penetration of social life, and to extending the medium concept as a way of understanding that process. Through the medium concept McLuhan outlined how media penetrated into existing forms of experience and interaction. He saw that the conditions Havelock identified as emerging from the emplacement of writing in oral cultures (fixing of speech, linearity and sequence, progressive separation, and privatizing of authorship and reading, etc.) were intensified in the mechanization of writing by print technologies (standardized typography, cheap paper, grammatical conventions, associated rights of ownership and expression). The effects, he believed, revealed themselves comparatively; in the contrast, for instance, between the informational mechanics of past oral societies and the residual forms that orality took in the contemporary world. Industrial modernity introduced a third modality in the form of the electronic, beginning with the telegraph. Following Innis, McLuhan argued that the electronic again impacted the mediation of social and personal experience, initially he believed by the reconfiguration of our shared sense of temporality. His claim was that the idea of time shifted as information circulation detached itself from modes of physical transportation; and as a result people for practical reasons needed to come to terms with how time in one community related to time in other places. In communities connected by the expanding railroad systems of the late nineteenth century, there were opportunities to use the railway telegraph stations to coordinate markets temporally, in effect creating markets that matched the availability of goods and resources at one location with demand at others. Other organized activities followed: formal commodity exchanges and futures trading, mail order systems for commercial goods, and new forms of systematic observation, such as the monitoring and pooling of local weather reports into regional outlooks. This integration of bodies and materials in time and space resulted in a new punctuation of social and work life.

Telegraphy impacted other media in turn. Information about distant events now moved with the speed of electric current and this immediacy disrupted the closed world of local communication and repositioned social experience within wider symbolic flows. Wire services, which early on developed in tandem with telegraphy, provided information about distant events to local newspapers, thus bypassing the need to await the arrival of city papers. Subsequent developments in electronic signaling would further configure these specificities of the medium, deepening the social investment in simultaneity and co-location as new forms of temporal and spatial experience.[9]

2 Mediation as social feedback[10]

Beginning in the 1970s, influenced in part by the growing sense of media's role in social change, a focus developed that would become broadly recuperative of the formative historical periods for mass media, from the printing press to all the subsequent components of the widening age of technologically-reproduced sound, vision, and data. This is where the theme of mediation intersects contemporary themes in social theory and social history.

From the 1960s onward, social theory had selectively tried to account for communications. Communicative rationality, for instance, grounds the social theory of Jürgen Habermas. While Habermas did not pursue a concept of the medium, his earliest work ([1962] 1989) deals directly with the question of the transitional space opened up by the new vehicles of print culture emerging in sixteenth century Europe (broadsheets, pamphlets, polemics, journals, newspapers, and books). As informal communities of text and talk formed around these vehicles, new sites of social comity appeared. It was through these sites (initially coffee houses, pubs, salons, booksellers, and other places apart from the prevailing authority of church and state) that Habermas located the forms of interaction constitutive of an emerging public sphere.[11]

Anthony Giddens's communications informed social theory draws explicitly on a medium concept. His outline of societal development as a dynamic of disembedding and re-embedding mechanisms looks to historical changes in media in accounting for the successful stretching of administrative statecraft over time and space ('time-space distantiation'); much as his conception of modern identity formation looks to the constitutive features of an interaction order mediated in and

---

9 Telegraph has become a major topic. See for instance, ‚Stephen Kern (1983), *The Culture of Time and Space*; Tom Standage (1998), *The Victorian Internet*, and James Gleick (2011), *The Information*, all of whom credit telegraphy with a seminal role in extending the informational nexus.

10 David Olson has been especially attentive to the value of this work and subsequent work by Goody for its contribution to literacy, learning and communication studies. See Olson (1994), *The World on Paper*.

11 For another take on the rise of the public sphere and the role of vernacular publishing, see Benedict Anderson (1991), *Imagined Communities*. An approach that shares some common ground with mediation theory and draws on the idea of communicative rationality and publics is Michael Warner (2002) 'Publics and Counter-publics.' See as well the recent collection of essays by Clifford Siskin and William Warner (2010) *This is Enlightenment*.

through available forms of symbolic exchange ('presence-availability'). If Habermas, at least initially, is attentive to the power of print in the early modern period, Giddens forcefully acknowledges the ways in which the post-mechanistic apparatus of electric signaling technologies is deeply implicated in the modern mediation of experience. Following Innis and McLuhan and others on telegraphy's impact on time/space relations, Giddens (1991) sees the telegraph as a proto-type for how locality, confronted by the spread of the railroads and the need to know how time worked in its expanding relations with other localities regionally, becomes repositioned within wider sets of experiential association and relations at a distance. This is the new punctuation that emerging media bring to social worlds, at first disruptive, then slowly normalized and at length seemingly naturalized.[12]

If this process seems to suggest something of a one-way influence, the turn toward social history – including every aspect of modernity's broad embrace of communication devices and systems – from the printed book through the age of mechanical reproductions of image and sound to the birth of the electronic – has led us in turn into an appreciation of society's role in giving the medium its particular social 'hum,' so to speak. Since Elizabeth Eisenstein's (1980) detailed reworking of McLuhan's print culture in *The Printing Press as a Agent of Change* and the work inspired by Lucien Febvre and Henri-Jean Martin's ([1957] 1976) epic blueprint for the commodification of print in *The Coming of the Book* we now know a great deal more about printing, reading and the culture of the book. Emblematic of this direction has been the work of Natalie Zemon Davis (1975, 1987, 1995), who was an early participant in the Toronto circle of scholars, and who subsequently has pieced together how proto-literacy penetrated the peasant oral society of pre-modern France and how oral culture in turn reshaped the uses of those printed materials. The work of Roger Chartier (1994) and Robert Darnton (1982) indicate other dimensions added to the specificity of the book as medium; Chartier through detailed attention to the reproduction process itself (papermaking to binding, standardizations of text, and the orchestration of conventions), and Darnton through expanding the model of the circuitry of published works to include in addition to authors, texts, and readers, a network of trades and practices devoted to making, shipping, trading, policing, collecting, and commenting on a maturing world in print.

Assemblages like these around the medium add historical context to the medium's specificity, how a medium comes to its codes and conventions and why within any given society there are so many interests arrayed around information activities. In the nineteenth century transition from a predominantly print based social order through multiple mechanical devices for optical and acoustic reproduction to electrification, ever-widening trades and practices opened up around

---

12 I mean feedback as a second-order phenomenon, following Stanley Salthe and Gregory Bateson's idea of an informed system able to classify information from a monitored environment.

new forms of electric signaling: first telegraphy, then telephony and broadcasting. Coming to grips with these configurations has led social historians to focus on the interactions around usage and how the discourse of media tradespeople and professionals regarding the observed behavior of users fed into decisions about development and design. Carolyn Marvin's (1987) *When Old Technologies Were New* and Claude S. Fischer's (1992) *America Calling* make clear how social users generate values in use and how these forms of social agency help shape media technology to culture.

Perhaps no event since the printed book has brought the institutional arrangements of society so directly into question as the development of the internet. Fittingly, Manuel Castells (2001) in *The Internet Galaxy* draws on social history and theory plus the medium concept to build a conceptual bridge to the formative processes of the internet and a provisional framework for understanding the unfolding effects and consequences of a new medium. He does this firstly, he suggests, by attending to how the internet puts into play temporality – that is, how a new sense of 'internet time' begins to punctuate the mediation of experience, such as occurred earlier with telegraphy. Secondly, he addresses the discourse of users and usage; because a new medium will be reflexively formed in its formative periods of use and shaped by responses, in the way that telephony was shaped by its largely unanticipated social uses. Finally, Castells follows the assemblages of actors as they work out the relationships of the new medium with other media in place. Constraints on existing media potentially fuel new media innovation, such as the way experimentation with early prototypes for 'e-mail' fed the development of new telecommunication protocols; not so far removed from the way the early telephone's experimentation with proto-broadcasting to the home identified uses to which emerging wireless radio protocols would subsequently be applied.

3 Intermediation

If circumstances like those outlined by Castells have propelled the internet into a viable electronic medium with global reach and implications, the time seems right to ask how mediation theory might inform our sense of these developments. Certainly the 'blurring' of once settled categories of what is print, image, and the televisual does raise questions about the status of the medium – whether or not the form and specificity of the contemporary internet will have legs – and points to issues with implications for the 'status quo' of governmental, corporate, and other institutional regimes built up around established media. Understanding this conundrum has already encouraged genealogical accounts of the diverse activities and technologies which this new electronic environment brings together. Interestingly, the medium concept is also once again in play.

The new electronic embodiments easily fit within Innis's proposal for thinking about embodiments: by taking account firstly, of the new media's ease of use/affordability; secondly, its speed/portability; and thirdly, its qualities of persistence/impermanence. Makers of desktops, laptops, tablets, and cell phones have moved rapidly to create increasingly affordable social tools suitable for general use; and electronic networks have driven down exponentially the costs of distribution. Information simultaneity and situations of co-presence and portability have all been at least augmented and probably enhanced by connected media technologies. Persistence remains the stalking horse, as struggles over platforms, standards, and intellectual property indicate. Even here, we can see the emergence of potential assemblages around the status and sustainability of online information through new forms of electronic curation. But the outcome of these latter issues aside, the conditional embodiments noted here suggest that we already face some distinct challenges with respect to how we construct relations informationally in time and space.

The perceived potential for a new participatory commons has also been retrieved by new media. The internet does reproduce a facsimile of print, but at the same time it breaks with some of the temporal achievements of print, such as print's enforced linearity, its sequential ordering, and most of all with the types of access that have been built around these temporal conventions of narrative organization. The limited portability of and speed of access to printed materials compared to the internet also raises issues of changing temporality. The adoption of hyperlinks for general use in the *World Wide Web* may be only one generic example of technics in the internet arsenal but the effect has been considerable. Wikipedia, for example, whatever its future, has largely abolished the centuries old tradition of printed encyclopedias; and kaleidoscopic online resources have now eclipsed print-based newspapers and even local television news as a primary source for the daily mosaic of newsworthy events. Moreover, the conventions associated with print culture that carried over as models for televisual developments – the narrative fictional forms of feature length films and serialized television programming, for instance, or the associated rights and covenants of intellectual ownership – are all again in flux, as they were during the long transition from oral to written culture with its ambiguities of authorship and its transitional figures facilitating access to textual talk and the rise of sites for participation and performance. Sounds familiar.

So how should we proceed in what are clearly transitional circumstances? Perhaps by paying greater attention to the shifting conditions of mediality as a second-order phenomena. Since publication of *The Mode of Information*, Mark Poster (1990) has insisted on viewing the communication media as 'forms of language wrapping' that have characterized the passage from orality to print and now to further stages of the electronic, arguing that at each stage these wrappings of the primary medium work to alter our relationship to symbols and to things.

This kind of reconceptualizing has exposed limitations in our past thinking about issues such as intertextuality – and proposed alternatives. In *Remediation*, Jay David Bolter and Richard Grusin (1999) claim that as we move closer to a world in which electronic symbolic exchanges become the primary vehicles of communication we will need a better sense of media interpenetration. Carrying forward formulations first broached by McLuhan and Edmund Carpenter they suggest every medium should be understood as 'that which remediates' – that all media normally work this way, translating, refashioning, and repurposing both the form and the content of other media.

Then there is the connected media of sound and image. Overwhelming in its implications, not least for ownership regimes that were established when other media formats predominated and must now contend with the new interplay of open source software and a cultural commons that resonates with the disruptive possibilities of the early age of printing. Worth noting here is the work of Vilem Flusser (1984, 2002) and related to his work a contemporary revival of German media thought that retrieves aspects of the earlier project of Marshall McLuhan, this time emphasizing the status of the image (Bolz and Mattson, 1999). If linearity arose as a key feature of a world in print, Flusser adds a systematic appreciation of the rise of the photographic image and shows us how this new technical image disrupts the linearity of text. For Flusser, our reading of these images introduces a different sense of temporality; an experience he sees akin to simultaneous reception, in which technical images must be 'discomposed' then reconstructed with the help of our prior 'understandings' of the world. In effect, Flusser sees the technical image and our responses to it as a model for how a new technics of the visual, raised to the level of systematic use, alter experience and behavior.

In *The Language of New Media*, Lev Manovich (2002) pushes appreciation of electronic mediations into other areas, notably touch and the haptic dimensions of new media opened up by our relationship with digital screens. As a new interface, digital screens borrow and rework features of earlier media: the printed page, the cinematic screen and the television screen, among others. Such borrowings, he argues, make computer screens an increasingly hybrid form, combining an information surface with a window into illusionary space with a control panel. As technics mature, the digital screen favors haptic relations, as something with which we physically interact – and through touch enact proxies for older forms of keyboarding, page turning, channel changing, bookmarking and so on.

Intermediation may not be the most elegant term to describe this nexus of changed and changing relationships to symbolic processes. Tentatively, however, it does help bring these newest embodiments of media within the conceptual reach of mediation theory.[13]

---

13 For additional background on the social and cultural turn in relation to mediation theory, see David Crowley and David Mitchell (1994), *Communication Theory Today*, especially the essays by John B. Thompson and Joshua Meyrowitz which expand on the medium concept as it relates to institutions and social order.

Further reading

Davidson, Donald. 2001. *Inquiries into Truth and Interpretation*. New York: Oxford University Press.
Goldberg, Ken (ed.). 2000. *The Robot in the Garden*. Cambridge, MA: MIT Press.
Latour, Bruno. 2011. *Hybrid Thoughts on a Hybrid World*. London: Routledge.

References

Anderson, Benedict R. O'G. 1991. *Imagined Communities: Reflections on the Origin and Spread of Nationalism*, revised and extended edn). London: Verso.
Bateson, Gregory. 1972. *Steps to an Ecology of Mind*. Chicago: University of Chicago Press.
Benjamin, Walter. 2008. *The Work of Art in the Age of its Technological Reproducibility and Other Writings on Media*. Jennings, Michael W., Doherty, Brigid and Levin, Thomas Y. (eds.). Cambridge, MA: Harvard University Press.
Bolter, Jay David & Richard Grusin. 1999. *Remediation*. Cambridge: MIT Press.
Bolz, Norbert & Michelle Mattson. 1999. Farewell to the Gutenberg-galaxy. *New German Critique* 78: 109–131.
Carey, James. 1989. *Communication as Culture*. New York and London: Routledge.
Castells, Manuel. 2001. *The Internet Galaxy*. New York: Oxford University Press.
Chartier, Roger. 1994. *The Order of Books*. Stanford, CA: Stanford University Press.
Crowley, David & David Mitchell (eds.). 1994. *Communication Theory Today*. Stanford, CA: Stanford University Press.
Darnton, Robert. 1982. *The Literary Underground of the Old Regime*. Cambridge, MA: Harvard University Press.
Darnton, Robert. 2000. An early information society: news and the media in eighteenth century Paris. *American Historical Review* 105. 1–35.
Eisenstein, Elizabeth. 1980. *The Printing Press as an Agent of Change*. New York: Cambridge University Press.
Febvre, Lucien & Henri-Jean Martin. [1958]. 1976. *The Coming of the Book*. London: Verso. First published Paris: Albin, Editions Michel.
Fischer, Claude S. 1992. *America Calling: A Social History of the Telephone to 1940*. Berkeley, CA: University of California Press.
Flusser, Vilem. 1984. *Towards a Philosophy of Photography*. Gottingen: European Photography.
Flusser, Vilem. 2002. *Writings*. Minneapolis, MN: University of Minnesota Press, 2002.
Fuller, Matthew. 2005. *Media Ecologies: Materialist Energies in Art and Technoculture*. Cambridge, MA: MIT Press.
Gentili, Bruno. 1988. *Poetry and its Public in Ancient Greece*. Baltimore: The Johns Hopkins University Press.
Giddens, Anthony. 1990. *The Consequences of Modernity*. Stanford, CA: Stanford University Press.
Giddens, Anthony. 1991. *Modernity and Self-Identity*. Stanford, CA: Stanford University Press.
Giedion, Siegfried. 1948. *Mechanization Takes Command*. New York: Oxford University Press.
Gleick,, James. 2011. *The Information: A History, A Theory, A Flood*. New York: Pantheon Books.
Goody, Jack & Ian Watt. 1963. The consequences of literacy. *Comparative Studies in Society and History* 5. 304–345.
Habermas, Jürgen. [1962]. 1989. *The Structural Transformation of the Public Sphere: An Inquiry into a Category of Bourgeois Society*. Cambridge, MA: The MIT Press. First published Neuwied: H. Luchterhand.

Havelock, Eric. 1963. *Preface to Plato*. Cambridge, MA: Harvard University Press.

Heyer, Paul. 2003. *Harold Innis*. Lanham, MD: Rowman & Littlefield Publishers Inc.

Innis, Harold. [1950]. 1975. *Empire and Communications*. Toronto: University of Toronto Press. First published Toronto: University of Toronto Press.

Innis, Harold. [1951]. 1995. *The Bias of Communication*. Toronto: University of Toronto Press. First published Toronto: University of Toronto Press.

Innis, Harold. [1952]. 2003. *Changing Concepts of Time*. Boulder, CO: Rowman & Littlefield. First published Toronto: University of Toronto Press.

Kern, Stephen. 1983. *The Culture of Time and Space, 1880–1918*. Cambridge, MA: Harvard University Press.

Latour, Bruno. 1994. On technical mediation. *Common Knowledge* 3. 29–64.

McLuhan, Marshall. 1962. *The Gutenberg Galaxy*. Toronto: University of Toronto Press.

McLuhan, Marshall. 1964. *Understanding Media*. New York: Signet.

Manovich, Lev. 2002. *The Language of New Media*. Cambridge, MA: MIT Press.

Marvin, Carolyn. 1987. *When Old Technologies were New*. New York: Oxford University Press.

Molella, Arthur P. 2002. Science moderne: Siegfried Giedion's Space, Time and Architecture and Mechanization Takes Command. *Technology and Culture* 43. 373–389.

Mumford, Lewis. 1934. *Technics and Civilization*. New York: Harcourt, Brace and Company.

Murray, Oswyn. 1980. *Early Greece*. London: Fontana.

Olson, David R. 1994. *The World on Paper*. New York and Cambridge: Cambridge University Press.

Poster, Marc. 1990. *The Mode of Information*. Chicago: The University of Chicago Press.

Salthe, Stanley N. 2011. Naturalizing information. *Information* 2. 417–425.

Schramm, Wilbur, Jack Lyle & Edwin B. Parker. 1961. *Television in the Lives of Our Children*. Berkeley, CA: University of California Press.

Simon, Herbert. 1962. The architecture of complexity. *Proceedings Of The American Philosophical Society* 106. 467–482.

Siskin, Clifford & William Warner (eds.). 2010. *This is Enlightenment*. Chicago: University of Chicago Press.

Strade, Lance & Casey Man Kong Lum. 2000. Lewis Mumford and the ecology of technics. *New Jersey Journal of Communication* 8. 60–78.

Standage, Tom. 1998. *The Victorian Internet*. London: Weidenfeld and Nicolson.

Theall, Donald. 2001. *The Virtual Marshall McLuhan*. Montreal: McGill-Queen's University Press.

Tylor, Edward Burnet. 1964. *Researches into the Early History of Mankind*. Chicago: The University of Chicago Press. First published London: John Murray [1865].

Warner, Michael. 2002. Publics and counter-publics. *Public Culture* 14: 49–89.

Zemon Davis, Natalie. 1975. *Society and Culture in Early Modern France: Eight Essays*. Stanford, CA: Stanford University Press.

Zemon Davis, Nathalie. 1987. *Fiction in the Archives: Pardon Tales and their Tellers in Sixteenth Century France*. Stanford, CA: Stanford University Press.

Zemon Davis, Natalie. 1995. *Women on the Margins: Three Seventeenth-century Lives*. Cambridge, MA: Harvard University Press.

Kim Christian Schrøder

18 Socio-cultural models of communication

Abstract: This chapter illuminates the core mind-set of socio-cultural models of communication by tracing the scholarly debates that took place around a significant moment of cultural studies, when in 1973 Stuart Hall published his canonical article about the processes of encoding and decoding media messages. Socio-cultural models as seen by Hall and the equally seminal Raymond Williams are holistic, they conceptualize discursive sense-making practices, and they insist on the formative role of situational and social contexts. The model's implications for scholarly analytical practices are demonstrated through short overview profiles of two central research traditions during four decades: 1. audience and reception research and 2. discourse analytical approaches.

Keywords: Cultural studies, sense-making, audience, reception, discourse analysis, representation, ethnography, cultural industries

If one can be so audacious as to characterize the current stage of socio-cultural approaches to media and communication as 'mature,' we can find many of these approaches at a stage of 'birth' or 'infancy' if we go back to the year 1973 – the year in which cultural theorist Stuart Hall published, in the form of a 'stenciled occasional paper,' one of the most seminal and canonical scholarly texts in the area of communication and media studies (Gurevitch and Scannell 2003). This paper, titled 'Encoding and decoding in the television discourse' (Hall 1973), encapsulates, in a nut shell, the theoretical tenets which have been developed and refined by socio-cultural communication scholars through the following decades, and which have retained their scientific validity ever since.

These tenets define media and communication research in terms of three interrelated perspectives: first, communication is a holistic enterprise, in which the researchers must, when defining and operationalizing their research objectives, conceptualize *the ensemble* of actors and processes involved in the communicative process from senders to receivers; secondly, the communicative process should be seen as consisting of *discursive sense-making practices* and be based on a social theory of signs; and thirdly, communication research should include *the situational and socio-cultural context* in the widest possible sense, as a co-shaper of the communicative processes. Especially the third of these perspectives is indebted to the pioneering theoretical interventions of Hall's contemporary Raymond Williams (1958, 1961), whose theory of culture as 'a whole way of life' was equally seminal for socio-cultural approaches to communication analysis.

This chapter offers an analytical account of the emergence of the holistic, meaning-oriented socio-cultural mind-set, by situating it chronologically and contextually in the intellectual and scientific landscape of media and communication research of the 1970s, and by positioning it in relation to the 'significant others' of this scientific landscape. The chapter then demonstrates how one particular scholarly framework – that of media audience reception studies – has applied this mind-set over the following decades. The chapter also considers how a similar mind-set has developed within the related area of language and discourse studies.

1 The study of culture and society – 'cultural studies'

In the 1973 paper, Stuart Hall, who was then Director of the Centre for Contemporary Cultural Studies at the University of Birmingham, cautiously suggests that the paper is the harbinger of a new era in cultural analysis (Hall 1973/1980: 131). Hall's model was a deliberate attempt to dethrone the then 'dominant paradigm' of social science communication research (Gitlin 1978), a positivistic, behavioral approach concentrating on the measurement of media 'effects,' which – with some evolutionary adjustments – had been unchallenged since the early days of Anglo-American communication research in the 1920s.

But the paper was also pitched against a dominant paradigm in the humanities, more specifically in the area of English literary studies. The critique of humanistic approaches was directed against the belief that literary analysis gave its practitioners direct access to the textual meaning. The model also seems to have been intended as a superior alternative to approaches to the analysis of culture (including the Frankfurt School, see Section 2.1) which championed the text as the repository of a fixed ideological meaning that would make a direct, seductive impact on the individual mind.

Finally, the theoretical paradigm incorporated in the encoding/decoding model was founded on a critical Marxist political agenda, characteristic of the human and social sciences in the 1960s and 1970s. Within the Marxist orientation, Hall, Williams and the Birmingham school took up a position which, unlike some other Marxist approaches, accorded a relatively autonomous role to the cultural sphere in society. But, most importantly, the model insists that the explanatory power of cultural analysis depends on our allegiance to the notions of *holism*, i.e. analytically holding together the different actors, institutions, practices, and contexts of the communicative process, and the indeterminacy and *complexity* of meaning, i.e. seeing encounters with media and cultural practices as being based on semiotic and communicative repertoires, and therefore having non-predictable outcomes.

The theory emanated from an intellectual environment in which many separate streams were slowly working their way towards the river that became modern cultural studies. Hall himself, in a reflective essay (Hall 1980), pointed out that cultural studies arose at the confluence of two major theoretical currents, culturalism and structuralism. The culturalist mindset came out of the British post-war intellectual environment, the key members being the cultural historian Richard Hoggart (1957), historian of the English working-class E. P. Thompson (1963), and notably cultural theorist Raymond Williams (1958, 1961, 1977). The other, structuralist, mindset came, for Hall, from a European continental tradition which he believed started with the Swiss linguist Ferdinand de Saussure, whose theories of signification and projection of a science called semiology (see Chapter 12, Cobley) informed the anthropological theories of Claude Levi-Strauss (1958), the Marxist political sociology of Louis Althusser (1971), and the literary and historical scholarship of the Italian semiotician Umberto Eco (1979).

2 Precursors in the social sciences

Although the actual media and communication research conducted under its regime was fairly complex, nevertheless the 'dominant paradigm' in media sociology manifested itself as an inescapable straitjacket that defined worthwhile research objects in strict behavioral terms and prescribed the use of quantitative research methods.

2.1 The argument about media effects

More specifically, the dominant paradigm can be characterized by its key interest in communication 'effects,' i.e. the belief of early 'effects' researchers that the media influence on the individual human organism is immediate, direct and strong. To a critical British observer within the social sciences in 1970, the "early view of mass communication assumed that people could be persuaded by the media to adopt almost any point of view desired by the communicator. Manipulation, exploitation and vulnerability were the key words" (Halloran 1970: 18). This view leaned on influential sociological theories about the lonely, vulnerable and easily manipulable individual in mass society (Riesman et al. 1950), and on the critical analysis of the cultural industries of the German Frankfurt School (Adorno and Horkheimer 1947a) (see Section 3).

In the late 1940s and early 1950s, doubt was cast on the theory of strong effects by a series of large-scale empirical studies in the US, which investigated the effects of media messages on the decision-processes of consumers and citizens (Lazarsfeld et al. 1948; Katz and Lazarsfeld 1955; Katz 1957). These researchers found that consumers' choice of products as well as the way citizens cast their votes in elections depend more on their interpersonal relations to significant others than on direct exposure to commercial and political messages in the media. Media effects were therefore reconceptualized as indirect and perhaps limited (see also Chapters 2, Eadie and Goret, 3, Craig, 16, Moy, 19, Self, 20, Hample, 21, Shoemaker and Johnson, 22, Bolchini and Lou).

However, the critical stance of cultural studies scholars towards the dominant paradigm and effects theory was not dependent on such fluctuations within the paradigm between notions of strong versus limited effects. For cultural theorists, the obsession with short-term media effects as such was misconceived and myopic. Williams, for instance, pointed out that the concern with behavioral effects only served to ignore other, perhaps long-term, socializing and culturally shaping media influences on society. Considering the alleged effects of TV on people's perceptions of sex and violence, or on political values and behavior, Williams observed that these phenomena were so general and complex "that it ought to be obvious that they cannot be specialized to an isolated medium but, in so far as television bears on them, have to be seen in a whole social and cultural process" (Williams 1977: 119). Further, he argued that the focus on individual effects, in isolation from the meaning structures of the visual and verbal elements of television supposedly carrying that effect, prevented investigators from understanding the real, semiotic and collective nature of the effects they were studying. Similarly, Hall criticized effects research for its conceptualization of the process of communication as a series of "isolated elements," which were analyzed in isolation from each other (Hall 1973: 128).

Williams also targeted the methodological shortcomings of the quantitative approach as leading to results with dubious validity (Williams 1977: 119). This lack of scientific quality made it even more deplorable that this paradigm had assumed a position of scientific hegemony, and with its "particular version of empiricism (...) claims the abstract authority of 'social science' and 'scientific method' as against all other modes of experience and analysis" (Williams 1977: 121).

2.2 The argument with Uses-and-Gratifications research

Uses-and-gratifications (U+G) research turned the key question of effects research ('What do the media do to people?') upside down for the benefit of a reverse knowledge interest in 'What do people do with the media?' In this way, U+G scholars brought the notion of 'active audiences' into communication studies, a notion which chimed well with the 'culturalist' perspective of cultural studies founders, according to which ordinary people were held to play a shaping role in their own life circumstances.

Nevertheless, Hall targeted the U+G researchers, in the form of James Halloran's media research group at Leicester University, as his primary opponents, because they considered people's media use to be a result of individual psychological needs, ignoring the role played by the contextual, structural conditionings of the wider social formation. Also the U+G researchers chose to stay inside the methodological orthodoxy of the dominant paradigm with its prescription of quantitative methods (Zillman 1985: 225; Lull 1985).

For Hall, who believed that "the discursive form of the message has a privileged position in the communicative exchange" (Hall 1973: 129), the U+G researchers committed a major sin in ignoring the textual meanings which people 'did things with.' The main reason why the signifying processes of the media text were a core concern for cultural studies was that these texts 'represent' the social and natural world through language and other semiotic modalities. Media texts do not bring to recipients a transparent reflection of the world; they construct – or 'articulate' – the world in discourse, producing a 'version' of reality according to the specific ideological perspective or vested interest of the encoder of the message (Hall 1973: 131–2).

In a capitalist class society such media versions of reality are bound to be saturated with particular class interests, and therefore media representations of, for instance, industrial conflicts (Glasgow University Media Group 1976), or police behavior and law and order, are not neutral representations of social reality (Hall et al. 1978). Similarly, media portrayals of women are likely to reproduce the norms and ideals of a patriarchal society (Goffman 1976; Williamson 1978; McRobbie 1978). Nevertheless, such representations are likely to convey the impression of being natural depictions of social phenomena, taken-for-granted pictures of what the world is like (cf. Vigsø 2010).

For Hall, representation and ideology are pervasive, inescapable conditions of being human, not the result of 'false consciousness' (Hall 1994: 259), and he also pointed out how scholars who are working without an understanding of representation may end up with invalid findings:

> We know (...) that representations of violence on the TV screen are not violence but messages about violence: but we have continued to research the question of violence, for example, as if we were unable to comprehend this epistemological distinction (Hall 1973: 131).

Before leaving the adversarial relation of Hall's cultural studies agenda and the U+G approach, it should be considered, from the perspective of a different time and age, that James Halloran's research group at Leicester University appears to have served as a convenient target for the Birmingham School's efforts to invent a new scientific paradigm, rather than as the genuine enemy. Halloran was overtly critical of American effects research for being atheoretical and excessively quantitative, and advocated a research agenda that resembled Hall's on several counts, as Halloran recognized (Halloran 1970: 15).

Boasting research that questioned simplistic effects perspectives, Halloran and colleagues analyzed media content critically and politically (Halloran et al. 1970), rehabilitated the cultural value of popular TV programs (Brown 1970), and looked at the micro-dynamics of television production (Elliott 1972). The research conducted at the Leicester School can thus hardly be said in retrospect to be a genuine representative of the dominant behaviorist paradigm. However, the fact that the encoding/decoding paper was intentionally born as a 'polemical' attack on the Leicester researchers testifies to the extent to which political tensions and struggles were an integral part of the structure of feeling in the humanities in the early 1970s. In the eyes of the Birmingham School it was unforgivable that the Leicester School wanted to give their research a functionalist *raison d'etre*, feeling "an obligation to contribute to the solution of social problems" (Halloran 1970: 21), rather than critiquing the kind of society which had caused the social problems to emerge in the first place.

3 Precursors in the humanities

The struggle of the fledgling cultural science against scholarly environments characterized by cultural elitism and text-centrism involved more entrenched adversaries. The British Leavisite practitioners of literary criticism and the German Frankfurt School of cultural critique had to be countered through a sustained theoretical argument in order to break their firm grip on widespread ways of thinking about cultural value, and methods to insight about such value.

As reflected in the title of his authoritative, culturally conservative *The Great Tradition* about the history of the English novel, Leavis's (1948) work was characterized by a cultural elitism according to which only a select few novels would stand the quality test of discriminating literary judges and become part of the great tradition of English novels. Such quality criteria led to the exclusion of all forms of popular and media culture from the field of scholarly vision, because the verdicts on cultural quality "derived from an institutionalized and class-based hierarchy of taste" (Barker 2000: 41).

A similar elitism, but located on the political left wing, characterized the Frankfurt School which, as mentioned in Section 2.1, can be seen as the common denominator of unmitigated Marxist cultural pessimism against which cultural studies reacted (Strinati 1995; Storey 1996: 4; Barker 2000: 45). The school was founded by Theodor Adorno and Max Horkheimer and others in Germany during the early interwar years under the shadow of authoritarian capitalism in the form of Nazism, and was consolidated while the key figures experienced the full blast of the commercial culture industries during their exile in the United States during WWII (Adorno and Horkheimer 1947b).

The received view of what the School gradually came to stand for during the post-WWII years was

1. an acerbic *cultural pessimism* which saw little hope of emancipation for a humanity ideologically seduced by the products of the cultural industries;

2. a confident *cultural paternalism*, and
3. a determined elitism insisting on the superiority of aesthetically difficult high art, with a logically following vehement condemnation of the products of mass culture.

The causal explanation of these devastating effects on culture relies on a crude form of economic determinism, which holds that the logics of capitalist production inevitably have these consequences in the cultural realm. In media studies, the later 'political economy' approach to cultural analysis can be seen as a less radical version of Frankfurt School thinking about culture (Schiller 1971; Herman and Chomsky 1988; Mosco 1996; McChesney 2008; see Hesmondhalgh 2007 for an innovative, non-dogmatic approach to the analysis of the cultural industries).

As implied in the title of one of the authoritative theoretical documents produced by the School, the essay 'The culture industry: Enlightenment as mass deception' (Adorno and Horkheimer 1947b), the Frankfurt approach rejects the notion of even minimally discriminating audiences: on the contrary, "the deceived masses (...) insist on the very ideology which enslaves them" (359) – an ideology which deprives them of "the last remaining thought of resistance" (367).

3.1 Raymond Williams's anti-elitist intervention: culture as a whole way of life

For Hall and Williams the challenge consisted, on the one hand, in devising a theoretical and analytical mindset that would enable them to acknowledge the potential meaningfulness and value of the mediated popular culture, and ordinary people's capacity for negotiating and sometimes resisting the dominant ideology disseminated by the mass media; on the other hand, they wished to retain a clear sense that the class-biased representations of society offered by the culture industries did have the hegemonic consequence of naturalizing the existing social arrangements in a way that was not in ordinary people's best interest in the long term.

In order to fully understand the anti-elitist thrust of early cultural studies, it is necessary to realize that the arts faculties in post-WWII Europe *were* really ivory towers for the culture of the educated classes, whose language and fine arts were studied as something elevated above the trivial cultural pursuits of ordinary people's life worlds. *The Uses of Literacy*, Hoggart's seminal analysis of "changes in working-class culture during the last thirty or forty years, in particular as they are being encouraged by mass publications" (Hoggart 1957: 9), was first of all an attempt to rehabilitate working-class culture as a legitimate academic research object, and "to 'read' working class culture for the values and meanings embodied in its patterns and arrangements as if they were kinds of 'texts'" (Hall 1980: 57).

Hoggart's perceptive analyses were inspired by a concern for the way working-class life and culture was adversely transformed by the emergence of mass society (Hoggart 1957: 340). However, Hoggart was far from as pessimistic as the Frankfurt School, retaining some confidence in the cultural resilience of the working class (Hoggart 1957: 345).

It was Raymond Williams's achievement to produce a more theoretically coherent alternative approach to the analysis of culture (Williams 1958, 1961). Williams is normally celebrated for defining culture in non-elitist terms as "a whole way of life"; however, although he was thus struggling to position everyday culture as a legitimate form of culture, he explicitly stressed that culture consisted of a number of equally necessary dimensions, ranging (with a tongue-in-cheek intertextual reference to Matthew Arnold) from "the best that has been thought and written in the world," to literary works that may be of lesser value, but which may throw significant light on "the particular traditions and societies in which they appeared" (Williams 1961: 56). The crucial, truly 'culturalist,' anthropological form of culture, he defined as "a particular way of life, which expresses certain meanings and values not only in art and learning but also in institutions and ordinary behaviour" (Williams 1961: 57).

Unlike the Marxist scholars of culture, who would insist that all aspects of culture are determined by and derivatives of the economic base and the class relations of capitalist society, Williams pointed out that it would be "an error to suppose that the social explanation is determining," because since culture is an integral part of the society, "there is no solid whole, outside it, to which (...) we concede priority" (Williams 1961: 61). The purpose of doing cultural analysis of such a relatively autonomous culture is to understand culture as a lived experience: what it feels like to be a member of that culture and to participate in its everyday pursuits. This goal, while always a challenge, poses a particular difficulty when we are not studying aspects of contemporary society, tending to see literary works of the past not in terms of their own *zeitgeist*, but "through our own experience, without even making the effort to see it in something like its original terms" (Williams 1961: 69) (for an early study which did try to make this effort when analyzing English children's magazines from the eighteenth to the twentieth century, see Drotner 1988).

In the contemporary world, we can at least visit and experience cultural domains 'live.' For instance, as the early cultural studies researchers did, we may observe and talk to the members of a contemporary youth subculture and try to understand their 'structure of feeling,' as Williams famously labeled it (Williams 1961: 64; Williams 1978: 128–135). This would consist in seeing them as agents who collectively build rituals and styles, by recombining existing and innovative cultural signs as a way to recreate a meaningful identity with which to replace older working-class identities, which were being eradicated by industrialization (Hall et al. 1976; Hebdige 1979; Willis 1977).

3.2 Hall's intervention: the relative autonomy of media audiences

In a capitalist democracy, the media are the political vehicles of ruling-class ideology that convey a naturalizing picture of a social order based on class domination; but the dominated classes, from their structurally subordinated position, can contest the social order that disadvantages them. Similarly, a text does have a shaping influence on what readers take from the text, but people's sense-making codes, or interpretive repertoires, may enable them to contest the intended meaning. Or rather, texts should be seen as in principle 'polysemic,' i.e. as having plural sense-making affordances. This political-textual circumstance logically entails that no cultural analyst, whether literary scholar or media critic, can speak authoritatively about the meaning of a text: a reception analysis is necessary in order to determine what meanings are actualized by different audiences, and how their readings may affect the ways in which they construct their views of the social world.

Hall's encoding/decoding model offered an economical framework for understanding the complex signifying relationships between three "linked, but distinctive moments" of mediated meaning-making: production, text, and consumption. His notion that the media text has a dominant, 'preferred meaning' is designed to solve the seeming paradox of textual determination and relative audience autonomy:

> We say *dominant*, not 'determined,' because it is always possible to order, classify, assign and decode an event within more than one 'mapping'. But we say 'dominant' because there exists a pattern of 'preferred' readings, and these (...) have the institutional/political/ideological order imprinted in them (Hall 1973: 134).

However, there may be a "lack of fit" between the codes of the encoder and the recipient (Hall 1973: 131). Hall suggests that we may usefully distinguish between three decoding positions, which are structurally related to three political-ideological stances which working-class people may adopt towards the capitalist social order: dominant, negotiated, and oppositional readings. A dominant, or hegemonic, reading occurs when the message is decoded in terms of the reference code in which it has been encoded. Negotiated readings take place when there is any level of partial acceptance of the reference code. Oppositional readings occur when there is thoroughgoing rejection of the reference code.

For Hall, and for David Morley (1980), who framed his reception study of the UK current affairs TV program 'Nationwide' in compliance with Hall's tripartite typology (derived from a similar typology proposed by the sociologist, Frank Parkin), these reading strategies originated from people's class position. Later reception research, inspired by theories of 'interpretive communities' (Fish 1980; Schrøder 1994), found reading patterns which corresponded clearly with people's ethnic and gender identities (Hobson 1982; Brown and Schulze 1990; Jhally and Lewis 1992).

4 The research practice of socio-cultural models: the case of audience reception research

The immediate result of Hall's 1973 paper was the gradual emergence and consolidation through the 1980s and 1990s of a new tradition of qualitative media audience research, founded on the key tenets of Hall's paper: the need to study media/audience relations holistically in terms of meaning and sense-making in communications, not behavior or effects, and the need to anchor these sense-making processes in the life-world of audience as well as in wider social contexts.

A few studies, such as Gripsrud's analysis of the American soap opera *Dynasty* (Gripsrud 1995) and Corner et al.'s analysis of news and documentary accounts of the risks of nuclear energy (Corner et al. 1990), fully met the holistic challenge and followed the meaning processes of mass mediated products from the moment of production to the moment of reception (see also Gavin 1998). However, during the first decades, the empirical gaze of reception research remained focused on the heavily under-researched nexus of media texts and audience 'readings,' under the motto of "audience-cum-content analysis" (Jensen 1988), while the empirical investigation of the moment of encoding and its relation to the other key 'moments' was postponed. Reception researchers largely accepted, in a general manner, the existing findings of political economy research about cultural production – that the production logics of the information and cultural industries did result in a popular media fare that was standardized, impoverished, and ideologically biased. However, a few studies did adopt an ethnographic fieldwork approach to researching the actual behind-the-scenes mechanics of prime-time television serial production; they found that nuanced, critical analysis of the creative, organizational and economic processes of mass cultural production provided complex insights not obtained through the political economy approach (Gitlin 1983; Feuer et al. 1984). The distinctive dearth of holistic media analyses was addressed theoretically as well as empirically by Deacon et al. (1999) in their eminently holistic study of "the natural history of a news item" from inception to reception, which aimed to restore and empirically investigate Hall's original focus on the complete and complex relationships in communication between messages, their sources, their journalistic encoders and their receivers.

The first waves of reception research showed a predilection for television news/current affairs programmes, and for print and televised serial fiction (for reception studies of advertising, see for instance Mick and Buhl 1992 and O'Donohue 1997). Reception studies of TV fiction were often directed towards an attempt to rehabilitate despised trash genres like romance novels, soap operas or women's magazines (Radway 1984; Hobson 1982; Ang 1984; Schrøder 1988; Hermes 1995), arguing that although these genres were "easily put down," as Hermes word-played about women's magazines, they nevertheless could be seen to hold quality for their regular users and fans. Liebes and Katz's (1990) ground-breaking simulation of the different readings produced by the global audiences of the American soap opera *Dallas* demonstrated how the diverse actualized meanings of such serials were rooted in and generated by the national-ethnic 'interpretive communities' (Fish 1980) of the viewers (see also Biltereyst's 1991 study of Belgian audience readings of US sitcoms). Radway's seminal ethnographic study of romance novels among American women showed that the melodramatic storylines invited readers to acquiesce in an oppressive patriarchal social order, while the social act of reading provided women with a legitimate, and liberating, excuse for a temporary leave of absence from their domestic obligations. Her study thus served as a reminder that reception research should maintain a dual focus on both the readers' decoding of textual meaning and on the contextual uses to which such decodings are put.

Deviating slightly from Hall's recipe, some reception researchers left audience decoding processes in the background and instead directed their torchlight towards the situational uses of media, particularly television. The pioneering study in this category, James Lull's (1980) ethnography of the social uses of television in 200 American families, analyzed how television is used by family members to puncture the day between meals, work, and leisure activities ('structural uses'), and how television viewing is also used to manage interpersonal communicative and affective relations between spouses and between parents and children ('relational uses'). In similar vein, but using qualitative interviews rather than participant observation, David Morley's (1986) study of 'family television' analyzed the gendered power relations around the TV set in a small number of British households, noting for instance how the remote control – labeled "Daddy's thing" – was often wielded as a tool of patriarchal authority. Gray (1992) studied the ways in which British housewives used the then new technology of video recorders for circumventing male definitions of appropriate cultural tastes. Gillespie's ethnographic study of the uses of television among Punjabi youth cultures in London emphasized the ways in which media may serve diasporic functions for ethnic subcultures, as they negotiate religious, cultural and national identities (Gillespie 1995).

A third variant of reception research considers how audiences may use media as resources for action (Jensen 2012a: 171–184). In the area of mediated citizenship and democracy, Schrøder (2012) suggests that reception studies of media as resources for citizenship can be divided into five stages. During the first stage, *hegemonic citizenship*, researchers like Stuart Hall (1973) and David Morley (1980) were concerned with the analysis of the formation of political consciousness in a class society (cf. above), exploring audience readings of political news in terms of the balance between the forces of hegemony and emancipation. John Fiske (1987) proposed that the pleasure of popular television for working-class viewers resided in the offer of symbolic resistance, through identification with underdog protagonists, to the hegemonic power of the system. Looking through the lens of *monitorial citizenship*, reception researchers like Klaus Bruhn Jensen (1986, 1990) and Justin Lewis (1991) during the second stage considered whether news media enable citizens to monitor events and processes in their surrounding world, so as to enable them to function as enlightened citizens. Even when this does occur, citizens were found not to use the acquired information as a resource for democratic participation, leading the researchers to suggest remedies like an increased educational effort to build higher levels of media literacy. During the third stage, *popular citizenship*, the analytical target was to establish whether the then new TV genre of studio debate programs served to provide audiences with the prerequisites of citizenship through the dialogical televisual public sphere. Livingstone and Lunt (1994) – pioneering a combination of qualitative and quantitative methods (Livingstone et al. 1994) – found that audiences were appreciative of the multivocal lay voices appearing on these programmes, and that studio debate programmes were a genuine vehicle of popular citizenship. After the emergence of new digital affordances for participation through the 'convergence culture' (Jenkins 2006), reception researchers started to investigate *participatory citizenship*. This occurred when audiences were not just reading news media, but adopting intervention strategies in the form, for instance, of user-generated content. Wahl-Jørgensen et al. (2010) found that when news audiences encounter user-generated content in the news, they have mixed feelings about it: while they appreciate authentic, eye-witness accounts from non-journalists, they tend – paradoxically from a democratic public sphere point of view – to resent the more deliberative have-your-say contributions of the lay public.

Finally during the fifth stage of *ubiquitous citizenship* reception researchers are responding to recent retheorizations of politics, according to which politics is not confined to a particular sphere in the social formation; on the contrary, "we engage politics everywhere, all the time, and the media are central to that engagement" (Jones 2006: 379). Ubiquitous citizenship has been researched in a wide-ranging cross-media multi-method study by Couldry et al. (2007), in which they mapped the extent to which citizens could be said to have, or not have, 'mediated public connection' leading to democratic engagement. Graham and Hajru (2011) in a netnographic form of reception research about reality TV shows analyzed viewers' spontaneous, unsolicited discussions about the characters and topics of these programs in online chat fora, finding that conversations that lack any overt political purpose often turn into serious political issues (for an early reception study of internet fora, see also Baym 2000).

For reception research as a democratically committed scholarly pursuit, the emerging ubiquity of potentially interactive mediated citizenship poses new challenges: from now on, programmatically and conceptually, media experiences with democratic implications are to be explored intertextually across the ensemble of media (Hasebrink and Popp 2006). Moreover, reception research is compelled to incorporate participatory audience practices under its scientific remit (Mascheroni 2010; Carpentier 2011), and seek to understand how mediated dormant citizenship may transform into mediated engaged, or interventionist citizenship: how latency becomes agency. Similar cross-media and participatory challenges are facing reception analyses of digital entertainment genres, such as theatrical films (Barker and Mathijs 2008, which also addresses the challenges of cross-cultural audience research) and online drama (Hardy et al. 2011).

5 The research practice of socio-cultural models: the case of discourse analysis

As mentioned at the beginning of this chapter, the field of discourse analysis has undergone a similar development to the one traced above in the field of cultural studies – from the media analyses of 'critical linguistics' based on a text-centric approach (Fowler et al. 1979), through a holistic phase in which the crucial role of textual production and reception was gradually acknowledged (Fairclough 1995), to the current situation in which some discourse analysts are adopting multi-method research designs and combining insights provided by textual and fieldwork methods (Scollon 2002; Oberhuber and Krzyzanowski 2008).

Through the 1970s, the practitioners of 'critical linguistics' developed an analytical procedure and perspective which were strongly akin to the ideological critique of the Frankfurt School. But whereas the latter often remained impressionistic and unsystematic, it was the great achievement of critical linguistics to devise an arsenal of linguistic concepts and features, derived from the functional linguistics and social semiotic of M. A. K. Halliday (1973, 1978). These linguistic concepts could be systematically and cumulatively applied to the analysis of media (and other) texts, in order to demonstrate their propagation of ideologically invested meanings. However, these analyses assumed that there existed a direct relation between the media representations of social reality and the ideological impact on the members of the social formation, i.e. readers anchored in the grip of social class identities, and the journalistic processes generating the report. The sense-making activities applied by readers lay outside the scope of critical linguistic analysis.

The first steps towards a more communicative, holistic approach to discourse analysis were taken by a number of scholars under the banner of 'social semiotics' (Hodge and Kress 1988). However, it is fair to credit the British linguist Norman Fairclough (1989, 1992) with the invention of a new theoretical framework which insisted on including – between the textual object and the sociocultural environment around it – the discursive processes of textual production and reception as central analytical objects (Fairclough 1995: 57). For Fairclough, who acknowledged the inspiration from reception research (Fairclough 1995: 49–50), these processes are crucial because they mediate between the other two levels of analysis:

> (...) the link between the sociocultural and the textual is an indirect one, made by way of discourse practice: properties of sociocultural practice shape texts, but by way of shaping the

nature of the discourse practice, i.e. the ways in which texts are produced and consumed, which is realized in the features of texts (Fairclough 1995: 59–60).

While this is an unequivocal acknowledgement of the need for holism, the last clause of the quotation reveals that for Fairclough the study of textual production and reception does not require empirical fieldwork, in which the analyst engages the real people involved in these activities, in order to unravel their communicative intentions and sense-making logics. The text itself is accorded the status of a royal road to understanding the discursive agents around it. Fairclough's analytical holism is thus a half-hearted non-empirical one, and even though he and other discourse analysts may achieve striking insights by deducing properties of production and reception from the media text itself, the indeterminacy of textual meaning becomes an obstacle to achieving deeper explanatory insights (Philo 2007).

Other scholars in discourse analysis have taken a more empirical turn. Swales and Rogers (1995) in their analysis of corporate mission statements argued that "(...) any interpretation of discourse that relies principally on only the <text> is likely to be incomplete and perhaps suspect" (Swales and Rogers 1995: 225). In an early discourse analytical study of the media/audience nexus, Bell (1994) compared media and citizen discourses about climate change.

During the last decade, a number of discourse scholars have led a more decisive and theoretically coherent attempt to innovate the inherited text-centered framework of discourse analysis. The *discourse-historical approach*, which traces interdiscursive and intertextual relations, such as the historical continuities and discontinuities of the climate debate, in a systematic diachronic perspective, often engages in fieldwork in the form of interviews with key actors (Abell and Myers 2008; Krzyzanowski 2008). *Discourse ethnography* acknowledges that existing discourse data often do not suffice and therefore supplement textual data with discourse data constructed through fieldwork (Oberhuber and Krzyzanowski 2008; Wodak 2000). Finally, Ron Scollon has developed an ethnographically committed, situated and agency-oriented approach to discourse analysis under the title *mediated discourse analysis* (Scollon 2002; Scollon and Scollon 2004). Frequently these types of discourse analysis, while according pride of place to linguistic representations, are adopting a multimodal approach, which takes into account the multi-semiotic nature of mediated communication (Kress and van Leeuwen 2001; O'Halloran 2011), emphasizing particularly the analysis of visual dimensions of mediated communication (Rose 2007).

6 'Reworking' the model: towards a more participatory media culture

Since the seminal years in which the foundations of the socio-cultural model of communication were laid, the paradigm has developed under the influence of internal and external dialogues and critiques. This chapter has concentrated on presenting a congenial interpretation of the founding mindset of cultural studies, leaving it to others to trace the insufficiencies and blind alleys that characterize the development of any scholarly approach.

For instance, Marjorie Ferguson and Peter Golding's (1997b) edited volume, *Cultural Studies in Question* can be seen in some ways as a the-political-economy-empire-strikes-back effort (cf. Golding and Murdock 2005). The volume's contributors argued that cultural studies would benefit from incorporating significant social science issues and debates into its overwhelmingly humanities agenda which overlooks the importance of "changing media technology, ownership, regulation, production and distribution" (Ferguson and Golding 1997a: xiv).

In his comprehensive re-theorization of cultural industries analysis, David Hesmondhalgh (2007) transcends the conflictual debates between the political economy and cultural studies approaches, as he traces the patterns of change as well as the continuities in the way the cultural industries have entered the age of the experience economy since the 1980s. Hesmondhalgh argues that while the analysis of the ownership and control of the cultural industries is indispensable to the analysis of media and culture, the cultural studies approach will "complement the cultural industries approach by asking us to consider more carefully how what people want and get from culture shapes the conditions in which these industries have to do business" (Hesmondhalgh 2007: 43).

A distinctive shortcoming of Hall's model was due to its mono-dimensionality, i.e. its time-bound concern with the ideological dimension of audience readings. Schrøder (2000), taking his lead from 'classic' critiques of the encoding/decoding model (Morley 1981; Wren-Lewis 1983), proposed a multi-dimensional model of audience readings (see also Michelle 2007), suggesting that audience readings should be seen in terms of five additional sense-making dimensions, including 'motivation,' 'comprehension,' and 'aesthetic discrimination.'

On a more methodological note, cultural studies for many years suffered from a strong aversion to the use of quantitative methods, because of the fierce epistemological struggles against the dominant paradigm, and because of the need to apply qualitative methods in order to study the ambivalences of sense-making and the ambiguities of structures of feeling. Since the mid-1990s, however, quantitative methods have been making their way into cultural studies, as Lewis (1997) argued that we should abandon "the lingering suspicion of numerical data," and that qualitative studies could often benefit from insights provided by numbers; for instance, "it is important for us to know, roughly, the number of people who construct one reading rather than another" (Lewis 1997: 87). Similarly, Klaus Bruhn Jensen (2012b) has argued forcefully for the "complementarity of qualitative and quantitative methods."

The foundations of cultural studies were laid almost forty years ago, in a society that was very different in terms of its technological, political, and cultural constituents. One challenge today consists in fully aligning cultural studies, poised between the culturalist and structuralist perspectives, with a digital convergence society and a participatory culture, in which people are not just active audiences but, in increasing numbers, using digital mobile technologies to *participate actively* in practices of collective intelligence and creativity (Jenkins 2006).

Some propose that a contemporary 'cultural science' should add to the conventional procedures drawn from the humanities "a much greater attention to robust empirical methodology than has been evident to date," in the form of for instance "computational research power" and "large-scale data-collection" (Hartley 2010: 104).Whether this should be one ingredient of the recipe in a different age for rejuvenating the original concerns and agendas of the socio-cultural model of communication, as envisaged by Raymond Williams and Stuart Hall, is for the contemporary practitioners of cultural studies to decide as they perform cultural research in accordance with, or deviation from, the heritage of their discipline, as they see fit.

Further reading

Deacon, David, Natalie Fenton & Alan Bryman. 1999. From inception to reception: The natural history of a news item. *Media, Culture & Society* 21. 5–31.

Gurevitch, Michael & Paddy Scannell. 2003. Canonization achieved? Stuart Hall's 'Encoding/Decoding'. In: Elihu Katz, John D. Peters, Tamar Liebes and Avril Orloff (eds.), *Canonic texts in media research. Are there any? Should there be? How about these?* Cambridge: Polity Press.

Hesmondhalgh, David. 2007. *The cultural industries*, 2nd edn. Los Angeles: Sage.

Jensen, Klaus B. 2012. Media reception: qualitative traditions". In: Klaus Bruhn Jensen (ed.), *A handbook of media and communication research*, 2nd edn, 171–185. London: Routledge.

O'Halloran, Kay L. 2011. Multimodal discourse analysis. In: K. Hyland and B. Paltridge (eds.), *Continuum Companion to Discourse*. London and New York: Continuum.

References

Abell, J. & Greg Myers. 2008. Analyzing research Interviews. In: Ruth Wodak and Michael Krzyzanowski (eds.), *Qualitative Discourse Analysis in the Social Sciences*. Basingstoke: Palgrave Macmillan.

Adorno, Theodor W. & Max Horkheimer. 1947a. /1972. *The dialectic of enlightenment*. New York: Herder and Herder.

Adorno, Theodor W. & Max Horkheimer. 1947b. /1977. The culture industry: Enlightenment as mass deception. Abridged version published in James Curran, Michael Gurevitch and Janrt Woolacott (eds.), *Mass communication and society*, 349–383. London: Edward Arnold 1977.

Althusser, Louis. 1971. *Lenin and Philosophy and Other Essays*. London: Monthly Review Press.

Ang, I. 1984. *Watching Dallas: soap opera and the melodramatic imagination*. London: Routledge.

Barker, Chris. 2000. *Cultural studies: theory and practice*. London: Sage.

Barker, Martin & Ernest Mathijs (eds.). 2008. *Watching The Lord of the Rings*. New York: Peter Lang.

Baym, Nancy K. 2000. *Tune in, log on: Soaps, fandom and online community*. London: Sage.

Bell, Alan. 1994. Climate of opinion: Public and media discourse on the global environment. *Discourse & Society* 5 (1). 33–64.

Biltereyst, Daniel. 1991. Resisting the American hegemony: A comparative analysis of the reception of domestic and US fiction. *European Journal of Communication* 6. 469–497.

Brown, Jane D. & Laurie Schulze. 1990. The effects of race, gender, and fandom on audience interpretations of Madonna's music videos. *Journal of Communication* 40 (2). 88–102.

Brown, Roger L. 1970. Television and the arts. In: Halloran (ed.) 1970.

Carpentier, Nico. 2011. *Media and Participation. A Site of Ideological-Democratic Struggle*. Bristol: Intellect.

Corner, John, Kay Richardson & Natalie Fenton. 1990. *Nuclear reactions. Form and response in 'public issue' television*. London: John Libbey.

Couldry, Nick, Sonia Livingstone & Tim Markham. 2007. *Media Consumption and Public Engagement. Beyond the Presumption of Attention*. Basingstoke: Palgrave Macmillan.

Deacon, David, Natalie Fenron & Alan Bryman. 1999. From inception to reception: The natural history of a news item. *Media, Culture & Society* 21. 5–31.

Drotner, Kirsten. 1988. *English children and their magazines 1751–1945*. New Haven: Yale University Press.

Eco, Umberto. 1979. *The Role of the Reader*. Bloomington: Indiana University Press.

Elliott, Philip. 1972. *Making of a Television Series. A case study in the sociology of culture*. London: Constable.

Fairclough, Norman. 1989. *Language and power*. London: Longman.

Fairclough, Norman. 1992. *Discourse and Social Change*. Cambridge: Polity Press.

Fairclough, Norman. 1995. *Media Discourse*. London: Edward Arnold.

Ferguson, Marjorie & Peter Golding. 1997a. Cultural studies and changing times. An introduction. In: Marjorie Ferguson and Peter Golding (eds.).

Ferguson, Marjorie & Peter Golding. 1997b. *Cultural studies in question*. London: Sage.

Feuer, Jane, Paul Kerr & Tise Vahimagi (eds.). 1984. *MTM: 'Quality television*. London: British Film Institute.

Fiske, John. 1987. *Television culture*. London: Methuen.

Fish, Stanley. 1980. *Is there a text in this class? The authority of interpretive communities*. Cambridge, MA: Harvard University Press.

Fowler, Roger, Robert Hodge, Gunther Kress & Tony Trew. 1979. *Language and Control*. London: Routledge and Kegan Paul.

Gavin, N. T. (ed). 1998. *The economy, media and public knowledge*. London: Leicester University Press.

Gillespie, Marie. 1995. *Television, Ethnicity, and Cultural Change*. London: Routledge.

Gitlin, Todd. 1978. Media sociology: the dominant paradigm. *Theory and Society* 6. 205–253.

Gitlin, Todd. 1983. *Inside prime time*. New York: Pantheon.

Glasgow University Media Group. 1976. *Bad News*. London: Routledge and Kegan Paul.

Goffman, Erving. 1976. *Gender Advertisements*. Society for the Study of Visual Communication (USA). Published in the UK 1979. by Macmillan Press.

Golding, Peter & Graham Murdock. 2005. Culture, communication and political economy. In: James Curran and Michael Gurevitch (eds.), *Mass media and society*, 4th edn, 60–83. London: Arnold.

Graham, Todd S. & Auli Hajru. 2011. Reality TV as a trigger of everyday political talk in the netbased public sphere. *European Journal of Communication* 26 (1). 18–32.

Gray, Ann. 1992. *Video playtime: The gendering of a leisure technology*. London: Routledge.

Gripsrud, Jostein. 1995. *The Dynasty years*. London: Routledge.

Gurevitch, Michael & Paddy Scannell. 2003. Canonization achieved? Stuart Hall's 'Encoding/ Decoding'. In: Elihu Katz, John D. Peters, Tamar Liebes and Avril Orloff (eds.), *Canonic texts in media research. Are there any? Should there be? How about these?* Cambridge: Polity Press.

Hall, Stuart. 1973. Encoding and decoding in the television discourse. Stenciled occasional paper, Media Series No.7, Centre for Contemporary Cultural Studies, University of Birmingham. Abridged version. In: S. Hall (eds.) 1980.

Hall, Stuart. 1980. Cultural studies: Two paradigms. *Media, Culture & Society* 2. 57–72.

Hall, Stuart. 1994. Reflections upon the encoding/decoding model: An interview with Stuart Hall. In: J. Cruz and J. Lewis, *Viewing, reading, listening*. Boulder, CO: Westview Press.

Hall, Stuart & Tony Jefferson (eds). 1976. *Resistance through rituals*. London: Hutchinson. First published 1975.

Hall, Stuart, Chas Critcher, Tony Jefferson, John Clarke & Brian Roberts. 1978. *Policing the crisis. Mugging, the state, and law and order*. London: Macmillan.

Hall, Stuart, Dorothy Hobson, Andrew Lowe & Paul Willis (eds). 1980. *Culture, media, language*. London: Hutchinson.

Halliday, Michael A.K. 1973. *Explorations in the functions of language*. London: Edward Arnold.

Halliday, Michael A.K. 1978. *Language as Social Semiotic. The social interpretation of language and meaning*. London: Edward Arnold.

Halloran, James (ed.). 1970. *The effects of television*. London: Panther.

Halloran, James, Philip Elliott & Graham Murdock. 1970. *Communications and demonstrations*. Harmondsworth: Penguin.

Hardy, Ann, Craig Hight & Carolyn Michelle. 2011. 'Reservoir Hill' and audiences for online interactive drama. *Participations* 8 (2). 616–643.

Hartley, John. 2010. Where money and meanings meet: theorizing the emergence of new values in media and education. In: Kirsten Drotner and Kim C. Schrøder (eds.), *Digital content creation. Perceptions, practices and perspectives*. New York: Peter Lang.

Hasebrink, Uwe & Jutta Popp. 2006. Media repertoires as a result of selective media use. A conceptual approach to the analysis of patterns of exposure. *Communications* 31. 369–387.

Hebdige, Dick. 1979. *Subculture. The meaning of style*. London: Methuen.

Herman, Edward S. & Noam Chomsky. 1988. *Manufacturing consent: the political economy of the mass media*. New York: Pantheon Books.

Hermes, Joke. 1995. *Reading women's magazines: An analysis of everyday media use*. Oxford: Polity Press.

Hesmondhalgh, David. 2007. *The cultural industries*, 2nd edn. Los Angeles: Sage.

Hobson, Dorothy. 1982. *Crossroads: the drama of soap opera*. London: Methuen.

Hodge, Robert & Gunther Kress. 1988. *Social Semiotics*. Cambridge: Polity Press.

Hoggart, Richard. 1957. *The uses of literacy*. Harmondsworth: Penguin.

Jenkins, Henry. 2006. *Convergence culture: Where old and new media collide*, New York: New York University Press.

Jensen, Klaus B. 1986. *Making sense of the news*. Aarhus, Denmark: Aarhus University Press.

Jensen, Klaus B. 1990. The politics of polysemy: Television news, everyday consciousness and political action. *Media, Culture & Society* 12. 74–90.

Jensen, Klaus B. 1988. Answering the question: What is reception analysis? *Nordicom Review 9* (1). 2–5.

Jensen, Klaus B. 2012a. Media reception: qualitative traditions. In: Klaus Bruhn Jensen (ed.), *A handbook of media and communication research*, 2nd edn. London: Routledge.

Jensen, Klaus B. 2012b. The complementarity of quantitative and qualitative methodologies in media and communication research. In: Klaus Bruhn Jensen (ed.), *A handbook of media and communication research*, 2nd edn. London: Routledge.

Jhally, Sut & Justin Lewis. 1992. *Enlightened racism: the 'Cosby Show', audiences and the myth of the American dream*. Boulder, CO: Westview Press.

Jones, Jeffrey P. 2006. A Cultural Approach to the Study of Mediated Citizenship. *Social Semiotics* 16 (2). 365–383.

Katz, Elihu. 1957. The two-step flow of communication. *Public opinion quarterly* 21:61–78.

Katz, Elihu & Paul Lazarsfeld. 1955. *Personal influence: The Part Played by People in the Flow of Mass Communications*. Glencoe, IL: Free Press.

Kress, Gunther & Theo van Leeuwen. 2001. *Multimodal Discourse. The Modes and Media of Contemporary Communication*. London: Edward Arnold.

Krzyzanowski, Michael. 2008. Analyzing focus group discussions. In: Ruth Wodak and Michael Krzyzanowski (eds.), *Qualitative Discourse Analysis in the Social Sciences*. Basingstoke: Palgrave Macmillan.

Lazarsfeld, Paul F., Bernard Berelson & Hazel Gaudet. 1948. *The People's Choice: How the Voter Makes Up His Mind in a Presidential Campaign*. New York: Columbia University Press.

Leavis, Frank R. 1948. *The great tradition*. London: Chatto and Windus. Reprinted 1962.

Levi-Strauss, Claude. 1958. *Anthropologie structural*. Paris: Plon.

Lewis, Justin. 1991. *The ideological octopus. An exploration of television and its audience*. New York: Routledge.

Lewis, Justin. 1997. What counts in cultural studies. *Media, Culture & Society* 19 (1). 83–97.

Liebes, Tamar & Elihu Katz. 1990. *The Export of Meaning*. New York: Oxford University Press.

Livingstone, Sonia & Peter Lunt. 1994. *Talk on television*. London: Routledge.

Livingstone, Sonia, Mallory Wober & Peter Lunt. 1994. Studio audience discussion programmes: An analysis of viewers' preferences and involvement. *European Journal of Communication 9*. 355–379.

Lull, James. 1980. The social uses of television. *Human communication research* 6. 197–209.

Lull, James. 1985. The naturalistic study of media use and youth culture. In: K. E. Rosengren 1985.

McChesney, Robert W. 2008. *The political economy of media: enduring issues, emerging dilemmas*. New York: Monthly Review Press.

McRobbie, Angela. 1978. Working class girls and the culture of femininity. In: *Women take issue. Aspects of women's subordination*, 96–108. The Women's Studies group, Centre for contemporary cultural studies, University of Birmingham. London: Hutchinson.

Mascheroni, Giovanna. 2010. Remediating participation and citizenship practices on social network sites. *Medien Journal* 3. 22–35.

Michelle, Carolyn. 2007. Modes of reception: A consolidated analytical framework. *The Communication Review* 10 (3). 181–222.

Mick, David G. & Claus Buhl. 1992. A meaning-based model of advertising experiences. *Journal of consumer research* 19. 317–338.

Morley, David. 1980. *The 'Nationwide' audience*. London: British Film Institute.

Morley, David. 1981. 'The Nationwide Audience' – A critical postscript. *Screen Education* 39. 3–14.

Morley, David. 1986. *Family Television*. London: Comedia.

Mosco, Vincent. 1996. *The political economy of communication: rethinking and renewal*. London: Sage.

Oberhuber, Florian & Michal Krzyzanowski. 2008. Discourse Analysis and Ethnography. In: Ruth Wodak and Michal Krzyzanowski (eds.), *Qualitative Discourse Analysis in the Social Sciences*. Basingstoke: Palgrave Macmillan.

O'Donohoe, Stephanie. 1997. Leaky boundaries: Intertextuality and young adult experiences of advertising. In: M. Nava, (ed.), *Buy This Book: Studies in Advertising and Consumption*. London: Routledge.

O'Halloran, Kay L. 2011. Multimodal discourse analysis. In: K. Hyland and B. Paltridge (eds.), *Continuum Companion to Discourse*. London and New York: Continuum.

Philo, Greg. 2007. Can discourse analysis successfully explain the content of media and journalistic practice? *Journalism Studies* 8 (2). 175–196.

Radway, Janice. 1984. *Reading the romance: women, patriarchy and popular literature*. Chapel Hill: University of North Carolina Press.

Riesman, David, Nathan Glazer & Reuel Denney. 1950. *The lonely crowd: a study of the changing American character*. New Haven: Yale University Press.

Rose, Gillian. 2007. *Visual Methodologies. An Introduction to the Interpretation of Visual Materials*. London: Sage.

Rosengren, Karl Erik, Lawrence A. Wenner & Phillip Palmgreen (eds.). 1985. *Media gratifications research*. Beverly Hills: Sage.

Schiller, Herbert I. 1971. *Mass communication and American empire*. Boston: Beacon Press.

Schrøder, Kim C. 1988. The pleasure of *Dynasty*. In: Philip Drummond and Richard Paterson (eds.), *Television and its audience*. London: British Film Institute.

Schrøder, Kim C. 1994. Audience semiotics, interpretive communities and the 'ethnographic turn' in media research. *Media, culture & society* 16. 337–347.

Schrøder, Kim C. 2000. Making sense of audience discourses: Towards a multidimensional model of mass media reception. *European Journal of Cultural Studies* 3 (2). 233–258.

Schrøder, Kim C. 2012. From semiotic resistance to civic agency: Viewing citizenship through the lens of reception research 1973–2010. In: Helena Bilandzic, Geoffroy Patriarche and Paul J. Traudt (eds.), *The Social Use of Media. Cultural and Social Scientific Perspectives on Audience Research*. London: Intellect.

Scollon, Ron. 2002. Action and text. Toward an integrated understanding of the place of text in social (inter)action, mediated discourse analysis and the problem of social action. In: Ruth Wodak and Michael Meyer (eds.), *Methods in Critical Discourse Analysis*. London: Sage.

Scollon, Ron & Suzie Wong Scollon. 2004. *Nexus Analysis. Discourse and the Emerging Internet*. London: Routledge.

Storey, John. 1996. *What is cultural studies? A reader*. London: Arnold.

Strinati, Dominic. 1995. *An introduction to theories of popular culture*. London: Routledge.

Swales, John M. & Priscilla S. Rogers. 1995. Discourse and the projection of corporate culture: the mission statement. *Discourse and Society* 6 (2). 223–242.

Thompson, Edward P. 1963. *The making of the English working class*. London: Victor Gollancz.

Vigsø, Orla. 2010. Naming is framing: Swine flu, new flu, and A(H1N1). *Observatorio* 4 (3). 229–241.

Wahl-Jørgensen, Karin, Andrew Williams & Claire Wardle. 2010. Audience views on user-generated content: Exploring the value of news from the bottom up. *Northern Lights 8, Yearbook of Film and Media Studies*, 177–194. Bristol, UK: Intellect Press.

Williams, Raymond. 1958. *Culture and society*. London: Chatto and Windus.

Williams, Raymond. 1961. *The long revolution*. London: Chatto and Windus. Published by Pelican Books 1965.

Williams, Raymond. 1977. *Marxism and literature*. Oxford: Oxford University Press.

Williamson, Judy. 1978. *Decoding Advertisements. Ideology and Meaning in Advertising*. London: Marion Boyars.

Willis, Paul. 1977. *Learning to labour: How working class kids get working class jobs*. London: Saxon House.

Wodak, Ruth. 2000. Recontextualization and transformation of meanings: A critical discourse analysis of decision-making in EU meetings about employment policies. In: Srikant Sarangi and Michael Coulthard (eds.), *Discourse and Social Life*, 185–207. London: Longman.

Wren-Lewis, Justin. 1983. The encoding/decoding model: Criticisms and redevelopments for research on decoding. *Media Culture & Society* 5 (2). 179–197.

Zillman, D. 1985. The experimental explorations of gratifications from media entertainment. In: Dolf Zillman and Jennings Bryant (eds), *Selective exposure to communication*, 225–239. Hillsdale, NJ: Laurence Erlbaum.

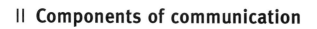

II Components of communication

Charles C. Self
19 Who

Abstract: Early in the twentieth century, the media communicator was assumed to exercise 'strong effects' on isolated individuals in mass society. By mid-century, research conducted in the emerging disciplines of communication science had found that the communicator had 'limited effects' on the behavior and attitudes of socially connected individuals. After 1960, research from structural, semiotic, and cognitive-schemata paradigms envisioned the communicator as a societal force with powerful 'structural effects' on economic, political, cultural, and social formations. At the turn of the twenty-first century, the communicator was understood as a shifting node within fluid networks of textual, technical, and social relationships producing 'semiotic effects' on economic, political, cultural, and social life. This chapter reviews the evolution of these changes.

Keywords: Strong effects, limited effects, cybernetics, structuralism, cognitive-schemata theory, cultural theory, semiotics, network theory, Actor Network Theory, post-structuralism

Twentieth century communication 'science' might be seen as a struggle to understand how much power a communicator can exercise in society. The century opened with a vision of a strong individual or media communicator exercising powerful social influence. By mid-century communication science had modified the vision to an isolated, discrete communicator who exerted limited effects on individual recipients. In the second half of the century, the communicator evolved again into a structural semiotic force shaping social reality. By the twenty-first century the communicator had become a shifting node within semiotic, cybernetic, or social network relationships.

1 The strong effects base (until 1939)

Traditions competed for legitimacy in early communication science in Europe and the United States: historical/rhetorical traditions, cultural/analytical/sociological traditions, and positivist/empirical/psychological traditions. All were well established in Europe by the end of the nineteenth century. All had been exported into the United States early in the twentieth century. All influenced the early conceptions of a powerful communicator influencing society (Rogers 1994: 129–130).

The rhetorical traditions can be traced back through medieval scholastic studies to Plato, Aristotle, and Socrates (Oates 1948: 36). The analytical traditions traced their lineage through European sociology and Marxism to German Idealism and speculative philosophy (Hardt 1979: 18 and 67; Delia 1987: 70). The empirical traditions can be traced back through experimental behavioral psychology to British Empiricism and French and Scottish Positivism (Boring [1929] 1957: 179–216). Early American academic studies in journalism and speech departments reflected these traditions (Delia 1987: 73–85; Rogers 1994: 280–284).

Hanno Hardt has demonstrated that many American scholars "whose training or background included encounters with the German tradition of the social sciences and whose scholarship – labeled 'American science'" in Germany – included similar notions concerning the importance of communication and mass communication in a modern society" (Hardt 1979: 36–37).

At the time Lasswell wrote his 'model' of the communication act, the empirical approaches often applied that scholarship for political, commercial, and government agency interests (Delia 1987: 46–54). This scholarship saw the communicator as a strong, discrete entity influencing a mass of disconnected and isolated individuals characteristic of the modern societies. This vision of a 'strong effects' communicator grew from nineteenth century European sociological literature (Hardt 1979: 17), propaganda analysis after WWI (Lasswell 1927: 1–13), propaganda successes of the Nazis (George 1959; Ellul 1965), and commercial and political applications of polling data (Delia 1987: 46–54).

The communicator of the Enlightenment had sought knowledge to empower himself (Klein 2001: esp. 153–162) in the 'public sphere' (Habermas 1991: 181–186; see also Habermas 1985). However, in the late nineteenth century, the emphasis shifted back to the communicator's power to persuade (Habermas 1991: 186–195). The European sociology of Ferdinand Tönnies, Max Weber, Georg Simmel, Albert Schäffle, and others spurred an interest in what shaped mass audiences (Hardt 1979: 36). By the early twentieth century the emphasis in United States scholarship was upon helping the communicator persuade his mass audience.

By the time Lasswell began his studies in propaganda, the view of a strong communicator with powerful influence had become established as the 'magic bullet' (Klapper 1960: 11; Gitlin 1978: 209–210; DeFleur and Ball-Rokeach 1989), 'hypodermic needle' (Berlo 1960: 27–28), or 'strong effects' model of mediated communication (Schramm 1957: 26–32). That view helped shape Lasswell's research in communication as propaganda and public opinion.

Media industries were interested in propaganda and the emerging radio audience as well as public opinion polling (Rogers 1994:205; Lasswell 1980: 525–528; Cantril and Allport 1935; Smith 1969: 42–89; Erskine 1970).

2 The limited effects communicator (1940–1959)

In the late 1930s, Harold Lasswell's description of communication as a linear process had helped establish the role of the communicator as the force driving communication for the emerging scientific study of communication. That perspective sought to solve 'problems' of 'effective' communication for institutional sponsors of major research initiatives in the 1930s and 40s (Lasswell 1941: 71; Delia 1987: 22–29; Gitlin, 1978: 210). However, it described a series of discrete components of a communication 'act' and researchers quickly found that these components could limit the communicator's ability to have effects on individuals who were socially connected to each other rather than isolated and dependent upon the strong communicator. The studies that described these limiting variables created a communication discipline in search of theoretical foundations.

Lasswell's description of 'an act of communication' was first articulated in 1939 as part of his work with the Rockefeller Communication Seminar (Rogers 1994: 221) and was published in 1948 at a moment of intense interest in the 'science' of communication (Hardt 1979: 17–24). Lasswell's 'model' of communication was deceptively simple: Who, Says What, In Which Channel, To Whom, With What Effect? (Lasswell 1948: 37). It embraced the 'administrative research' dominant among the pioneers of communication at the time (Gitlin 1978: 205; Slack and Allor 1983: 209). It focused on control and persuasion. "Scholars who study the 'who,' the communicator, look into the factors that initiate and guide the act of communication," Lasswell wrote. "We call this subdivision of the field of research *control analysis*" (emphasis his)(Lasswell 1948: 37).

The 'founding fathers' of communication science research brought European science to the study of communication in the United States in the 1930s and 1940s: Paul Lazarsfeld (social effects research), Kurt Lewin (group dynamics research), Carl Hovland (experimental psychological effects research), and Harold Lasswell (propaganda and persuasion research) (Schramm 1963: 2–5; Rogers 1994: xi). Lazarsfeld had labeled this approach administrative research because it was carried out on behalf of administrative agencies. He was trying to distinguish it from European critical traditions manifest in Frankfurt School theorists Max Horkheimer at Columbia University and Theodor Adorno, whom Lazarsfeld had asked to join him at the Princeton University Radio Project in 1938 (Slack and Allor 1983: 209–210).

The introduction of social psychological approaches into the study of communication transformed the notion of the influence of the communicator on individual recipients. It suggested that individual recipients were more resistant to mass media and strong communicators than had been thought. Administrative research thus focused on how the communicator should construct the message in order to realize specific effects (Berelson [1960] 1972: 342–543). The model assumed that the core problem was making the connection between the communicator and the individual recipient with a persuasive message. Little attention was given in the perspective to the underlying motives of the communicator or to power relationships underlying the communicative act that had been important in European sociology (Gitlin 1978: 225–233; Slack and Allor 1983: 215–217; Rogers 1994: 311–314).

This emphasis served the needs of radio and newspaper owners and advertisers (Schramm 1983: 7). It served politicians and political parties trying to influence voting behavior (Hurwitz 1988; Erskine 1970). It also served government agencies measuring the effectiveness of propaganda in the lead up to war (Rogers 1994; Gitlin 1978; Schramm 1983: 7).

2.1 Limiting the power of the 'who'

Schramm's 'founding fathers' used empirical techniques to help media, advertisers, and government planners to solve the problems of connecting the persuasive message with the individual recipient.

The research efforts fell into four major categories: (1) credibility and learning effects (pioneered by Hovland), (2) social effects (pioneered by Lazarsfeld), (3) congruity and attitude change (pioneered by Lewin); and (4) propaganda content effects (pioneered by Lasswell).

2.1.1 Credibility and learning effects

Hovland applied experimental behavioral psychology to understanding when audiences would trust the communicator. Aristotle had argued that character was an effective means of persuasion. He suggested that communicators were credible because the audience perceives the 'rightness' of the message, the speaker knows how to reveal himself to particular audiences, and the character of the audience makes it credulous of the message (Self 2009: 437). Hovland's research set out to systematically test these assertions (Hovland et al 1953).

Hovland and his colleagues defined *credibility* as 'trustworthiness' and 'expertise' (Hovland et al. 1953; Hovland and Weiss 1951–1952). They presented positive and negative messages from high credibility and low credibility sources to audiences and measured whether the information was learned and whether it changed attitudes. They measured whether the same participants retained the information four months later. Hovland found that high credibility sources changed attitudes more than low credibility sources, but that information was learned about equally well from both source types. An unanticipated *sleeper effect* was found in follow-up studies four months later. Even those who initially were skeptical about the credibility of the source showed higher levels of persuasion after time passed (Hovland et al. 1949; Hovland and Weiss 1951–1952). Hovland's research demonstrated that perceived credibility, repetition, and reinforcement limited and shaped how a communicator might influence attitude change in individuals (Hovland 1959).

2.1.2 Social effects

Lazarsfeld's early research of social effects had an even more powerful influence on the understanding about the communicator. It was developed from Lazarsfeld's 1940 Erie County study of voting decisions in the U.S. presidential elections published as *The People's Choice* (Lazarsfeld et al. [1944] [1948] 1968; Lazarsfeld et al. [1960] 1972) and his later Decatur, Illinois, study of how 800 women obtained information and made decisions about buying and voting published as *Personal Influence* (Katz and Lazarsfeld 1955). These two studies spawned many others at the Radio Research Project and the Bureau of Applied Social Research by Lazarsfeld and his students. They transformed the notion of powerful, direct effects of the 'hypodermic needle' model by discovering 'limits' to those effects (De Sola Pool 1963: 134–135). Lazarsfeld's research suggested that 'opinion leaders' filtered media messages through interpersonal relationships (Lazarsfeld and Menzel 1963: 96). This 'two step flow' of information limited the concept of a powerful communicator with a model of shared social influence (Katz [1960] 1972: 346–347). It connected the idea of limited effects to Lewin's concepts of group influence on individual persuadability.

2.1.3 Congruity and attitude change

Kurt Lewin proposed a 'field theory' of social science. His field theory and his emphasis upon the influence of groups on individual behavior contributed to the field of social psychology and its application to communication research. This work introduced the idea that social groups shaped the individual's 'perception' of the communicator effectively rendering any message to be changed depending upon the influences of the social group to which an individual receiver belonged.

2.1.4 Propaganda effects

Lasswell incorporated these lines of research into his own interests in communication, propaganda, and Freudian psychology (Lasswell 1980). He was interested in how newspapers, pamphlets, and other forms of communication influenced audiences (Lasswell 1941). He applied content analysis in his War-Time Communications Project to help the military craft persuasive messages. This method came to be widely adopted to examine the effects of mediated communication messages (Rogers 1994: 232–233).

Lasswell, in trying to understand how media shaped the way individuals thought about issues, therefore promoted the idea of a strong communicator, but one limited by the mediated communication process itself.

3 The concept shifts: the structural effects communicator (1960–1989)

By 1960 researchers were seeking new approaches that would go beyond the 'limited effects' notion of the communicator. Lazarsfeld's colleague, Elihu Katz (1983: 52) commented, "It is curious that so little work has been done on these institutional aspects; Lasswell's 'who' appears to have been poorly conceptualized," he wrote. He said that critics of limited effects fell roughly into three groups that envisioned the 'who' of communication in terms of "direct and/or powerful effects instead" (Katz 1987: S27). He labeled them 'institutional (or political or cognitive), critical, and technological' perspectives (cf. Grossberg 1979, Carey 1983: 311 and 312; Delia 1987: 69).

3.1 Re-empowering the communicator as structural force

Thus, this period produced competing paradigms about the power of the communicator and the competing visions created 'ferment in the field' after 1970 (Gerbner 1983). Here they will be labeled critical/cultural theories, technological theories, and structural/cognitive theories. All of these approaches found that the communicator was more powerful in shaping society than the individual effects studies had found. They recognized power relationships within communication structures and replaced the idea of a discrete individual or institutional communicator with the idea of a social, technological or structural force.

3.2 Critical/cultural/semiotic theories

By the 1960s, when critical approaches including Marxist approaches had claimed a central place in the science of communication (Garnham 1983: 317–321) and rhetorical perspectives (Burke 1966) and structural/systems approaches (Lévi-Strauss 1963; Foucault 1970; Lacan 1988) were also reasserting themselves, there was a shift in thinking about the communicator. If early twentieth century research had been about individual institutional power and mid-century research had been about limited effects, research which implicated the 'who' of communication after 1960 was about social, structural, economic, and semiotic formations of power. It examined media and the communicator as a social/institutional manifestation of cultural structures of signification with social, political, and economic consequences (Slack and Allor 1983: 214).

Roland Barthes ([1957] 1973), Umberto Eco (1986) and Stuart Hall (1982) rejected the linearity of the social effects paradigm with its discrete sender and individual receiver. They suggested that the communicator was a point of cultural negotiation over politics, economics, and power. The concern about symbols, language, and the production of meaning was reflected in the work of many cultural and language theorists. In a related way, structuralism in the human sciences – particularly the structural linguistics of Ferdinand de Saussure (1959), the structural anthropology of Claude Lévi-Strauss (1963), the philosophy of Michel Foucault (1970), and the psychology of Jacques Lacan (1988), all of which were influential in the 1970s and 1980s – argued that structural relationships shape ideology and meaning. The communicator thus appeared as a surface manifestation of underlying structural and power relationships. In this sense, structuralism destabilized the notion of the communicator as a discrete agent and broadened the communicator into a structural relational force, a bearer of social and meaning structures rather than a controller of them.

Other theorists in this period also focused on language and cultural dynamics as the basis for understanding the communicator. They included such diverse scholars as John Searle with his 'speech act theory' (Searle 1983), the linguistic relativism of Edward Sapir and Benjamin Whorf (Sapir 1983), S. I. Hayakawa and Alfred Korzybski (Hayakawa 1964), Charles Morris, Jürgen Ruesch, Gregory Bateson and Jean Piaget (1952). Again, these theorists were less concerned about how the media or a communicator produces specific individual effects than they were about the role of the language and symbols as cultural forces in creating, negotiating, or expressing cultural meaning. Giddens's Structuration Theory (Giddens 1986) represents a further example of this tendency. It is concerned with the 'duality of structure,' and the webs of language created within the nexus of human and social agency.

Critical theory, too, manifested this shift away from the communicator as an autonomous, self-identifying entity (Nordenstreng 2004). In general, it saw the role of the communicator as determined by shifts of power. Altschull ([1984] 1994) suggested that communication systems consisted of three types of structures, all with their consequences for determining the way that the communicator is suspended in power relations: market, communitarian (socialist) and advancing (developing countries) understandings of power relationships. Another way that communication scholarship has figured in this understanding of communication systems is with reference to Antonio Gramsci's concept of cultural hegemony in which the communicator is riven by the conflicting interests among social classes and attempts to win consent to messages and/or social programmes (Hall 1986).

Although not addressing the issue of hegemony directly, James Carey (1983) pointed out that cultural studies were also concerned with structures and how communicators produced and reproduced cultural symbols and meaning. For him, societies, as complex interactive wholes, are threaded throughout by culture: the production and reproduction of systems of symbols and messages (1983: 313).

He referred to Geertz's notion of 'thick description' to understand the interplay of the communicator, culture, and meaning, indicating that the relations among of them are embedded in very specific cultural contexts which are difficult to understand from outside that context. This perspective lies in stark contrast to the linear notion of effects in which the role of the communicator in relation to the production and reception of meaning is taken to be clear to any observer standing outside of that context (Carey 1989: 38–40; Carey 1982). This is acknowledged, to some extent, by other perspectives; for example, 'normative theories' (Siebert et al. [1956] 1963) advanced the notion that the communication media were shaped by the political systems within which they operated.

3.3 Technological theories

Where critical and cultural studies insist on socio-cultural and political dimensions as crucial to understanding the communicator, they sometimes run the risk of neglecting the shaping role of technology. In 1949, Shannon and Weaver introduced cybernetics into communication research with their mathematic model of communication. The model, seemingly linear in character, included a 'feedback loop' to monitor the status of structural components of the communication environment, including the communicator (Shannon and Weaver 1949; Wiener 1950). As such, the communicator – even if human – was to be figured as a systemic feature interacting with the other technological components of the communication process.

Versions of technological structures immersing the communicator had sprung up almost as Lasswell was publishing his own model. Norbert Wiener's cybernetics was applied to communication as communication researchers embraced Information Theory. Cybernetics offered an influential means of reintroducing structural power into mainstream communication research. But, as with other structural models, it was based on assumptions that what the communicator was and did were shaped by the structural elements of the communication environment.

General Systems Theory also had an impact on thinking about the structural elements surrounding the communicator (von Bertalanffy 1974). It tapped into growing evidence in biology and other fields of structural relationships within both closed and open systems that exhibited homeostasis and internal regulation (see Chapter 5, Baecker). It suggested that the manifestation of meaning in communication was driven not by the isolated, controlling character of the communicator, but by the nature of the inputs, outputs, and structural relationships required to maintain communication systems in some kind of steady state. Allied to this was a perspective in which the very role of the communicator was, for theoretical purposes, effectively eradicated. In the 1960s, the Canadian theorist Marshal McLuhan inspired a generation of scholars and media practitioners to conceive of media technology itself as the driving force of communication (McLuhan 1962, 1964). He famously suggested that the communicator and the communication medium itself was the message of the communication, that technology changed culture, and implied that the human communicator was subordinate to these technological processes.

3.4 Institutional/cognitive visions of power

Much communication theory in the period after the Second World War was devoted to the idea that the communicator could be not just one, singular entity, but a collective one. In 1954, Bruce Westley and Malcolm MacLean published their 'process' model of communication (Westley and MacLean 1957). It imported holistic structural cognitive relationships into studies of communication bringing assumptions from Gestalt psychology and American Pragmatism into thinking about the communicator. Central to their model was the idea that the workings of different kinds of groups effect the communication process. Likewise, Kurt Lewin's research introduced holistic structures based on the study of group dynamics into the basic model of communication. Drawing on Heider's (1944, 1946) POX model and his broader Attribution Theory (1958) and Festinger's (1963) Theory of Cognitive Dissonance, these 'group' approaches to the communicator resulted in Osgood and Tannenbaum's (1955) Congruity Theory and reached their zenith in Westley and MacLean's ABX model (Westley and MacLean 1957). In general, these approaches broadened the idea that social groups influenced communicator effects on individuals. They suggested that the communicator both represented the product of the general social environmental structure and a powerful force producing and shaping social structures and expectations. The cognitive 'schemata' structures of media communicators became of special interest in 'institutional' communication research as repositories of social schema structures influencing and influenced by media. In this sense, 'effects' were redefined as broad structural social effects rather than as individual effects (see Ausubel 1965: 67–70).

The media communicator at the point of such structural negotiations was also central to the work of George Gerbner and his colleagues (Gerbner et al. 1986) at the University of Pennsylvania, particularly the 'cultivation' hypothesis. Their studies focused on media production processes and how media messages from a communicator 'cultivated' general predispositions and conceptions of social reality. Another line of reasoning within the structural institutional paradigm was agenda setting theory (McCombs and Shaw 1972) and the evolution of Erving Goffman's (1959) framing theory into Entman's complimentary strong effects framing perspective (Entman 1993; McCombs and Ghanem 2001). That work produced a series of studies of media professional practices and the idea of the social construction of meaning. This Social Constructionism (Berger and Luckmann 1966) argued that social practices of communicators shaped the messages they produced as well as the social signification of the messages defining social meaning for individuals and groups as described in the parallel Theory of Social Constructivism (Tuchman 1978).

Other theories that dealt with the duality of the communicator as a structural point of social negotiation of meaning include:
- Social Cognitive Theory (Bandura 1962, 1989);
- expanding versions of Social Judgment Theory (Sherif et al. 1965);
- Knowledge Gap Hypothesis (Tichenor et al. 1970);
- Media Systems Dependency Theory (Ball-Rokeach and DeFleur 1976); and the
- Heuristic-Systematic model of information processing (Chaiken 1980).

The core notion of social structure also influenced:
- Uses and Gratifications Theory (Katz 1959);
- Diffusions of Innovation (Rogers [1962] 1983);
- Inoculation Theory (McGuire 1961; Pfau 1997);
- Third Person Effect (Davison 1983);
- the Elaboration Likelihood Model (Petty and Cacioppo, 1981);
- Spiral of Silence (Noelle-Neumann 1993)

and many other studies in the late twentieth century. The broadly Social Constructionist perspective also influenced a range of public relations theories flowing from
- Grunig's Situational Theory of Publics, clearly grounded in the American Pragmatic social tradition,
- his Excellence Theory of symmetrical communication (Grunig 1997), and
- Kent and Taylor's (2002) Dialogic Theory.

These approaches assume that effective communication is not unidirectional, from communicator to target, and depends upon contextualized relationships among participants in the communicative situation.

4 The twenty-first century: the 'semiotic effects' communicator (1990 and after)

Before Lasswell, the communicator was conceived to be a strong and persuasive force for audiences of isolated individuals (Lasswell 1941), producing specific 'effects'. At mid-century the communicator was reconceived as a weak force limited by social, psychological, and group variables (Klapper 1960), producing limited effects. After 1960, the communicator was reconceived once more as a strong structural and semiotic force embedded within social, cultural, institutional, technological, political and economic systems (Cobley 2006, 2010).

As the twenty-first century arrived, the communicator was again being reconceived. Three forces were driving this re-conceptualization: Post-structuralism (and Postmodernism), the Internet, and the re-emergence of network science. In the emerging paradigm, the communicator was less a component of a structure than it was itself a shifting node in a fluid semiotic network of relationships.

Post-structuralist writers such as Michel Foucault (1970), Jacques Derrida ([1974] 1976; 1982), Jean-Francois Lyotard (1984) and Jean Baudrillard (1994) had offered a critique of stable systems of knowledge including metaphysics, phenomenology, and structuralism. They suggested that these grand narratives had collapsed into local narratives grounded in 'readings' of the 'signs' or 'texts' that constitute meaning within a local situation. Barthes (1977) declared the 'death' of the 'author' or communicator and the ascendency of the 'reader' who interprets a shifting fabric of text based on layers of meaning from multiple centers of culture (see also Foucault 1984: 101–102). The post-structural writers argued that the communicator was no more in control of the text than was the reader. Both were produced by shifting cultural relationships.

At the opening of the twenty-first century, the Internet offered technological evidence of this notion of the communicator as constituted by shifting relationships, rather than as a fixed author. The complexity of sourcing on the Internet was often unclear (Castells 2000a; McNair 2006; Jenkins 2006, Bignell 2000). The origins of meaning seemed to 'flow' across a worldwide communication network including digital and wireless media. 'Mash-ups' (Shirky 2008) and the anonymity of 'murky' sourcing shrouded in ambiguity (Sundar 2008; Sundar and Nass 2001) left the notion of authorship and the stability of authorship in question. Messages could easily be passed among multiple sources and continuously modified intentionally or unintentionally. The development of social networking in particular offered group sourcing for communication messages and information (Winograd and Hais 2009: 156–173; Sunstein 2006; Wellman 2001). The communicator came to be understood as the 'play' of social, political, corporate, or ideological power relationships shaping the semiotic sense of reality.

The third major trend was the reemergence of Network Theory, which could trace its roots to Gestalt psychology, Lewin's Field Theory, and graph theory (Scott 2000: 7–13). It, too, offered a concept of signification emerging from shifting relationships, rather than from a discrete communicator. Social network analysis and its accompanying theoretical postures suggested a shifting pattern of relationships among 'nodes' in social networks – some dense and tightly connected, some bridging more distant sub-networks. The work found 'cliques,' structural holes, power law distributions, and a range of internal network dynamics across apparently widely diverse network types (White 2008; Monge and Contractor 2003; Castells 2000a, b, 2008, 2011). In one of many examples, Chang, Himelboim and Dong explored the relationships between political economy and international hyperlink networks of news flows (Chang et al. 2009: 140–144). Monge and Contractor

(2003: 4) suggested that these cultural and communication processes "are built around material and symbolic flows that link people and objects both locally and globally without regard for traditional national, institutional, or organizational boundaries." Castells (2000c) argued that cultural battles across international informational networks are the power battles of the information age and that they are fought primarily in and by communication media but that the media communicators are no longer the power holders. Rather, power lies in the networks of information exchange and symbol manipulation.

> Power...is no longer concentrated in institutions (the state), organizations (capitalist firms), or symbolic controllers (corporate media, churches). It is diffused in global networks of wealth, power, information, and images, which circulate and transmute in a system of variable geometry and dematerialized geography....
> *The new power lies in the codes of information and in the images of representation around which societies organize their institutions and people build their lives and decide their behavior. The sites of this power are people's minds.* This is why power in the information age is at the same time identifiable and diffused. We know what it is, yet we cannot seize it because power is a function of an endless battle around the cultural codes of society...But victories may be ephemeral, since the turbulence of information flows will keep codes in a constant swirl. (Castells 2000c: 424–425; emphasis in original)

The Actor Network Theory of Michel Callon, Bruno Latour, and John Law (Latour 1993; Law 1999) offered another theoretical approach to the communicator grounded on what Law called a "semiotics of materiality...the semiotic insight... that they are produced in relations, and apply this ruthlessly to all materials – and not simply those that are linguistic" (4) The theory encompassed non-human actor patterns, or what Latour called 'hybrids' as participants in the notion of the communicator (Latour 1993: 10–12). As such, the communicator could not be conceived as just human, or even just machine, but rather a result of the relations of both. Similarly, 'posthumanism' has problematized the human communicator, seeing, instead, the rise of the cyborg and recognising the human communicator's "imbrication in technical, medical, informatic, and economic networks" (Wolfe 2010: xv) as well as its animal status. Others have pointed out that biosemiotics and cybersemiotics manifest similar structural interpretations that do not depend upon the centrality of a human communicator to the production of meaning within the system (Cobley 2006: 28–29; Cobley 2010: 9 and 199–200).

Thus, at the beginning of the twenty-first century the powerful communicator remains but has been repositioned into larger constellations of social, structural, and semiotic forces that lie beyond any individual or institution. The communicator has come full circle. The communicator is again thought to be powerful, but this communicator is the semiotic product of the shifting texts and networks of human and non-human relationships that produce the constantly changing currents of meaning that define and redefine twenty-first century life.

Further reading

Cobley, Paul (ed.). 2006. *Communication Theories, Vol. 1–4*. New York: Routledge.
Delia, Jesse G. 1987. Communication research: a history. In: Charles R. Berger and Steven H. Chaffee (eds.), *Handbook of Communication Science*, 20–98. Newbury Park, CA: Sage.
Gerbner, George (ed.). 1983. *Ferment in the field: Journal of Communication* (Special Issue). 33 (3).
Gitlin, Todd. 1978. Media sociology: the dominant paradigm. *Theory and Society* 6 (2). 205–253.
Rogers, Everett M. 1994. *A History of Communication Study: A Biographical Approach*. New York: The Free Press.

References

Ausubel, David P. 1965. A cognitive structure view of word and concept meaning. In: Richard C. Anderson and David P. Ausubel (eds.), *Readings in the Psychology of Cognition*, 58–76. New York: Holt Rinehart and Winston.
Altschull, J. Herbert. [1984]. 1994. *Agents of Power: The Media and Public Policy*, 2nd edn. New York: Allen and Bacon.
Ball-Rokeach, Sandra J. & Melvin L. DeFleur. 1976. A dependency model of mass-media effects. *Communication Research* 3. 3–21.
Bandura, Albert. 1989. Human agency in social cognitive theory. *American Psychologist* 44. 1175–1184.
Bandura, Albert. 1962. *Social Learning through Imitation*. Lincoln, NE: University of Nebraska Press.
Barthes, Roland. [1957]. 1973. *Mythologies*. Lavers, A. (trans.). London: Paladin.
Barthes, Roland. 1977. *Image, Music, Text*. Heath, Stephen (trans.). New York: Hill and Wang.
Baudrillard, Jean. 1994. *Simulacra and Simulation*. Glaser, Sheila Faria (trans.). Ann Arbor: University of Michigan Press.
Berelson, Bernard. [1960]. 1972. Communications and public opinion. In: Wilbur Schramm (ed.), *Mass Communications*, 527–543. Urbana: University of Illinois Press.
Berger, Peter L. & Thomas Luckmann. 1966. *The Social Construction of Reality: A Treatise in the Sociology of Knowledge*. Garden City, NY: Anchor Books.
Berlo, David K. 1960. *The Process Of Communication*. New York: Holt, Rinehart, and Winston.
Bignell, Jonathan. 2000. *Postmodern Media Culture*. Edinburgh: Edinburgh University Press.
Boring, Edwin G. [1929]. 1957. *A History of Experimental Psychology*, 2nd edn. New York: Appleton-Century-Crofts Meredith Corporation.
Burke, Kenneth. 1966. *Language as Symbolic Action*. Berkeley, CA: University of California Press.
Cantril, Hadley & Gordon Allport. 1935. *The Psychology of Radio*. New York: Harper.
Carey, James W. 1989. Mass communication and cultural studies. In: *Communication as Culture*. Oxford: Routledge.
Carey, James W. 1983. The origins of the radical discourse on cultural studies in the United States. *Ferment in the Field: Journal of Communication* (Special Issue). 33 (3). 311–313.
Carey, James W. 1982. The mass media and critical theory: an American view. In: Michael Burgeon (ed.), *Communication Yearbook 6*, 18–33. New York: Sage.
Castells, Manuel. 2011. *Communication Power*. Oxford: Oxford University Press.
Castells, Manuel. 2008. The new public sphere: global civil society, communication networks, and global governance. *The ANNALS of the American Academy of Political and Social Science* 616. 78–93.

Castells, Manuel. 2000a. The network enterprise: the culture, insinuations and organizations of the informational economy. In: *The Rise of The Network Society*. 2nd edn. Oxford: Blackwell.

Castells, Manuel. 2000b. Toward a sociology of the network society. *Contemporary Sociology*, 29 (5). 693–699.

Castells, Manuel. 2000c. *End Of Millennium*. 2nd edn. Oxford: Blackwell Publishers.

Chaiken, Shelly. 1980. Heuristic versus systematic information processing and the use of source versus message cues in persuasion. *Journal of Personality and Social Psychology* 39 (5). 752–766.

Chang, Tsan-Kuo, Itai Himelboim & Dong Dong. 2009. Open global networks, closed international flows: world system and political economy of hyperlinks in cyberspace. *International Communication Gazette* 71. 137–159.

Cobley, Paul (ed.). 2010. Introduction. In: *The Routledge Companion to Semiotics*, 3–12. New York: Routledge.

Cobley, Paul (ed.). 2006. General Introduction. *Communication Theories, Volume 1*, 1–33. New York: Routledge.

Davison, W. P. 1983. The third-person effect in communication. *Public Opinion Quarterly* 47 (1). 1–15.

de Saussure, Ferdinand. 1959. *Course in General Linguistics*, Bally, Charles and Sechehave, Albert (eds.). New York: Philosophical Library.

Delia, Jesse G. 1987. Communication research: a history. In: Charles R. Berger and Steven H. Chaffee (eds.), *Handbook of Communication Science*, 20–98. Newbury Park, CA: Sage.

DeFleur, Melvin & Sandra Ball-Rokeach. 1989. Mass society and the magic bullet theory. In: *Theories of Mass Communication, 5th Edition*, 145–167. White Plains, NY: Longman.

Derrida, Jacques. 1982. Différance. In: *Margins of Philosophy*. Alan Bass (trans.), 1–27. Chicago: The University of Chicago Press.

Derrida, Jacques. [1974]. 1976. *Of Grammatology*. Spivak, Gayatri Chakravorty (trans.). Baltimore: the Johns Hopkins University Press.

De Sola Pool, Ithiel. 1963. The effect of communication on voting behavior. In: Wilbur Schramm (ed.), *The Science Of Human Communication*, 128–138. New York: Basic Books.

Eco, Umberto. 1986. *Travels in hyperreality*. Weaver, W. (trans.). New York: Harcourt Brace Jovanovich.

Ellul, Jacques. 1965. *Propaganda: The Formation of Men's Attitudes*. New York: Knopf.

Entman, Robert. 1993. Framing: toward clarification of a fractured paradigm. *Journal of Communication* 43 (4). 51–58.

Erskine, H. G. 1970. The polls: opinion of the news media. *Public Opinion Quarterly* 34 (4). 630–643.

Festinger, Leon. 1963. The theory of cognitive dissonance. In: Wilbur Schramm (ed.), *The science of human communication*, 17–27. New York: Basic Books.

Foucault, Michel. 1984. What is an author? In: Paul Rabinow (ed.), *The Foucault Reader*, 101–120. New York: Pantheon Books.

Foucault, Michel. 1970. *The Order of Things: An Archaeology of the Human Sciences*, 1st American edn. New York: Pantheon Books.

Garnham, Nicholas. 1983. Toward a theory of cultural materialism. *Ferment in the Field: Journal of Communication (Special Issue)* 33 (3). 314–329.

George, Alexander L. 1959. *Propaganda Analysis; A Study of Inferences Made From Nazi Propaganda in World War II*. Evanston, IL: Row, Peterson.

Gerbner, George, Larry Gross, Michael Morgan & Nancy Signorielli. 1986. Living with television: the dynamics of the cultivation process. In: Jennings Bryant and Doff Zillman (eds.), *Perspectives on Media Effects*, 17–40. Hillsdale, NJ: Lawrence Erlbaum Associates.

Giddens, Anthony. 1986. *Constitution of Society: Outline of The Theory of Structuration*. Berkley: University of California Press.

Gitlin, Todd. 1978. Media sociology: the dominant paradigm. *Theory and Society* 6 (2). 205–253.

Goffman, Erving. 1959. *The Presentation of Self in Everyday Life*. New York: Anchor.

Grossberg, Lawrence. 1979. Language and theorizing in the human sciences. *Studies in Symbolic Interaction* 2. 189–231.

Grunig, J. E. 1997. A situational theory of publics: conceptual history, recent challenges and new research. In: D. Moss, T. MacManus and D. Vercic (eds.), *Public Relations Research: An International Perspective*, 3–48. London: International Thomson Business Press.

Habermas, Jürgen. 1991. *The Structural Transformation of The Public Sphere: An Inquiry into a Category of Bourgeois Society*. Burger, Thomas (trans.) with Lawrence, Frederick (asst.). Cambridge, MA: The MIT Press.

Habermas, Jürgen. 1985. *Theory of communicative action* (two volumes). McCarthy, Thomas (trans.). Boston: Beacon Press.

Hall, Stuart. 1986. The problem of ideology – Marxism without guarantees. *Journal of Communication Inquiry* 10 (2). 28–44.

Hall, Stuart. 1982. The re-discovery of 'ideology': return of the repressed in media studies. In: M. Gurevitch (eds.), *Culture, Society and The Media*. London: Methuen.

Hardt, Hanno. 1979. *Social Theories of The Press: Early German and American Perspectives*. Beverly Hills: Sage.

Hayakawa, S. I. 1964. *Language in Thought and Action*, 2nd edn. Boston: Harcourt.

Heider, Fritz. 1958. *The Psychology of Interpersonal Relations*. New York: John Wiley and Sons, Inc.

Heider, Fritz. 1946. Attitudes and cognitive organization. *Journal of Psychology* 21. 107–112.

Heider, Fritz. 1944. Social perception and phenomenal causality. *Psychological Review* 51. 358–374.

Hovland, Carl I. 1959. Reconciling conflicting results from experimental and survey studies of attitude change. *American Psychologist* 14. 8–17.

Hovland, Carl I., I. L. Janis & H. H. Kelley. 1953. *Communication and Persuasion*. New Haven, CT: Yale University Press.

Hovland, C. I., Arthur Lumsdaine & Fred D. Sheffield. 1949. *Experiments On Mass Communication: Studies In Social Psychology In World War II, Volume 3*. New Haven: Yale University Press.

Hovland, C. I. & W. Weiss. 1951–1952. The influence of source credibility on communication effectiveness. *Public Opinion Quarterly* 15. 635–650.

Hurwitz, Donald. 1988. Market research and the study of the United States radio audience. *Communication* 10 (2). 223–241.

Jenkins, Henry. 2006. *Convergence Culture: Where Old and New Media Collide*. New York: New York University Press.

Katz, Elihu. 1987. Communications research since Lazarsfeld. *The Public Opinion Quarterly* 51 (Part 2: Supplement: 50th Anniversary Issue). .

Katz, Elihu. 1983. The return of the humanities and sociology. *Ferment in the Field: Journal of Communication* (Special Issue). 33 (3). 51–52.

Katz, Elihu. [1960]. 1972. The two-step flow of communication. In: Wilbur Schramm (ed.), *Mass Communications*, 346. Urbana: University of Illinois Press.

Katz, Elihu. 1959. Mass communication research and the study of culture. *Studies in Public Communication* 2. 1–6.

Katz, Elihu & Paul F. Lazarsfeld . 1955. *Personal Influence: The Part Played by People in the Flow of Mass Communication*. New York: Free Press.

Kent, Michael & Maureen Taylor. 2002. Toward a dialogic theory of public relations. *Public Relations Review* 28. 21–37.

Klapper, Joseph. 1960. *The Effects of Mass Communication*. Glencoe, IL: The Free Press.

Klein, Lawrence E. 2001. Enlightenment as conversation. In: Keith Michael Baker and Peter Hanns Reill (eds.). *What's Left of Enlightenment?: A Postmodern Question*. Stanford, CA: Stanford University Press.

Lacan, Jacques. 1988. *The Seminar of Jacques Lacan*. Miller, Jacques-Alain (ed.). New York: Norton.

Lasswell, Harold D. 1980. The future of world communication and propaganda. In: Harold D. Lasswell, Daniel Lerner and Hans Speier (eds.), *Propaganda and Communication in World History: Volume 2. Emergence of Public Opinion in the West*. Honolulu: University Press of Hawaii.

Lasswell, Harold D. 1948. The structure and function of communication in society. In: Lyman Bryson (ed.), *The Communication of Ideas*, 37–51. New York: Institute for Religious and Social Studies and Harper and Brothers.

Lasswell, H. D. 1941. *Democracy Through Public Opinion*. Manasha, Wisc: George Banta Publishing Company.

Lasswell, Harold D. 1927. *Propaganda Technique in The World War*. New York: Knopf.

Latour, Bruno. 1993. *We Have Never Been Modern*, Porter, Catherine (trans.). Cambridge, MA: Harvard University Press.

Law, John. 1999. After ANT: complexity, naming and topology. In: John Law and John Hassard (eds.), *Actor Network Theory and After*. Oxford: Blackwell Publishers/The Sociological Review.

Lazarsfeld, Paul F., Bernard Berelson & Hazel Gaudet. [1960]. 1972. Radio and the printed page as factors in political opinion and voting. In: Wilbur Schramm (ed.), *Mass Communications*, 513–526. Urbana: University of Illinois Press.

Lazarsfeld, Paul F., Bernard Berelson & Hazel Gaudet. 1944. /1948. /1968. *The People's Choice: How the Voter Makes Up His Mind in a Presidential Campaign*. New York: Columbia University Press.

Lazarsfeld, Paul F. & Herbert Menzel. 1963. Mass media and personal influence. In: Wilbur Schramm (ed.), *The Science of Human Communication*, 94–115. New York: Basic Books.

Lévi-Strauss, Claude. 1963. *Structural Anthropology*. Jacobson, Claire and Grundfrest Schoepf, Brooke (trans.). New York: Basic Books.

Lyotard, Jean-Francois. 1984. *The Postmodern Condition: A Report on Knowledge*, Bennington, Geoff and Massumi, Brian (trans.). Minneapolis: University of Minnesota Press.

McCombs, Maxwell & Salma I. Ghanem. 2001. The convergence of agenda setting and framing. In: Stephen Reece, Oscar H. Gandy, and August E. Grant (eds.), *Framing Public Life,* 67–81. Mahwah, New Jersey: Lawrence Erlbaum.

McCombs, Maxwell E. & Donald L. Shaw. 1972. The agenda-setting function of mass media. *The Public Opinion Quarterly* 36. 176–187.

McGuire, W. J. 1961. The effectiveness of supportive and refutational defenses in immunizing defenses. *Sociometry* 24. 184–197.

McLuhan, Marshall. 1964. *Understanding Media: The Extensions of Man*. New York: McGraw-Hill.

McLuhan, Marshall. 1962. *The Gutenberg Galaxy: The Making of Typographic Man*. Toronto: University of Toronto Press.

McNair, Brian. 2006. *Cultural Chaos: Journalism, News, and Power in a Globalised World*. London: Routledge.

Monge, Peter R. & Nashir Contractor. 2003. *Theories of Communication Networks*. Oxford: Oxford University Press.

Noelle-Neumann, Elisabeth. 1993. *The Spiral of Silence: Public Opinion–Our Social Skin*. Chicago: University of Chicago Press.

Nordenstreng, Kaarle. 2004. Ferment in the field: notes on the evolution of communication studies and its disciplinary nature. *Javnost–the Public* 11 (3). 5–18.

Oates, Whitney J. 1948. Classic theories of communication. In: Lyman Bryson (ed.), *The Communication of Ideas*, 27–36. New York: Institute for Religious and Social Studies and Harper and Brothers.

Osgood, Charles E. & Percy H. Tannenbaum. 1955. Attitude change and the principle of congruity. In: Wilbur Schramm (ed.), *The Process And Effects of Mass Communication*, 251–260. Urbana: University of Illinois Press.

Petty, R. E. & J. T. Cacioppo. 1981. *Attitudes and Persuasion: Classic and Contemporary Approaches*. Dubuque, IA: Wm. C. Brown.

Pfau, M. 1997. The inoculation model of resistance to influence. In: F. J. Boster and G. Barnett (eds.), *Progress in Communication Sciences, Volume 13*, 133–171. Norwood, NJ: Ablex.

Piaget, Jean. 1952. *The Origins of Intelligence in Children*, Cook, Margaret (trans.). New York: W. W. Norton and Company.

Rogers, Evertt M. 1994. *A History of Communication Study: A Biographical Approach*. New York: The Free Press.

Rogers, Everett M. [1962]. 1983. *Diffusion of innovations*. New York: Free Press.

Sapir, Edward. 1983. *Selected Writings of Edward Sapir in Language, Culture, and Personality*. Mandelbaum, David G. (ed.). Berkley: University of California Press.

Schramm, Wilbur. 1983. The unique perspective of communication: a retrospective view. *Ferment in the Field: Journal of Communication* (Special Issue). 33 (3). 6–17.

Schramm, Wilbur. 1963. Communication research in the United States. In: Wilbur Schramm (ed.), *The Science Of Human Communication*, 1–16. New York: Basic Books.

Schramm, Wilbur. 1957. *Responsibility in Mass Communication*. New York: Harper and Row.

Scott, John. 2000. *Social Network Analysis: a handbook*. New York: Sage.

Searle, John R. 1983. *Intentionality, an Essay in the Philosophy of Mind*. New York: Cambridge University Press.

Self, Charles C. 2009. Credibility. In: Don W. Stacks and Michael B. Salwen (eds.), *An Integrated Approach to Communication Theory and Research*, 2nd edn, 435–456. New York: Routledge.

Shannon, Claude E. & Warren Weaver. 1949. *A Mathematical Model of Communication*. Urbana, IL: University of Illinois Press.

Sherif, C. W., M. S. Sherif & R. E. Nebergall. 1965. *Attitude and Attitude Change*. Philadelphia: W.B. Saunders Company.

Shirky, Clay. 2008. *Here Comes Everybody: The Power of Organizing Without Organizations*. New York: The Penguin Press.

Siebert, Fred, Theodore Peterson & Wilbur Schramm. [1956]. 1963. *Four Theories of the Press: The Authoritarian, Libertarian, Social Responsibility and Soviet Communist Concepts of What the Press Should Be and Do*. Urbana, IL: University of Illinois Press.

Slack, Jennifer Daryl & Martin Allor. 1983. The political and epistemological constituents of critical communication research. *Ferment in the Field: Journal of Communication (Special Issue)* 33 (3). 208–218.

Smith, B. L. 1969. The mystifying intellectual history of Harold D. Lasswell. In Rogow, A. A. (ed.), *Politics, Personality, and Social Science in The Twentieth Century: Essays in Honor of Harold D. Lasswell*, 41–105. Chicago: University of Chicago Press.

Sundar, S. S. 2008. Self as source: agency and customization in interactive media. In: E. Konijn, S. Utz, M. Tanis and S. Barnes (eds.), *Mediated Interpersonal Communication*, 58–74. New York: Routledge.

Sundar, S. Shaym & C. Nass. 2001. Conceptualizing sources in online news. *Journal of Communication* 51 (1). 52–72.

Sunstein, Cass R. 2006. *Infotopia: How Many Minds Produce Knowledge*. Oxford, England: Oxford University Press.

Tichenor, P. J., G. A. Donohue & C. N. Olien. 1970. Mass media flow and differential growth in knowledge. *Public Opinion Quarterly* 34 (2). 159–170.

Tuchman, Gaye. 1978. News as constructed reality. In: *Making news*, 182–217. New York: The Free Press, 1978.

von Bertalanffy, Ludwig. 1974. *Perspectives on General System Theory*. Taschdjian, Edgar (ed.). New York: George Braziller.

Wiener, Norbert. 1950. *The Human Use of Human Beings*. Boston: The Riverside Press (Houghton Mifflin).

Wellman, B. 2001. Computer networks as social networks. *Science* 293. 2031–2034.

Westley, Bruce H. & Malcolm S., Jr. MacLean. 1957. A conceptual model for communications research, *Journalism Quarterly* 34 (1). 31–38.

White, Harrison C. 2008. *Identity and Control: How Social Formations Emerge*, 2nd edn. Princeton, NJ: Princeton University Press.

Winograd, Morley & Michael D. Hais. 2009. *Millennial Makeover: Myspace, Youtube, and the Future of American Politics*. New Brunswick, NJ: Rutgers University Press.

Wolfe, Cary. 2010. *What is Posthumanism?* Minneapolis: University of Minnesota Press.

Dale Hample
20 What

Abstract: This chapter is concerned with the message, and particularly with its content. The purpose of a message is to alter the audience in respect to its beliefs, attitudes, intentions, values, feelings, and/or behaviors. This is done by supplying content that creates, changes, or reinforces those things. A fundamental element of a message's content is its argument, and so the chapter focuses on how to analyze, reconstruct, and create arguments. Attention is also given to organization and style, especially as they connect to the message's arguments.

Keywords: Message, content, argumentation, enthymeme, metaphor, narrative, style, organization, delivery

In a standard summary of the conceptual topics in communication, we ask 'who says what to whom, in what channel, and with what effects?' This chapter concerns the first 'what,' that is, the message and its content.

Singling out 'what' is of course merely an intellectual move. In reality, the message is not sharply distinguishable from its source, its audience, its form, or its results. A person who enacts a message adds meaning to it from his or her identity, presence, and performative behaviors. Meanings vary from audience to audience: the same statement can be funny to one group and evidence that the source's character is deficient to another assembly. The channel also modifies the message's apparent meaning, as is evident if one compares two statements that a romantic relationship is over, one made via email and another conveyed with a scrawled note attached to a door with a knife. The same message can be enraging or satisfying depending on its moment and setting; those effects are thought to be descriptive of the message itself, as when we say that a message is persuasive, or offensive, or loving. In short, every message is motivated, situated, and heard. These brute facts can be held to be external to the message, and this is convenient for thinking about one facet of communication at a time. But that is merely an analytic handiness, and as we look inward to the message's content in this chapter we should remember that the message is also constituted outwardly, causing and being caused by its companion components: source, audience, form, setting, and consequences.

The classical canons of rhetoric are invention, organization, style, memory, and delivery (Kennedy 1962). The first three canons pertain most immediately to the planned message and so will be our preoccupations here, although we will mention delivery briefly. Invention refers to the development of content for the message, organization concerns how the content is ordered, and style has to do with its phrasing. This chapter is most concerned with the first canon but will comment on organization and style as well. Even though the canons were developed with public speeches in mind, they illuminate interpersonal, computer mediated, and mass mediated communication just as well.

1 Invention

Messages are intended and received as vehicles to create, reverse, modify, or reinforce meanings for the audience. This is done by content. Messages give or imply reasons for those changes in meaning, and this is why we recognize that arguments are central to the first canon (Hample 2009).

The meanings of messages have substantial effects on whether they are transformed from private thought to public event. A speaker will be spontaneously motivated by the wish to express a particular meaning, of course. When the message needs to survive various filters in order to appear in mass media, research indicates that editors register meanings as being consonant with editorial expectations or not, as matching the interests of elites or not, as connecting with ongoing media preoccupations or not, as being entertaining or not, and many other factors (Galtung and Ruge 1965; Harcup and O'Neill 2001; Venables 2005). All of these have mainly to do with meanings, conveyed verbally or nonverbally, so let us examine content in detail.

1.1 Enthymemes

Most real-world arguments are not fully developed as expressed, and they leave important elements unsaid (Aristotle 1984). In other words, messages are enthymematic (Bitzer 1959): some parts of the argument are conveyed by its source and others are supplied by the audience. The explicit argument 'Jones is smart, so you should vote for her' leaves the audience to contribute 'Anyone smart deserves my vote,' and is therefore an example of an enthymeme.

Even in the case of slogans whose arguments are superficially absent, we can see enthymemes asserting themselves. For instance, Nike's "Just do it" does not make any immediate or explicit reference to shoes. On reflection, however, we can see that an enthymeme is at work. The slogan means roughly "You can do whatever you want to do and should try to achieve any goal you choose; because we said that, you can see that this is what our company stands for; therefore you can be confident that we have made sure our shoes make it possible for you to accomplish any of your goals; so Nike shoes match your personality and aims, and you should buy them." Although this reconstruction is labored, we can see that it does imply a claim about Nike shoes: the company has just left the audience to supply all the questionable material.

Other messages are even less obviously argumentative than Nike's slogan. For instance, a first step in a political campaign is to achieve name recognition, and this is often accomplished by putting up signs and displaying the candidate's name. We should understand this as preliminary to the later messages in which the candidate's virtues and views are exhibited, in much the same way that a smile might set up a request for a favor. This is an example of how one element of a large-scale campaign only exhibits its argumentative role when the rest of the campaign is taken into account.

1.2 Analysis of message content

Quite a few analytic methods have been developed to elaborate, understand, and critique a message's argumentative content. The first of these was formal logic. This approach is not used by most argument critics today because logic's artificiality requires that real-world arguments must be translated into precise propositional form prior to analysis. Other methods better adapted to ordinary discourse have been developed. These include the Toulmin model, the acceptability-relevance-sufficiency standards in informal logic, and argument reconstruction.

1.2.1 The Toulmin model

Toulmin (1958) offered an alternative to formal logic, one that has become known as the Toulmin model (see also Chapter 9, Tindale). A distinctive feature of his treatment is that a message need not be transformed before analysis, although it does have to be understood, which is not an analytically neutral task. Toulmin distinguished six elements of an argument, which are omitted or called into play depending on the arguers' momentary understandings. Central is the claim (conclusion), which expresses the point of the argument. The claim (C) is directly supported by the data (D), or evidence. This must be an agreeable starting point, something that the message's recipient regards as secure. If it is not, the data portion of one argument must be established as the claim of an earlier one. Assuming that this has been done, the data give support to the claim. This relationship (the 'supporting') may be obvious in the moment and so will not require expression, but the data-claim connection is always mediated by what Toulmin called the warrant (W). A warrant expresses the reason that the data support the claim. Somehow it fulfills the function of assuring the recipient that if the data are accepted, the claim should be accepted as well. This D-W-C unit is the base part of the argument. For example: We need to get off this planet (C) because we will add another billion people in the next ten or 12 years (D), and one planet's finite resources cannot handle this population growth for very long (W).

The other three elements of the Toulmin model bear on the first three. Next is the backing (B), which gives support to the warrant. The warrant can be construed as a claim itself, and if the audience is reluctant to accept it, data-like material must be supplied to strengthen it. In our example, the backing might be: water and energy sources are becoming scarce (B). Also bearing on the warrant is the next element, reservations (or rebuttals). Given that the warrant is generally applicable, a reservation (R) expresses some condition in which a normally acceptable warrant must be set aside. For example, a reservation to the warrant above might be: unless we continue to make technological advances in agriculture, energy, and conservation that are so substantial that they outstrip population growth (R). The final part of the model is one of the most important: the qualifier. Qualifiers (Q) attach to the claim and are intended to reflect the strength of the argument as a whole. A very strong argument might support a qualifier such as 'almost certainly:' We almost certainly (Q) need to get off this planet (C). If the argument seems weaker, the qualifier should reflect that, and we might see qualifiers such as 'maybe,' 'probably not,' or 'if we can't think of anything else.' Some things really are uncertain, and an argument that clearly proves that can be a good one. This highlights the importance of proper qualification, not over- or under-claiming what one has proved.

1.2.2 Informal logic

Informal logic is a theoretical and pedagogical movement that reacted to students' view of formal logic as arid and unsatisfying, by developing ways of analyzing argument quality without resort to syllogisms (van Eemeren et al. 1996: chapter 6). Two of the founders of the movement, Ralph Johnson and Anthony Blair, developed an apparently simple way to evaluate arguments. They proposed three criteria: acceptability, relevance, and sufficiency (Govier 1999: chapter 7). These are applied to an argument's premises and their connection to the conclusion.

Acceptability means that the premise material must be unobjectionable on factual grounds. It does not refer to whether the argument recipient agrees with the material, however. This criterion, like the other two, is applied by the analyst, who is expected to research and think carefully about matters that might pass by unremarked in ordinary discourse. The point here is not to estimate whether the argument will be effective; rather the idea is to give an analytical evaluation that does not depend on who the actual arguers might have been.

Supposing the premises to be acceptable, the further questions are whether they are relevant to the conclusion and whether they are collectively sufficient to prove it. Relevance is not as simple an idea as in ordinary talk. Suppose someone says, "Smith is a bad professor because he's ugly." Our instinct is immediately to say that ugliness is irrelevant, but that has to be reasoned out. The analyst would need to define 'bad' and 'professor' in concert, establishing the criteria for badness in a professor. Then the criteria would have to be inspected to see if ugliness addresses any of them, either directly or by means of what it might imply. Only if this results in a null match can the analyst say the premise is irrelevant. In practice, relevance is often a matter of degree and so we might say that ugliness is at most weakly relevant.

Sufficiency, the third standard, refers to whether the premises taken together prove the point. Suppose one made a point by offering several examples. Each example might individually be insufficient, but together they might make a satisfactory case. Circumstantial evidence in a criminal case can have this nature: perhaps each bit of suggestive data can be explained away individually, but eventually the jury may have to decide between one conclusion (guilt) or dozens of independent conclusions (he looks like lots of people, anyone might buy a knife, many people wear size 12 shoes, and so forth). They might decide that many individually flawed proofs add up to one sufficient case. In orchestrated political actions, sometimes various spokespeople are given individual points to make; only when these are collected in comprehensive news accounts might the full argument be apparent and sufficient.

The standards of acceptability, relevance, and sufficiency all have to do with the argument as presented. Johnson (2000) proposed an additional criterion that is somewhat external. He said that arguments must also be evaluated on the dialectical tier. By this he meant that the analyst should consider what objections to the argument might be made, even if they weren't made in the actual moment of argument. If the arguers miss some point in their email exchange, or if the audience doesn't notice some questionable assumption in a televised appeal, the analyst is expected to do the noticing for them, and evaluate how the argument should work out if it were answered and defended as well as possible.

Arguments that have premises that are individually acceptable and relevant, that are collectively sufficient, and that survive exposure to the dialectical tier are good arguments. Argument quality is a matter of degree, and so nuanced judgments are expectable.

1.2.3 Argument reconstruction

Arguments in ordinary use work out of and create their own substantive contexts. Not everything that is meant or understood is said. The whole argument – not merely what is explicit – has to be reconstructed before the argument can be analyzed and evaluated (van Eemeren et al. 1993).

Arguments are composed of speech acts, and every speech act has various felicity conditions. For example, "shut the door" is a command, and one of the felicity conditions for a command is that the speaker must have the right to impel the hearer to do something. One could object to this command on the grounds that there is no door, thus working at the level of surface meanings. Perhaps more likely, however, would be a counter-argument such as "you're not the boss of me," which responds not to the surface meaning but to the underlying assumption of superiority. This latter reply is entirely legitimate because merely giving the command *committed* the speaker to the proposition that he or she was superior to the hearer, and that commitment is part of what is arguable.

Reconstruction of an argument adds commitments and assumptions to what is actually said, so that the whole argument and its implications are available for analysis and critique. Full reconstruction on the van Eemeren et al. (1993) plan is quite detailed, and proceeds from theoretical statements about what the stages of a critical dispute are, what speech acts are required, and what felicity conditions those speech acts have.

This chapter is too short to go into that much development, but there are several over-arching commitments that should be mentioned. Every argument is assumed to be a step toward a reasoned conclusion, and this involves certain conditions that need to be fulfilled. First-order conditions involve the idea that the arguer is proceeding constructively in a way that allows full exchange of reasons. For instance, arguers implicitly contract to answer objections, to allow the other party to counter-argue, to express themselves clearly, and so forth. Second-order conditions for proper arguing include being genuinely open to the force of reason (i.e., being willing to be persuaded away from one's original position) and being capable of good arguing (e.g., being able to recognize that one argument is better than another). Third-order conditions specify that both parties are unconstrained: that in practice they both have the same access to information, have the same rights to argue, and have the same access to the relevant channels of communication. In other words, all parties should have the same opportunity to create and respond to messages.

Reconstructing all of this results in defining the "disagreement space" for the argument. This refers to all the points that are potentially arguable. The claims explicitly made by the expressed argument are in the disagreement space, of course, but so are all of the assumptions those statements make, all of the commitments required by those speech acts, and the question of whether each of the first-, second-, or third-order conditions is being satisfied. A good argument is one that passes critical tests of all these kinds. A flawed argument will be open to serious criticism on one or more of these criteria.

The disagreement space of an argument turns out to be quite a bit more expansive than just the expressed content. Once the reconstruction has been done, analysts can apply many standards of judgment. The argument's elements can be examined in their internal context, as with the Toulmin model; statements and assumptions can be evaluated as to their acceptability, relevance, and sufficiency; the dialectical tier can be entered by considering pertinent content outside the immediate textual context; and assumptions, commitments, and higher-order conditions can be identified and evaluated. A message's content can be understood in considerable detail, either at the stage of producing a message or at the stage of receiving it.

1.3 Content and relational levels of meaning

Messages are more than content, however. Watzlawick et al. (1967) explain that every message has two levels of meaning, content and relationship. The content level is roughly what we have been examining so far: the statements, their literal meanings, their implications and assumptions. The relationship level of meaning has to do with projecting definitions of identity and relationship among the source and recipients of the message. Inescapably, every message conveys both sorts of meaning.

Suppose a televised public health campaign features an official who tells viewers that parents should get vaccines for their children. The content level of meaning has to do with children, parents, responsibility, vaccines, health, and so forth, and would be analyzed in the ways already mentioned. But such a message conveys a lot of relational meaning as well. First, consider the public health official's projected identity. He or she is claiming a position superior to the audience, because this is implied in the act of advising. The official might be introduced as "Dr. Smith" or as "Jim Smith," and these choices project different identities (professional or friendly) and aim at different relationships with viewers. Second, consider the identity the official is projecting onto the audience. One only advises people who need advice, and so the audience is being construed as a group of people who lack the information, intelligence, ability, or motivation to do the right thing on their own. Given the assumption of superiority implicit in advising, the audience is thereby being offered the identity of people who are subordinate and somewhat incapable. Finally, consider the definition being projected for the relationship between official and audience. It is asymmetrical, with the official dominating. This can be modified in some degree but the essential asymmetry is inevitable in advising.

Many messages and campaigns have a persuasive goal, and these relational meanings inhere to the act of persuading, which always aims to constrict a hearer's freedom and therefore affront his or her 'negative face' (Brown and Levinson 1987). A natural response to such an affront is stubbornness or reactance (Brehm 1966). Consequently an elaborate appeal or public campaign might concentrate on giving information rather than advice, at least in its early stages, to avoid these reactions.

Relational meanings are often conveyed nonverbally, and here we touch on the final canon, delivery. Facial expression, tone of voice, and gesture convey identities and relationships face to face. Camera angles, establishment of settings, background music, and the length of cuts are analogous techniques in video production. This nonverbal nature results in relational meanings being hard to pin down in a critiqueable way, and so they often are left merely to resonate or not.

1.4 Narratives

To this point, the chapter has assumed that messages convey content by means of arguments that take a linear form: a series of premises that lead to a conclusion. However, arguments can also be nonlinear (Bosanquet 1920). A common nonlinear form is the story. A narrative can make a point, and so can be regarded as an argument that makes or modifies meanings. Stories are a common way of summarizing litigations (Bennett and Feldman 1981). A contested criminal trial can be seen as a choice between two stories: in the prosecution's story, the defendant is a character encased in a plot that makes him or her guilty; in the defense's story, the crime occurred in a way that did not involve any illegal actions by the defendant. Entertainment-education is an approach to public health that uses televised entertainment programming to display recommended behaviors, attitudes, and beliefs. This media strategy has been used throughout the world on a variety of health topics (e.g., Brodie et al. 2001; Hether et al. 2008).

To see that a story is making an argument in the first place, one must be able to discern its conclusion and its reasons. In principle, therefore, a narrative can be analyzed in the ways already described. However, the problem of translation into analytically useful terms is daunting because the story's argumentative premises and conclusions might all be implicit. Watching a soap opera character go to the doctor models the argument rather than making it in propositional detail.

This problem of how to analyze a narrative's argumentative content has been addressed by Fisher (1987). He said that two standards can be used to evaluate a narrative. These are coherence and fidelity, and both join together to produce an estimate of whether a story is probable or not. Narrative coherence is internal to the story, and it refers to whether the story's elements hang together or not. Do characters act consistently from one part of the narrative to another? Narrative fidelity, in contrast, is external to the story. Here, the audience checks the story against their understanding of the world. Do people actually act that way? Is this what happens when that sort of act occurs? A story that has both coherence and fidelity results in a trusted mental model of whatever the story is about, and people will naturally draw inferences from their models. These two standards can be used to generate useful judgments of the narrative as a whole.

1.5 Conclusions about invention

This section, the largest of the chapter, has concentrated on the first canon of rhetoric, the task of finding and creating meaning for a message. Most often, a message's content will be its primary reason for existing, although sometimes a message may be created in order to define or redefine an identity or relationship. Content and argument are quite closely connected, and so various ways of understanding an argument have been reviewed: Toulmin's approach, informal logic, and reconstruction. Whether linear or narrative in form, a message's content can be closely examined and assessed.

2 Organization

The second canon of rhetoric is organization, or arrangement. Given a collection of content that someone wants to convey, it must be put in some order. Successful message forms must look toward a match with the patterns that already exist in their audiences.

Kenneth Burke (see Heath 1979) wrote extensively on form for many years. Form is important, he said, for two reasons: it reflects people's schematic understandings and it emerges out of language's own structure. The first point explains how a message can resonate or not: if it orders things in a familiar way, it will be easily received. The second point is related to the first, in that people know language and therefore anticipate, for instance, where a sentence or slogan or novel should end, given how it started. A message can have any internal order, even a random one, but a good arrangement will match audience psychology and linguistic practice. Sometimes disordering can be used for effect, as when a joke jolts the hearer into an unexpected realization.

Only a few organizational matters have been well researched. One of these is ordering arguments by strength. Classical writers sometimes recommended that a rhetor's strongest argument be put first in a sequence of arguments, and other authorities said the strongest argument should be last. Modern research on primacy and recency effects has also taken up this question, but with no more conclusive an answer than was available in the Roman Empire (see O'Keefe 2002). The most secure recommendations are that one's best argument should be clearly featured, probably by putting it first or last, and that one's weakest arguments should be buried in the middle of a message or campaign (assuming that the weak arguments need to be made at all, which will happen, for example, if an opponent is pressing an issue).

More decisive work has examined various series of messages in the context of persuasion (see O'Keefe 2002; Stiff and Mongeau 2003). Among the sequences for which there is good evidence of effectiveness are three. 'Door in the face' involves first making an outrageously large request, which is normally rejected. This is followed by making a more modest request, which is accepted at higher levels than if it were made by itself. A companion sequence is 'foot in the door.' Here, the persuader begins by making a minor request that is accepted, and then follows by making a larger request. As before, the second appeal is more successful than if it is made alone. The 'low-ball' technique involves obtaining agreement at one level of cost, and then raising the price. This works as well, although it has an obvious exposure to ethical objections and long-term relationship problems. Other persuasive sequences have been studied less thoroughly, but these three are enough to emphasize that effect depends in part on context. Every appeal has a place in an order, and message producers should attend to their orderings. The ordering can be entirely controlled by one agency, or it may be a joint production of several parties addressing the same set of issues, possibly at cross purposes.

A final organizational matter has to do with the positioning of one's point within a message. In the West, the usual form involves placing one's point early in the appeal. In Asia, the point is often withheld until the end, and possibly abandoned without expression if the interlocutor does not display uptake. Young (1982) analyzed conversations between Chinese and Western businessmen and found confusion on the part of Westerners (whose conversational partners seemed to be talking pointlessly) and discomfort on the part of Chinese businessmen (whose partners seemed unreasonably aggressive).

Young's study returns us to where we began, to the necessity of knowing what forms are expected and natural. That there might be cultural differences is not surprising since various languages have different forms and politeness enactment norms differ throughout the world. Organization is consequential, whether we are examining sequences of messages or considering the sequence of elements within a single message. The effectiveness – and thus the meanings – of messages are affected by their contextual place and internal organization.

3 Style

Style, too, affects meaning. A common misunderstanding holds that there is some sort of base way of expressing things, and figurative language can just be pasted on for the purpose of embellishment. The implication is that rhetorical figures do not really alter the meaning of the real message; they are just flourishes that show off some element of the source's identity or exploit the hearers' feelings. This is wrong.

According to Burke, the metaphor is one of the core figures, and quite a few other sorts of figurative expression are versions of it. Metaphors are argumentative. To see this, consider Perelman and Olbrechts-Tyteca's (1969) explanation of the relationship between metaphor and analogy (the latter being widely understood as a sort of argument) (see also Chapter 9, Tindale). An analogy orders four terms and equates two ratios. For instance, "As dessert is to a full meal, so is a child to a marriage." The analogy is arguing that children are a treat, one that fulfills and completes a family. A metaphor is a "condensed analogy" (Perelman and Olbrechts-Tyteca 1969: 399). The metaphor here would be "children are a family's dessert." A real claim is being made in that expression, and a reason is being suggested. This metaphor is not a meaningless embellishment of something else;

it can stand on its own as an argument. Fahnestock (1999) explored the argumentative role of rhetorical figures in scientific discourse, a place where one might suppose the case would be hard to make. Her careful analysis of dozens of distinguishable figures showed that they do, in fact, have argumentative functions.

How far from unembellished propositional language can an arguer go without forfeiting any claim to the pursuit of rationality? The answer is that a certain amount of 'strategic maneuvering' is legitimate, so long as it does not actually stray into the domain of fallacy (van Eemeren 2010). Sources are entitled to select only certain material to argue about, they are entitled to present their material in a way that is pleasing to hearers, and – this is the immediate point – they are entitled to use presentational devices in strategic ways. The work of van Eemeren and his colleagues goes into detail about what particular maneuvers are legitimate and which are fallacious, but for our present purposes it is enough to see that stylistic imagination can forward good arguments, and not merely disguise bad ones.

Figuration should not be at the price of clarity. O'Keefe (2002) has completed several meta-analyses that tested how much of an enthymeme can be unexpressed. He compared studies in which conclusions were stated explicitly with those that left the conclusion implicit, studies that made supporting evidence explicit with those that did not, and studies that gave explicit behavioral recommendations with those that merely implied them. In all three cases, he reports that the clearer messages – those with the explicit elements – are more effective. Unmistakable expression gives better control of the message's meaning. Rhetorical figures need not interfere with clarity, however, and can even make points stand out more starkly.

Figurative expression is flourish, but not merely so. Remarkable presentation can affect listeners' impressions of a speaker, can make certain thoughts stand out in the moment, can move an audience emotionally, can enhance listeners' motivation, and can make ideas memorable. But all the while these things are happening, arguments are being made and meanings shaped in ways that would have occurred differently with different expression. Nor must figures be merely linguistic: in various media, parables can be acted out, symbols can be personified, and similes can be performed (e.g., Littlefield 1964; Wilson 2007).

4 Conclusions

This chapter has been about the message, considered mostly in terms of the first three canons of rhetoric – invention, arrangement, and expression. These are no more independent of one another than a message is really independent of its source, or its audience, or its channel. All the elements of communication come together to create, change, or reinforce meaning. Since meaning management is the province of argumentation, it has been convenient to use arguments as the touchstone in this discussion. Arguments harness prior meanings to make new ones. The strength and legitimacy of arguments are well understood, from several different viewpoints.

Whether one is considering a message (or series of messages) from the stance of designing one, or analyzing one, or receiving one, the central preoccupation should be meanings. Messages should, with intention and intelligence, shape recipients' meanings by means of good arguments founded on secure grounds.

Further reading

Greene, John. O. (ed.). 1997. *Message production: Advances in communication theory*. Mahwah, NJ: Lawrence Erlbaum Associates.

Howell, Wilbur Samuel. 1971. *Eighteenth-century British logic and rhetoric*. Princeton, NJ: Princeton University Press.

Kaid, Lynda Lee (ed.). 2004. *Handbook of political communication research*. Mahwah, NJ: Lawrence Erlbaum.

Wasko, Janet, Graham Murdock & Helena Sousa (eds.). 2011. *The handbook of political economy of communications*. Malden and Oxford: Wiley Blackwell.

Wilkins, Lee & Clifford G. Chrisians (eds.). 2009. *The handbook of mass media ethics*. New York: Taylor & Francis.

References

Aristotle. 1984. *Rhetoric*. Roberts, W. R. (trans.). In: J. Barnes (ed.), *The complete works of Aristotle*, 2 vols. Princeton, NJ: Princeton University Press.

Bennett, W. Lance & Martha S. Feldman. 1981. *Reconstructing reality in the courtroom: Justice and judgment in American culture*. New Brunswick NJ: Rutgers University Press.

Benoit, William L., Dale Hample & Pamela. J. Benoit (eds.). 1992. *Readings in argumentation*. Berlin: Foris Publications.

Bitzer, Lloyd. F. 1959. Aristotle's enthymeme revisited. *Quarterly Journal of Speech* 45. 399–408.

Bosanquet, Bernard. 1920. *Implication and linear inference*. London: Macmillan.

Brehm, Jack W. 1966. *A theory of psychological reactance*. New York: Academic Press.

Brodie, Mollyann, Ursula Foehr, Vicky Rideout, Neal Baer, Carolyn Miller, Rebecca Fluornoy & Drew Altman. 2001. Communicating health information through the entertainment media. *Health Affairs* 20. 192–199.

Brown, Penelope & Stephen C. Levinson. 1987. *Politeness: Some universals in language usage*. Cambridge, UK: Cambridge University Press.

Burke, Kenneth. [1945]. 1969. *A grammar of motives*. Berkeley CA: University of California Press.

Burke, Kenneth. [1966]. 1968. *Language as symbolic action*. Berkeley CA: University of California Press.

Burke, Kenneth. 1969. *A rhetoric of motives*. Berkely CA: University of California Press. [1950].

Fahnestock, Jeanne. 1999. *Rhetorical figures in science*. Oxford: Oxford University Press.

Fisher, Walter R. 1987. *Human communication as narration: Toward a philosophy of reason, value, and action*. Columbia, SC: University of South Carolina Press.

Galtung, Johan & Mari Holmboe Ruge. 1965. The structure of foreign news. *Journal of Peace Research* 2. 64–91.

Govier, Trudy. 1999. *The philosophy of argument*. Newport News VA: Vale Press.

Hample, Dale. 2005. *Arguing: Exchanging reasons face to face*. Mahwah, NJ: Erlbaum.

Hample, Dale. 2009. Argument: Its origin, function, and structure. In: D. S. Gouran (ed.), *The functions of argument and social context*, 1–10. Alta, UT: National Communication Association.

Harcup, Tony & Deirdre O'Neill. 2001. What is news? Galtung and Ruge revisited. *Journalism Studies* 2. 261–280.

Heath, Robert L. 1979. Kenneth Burke on form. *Quarterly Journal of Speech* 65. 392–404.

Hether, Heather J., Grace C. Huang, Vicki Beck, Sheila T. Murphy & Thomas W. Valente. 2008. Entertainment-education in a media-saturated environment: Examining the impact of single and multiple exposures to breast cancer storylines on two popular medical dramas. *Journal of Health Communication* 13. 808–823.

Johnson, Ralph H. 2000. *Manifest rationality*. Mahwah NJ: Erlbaum.

Kennedy, George. 1963. *The art of persuasion in Greece*. Princeton NJ: Princeton University Press.

Kennedy, George. 1962. *The art of rhetoric in the Roman world 300 B.C. – 300 A.D.* Princeton NJ: Princeton University Press.

Littlefield, Henry M. 1964. The Wizard of Oz: Parable on populism. *American Quarterly* 16. 47–58.

O'Keefe, Daniel J. 2002. *Persuasion: Theory and research*, 2nd edn. Thousand Oaks CA: Sage.

Perelman, Chaim & Lucy Olbrechts-Tyteca. 1969. *The new rhetoric: A treatise on argumentation*. Wilkinson, J. and Weaver, P. (trans.). Notre Dame, IN: University of Notre Dame Press.

Stiff, James B. & Paul A. Mongeau. 2003. *Persuasive communication*, 2nd edn. New York: Guilford Press.

Toulmin, Stephen. 1958. *The uses of argument*. Cambridge: Cambridge University Press.

van Eemeren, Frans H. 2010. *Strategic maneuvering in argumentative discourse*. Amsterdam: John Benjamins.

van Eemeren, Frans H., Rob Grootendorst, Sally Jackson & Scott Jacobs. 1993. *Reconstructing argumentative discourse*. Tuscaloosa AL: University of Alabama Press.

van Eemeren, Frans H., Rob Grootendorst & Francisca Snoeck Henkemans. 1996. *Fundamentals of argumentation theory: A handbook of historical backgrounds and contemporary developments*. Mahwah NJ: Erlbaum.

Venables, John. 2005. *Making headlines: News values and risk signals in journalism*. Huntingdon UK: Elm Publications.

Watzlawick, Paul, Janet H. Beavin & Don D. Jackson. 1967. *Pragmatics of human communication*. New York: Norton.

Wilson, Dominique. 2007. Christianity in Narnia. *Sydney Studies in Religion* 6. 173–187.

Young, Linda Wai Ling. 1982. Inscrutability revisited. In: John J. Gumperz (ed.), *Language and social identity*, 72–84. Cambridge: Cambridge University Press.

Pamela J. Shoemaker, Jaime Riccio and Philip R. Johnson
21 Whom

Abstract: There are many audiences, but which did Lasswell have in mind in whom? We conclude that, over time, there is not a 'newer' or 'improved' understanding of the audience. Researchers rarely acknowledge the audience or define it. There is no one audience, but rather many audiences who form and reform for big and small reasons. As audience members create content at the same time as journalists and producers, the entire information world is changed. What audiences will be like 20 years from now – or even whether anyone uses the term audience – is not known, but as theorists and researchers we must give more attention to the recipients of messages.

Keywords: Lasswell, audience, receivers, creators, individuals, active audience, hyperactive audience, messages, content, media reality

1 Introduction

In Lasswell's (1948) definition of communication, whom is perhaps the most important pronoun (apologies to who) in all of the discipline, because whom refers to the receiver of the message (Shannon 1948). There are different types of receivers; for example, receivers of mass communication messages are called audiences, whereas in a conversation people are alternately sender and receiver. In either case, whom is defined as the people who receive the output of communicators and as a result may learn, change their opinions, or behave in various ways. Although the audience is an entity, composed of individuals, it should also be studied as a theoretical construct that is carefully conceptualized. External forces such as social and individual factors act on receivers of messages, reflecting Lasswell's use of the preposition: to whom.

In this chapter, we take *whom* from the Reformation to Twitter, a varied discourse on a largely hidden construct. We have been surprised that little scholarship has addressed *whom* by any name at all. Scholars who study *producers and their content*, the *effects of content*, and *exposure to content* could be more successful if they defined the audience in more detail. *Audience* is usually treated as a primitive construct around which scholars study, but rarely mention by name. In communication scholarship, receivers are simultaneously crucial and invisible in studies of media *effects*. Studies test hypotheses that show the audience has been affected by exposure to communication messages, but the audience is rarely conceptualized. Instead such studies operationalize characteristics of the audience, such as controlling for gender or ethnicity. Statistically controlling for characteristics of receivers may be useful in data analysis, but lack information that will enhance interpretation of statistical results. Explaining why media exposure influences its effects on receivers would be greatly aided by theoretically defining *whom*, whether individual, publics, audiences, or consumers.

Exceptions include Leo Bogart's 1989 book *Press and the Public*, in which he defines the audience as "anyone who ever looks at a newspaper" (75). A fuller definition is offered by James Ettema and Charles Whitney in their 1994 edited volume *Audiencemaking*. They write that "receivers are constituted – or, perhaps, reconstituted – not merely as audiences but as *institutionally effective audiences* that have social meaning and/or economic value within the system" (Ettema and Whitney 1994: 5). They conceptualize three types of audiences: Measured audiences are created by data collected by the media research in order to sell to advertisers. Specialized or segmented audiences either shape media content or are themselves shaped by it. Hypothesized audiences are protected by media regulators. These all "exist *as* relationships within the media institution" (6).

2 *Whom* as the Passive Audience

Robert Snyder (1994) has proposed that Vaudeville performances created the first mass audience in the United States around 1900. To appeal to people's common interests, Vaudeville programming became less controversial and more homogeneous. Snyder concluded that Vaudeville made individuals into "a mass audience" (228).

The construct *audience* is often thought of as a manifestation of the nexus between the development of capitalism and the growth of the mass media. In the United States the mass audience did not exist until factories were built and towns grew around them; previously rural workers became city dwellers, and the mass media took up the job of providing them with information about their new environments.

2.1 Propaganda

During the twentieth century's two World Wars, the warring powers used propaganda as a weapon. Lasswell (1937: 521–522) defined propaganda broadly, as the "manipulation of representations" in order to influence 'human action.' The audience was considered passive, with few defenses against manipulative messages.

During both World War I and II, propaganda leaflets were dropped by air on both military and civilian populations. Although billions of propaganda leaflets were dropped by air, there is only anecdotal evidence about its effectiveness (Lowery and DeFleur 1988: 188–189).

In 1962 Jacques Ellul (1965: xiii; French edition 1962) defined propaganda as also involving routine

> public and human relations:... These activities are propaganda because they seek to adapt the individual to a society, to a living standard, to an activity. They serve to make him conform, which is the aim of all propaganda.

For Ellul, individuals could be influenced by the whole, but propaganda was effective only when individual opinions joined into an ideologically cohesive collective. No matter how large, a group of disconnected individuals was not to be considered an audience.

2.2 Media reality, social reality

In 1938 Orson Welles surprised his US radio audience with a realistic drama about Martians invading Earth, and the aftermath suggested mass hysteria on part of the "common man" (Cantril 1940; in Schramm and Roberts 1971: 579). An analysis by Hadley Cantril revealed that of the six million people who listened to the show, one million reported being frightened by it. Cantril concluded that those scared lacked the ability to critically analyze what they heard (589–593). What was originally thought to be the result of "shock and terror" (580) on the part of the mass audience was explained by audience members' individual characteristics. The radio audience may have passively received the message at first, but many actively tried to verify the information afterward. Cantril was one of the earliest social scientists to verify the importance of audience members' individual characteristics in moderating the effects of exposure to one strong mass media message.

Long-term exposure to the mass media was called the 'narcotizing dysfunction' by Paul Lazarsfeld and Robert Merton (1948). They proposed that people were narcotized when they spent more time consuming media than taking social action. These passive individuals congratulated themselves on being knowledgeable, but they had substituted knowing for doing.

Another approach to audiences' responding to television content was proposed by George Gerbner. Cultivation theory (Gerbner 1969) conceived of the audience as passive consumers of shows, such as dramas, situation comedies, and cartoons. The metaphor of cultivation suggests that the audience passively consumed televised images, although there were some differences explained by demographic variables (Gerbner and Gross 1976; Signorelli and Gerbner 1988).

Also looking at media effects over time, the knowledge gap hypothesis suggests that individuals in a social system learn as a function of time passing (Tichenor et al. 1970). Although individuals' knowledge was measured, knowledge was aggregated within the social system. The use of time as the independent variable emphasized the social system. The theory was less about how individuals learned and more about how information diffused through a social system.

3 *Whom* as the Active Audience

Audience is a modern term. In the Reformation (1500–1550), a collective of non-elites was known as *the people*, a group of ignorant individuals who threatened political institutions (Martín-Barbero 1993). In the Enlightenment (1700–1800), Rousseau described the people as "the very opposite of 'reason'" (cited in Martín-Barbero 1993: 7). Romanticism (1760–1850) recognized the revolutionary power of individuals, in that common people could form a "social collectivity" that could be powerful if a leader stepped forward (Martín-Barbero 1993: 9).

Masses became a popular term in the nineteenth century. Aristocrats disliked the great unwashed, but disdain was turned into fear of the mob by the 1848 French Revolution (Martín-Barbero 1993). Scholars concluded that although the crowd/public is comprised of individuals, they are less important than the actions of the collectives. In 1895 Gustave Le Bon alternately used the terms the *mob* and the *crowd*. In the crowd, diverse individuals were "given a collective soul" (Martín-Barbero 1993: 27). In 1901, Gabriel Tarde emphasized the role of communication and the press in the actions of the crowd. Tarde reconceptualized the masses from an unruly collective into *the public*.

The early part of the twentieth century brought war (World War I), revolution (in Russia), and the growth of fascism in Europe. During this time, *the public* required redefining. The growth of Marxism led to the replacement of the term *people* with the *proletariat* (Martín-Barbero 1993: 14), as a collective of individuals who would change the basic structure of society.

By 1927, John Dewey argued that individual opinions were less important than the construct public – a shared intelligence that rose as a result of technology (the telegraph) and the news media (Carey 1991: 37). A public was created whenever individuals talked about things they needed or wanted. A public could not be maintained without interactions among individuals.

3.1 The public has opinions

Who was the 'public' in *public opinion*? From the seventeenth and eighteenth centuries, the term had the connotation of "collective judgments outside the sphere of government that affect political decision making" (Price 1992: 8). In the early twentieth century some scholars defined the public as a social entity, consistent with fear of crowds and other mass audiences. In contrast, Blumer (1946) argued that a public existed when a group of people were divided over an issue and discussed (as cited in Price 1992).

Before the United States entered the Second World War, American social scientists wanted to know if political propaganda could influence the outcome of presidential elections. In 1932, George Gallup conducted a poll to assess public support for his mother-in-law's candidacy to be Secretary of State in Iowa, and in 1936 he and other pollsters successfully predicted the winner of the election by adopting advances in sampling and survey research methodology. Although Gallup's business was called *public opinion* polling, the opinions he sold were not characteristics of the public-as-collective, but rather the aggregate of individual opinions.

In their 1944 book *The People's Choice*, Paul Lazarsfeld, Bernard Berelson, and Hazel Gaudet specified their goal – "a large-scale experiment in political propaganda and public opinion" (Lazarsfeld et al. 1944: 1). They decided to study how the area's political propaganda would affect people's vote intentions in the 1940 election in Erie County, Ohio. But they found that "campaign propaganda ... [produced] ... no overt effect on vote behavior at all" that the media, at most, reinforced people's prior decisions (87). The mass audience was fragmented into "politically homogeneous" social groups (Lazarsfeld et al. 1944: 148), and opinion leaders from these groups were active in forming political attitudes.

Lazarsfeld, Berelson and Gaudet suggested that audiences might protect themselves from propagandist messages. Just how the audience might actively defend against political propaganda, however, was uncertain until Katz and Lazarsfeld reanalyzed the 1940 election data. In their 1955 book *Personal Influence* they concluded that voters actively guarded themselves against political propaganda and that the media's main effect was to reinforce individuals' original voting intentions. This 'personal influence' suggested the various interpersonal contexts that resulted in different effects being had on different people. Lazarsfeld et al.'s 1954 book *Voting* described their 1948 study in Elmira, New York, and reinforced the idea that people used their "perceptual opportunities as a defense or protection against the complexities, contradictions, and problems of the campaign" (230). Those who were cross-pressured had to somehow reduce the stress that the campaign created. "If the voter finds himself holding opinions championed by opposing parties.... He [sic] can perceptually select, out of the somewhat ambiguous propaganda of the campaign, those political cues which remove the problem by defining it away" (231).

This is consistent with Leon Festinger's (1957) interpersonal theory of cognitive dissonance. Festinger argued that people would not only selectively expose themselves to information, but also would selectively perceive and retain only desired or congruent information. Lazarsfeld and colleagues' findings had consequences for media 'effects' research, especially on the field's first doctorates, graduated in the 1950s and 1960s. They learned that the media reinforced pre-existing attitudes and behaviors, making individual members of the audience much more active than anyone had thought. So scholars turned their attention to studying the media audience (McQuail 1991).

3.2 The public as a group of individuals

In their classic study of a college football game, Albert Hastorf and Hadley Cantril (1954) concluded that "there is no such 'thing' as a 'game' existing 'out there' in its own right which people merely 'observe'" (1954: 132–133). In other words, people are not simply observers, but actively engage with their surroundings and create meanings from them – often different meanings. Constructivists such as Jean Piaget (1971) and Lev Vygotsky (1978) believed, as in the case of a football game, that reality was socially constructed by members of society, in part with the help of the media. Much as in George H. Mead's (1934) symbolic interactionist approach to interpersonal communication, people create their own meanings from messages, and their motivation to attend to different messages is based on the socially determined meanings they assign a message through interactions with others.

By mid-century, several such approaches made individual audience members and the construct motivation important in studying people's use of the media, and 'effects' research of the mass audience was mostly left behind. In 1964, Raymond Bauer interpreted communication to be transactional, an exchange in which "each gives in order to get" (1964; from Schramm and Roberts 1972: 345). Although people chose from among media messages, the messages had been created to attract the audience. Katz et al. (1974) echoed Bauer's transactional approach, in which individuals evaluated the media and actively selected content that most pleased them (McQuail 1991). In 1991, Peter Golding and Graham Murdock wrote about this transaction and about audiences as commodities – the mass media "exchange… audiences for advertising revenue" (Golding and Murdock 1991: 20). The cultural studies perspective, however, maintained that audiences were active enough to make their own meaning from media content, what Stuart Hall (1980) called reverse decoding.

Although not strictly audience-based, Albert Bandura's (1962) work in cognitive psychology became crucial to the development of theories based more on cognition than motivations. Bandura asserted that human beings are cognitive entities who see, think, and learn by watching television or films (Bandura 1962). This perspective emphasized that individual differences between people were important, opening the door for more research on media effects. But the microscopic audience he studied was a bunch of idiosyncratic individuals who were more important separately than together.

Bernard Cohen (1963) also gave hope to those interested in studying individuals' cognitive influence on media effects by stating that the mass media could more easily teach people what to think about rather than to shape their opinions. Maxwell McCombs and Donald Shaw (1972) redefined this idea in their agenda setting theory, bringing cognitive theory back into mass media research. They showed that the prominence with which a newspaper covered topics was positively related to how important people in the community thought the topics were. Measurement was at the individual level, but the theory had ramifications for the audience as a whole. As in many studies of public opinion, the aggregation of individual opinions was interpreted as a measure of the collective – the public. These psychological approaches to public opinion favored individuals' concerns and not the concerns of society.

3.3 The audience as consumers

This idea developed in the middle of the twentieth century, when the mass audience became central to the economic role of society. *Individuals* became important as *buyers* of consumer products and services.

Originally, however, consumer research conceived of the individual consumer as passive – a person whose attitudes and 'purchase' decisions could be manipulated by advertisers and public relations. Hovland, Lumsdaine, and Sheffield took this approach in 1949 during their study of the effects of the *Why We Fight* films on World War II soldiers. They were largely a passive media audience who were to be persuaded rather than conceived as actively participating (Roberts 1954: 2–4).

In 1948 Bernard Berelson wrote that producers and consumers saw each other as engaging in a more active, two-part process: "The audience selects the communications which it finds most congenial, and the producers select people with 'the right viewpoint' to prepare communications for other people with 'the right viewpoint'" (cited in Schramm 1960: 530). He asserted that audience members were more actively involved in the communication process than originally anticipated. So, have the mass media really influenced the audience? Berelson answered: "Some kinds of *communication* on some kinds of *issues*, brought to the attention of some kinds of *people* under some kinds of *conditions*, have some kinds of *effects*" (Schramm 1960: 531).

The work of Herbert Kelman expounded upon Berelson's findings and laid a path for future studies into an active audience, showing that internalization of a message and attitude change could occur when it was congruent with audience members' pre-existing values (Kelman 1958: 55). The role of attention was more important than the individual's backgrounds and experiences (Hovland and Weiss 1951; Kelman and Hovland 1953; Hovland 1957). By the end of the 1960s, the study of attitude change had shifted more toward audience members' cognitive behaviors rather than the abilities of message sources and senders (Greenwald 1968).

4 *Whom* as the Hyperactive Audience

Historically, media theory has been saturated with discussions of the content and effects of television, radio and the print media. It has focused on either a passive, impressionable audience (Lasswell 1948; Gerbner 1969; McCombs and Shaw 1972), a reactive, mass audience (Cantril 1940; Lazarsfeld 1948) or individuals with specific reasons for media use (Festinger 1957; Katz, Blumler and Gurevitch 1974). The advent of digital media, however, allowed *whom* to enter the sphere of media creators – as not only co-determinants of media outcomes, but themselves as message creators and influencers.

The new *hyperactive* audience – is comprised of people who read, view, and listen, as well as post, tweet, and comment. They make personal connections that tie individuals into groups (Yus 2011). Individuals shape their online identities so that they will appeal to social groups.

4.1 Digital media and interpersonal theory

New digital technologies have provided, for the first time, a true intersection of mass and interpersonal communication. Social media have allowed the simultaneous existence of a mass audience and an individual collective. As discussed previously, interpersonal approaches belonging to scholars such as Elihu Katz, Paul Lazarfeld and Leon Festinger have been utilized in earlier studies of an active audience, but a *hyperactive* audience involves a greater degree of individual-level interactions.

In the Lasswellian model, the 'effect' is seen as the destination, rather than the process of interactions leading to a final conclusion. Kenneth Burke included the idea of 'scene' in Lasswell's model, bringing the importance of context, including interpersonal interactions and cultural influences, to the forefront of communication theory (Foss et al. 1991). This context becomes increasingly important in the world of digital media, where technological advances blur traditional boundaries between mass and interpersonal communication. For digital and social media, *whom* may differ greatly if the receivers are in the form of a mass audience or face-to-face interaction.

Homans's (1958) theory of social exchange argues that the major force in interpersonal relationships is the satisfaction of both people's self interest. This can be applied to the world of digital media, wherein this self-interest influences not only how media is selected and received, but also leads to greater investment in the types of information available – sometimes resulting in the creation of one's own messages (a level of *hyper*activity in the form of viral videos, blog posts or tweets). All of this is based on a perceived level of rewards and costs.

The norms and mores of a digital setting are different from those in personal interactions of the real world, and also differ from the traditional mass communication spectrum on which print, television, radio and film operate. The growth of control and convenience in online communication necessitates a rethinking of the standards of interaction. Because individuals rely on previous experiences to determine which set of rules to apply to a communication setting (Pearce and Cronen 1980), scholars must account for the lack of previous experiences to apply to the hyperactive audience of social media; the rules are constantly being created and recreated.

4.2 The many roles of the hyperactive

The hyperactives are not exclusively young people, but most young people are active in the digital world. They email online articles to friends while reading a paper newspaper. They listen to satellite radio and watch movies on their laptops or tablets. They tweet about broken washing machines and get quick service from the company. They create new selves on Facebook and post videos to YouTube that could reach millions of people. Smart phones are now powerful computers allowing people to read online books while waiting in line, to schedule appointments, to keep in touch with grandparents, and to enjoy surfing from one internet site to another.

People send and receive, encode and decode. They tap out text messages on their phones' tiny screens. They read the *New York Times*, the *Huffington Post* and their favorite blog while listening to music. They watch a video on one device, while talking or texting on another, and browsing the internet on a third. They comment on articles they like and dislike and send links to other people. They watch a missed episode of a television program while using their tablets' documents and ebooks to study for an exam. Their mobile phones are nearby at all times.

The hyperactive form a multitude of audiences, from huge to miniscule. Individuals form both small and large audiences that, like oil in water, can change configuration rapidly. Digital audiences are fluid, having no pre-determined form and changing at the slightest nudge.

Their dual role as media users and content creators gives audience members the option of changing or redirecting media content to fit their needs. Hyperactive audience members are simultaneously the producers of information who "contribute to the collectivity" of the internet and the cognitive acrobats who make sense of its endlessly available user-generated content (Yus 2011: 93–94).

Digital media audiences are primarily economic entities (Kozinets et al. 2010; Lieb 2011), with research addressing the practical uses of social media as a marketing tool. In some cases the digital media have made more traditional media subject to the push and pull of hyperactive audiences: reality show producers, for example, have used audience feedback from social media to plan the next episode or season

(Holmes 2004, McClellan 2010). Thus hyperactive audiences are powerful, contributing to the success or failure of many types of media outlets. The diversity of social media users helps explain the fluidity of audience composition across time, topic, and technology. When individuals join and rejoin in temporary and virtual audiences, they tend to consume more media. They are never far from their communication devices and regularly use them, giving them an influence on media decision-making at all levels, sometimes directly and sometimes more subtly.

5 Conclusions

Michael Schudson (1991: 58) has written: "The audience... has been (like the weather), something that everybody talks about and nobody does anything about." It turns out that the audience is itself a social construction. In his 1992 book *Public Opinion,* Vincent Price concluded that

> the public is a difficult entity to define precisely. It is loosely organized through communication surrounding an issue, it includes both active and passive strata, it changes in size and shape as it develops, and it passes into and out of existence along with an issue (Price 1992: 33).

In this time of great change in all media, the terms "traditional," "social," and "digital" media are blending, no longer having discrete and different audiences. As they blend, the audiences expect constant monitoring of the world minute by the minute, use of the internet's huge resources, and innovation in message technology. Yesterday's gossip is on today's web news site, sometimes put there by a 'journalist' and many other times by a 'blogger' – who could be the same person.

The media must feed the voracious appetite of the world's audiences and collect information from sources beyond the 'insider' crowd. Someone is always awake somewhere, both needing information and creating or producing information. Individuals must encode and decode information more quickly than ever before, making the information world seem chaotic, even to hyperactive audiences.

Both the 'traditional' and 'social media' operate according to the demands of multiple hyperactive audiences. Will the media play the same role? No one knows – not the individuals who send and receive and not the aggregations of individuals that we still call audiences. Perhaps one worldwide audience will exist for important messages, with converging and diverging audiences for smaller interest groups.

We need a comprehensive study of the audience, including variations that occur in the many information worlds we live in. This chapter has identified many audiences, but it is only the beginning of an ongoing theoretical journey. We need to enhance our knowledge about the audience, both historically and currently, to understand both how audiences create media and media create audiences. We know that journalists create content, but for whom? Watching violence makes some children more aggressive, but which children? The time spent with the media can change political opinions or cultivate ideas about what the world is like, but for whom? Digital or social media occupy youngsters' lives, but which youngsters? Studies on these and many more media topics rarely address the audience by name. It is assumed to be there, but not defined, regardless of the theory or methodology used. The audience is taken for granted, but when assumptions are neither investigated nor written, we can misunderstand theory and data analysis.

Further reading

Bandura, A. 1986. *Social foundations of thought and action: A social cognitive theory.* Englewood Cliffs, NJ: Prentice-Hall.

Conville, R. L. & L. E. Rogers. 1998. *The meaning of "relationship" in interpersonal communication.* Westport, CT: Praeger.

Gerbner, G. & M. Morgan. 2002. *Against the mainstream: The selected works of George Gerbner.* New York: Peter Lang.

McQuail, D. 1997. *Audience analysis.* Thousand Oaks, CA: Sage.

Noor Al-Deen, H. S. & J. A. Hendricks. 2012. *Social media: Usage and impact.* Lanham, MD: Lexington Books.

References

Bandura, A. 1962. *Social learning through imitation.* Lincoln, NE: University of Nebraska Press.

Bauer, R. 1964. The obstinate audience: The influence process from the point of view of social communication. *American Psychologist* 19 (5). 319–328.

Berelson, B. 1948. Communications and public opinion. In: W. Schramm (ed.), *Communications in Modern Society,* 167–185. Urbana: University of Illinois Press.

Blumer, H. 1946. Collective behavior. In: A. M. Lee (ed.), *New outlines of the principles of sociology,* 167–222. New York: Barnes and Noble.

Bogart, L. 1989. *Press and the public: Who reads what, when, where, and why in American newspapers.* Hillsdale NJ: Lawrence Erlbaum Associates.

Cantril, Hadley. 1940. *The invasion from Mars: A study in the psychology of panic.* Princeton, NJ: Princeton University Press.

Carey, J. 1991. Communications and the progressives. In: R. Avery and D. Eason (eds.), *Critical perspectives on media and society,* 28–48. New York: The Guilford Press.

Cohen, B. C. 1963. *The press and foreign policy.* Princeton: Princeton University Press.

Dewey, J. 1927. *The public and its problems.* New York: Henry Holt.

Ellul, J. 1965. *Propaganda: The formulation of men's attitudes.* K. Keller and J. Lerner (trans.). New York: Alfred A. Knopf, Inc.

Ettema, J. S. & D. C. Whitney. 1994. The money arrow: An introduction to audiencemaking. In: J. S. Ettema and D. V. Whitney (eds.), *Audiencemaking: How the media create the audience* (1–18). Thousand Oaks CA: Sage Publications.

Festinger, L. 1957. *A theory of cognitive dissonance.* Stanford, CA: Stanford University Press.

Foss, F., K. Foss & R. Trapp. 1991. *Contemporary perspectives on rhetoric*, 2nd edn. Prospect Heights, Illinois: Waveland Press.

Gerbner, G. 1969. Toward 'cultural indicators': The analysis of mass mediated message systems. *AV Communication Review* 17 (2). 137–148.

Gerbner, G. & L. Gross. 1976. Living with television: The violence profile. *Journal of Communication* 26. 172–199.

Golding, P. & G. Murdock. 1991. Culture, communications, and political economy. In: J. Curran and M. Gurevitch (eds.), *Mass media and society*, 15–32. London: Edward Arnould.

Greenwald, A. G. 1968. Cognitive learning, cognitive response to persuasion and attitude change. In: A. G. Greenwald, T. C. Brock and T. M. Ostrom, *Psychological Foundations of attitudes*, 147–170. San Diego, CA: Academic Press.

Hall, S. 1983. The problem of ideology – Marxism without guarantees. In: B. Matthews, (ed.), *Marx: One hundred years on*, 57–85. London: Lawrence Wishart.

Hastorf, A. H. & H. Cantril. 1954. They saw a game: A case study. *Journal of Abnormal and Social Psychology* 49 (1). 129–134.

Holmes, S. 2004. "But this you choose!": Approaching the 'interactive' audience in reality TV. *International Journal of Cultural Studies* 7 (2). 213–231.

Homans, George C. 1958. Social behavior as exchange. *American Journal of Sociology* 63. 597–606.

Hovland, C. I. 1957. *The order of presentation in persuasion*. New Haven, CT: Yale University Press.

Hovland, C. I., A. A. Lumsdaine & F. D. Sheffield. 1949. *Experiments on mass communication: Studies in social psychology in World War II: Volume III*. Princeton: Princeton University Press.

Hovland, C. I. & W. Weiss. 1951. The influence of source credibility on communication effectiveness. *Public Opinion Quarterly* 15. 635–650.

Katz, E. & P. Lazarsfeld. 1955. *Personal influence*. New York: Free Press.

Katz, E., J. G. Blumler & M. Gurevitch. 1974. Utilization of mass communication by the individual. In: J. G. Blumler and E. Katz, *The uses of mass communications: Current perspectives on gratifications research*, 19–32. Beverly Hills: Sage.

Kelman, H. C. & C. I. Hovland. 1953. "Reinstatement" of the communicator in delayed measurement of opinion change. *Journal of Abnormal and Social Psychology* 48. 327–335.

Kelman, H. C. 1958. Compliance, identification, and internalization: Three processes of attitude change. *Journal of Conflict Resolution* 2 (1). 51–60.

Kozinets, R., K. de Valck, A. Wojnicki & S. Wilner. 2010. Networked narratives: Understanding word-of-mouth marketing in online communities. *Journal of Marketing* 74 (2). 71–89.

Lasswell, H. D. 1937. Propaganda. In: E. R. A. Seligman and A. Johnson (eds.), *Encyclopedia of the Social Sciences, Vol. 12*, 521–528. New York: Macmillan.

Lasswell, H. D. 1948. The structure and function of society. In: L. Bryson (ed.), *The Communication of Ideas*. New York: Institute for Religious and Social Studies.

Lazarsfeld, P. F., B. Berelson & H. Gaudet. 1944. *The people's choice: How the voter makes up his mind in a Presidential campaign*. New York, NY: Columbia University Press.

Lazarsfeld, P. F. & R. K. Merton. 1948. Mass communication, popular taste and organized social action. In: L. Bryson (ed.), *The Communication of Ideas*. New York: Institute for Religious and Social Studies.

Lazarsfeld, P. F., B. Berelson & W. N. McPhee. 1954. *Voting*. Chicago: University of Chicago Press.

LeBon, G. 1895. *La Pschologic de foules (the crowd)*. London: T. Fisher Unwin.

Lieb, R. 2011. Ad targeting gets social. *Advertising Age* 82 (14).

Lowery, S. A. & M. L. DeFleur. 1988. *Milestones in mass communication research*, 2nd edn. White Plains, NY: Longman.

Martín-Barbero, Jesús. 1993. *Communication, culture and hegemony: From the media to mediations*. London: Sage.

McClellan, S. 2010. "Watercooler" chats spread to the home. *Adweek* 51 (13).

McCombs, M. E. & D. L. Shaw. 1972. The agenda-setting function of mass media. *Public Opinion Quarterly* 36. 176–187.

McQuail, D. 1991. Reflections on uses and gratifications research. In: R. Avery and D. Eason (eds.), *Critical perspectives on media and society*, 9–27. New York: The Guilford Press.

Mead, G. H. 1934. *Mind, self and society*. Chicago: University of Chicago Press.

Pearce, W. B. & V. E. Cronen. 1980. *Communication, action and meaning: The creation of social realities*. Westport, CT: Praeger.

Piaget, Jean. 1971. *Biology and knowledge: An essay on the organic regulations and cognitive processes*. Chicago: University of Chicago Press.

Price, V. 1992. *Public opinion*. Thousand Oaks CA: Sage Publications.

Roberts, W. R. (trans). 1954. *Rhetorica: The works of Aristotle, Vol. 11*. Oxford: Clarendon Press.

Schramm, W. 1960. *Mass communications*. Urbana: The University of Illinois Press.

Schramm, W. & D. F. Roberts. 1971. *The processes and effects of mass communication*. Urbana: The University of Illinois Press.

Schudson, M. 1991. The new validation of popular culture. In: R. Avery and D. Eason (eds.), *Critical perspectives on media and society*, 49–68. New York: The Guilford Press.

Schudson, M. 1996. *The power of news*. Cambridge: Harvard University Press.

Signorelli, N. & G. Gerbner. 1988. *Violence and terror in the mass media: An annotated bibliography*. New York: Greenwood Press.

Shannon, C. E. July 1948. *A mathematical theory of communication*. Reprinted with corrections from *The Bell system technical journal* 27. 379–423.

Snyder, R. W. 1994. *The Vaudeville Circuit*: A prehistory of the mass audience. In: J. S. Ettema and D. C. Whitney (eds.), *Audiencemaking: How the media Create the Audience* (215–231). Thousand Oaks CA: Sage Publications.

Tarde, G. 1901. *L'Opinion et la foule (crowd)*. Paris: Felix Alcan.

Tichenor, P. J., G. A. Donohue & C. N. Olien. 1970. Mass media flow and differential growth in knowledge. *Public Opinion Quarterly* 34. 159–170.

Vygotsky, L. S. 1978. *Mind in society: The development of higher psychological processes*. Cambridge: Harvard College Press.

Yus, F. 2011. *Cyberpragmatics: Internet-mediated communication in context*. Philadelphia: John Benjamins.

Davide Bolchini and Amy Shirong Lu

22 Channel

Abstract: Communication relies on an essential instrumentation to enable its message to emerge as perceivable in our experience. This instrumentation, which comprises material and immaterial elements (from air waves to senses to media forms), is traditionally conceptualized as the communication channel. This chapter provides a novel lens to read the theoretical models that explain the nature of a communication channel, from its fundamental elements to its functions. We paint a broad picture of the relations between existing constructs and project them on the changing roles of channel in today's communication, from the web to interactive media.

Keywords: Communication channel, medium, user, interactivity

1 Introduction

Far from being a comprehensive recollection of all the communication literature on the notion of channel and medium, this chapter has two specific aims. First, we discuss a succinct yet expressive conceptual framework that models and interrelates the key facets of a communication channel as approached by some of the major traditions of communication models. This framework illustrates the complexity of the topic of communication channel and its fundamental relevance for a meaningful conceptualization of traditional and modern communication. On the other hand, we enrich and actualize our theoretical analysis with fresh, state-of-the-art examples from the pervasive panorama of modern communication practice. Tightly connected to this discussion, the second aim of our chapter is to review some of the fundamental characterizations of the notion of interactive communication channel from the perspective of interactive media theories, mainly emphasizing the role of the different agents in shaping the nature of the channel. Our theoretical analysis is nurtured with state-of-the-art examples from the Internet, the Web, ubiquitous communication, mobile devices, and social networks.

We hope that the reader will gain a theoretically grounded and synthetic perspective on the topic, and that this could help gain a better understanding of the complexity, roles, and interrelationships of the communication channels that shape the fabric of our society.

2 The concept of channel in traditional communication models

The notion of channel has been theoretically addressed and recognized since the early models of communication, starting with Lasswell (1948). In Lasswell's conception – primarily concerned with mass communication – a channel is simply what carries the message; in other words, the channel is intended as the perceivable modality (e.g. airwaves for radio message, or touch when tapping a friend's shoulders) used to convey the message to the intended audience. Already in this basic proposition, it is clear the fundamental role of the channel in the communication process. Any communication act, in fact, is made possible by some form of *concrete reification* of the message, which, at its most elementary level, must abide by physical laws to exist and take shape.

Imagine a blind person wishing to browse a website. The message is there (the website content), sender (the website designer) and receiver (the user) are ready to communicate, but something is missing. The proper channel is not in place. The message is conveyed through the visual channel, which obviously cannot be perceived by a person with visual impairment. This is why, for example, a number of additional channels have been created to enable this type of communication: from Braille displays (supporting tactile communication) to software that 'read aloud' web pages (unleashing aural communication). It is as if, when the channel is not there or does not work, the message itself is not perceivable, i.e. it still does not exist for the person waiting for it. This simple example already elucidates the function that corresponds to the broad notion of channel. The channel is the enabling factor that allows a message to take concrete form, be properly conveyed to the receiver, as well as be accessed, perceived, manipulated, and processed.

From this consideration, we can take at least two perspectives to discuss the general notion of channel, one passive and one active. On the one hand, a channel can be considered a fundamentally 'limiting' factor on the communication process, an objective constraint that we cannot remove, but to which we must submit our communication effort. Being forced to modulate our communication through a channel (even if we can choose one of many) implies the necessary consideration of the rules inherent to the channel (e.g. time, posture, style, genre, rapport with the receiver) and the adaptation of what we ideally would like to communicate to these constraints. We as humans still need to contaminate our thoughts with concrete, physical elements (sounds, visual cues, and writing, for example) to make these messages perceivable by others. On the other hand, moving from a passive to an active, or proactive perspective, the necessity of using a channel can be considered an 'exalting' factor in human communication. Using a specific channel (e.g., talking, writing an email, writing a text message, calling, or using an instant messaging system) can be considered an intentional condition which enables us to clarify, fulfill, and give coherent shape to thoughts and ideas, which would be otherwise unformed, scattered, and inaccessible first and foremost by the sender.

This active perspective opens the possibility to see that there are functions of a channel that go much beyond the pure transmission of the message. For example, choosing a specific channel (e.g. talking face to face with one's own students) instead of another (using email) over time could help build a stronger rapport and better convey trust. On the other hand, using social networking sites such as Facebook.com as the only communication channel with real life friends could facilitate multi-tasking in carrying out everyday activities, but it could limit the opportunities to engage in articulate, meaningful, and prolonged conversations.

As a more recent example, the Google Art Project (Google 2011) is a website that enables users for the first time in history to browse and visualize world renowned works of art at such a degree of visual detail that has never been possible before, and that is nowadays not even possible in a real museum for a visitor. The site enables the user to look at the composition of the painter's single paintbrush (as visitors would stand their eyes at one inch of distance from the painting), and appreciate the thickness, shape, and structure of the atomic elements that make up such an impressive texture of colors. The museum chooses a channel (the Web), which thus imposes a number of limitations over the real-life experience of a work of art: the experience of presence, atmosphere of awe, physical sequencing of the painting and actual perception of the size of the work are not there, and will probably never be on the Web. The experience that such a website unleashes, however – given the unique characteristics of this technological channel – has the potential to enrich and exalt the appreciation of a work of art at a level of depth and quality that is unparalleled in any other modality of communication. These examples show that using a channel can open new opportunities within the given constraints. In other words, the same constraints that define a channel in its distinctive characteristics are the same factors that make those channels desirable forms of communication for specific purposes.

It is thus clear that a channel is a rather complex and composite element of a communication process, which deserves an in-depth characterization. To provide a coherent perspective on the various facets of the notion of channel, we introduce here a tripartite model (Fig. 1), which serves two aims. First, it provides a synthetic view to conceptualize the complexity of what a channel is at the proper level of granularity and relevance for understanding modern communication. Second, it offers a perspective to illustrate how the notion of channel has been conceived and analyzed in different ways by some of the most famous communication models, namely Lasswell's (Lasswell 1948), Shannon's (Shannon and Weaver 1949), Schramm's (Schramm 1954) and Berlo's (Berlo 1960). In particular, the 3-layered conceptualization of the notion of communication channel is comprised of the following levels: the consideration of channel as transportation device (1), as sensorial stimulus (2) and as form of the experience (3).

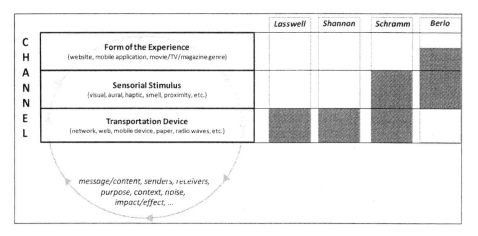

Fig. 1: The anatomy of the notion of communication channel (left) and the focus of early communication models (right)

2.1 Channel as 'transportation device'

The most elementary and basic characterization of a communication channel is the consideration of the channel as physical carrier of the message, or transportation device. This aspect captures the fundamental function of the channel as the basic physical and technical infrastructure that supports the proper and continuous movement of messages between a sender and a receiver. Like a freight train transporting goods from the production source to destination markets, a channel acts as a carrier whose primary mission is to take in incoming messages from the sender, preserve it as intact as possible throughout the journey, and bring it to the receiver. As stated by Shannon in his groundbreaking theory of communication, "the fundamental problem of communication is that of reproducing at one point either exactly or approximately a message selected at another point" (Shannon and Weaver 1949: 1).

Both Shannon and Lasswell, from different disciplinary standpoints, assume this primary transportation function of the channel. In Lasswell's view, in fact, mass communication relies on devices such as radio and newspapers as fundamental carriers of messages. Encompassing the spectrum of communication channels from the early models until today, it is interesting to notice that one of the most important transportation functions of the channel stems from its capability to 'spread out' the message. Channels have the potential to reach out to a multitude of people and to do so efficiently. So, whereas a superficial consideration of the early communication models may state that they characterize one-to-one communication process (one sender communicates a message through a channel to one receiver), it is critical to acknowledge that one-to-many, or many-to-many communication is the most common paradigm for mass communication.

This is why the consideration of the channel must also become articulate and include a 'network' of branches that can reach out to multiple target audiences in capillary ways. In this perspective, some of the fundamental characteristics of communication channels as transportation devices are their *reusability* and *efficiency*. Thanks to its multiple, physical ramifications (let us think about a telecommunication network), a multitude of messages can be carried out over the same physical channel over and over again at a minimal incremental cost. Shannon emphasizes the notion of reusability of the channel by stressing the fact that engineering the channel must be independent of the consideration of the specific instances of the messages that will be transported over it. The separation of concerns between the semantics of the message and the function of the channel is clearly explained in the following passage from his theory of communication:

> Frequently the messages have meaning; that is they refer to or are correlated according to some system with certain physical or conceptual entities. These semantic aspects of communication are irrelevant to the engineering problem. The significant aspect is that the actual message is one selected from a set of possible messages. The system must be designed to operate for each possible selection, not just the one which will actually be chosen since this is unknown at the time of design. (Shannon and Weaver 1949: 1)

In Shannon's view – built over very early work by Nyquist (1924) and Hartley (1928) – abstractions of physical devices such as electrical circuits, wires, cables, and transmission tools fulfill the basic function of the channel, as the device that enables the conduction of the encoded message to a receiver. In his perspective, "the channel is merely the medium used to transmit the signal from transmitter to receiver. It may be a pair of wires, a coaxial cable, a band of radio frequencies, a beam of light" (Shannon and Weaver 1949: 2).

This level of abstraction in modeling the characteristics of communication enabled Shannon to introduce the fundamental, groundbreaking innovations in the history of telecommunication that made him famous: the invention of digital signals (to decode an analog message into binary digits that can be very easily amplified throughout the channel), signal compression, channel capacity (bit per second that can be transmitted), channel noise (or equivocations), and entropy (a measure of the uncertainty of the information being transmitted).

2.2 Channel as 'sensorial stimulus'

Moving from an infrastructure-centric perspective of the communication channel to a more human-centric perspective, we encounter other two models of communication, namely Berlo's (Berlo 1960) and Schramm's (Schramm 1954). In these frameworks, an emerging characterization of the channel revolves around the sensorial, perceptual form of the message. A channel is therefore conceptualized as the reification of the message that allows us to perceive it through our senses. According to these frameworks, the available channels are therefore the physiological capacities that we possess and that provide input to perception: sight, hearing, touch, smell, and taste. This level of the characterization of the communication channel is of great importance because the sensorial channels are the ones enabling the message to emerge as part of our experience.

In particular, by expanding on Shannon and Weaver's stance, Berlo in 1960 introduces the Sender-Message-Channel-Receiver (SMCR) Model of Communication. Although the high-level components of the communication process appear similar in nature to the ones first introduced by Shannon and Weaver, the actual content and interpretation of each part of the model reveal a more complex and comprehensive conception. In Berlo's model, the source of the message and the receiver goes beyond a purely technical network equipment, but it includes the attitudes, knowledge, communication skills, as well as the social and cultural context of the sender. Similarly, the channel assumes a highly *human-centered* perspective; a channel is conceived as consisting of the various sensorial modalities by which we can perceive a message (hearing, seeing, touching, smelling and tasting).

Extending the original Berlo's conception with examples of modern communication channels, such as the ones afforded by Information and Communication Technologies (ICT), we can clearly see the interplay between these sensorial elements, both as input and output modalities. If we map the available channels for sensorial input that we can use to mediate (mainly through ICT) our communication, we can see many of the emerging channels used in everyday life (Table 1).

Modern ICT unleash a spectrum of communication channels relying on a variety of sensorial input and output. By simply considering an example of today's mobile phones, or the so-called 'smart phones,' we can see at play a channel which relies on the human ability to directly interact with objects by touching them (touch screens as input), combined with the visual (typical of graphical user interfaces) and the aural channel (listening to a phone call, but also listening to screen labels being read aloud by a software) as output modalities. Eye-tracking

Table 1: Examples of communication channels relying on a variety of sensorial input/output combinations

Input / Output	Sight	Hearing	Touch	Smell
Sight	Eye-tracking technologies	...with acoustic displays	...with haptic interfaces	...with smell-output devices
Voice	Voice-access technologies	...with acoustic displays	...with haptic interfaces	...with smell-output devices
Touch	Touch screens	...with acoustic displays	...with haptic interfaces	...with smell-output devices

devices are able to track the gaze of a person while looking at a screen, and there-fore – through properly defined rules – infer the intention of selecting a specific interface element. This use of sight as the input channel is particularly important for people with disabilities or illnesses that do not allow them to move their arms and hands. The systematic use of other sensorial channels in ICT (e.g. smell) is still a focus of highly innovative research labs rather than part of the mainstream communication.

Finally, considering the channel as 'sensorial stimulus,' we can also character-ize higher level perceptual elements of the communication channel (which may involve a variety of senses at the same time to satisfy the users' increasing demands for enhanced mediated communication). Let us consider, for example, the case of distance (proximity) between the sender and the receiver. Interestingly, the relative position of the sender and receiver – clearly varying from culture to culture – can be considered a vehicle of a communication message *per se*, which runs in parallel to the actual, explicit (e.g. verbal) messages to be conveyed. Getting physically closer and closer to a person may well indicate an increasing level of intimacy or the intention to start a conversation (and the level of privacy of this conversation). Moreover, the proximity channel can involve sight (e.g. I can clearly see the other coming closer to me), but also touch (e.g. tapping on shoulders), hearing, and – in some cultures – smell.

2.3 Channel as 'form of the experience'

Technology is neither good nor bad; nor is it neutral (Kranzberg 1986: 545).

At the highest level of our channel conceptualization model (see Fig. 1), we con-sider a communication channel as a coherent architecture of elements that funda-mentally shape the experience of the message. Whereas both the transportation function of the channel and its sensorial stimuli are essential for communication to happen, a channel is much more than its physical infrastructure and sensorial perception. It involves a designed architecture of ingredients that may include the size, length, structure, dynamics, and control mechanisms of the experience, as well as the constraints imposed on the context in which we experience the mes-sage. Let us consider the following example to introduce us into the ways a channel shapes the form of our communicative experience. We can well argue that the newspaper delivered every morning at our doorstep conveys – approximately – the same types of messages of the newspaper website that we may browse during the day on a lunch break. On the same basis, it is easy to see the substantial difference in the type of expected and actual experience that we engage in while using these channels. These differences concern many different levels, which we summarize in three key aspects: the impact of the sensorial experience (1), the channel as modi-fier of the message (2); the channel and the context of the experience (3).

First, the sensorial elements of the channel are a primary characteristic that determines an important difference between holding in our hands, manipulating, flipping the pages, folding and sharing a paper-based newspaper and reading the same news on a webpage on a computer screen. The viscerality of the paper experience is still unparalleled by any virtual experience, and this can have further consequences. One can easily spill coffee on a newspaper without much damage to the reading experience, whereas one has to pay particular attention to the way we hold, manipulate, and touch an electronic reading device. Moreover, by holding a physical object (although articulate and complex as a daily newspaper), one can immediately get a sense of how much there is to read, how much one has read and how much is left. In other words, the physicality of the object enables the reader to immediately conceptualize its boundaries, even if as simple quantity of messages being conveyed (and therefore projected time needed to experience them).

Second, the choice of a channel over another affords types of experience that modifies the message itself. A newspaper website typically provides additional, dynamic, in-depth information on a topic by following the last-minute updates (impossible to obtain in the morning edition of the newspaper, which contains by definition 'static' messages). Besides being updated frequently (possibility afforded by the web channel), the newspaper website offers a network of navigation paths enabling the reader to access connected websites, resources and background information, which may be useful to better frame or understand a news story. Finally, the multimedia possibilities offered by the electronic channel (watching video interviews or reportage rather than reading text articles only) expand the realm of messages available to the audience.

Finally, we need to consider that the channel shapes the context (broadly defined) in which the message may be experienced. Today, the same generic channel (e.g. the newspaper in its website version) can be experienced through a variety of specific channels: one can read the news on the home computer, on the mobile phone on the go, or on the iPad during a boring business meeting. A paper-based newspaper would afford different experiences in different social and physical contexts.

3 Media use and interactive communication channels

The passive notion of communication channel, i.e., an objective constraint that we cannot remove, but to which we must submit our communication effort, applies primarily to traditional media such as newspaper, radio, film, or television. Since these media are often the carriers of message, there is little user involvement regarding the creation, transmission, and manipulation of the mediated information. With the development of interactive media, the channels of communication should no longer be treated as an isolated concept separated from the users, who should be conceptualized as active participants in the communication process. Therefore, the active perspective of communication channel, i.e., the channel's function would go much beyond the pure transmission of the message, informs the conceptualization of the interactive communication channel.

Interactivity is one of the key variables for new media and communication research. It refers to a process of reciprocal influence (Pavlik 1996: 135) and was used as a criterion to decide if a channel is interactive (Durlak 1987; Heeter 1989; Rafaeli 1988). Interactivity thus became a standard to judge a specific communication channel. Interactive channels help to enable audiences as active participants by controlling the state, shape, location, etc. of the message. Take a painting displayed in a museum for example, the frame, the canvas, the oil paint make up a static channel through which an artist conveys to the world her perception and ideas. The painting does not allow the audience members' active participation or control of its state, shape, or texture. The only 'adjustment' the audience members are able to do would be physically moving around the painting to adjust the relative spatial relationship with it. Even if the painting has been reproduced on a postcard, a coaster, or a carpet in the museum's store, the variety of interactions is as limited as the original painting. On the other hand, a touch-screen photo viewer containing the image of the painting would allow the audience members more control via different levels of input. They can enlarge and adjust the size of the painting as well as touch on specific items in the painting to get detailed introduction by just using their fingers without having to adjust their physical distance.

In their explication of interactivity, Sundar et al. (2003) presented two perspectives of interactivity: the functional view and the contingency view. The functional view is concerned with whether a communication channel would go beyond enabling the interaction with a user by offering the opportunity to create some dialogue or mutual discourse (Roehm and Haugtvedt 1999). Following this line of thought, the level of channel interactivity depends on the number of functional features embedded in the channel. A user's actual utilization of the functional features to serve the goals of communication, though, is not taken into consideration. For example, a website with many bells and whistles such as a discussion forum, a chat room, a live video cam, a guestbook, etc. may be easily labeled as an 'interactive' channel according to the functional perspective. On the other hand, the site visitors might have failed to utilize any of the special features due to the poor usability of the site design. Although the website provides the opportunity for an interactive form of experience through various types of sensorial stimuli on multiple transportation devices, as a channel, that website is not truly interactive (as it fails to realize its interactivity potentials).

An alternative perspective, or contingency view, adds to the functional view an additional layer of the user experience of the interactive features, i.e., an interactive channel should not only possess the necessary hardware for interactivity but also ensure the interconnection, or interdependence, of the messages for communication. Rafaeli (1988) has conceptualized interactivity to be "an expression of the extent that in a given series of communication exchanges, any third (or later) transmission (or message) is related to the degree to which previous exchanges referred to even earlier transmissions (11)." An interactive channel, therefore, should be conceptualized as a communication process that involves continuous messages exchanged among users that are related to one another, i.e., the subsequent messages need to be contingent on the previous ones. For example, an online discussion forum can be considered as an interactive channel when users' discussion revolves around the previous input of other users or their earlier posts. Interactive channels do not have to involve more than one user to participate. In the previous example, any further interaction of the museum visitor with the touch-screen photo viewer is related to the earlier interaction with the system. If the visitor has enlarged part of the painting to watch the details and would like to switch back to a panoramic view, he would need to start with the already enlarged portion of the painting with a new input.

The contingency perspective helps to characterize channels with an interactive flavor. More importantly, interactivity has invited users to actively facilitate the channel's function to convey messages. It also helps to incorporate the roles of active communication agents as well as the means of message delivery into the concept of communication channels. This type of conceptualization echoes the media richness theory that shares some of similar perspectives on people's choice of different communication channels: the users' perceptions of the channel's richness (Daft and Lengel 1986) and their ability to use the channels to satisfy their needs (Dobos 1992) serve as predictors of user's choice of communication channels. In addition, the contingency view also adds another layer in the communication process by making the channel itself an active communication agent, who could interact with the users independently from the message creators. The touch-screen photo viewer system, when programmed to offer full interactive experience, could create a unique interactive experience with each different user to help them fully appreciate the painting. In other words, such interactive experience is offered to the users on behalf of the painter, who may have created the original painting but who may not be the author of the interactive haptic experience afforded to each unique audience member.

Consequently, the contingency perspective helps to bring several new dimensions to define interactive communication channels. Many of these dimensions involve the interaction between the channel and the participatory users. These dimensions include: message flow (number of agents and directionality), input/output modality, temporal simultaneity, spatial relations, and privacy of space. Table 2 offers a rough categorization of various interactive channels. It is worth noting that the distinctions among the channels are based on some typical usage scenario.

Table 2: Interactive media channels

Interactive Channels	Message Flow		Input/Output Modality	Temporal Simultaneity	Spatial Relationships	Privacy of Space
	Number of Agents	Directionality				
Email	1 : 1 or n	⟨┄┄⟩	Sight	Asynchronous	Dislocated	Private
Instant Messaging	1 : 1 or n	⟨┄┄⟩	Sight	Synchronous	Dislocated	Private
Chat Rooms	1 : 1 or n	⟨┄┄⟩	Sight/Hearing	Synchronous	Dislocated	Public
Discussion Forums	1 : n	⟨┄┄⟩	Sight	Asynchronous	Dislocated	Public
Personal Blogs	1 : n	⟨┄┄⟩	Sight	Asynchronous	Dislocated	Public
Social Network	n : n	⟨┄┄⟩	Sight	Asynchronous	Dislocated	Semi-private
MMORPG	n : n	⟨┄┄⟩	Sight/Hearing	Synchronous	Dislocated	Public
Touch-Screen Display	1	┄⟩	Sight/Hearing/Touch	Synchronous	–	Public/Private
Console Games	1	┄⟩	Sight/Hearing	Synchronous	–	Private
Virtual Reality	Depends	⟨┄┄⟩	Sight/Hearing/Touch	Synchronous	Co-located/Dislocated	Private/Public

Message flow refers to the transfer or exchange of information within, between, or among communication agents. It is characterized by the number of agents involved in communication process and the directionality of the message flow. For example, e-mails, instant messaging, and online chatting are usually initiated by one person and the other participants can range from one to more. Discussion forums and personal blogs typically would start with the input from one user followed by more users. Social networking sites and massively multiplayer online role-playing games (MMORPG), would involve input from multiple users due to their social networking nature. Single-player console games and touch-screen displays typically would involve one user's continuous input. The direction of message flow could also be an indicator of the friendliness of the online communication. For example, a common interactive chatting communication, or social networking condition, should allow mutual message exchanges among different communication agents. When the direction of the message flow becomes mostly directed to a few 'targets' from many other users, such condition may indicate, for example, the existence of online bullying.

Input / output modality is related to the sensorial elements associated with the user's input and output modalities during the communication process. Sight has been one of the most common modalities and can be found within almost all interactive channels. Users will not be able to fully utilize the communication channel unless applying their visual perceptions to facilitate the message creation and exchange. While sight dominates interactive communication channels, sound provides additional affordances to the communication process. It can be found across channels such as chat rooms, MMORPGs, and console games. Touch-screen display and virtual reality call for users' participatory actions such as touching and feeling the components or elements of channel. Well integrated, these channels provide more modalities and enable a richer message exchange experience.

Temporal simultaneity refers to whether the transfer or exchange of information is synchronous or asynchronous. It is about the temporal relationship among the exchanged messages. While an interactive channel emphasizes the interconnectedness of the messages, the temporal relationships among the messages are not uniform. Instant messaging, chat rooms, MMORPG, and console games where the message exchanges usually occur at the same time with very little delay. Extended delays will either hamper the perception of communication quality or reduce the enjoyment of entertainment media. Email, discussion forum, personal blogs, and social networking sites, on the other hand, allow delays for message exchange. Proper delays within the channel should facilitate the subsequent message exchanges within users. For example, a political candidate may opt for an online personal blog to interact with the public and to promote his political agenda. When he posts something to his blog, he would not expect the immediate occurrence of numerous thoughtful comments from the users. Instead, there should be some time intervals between the comments to the posted message.

Spatial relationships refer to the relative location of communication agents, who can be co-located or dislocated. Interactive channels allow the communication process to go beyond the geographical limitations and thus the users can be located in different parts of the globe while still able to maintain an active message exchange. Console games and touch-screen displays are slightly different from the other interactive channels because the channels can be considered as stand-alone communication agents interacting with the users. Therefore they should be co-located to allow the interaction to occur.

Lastly, *privacy of space* refers to the environment where the channels are utilized. Emails, instant messaging, and console games are considered private channels as the communication process and message exchange either require user's log-ins or could occur in a private space. On the other hand, chat rooms, discussion forums, personal blogs, MMORPGs are more open regarding the message exchange. Other users will be able to sense the message exchange in these channels. Social networking sites fall in between, since a user would be able to communicate private messages to other users while the user is also able to see other user's input. Therefore, such channels offer users a semi-private message exchange space.

4 Conclusion

In this chapter, we have described an integrated conceptual model for communication channels by drawing from classic communication scholarship. We continued to expand the conceptual model to the notion of interactive communication channels. With the evolution of communication technologies, which offer increasing opportunities for users to engage in the communication process, the notion of channels should be updated in accordance with the audience's active participation. Interactive channel is a good start since its intrinsic characteristics assumes the role of the users in the communication process. Our explorations also raise several questions: with the roles of channels and media becoming similar to each other in the communication process, what would distinguish one from another? Marshall McLuhan (1964) has considered the medium to be the message. How would people as active users or audience members be situated in this process when the traditional boundaries are disappearing? Will they become part of the channel or an extended of the media? How would their message exchange affect the communication process? These are probably some of the initial questions to ask to refresh our conceptualization of communication channels.

Further reading

Berlo, David. 1960. *The process of communication: An introduction to theory and practice.* New York: Holt, Rinehart and Winston.

Durlak, Jerome T. 1987. A typology for interactive media. In: M. McLaughlin (eds.), *Communication Yearbook 10.* 743–757. Newbury Park, CA: Sage.

Pavlik, John. 1996. *New media technology: Cultural and commercial perspectives.* Boston: Allyn & Bacon.

Roehm, Harper A. & Curtis P. Haugtvedt. 1999. Understanding interactivity of cyberspace advertising. In: D. W. Schumann and E. Thorson (eds.), *Advertising and the World Wide Web*, 27–39. Mahwah, NJ: Lawrence Erlbaum.

Schramm, Wilbur. 1954. How communication works. In: Wilbur Schramm (ed.), *The process and effects of mass communication.* Urbana, IL: University of Illinois Press.

References

Berlo, David. 1960. *The process of communication: An introduction to theory and practice.* New York: Holt, Rinehart and Winston.

Daft, Richard L. & Robert H. Lengel. 1986. Organizational information requirements, media richness and structural design. *Management Science* 32 (5). 554–571.

Dobos, Jean. 1992. Gratification models of satisfaction and choice of communication channels in organizations. *Communication Research* 19. 29–51.

Durlak, Jerome T. 1987. A typology for interactive media. In: M. McLaughlin (eds.), *Communication Yearbook 10.* 743–757. Newbury Park, CA: Sage.

Google. 2011. *Google Art project.* http://www.googleartproject.com/ (accessed on February 14, 2011).

Hartley, Ralph V. L. 1928. Transmission of Information. *Bell System Technical Journal.*

Heeter, Carrie. 1989. Implications of new interactive technologies for conceptualizing communication. In: J. Salvaggio and J. Bryant (eds.), *Media in the information age: Emerging patterns of adoption and consumer use,* 217–235. Hillsdale, NJ: Lawrence Erlbaum.

Kranzberg, Melvin. 1986. Technology and History: 'Kranzberg's Laws'. *Technology and Culture* 27 (3). 544–560.

Lasswell, Harold D. 1948. The structure and function of communication in society. In: L. Bryson (ed.), *The communication of ideas.* New York: Harper.

McLuhan, Marshall. 1964. *Understanding media: the extensions of man.* New York: McGraw-Hill.

Nyquist, Harry. 1924. Certain Factors Affecting Telegraph Speed. *Bell System Technical Journal.*

Pavlik, John. 1996. *New media technology: Cultural and commercial perspectives.* Boston: Allyn and Bacon.

Rafaeli, Sheizaf. 1988. Interactivity: From new media to communication. In: R. Hawkins, J. Weimann, and S. Pingree (eds.), *Advancing communication science: Merging mass and interpersonal processes,* 110–134. Newbury Park, CA: Sage.

Roehm, Harper A. & Curtis P. Haugtvedt. 1999. Understanding interactivity of cyberspace advertising. In: D. W. Schumann and E. Thorson (eds.), *Advertising and the World Wide Web,* 27–39. Mahwah, NJ: Lawrence Erlbaum.

Schramm, Wilbur. 1954. How communication works. In: Wilbur Schramm (ed.), *The process and effects of mass communication.* Urbana, IL: University of Illinois Press.

Shannon, Claude & Warren Weaver. 1949. *The mathematical theory of communication.* Urbana, IL: University of Illinois Press.

Sundar, Shyam S., Sriram Kalyanaraman & Justin Brown. 2003. Explicating website interactivity: Impression-formation effects in political campaign sites. *Communication Research* 30 (1). 30–59.

Mary Beth Oliver, Julia K. Woolley and Anthony M. Limperos
23 Effects

Abstract: The purpose of this chapter is to provide an overview of scholarship on effects of media communication. To organize this vast literature, this chapter highlights three broad classes of effects: those that reflect cumulative, gradual exposure to messages; those that occur in the immediate viewing context; and those related to audience use, interpretation, and response. We end the chapter by examining what newer technologies imply for effects-related theories, as well as suggesting possible directions for future research.

Keywords: Media psychology, media effects, cultivation, agenda setting, priming, uses and gratifications, media enjoyment

Within the field of communication, the examination of the effects of communication messages can be found in a diversity of sub-areas, including interpersonal communication, organizational communication, and small-group communication, among others. With these areas of research noted, however, in this chapter we focus our attention specifically on the effects of media. The examination of effects, which has been central to research in mass communication, constitutes a vast body of scholarship commonly referred to as "media effects."

The phrase "media effects" is frequently employed to signify research that employs a social-scientific approach to examining the viewer-media relationship. Although this phrase has drawn some critical attention by implying to some scholars that this approach favors an overly simplistic perspective on media influence (for example, see Lang et al. 2008), in this chapter we instead endorse the idea that media effects is a phrase generally understood more broadly. That is, like many other scholars, we use the phrase media effects to refer not only to the social and psychological outcomes that accrue from media consumption, but also the processes that help to explain and predict such effects, as well as the predictors of viewers' perceptions and selections of media content that may initiate media consumption in the first place (Nabi and Oliver 2009).

Within the last several decades, a number of scholars have attempted to synthesize the "state" of media-effects theories in the discipline of communication. Some of these synthesis pieces have served to identify the theories most frequently employed (Bryant and Miron 2004), others have bemoaned the general lack of theory development resulting from a dearth of "milestone" research (DeFleur 1998), others have called for a "paradigm shift" by suggesting a need for a greater focus on process and dynamic media-viewer relations (Lang 2011), and still others have pointed out the need for theoretical revision in light of newer technologies that lead us to question the applicability of extant assumptions concerning content, receivers, and channels which may no longer be relevant (Chaffee and Metzger 2001).

Given the variety of theoretical perspectives one might find useful in exploring media effects, it stands to reason that a diversity of organizing schemes have been employed in attempts to present the literature in a coherent form. Perhaps most common are schemes that focus on the type of content in question (e.g., entertainment, news), the intended effects of media exposure (e.g., persuasion), or the target audience (e.g., children) (Bryant and Zillmann 2002). In this chapter, rather than providing an historic overview of notable examples of media-effects studies (e.g., the Payne Fund Studies, Bandura's bobo doll studies), we take a different approach that reflects our broad characterization of what constitutes effects research. Namely, our goal in this chapter is to provide a heuristic template using an organizing scheme that reflects one typology of how effects are thought to occur. Specifically, we begin our chapter by considering theoretical approaches that conceptualize effects in terms of cumulative or long-term exposure principles. In Section 2 we turn to approaches that conceptualize effects in terms of immediate influence reflecting media instigation of emotion and of already-existing cognition. Section 3 then acknowledges the theoretical perspectives emphasizing the active role of the viewer in initiating media consumption and in responding to media content. Further, within each of these three sections, when applicable, we consider the anticipated length of the effects (short-term, long-term) that are predicted by the various theoretical perspectives. Finally, our chapter ends with suggested directions for future research.

1 Effects from cumulative exposure

The widely held perception of media as socializing agents is consistent with the notion that media effects can best be conceptualized as the result of long-term, cumulative exposure to media content over the course of extended periods of time, including over the course of a lifetime. From this perspective, media effects happen gradually and can serve to aid in the development of stable attitudes and perceptions, in much the same way that parents, peers, or educational environments exert formative influences.

Perhaps one of the earliest theoretical perspectives reflecting a cumulative-exposure perspective is agenda-setting. Agenda-setting theory holds that by covering certain topics with more frequency than others, news media make certain issues more salient to audiences than other issues (McCombs and Shaw 1972). Effectively, this means that the news media tell audiences "what to think about." This general effect on perceived issue importance is referred to as "first-order agenda-setting." Second-order agenda-setting, or "attribute agenda-setting," is a process whereby the frequency of media emphasis on certain *attributes* about an issue, object, or person determines their relative importance (see McCombs and Reynolds 2008). Therefore, the news media not only make certain issues salient, but also which attributes of that issue are the most important. In this regard, second-order agenda setting shares many similarities with framing theory. Namely, framing theorists also examine how the news media present certain topics, specifically in terms of how the issues or attributes of an issue are given meaning (Iyengar 1990; Tewksbury and Scheufele 2008).

We include agenda-setting scholarship in this section representing cumulative effects, as research in this area generally conceptualizes influence as resulting from consumption of media coverage over time. As a result, scholarship in this area has generally tended to employ panel designs in which media coverage and public opinion are examined over time (McCombs and Shaw 1972), or has made use of archival data that allows for the examination of trends in public opinion over years or even decades (Lowry et al. 2003). However, we note that some scholars have examined similar perceptual outcomes using more abbreviated experimental approaches (Iyengar and Kinder 1987).

Whereas agenda-setting has traditionally focused specifically on news, additional theories reflecting assumptions of cumulative influence are much broader in terms of the content they consider. Namely, cultivation theory, arguably one of the most widely referenced and researched theories in the discipline, argues that television programming in general tells consistent and repetitive stories across different types of content. Originating from the work of George Gerbner (1969) and the Cultural Indicators Project, cultivation theory assumes that we live in a media-saturated environment in which certain themes or narratives are consistently emphasized, with little diversity of content and little real choice or selectivity on the part of viewers. Over time, this process is thought to create a cultivation effect whereby viewers' beliefs about the real world become consistent with those espoused in the mass media (see also Morgan and Shanahan 2010). One of the most frequently cited cultivation effects is that of the "Mean World Syndrome," or the notion that entertainment media typically present the outside world as one that is threatening, hostile, and violent (Gerbner and Gross 1976).

The methodology usually employed to measure cultivation effects is a comparison of perceptions of reality with real-world facts and hours of television watched. However, consistent with the notion that cultivation is an outcome of cumulative and long-term exposure, recent research has shown that social-reality perceptions are more strongly correlated with estimates of television viewing over a lifetime than with current television usage patterns (Riddle 2010). Despite various criticisms of cultivation research (e.g., Doob and Macdonald 1979; Hirsch 1980), years of scholarship suggest that television viewing does indeed have a stable, albeit small, effect on real-world judgments.

2 Effects from media instigation

In addition to recognizing that media influence can result from gradual, long-term exposure, some theories of media influence point out that media effects can also be observed immediately in response to a single media exposure. Further, unlike models assuming cumulative exposure, instigational models generally predict that media influence is relatively short lived or transitory. To illustrate this perspective in media effects, we discuss two theories: one pertaining to the arousal of emotional states, and one to the instigation of attitudes or beliefs that may already be present.

Media undoubtedly are successful in eliciting a host of emotions, including fear from horror films, sadness from tear-jerkers, or humor from comedies. Excitation transfer is one prominent theory of media effects that identifies media effects on emotion as immediate and short-lived (Bryant and Miron 2003; Zillmann 1971). Briefly, excitation-transfer theory notes that affective reactions are composed of both cognitive appraisals of events (i.e. the meaning of the event for the self) which determine affect type (e.g. happiness or sadness), and a level of physiological excitation or intensity. Because sympathetic excitation is not strongly differentiated between affect types, increased arousal in response to one situation (e.g., anger) may serve to intensify one's response to a second situation (e.g., fear) if the subsequent situation occurs before the arousal from the first situation has returned to baseline levels. Applied to media contexts, this theory suggests that affect in response to any arousing stimulus (e.g., sexual portrayals) may serve to intensify subsequent affect in response to a second stimulus, even if that subsequent affect is of a different type than the original (e.g., aggression) (for an overview, see Bryant and Miron 2003). As a result, this theory provides interpretations for a wide variety of media experiences, including elation when a beloved sports team wins after the agony of a close match (Zillmann et al. 1989), or euphoria when an endangered heroine in a thriller movie manages to narrowly escape from the evil villain (Zillmann 1991b). However, given that the primary mechanism at work in this theory is elevated arousal, this theory generally suggests only short-term effects, as any influence due to arousal should cease once the arousal has dissipated.

Associative priming is an additional widely employed theory in media psychology reflecting instigational effects (Berkowitz 1984). At the broadest level, priming generally refers to the idea that media messages (or any environmental stimuli) can serve to activate cognitions, affect, or even behavioral tendencies associated with exposure to those stimuli. This activation then spreads to and activates semantically similar cognitions. As a result of this activation, when ambiguous stimuli are encountered in the environment, these stimuli are perceived or interpreted through the lens of the cognitions that have been previously activated (for overviews, see Jo and Berkowitz 1994; Roskos-Ewoldsen and Roskos-Ewoldsen 2009). For example, a person who has recently viewed media violence may have a host of violent cognitions that have been activated. As a result, the person may erroneously perceive a threat when encountering an unknown individual while walking down a dark street.

Like excitation transfer, priming is generally thought to be a rather short-lived effect, as activation of cognition is thought to dissipate rather quickly (in a matter of minutes). However, there are at least two ways in which associative priming may also be relevant to longer-term media influences as well. First, scholars have noted that although the activation of cognitions may be generally transitory in many circumstances, for some individuals or under some circumstances, the activation of cognitions may be more persistent (Bargh et al. 1986). This notion of "chronic accessibility" implies that media, by repeatedly priming certain concepts (e.g., violence), may make these concepts readily available for much longer than a single media experience.

A second way that priming may have long-term implications is via what Jo and Berkowitz (1994) referred to as "context cues." Specifically, these authors noted that otherwise "neutral" stimuli can become part of a person's cognitive network via processes such as classical conditioning during media viewing. As a result, future encounters with the "neutral object" outside of a media-viewing context can serve to prime related cognitions (see Josephson 1986). For example, as a result of watching a large number of television crime dramas, Italian men may become an element in a person's cognitive network concerning the mafia. Consequently, at some distant future time, exposure to an Italian man may prime thoughts of crime. In this regard, then, priming may be of relevance in more situations than the immediate viewing context.

3 User selection and interpretation

The final element of our template for organizing the focus of media effects inquiry pertains to user selection and interpretation of media content. Although it may seem odd to characterize user selection as an example of a media effect, we believe it plays a crucial role in the media-effects process. First, a great deal of media exposure obviously occurs as a result of user selection, making audience activity a central element in the media-effects process. Second, how an individual responds to media content will ultimately depend on how that content is understood or interpreted by the individual, making individuals' perceptions a crucial variable in predicting media influence. Finally, we believe that the distinction between user response (e.g., audience enjoyment) and media effects (e.g., effects of humorous content on viewers) is often blurred, reflecting more of a semantic difference than one that is theoretically driven. With this rationale in mind, this section considers both short-term or immediate audience selection and interpretation, and more enduring effects involving audience activity.

The theoretical conceptualization of the audience in active terms is undoubtedly most closely associated with the uses and gratifications (U&G) perspective. Although early media research focused on how people react to media, U&G research has primarily focused on exploring questions of how people select and use media (Kim and Rubin 1997; Swanson 1979). Accordingly, U&G research suggests that selection of media genre and forms, as well as gratifications and consequences of media use, are largely determined by motivations or goals of media users, and that these motives are often constrained by social and psychological circumstances (Katz et al. 1974; Rubin 2009).

Early television research guided by U&G focused on exploring how basic demographic variables (e.g., age, gender, and education) were related to motives for viewing television (Greenberg 1974; Rubin 1979; Rubin and Rubin 1982). In addition to observing how demographic information is linked to media selection across a variety of contexts, U&G researchers have also found relationships between individual psychological differences and media selection, motives, and effects. For example, Krcmar and Greene (1999) found that disinhibited individuals were more likely to report watching violent television than their counterparts, and Haridakis (2002) and Haridakis and Rubin (2003) found that locus of control was linked to motives for watching, and effects of, violent television. U&G research has also been instrumental in understanding which social and psychological factors influence the selection of newer media such as the Internet (Lin 2001; Pappacharissi and Rubin 2000), video games (Sherry et al. 2006), and even social-networking websites (Raacke and Bonds-Raacke 2008). To summarize, since its inception, U&G research has provided much insight into how people use media and communication technologies by linking individual differences with motivations and selection of media, as well as outcomes of media use.

Whereas uses and gratifications tends to conceptualize audience motivations and preferences in more enduring or trait-like terms, other perspectives recognize that media preferences may change quickly over time, reflecting state-like inclinations. In this regard, mood-management is a notable example of a theory of audience selection that recognizes the variability of media selection within individuals at any given moment in time. Specifically, mood-management theory is based on the hedonic premise that audiences are motivated to seek pleasure and avoid displeasure (Zillmann 1988). Put simply, mood-management holds that individuals are motivated to use media to prolong and intensify positive moods and terminate or diminish negative moods. Individuals will then arrange and rearrange their exposure to entertainment media in order to meet these ends. Media content is thought to vary in its effectiveness in the mood-management process based on several characteristics: its excitatory potential (how arousing the content is), absorbing potential (how involving the content is), behavioral affinity (how similar the content is to one's own present circumstances), and hedonic valence (whether the content is positively or negatively valenced). In terms of methodology, mood-management theorists typically rely on experimental designs which manipulate antecedent mood and/or content of the stimulus. Such research has provided a good deal of empirical evidence in support of the theory (e.g., Bryant and Zillmann 1984; Knobloch and Zillmann 2002)

Both uses and gratifications and mood-management are ultimately theories of media selection, though both imply that individuals are likely to select content that is gratifying or enjoyable. However, a host of additional research regarding audience response focuses specifically on notions of audience enjoyment. In general, research examining audience enjoyment has tended to examine individuals' reactions to a specific media experience, such as their evaluations of a movie, their reactions to a television drama, or their engagement with a video game. As a result, many theories of audience enjoyment tend to focus on short-term or immediate reactions that are largely contained to the media experience while it is ongoing. One prominent theory in explaining audience enjoyment is disposition theory (Zillmann 1991a). Disposition theory holds that audience enjoyment of entertainment content is based largely on a viewer's affective disposition toward story characters and outcomes for those characters. In the original formulation of the theory, this affective disposition was thought to result from a moral evaluation of the character (Zillmann and Bryant 1975). However, more recent reformulations of the theory (Raney 2004) suggest that moral evaluations of characters may follow (rather than precede) the decision to like or dislike a character. In any event, audiences are then thought to experience enjoyment if there are positive outcomes for liked characters and negative outcomes for disliked characters (Bryant and Miron 2002; Raney 2003). Empirical support for disposition theory has been strong (e.g., Raney and Bryant 2002; Zillmann and Cantor 1977; Zillmann et al. 1998).

Finally, related to enjoyment responses, media effects scholars have also gone beyond examining perceptions of media characters to highlight the importance of audience *interactions* with media characters as an important element in the media effects process. In this regard, both short-term and long-term conceptualizations have been noted. For example, the concept of identification with media characters is generally understood as being a short-term response that individuals have to media content during viewing. More specifically, identification can be understood as a process of temporarily adopting the identity and perspective of a media character, made up of cognitive, empathetic, motivational, and absorption components (Cohen 2001). However, viewers' more enduring or long-term relationships with media characters have also been noted, with scholars using the phrase "parasocial relationships" to refer to the imagined, interpersonal connections that users sometimes develop with media personae (Horton and Wohl 1956). Although long-term exposure to a particular media content can be enough to cause audience members to develop parasocial relationships with media characters, scholars have shown that certain motives (e.g, social interaction), perceptions about life positions (e.g., loneliness and hopelessness), and orientations toward media personalities to be significant predictors in the development of parasocial interactions among media users (Chory-Assad and Yanen 2005; Giles 2002; Rubin and Perse 1987). Therefore, while media users can identify with particular media characters in the short-term, parasocial relationships tend to be a bit more enduring and are often tied to individual psychology and social circumstances.

To summarize, theoretical conceptualizations of audience activity in the selection of and response to media content holds an important place in media-effects processes. These conceptualizations recognize that users have both enduring and immediate motivations for using media to fulfill their needs, and that they can form relationships with media characters during the course of consuming media content and long after that content has been viewed.

4 Future directions in media effects

As the media landscape continues to evolve at lightning speed, it is obvious that existing theoretical approaches to media effects must contend with new variables, new contexts, and more complex processes that may not have been relevant in the not-too-distant past. We end this chapter by considering several directions for research that we believe may be particularly fruitful for scholars to examine.

First, in the previous section we highlighted the importance of media selection in the effects process. As newer technologies continue to allow for greater selectivity and more varied options of both content and delivery, we believe the issue of selectivity will become increasingly important in understanding media effects. Specifically, we predict that dynamic models that recognize the mutual influence of audience selection/perception and media influence will become ever more relevant and applicable. Such "spiral models" have been present in communication scholarship since early work on the spiral of silence (Noelle-Neumann 1974), but more recently have been applied to additional content and technologies, including media violence (Slater 2007), and the implications of Internet news for political polarization (Iyengar and Hahn 2009; Sunstein 2001).

Second, we also recognize the importance of newer technologies which function as more than merely a means of delivering content. Specifically, most technologies now not only allow for individuals to respond to media content via user comments and user ratings, but they also allow individuals the opportunity to engage in social sharing. The notion of sharing important information or media messages via personal relationships is an idea that can be found in early mass communication research. The two-step flow of mass communication, as originally elaborated by Katz and Lazarsfeld (1955), suggests that media influence occurs through interpersonal conversations with opinion leaders rather than directly from original media messages. Recently, computer-mediated communication and mass communication scholars have advocated revisiting some of the general ideas which emanated from early two-step flow approaches in light of new communication technologies such as Internet forums, blogs, and social-networking websites (Nisbet and Kotcher 2009; Walther et al. 2010) Because there are so many ways to share, create, and spread information in today's media environment, discerning exactly how these activities affect or impact individuals is likely to be a complex, yet fruitful area for future effects research and scholarship.

Third, we believe that the increasing mobility of media content will have profound implications in a diversity of contexts. First, mobile communication and "smart" technologies allow individuals to routinely carry with them a constant access to media messages. Listening to the radio while walking downtown, watching a sitcom while riding a bus, or using Facebook while sitting in a restaurant are now commonplace occurrences. Importantly, too, as technologies continue to develop, individuals will not only take their media with them, but media messages will "follow" individuals. Specifically, location-based and context-aware content such as advertising can now use built-in GPS devices to detect an individual's location and to push media content that is thought to be most relevant at that moment.

In addition to changing the way individuals access media messages, mobile communication also has implications for activities and interactions that have, until recently, occurred in contexts that were generally free from potentially distracting entertainment possibilities. Now, however, YouTube videos, Facebook postings, and mobile games are readily available everywhere, including in contexts where they might be considered inappropriate or distracting (e.g., classrooms, work-related meetings, dinner with companions). Although research is beginning to emerge on issues such as the influence of multi-tasking on cognitive ability (e.g., Ophir et al. 2009) or the effects of mobile-media use on interpersonal perception (Campbell 2007), there are obviously a multitude of potential additional effects that await exploration, as well as systematic theory development.

5 Concluding comments

Research on the effects of media on users' cognitions, behaviors, and emotions is arguably a relatively young area of study. Yet during the last century, a variety of theoretical approaches in media psychology have been formulated that help us to understand the effects of media content on both individuals and on society at large. We hope that by providing a template for categorizing the effects in terms of cumulative influence, instigational effects, and user selection and interpretation, this chapter will supply readers with a way of understanding and organizing a broad and growing body of literature. We further hope that readers recognize the importance of continued research on effects, as technological developments have resulted in profound changes in both the media landscape itself, as well as the integration of media into the daily lives of individuals and of our culture.

Further reading

Bryant, Jennings & Dorina Miron. 2004. Theory and research in mass communication. *Journal of Communication* 54 (4), 662–704.

Bryant, Jennings & Mary Beth Oliver (eds.). 2008. *Media effects: Advances in theory and research*, 3rd edn. New York: Routledge.

Nabi, Robin & Mary Beth Oliver (eds.). 2009. *Handbook of media processes and effects*. Thousand Oaks, CA: Sage.

Nabi, Robin & Mary Beth Oliver. 2009. Mass media effects. In: C. Berger, M. Roloff, and D. Roskos-Ewoldsen (eds.), *Handbook of communication science*, 2nd edn, 255–272. Thousand Oaks, CA: Sage.

References

Bargh, John A., Ronald N. Bond, Wendy J. Lombardi & Mary E. Tota. 1986. The additive nature of chronic and temporary sources of construct accessibility. *Journal of Personality and Social Psychology* 50. 869.

Berkowitz, Leonard. 1984. Some effects of thoughts on anti- and prosocial influences of media events: A cognitive-neoassociation analysis. *Psychological Bulletin* 95. 410–427.

Bryant, Jennings & Dorina Miron. 2002. Entertainment as media effect. In: Jennings Bryant and Dolf Zillmann (eds.), *Media effects: Advances in theory and research*, 549–582. Mahwah, NJ: Lawrence Erlbaum Associates.

Bryant, Jennings & Dorina Miron. 2003. Excitation-transfer theory and three-factor theory of emotion. In: Jennings Bryant, David Roskos-Ewoldsen and Joanne Cantor (eds.), *Communication and emotion: Essays in honor of Dolf Zillmann*, 31–59. Mahwah, NJ: Lawrence Erlbaum Associates.

Bryant, Jennings & Dorina Miron. 2004. Theory and research in mass communication. *Journal of Communication* 54. 662–704.

Bryant, Jennings & Dolf Zillmann. 1984. Using television to alleviate boredom and stress: Selective exposure as a function of induced excitational states. *Journal of Broadcasting* 28. 1–20.

Bryant, Jennings & Dolf Zillmann. 2002. *Media effects: Advances in theory and research*, 2nd edn. Mahwah, NJ: Lawrence Erlbaum Associates.

Campbell, Scott W. 2007. Perceptions of mobile phone use in public settings: A cross-cultural comparison. *International Journal of Communication* 1. 738–757.

Chaffee, Steven H. & Miriam J. Metzger. 2001. The end of mass communication? *Mass Communication & Society* 4. 365–379.

Chory-Assad, Rebecca M. & Ashley Yanen. 2005. Hopelessness and loneliness as predictors of older adults' involvement with favorite television performers. *Journal of Broadcasting & Electronic Media* 49. 182–201.

Cohen, Jonathan. 2001. Defining identification: A theoretical look at the identification of audiences with media characters. *Mass Communication & Society* 4. 245–264.

DeFleur, Melvin L. 1998. Where have all the milestones gone? The decline of significant research on the process and effects of mass communication. *Mass Communication and Society* 1. 85–98.

Doob, Anthony N. & Glenn E. Macdonald. 1979. Television viewing and fear of victimization: Is the relationship causal? *Journal of Personality and Social Psychology* 37. 170–179.

Gerbner, George. 1969. Toward "cultural indicators": The analysis of mass mediated public message systems. *Educational Technology Research and Development* 17. 137–148.

Gerbner, George & Larry Gross. 1976. The scary world of TV's heavy viewer. *Psychology Today* 9. 41–45.

Giles, David C. 2002. Parasocial interaction: A review of the literature and a model for future research. *Media Psychology* 4. 279–305.

Greenberg, Bradley S. 1974. Gratifications of television viewing and their correlates for British children. In: Jay G. Blumler and Elihu Katz (eds.), *The uses of mass communications: Current perspectives on gratifications research*, 71–92. Beverly Hills, CA: Sage.

Haridakis, Paul M. 2002. Viewer characteristics, exposure to television violence, and aggression. *Media Psychology* 4. 323–352.

Haridakis, Paul M. & Alan M. Rubin. 2003. Motivation for watching television violence and viewer aggression. *Mass Communication and Society* 6. 29–56.

Hirsch, Paul. 1980. The "scary world" of the non viewer and other anomalies: A reanalysis of Gerbner et al.'s findings on cultivation analysis, Part I. *Communication Research* 7. 403–456.

Horton, Donald & R. Richard Wohl. 1956. Mass communication and para-social interaction. *Psychiatry* 19. 215–229.

Iyengar, Shanto. 1990. Framing responsibility for political issues: The case of poverty. *Political Behavior* 12. 19–40.

Iyengar, Shanto & Kyu S. Hahn. 2009. Red media, blue media: Evidence of ideological selectivity in media use. *Journal of Communication* 59. 19–39.

Iyengar, Shanto & Donald R. Kinder. 1987. *News that matters: Television and American opinion*. Chicago: University of Chicago Press.

Jo, Eunkyung & Leonard Berkowitz. 1994. A priming effect analysis of media influences: An update. In: Jennings Bryant and Dolf Zillmann (eds.), *Media effects: Advances in theory and research*, 43–60. Hillsdale, NJ: Lawrence Erlbaum Associates.

Josephson, Wendy L. 1986. Television violence and children's aggression: Testing the priming, social script, and disinhibition predictions. *Journal of Personality and Social Psychology* 53: 882–890.

Katz, Elihu, Jay G. Blumler & Michael Gurevitch. 1974. Utilization of mass communication by the individual. In: Jay G. Blumler and Elihu Katz (eds.), *The uses of mass communications: Current perspectives on gratifications research*, 19–32. Beverly Hills, CA: Sage.

Katz, Elihu & Paul Felix Lazarsfeld. 1955. *Personal influence: The part played by people in the flow of mass communication*. Glencoe, IL: Free Press.

Kim, Jungkee & Alan M. Rubin. 1997. The variable influence of audience activity on media effects. *Communication Research* 24. 107–135.

Knobloch, Silvia & Dolf Zillmann. 2002. Mood management via the digital jukebox. *Journal of Communication* 52. 351–366.

Krcmar, Marina & Kathryn Greene. 1999. Predicting exposure to uses of television violence. *Journal of Communication* 49 (3). 24–45.

Lang, Annie. 2011. *The shifting paradigm of mass communication research?* Paper presented at the International Communication Association, Boston.

Lang, Annie, Rob. B. Potter & Paul Bolls. 2008. Where psychophysiology meets the media: Taking the effects out of mass media research. In: J. Bryant and M. B. Oliver (eds.), *Media effects: Advances in theory and research*, 207–227. New York: Routledge.

Lin, Carolyn. 2001. Audience attributes, media supplementation, and likely online service adoption. *Mass Communication and Society* 4. 19–38.

Lowry, Dennis T., Tam Ching, Josephine Nio & Dennis W. Leitner. 2003. Setting the public fear agenda: A longitudinal analysis of network TV crime reporting, public perceptions of crime, and FBI crime statistics. *Journal of Communication* 53. 61–73.

McCombs, Maxwell E. & Donald L. Shaw. 1972. The agenda-setting function of the mass media. *Public Opinion Quarterly* 36. 176–187.

McCombs, Maxwell & Amy Reynolds. 2008. How the news shapes our civic agenda. In: Jennings Bryant and Mary Beth Oliver (eds.), *Media effects: Advances in theory and research*, 1–16. New York, NY: Routledge.

Morgan, Michael & James Shanahan. 2010. The state of cultivation. *Journal of Broadcasting & Electronic Media* 54. 337–355.

Nabi, Robin L. & Oliver, Mary Beth. 2009. Introduction. In: Robin L. Nabi and Mary Beth Oliver (eds.), *Sage handbook of media processes and effects*, 1–5. Thousand Oaks, CA: Sage.

Nisbet, Matthew C. & John E. Kotcher. 2009. A two-step flow of influence? Opinion-leader campaigns on climate change. *Science Communication* 30. 328–354.

Noelle-Neumann, Elisabeth. 1974. The spiral of silence: A theory of public opinion. *Journal of Communication* 24. 43–51.

Ophir, Eyal, Clifford Nass & Anthony D. Wagner. 2009. Cognitive control in media multitaskers. *Proceedings of the National Academy of Sciences* 106. 15583–15587.

Pappacharissi, Zizi & Alan M. Rubin. 2000. Predictors of Internet use. *Journal of Broadcasting & Electronic Media* 44. 175–196.

Raacke, John & Jennifer Bonds-Raacke. 2008. MySpace and Facebook: Applying the uses and gratifications theory to exploring friend-networking sites. *Cyberpsychology & Behavior* 11. 169–174.

Raney, Arthur A. 2003. Disposition-based theories of enjoyment. In: Jennings Bryant, David Roskos-Ewoldsen and Joanne Cantor (eds.), *Communication and emotion: Essays in honor of Dolf Zillmann*, 61–84. Mahwah, NJ: Lawrence Erlbaum Associates.

Raney, Arthur A. 2004. Expanding disposition theory: Reconsidering character liking, moral evaluations, and enjoyment. *Communication Theory* 14. 348–369.

Raney, Arthur A. & Jennings Bryant. 2002. Moral judgment and crime drama: An integrated theory of enjoyment. *Journal of Communication* 52. 402–415.

Riddle, Karyn. 2010. Remembering past media use: Toward the development of a lifetime television exposure scale. *Communication Methods and Measures* 4. 241–255.

Roskos-Ewoldsen, David R. & Beverly Roskos-Ewoldsen. 2009. Current research in media priming. In: Robin L. Nabi and Mary Beth Oliver (eds.), *Sage handbook of media processes and effects*, 177–192. Thousand Oaks, CA: Sage.

Rubin, Alan M. 1979. Television use by adolescents and adults. *Human Communication Research* 5. 109–120.

Rubin, Alan M. 2009. The uses-and-gratifications perspective on media effects. In: Jennings Bryant and Mary Beth Oliver (eds.), *Media effects: Advances in theory and research*, 165–184. New York, NY: Routledge.

Rubin, Alan M. & Elizabeth M. Perse. 1987. Audience activity and soap opera involvement: A uses and effects investigation. *Human Communication Research* 14. 246–268.

Rubin, Alan M. & Rebecca B. Rubin. 1982. Contextual age and television use. *Human Communication Research* 8. 228–244.

Sherry, John L., Bradley S. Greenberg, Kristen Lucas & Ken Lachlan. 2006. Video game uses and gratifications as predictors of use and game preference. In: Peter Vorderer and Jennings Bryant (eds.), *Playing video games – Motives, responses, and consequences*, 213–224. Mahwah, NJ: Lawrence Erlbaum Associates.

Slater, Michael D. 2007. Reinforcing spirals: The mutual influence of media selectivity and media effects and their impact on individual behavior and social identity. *Communication Theory* 17. 281–303.

Sunstein, Cass R. 2001. *Republic.com*. Princeton, NJ: Princeton University Press.

Swanson, David L. 1979. The continuining evolution of the uses and gratifications approach. *Communication Research* 6. 3–7.

Tewksbury, David & Dietram A. Scheufele. 2008. News framing theory and research. In: Jennings Bryant and Mary Beth Oliver (eds.), *Media effects: Advances in theory and research*, 17–33. New York, NY: Routledge.

Walther, Joseph. B., Calab Carr, Scott Choi, David DeAndrea, Jinsuk Kim, Stephanie Tom Tong & Brandon Van Der Heide. 2010. Interaction of interpersonal, peer, and media influence sources online: A research agenda for technology convergence. In: Zizi Papacharissi (ed.), *A networked self: Identity, community and culture on social network sites*, 17–38. New York, NY: Routledge.

Zillmann, Dolf. 1971. Excitation transfer in communication-mediated aggressive behavior. *Journal of Experimental Social Psychology* 7. 419–434.

Zillmann, Dolf. 1988. Mood management through communication choices. *American Behavioral Scientist* 31. 327–340.

Zillmann, Dolf. 1991a. Empathy: Affect from bearing witness to the emotions of others. In: Jennings Bryant and Dolf Zillmann (eds.), *Responding to the screen: Reception and reaction processes*, 135–167. Hillsdale, NJ: Lawrence Erlbaum Associates.

Zillmann, Dolf. 1991b. The logic of suspense and mystery. In: J. Bryant and D. Zillmann (eds.), *Responding to the screen: Reception and reaction processes*, 281–303. Hillsdale, NJ: Lawrence Erlbaum Associates.

Zillmann, Dolf & Jennings Bryant. 1975. Viewer's moral sanction of retribution in the appreciation of dramatic presentations. *Journal of Experimental Social Psychology* 11. 572–582.

Zillmann, Dolf, Jennings Bryant & Barry S. Sapolsky. 1989. Enjoyment from sports spectatorship. In: Jeffrey H. Goldstein (ed.), *Sports, games, and play: Social and psychological viewpoints*, 241–278. Hillsdale, NJ: Lawrence Erlbaum Associates.

Zillmann, Dolf & Joanne R. Cantor. 1977. Affective responses to the emotions of a protagonist. *Journal of Experimental Social Psychology* 13. 155–165.

Zillmann, Dolf, Kay Taylor & Kelly Lewis. 1998. News as nonfiction theater: How dispositions toward the public cast of characters affect reactions. *Journal of Broadcasting & Electronic Media* 42. 153–169.

Biographical sketches

Dirk Baecker is a sociologist and Professor for Cultural Theory and Analysis at the Department for Communication and Cultural Studies at Zeppelin University in Friedrichshafen, Germany. He studied economics and sociology at the universities of Cologne and Paris-IX (Dauphine) and did his dissertation and habilitation in sociology at the University of Bielefeld. He was a visiting scholar at Stanford University, California, the London School of Economics and Political Sciences, and Johns Hopkins University, Baltimore, Maryland. His research areas cover sociological theory, culture theory, economic sociology, organization research, and management education. Among his books is *Form und Formen der Kommunikation* (Frankfurt am Main: Suhrkamp, 2005). Internet addresses: www.zu.de/kulturtheorie and www.dirkbaecker.com.

Adrian Bangerter is a Professor of Work Psychology at the University of Neuchâtel, Switzerland. He does research on coordination processes in conversation, especially coordinating parallel activities and interruptions and the relationship between pointing gestures and language. He also does research on interactions between recruiters and applicants in personnel selection, and the cultural transmission of knowledge and popular beliefs.

Davide Bolchini is Assistant Professor and Director of the Human-Computer Interaction Program at Indiana University-Purdue University Indianapolis (IUPUI) School of Informatics. Through over 100 publications, his research spans human-computer interaction, communication design, and web engineering, and investigates novel conceptual tools to structure design reasoning for web and content-intensive interactive applications. Dr. Bolchini received his Licentiate and PhD degree in Communication Science from the University of Lugano (Switzerland).

Brandon Bosch (Ph.D., University of Washington) is a lecturer in sociology at the University of Nebraska-Lincoln. His research focuses on political communication and media effects.

Paul Cobley, Professor of Semiotics and Communications in the Faculty of Social Sciences and Humanities at London Metropolitan University, is the author of a number of books, including *The American Thriller* (2000) and *Narrative* (2001). He is the editor of *The Communication Theory Reader* (1996), *Communication Theories* 4 vols. (2006), *Realism for the 21st Century: A John Deely Reader* (2009), *The Routledge Companion to Semiotics* (2010), *"Semiotics Continues to Astonish": Thomas A. Sebeok and the Doctrine of Signs* (2011) among others.

Robert T. Craig is a Professor of Communication at the University of Colorado Boulder, USA. A fellow and past president of the International Communication Association (ICA), he was founding editor of the ICA journal *Communication Theory* and currently serves as series editor of the *ICA Handbook Series*. His published research has addressed a range of topics in communication theory and philosophy, discourse studies, and argumentation. Recent work has focused on meta-discursive arguments about communication in public discourse and developing the methodology of grounded practical theory.

David Crowley has taught at the University of Toronto and at McGill University in Montreal, where he was Director of the Graduate Program in Communication. He is a current associate of Media@McGill and a principal with the InterNet Communications Group. The sixth edition of *Communication in History: Technology, Culture, Society* (with Paul Heyer) was published in 2011.

Jonathan Delafield-Butt is Lecturer in Early Years at the University of Strathclyde. His work examines early development of the embodied infant mind, with attention to affective consciousness, development of prospective motor control, and social intentions communicated in movement. He completed his PhD in Developmental Neurobiology at the University of Edinburgh followed by clinical and basic research in Psychology at the Universities of Edinburgh and Copenhagen.

Elizabeth Dorrance Hall is a PhD student in the Brian Lamb School of Communication at Purdue University. Her research focus is on interpersonal communication in families and other close relationships.

William F. Eadie is Professor in the School of Journalism and Media Studies at San Diego State University. He is a former Associate Director of the National Communication Association (NCA), where his portfolio included the promotion of communication and media scholarship to a variety of audiences. He currently serves as Editor of the *Western Journal of Communication*. He edited *21st Century Communication: A Reference Handbook* for Sage Publications, and his forthcoming book is titled, *When Communication Became a Discipline*.

Robin Goret holds two master's degrees from San Diego State University, in Communication and Theater Arts. She is currently on staff at San Diego State University in the School of Journalism and Media Studies and has lectured on media and culture. She owns her own business, Corner of the Sky Communication Group, and produces web content for the San Diego State's College of Extended Studies Digital and Social Media website.

John O. Greene is a Professor in the Brian Lamb School of Communication and a Faculty Associate of the Center for Aging and the Life Course, both at Purdue University. He is former Editor of *Human Communication Research*, and is presently the Director of the Publications Board of the National Communication Association. He is a previous recipient of NCA's Charles H. Woolbert Award.

Cees J. Hamelink is Emeritus Professor of International Communication at the University of Amsterdam. He is currently Professor for Information Management at the

University of Aruba, and Professor of Human Rights and Public Health at the Vrije Universiteit of Amsterdam. He is also the Editor-in-chief of the *International Communication Gazette* and Honorary President of the International Association for Media and Communication Research. He is author of 17 monographs on communication, culture, and human rights.

Dale Hample is an Associate Professor of Communication at the University of Maryland (College Park MD, USA). He has published more than 100 chapters, journal articles, and books. His primary research area is interpersonal argumentation, and that interest has led him to do work in message production, interpersonal communication, persuasion, and conflict management. His most substantial work is *Arguing: Exchanging Reasons Face to Face* (Erlbaum, 2005), for which he won the Gerald R. Miller book award from the interpersonal division of the National Communication Association.

Richard L. Lanigan is University Distinguished Scholar and Professor of Communicology (Emeritus) at Southern Illinois University; currently Director, International Communicology Institute in Washington, DC, USA. He was Vice President of the International Association for Semiotic Studies, Senior Fulbright Fellow (P.R. China 1996; Canada 2007), President of the Semiotic Society of America, Editor of *The American Journal of Semiotics*, founding Chair of the Philosophy of Communication Division of the International Communication Association. Publications include *Speaking and Semiology* (1972; 1991), *Speech Act Phenomenology* (1977), *Semiotic Phenomenology of Rhetoric* (1984), *Phenomenology of Communication* (1988), and *The Human Science of Communicology* (1992).

Philip R. Johnson is Assistant Professor in the Public Relations and Communication Departments at the S. I. Newhouse School of Public Communications at Syracuse University. His areas of work are media sociology, new communication and information technology, public relations and research methods. Recent publications are concerned with gatekeeping, international news and blogs in crisis communication.

Philip Lieberman is George Hazard Crooker University Professor, Emeritus, Brown University, Department of Cognitive, Linguistic and Psychological Sciences. He won his BS and MSEE at MIT in 1958 and a PhD Linguistics in 1966. He held a position on the Research Staff, Air Force Cambridge Research Laboratories, 1959–1972 and was a Professor, University of Connecticut, Department of Linguistics and Research Staff, Haskins Laboratories, 1972–1978; then at Brown University 1978–2012. He is a Fellow of the American Association Advancement of Science, American Psychological Association, American Anthropological Association. His books include *The Biology and Evolution of Language* (1984), *Human Language and Our Reptilian Brain: The Subcortical Bases of Speech, Syntax and Thought* (2000), *Towards an Evolutionary Biology of Language* (2006), and *The Unpredictable Species: What Makes Humans Unique* (2013). Listed in *Who's Who* and in *Who's Who* *in American Art,* for photography. Documentation of Himalayan and Tibetan culture, see www.THDL.org.

Anthony M. Limperos is an Assistant Professor in the School of Journalism and Telecommunications and the Division of Instructional Communication at the University of Kentucky. Broadly, his research focuses on media uses and effects, with an emphasis in understanding the psychology and behavioral impacts of new communication technologies and video games in health, instructional, and entertainment contexts. His work has been published in *Cyberpsychology, Behavior, and Social Networking, Communication Yearbook,* and *Mass Communication and Society.*

Amy Shirong Lu is a Assistant Professor in the Department of Communication Studies of the School of Communication and a member of the Robert H. Lurie Comprehensive Cancer Center at Northwestern University. She studies the persuasive mechanisms and psychological, physiological, and behavioral effects of media technology and has written widely on interactive media and their effects on children's dietary intake and physical activity behaviors. She received her PhD in mass communication and MA in communication studies from the University of North Carolina, Chapel Hill.

Eric Mayor is a post-doctoral researcher at the University of Neuchâtel, Switzerland. His research interests include interpersonal communication in natural and experimental groups, correlates of cognitive appraisal and risk perception, and lay explanations for societally relevant issues. He investigates how text, discourse and nonverbal actions inform us about collaboration, values and opinions, as well other social processes.

Patricia Moy (Ph.D., University of Wisconsin) is the Christy Cressey Professor of Communication and Adjunct Professor of Political Science at the University of Washington. Her research focuses on communication and citizenship, public opinion, and media effects. She is editor of *Public Opinion Quarterly* and editor-in-chief of *Oxford Bibliographies: Communication.*

Mary Beth Oliver is a Distinguished Professor and Co-Director of the Media Effects Laboratory in the College of Communications at Penn State University. Her research is in the area of media psychology, with an emphasis on emotion and social cognition. She is co-editor of *Media Effects: Advances in Theory and Research* (with Jennings Bryant) and *Handbook of Media Processes and Effects* (with Robin Nabi).

Jaime R. Riccio is a doctoral student in the Mass Communication program at the S.I. Newhouse School of Public Communications at Syracuse University. She has been working with Pamela Shoemaker since early 2011 and has co-authored a number of pieces as Dr. Shoemaker's research assistant. Riccio's research examines the power of the audience in mediated contexts. She is currently studying self-performance in online social settings and is working on a piece titled "All the Web's a Stage: The Dramaturgy of Young Adult Social Media Use."

M. Bjørn von Rimscha is Senior Research and Teaching Associate in the field of media economics and media management at the Institute of Mass Communication and Media Research of the University of Zurich. His research interest is in structural and individual influences on media production. His work has been published among others in *Media, Culture & Society*, the *Journal of Cultural Economics* and the *International Journal on Media Management*.

Kim Christian Schrøder is Professor of Communication at the Department of Communication, Business and Information Technologies at Roskilde University, Denmark. His co-authored and co-edited books in English include *Researching audiences* (2003), *Media cultures* (1992), *The Language of Advertising* (1985) and *Digital Content Creation* (2010). His interests comprise the theoretical, methodological and analytical aspects of audience uses and experiences of media.

Peter J. Schulz is Professor for Communication Theories and Health Communication at the Faculty of Communication Sciences and Director of the Institute of Communication and Health at the Università della Svizzera italiana (USI), and a Guest Professor at Virginia Tech University, USA. Recent research and publications have focused on consumer health literacy and empowerment, argumentation in health communications, and cultural factors in health. He is author of more than 60 articles and has published nine books, most recently *Theories of Communication Sciences* (four volumes, Sage, London, 2010). Since 2010 he has been Associate Editor, then Deputy Editor-in-chief of *Patient Education & Counseling* (Elsevier). Since October 2011 he has been a member of the National Research Council of the Swiss National Science Foundation.

Charles C. Self is Professor and Director of the Institute for Research and Training and Gaylord Chair of Journalism at the University of Oklahoma. He was Founding Dean of the College. He has been President of the U.S. Council of Communication Associations, the Association for Education in Journalism and Mass Communication, and the Association of Schools of Journalism and Mass Communication. His PhD is from the University of Iowa. He studies communication theory, international communication, media technology, and civil society.

Lijiang Shen (Ph.D., University of Wisconsin-Madison, 2005) is an Associate Professor in the Department of Communication Studies at the University of Georgia. His primary area of research considers the impact of message features and audience characteristics in persuasive health communication, message processing and the process of persuasion/resistance to persuasion; and quantitative research methods in communication. His research has been published in major communication and related journals. He is the co-editor of the *Sage Handbook of Persuasion* (2nd ed., with James P. Dillard).

Pamela J. Shoemaker is the John Ben Snow Professor at the S. I. Newhouse School of Public Communications at Syracuse University. Her work focuses on media content and the forces that shape it. Publications include *Gatekeeping Theory* (with T. Vos, 2009), *How to Build Social Science Theories* (with J. Tankard and D. Lasorsa, 2004) and *Mediating the Message: Theories of Influences on Mass Media Content* (with S. Reese, 1996). Shoemaker has been editor (with Michael E. Roloff) of *Communication Research*, for many years and was associate editor of *Journalism & Mass Communication Quarterly*.

Gabriele Siegert is Professor of Communication Science and Media Economics at the University of Zurich and Director of the IPMZ-Institute of Mass Communication and Media Research. Her research focuses on media economics, media management and advertising. Recent publications deal with the comparison of advertising markets, commercial audience research or media brands.

Christopher W. Tindale is Professor of Philosophy and Director of the Centre for Research in Reasoning, Argumentation, and Rhetoric (CRRAR) at the University of Windsor, Canada. He publishes and teaches in the areas of argumentation, Greek philosophy, and ethics. Among his key publications are: *Good Reasoning Matters* (with Leo Groarke Oxford, 1989/5th ed. 2012), *Acts of Arguing* (SUNY, 1999), *Rhetorical Argumentation* (Sage, 2004), *Fallacies and Argument Appraisal* (Cambridge, 2007), *Reason's Dark Champions* (South Carolina, 2010).

Colwyn Trevarthen is Emeritus Professor of Child Psychology and Psychobiology at the University of Edinburgh, a Fellow of the Royal Society of Edinburgh, and a Vice President of the British Association for Early Childhood Education. He worked with Roger Sperry on the 'split brain' before moving to infancy research at with Jerome Bruner at Harvard in 1967. He has published on vision and movement, brain development, infant communication, early education and emotional health, and on the psychology of musical communication.

Tim Wharton is Lecturer in Linguistics in the School of Humanities, University of Brighton, UK. He specializes in pragmatics, the study of utterance interpretation. In particular, his research explores how 'natural', non-linguistic behaviours – tone of voice, facial expressions, gesture – interact with the linguistic properties of utterances. His main theses are outlined in his 2009 book, *Pragmatics and Non-Verbal Communication*, which charts a point of contact between pragmatics, linguistics, philosophy, cognitive science, ethology and psychology.

Julia K. Woolley is an Assistant Professor of Communication Studies at California Polytechnic State University, San Luis Obispo. Her research examines media processes and effects in the areas of entertainment psychology and new communication technologies. Notable achievements include co-authored articles published in *Mass Communication and Society*, *Human Communication Research*, and *Cyberpsychology, Behavior, and Social Networking*.

Index

19475180R00268

Printed in Poland
by Amazon Fulfillment
Poland Sp. z o.o., Wrocław